Red Shirt

Red Shirt

The Life and Times of
Henry Lafayette Dodge

Lawrence D. Sundberg

SUNSTONE PRESS
SANTA FE

© 2013 by Lawrence D. Sundberg
All Rights Reserved.

No part of this book may be reproduced in any form or by any electronic or mechanical means including information storage and retrieval systems without permission in writing from the publisher, except by a reviewer who may quote brief passages in a review.

Sunstone books may be purchased for educational, business, or sales promotional use. For information please write: Special Markets Department, Sunstone Press, P.O. Box 2321, Santa Fe, New Mexico 87504-2321.

Book and Cover design › Vicki Ahl
Body typeface › Rotis Semi Sans
Printed on acid-free paper
∞

Library of Congress Cataloging-in-Publication Data

Sundberg, Lawrence D., 1952-
  Red shirt : the life and times of Henry Lafayette Dodge / by Lawrence D. Sundberg.
       pages cm
  Includes bibliographical references.
  ISBN 978-0-86534-949-0 (softcover : alk. paper)
  1. Dodge, Henry Lafayette, 1810-1856. 2. Indian agents--New Mexico--Biography. 3. Navajo Indians--New Mexico--History--19th century. 4. Navajo Indians--Government relations--History--19th century. 5. Frontier and pioneer life--New Mexico. 6. New Mexico--History--19th century. 7. Dodge, Henry, 1782-1867--Family. 8. New Mexico--Biography. I. Title.
  F801.D63S86 2013
  978.9004'9726092--dc23
  [B]
                                                        2013028143

WWW.SUNSTONEPRESS.COM
SUNSTONE PRESS / POST OFFICE BOX 2321 / SANTA FE, NM 87504-2321 /USA
(505) 988-4418 / ORDERS ONLY (800) 243-5644 / FAX (505) 988-1025

This book is dedicated to my mother, H. Eileen Sundberg, whose patience, support and suggestions made this work possible.

CONTENTS

INTRODUCTION 9

1. A Turn of Fortune 13
2. I Regret To Inform You 18
3. A Matter of Honor. 24
4. Damn'd Rascals. 32
5. The Devil Take All 42
6. Sainte Genevieve 50
7. A Nasty Little War. 61
8. Non Est 69
9. Fever River 76
10. Captain of an Aggressive
    Civilization. 87
11. A Nastier Little War 94
12. A Soft-Shelled Breed 102
13. Army of the Frontier 109
14. Kill the Nits, Then You'll Have
    No Lice 120
15. Politics Again 127
16. The Devil's Foothold. 137
17. Mineral Point 146
18. Absquatulated 154
19. Army of the West 162
20. Montezuma's Fire 172
21. Rebellion. 184
22. Indians. 194
23. Expedition. 204
24. Into De Chelly. 215
25. El Morro 228
26. Cebolleta. 239
27. An Extremely Violent Contest . . 252

28. Chupadero 263
29. Fort Defiance 1851. 274
30. Wild as Hawks. 286
31. Hearth and Home 297
32. Navajo Agent 306
33. On the Brink 318
34. Unfit For Civilized Man 330
35. Blessings of a Christian
    Civilization. 342
36. Pass Washington 351
37. In a House Made of Dawn 361
38. Stern But Needful Justice 372
39. Taking Up The Cross 384
40. Best Friends. 396
41. Laguna Negra 407
42. For Amigos 420
43. Madness In The Extreme 430
44. An Ounce of Fear. 441
45. A Moot Point 454
46. Reconnaissance 459
47. Zuni Salt Lake. 461
48. Every Exertion. 465
49. A Wanton Act Inexplicable. . . . 469
50. The Worst of News 477
51. With Due Solemnity. 481
52. Of Greater Use to the Indians . . 488

NOTES. 497
BIBLIOGRAPHY 585

Marie Therese, born in 1839, would have been six years of age in 1845 when her father probably 'went west.' She always, all her life, had a feeling of sadness and longing where her father was concerned. It was undoubtedly because of this intense feeling that she made me promise that I would someday find his grave at Fort Defiance and take some earth from his grave and put it on her own. She lived to be 93.
  —Sheridan Spearman to Frank McNitt, January 3, 1972

INTRODUCTION

Although Henry L. Dodge has long been a familiar name to American Southwest historians and ethnologists, a comprehensive biography of him had never been done until I undertook the task. Indeed, does his life even justify one? Obviously, I believe it does. Henry L. Dodge's story gives a personal view of not only a life, but how that life reflects and reveals the attitudes and circumstances which shaped crucial events of 19th century New Mexico and of the American West in general. Acknowledging that, my first and most durable reason for writing the book was that I liked Henry L. Dodge, despite—or perhaps because of—his flaws, and I am convinced his life makes a good story that captures the irreverent and boisterous vitality of the man and his times.

The work has been many years in the making. I began the book in 1994, and through nearly two decades of weaving it through the demands of life, countless evenings and weekends in archives and libraries, hovering for hours above the glare of microfilm readers, hours surrounded by musty and crumbling documents, and days on the road, I've managed to nearly complete it. Complete, that is, but for one last section, often the least read but probably the most important part of a history, in my mind at least; the acknowledgements of people, usually representing institutions, who made history such as this possible. There were so very many of them, from Arizona to Wisconsin, Albuquerque to Des Moines, Laguna Nigel to Washington, DC. For these are the folks who are preserving us—who we are as people and a nation—each day and every day, as they pour through collections of letters and books and photographs, patiently categorizing and filing them, down to the most trivial minutia, such as unused postage stamps, so that nothing of that niche of history is lost. For much of history is lost already, through fire or flood or war, and most often from simple neglect. It is these people who labor to rescue it, and who make the telling of history a possibility.

That said, simple neglect, the passage of the years, and a spotty memory, compel me to confess that I have lost so many of these individuals' names. Many of them, I'm sure, are gone now. First, I must thank my late mother, H. Eileen Sundberg, for her support and encouragement and her invaluable assistance in editing. When you needed me, Mom, I found that I needed you, and I'll always love you for that.

I'd be remiss if I didn't also thank my brother, Dr. Fredrick Sundberg, and sister-in-law Debbie Whitney Sundberg, for their support, not only for putting up with me, but putting me up not once, but twice, at their home in Manassas Junction so that I could continue research at the National Archives in Washington, DC.

As to individuals to whom I owe expressions of gratitude, I'd like to specifically thank Lucille Basler of the Ste. Genevieve Historical Society; Eugene Beckett of the Mississippi Valley French Research; David M. Brugge of Albuquerque; Ward Churchill of UC Boulder; Dean Conners of Foundry Books in Mineral Point; Betty Danielson of Albuquerque; Dodge descendants Henry and Brenda Dodge of Apache Junction, Arizona; Curator Mary Freymiller and Archive Assistant Tara Teesch of the Wisconsin Room at the University of Wisconsin, Platteville for their invaluable guidance; and Neil Giffey of the Iowa County Historical Society, Dodgeville for all his insights, expertise and advice as well as for having bought me lunch.

As to the contributing institutions, they must stand in place of the actual individuals, of which there were many, who made the book possible. In alphabetical order, I am indebted to the Angelico Chavez History Library, Palace of the Governors, Santa Fe; the Arizona State Department of Library Archives and Public Records, Phoenix; the Catholic Archdiocese of Santa Fe and Gallup; the Center for Southwest Research, Zimmerman Library, University of New Mexico, Albuquerque; El Morro National Monument, National Parks Service, Department of the Interior, Ramah, New Mexico; the Family History Libraries, Church of Jesus Christ of Latter Day Saints, Albuquerque and Colorado Springs; the Hayden Library Department of Archives and Manuscripts, Arizona State University, Tempe; the Henry E. Huntington Library and Art Gallery, 1151 Oxford Road, San Marino; the Iowa State Historical Society Library and Archives, Des Moines; the Kansas Heritage Center, Dodge City; the Kraemer Library, University of Colorado, Colorado Springs; the Mineral Point Room of Local History, Mary Alice Moore, Curator, Mineral Point Public Library, Mineral Point, Wisconsin; Mississippi Valley French Research, Eugene Beckett, Genealogist, Cambria, Illinois; the Missouri State Archives and Museum, Jefferson City, Missouri; the Moise Memorial Library, Santa Rosa, New Mexico, the National Frontier Trails Center, Independence, Missouri; the Iowa County Historical Society, Dodgeville, Wisconsin; the New Mexico State Records and Archives Center and the New Mexico History Library, Santa Fe; the Pendarvis Historic Site, Mineral Point, Wisconsin; the East Library and Penrose Carnegie Special Collections Library at the Pikes Peak Public Library, Colorado Springs; the Santa Fe Trail Center Historical Museum and Library, Larned, Kansas; the St. Louis Genealogical Society, St. Louis; the St. Rose of Lima Catholic Parish in Santa Rosa, New Mexico; the State Historical Society of Missouri;

the Ste. Genevieve County Courthouse; the Ste. Genevieve Historical Society; the Denver and Laguna Nigel Regional Centers of the United States National Archives and Records Administration; the United States National Archives at Washington, DC and College Park, Maryland; the Wisconsin Room, Karrmann Library, University of Wisconsin, Platteville; the Valencia County Courthouse, Los Lunas, New Mexico, the Western Historical Manuscripts Collection, University of Missouri, Columbia; and the Wisconsin State Historical Society, Madison, Wisconsin.

To all of those patient and helpful people who, through their tireless quest to preserve history, made my work and that of so many others possible, I gratefully offer my appreciation.

—Lawrence D. Sundberg

1

A TURN OF FORTUNE
NOVEMBER 1856

The instant he emerged from the arroyo and rounded that gnarled clump of juniper trees, Henry knew he was in trouble. By all accounts, that crisp November day of 1856 had been a leisurely and carefree one. Moments before he'd been riding along, comfortable in his easy familiarity with the terrain, his mundane thoughts wandering aimlessly as he tracked deer. But suddenly...

What was it like to abruptly come face to face with death, to be placed on the edge of destruction by a combination of obscure events that—at least up to that moment—had held no relevance whatsoever? Henry L. Dodge had probably pondered such circumstances on more than one occasion. In a heartbeat, seemingly languid 19th century New Mexico could become a truly murderous place. Certainly incidents of violence were relatively sporadic, but frequent enough to goad one into contemplating one's own mortality. It wasn't uncommon to come across the bloated corpse of some anonymous soul waylaid along the trail, his skull split and his brains bulging out in a halo of flies—abandoned and forgotten by all but the appreciative coyotes and ravens—his only fault perhaps having possessed a pair of attractive boots, or a new hat, or a fine riding mule. Men had been butchered for far less. So most conceded that, between the violence of man and the violence of nature, surviving in the New Mexico outback required skill, caution and luck—a lot of luck.

For Henry L. Dodge, Agent to the Navajo, 1856 had been a tense and foreboding year, but that particular week his prospects had been encouraging. Three days earlier, he had left Fort Defiance in the company of some forty United States soldiers. Although it was officially a military reconnaissance, Dodge's presence on this particular trip was happily unofficial. Seldom refusing an opportunity get out and about the countryside, he had joined the expedition as a lark.

For Major Henry Kendrick who commanded the reconnaissance, it was a most serious matter. Hostile Coyotero and Mogollon Apache were rumored to be active in the Zuni Pueblo area. There had been a long pattern of conflict between American troops and Apaches, most recently a skirmish earlier that spring between Major Chandler's troops out of Fort Thorn and a band of Mogollon, in which several Indians were killed. But it was the events of the previous month that most concerned

Kendrick. In early October, a party of Coyotero Apaches had raided Zuni, killing a shepherd and running off his flock. Zuni warriors, notoriously tenacious fighters, gave pursuit and took the raiders completely by surprise, killing one Apache and recovering the sheep. The defeat had been a complete humiliation for the Apache and Kendrick knew it was an embarrassment that demanded revenge at the first opportunity. When news that the Coyotero were out to even the score blew through his post, the major decided to assess the situation first hand.

Consequently, on the morning of November 16th, 1856 a scouting detail of the 2nd Artillery and 3rd Infantry departed Fort Defiance. The column headed south along Black Creek, Kendrick in command, with 2nd Lt. R. V. Bonneau at his side and Henry Dodge, Navajo Agent, along for the ride. If the weather portended any dangers, the omens were missed. It wasn't especially balmy or pleasant, but the weather wasn't singularly cold, either. It was, well, a normal, bracing November day. Although snow frosted the Defiance Plateau to the west, Kendrick's men found little to impede their brisk pace as they jounced along. All in all it was capital riding weather. Dodge had enlisted his friend Navajo headman Armijo and roughly twenty of his band to accompany the detail as guides and auxiliaries. Dodge had a relaxed and generous manner with the Navajo that seemed to come naturally. Unlike their previous agent, it was clear to the Indians that Henry actually enjoyed their company. As a result, he was quite popular. Although that popularity had proven indispensible in preserving a precarious peace between the Navajo and the Americans, Henry Dodge could absolutely exasperate his Indian Service superiors and the stern Major Kendrick himself. Too often he couldn't be found when he was needed. He spent far too much time hobnobbing with his Indians, going to their ceremonial get-togethers, and taking off on hunting trips. Dodge seldom filed reports. If he were weak on paperwork, he was worse with money. It wasn't that he didn't take his job seriously. He just wasn't very business-like. Kendrick dutifully endured all these foibles. Being the discreet and morally proper New England soldier, he must have particularly abhorred Dodge's propensity for . . . as the good major might have delicately put it . . . fraternizing with his charges, and secretly acknowledged the scandalous probability that several of Armijo's Navajos riding with them that day were not merely Henry's official charges but his in-laws. Henry Dodge, the major suspected, had many in-laws.

The soldiers proceeded south through the low wooded mesas without incident and made their first night's camp on the north banks of the muddy Puerco River. The following day's ride proved to be as uneventful as the first. Crossing Whitewater Arroyo, near the present day Arizona-New Mexico state line, the column angled southeast towards the Zuni River. Following the stream, Kendrick's expedition arrived at Zuni Pueblo that evening. They stayed long enough to beef up their detachment with a handful of warriors led by Salvador, the Zuni war captain. The major wasn't taking any chances. Granted there was the real possibility that they'd not see a single hostile. Still, if the Apache were in the area, he hoped the appearance of such substantial force would make them think twice about raiding the pueblo.

They left Zuni early on the 18th and began the long climb up the crimson mesas rising behind the pueblo. The final destination was to be Laguna Sal, the sacred Zuni Salt Lake, some two-day's ride due south. Kendrick expected to make half that distance by evening. An exhaustingly brisk pace for both men and mounts would be required, as well as a good road. Fortunately, such a road existed. The Zuni Salt Trail was not only a clear and direct route, but it was reputed to be a safe one. Apache, Navajo and a variety of Pueblos used the trail to ritually gather salt at Laguna Sal and there was an unspoken agreement among antagonists to observe a right of safe passage. Anyone could travel the sacred Salt Trail in peace—provided one stayed on the trail.

True to expectations, Kendrick's detachment made excellent time. The morning passed into afternoon as the column wound its way through the piñon pines and sage of the upland. When the column began the long, gentle descent into the broad Jaralosa Valley, dusk was already gathering. Under the mantle of night, Kendrick, Dodge and their weary companions pitched camp where the Zuni Salt Trail dropped down a wall of volcanic cliffs, at the entrance to Atarque Canyon. Major Kendrick would later refer to the spot as Cedar Springs, some thirty miles south of Zuni. Lt. O. L. Shepherd, who served with Kendrick in 1856 but would not pass by the region for another three years, referred to it as a site with good water, wood and grass. He noted in some detail that on the cliff tops above the camp were the crumbling but still impressive basaltic walls of a pueblo ruin. Curious remnants of Anasazi outposts dotted the valley, silent relics of thriving towns and inhabitants long since gone to dust. Petroglyphs covered the cliffs and boulders marking the Old Salt Trail, subtle reminders of the generations of Indian feet that had passed by.

Although Shepherd found the pueblo's basaltic construction noteworthy, it was hardly surprising. The country was cluttered in volcanic rubble. Long before humans had etched their first feeble marks on the land, massive blankets of lava had smothered the region. It had taken fifteen million years of relentless upheaval and erosion to exhume it, leaving a fortification of basalt cliffs stretching the entire length of the valley. This then was the awesome Mal Pais, or the 'Bad Country', where the igneous rocks could slice through leather boots and hidden crevices swallow up pack mules. Yet, undetected by those small souls kindling campfires at its base that night, the cliff itself was imperceptibly cascading a chunk at a time into the canyon. Even the Malpais would eventually, inexorably surrender to time.

Such musings were a convenience of leisure, a scarce commodity for the trail-beaten soldiers just setting their horses out to graze beyond the firelight that frigid evening. For Henry Dodge, it was a typical camp, the kind to which he had cheerfully accommodated himself since his youthful years in Wisconsin. Reconnoitering offered few camp luxuries. There were no tents, few rations, and scant bedrolls to fend off autumn's chill. But it was a relaxed camp. Soldiers and Indians alike clustered around the paltry warmth of their campfires. The less weary chatted and ate. The exhausted huddled under striped Navajo blankets or great coats, their shoulders stooped and heads already nodding in sleep. On the edges of this small circle of relative comfort, petroglyphs marking the canyon walls danced in the firelight and beyond that a vast, dark and absolute silence.

The groaning and hacking of Kendrick's men in the predawn light ushered in the day of November 19th. Camp Cedar Springs soon rattled with the clatter of carbines, tin cups, and stirrups. The major was eager to get underway. The day's ride promised to be as demanding as the previous one if they were to reach Laguna Sal by evening. The day dawned cold but, with the exception of some high clouds and a cutting breeze, it was clear. While the men began stowing their meager camp equipage, Agent Dodge and Armijo saddled their horses. The two had decided to take advantage of the day to do some hunting. It would be a diversion from the tedium of the trail and fresh venison would be a welcome supplement to troop's typical fare of hardtack and salt pork. After bagging a deer or two, they planned to rejoin Kendrick's column along the route later that day. Bidding the troops farewell, Dodge and Armijo trotted off in a southwesterly direction into the flat expanse of Jaralosa Valley, their destination, the distant ramparts of Zuni Plateau.

Seen from the cliff tops of Atarque Canyon, the vastness of the Jaralosa was awesome enough, but once the two riders entered valley, its emptiness seemed to overwhelm them. As flat as a griddle, the valley's uniform brownness stretched out in every direction, trivializing the heights of mesas previously thought to be grand. Dodge and Armijo rode some four or five miles, roughly paralleling the Salt Trail. Wildlife sprang up around them as they ambled along to the comforting sound of creaking saddle leather; jackrabbits bounding away, a herd of antelope tearing across the grassland in a streak of dust and white tails, while red-tailed hawks overhead screeched at the men's irritating intrusion. Initially, signs for a successful hunt were good. The signs improved as they approached the southern edge of the valley. The piñon crowned cliffs of Zuni Plateau seemed to expand before them as Dodge and Armijo moved into the foothills. They got their first deer among the junipers and yucca there, the fact announced by a gunshot reverberating throughout the Jaralosa. Armijo volunteered to dress the carcass and take it back to the troops. Encouraged by their success, Dodge was reluctant to surrender so soon to Kendrick's dreary march. The Zuni Plateau was reputed to have the best hunting, that up among the piñon and ponderosa on the summit, prize bucks were plentiful. The day was still young and the prospect of a second killing promising, so he told the Navajo headman he would go ahead alone, then double back and rejoin the column later. Thus Henry L. Dodge and Armijo parted.[1]

Being utterly alone in the wilderness didn't bother Henry Dodge. He'd often traveled alone. He was a skilled woodsman and as comfortable in the New Mexico wilds as he was in his own boots. True, over the years he'd lost some of his resilience. He was forty-six years old then and, through the trail dust, his dark hair appeared receding and splashed with a hint of silver about the temples. The high coloring of his face, once clear and quick to flush with youthful zeal, was creased and burned brown by the sun, his blue eyes mellowed to a more patient, less passionate gray. Despite the weathering of the years, standing five feet ten inches tall, Henry was still convincingly robust. More over he had retained an unflagging sense of rugged self-confidence. Major Kendrick might have characterized it as a fortuitous but potentially unhealthy balance of bravado, rashness and luck.

Visibility markedly decreased as Henry worked his way up through the broken terrain towards the sandstone heights of Zuni Plateau. On the other hand, the view from the top of that plateau to the foothills below was excellent. To whoever might have been watching, Dodge would have appeared as a tiny but conspicuously moving speck, one moment vanishing behind a screen of cedar, then appearing along an eroded hillside or in a sandy wash, his path completely consistent with that of a hunter stalking deer. Occasionally Henry would halt to check for signs of game and reaffirm his bearings. Off to Henry's right, secluded in one of the many canyons that fractured the plateau, was Cantalero Spring. The cluster of vegetation indicated there might be a small pool and possibly a route upward into the mesa heights.

In the distance directly to his left, Dodge could make out the Salt Trail meandering southward across the valley before climbing into the evergreen summits of Mesa Santa Rita. By then, it was early afternoon and there was no sign of Kendrick's column. The trail was empty. Half a day had slipped by since Dodge had left Armijo, so he had little doubt the Navajo headman had rejoined the column. At the very least Kendrick's men had begun the ascent of Santa Rita. If the boys were up to the major's pace, they were probably already on top. Dodge was well aware of Henry Lane Kendrick's often excruciating efficiency in all matters, however slight. The major insisted on making good time, particularly when late autumn so constrained the hours of daylight. No matter. Dodge would get his deer and then meet them further down the trail. Unconcerned, Henry urged his horse onward.

Then he rounded that last clump of junipers and was suddenly brought up short by the specter of his own mortality.

2

I REGRET TO INFORM YOU . . .

Fort Defiance was a modest post, hardly as intimidating as perhaps a fort wedged in the hostile depths of Navajo country should have been. It had the dubious distinction of being the most isolated garrison in New Mexico Territory, inspiring one officer to describe it as "so far west that the waters of the neighbourhood flow into the Pacific." Two rough track military roads led out of the post, one eastward to Santa Fe via Laguna and Albuquerque and the other southward to Zuni. Santa Fe's alluring charms and corrupting vices were two hundred miles distant. As for Zuni, there was no allure. The only other settlements in the vicinity, should anyone ever wish to go, were at Hopi, to which there was no reliable road.

Fort Defiance's isolation was no accident. Colonel E. V. Sumner established the post in 1851 to restrain Navajo raids on New Mexican settlements and to intimidate the Indians into observing a "firm and lasting peace." To shore up its effectiveness, crack units of the 3rd United States Infantry of Revolutionary War fame, garrisoned Defiance. When Colonel J. K. F. Mansfield inspected the fort in 1853, he praised it as being the most beautiful and interesting post in the territory. Members of the famed Old Guard, compelled to remain on that barren, windswept edge of 19th century America, were less enthusiastic. They had nicknamed Defiance "Hell's Hollow." Perpetually dusty in the summer or muddy in the winter, it was a tight-fitted post, a compact cluster of sagging adobe and rough-hewn log buildings arranged around the traditional parade ground, if the small sandy plaza marked by a flag pole could be so flattered with the term. As with most western Army posts of that day, there was no defensive wall or picketed stockade reminiscent of the earlier Revolutionary forts: no sally ports, no imposing block houses, and no gates. In the words of one reminiscing soldier, Defiance was as open as any quaint New England village.

The lack of a stockade must have been acutely felt when tensions with the Navajos ran high, particularly considering where Fort Defiance had been erected. Like some orphaned whelp, the post was snuggled up to the underbelly of Defiance Plateau. Mesa cliffs overlooked the fort on three sides. Directly to the east there was a rocky ridge commanding the parade ground at a perfect elevation for sending musket shot onto the troopers' heads below, should a stealthy Navajo force so choose. Despite Mansfield's suggestion that a couple of blockhouses be erected there to secure the heights, none were ever built and the ridge remained empty and undefended. Fortunately the Navajo had reacted to Defiance's presence in their county with disgruntled complacency and had up to that time threatened neither the heights nor the fort.

Dirty, drafty, drab, and depressing—that was Fort Defiance. And, on the evening of November 25th, when Major Henry Lane Kendrick and his trail-beaten dragoons first caught a glimpse of it through the gray shroud of snow flurries, it was never a more welcomed sight.

The following morning, in the relative comfort of his log and mud quarters, Kendrick settled into his desk chair and pondered the dispatch he would send to Colonel Bonneville at headquarters in Santa Fe. He'd sent one letter already, a hastily scrawled note penned shortly after his column had returned to Zuni on the 22nd, an express to Major Van Horne at Fort Craig on the Rio Grande. Its brevity testified to the desperation of events and to the major's utter exhaustion. Now in familiar surroundings and somewhat recovered, Major Kendrick formed his thoughts, arranging the details meticulously as was ever his nature, and dipped his quill in the ink well.

"Head Quarters, Fort Defiance N.M.
November 26, 1856
"Major—
"I regret to have to inform you that Captn. H. L. Dodge Navajoe Indian Agent, left our camp, some thirty miles southwards of Zuni, on the morning of the 19th of this month, for the purpose of hunting along the route, & has not since been seen by us.

"Although at our night's camp of the 19th at the "Laguna Sal" we employed the usual means of attracting attention, yet knowing his intelligence as a good woodsman & having during the march seen no signs of Indians other than the friendly Navajoes & Zunis, who accompanied us, his absence from camp gave to these Indians & to ourselves no other anxiety than the fear that he might suffer from the cold before finding us.

"In the morning, however, when we found that several animals of the Indians, & others that had been permitted to graze at large, had been stolen, our apprehensions were awakened for Capt. Dodge's safety & the Indians were sent to find his trail, & to follow it back until something definite could be ascertained respecting him..."

Kendrick recalled Dodge and Armijo's confident departure the morning of the 19th. They'd left Cedar Camp in the dawn light at an easy pace, the tails of their ponies waving a lackadaisical farewell. Then they were gone, absorbed into the gloom. The two men had a head start on the major's column, but not much of one. Kendrick's detachment soon snapped to and was off, loping through the dawn southward along the Salt Trail. Again, the trip had revealed nothing of a threat by hostiles and very little even of interest. They crossed the Jaralosa, eventually turning into Rincon Hondo wash, where the mesas finally began to encroach. The climb into the piñon and cedar forests above was relatively mild and the trail was in excellent condition.

Late that morning Armijo had rejoined them, bringing in a deer and news that Dodge had gone into the heights and would meet the column later. The trail across Santa Rita and Zuni Mesas was true to the Spanish term—flat. From the mesa top, it seemed as if one could see clear into Mexico. By mid-afternoon they began to descend the southern face. Below them appeared a barren plain that, incredibly, seemed to dwarf the Jaralosa. Beyond that plain ten or so miles to the southeast was their destination for the night, a low set of hills backed by uplands that cradled the murky Zuni Salt Lake. They were making better time than even Kendrick had hoped. If Dodge was going to meet them along the trail, he'd better hurry.

As Kendrick's column moved downward onto the flat, the piñons gave way to yucca and dwindling juniper. The character of the valley floor changed as it flattened out: initially rock strewn then gradually growing sandy. It wasn't the red, pristine sand typical of Navajo country, but a dirty sand, the powdery pulverized refuse of ancient lake deposits, the type that blows into everything—your coffee, your boots, your nose—and when wet congeals into a sucking mud that cannot be removed without the diligent use of a bayonet.

A biting wind had risen and a steely gray overcast the sky as they arrived at their campsite. As the name implied, brackish Laguna Sal was completely undrinkable, lying as it did in the lowest spot in the valley. A disappointing stop, certainly, but at least Kendrick's men had the three essentials: water, wood and grass. Just past Salt Lake, a fresh spring trickled from a line of basaltic cliffs. There was abundant firewood in the clustered cedars above and enough grass in the vicinity for their animals. They would have to hobble their horses and set them out to graze during the night. Lacking any evidence whatsoever of Apaches in the area, Kendrick thought it a reasonable risk.

The weather, however, was threatening to turn nasty. It had grown cold during the evening and with sunset the temperature dropped precipitously. Still, Dodge had not appeared. Those soldiers who strayed a few steps from their fires were immediately seized by a fierce cold. Imagining Dodge stumbling alone in the dark, shoulders stooped against the cutting wind, perhaps disoriented, Kendrick had his men set signal fires on top of the hills surrounding Laguna Sal. The bonfires were easily visible from nearly every direction that night. If Dodge had been anywhere in the area, whether on top of Zuni Plateau or in the valley below, he couldn't have failed to see them. Yet Dodge did not come. Was he actually lost? The canyons congenial by day could become a black labyrinth by night. Kendrick's concern grew. He instructed his men to fire shots into the air, believing Dodge, for some inexplicable reason, was unable to see the fires. They kept up a deafening racket for a good hour without attracting anyone's attention . . . or so it had seemed at the time.

The morning of the 20th brought a disturbing discovery. When the soldiers went to retrieve their hobbled horses, they had found several of the animals were missing. Kendrick sent out a detachment under Lieutenant Bonneau to locate them. Shortly after leaving camp, Bonneau made another disturbingly incongruous find. As the troopers approached a line of cliffs, a bedraggled Mexican lad abruptly emerged from among the boulders. He was worn out but visibly relieved to see the soldiers. The soldiers took him up and returned to camp, where the twelve-year-old boy explained in Spanish that he had been held captive by a group of Apache camping in the cedars near the Laguna Sal. After managing his escape in the darkness, he had been drawn towards Kendrick's camp by the bonfires and gunshots before hiding among the rocks.

Kendrick mulled over this grim news. Incredulously, there was irrefutable evidence that there were Apache hostiles in the vicinity, yet not one of his company

. . . not he, not Bonneau, not his Navajo guides, not the Zuni . . . had detected the slightest hint of their presence. Henry Dodge's tardiness had always been a mild nuisance to Kendrick. Now it had become a real anxiety. He immediately sent Armijo and a group of Navajo and Zuni back up the trail to find Dodge's track. Meanwhile, the major regrouped his thoughts, organized his column and undertook the march northward back up the Salt Trail.

It wasn't until noon of the following day, the 21st of November, when they discovered evidence of what had happened. Four or five miles south southwest of Cedar Springs, where the soldiers had camped on the 19th, the Indian trackers discovered Dodge's boot prints in the sand, in company with several moccasin prints. Both Armijo and Salvador immediately asserted them to be, rather than Coyotero Apache, Mogollon or Gileño. There had been no sign of bloodshed or a struggle. No torn body, no scattered limbs, no stray hanks of bloodied hair. That was both encouraging and surprising. The Apache often took women and children captive, but seldom failed to kill the men. The Mexican boy, having lived with the Mogollon and presumably knowledgeable, suggested that since no violence had been used against Henry in the first place, then none would probably be used later. Kendrick hoped the lad was right.

The pattern of tracks in the sand certainly sketched a peculiar scene. Dodge's boot prints moved to and fro, indicating he was not only alive, but had been standing and having what appeared to be an idle conversation with his captors. On reflection, that wasn't particularly incongruous. The gregarious Dodge was well known throughout the territory. He enjoyed wandering the countryside, taking tours of Navajo country, tramping around Zuni and Acoma, Laguna and Cebolleta, Santa Fe and Albuquerque and he often went—most injudiciously—alone. Studying the prints, Kendrick and Bonneau determined that Dodge and the Apache had conversed for some time, then had mounted their horses and galloped off to the southeast toward the Gila Wilderness.

If the Apache had kidnapped Dodge, it could only have been because the hostiles had recognized him and planned to ransom him. In spite of his rugged appearance, Henry L. Dodge was not the typical captive. He was a government agent to the Navajo, an Army officer of sorts, and a widely-known trader, not to mention the first-born son of the influential Senator Henry Dodge of Wisconsin. He would be worth more to the Indians alive than dead. In addition, Dodge's savvy for getting along with the natives, being acquainted as he was with the principal Chiricahua Apache leader Mangas Coloradas and being able to speak to his captors in fluent Spanish would improve Henry's situation considerably. The Mexican lad confidently predicted that once Mangas or his brother learned of Dodge's capture, they would arrange for his release.

Perhaps, the Major mused as he momentarily studied the tip of his pen quill, Dodge had luck on his side. He had certainly been lucky before. He dipped the pen into the ink once more.

> "All attempts at pursuit, if they had not been otherwise injudicious, would have been useless, as well from the lapse of time as from the snow storm then coming on, & which proved so heavy that our guide lost the trail where he was best acquainted with the country...."

Considering the circumstances, even if he'd had the opportunity of giving prompt pursuit in good weather rather than a delayed pursuit in snow, going after Dodge would have been futile, if not down right dangerous. There was a strong chance that he'd have simply got Henry Dodge killed and his own small command shredded in the bargain.

> "Under these circumstances, I see no other way at present to procure Captn. Dodge's release, but by negotiation. Accordingly I sent a special express from Zuni, on the 23rd Novbr. to Major Van Horne, at Albuquerque, requesting him to forward the information of Captn. Dodge's capture to Dr. Steck, Agent for the Indians, near where the former is now supposed to be, as quickly as possible, & also to send the same information to Depmt. Head Quart., & to the Governor of the Territory.

"I have the honor to be, major, very respectfully,
Your obedient servant
H. L. Kendrick
Captn. 2nd Artilry & Bmajor
& Commanding Post."[1]

It was with this fervent hope that Major Henry Lane Kendrick concluded his report and sent it off, perhaps pondering as the express thundered away how Henry's father, Senator Dodge might receive the news. Would it come in sympathetically chosen words from family acquaintances? No. News like that always arrived in the impersonal, bland jargon of military duty.

Dear Senator Dodge ... I regret to inform you...

Senator Dodge, I just this last evening received the painful intelligence of....

The Honorable Senator H. Dodge: We regret to notify you that, on or about the 19th of November 1856, your son, Captn. Henry L. Dodge, Navajoe Indian Agent, was reported missing....

However grim the news, some hope remained. With certainty, Kendrick knew that no expense would be spared to either win Dodge's release or, in the very worst case, exact a harsh revenge on his captors. And Kendrick knew Dodge. Of all the characters in the territory, Henry L. Dodge was one of the best suited to finagle his way out of a tight spot not only alive, but wearing an absurd smile on his face.

3

A MATTER OF HONOR

Senator Henry Dodge pulled the two letters his wife had given him from a coat pocket and slowly unfolded them. As his rugged hands smoothed the papers out across the desktop, he pondered the melancholy event that had placed those letters in his pocket. Senator Dodge was not particularly tall but at seventy-four years he yet displayed the posture of one long accustomed to leadership and influence. He was no stranger to Washington. He had been Senator for Wisconsin some eight years and had previously served as Wisconsin's territorial delegate to Congress. Upon his arrival in 1848, he had embraced Washington politics with Jacksonian exuberance. Now the damp Potomac winter of early 1857 reflected the spreading gloom in the Capitol. Like chunks of plaster dropping from a rotting ceiling, the country was slowly falling apart. There had been bloody civil war in Kansas, violence on the floor of the Senate and serious talk of secession in the halls of Congress. Dodge gazed down at the letters before him. Now on top of the political tragedy the senator had received news of a personal one.

Indians had abducted his eldest son Henry Lafayette Dodge.

The news conjured up the most disturbing images, but the old man's face betrayed no alarm. Senator Dodge's stern visage and gray eyes were etched by a long and tumultuous career in pioneer affairs and politics. He was the quintessential American frontiersman. Riding the swell of the westward movement in his younger years, he had been a miner, a marshal and a military man, an opportunist, entrepreneur and Indian fighter. As captain of the Sainte Genevieve militia, he'd fought Indians in Missouri with Daniel Boone during the War of 1812. In Wisconsin he had crushed the 1827 Winnebago revolt and in 1832 earned General Atkinson's effusive gratitude by decimating Black Hawk's band of Sauk at the Battle of Bad Axe. It was Colonel Dodge who President Jackson had chosen to lead the newly formed First U. S. Dragoons. He had commanded the Great Plains Reconnaissance of 1834 and the Rocky Mountain Expedition of 1835. All had left their stamp on him, physically and philosophically. Through it all, nothing had shaken his faith in his own self-confidence, the rights of the homesteader and the superiority of American civilization and its inevitable domination of the continent.

Success in business and war brought success in politics. Henry Dodge was a staunch, life-long Jacksonian Democrat. Such loyalty gave him with his share of ups and downs, but through it all he'd remained on top. He had helped usher Missouri into the Union in 1821 and could rightfully claim to be among the founding fathers of Wisconsin. As that territory's first governor, Henry Dodge had robustly defended the land rights of Wisconsin settlers and lead miners. As Superintendent of Indian Affairs of the territory he assured those rights by relieving the Wisconsin Indian tribes of vast tracts of land. Dodge's career hit a bump when the Whig victory in 1840 temporarily bounced him out of office. President Harrison replaced him with Dodge's political nemesis, that Green Bay Whig, James D. Doty. No matter. His faithful Democratic legislature promptly appointed him Wisconsin territorial delegate to Congress. For the next four years, Dodge labored untiringly to aggravate Governor Doty's agenda in Washington. Four years later the Democrats regained the White House and Dodge found himself back in the governor's seat.

In 1848, Wisconsin became a state and Dodge was elected senator. His credentials were presented to him on the Senate floor by none other than his old friend, the eminent Senator Thomas H. Benton of Missouri. Dodge's enthusiasm for his first term in the Senate had been boundless. Ahead lay a distant and radiant horizon. He had been chosen to help direct the course of American civilization and forge the nation's destiny with such legendary statesmen as Daniel Webster, John C. Calhoun, and Henry Clay. Nothing, he believed, could restrain the nation's ambitions ... or his own. When Polk engineered a war with Mexico in 1846, Dodge supported him, later pronouncing that the President had rightfully earned the thanks of every true American and the lasting gratitude of his country. Only when it was too late would the country realize their gratitude had been hastily bestowed. That radiant horizon of promise they had beheld in 1848 prophesied the national conflagration of 1861 and the territories seized during the Mexican War would help stoke the inferno.

Congress had long struggled to quell the growing antagonisms between North and South over sectionalism and slavery. Through repeated compromise, Webster, Calhoun and Clay hoped to placate both sides and preserve a precarious balance. By 1854, however, the great compromisers were dead. Senator Henry Dodge had been among the pallbearers who consigned the old Kentuckian Clay to his grave. As if mocking Clay in his tomb, the year produced one last fatal compromise. It was the Kansas-Nebraska Act. Ironically, the intent of the Kansas-Nebraska Act had been to maintain that balance between North and South by applying the sacred American principle of popular sovereignty. Sprawling Nebraska Territory would be divided into sister territories: Nebraska to the north and Kansas to the south. Without a doubt, Nebraskans would vote to outlaw slavery. Kansans, neighboring the slave holding state of Missouri, would most likely vote to embrace it.

That was the assumption. It was a bad one. The politicians, including Senator Dodge, fatally underestimated the depth of the people's resolve, North and South. Pro and anti slavery forces flooded Kansas, intent on securing it for their cause by any and all means. Kansas exploded in a crescendo of violence, spattering with gore even the fine marble and ornate carpet of the Senate chambers. Taking exception to a fiery speech by Massachusetts Senator Charles Sumner, Preston Brooks of South Carolina had savagely pummeled him into bloody unconsciousness with his walking stick. It seems that Sumner had offended the honorable Brooks by characterizing the Kansas proslaverites as the "drunken spew and vomit of an uneasy civilization."[1]

The potential for violence in Congress was nothing new. Duels remained an accepted reply to the challenge of one's honor. During many a heated debate, the bloodletting instinct often tore through that thin screen of civility and refinement. For their own protection, congressmen carried knives and pistols into the very halls of government. In 1850, even Senator Benton had been nearly dispatched by a pistol-packing Senator Henry Foote. As Foote lifted his gun, Dodge had rushed forward to shield Benton, who seemed intent on suicide as he swaggered toward Foote exclaiming, "Let him fire! I have no pistols! Stand out of the way! I disdain to carry arms!"[2] Foote was dissuaded from pulling the trigger and Dodge moved to form a committee to investigate the incident. No disciplinary action was ever taken, though the committee recommended that the Senators refrain from carrying arms in the Senate. Senator Dodge later expressed hope that an end to such disreputable behavior would vindicate the Senate. It was a curiously ironic position, for Dodge was widely known to carry a bristling array of weapons.

The senator from Wisconsin was not so much concerned over the sporadic mayhem in Congress, but the insidious disintegration of the Democrats. Loyalties in Congress were no longer drawn along the party line but along the Mason-Dixon Line, and it was eviscerating the party of Jackson. Though Dodge had strong ties to Missouri and the South and disdained abolitionists, he was no fire-eater. He saw himself as a moderate, somewhat akin to Stephen A. Douglas of Illinois. In his eyes, slavery was an economic issue and should be left as such. He himself had held slaves in Missouri. He also supported the Kansas-Nebraska bill. All that didn't matter to Henry Dodge. It was his sacred duty to vote the conscience of his state legislature rather than his own. When the Wisconsin legislature instructed him to vote against the Kansas-Nebraska Bill because it was viewed as an expansion of slavery, he did so without hesitation. It was simply a matter of honor.[3]

As a result, the Democratic Party was torn in two. In an introspective glance back, Senator Dodge may have realized his honor had been an accomplice in that destruction.

Nevertheless, however gloomy the present atmosphere in Washington was, life had been fortuitous for Henry Dodge and his family. The Senator's business ventures in mining and land speculation had been prosperous, while his long tenure in Washington, though hardly stellar, had been satisfyingly productive. The Dodge family held considerable prestige and influence in Wisconsin. Loved or hated, they were respectable and respected. They could count among the children, grandchildren and cousins numerous rising stars in the family's firmament. The most meteoric had been Senator Dodge's own son, his second son, Augustus Caesar. Augustus had demonstrated an uncanny adeptness at shadowing his own father's footsteps. In 1840, at the age of twenty-eight, Augustus became Iowa Territory's delegate to Congress. Eight years later he had become that state's first senator and, like his father, hit a bump in the road. It was Senator Augustus C. Dodge of Iowa who had introduced the infamous bill that would later emerge as the Kansas-Nebraska Act, glowingly praising it as "the noblest tribute which has ever yet been offered by the Congress of the United States to the sovereignty of the people." Augustus would abruptly fall victim to that sovereignty. Iowans, horrified by the butchery in Kansas, tossed him out of the Senate in 1855. In typical Dodge fashion, he simply rebounded. President Franklin Pierce promptly appointed Augustus C. Dodge as the

United States Minister to Spain. After a few years in Madrid and Europe, Augustus Caesar would return with the prospect of outdoing even his father. A cabinet post or even the presidency; nothing was beyond his reach. Henry Dodge was immensely proud of his boy. All the Dodges were. Augustus Caesar had become the dazzling diamond in the family crown.

Then there was Henry Lafayette, Dodge's first son.

Both Lafayette and Augustus had equally promising beginnings. The crucible of frontier life had shaped them in remarkably similar ways. Like their father, the boys had been tutored by the harsh realities of pioneer existence, their rowdy roughness smoothed somewhat by a smattering of formal education. Lafayette and Augustus had seen military duty during the Winnebago and Black Hawk conflicts. Both had taken up the reins of the family businesses in mining, land and mercantile. Neither shied from confrontation, verbal or physical. Passionate and headstrong Democrats, they were each politically savvy and each had known the fruits of political success. A. C. had been Iowa's Registrar of Public Lands. Lafayette had served as postmaster and sheriff of Iowa County in Wisconsin. Both had married well, Lafayette to Adele Bequette, a daughter of the influential Bequettes of Sainte Genevieve, Missouri and Augustus to the daughter of Dr. Hertich, professor of the small but prestigious Sainte Genevieve school known as The Asylum. In each case, Lafayette had seemed to take the lead over Augustus. Being the older brother, that was as it should have been.

In that lay the paradox. Somewhere along the journey Lafayette had fallen to the wayside. Both boys had been passionate but, of the two, Lafayette proved the less prudent and responsible. Life was a serious business and men were duty bound to carry it through and end it with honor. As a businessman and a family man, Augustus had been ever practical and circumspect. Lafayette on the other hand had been a disappointment. While Augustus was hammering out history in the exalted halls of Congress, Henry Lafayette remained exiled in distant, dusty New Mexico, denigrated to a second rate job drawing a paltry salary in the Indian Service. Granted the vindictiveness of petty politics had played a hand in that misfortune, but the yoke of the blame rested squarely on Lafayette's shoulders. While the family back in Wisconsin was full of Augustus' accomplishments, little was ever so much as whispered regarding Lafayette. His fall from grace just wasn't discussed, most particularly around Adele and the children. Senator Dodge had kept some contact with his son through the years, loaning him money on occasion and making discreet inquiries into his condition, but he could hardly guess what he was up to. Regular correspondence was difficult, even if Henry Lafayette had been predisposed to write.

Mail was painfully slow from that far outpost, taking a month or more to reach the east coast, provided it wasn't robbed in transit.

A month or more ... for Senator Dodge that delay seemed at that moment ever more so abysmal. Two letters had arrived simultaneously in Washington by express on January the 2nd, 1857, one addressed to the War Department, the second to the Department of the Interior. Both contained Brevet Major Henry L. Kendrick's reports detailing his son's abduction by the savages in November. As Secretary of War Jefferson Davis was forwarding his copy to Secretary of the Interior McClellaude, McClellaude was forwarding his to Jeff Davis.[4] Doubtlessly their respective couriers passed one another in the hallway that day.

"1857, Jan. 3
Department of the Interior, Washington, DC
Jefferson Davis Secretary of War

"Sir—

"I have the honor to enclose, herewith, a copy of a communication from Governor Merriwether of New Mexico, and accompanying papers in relation to the capture of Agent H. L. Dodge, by the Indians.

"As the War Department may not have received dispatches from its officers, containing the information in reference to the capture, the papers are referred, with the request that the proper officers of the Army, in New Mexico, may be instructed to aid the officers of this Department in that territory in their endeavors to release Agent Dodge from captivity.

I am—Very respectfully,
Your Obd. Servant
R. McClelland"[5]

What could Senator Dodge do but receive such news with stoic fatalism? In such circumstances worry was wasted emotion. The damned letter had been in transit for better than a month. What <u>might</u> be had already <u>been</u> and the future already consigned to the past. Whether joyous or tragic, the outcome was cruelly irrevocable. Damn the mail. Still the old insistence on action prodded the Senator. He had to do something, even if merely a gesture of reaching out to his son. He glanced at the letters on his desk. They were not the formal dispatches from New Mexico.

They were two letters, two Christmas letters Lafayette's daughters had written to their grandmother, Senator Dodge's wife Christiana. The contents were fairly inconsequential, prattlings about the weather, the many relatives, their schooling ... sharing the most mundane domestic joys that Lafayette hadn't experienced in years. Of the two letters, that of the oldest girl, seventeen year old Mary Therese, was longer and more in depth. Mary had turned seventeen the previous May. She began the letter "My Dear Grandma."

"Dodgeville, Nov. 27th

"My Dear Grandma,

"It has been some time since I have written to you but it is not from a want of inclination for I take great pleasure in writing to you but I do not have any-thing of interest to write about. I wrote to you and directed my letter to Poughkeepsie but do not know whether you received it or not..."

That may have elicited a grandfatherly smile from the senator. His gazed moved across his granddaughter's neat handwriting.

"... I received a letter from Kitty not long since. She and Fanny were quite well. Aunt Black is quite sick but I hope she will be better soon. I believe it is a bilious attack. Cousin Delia Maddin was here this afternoon. All of the family are well. We have had very disagreeable weather for the last two or three weeks. It has rained and snowed which made it very unpleasant. It is more settled now, however. The schools have commenced here and Linn is attending ..."

Christiana, or "Kitty," was her little sister, attending school away from home. She was thirteen years old and studying at St. Joseph's Academy in Dubuque, Iowa with her cousin Fanny. Lafayette's youngest, ten year old Linn, was in school at Dodgeville. The letter continued.

" ... I applied for the small school but could not get it. The Superintendents of the school would not take anyone that lived in town so I could not get it. It would have been a great help to us if I could have got it. We are all quite well, Ma. Grandma, George, Linn and all our friends send much love to you and dear Grandpa. Is Uncle Hayden in Washington? My love to Cousin Henry and little Christy. Believe me Dear Grandma to be your affectionate Grandchild.

Mary T. Dodge"[6]

Neither Kitty nor Linn probably remembered their father. Mary Therese did. However much she may have missed Lafayette, there was no hint of him in her letter. Perhaps she secretly blamed him for their tribulations. Particularly stinging was Mary's reference to her failure to get a teaching job. Adele and the family were struggling financially, taking in boarders and doing odd jobs. True, there was no mention of her father, but he was indelibly etched there in her fine pen strokes. Senator Dodge turned to the next letter, also addressed to his wife, from the little one, 'Kitty', as she was affectionately called. It was considerably shorter. Smaller children struggled more to pen important things to say. Dated December 6th, 1856, the news was again about the most normal things, but in abridged form. The weather was very cold, the snow quite deep. Studying hard and Merry Christmas and very happy New Year and would write a long letter but have nothing to write about. Love.[7]

Lafayette had four children, at least four children relatives could acknowledge without embarrassment. George Wallace Jones Dodge was the eldest, then Mary Therese and Christiana Adel and lastly Louis Fields Linn Dodge. Their father hadn't seen any of them since his departure for New Mexico ten years before. The Senator had helped Adele when he could. Over the years, the children had spent much of their time in the shelter of The Grove, Senator Dodge's Wisconsin residence. His thoughts turned nostalgically toward home. For better or worse, Lafayette's departure had ensured that the sprawling two story frame home would never lack for the clatter of children's footsteps up the stairs or across the kitchen's stone flooring.

In spite of the frenetic political activity that drove and defined him, Senator Dodge had played both father and grandfather to the youngsters. He took an active interest in his grandchildren's education, tutoring them in the classics and on Sundays the Bible. He encouraged Mary to practice long hours on their old piano brought up Missouri those many years past by enticing her with a silver coin, placed there on the piano. Mary had so enjoyed toying with the bells attached to a fur pelt on a wall. Indeed, the hallway was adorned with Indian paraphernalia, hung like trophies of the hunt. How very pleasant it would be to drink in the simple sounds of domestic life again, to overhear the women talking at the stair top window or to enjoy the shaded cool of the springhouse in summer. How he regretted that Lafayette was deprived of such happiness.[8]

Emerging from his reverie, Senator Dodge folded the letters together. He wrote his wife's name Mrs. Christiana Dodge on the back letter, then slipped them into an envelope franked with his name and sealed it. In a firm hand he wrote on the envelope: "Capt. Henry L. Dodge, U. S. Indian Agent, Santa Fe, New Mexico, Care of Gov. Merriwether."

He would send it postage free from Washington City and trust his friend David Meriwether to get it to his son. It would be perhaps a meaningless gesture, but a gesture nevertheless of hope and reconciliation. With luck and the blessing of Providence, Meriwether would be able to deliver it to his obstreperous son.

4

DAMN'D RASCALS

It was hardly surprising that Henry Lafayette Dodge might be seen as obstreperous. He was a Dodge, after all, and the Dodges had always been a cantankerous lot. Admittedly that made them typical Americans. It took a certain streak of obnoxious self-serving independence to undertake a future in frontier America, as Lafayette's first American forbearer, Tristram Dodge, discovered when he stumbled pale and sickened onto American shores in 1661. Tristram and his family had sailed on *The Lion's Whelp* from their home near River Tweed in England. For better than a month they endured the dark and clammy creaking quarters below, the incessant rolling and pitching, the stench of sweat and urine and vomit and the gnawing of hunger and disease. Thus the dreary hours passed in company with equally dreary companions. The distinctly American characteristic of self-reliance may have been conceived during that tense, gloomy passage as the cramped immigrants increasingly took boisterous offense against any perceived trespass by their cabin mates. Tristram quickly learned that asserting one's independence enhanced one's chances for survival.

Tristram Dodge and his family did survive. In April of 1661, he and fifteen other families started a settlement at Block Eylandt, just south of the main shore of Rhode Island. With equal contributions of work, audacity and luck, Tristam's descendants prospered and grew. The Dodge progress was marked through the generations by a succession of Israels and Johns.[1] Of them all, two brothers would stand to the fore as being the quintessential Dodges. John born in 1749 and Israel born in 1760, both hailed from Connecticut. Young Henry Lafayette Dodge never knew them, but they would indelibly shape him. Neither famous frontier trailblazers nor exalted statesmen, John and Israel Dodge were common men who would like so many others carved a niche for themselves out of the Illinois wilderness. The Dodge brothers would prove a force with which to be reckoned, to the consternation of the Indians, the colonial French and certain authorities of a fledgling United States of America.

John and Israel were probably the first of the Dodge clan to go west. They were apt examples of how European competition over New World possessions not only forged and shattered imperial aspirations but also hammered out the destinies of ordinary men. The most recent squabble had been the French Indian War and a bloody one it had been. Increasingly alarmed by English colonial encroachments westward into the Ohio Valley, the French constructed a series of forts along the Ohio River. In response the governor of Virginia dispatched one hundred fifty militiamen to demand the French depart. A young George Washington led the force. Regrettably the haughty Virginia boys delivered the demand with musket shot, plunging the colonies into six years of butchery. Initially the French and their Indian allies held the advantage. Their familiarity with the wilderness and their adeptness at waging guerrilla warfare regularly chewed up the colonials. Yet French advances began to evaporate under the steady flow of English troops pouring into the fray. The British capture of Montreal in 1760 all but snuffed out France's immediate ambitions in the New World. The Treaty of Paris in 1763 gave England jurisdiction over Canada and all lands from the Mississippi River eastward.

Indian tribes and French settlers and traders heretofore allied with France now owed their allegiance to the Union Jack. At first this change had little direct impact on the Indian and French settlements strung along the Mississippi. The French citizens remained in their towns and trading posts hoping to forget the bitter antagonism of the past and continue on. At the very least, the royalist French could take solace in knowing that a monarch yet ruled them albeit an Anglais king. That would be a short-lived consolation. Despite its brutality, the French Indian War had been a windfall for the land-hungry colonists. With the French conveniently dispatched and their Indian allies swept aside in confusion, Americans began moving over the Appalachians and into the Ohio Valley, drawn by the promise of profit and prosperity. In an attempt to choke back the rising flood, King George issued the Proclamation of 1763. Henceforth colonists were forbidden to settle the recently conquered lands. The proclamation proved ineffective. The land beyond the Alleghenies was free, bountiful and beckoning. Ambitious settlers and land speculators would not be denied the American birthright to subdue the wilderness. They defied the law and surged into the Ohio. In the end, Great Britain would pay a high price for their victory over the French. The patronizing relationship England had nurtured with its colonials was beginning to crumble. Colonists increasingly opposed British attempts to control and restrain them. Sedition had become fashionable and, with sedition, revolution.

At the close of the French-Indian conflict, the now humdrum states of Ohio, Illinois, and Indiana were the unsettled frontier. It took the Americans, including John and Israel Dodge, to make it the Wild West. John Dodge first moved west in 1770. He settled at the Wyandot Indian villages near Sandusky and took up trading with the natives. What qualified him for this particular avocation remains a mystery. When revolution erupted in the colonies, John's influence among the Indians at the very least kept the Wyandot neutral. In 1776 he was arrested by the British for sedition. He spent the opening two years of the Revolution imprisoned in Detroit and later Quebec before managing his escape. Upon his return to the colonies, he found time to write a book about his incarceration, pry a land grant out of Congress to compensate his losses and prevail on a brief acquaintance with General Washington to recommend him to the governor of Virginia, Thomas Jefferson. In 1779, John was rewarded with an appointment as agent of Indian affairs in what would later be known as Illinois.[2]

Up to that time, Israel's life had been every bit as interesting as his older brother's, if not more so. As a youth, Israel reputedly had traveled to Africa on a commercial slaver. Upon his return, he cast his lot as a patriot in the Revolutionary Army. While older brother John was cooling his heels in a British dungeon, younger brother Israel, barely out of puberty, was seeing the Revolution from uncomfortably close proximity. During the close quarter slaughter at the Battle of Brandywine Creek in 1777, Israel was skewered by British bayonet. Coincidentally, as the story went, the dashing Marquis de Lafayette was also wounded, hit in the leg with a musket ball. Both men would survive. Although the Marquis probably took no notice of the adolescent patriot, the young Dodge considered their shared baptism by fire a patriotically sacred event. He affectionately looked upon the bold French nobleman as a blood brother of sorts. The Marquis would go on to see Cornwallis surrender at Yorktown and Israel Dodge would move west with his brother John, carrying that affection forever in his heart.[3]

Both Israel and John were Eastern boys, but they quickly took on the rugged exterior of frontiersmen of the period. In 1780, Israel married a true frontier girl, Nancy Ann Hunter of early Kentucky pioneer blood, at a tiny military station in Iron Banks, Kentucky. For a time, they lived on the Falls of the Ohio near present day Louisville. Some time after the birth of a son and a daughter, Israel left Nancy and his family to join John at a little backwater French town on the east banks of the Mississippi, called Kaskaskia. Kaskaskia had long been a center of French Mississippi life. It had modest beginnings in 1703 as a Jesuit Catholic mission to the Kaskaskia Indians. The French settlers who followed the Jesuits farmed the vast Mississippi bottomlands below the eastern bluffs. Several of the well-to-do families held slaves, both African and Indian. Others engaged in trading with the natives or trapping furs. It wasn't until the French Indian War that the inhabitants of the town felt compelled to build a stockade on the bluffs at their backs to stand against the British, in the end a futile effort.[4]

The Pontiac War delayed the actual British occupation of Kaskaskia by two years. Once the British arrived, they paid little attention to the development and defense of the region, much to the disgust and dismay of the French citizenry. When Revolutionary General George Rogers Clark's ragged force of 175 Virginians and Kentuckians moved to seize the British settlements along the Ohio and Mississippi in 1778, they encountered little resistance from English forces and considerable encouragement from the former subjects of the King of France. Two notable men aided Clark's expedition. The influential French priest Father Gibault persuaded his Gallic countrymen to swear allegiance to Clark and the Americans. The second man was one Thomas Bentley, an Englishman originally hailing from London. A practical fellow, Bentley observed more loyalty to his business than to his crown. He had lived in Kaskaskia since the early 1770s' and had married the daughter of a prominent French Creole family, Margaret Beauvais. With his knowledge of the terrain and his French connections, he was invaluable to Clark. Regarding the later activities of John and Israel Dodge, however, Gibault, Bentley and Madame Beauvais would have a parting of the ways.[5]

Clark's army occupied Kaskaskia in July of 1778. Shortly thereafter and to the consternation of the old French families there, American settlers from neighboring Kentucky began to trickle in. The residents of Kaskaskia had loathed the British and celebrated their defeat, but at best they distrusted the Americans. After all, the influential French families of the region were staunch monarchists. A British king was bad enough but at least it was a king. They viewed republicanism as thinly veiled anarchy. American frontier democracy, they feared, would be the epitome of rule by the mob and they disdained the rambunctious and rash behavior of their new Yankee neighbors. The French of Kaskaskia would get more than their fill of those qualities from John Dodge and his brother Israel.

John seldom hesitated to be intimidating and violent when enforcing his brand of justice at Kaskaskia. Some would refer to him as the boldest and ablest pioneer of the frontier. Others would brand him a petty tyrant and pirate. With Israel's aid, John soon established himself as the unofficial power over this new brand of Yankee democracy and the uncontested leader of the growing American faction. Between the years 1780 and 1786, the Dodges routinely acquired lands and exacted subservience from the French of Kaskaskia. As if to symbolize his domination, John and his followers occupied the ruins of the old French fort on the bluffs commanding the town. Dodge's men threw up a stockade and renamed the site Fort Gage. Two cannon glared threateningly down on Kaskaskia from the fort walls, guaranteeing John's assumption of power. One of Dodge's first efforts, in partnership with Thomas Bentley the entrepreneurial Englishman, was to buy up local French claims to Congress for their losses at the hands of the Americans during the Revolution. Any resident of Kaskaskia showing damages could petition Congress for restitution. As any trip back east could be at the least long, physically and financially exhausting, astute middlemen acting as the claimant's agents bought the claims at cut rate prices, thereby saving them the trip. Once a substantial number of claims had been purchased, the agent undertook the trip, submitted the claims to Congress and received their full value . . . if they were lucky. Still, it seemed a reasonable gamble. All one needed was enough cash. Where Dodge and Bentley got the backing for such an undertaking is a matter of some curiosity. During his tenure as Indian agent, John Dodge was accused in several written complaints of misappropriation and mismanagement of public goods, and was taken to court for refusing to appropriate shirts for soldiers in 1781. In response to these complaints, Thomas Jefferson did not remove him, but instructed George Rogers Clark to keep an eye on his activities.[6]

Dodge and Bentley's business enterprise was the first shot in what would become a long fight between the Dodges and the French of Kaskaskia. By May of 1781, the exasperated residents were sending off petitions to Congress and Governor Jefferson protesting Dodge's usurpation of power, how he incessantly bullied the inhabitants, illegally misappropriated property and imprisoned anyone who raised his ire, irrespective of age and position. When a mere boy had the temerity to challenge John Dodge's right to expropriate some poor Frenchman's wood stack, he had the lad tossed into a cell. According to the French, the best inhabitants of Kaskaskia were fleeing across the river into Spanish Louisiana rather than suffer such despotism. When their pleas seemed to go unanswered, it was rumored that John Dodge had had the couriers murdered.[7]

Father Gibault and the local priest, Father de la Valiniére regularly condemned John Dodge's rule to the authorities. In direct reference to the Dodges, Gibault wrote that the "... breaking of limbs, murder by means of a dagger, sabre or sword ... are common, and pistols and guns are but toys in these regions ... the most solemn feasts and Sundays are days given up to dances and drunkenness ... with girls suborned and ravished in the woods, and a thousand other disorders which you are able to infer from these."[8]

In full fury over such piracy, Father de la Valiniére sacrificed many an hour and quill documenting in excruciating detail Dodge's outrages. Neither Frenchman nor American high or low was immune to John's attacks. De la Valiniére accused Dodge of openly defying some U.S. agents and subverting others with offers of room, board and strong drink; that he had illegally deported two Americans to a Spanish prison across the river; that he was violent, "... striking many with his sword, drawing the eyes from the head of another." In one memorable incident Dodge assaulted a notary clerk who was indiscreet enough to question his word and would have gouged his eyes out if an officer present had not cried out in protest. Almost as an afterthought, Valiniére penned the most damning indictment.

"I forgot the most horrid payment occasioned the 14 June 1784. by John Dodge, to a Trader named Daniel Murray to whom John Dodge was indebted. Instead of paying him his due, he quarreled him, and said to his associate in trade Mr. Timothée Mombrun who was chief justice or lieutenant of country, saying '... *that man will kill me give order to take him prisoner*' which order being granted."

Upon which, Dodge in company with Captain La Chance and a band of ruffians broke down Murray's door. When Murray opened fire, Dodge's party returned it, hitting Murray in the arm and shattering the bone. The wound was bad enough to cause Murray's death a short time later.[9]

Lieutenant Mombrun's unfortunate predecessor, Richard Winston, had earlier paid the price for being uncooperative with John Dodge. Winston was a local trader and had succeeded John Todd, who had left in disgust after proclaiming the region ungovernable. Winston's downfall began in 1781 in a dispute with Dodge over money. The feud climaxed a year later when John ordered brother Israel to arrest Winston and seize his property on the pretense of being "a dam^d' Rascal & no friend to the country." In delivering him up to the courts, John Dodge took the high moral ground.

> "Whereas M Richard Winston has been guilty of treasonable expressions Against the State and officer who have the hon^r of wearing Commission in the Service of their Country dam^nd them all and said they were all a set of thieves and Robers and only come to the Country for that purpose, The above crime being proved before. i now deliver him to you prisoner and request of you to Keep him in surety until he may be brought to justice ... "[10]

The fact Winston was the acting United States county lieutenant, and that his accusations rang true, did not appear to phase the Dodges, who claimed governmental authority of their own. Then there was the matter of Madame Margaret Beauvais, the estranged wife of John Dodge's crafty business partner Thomas Bentley. Bentley and Beauvais had been wed shortly before the outbreak of the American Revolution. Like Dodge, the British had imprisoned Bentley. Upon his return to Kaskaskia, he heard rumors that his wife, to put it delicately, had been courting the affections of other men. Whatever the truth, he cast her out. Thomas eventually appointed John Dodge as executor of his estate. When Bentley died, Dodge not only cut Margaret and her family out of the will but also moved to seize her property and slaves as part of the Bentley estate. He made his justification scandalously public.

> "Whereas Margret Beauvais alias Mrs. Bentley has by her infamous Conduct and Whoredom dissipated & squander'd away great part of the Estate of Mr. Thomas Bentley disseased & has forfited & lost all Right title Claim & Pretention to any part of said Estate except One dollar according to his express Will. . . . I do hereby forwarn all & every Person or Persons whomsoever from harbouring concealing or detaining on any Pretence whatsoever a Certain Mallattoe Woman named Genvievé with four Children also a Negro Man named Pereault as well as any other part of said Estate on pain of suffering the Rigour of the Law ..."

It was a gracious gesture from an old friend to a deceased partner. It was convenient, too. The Beauvais family had been vocal opponents of Dodge and his group. Dodge also sent a warning to Valiniére, stating that " ... Madame Bentleys Scribbler ... had better mind his own Business & have a little more Respect to the Cloth which some over sighted Clergy may have given him."[11]

The arrival of Lieutenant John Rice Jones in 1786 would be Dodge's undoing. Ironically, their first antagonistic meeting would resonate through the Dodge and Jones family descendents for decades thereafter. Lt. Jones was in most every way John Dodge's complete opposite. Born in Wales, educated at Oxford, he had practiced law in London before settling at Philadelphia in February of 1784. During the fall of 1786, Jones arrived in Kaskaskia as commissary agent for General Clarke, who at the time was undertaking a military expedition against the Indians of the Northwest Territory. It was the lieutenant's task to requisition wheat sufficient to supply Clarke's troops garrisoned in Vincennes. After some haggling and probably some coercion, Jones persuaded two Americans to deliver him a supply of wheat with a promise of future payment. The next day Lt. Jones brought up twenty carts to take delivery of the wheat. To his irritation he discovered that John Dodge had convinced the two Americans to renege. He had offered to help the men stand their legal ground and physically defend them with thirty of his own men if need be. Outraged, John Rice Jones returned to Vincennes. When he reappeared at Kaskaskia, it was in command of a contingency of troops. Stationing them outside Dodge's stockade, Jones threatened to cast Dodge out of his damn[d'] fort. Illegal or not Dodge realized the troops camped outside the fort cleaning their muskets were far more at hand than any protection of the courts. Lieutenant Jones got his wheat. It would be John Dodge's first stinging defeat. Lieutenant John Rice Jones departed Kaskaskia determined if at all possible to unseat Dodge and send him and his followers flying across the Mississippi into Spanish Louisiana along with all the other riff-raff.[12]

In the wake of this event John Dodge began to see his fortunes in Illinois country cloud over. Fortunately for him, the Spanish administration across the river in Louisiana distrusted the young United States more than they did Yankee émigrés like Dodge. To strengthen Louisiana against potential U.S. encroachment, the Spaniards were encouraging American settlement in the province. John and Israel Dodge saw the opportunity and took it. By the spring of 1787, John was liquidating his own assets and apparently the assets of others in preparation for his move across the river. Madame Beauvais-Bentley openly accused John Dodge of stealing her belongings and a female slave under the cover of darkness and petitioning Congress to have him arrested should Messer Dodge ever again appear on the east bank.[13]

At about that time Israel may have decided to distance himself from his brother. While John was closing up shop, Israel left Kaskaskia in 1787 to temporarily join his wife Nancy and their two children at the Falls Upon the Ohio, near present day New Albany. He would soon rejoin his older brother in Louisiana. In the meantime, John attached himself to a group of American colonists at New Madrid, and then headed north along the Mississippi banks to a small French farming community called Sainte Genevieve that seemed to promise the kind of elbow-room he was accustomed to.

Upper Spanish Louisiana in the 1780s was much like Illinois country on the east side of the Mississippi, except more remote. Originally occupied by the Missouri and Osage Indians, Missouri and the Mississippi River Valley had long held the interest, if not the commitment, of French national and commercial ventures. Out of Canada, Louis Jolliet and Jacques Marquette would explore the river as far as Arkansas in 1673. He was followed by La Salle nine years later, who christened the country Louisiana, in honor of King Louis XIV. France's interests were limited to finding precious metals, establishing mission settlements, and erecting trading posts to prop up the fur trade. The efforts brought minimal results. Increasing difficulties with Indians, particularly the Osage, spoke to the failure of mission work. After nearly sixty years, the number of permanent French settlements in Upper Louisiana could be counted on the fingers of one hand. Saint Louis would not be founded until 1764, when the French ceded Louisiana to their ally Spain, in part repayment for Spanish losses from the war against England and in part to maintain a buffer, albeit Spanish, against English expansionism.

Spain took a more aggressive stance than the French regarding Louisiana territory. When the American Revolution seemed to be unraveling the British New World possessions, the Spanish gleefully supported the revolutionaries in the west. The Spanish Lieutenant Governor, Fernando de Leyba offered Clark assistance upon his occupation of Kaskaskia and threw him and his officers a lavish reception in St. Louis. To thwart British expansionism, in 1778 the Spanish crown authorized granting land, grain, livestock and tools to any Catholic immigrant who might choose to relocate to Louisiana. The offer attracted many dissatisfied French and Indian inhabitants of Illinois as well as a few Americans, but the resulting exodus across the river was a modest one at best.[14]

With colonial independence, the Spaniards soon gained a new appreciation for the United States' appetite for territory. Hoping to bolster their province, Spain continued the policy of inviting immigration into Louisiana, now liberally extended to the Americans themselves. Spanish authorities believed that most western Americans had only a flimsy loyalty to their government and with the right incentives could be converted. That assessment was not completely unfounded. Western territories, feeling neglected by the federal government, were already speaking of secession. Once settled in Louisiana's lap of luxury the conventional Spanish wisdom held Americans would become loyal and constructive citizens, as had the Illinois French. All they need do to be warmly welcomed was swear allegiance to the Spanish crown and covert to Catholicism. In retrospect, it was an unwise policy, the inevitable results of which were not lost on Secretary of State Thomas Jefferson. Knowing that the mass immigration of Americans would conquer a territory far more effectively and more cheaply than any army, Jefferson confided with a chuckle, "I wish a hundred thousand of our inhabitants would accept the invitation."[15]

In his new home near Sainte Genevieve, John busied himself developing grist and saw mills, a brewery and a still. A year later he requested a license to ship agricultural goods downriver to New Orleans, no doubt to sell the farm goods he had been obliged to accept as payment for his holdings in Kaskaskia. But if his French antagonists on the east banks hoped that his new interests would restrain him from molesting the citizens of Kaskaskia, they would be sorely disappointed. To prod American settlers across the river to repatriate, the Spanish administration had secretly encouraged Indian tribes to terrorize and demoralize the Illinois pioneers, in effect driving them into Louisiana for safety. It was a golden opportunity for John Dodge, still simmering from his expulsion, to strike back. On October 8, 1789, he led an armed party of whites and Piankeshaw Indians across the Mississippi and into Kaskaskia. His purpose, bolstered by some flimsy legal pretense, was to seize the slaves of one of his long time enemies, a Mr. John Edgar, business associate of John Rice Jones. The sudden appearance of Dodge's rough group must have inspired a good amount of panic. John failed to get his slaves, but he and his entourage terrorized Kaskaskia, threatening to burn it to the ground before they finally departed. After that harrowing evening, a stream of rumors predicting attacks by the Delaware, the Shawnee, the Piankeshaw, and the Sauk regularly rattled the citizens of Kaskaskia. Coolly discounting them, James Rice Jones appreciated the rumors for what they were, mere tales invented by certain unnamed, disenchanted and expatriated American malcontents ranting on the Louisiana side of the river.[16]

5

THE DEVIL TAKE ALL

John and Israel settled at New Bourbon, a small ramshackle hamlet some three miles south of the old French town of Sainte Genevieve. Although founded by the French royalist Henri Peyroux de la Coudreniere, the settlement became a distinctly American community. Just up the road, the town of Sainte Genevieve was the regional center of economic activity and a stronghold of conservative French Creole ways. It was the oldest of the Missouri settlements, predating Saint Louis and outstripping her in population. It was conveniently nestled between two forks of the Gabourie River along a fine stretch of bottomland. There was an acceptable harbor at Eagle Rock where the north fork emptied into the Mississippi, deep enough to accommodate a variety of vessels bringing commodities from down the Ohio or transporting crops and lead ore down river to New Orleans.

The Indian trade, salt works and lead mining all contributed to Sainte Genevieve's prosperity, but agriculture was the townspeople's main pursuit. The notably rich Bois Brula bottomland extended some nine miles along the river. Flat as a tabletop, the vast field was surrounded by a common fence and divided into family gardens and orchards of various sizes, depending on the size and wealth of the family. Though important, agriculture was not intensively practiced. Planting and harvest times were the busiest. Plowing and planting began in April, turning the bottom into a scene of activity for about two weeks, as farmers and their slaves, plows, carts and horses move to and fro. But once the seed was in the ground, the crops were left to mature on their own, with little attention paid to weeds and the like. During the summer months, a large number of the farmers of Sainte Genevieve migrated inland to mine lead and to escape the oppressive conditions along the Mississippi.

Due to its flood-prone location Sainte Genevieve had a reputation for being singularly unpleasant, particularly in summer. The disdainful Illinois French across the river oft referred to Sainte Genevieve as *Misére* because of its infamously damp, muddy and fever racked location. Indeed, in 1785 the Mississippi nearly eradicated Sainte Genevieve with a flood so deep the boatmen were resigned to secure their craft by tying them to the chimney tops of their former homes. Once the waters subsided, most people took the hint and built a new settlement on higher ground. In the summer black clouds of mosquitoes bearing yellow fever and malaria habitually plagued Sainte Genevieve. The first of August to the end of September was known as the fever period. Malaria was seldom fatal, though once weakened by it a man might succumb to other diseases such as pleurisy or pneumonia.

Thus was life in lackadaisical Sainte Genevieve, a quiet backwater satellite of Kaskaskia that seemed to have little future. The Americans would change all that. Generally the French Creole of Sainte Genevieve shared their Kaskaskia cousins' sympathies. They viewed Americans with a mixture of alarm and disgust. If first impressions are lasting ones, then their skepticism could be understood. A rude introduction came when fifty American deserters from George Rogers Clark's Revolutionary army appeared at the town in 1778. They were so obnoxious that the Spanish Governor De Leyba characterized them to Clark as "turbulent and lawless fellows . . . going out to assassinate any countryman or soldier from the other side whom they might find wandering around." Americans were seen as hotheads and ruffians, one observer referring to them as the "Whiskey Boys." To the relief of many a proper French citizen, Americans tended to settle away from Sainte Genevieve itself, in the surrounding isolated areas that were more suitable for their unconventionally self-sufficient and independent life style.[1]

It was at about this time that a young, roughly clad teenager appeared in Sainte Genevieve asking for Israel Dodge. His name was Moses Henry Dodge, and he was looking for his father. Henry had been born on October 12, 1782 at Post Vincennes and had hardly known the man. According to the family history, Moses Henry Dodge was raised by his mother Nancy in Kentucky, on that "dark and bloody ground", where the "stealth and treachery of the Indians made the cultivation of the soil extremely hazardous." Adversity would be Henry's life long companion and it made his acquaintance early. Shortly after his birth a band of Piankeshaw Indians looking for trouble stopped at Nancy's cabin. In the course of trying to terrorize her, the Indian headman threatened her baby. The quick thinking of Nancy's neighbor saved the boy's life . . . or so goes the tale.

> ". . . a Piankeshaw chief came in, and said that it could not be allowed to live in their country, and he would dash out it's brains. The mother pleaded for the life of her first born. Moses Henry explained that it was the 'papoose' of a friend of his, while 'squaw' was sojourning in his house-that the child was born out of due time while the young mother was on her way to her people, and that they would soon go on their journey. These expostulations prevailed, the chief at the same time remarking, 'nits make lice; this little nit may grow to be a big louse and bite us . . .'"

43

In gratitude to Mr. Henry, Nancy named the boy after his benefactor. As to whether the Piankeshaw chief ever came to regret sparing the child is not known, but his purported parting remarks would become prophetic.

Another tale, similar to the first as being more consistent with fable than fact, illustrated both Moses Henry's bravery and his later propensity for getting entangled with Indians. As a lad of fourteen, Henry was strolling across the village square one day when he spotted an Indian brave hovering over a prostrate pioneer woman. In his barbarous hands was a butcher knife, with which he intended to lift her fair scalp. Energized by woman's screams, Henry snatched up a stone and struck the brave down. It was a legendary image, symbolic of the struggle between white civilization and Indian savagery, one that yet plays endlessly in the American psyche. Convinced that that the Indians would take revenge on her boy, Nancy sent Henry scurrying for his life. The teenager spent that night in a graveyard, and then linked up with a band of Louisiana bound pioneers. Gradually he made his way to New Bourbon and his father.[2]

It was here where Henry was initiated into the tumultuous world of Louisiana, where malaria, yellow fever and rambunctious Americans posed a greater danger than skulking Piankeshaws. Israel took the boy up readily. John Dodge would not live long enough to show an interest in his nephew. By November of 1797, hardly forty years of age, he was dead.[3] What dispatched him remains a mystery. Israel was living at New Bourbon as a Catholic.[4] A farmer by trade, he had a large cattle herd and was involved in salt mining below the mouth of Saline Creek. As the name Camp Rowdy indicated, it was an American establishment. It would later become the village of St. Mary's. Once Moses Henry matured, Camp Rowdy served as his home while he oversaw Israel's operation there.[5] Having built up some influence among the local Spanish authorities as an interpreter for the local commandants, Israel received a land grant upon which he built mills, breweries and distilleries.[6] When Henry arrived in New Bourbon, Israel was embroiled in a business dispute with one Hypolite Bolon, a long time Louisiana resident and an interpreter for several Indian tribes. In the heat of argument, Israel later claimed, Bolon threatened to have the Indians burn Israel's brewery to the ground and kill him in the deal. Doubtlessly he could have carried out the threat but he did not.[7] Such confrontations were the rule rather than the exception and the rigors of such a life toughened Henry's outlook as he grew into manhood, laboring side by side with his father and the family slaves in the fields, salt works and breweries.

In 1800 Henry Dodge married Christiana McDonald near St. Louis. He was all of eighteen years old. She was fifteen. He may have seen in his marriage an auspicious inaugural to a new life in a new century. The newborn 19th century would bring astonishing and unfathomable changes upon all of Louisiana and the West, and thereby upon the Dodges as well. American immigration into Louisiana continued during the closing years of the 18th century. In 1799 the icon of the American frontier spirit itself, Daniel Boone moved his family to Louisiana. By the new century it was quite clear to Spain that Louisiana was not worth the crown's trouble and expense. It was too vast to be administered effectively. Too late Spain realized their liberal immigration policies had all but delivered the territory into American hands. Any attempt to restrain the wave of Americans pouring into the realm would invite the United States to seize it outright. France's Napoleon Bonaparte provided the solution. He wanted to reestablish France in the New World. In exchange for a few French favors and Bonaparte's promise to preserve Louisiana as a protective buffer for Spanish Mexico, Spain surrendered Louisiana to France in 1800. Disgusted, the Spanish governor Charles Delassus proclaimed as he departed, "The devil take all!"[8]

The news of France's acquisition and the deployment of French troops in the Caribbean alarmed President Thomas Jefferson. While pondering a military alliance with England to counter Bonaparte's ambitions, Jefferson busily negotiated with French ministers to purchase New Orleans outright. Secretly, Jefferson hoped to acquire Louisiana territory in its entirety. Fortunes for Jefferson and the United States could not have been more kind. Napoleon's designs began to crumble. Yellow fever decimated his troops in the Caribbean and it became clear to him that Louisiana was a millstone about his neck. It was costly and vulnerable. To the utter dismay of his Spanish allies, Napoleon authorized the sale of not only New Orleans but the entire Louisiana province to the United States. He could use the money, over twenty three million dollars, to finance his war against the British elsewhere.

By 1804, six thousand out of the ten thousand residents of Louisiana Territory were Americans. There were roughly 1200 residents at Sainte Genevieve and six hundred in New Bourbon, most of them Yankees. Perhaps not so surprisingly, the news of this newest reversal was received with mixed feelings among both Creole French and Americans. Rather than giving a hearty hurrah for the stars and stripes, many American immigrants fretted over what effect this change would have over taxes and their claims to land under the old Spanish grant system. Given previous conflicts in Illinois, it could be assumed that Israel was counted among the fretters. The new American territory would be under the jurisdiction of Indiana Territory and Governor Henry Harrison. Many Louisiana Americans no doubt welcomed annexation, but Captain Daniel Bissell taking charge for the United States at New Madrid noted the locals expressed "the greatest grief" at the prospect of American rule. Israel and Moses Henry were on hand for the ceremony of transfer that March of 1803. Israel himself raised the Star Spangled Banner over Sainte Genevieve. If they both had their doubts, they never admitted it.[9]

The transfer proved a boon for the Dodges. Israel was appointed first sheriff of Sainte Genevieve. His son Moses Henry was made deputy. Inevitably, Henry's good fortune was darkened by tragedy. In 1802, Christiana gave birth to their first child, significantly a son. Henry named him Israel. His aspirations for his heir were short lived. Children of that era were especially vulnerable to accident and disease. Israel did not survive. He died in 1804 at the age of two years. Henry would wait through six years and the birth of two daughters before the next heir arrived. By 1805, Henry had succeeded his father as sheriff of Sainte Genevieve.[10]

Irrespective of his official status, Henry's actions were at times reminiscent of his late uncle John's. In March of 1805, Henry Dodge's name appeared on a grand jury list of six men indicted and convicted of assault and battery.[11] Henry would become involved in substantially more serious events of a treasonous nature. The year 1805 would test the man. That test began with newly appointed governor James Wilkinson's arrival at St. Louis.

The fact that Jefferson appointed Wilkinson, a man who had earlier conspired to create an independent state of Kentucky or at the very least depopulate the territory in favor of Spanish Louisiana, was an amazing contradiction. President Jefferson would later regret it. Wilkinson was a protégé of then Vice President Aaron Burr. Jefferson justified his appointment by expressing faith in the enigmatic general's ability to deal with difficulties of running a frontier post. The problems were many and complicated. On top of the political intrigues involving neighboring Spanish and British possessions, there were conflicts within the territory. The Sauk and Fox, earlier ejected by Henry Harrison from fifteen million acres of homeland, had declared a war on the Osage and had attacked settlers they believed were sympathetic to their enemy. Between the French Creole and recently arrived Americans there was an increasingly violent competition for lands, particularly in the lead mining district.

Hence before even stepping foot in St. Louis, Wilkinson was already beset by a myriad of problems. The political positioning by Americans and French for favors from the new governor was well underway before Wilkinson's inaugural reception in St. Louis. Israel and Henry Dodge supported one of most insistent lobbyists, land speculator John Smith T. Smith, a vain and volatile chap who had attached the final letter T to his name in honor of his home country of Tennessee. Like the Dodges,

John Smith T had been busily gobbling up land claims in the lead district and was not hesitant to back up his transactions with violence.

His greatest competitor and sworn enemy was Moses Austin. Austin had been in the territory since the late 1700s and made lead mining for the first time a really profitable affair. Having operated mines in Virginia, he convinced Spanish authorities that such mining would be profitable and in 1797 convinced them to grant him lands in the heart of mining country at Mine á Breton, later renamed Potosi. His efforts paid off handsomely and the rush was on. American speculators in the province elbowed and shoved one another for position in the lead fields. Previously, the mining country under the Spanish was open to anyone who might wish to prospect, but along the principle of exclusive rights and private property, Austin religiously evicted unauthorized persons from mining on his claim. When the late-comer John Smith T. claimed a lead rich tract dubbed New Diggings only two miles from Austin's stake, the stage was set for a fight. Both Austin and Smith actively recruited armed supporters to defend their claims. Hoping to make lead profitable for themselves, Israel and Henry sided with Smith. Indeed, when the inhabitants of Sainte Genevieve filed a petition with Governor Wilkinson in support of Henry for sheriff, it was signed by, among others, John Smith T.[12] Lead country was absolutely simmering.

In short order, Wilkinson found himself embroiled in the dispute. From Moses Austin's perspective, the governor appeared to favor his adversary and proclaimed Wilkinson was no friend of his. Governor Wilkinson did enjoy solid support from John Smith T., Israel, and Henry Dodge, among others. That perception further widened the rift between the two camps. To complicate matters, Wilkinson's mentor Aaron Burr appeared in St. Louis in September of 1805 with intrigue on his mind. After being discredited for his role to have New York secede from the Union and having killed Alexander Hamilton in a duel over the whole issue, Burr's conspiracy for creating a separate nation shifted from New York to the Mississippi Valley. Louisiana figured big in his grand scheme for a Trans Mississippi Empire, once he had managed to seize all of Mexico from Spain. It was a hair-brained plot but one he knew that Wilkinson might endorse. No doubt he was in St. Louis to enlist the new governor's support. He also counted on the support of the Americans who had earlier come to Louisiana and resented the United States' annexation of their territory.

Israel Dodge was probably sympathetic to such a scheme, but wouldn't be fit to be of help anyway. In his mid forties, his health was failing him. The young and upcoming Moses Henry succeeded him as sheriff in 1805 and was probably managing his businesses as well. The year before Israel had granted his son a hefty portion of his farmland at Prairie Gauthier, near New Bourbon.[13] Throughout 1805, Dodge continued to strengthen his holdings by purchasing real estate. Israel was able enough drawn up the plans for a stout jail to be placed on Sainte Genevieve's public square, but it would be one of his last acts. He died a year later in the fall of 1806 at the age of forty-seven, having not survived much longer than his brother John.[14] Henry was the executor of his estate.

On the heels of his passing, more bad news arrived. Jefferson had ignored several memorials signed by Henry Dodge and others in support of Governor Wilkinson and had ousted him. For a time he would be temporarily replaced by Joseph Browne, Burr's brother in law and the territorial secretary. That event didn't deter Dodge and John Smith T from continuing their assault on Austin Moses. At the time, Henry was both Sainte Genevieve sheriff and a lieutenant in the Sainte Genevieve District militia. John Smith T. served as justice of the peace and lieutenant colonel of the militia.[15] In August of 1806, frustrated with failed attempts to straighten out the mining mess, Austin was ready for a full scale war with Smith at Mine á Breton. When Sheriff Henry Dodge and John Smith T, presumably in an official capacity, showed up at the mine, Austin's militiamen fired a volley over both men's heads, causing Smith's horse to rear and throw him. Once reseated in the saddle, Smith demanded to know what the hell they were up to. Sarcastically, the men replied, "Mustering."[16]

At the close of December, 1807 Henry Dodge received news that Aaron Burr had put his scheme into motion. He and a hundred-man filibustering expedition were proceeding down the Ohio River. The expedition reached New Madrid on January 1st. Burr planned to move up the river to St. Louis to enlist support. Henry and John Smith T eagerly started with a group of would-be recruits to meet him in St. Louis. In route, their plans took an abrupt about face. News that Jefferson had issued an arrest warrant for Burr, the charge no less than treason, cooled everyone's enthusiasm. Smith and Dodge turned back towards home. A shock awaited them when they arrived at Sainte Genevieve. Both Henry Dodge and John Smith T were served their own arrest warrants, the charge also being treason.

Henry Dodge wisely submitted to arrest. John Smith T promptly drew his pistols and dared the authorities to take him. They did. How Henry reacted to his arrest and indictment is a matter of speculation. Being young and yet impressionable, he may have been horrified. Being a Dodge, he may have been outraged. According to one account, he was so offended at the accusation that after surrendering and posting bail, he "pulled off his coat, rolled up his sleeves, and whipped nine of the grand jurors. Henry Dodge was a tall man, over six feet high, as straight as an Indian, and possessed of great strength. He would have whipped every member of the grand jury if the rest had not run away."[17]

Accurate or not, it was a display of righteous obstreperousness completely consistent with the Dodge character.

Several of Burr's Missouri conspirators would lose their reputations and whatever official title they might have held due to their involvement. John Smith T was removed as Lt. Colonel of the militia and as justice of the General Quarter Sessions, as well as Commissioner of Pleas and Commissioner of Rates and levies for the district of Sainte Genevieve. If not exactly complementary, in Dodge's favor, Frederick Bates, who replaced Browne as secretary and acting governor of the territory in the absence of newly appointed governor, Meriwether Lewis, noted in a letter to Jefferson 1807 that factional fighting in the territory had subsided and that volunteer organizations had been formed to squash any residual treasonous activity. John Smith T had been stripped of official office. Bates recommended that the young sheriff Henry Dodge be treated more leniently.

> "He has not been dismissed because I believe the young man to be innocent... He is young-unhacknied in dissimulation-possesses good sense, spirit and frankness-and I hope, a love of country, and a reverence of its institutions. I do believe he has been misled by Col. Smith, and that, when liberated from the official control which that rash and impatient man has imperceptibly gained over him, he will repay confidence, by a prompt and honorable discharge of duty."[18]

Henry Dodge recovered from his misstep and remained in office as Sheriff of Sainte Genevieve. Legal facilities for upholding the law were meager. Through Israel's efforts there was a stout jail, but there was no courthouse. Court sessions were held in various private establishments, such as the Reverend Maxwell's parish home, or in John Price's tavern. Often they were held in Dodge's own home.[19] During the year of 1806, Sheriff Dodge found himself at acting in concert with the temporary governor Frederick Bates, an ally of Moses Austin, and against newly arrived American squatters. In a writ issued to Henry, Bates instructed the sheriff of Sainte Genevieve County to remove one John Harvey from his illegal homestead. Dodge investigated and wrote back "I have not found the within named John Harvey, his slaves, or any other persons making any improvements on the Publick Lands near the Mines of Arneau."[20] Between 1806 and 1807, Henry Dodge served as Lieutenant and Adjutant in the Sainte Genevieve Militia and then was appointed first Lieutenant and then Captain of the Sainte Genevieve troop of cavalry. He also displayed increasing interest in community affairs and politics. In 1807 he signed on as a subscriber to a new school in the town, Sainte Genevieve Academy, donating what was then a large sum of $75. When the school was incorporated the following year, he served on the board of trustees.[21]

By 1810, Dodge's future looked bright. He had inherited Israel's substantial estate. He had been able to shrug off accusations of treachery and treason with little ill effect. He'd survived flood and fever, not to mention the heated competition with Austin over lead. Henry was firmly established as a successful entrepreneur, a prosperous landowner, an influential citizen and a political infighter to be reckoned with.

6

SAINTE GENEVIEVE

On April 1st, 1810, Christiana Dodge gave birth to their third child and first surviving son, Henry Lafayette Dodge. After little Israel's premature death, two girls had followed; Nancy Adeline born in 1805 and Louisiana in 1808. Henry Dodge named his son Lafayette to honor his late grandfather Israel's admiration for the Marquis. In later years, it would be a name Henry Lafayette apparently came to dislike, acknowledging it only when necessary with the middle initial "L." As the eldest surviving son, Lafayette was first in line to inherit his father's name, fortune and legacy. He had one other brother would survive to adulthood, Augustus Caesar Dodge, born two years later. Over the next twenty years, Christiana would bear nine more children.

Henry Dodge had been appointed by acting governor Frederick Bates to conduct the census for the Sainte Genevieve district. Sheriff Dodge counted 4,620 inhabitants. American names represented a substantial portion of the district residents and their numbers were growing rapidly. It was a young and dynamic population. A full third of them, now including Dodge's own newborn son, were children under the age of sixteen, while those over forty-five years numbered barely three hundred. Nearly a fourth of the inhabitants were black slaves. Slavery had long been a part of Louisiana life prior to American annexation and continued to be represented in the farms and fields, in the lead mines and on the scaffolding of American-styled buildings being erected throughout the town.

In many ways, the Sainte Genevieve that Henry Lafayette came to know as a child appeared little changed from what his grandfather Israel had first seen. Due to its typical rambling French layout, from a distance the settlement appeared larger than it really was. At once cluttered yet paradoxically open, Sainte Genevieve was a patchwork of widely spaced residences, each one surrounded by a farm yard of private gardens and orchards, stables and barns and outbuildings, all enclosed by cedar picket or stone fences. Homes were built to endure rain, flood and steamy heat. They were constructed in the tropical fashion of the West Indies, *poteaux en terre* or post-in-ground, to slightly elevate the structure enough to lift it above high water . . . hopefully. The homes were one-story affairs, the walls constructed of vertical logs, chinked with adobe and properly whitewashed. The roof extended out beyond each wall, much like a wide-brimmed sun hat, to form a covered porch to protect from rain and snow in the winter and to soothe with cooling shade and breezes in the summer. Windows were scarce and glass windows scarcer. The less well-to-do inhabitants had to be contented with windowpanes of oiled skin or cloth. Homes were lit and heated by one or two fireplaces. In most houses the furnishing was austere. There might be a bedstead and bedding, some rough tables and chairs, a modest cupboard and a clothing chest.[1]

The narrow, rutted streets that meandered from one picketed farmyard to another wove these homesteads into the community tapestry. The rapid growth of population had fairly choked Ste. Genevieve's primitive avenues. In fair weather they were a cacophonous, dust-choked warren of merchants and hawkers, ore-wagons, mules, chickens, pigs, dogs and occasionally an abandoned cart plow or dead steer. In wet weather they deteriorated into such quagmires that pedestrians were obliged to take a horse for even the shortest of trips. Farming family plots in the Bois Brule river bottom, or what had become known as the American Bottom, remained the primary way of making a living for many in Ste. Genevieve. Both French and American farmers made the pilgrimage to the bottom for April plowing and planting, driving their stock and plows and oxcarts and slaves in the damp spring mornings.

By the time Henry Lafayette was old enough to run through those streets, the industrious Americans who called Ste. Genevieve home had dramatically transformed it. Where once the self-sufficient French had no need for a store, by 1811 there were no less than six of them. The American innovation of signs advertising each new establishment clustered along the walks and shingles hung from the storefronts. There was a large brickyard, a church and, on a rise the uncompleted edifice of a new school, the Sainte Genevieve Academy. On one end of the frenetic center of town stood the Southern Hotel, an American style two story brick building owned by John Donohue, boasting a billiard hall where spirited gambling went on around the clock. One impressed visitor remarked that he'd never seen a place where so many endeavored "with so much spirit and perseverance to win each other's money." Merchants, farmers, fur trappers, lawyers, doctors, boatmen, bureaucrats and lead miners—all congregated at the Southern for card games.[2] Given Lafayette's later propensity, one might suspect that he'd spent too much time as a youngster peering through the hotel windows at the gamblers. An early intimacy with the center of Ste. Genevieve came easily for him. He was a short dash across the main square from his own home, a comfortable two-story that became known as the Old Brick House. The family household proper was on the upper story. The lower story served as his father's sheriff office and on many occasions the town courthouse.[3]

In addition to transforming the town, Americans had revolutionized the traditional patterns of French farming along the American bottom. Driven by the Protestant moral, spiritual and economic obligation to toil, Americans spent a great amount of time working the fields, increasing their yield three fold over that of the more casual French farmer. Even this success was quickly eclipsed by a more profitable industry, its arrival heralded by behemoths rumbling down the once quiet rural roads; ox-drawn wagons carrying lead ore from the interior to the docks where the Gabourie River met the Mississippi.

This American-driven economic boom had made the old Creole village into the commercial and cultural crossroads of the region. In the stores, the bawdy houses and the banks, along the bottom lands, at the docks and among the keelboats, hummed a symphony of cultures, customs and languages. French yet remained the predominant voice, yet rising were voices of English, Spanish, and occasionally Shawnee and Peoria, all mingled in the daily domestic melody of life in Ste. Genevieve.

As a boy, Lafayette enjoyed considerably more security than had his father. At the age of twenty-eight, Henry Dodge had become a modestly affluent and respected citizen. His business interests were as lucrative as they were diversified. He ran the salt operations St. Mary's Landing on the Saline, formerly known as Camp Rowdy. It was no small enterprise. The operation boasted 100 to 150 rending kettles, each taking about 200 gallons of water to make 1 bushel of salt selling at $1.50, with an aggregate annual yield of some ten to fourteen thousand bushels of salt.[4] He owned a successful farm and cattle herd at New Bourbon, had bought several parcels of land along the river and in town with various partners. By the time Lafayette was ten, his father had bought and sold several home sites in the town, including the John McArthur home on the banks of the South Gabourie, which, along with the Old Brick House, would be a Dodge residence.[5]

Dodge also boasted holdings in the lead mining district; all affording him the luxury of purchasing a few slaves to help with work in fields at Prairie Gauthier. As sheriff of Sainte Genevieve County, Dodge also drew a salary. In addition, the county paid him a stipend for holding court in his home.[6] When, on June 4, 1812 Upper Louisiana was officially made the Territory of Missouri, Dodge was appointed United States Marshall. Doubtlessly his wife Christiana and children Nancy, Louisiana, Lafayette and the infant Augustus, were well provided for, although given his father's preoccupations, Lafayette probably didn't know the man's face particularly well.

This is not to say that living in Sainte Genevieve did not have its hazards. There were serious injuries from the rigors of farm and mining work. Children were particularly susceptible to diseases such as whooping cough, scarlet fever and pneumonia in the winter, while malaria and yellow fever were a constant threat during the summer months. The weather of the region could be brutal. With the humidity of the river valley, temperatures in July and August were often positively scalding. In contrast, winters might be exceedingly cold. In January of 1811, after a spate of unusually warm weather, the temperature plunged to minus 10 degrees. Twice during that winter the Mississippi was locked solid in ice. Such extreme conditions were infrequent, however. Writing as a visitor in 1818, Henry Rowe Schoolcraft noted that the climate of Ste. Genevieve could usually be counted on to be comfortably mild.[7]

There were also the unanticipated calamities. Yearly floods that replenished the American Bottom could as easily inundate field, farm and town. Then there were the earthquakes. Ste. Genevieve, clinging precariously along the Mississippi, rested just north of the New Madrid Seismic Zone. Between the months of December 1811 through February of 1812, several intense tremors, some as severe as magnitude 8, tore through the area, leveling trees, and rattling the landscape, for a time driving the Mississippi northward and ringing church bells as far away as Charleston and Boston. Predictably, New Madrid was hardest hit, while Sainte Genevieve suffered little more than some fallen chimneys and jittery nerves. Given the wide spread destruction, there was surprisingly little loss of life. Nevertheless, it was an unforgettably terrifying event.

The more mundane emergencies a young lad might experience, such as a broken toe, a slashed thumb, stomach cramps, cough or fever, were generally attended to at home. There were very few trained doctors in the territory. Mothers and grandmothers were the usual doctors and their skills, though at times highly esteemed, were limited to folk remedies such as homemade liniments, poultices and herb teas of questionable effectiveness.

Competent educators were also a rare commodity. Evidence of Lafayette's early education is illusive, though considering his later polish in writing and his father's steadfast support of education, it's reasonable to assume he was schooled. Schooling opportunities in the countryside were severely limited. Sainte Genevieve had had the good fortune of having schools from an early time. During the years of Spanish occupation, there had been a primary school, although it was closed in 1799.[8] In 1808, Henry Dodge and other prominent Sainte Genevieve men had attempted to create the Sainte Genevieve Academy, the first legally chartered school in the territory. It was an altruistic undertaking. The school would not only provide a general education, but school the indigent poor and Indian children for free. Basic instruction would stress reading, writing, spelling, and ciphering, with grammar and geography for the more gifted students, while French and English would be used throughout instruction.[9] The front edifice was eventually completed, but due to lack of government or private funding, the academy stood unfinished for years.

A more common form of education in American Missouri was the subscription school, where groups of families would contract and board any teacher who could be convinced to relocate to their remote outposts. The school year by necessity fit around the rural lives of the children, in session for most the winter and some of the spring, when the students weren't needed on the farms. Generally an educator's qualifications had to be taken at his word. The parents might believe they'd hired an educator, only to discover they were subsidizing a fraud. During a tour of the area, the Baptist missionary Timothy Flint wryly noticed the distasteful habit these would-be professors had for 'puffing,' the art of exaggerating much out of nothing. William S. Bryan described drawbacks of this system in his history of Missouri pioneer life.

> "... Now and then some pretentious pedagogue, with the title of professor, and pretending to be able to impart a knowledge of most of the languages and all the sciences, would straggle into a community and teach a three or four months' subscription school, in some disused cabin, hastily furnished as a school house, with split log benches and puncheon writing desks. To this 'academy' the youth of the community would be sent, to study

a little, and play a great deal more, while the teacher slept away the effects of too free an intercourse with his whisky bottle-for they nearly all drank freely."[10]

Clearly Lafayette had a smattering of formal education, more so than his influential father, who only wrote well enough to get his message across. In lieu of actually attending a school, Lafayette may have received the bulk of this education through a tutor, like many other local children. Although his sisters may have been educated as well, the common belief of the times was that a girl's complete education was mastering cooking, washing, spinning and weaving and being able to read the rudiments of the Bible.

In 1815 boys of the more prominent citizenry had an opportunity to attend a boarding academy just south of town called The Asylum. Contrary to the present-day connotations of its name, The Asylum was a first rate institution. It was founded by Dr. Joseph S. Hertich, a native of Switzerland and enthusiastic advocate of Pestalozzi methodology. Prior to opening his school, Hertich had run a store in Ste. Genevieve and tutored children in Israel Dodge's household. He was paid by Henry Dodge, as administrator of Israel's estate, "for his Services as Teacher—$50.00."[11] A gifted tutor well versed in the classics and fluent in French and German, Hertich molded a curriculum of stringent moral and academic standards with intellectual discovery. Before it closed in 1840, the school would graduate many future luminaries of Missouri, including Lafayette's little brother Augustus Caesar Dodge. When The Asylum first opened, Lafayette would have been five years old, so he may have had a brief opportunity to attend but, if he did, no record of it apparently survives.

If formal schooling gave young Lafayette valuable skills, his informal education proved all the more practical. The fields, streets and docks of Sainte Genevieve were his tutors. His childhood, though perhaps not as adventurous or daring as his frontier peers homesteading the interior, was entertaining enough. In day-to-day contact with the folk of Sainte Genevieve, he picked up aspects of French language and temperament, as well as Spanish. He became familiar with Indians. Groups of Shawnee, Delaware, and Peoria, driven from their lands by settlers, had settled around Ste. Genevieve, so Indian children were common playmates of Creole and American children. As a lad, Moses Austin's son, the famed Stephen A. Austin of Texas independence, romped with Shawnee chums at Mine à Breton. At Sainte Genevieve, Indian sidekicks taught a young Henry Brackenridge the bow and arrow. Henry's father in Pittsburgh had sent him to Louisiana purportedly to learn French and may not have approved his more indigenous tutoring. When fur trader Auguste

Chouteau's nine year old son Aristide was sent to school in Montreal, he became so lonely for his Indian playmates that he asked his father to send him his bow, a quiver of arrows, and his moccasins.[12]

The harbor on the Gabourie provided an interesting learning experience for a boy. It was a hectic place, with keel boats departing with the products of the area, whiskey and flour, corn, beef and pork, salt, butter, lumber and lead. The docks were a nest of conflict, where idle oarsmen and vagabonds spent their time drinking and gambling and fighting and engaging in such contests as trying to shoot objects off of one another's noggins. It was said that profanity was prolific, particularly among the Kentuckians. To a young lad like Lafayette, such an education was not only more practical, but infinitely more entertaining than enduring the drone of a pedantic pedagogue.

Early on Lafayette learned, as all boys did, an essential life skill; standing up for oneself. Doubtlessly, the political and economic struggles that characterized the country reinforced the importance of that lesson, for they certainly challenged the fortunes of his father and the family. Upper Louisiana had long had a reputation for being roughneck country. Settlers who came to the area were a tough and independent lot and so were their kids. They took immediate and volatile offense to any act perceived as trampling on their rights. Boys asserted their independence . . . with knuckles if need be . . . almost as soon as they could stand upright. Parents encouraged young boys to fight and praised them for their scrappiness. Henry Rowe Schoolcraft noted that the little ruffians not only resorted to fisticuffs, but frequently stabbed one another with pocketknives. Rather than punishing the boys, the older folks lauded it as "a promising trait of character." Schoolcraft was appalled.[13]

Predictably, fights among men were common place. It was as much form of entertainment as self defense, often the result of a favorite pioneer beverage, whiskey. Most settlers kept a small still and they drank without apology on most every occasion . . . men, women and children. Whiskey was abundant and most believed drinking it encouraged good health. A visitor coming to the door could expect to be welcomed with a draft from a gourd or horn cup. The failure to make such an offer was considered an insult. Men in local militias were enticed to show up for muster with a communal whiskey vat. Once drill was out of the way, the men, each armed with a long straw, squatted around the vat and drank themselves into a stupor.[14] Once the whiskey had sufficiently compromised inhibitions, fights inevitably erupted. The preacher Timothy Flint observed that the settlers were never happier than when engaging in "a scrimmage."

"... they generally devoted the day to the improving exercise of mashing noses, bruising faces, and gouging eyes; and it was an unusual thing for one of them to live to middle age without the loss of an eye, the disappearance of sundry teeth, or the total wreck of a nose."[15]

Lafayette's father certainly did not shrink from giving an antagonist a sound thrashing. A later daguerreotype of him in his dotage gives convincing testament to that fact, one that earlier portrait artists had graciously omitted. Henry Dodge had clearly had his nose busted. Repeatedly.

If at all possible, when the sultry summer arrived, people abandoned steamy Ste. Genevieve for the cooler interior of lead country. Westward from the Mississippi bottoms, the land pleasantly rose into a broken and rolling landscape cut by rivers and smoothed by lush valleys. Unconquered forests of sycamore, elm, mulberry, oak and yellow pine obscured the sky above and laid a deep, cooling shade over the ground below. It was feral land thick with daunting tangles of vines and shrubs. For those settlers who persevered, the countryside was a storehouse of natural harvests. Wild grapes, cherries, thorn berries, crab apples, walnuts and hazelnuts all grew in abundance. The hills were occasionally crowned in limestone cliffs that afforded majestic views of the Mississippi valley below. In Brackenridge's words, this exceedingly wild, picturesque and romantic land was the Lead District.

For all its charm, the essence of the violence and profanity that often characterized life in Louisiana Missouri could be readily observed in the Lead District and was therefore no place for a young lad. Schoolcraft described many of the early American miners as renegades or refugees from justice and that the mines were a scene of constant riot, disorder, depravity, and atrocity. Eventually the lower echelons of the riff-raff were driven off, but the mines continued to be a hotbed of strife.[16]

Under the French mining had been a seasonal pastime, a small endeavor, excavating with tools no more sophisticated than a pickaxe, sledgehammer and wood shovel. It was excruciatingly hard work for modest return. Miners burrowed until they struck a promising ore body or until the hole became too deep to throw more dirt out, at which time they moved to a new spot and began again. These prospectors were primarily French Creole, who, a sarcastic John Bradbury noted, "if I may judge from a single instance, retain as much fondness for showy dress as the most fopping of their ancestors."[17] Those fortunate enough to find a profitable ore body sold it to the owner of the land, usually for two dollars for every hundred pounds. The landowners extracted the ore in primitive smelters, another open pit into which logs and ore were thrown together and fired. That was under the best circumstances. More often than not, the individual prospector went away frustrated and disappointed.

The Americans were the first to make a real business of it. They soon demonstrated the profitability of year-round excavation, deep shaft mining and the use the more efficient ash and reverberating furnaces. By the time the United States took possession of the territory, there were at least five important mines being worked in the Missouri area as well as numerous small ones. Moses Austin started the first of these large operations. In 1797 he petitioned the Spanish government for a concession of near 6,000 acres near Mine à Breton and founded Potosi, named after the famous Spanish silver mining town in Bolivia. Austin and many other miners used African slaves to excavate the ore. At first, Austin hired black slaves from their masters, and then later purchased his own.[18] He soon demonstrated to the Spaniards that mining lead could deliver substantial and reliable profit.

By 1812, there were some forty-five working lead mines, including Austin's Mine à Breton, Mine Belle Fontaine, the Richwood Mines, Old Diggings and New Diggings and Elliot's Diggings. Most of the miners believed lead mining was essentially a healthy pursuit. The mines themselves might be polluted, but surrounding areas were riddled with fresh springs and creeks, while the airy and elevated terrain was free of the diseases commonly associated with the American bottom. Whether they recognized the potential toxicity of their labors or not, there was plenty of evidence of it around them. Smoke from the open furnaces belched out poisonous arsenic and sulfur and it wasn't uncommon to witness animals suddenly keel over dead.

> "There are, however, some losses annually sustained by the inhabitants of the mine tract, from the death of cattle, who die of the *mine sickness*. Cows and horses are frequently seen to die without any apparent cause. Cats and dogs are taken with violent fits, which never fail in a short time, to kill them...."[19]

That didn't deter the miners. Lead was always in demand in the East. It was shipped down to New Orleans or up the Ohio to Philadelphia and New York. Amazingly versatile, lead was used in oil paints, bullets, roofs and for lining bath tubs, house gutters and pipes, printers' types, glaze and enamels; buttons; boxes, weights; measures; toys; and castings.[20] The returns were well worth the risks.

But of all the dangers of lead mining, the greatest peril came from fellow miners. As word of the fortunes that could be made spread, both French and their

Johnny-come-lately American neighbors began to vie for ore-bearing lands. On many an occasion, claims real or imagined were vigorously defended, as Amable Partenay discovered. Having obtained a lease to a claim from the United States Government, he went out into the lead mines to stake his claim. No sooner had he put the notice up, a Mr. John Scott, Esquire promptly tore it down. He demanded that Partenay show him proof of authority, making use of "the most abusive Language at the same time, as well to Government as myself." John Scott was a lawyer who had moved to Ste. Genevieve from Vincennes in 1805. A graduate of Princeton, he was known to accent his logical and concise arguments with "genteel profanity."[21] Scott refrained from pummeling him only because Amable had taken the wise precaution of bringing two strapping men with him. On his next foray, a more confident Partenay went alone ... to his regret.

> "Yesterday, however, while I was by myself, peaceably riding through said Mines, in quest of a chain-carrier as I had began surveying, I was surrounded by Jno Scott and others, forcibly dragged off my horse, knocked down with a stick or club, and beat in a most shocking manner with clubs & sticks-John Scott who was the ringleader observing 'that was the way he would give possession.'"[22]

Henry Dodge held interests in lead mining, primarily in the Shibboleth Mines, located about ten miles from Mine à Breton in the hill country around Potosi. In partnership, the company of Dodge, Wilson & Craighead bought Shibboleth for six thousand dollars from the discoverers, then applied to the government land recorder, Frederick Bates, for a lease to legally mine. Dodge's first petition was approved in August of 1811.[23] That year Mine Shibboleth yielded five million pounds of crude ore, with an amazing net product of 3,125,000 pounds of lead, making it one of the richest mines in the area.

So it was particularly vexing that John Smith T claimed Shibboleth Mine as well, that he had secured it under a Spanish grant.[24] He asserted he'd actually leased the mine to Dodge.[25] Smith T promptly sued Dodge for trespass. To drive home his point, he had smelting furnaces erected on the land and installed his armed workforce of woodcutters, teamsters, blacksmiths, diggers and smelters.[26] Although Dodge and Company were supporting the miners, they instead were persuaded to deliver their ore to Smith T as the actual proprietor. In the end, Frederick Bates upheld Dodge's lease and ordered Smith off the property. Accepting the frustrating precedent that "possession was nine-tenths of the law" and knowing he'd be lucky to oust Smith, Henry petitioned to get out of the lease, claiming the United States had failed to protect what Dodge considered legally his. The damned government was asking far too much rent, anyway.

Henry Dodge's experience with Shibboleth Mine was the rule rather than the exception. Much of Dodge's activities at Shibboleth are outlined in a liturgy of lawsuits for trespass, which he brought against those who he saw as encroaching on his claim. Court dockets for the period overflowed with such suits. Dodge, Wilson and Craighead were targets as well, being sued by the Land Office for failure to pay what Recorder of Land Titles Frederick Bates estimated as about ten thousand dollars rent on his holdings at Shibboleth.[27]

Litigation was not the exclusive or final means of settlement. One could seek redress through the barrel of a pistol. When Bates had ruled in Dodge's favor, the trigger-happy Tennessean challenged the recorder to a duel. As one contemporary historian noted, Smith T was "as polished and courteous a gentleman as ever lived ... and as mild a mannered man as ever put a bullet into the human body." John Smith T was reputed to have killed several gentlemen in duels. Frederick Bates simply declined to be included in that list, brushing him off the way one would dismiss an irritating brat.

Such a challenge was a serious matter and dueling at all levels of government and society was common. It was the respected and respectable method expunging the blemish of some insult on one's honor. It was an honorable act, engaged in by the most honorable citizens. Of the many shootings, the most notable Missouri duel occurred in 1811, between the lawyer Thomas T. Crittenden and the well-liked Dr. Walter Fenwick, both of Sainte Genevieve, in which Henry Dodge was a second. The meeting took place on October 1, 1811, on Moreau's Island opposite Kaskaskia. It seems that the object of Crittenden's anger was not the good doctor at all, but his brother. As an honorable man, Dr. Fenwick took up the challenge to his brother. It was a fatal mistake. Crittenden shot him and Fenwick died the following day.[28]

In spite of a set back or two, Henry Dodge's investments in the Lead District, the American Bottom, and in the heart of Ste. Genevieve, grew and prospered as the territory prospered. Of course, all those business investments required a hefty amount of capital, and like so many others, Dodge borrowed heavily to finance his enterprises, piling up a debt that would very nearly be the family's undoing.

7

A NASTY LITTLE WAR

On June 4th, 1812, Congress and President James Madison granted upper Louisiana second-class territorial status. The grant provided for a territorial government, complete with a Governor, a legislative council and a three-judge superior court. Madison and the Senate selected John Scott as one of the members of the council. The people celebrated the act enthusiastically. Upper Louisiana had officially become the Territory of Missouri.[1]

The term Missouri was derived from the Indian tribe of the same name, roughly meaning "Town of the Large Canoes."

Two weeks later, the United States Congress formally declared war on Great Britain. Clearly unprepared for the conflict, the young republic experienced several serious setbacks almost immediately. These initial misfortunes alarmed Missourians, who suddenly felt utterly vulnerable to attack. They didn't fear British invasion and occupation. The region's isolation made that unlikely. Missourians feared the Indians. Tribes up and down the Mississippi and Ohio had remained steadfast allies of the British, understanding that the Americans had no place for Indians in the new country they were forging. In every practical sense, for the Indians and Americans of the Mississippi Valley, the War of 1812 began in 1804, when Old Glory was first hoisted on a Louisiana flagstaff.

For Henry Lafayette Dodge, contact with Indians would be a perpetual and formative experience and that contact began early in his life. Indians had long been an important part of a Missouri economy that revolved around the profitable fur trade. True, there was friction between Indians and whites, almost universally aggravated by Western civilization's inevitable bequest to native peoples—alcoholism. In 1792 Francois Valle complained of drunken Delaware threatening residents at the Saline, where they'd killed a calf and several pigs. In 1802, the people of New Bourbon petitioned the local commandant to stop the Peoria from coming within three miles of the town because of drunkenness and thefts of food. Perrin du Lac described the Delaware who came into Ste. Genevieve as "entirely destroyed by war, smallpox, and especially by strong liquor."[2] All the same, hostile behavior by the Indians was rare and paled in comparison to the violence rowdy miners or profane boatmen were capable of inflicting. It was far more common for Indians to peaceably enter the settlements and mining camps to trade furs, food, moccasins or other commodities. It was in their mutual interest. Granted the traders did not view Indians as their equals, but neither did they view them as animals worthy of extinction.

Indians had been living in the Mississippi Valley some 12 millennia before Europeans arrived. With the introduction of maize farming from Mexican civilizations in Mexico, the area's population exploded and civilizations arose. The Adena and Hopewell cultures were farming before 500 B. C. and had reached their apex between 300 and 400 A. D., their influence stretching from the Atlantic seaboard to the Great Plains. The Mississippian civilization commanded the region from 700 A.D. through 1500 A. D., erecting hundreds of trading centers and towns, each dominated by lofty temple mounds that centuries later would still brood down at the white man's passing flatboats. The metropolis surrounding the Great Mound of Cahokia was estimated to hold seventy-five thousand souls, dwarfing any 19th century American city and many European ones as well.[3] Eventually the far-flung Mississippian culture collapsed. Some theorized that European diseases, passed along the trade routes from Spanish Mexico, decimated the Mississippians long before their last descendants, the Natchez people, actually met a European. The Natchez themselves were effectively wiped out by the French in 1730 and with them the last remnants of Mississippian culture.[4]

When French explorers arrived at the confluence of the Mississippi, Ohio and Missouri Rivers, they had already traversed the homelands of several tribes. The Peoria, the Sauk and Fox, the Kaskaskia, the Illinois, Miami, Wea, Piankeshaw, and the Shawnee claimed lands up and down the river valleys. To the west along the tributaries of the Mississippi and Missouri were the Missouria, the Oto, the Kansa, Iowa and the Osage tribes, all of them horticultural hunters. The tribes vigorously protected their territories. Although they recognized a certain peace through parity—no one group was strong enough to drive another from their land—the Indian nations lived in mutual unease with one another. The American westward movement would aggravate this unease. As settlers overran Indian lands in the east, they pushed the vanquished tribes westward, which in turn displaced weaker Indian peoples as yet isolated from the colonials, who in turn infringed on tribes that at best had only a vague idea of what an American even was. The increasing availability of guns and devastation by disease accelerated this sinister domino effect. The Missouri people successfully defended their homelands around Grand River until the 1790s. After being ravaged by smallpox, the Missouri were so weakened that Sauk and Fox forced them to seek refuge with the Osage, the Kansa, and the Oto.

As a result, the tribe of the "Town of the Large Canoes" ceased to exist.[5]

The American victory in the Revolutionary War had been catastrophic for Indians. Powerful tribes formerly allied with England were ejected from their lands and cast across the Mississippi. In 1780 two hundred Peoria warriors and their families took sanctuary in Spanish Louisiana and settled near Ste. Genevieve. In the Ohio Valley, Louis Lorimier and his Shawnee shared a like fate. Lorimier was a Canadian-born trader with a Shawnee family, and had operated a trading post among them in Ohio. At war's outbreak, he had actually led the Shawnee against the Americans, at one point capturing Daniel Boone himself. It was a fleeting victory. In 1787, Lorimier, his family and roughly two thousand Shawnee and Delaware were compelled to flee the Ohio Valley and seek the protection of the Spanish crown in Louisiana. They, too, settled near Ste. Genevieve, along the Saline Creek south of town.

By 1797, the Shawnee, Delaware, Peoria, Illinois, Miami, Ottawa, Mascouten, Kickapoo and Potowatomie were all present in the territory, all expatriates. Given those circumstances, it is surprising that relations between Indian and white in Louisiana were as good as they were. Predictably, it wouldn't last. As the wave of American immigrants crested the Mississippi, tensions between white and Indian flared.[6] In 1802, thirty Osage warriors attempted to evict Moses Austin's miners from Mine á Breton. The beleaguered miners got little sympathy and less assistance from the nearby French Creole miners who witnessed the event. Moses Austin was their adversary and competitor. After all, the French had no quarrel with the Osage and business was business. To their disappointment, the Osage attempt failed.[7] At New Madrid, Mascouten Indians killed David Trotter and burned his house down after getting drunk on the whiskey he had sold them. The Americans in Ste. Genevieve mustered the militia, but before the Yankees could exact a sure vengeance, the Indians surrendered the murderer to the Spaniards, who promptly executed him by firing squad in hopes of pacifying the outraged Yankees.[8]

With the transfer of the vast territory of Louisiana to the United States in 1804, the Americans took up Indian relations and generally botched them. They had hoped to pacify the many Indian tribes with the promise of trade goods, as had the British, Spanish and French before them. This policy, however effective it had been previously, seemed to simply exacerbate jealousies among rival tribes. When the Americans appeared to favor the Osages, a party of disgruntled Sauks defiantly tied the U.S. flag to a horse's tail and dragged Old Glory through the dirt. They then declared war on the Osage and strongly hinted that they were contemplating an alliance with the hated British in Canada. As if to drive home the point, five Sauk attacked a settlement north of St. Louis, killing three settlers.[9]

Thomas Jefferson appointed the young governor of Indiana, William Henry

Harrison, to oversee the organization of the territorial government and to divest the Indians of their lands. Harrison wasted little time. He met with a delegation of Sauk and Fox and, after plying them with liquor, extracted the surrender of 15 million acres in Wisconsin, Illinois and Missouri. Hypolite Bolon, Israel Dodge's old nemesis, served as interpreter. Conversely, the main body of Sauk and Fox had not authorized the so-called delegates, drunken or sober, to make any such concession. Harrison, who was no friend of native peoples, probably knew it. As a result the infamous treaty inflamed relations between the Sauk and Fox and the Americans for thirty years, culminating in one of the bloodiest Indian wars to scar American history.[10]

By the summer of 1807, American paranoia over the Indian was simmering. Americans fretted that Shawnee leaders were forging a pan-Indian alliance with the British. They were not altogether delusional.[11] The Shawnee leader Tecumseh had nurtured a long and warm relationship with the English and had fought at their side during the American Revolution. When Governor Harrison persuaded a handful of chiefs in 1809 to surrender three million acres of Shawnee land in the Treaty of Fort Wayne, Tecumseh was livid. In partnership with his brother the Prophet Tenskwatawa, he exhorted all tribes to unite, reject American religion, customs and vices, most notably alcohol, and to return to traditional ways. Harrison immediately perceived a greater threat than a simple revival and he would not hesitate to crush it.

Meriwether Lewis, of Lewis and Clark fame, had been appointed to succeed James Wilkinson as the new governor of Upper Louisiana. A manic-depressive, he was hardly the man for ironing out Indian troubles, much less his own. He arrived in St. Louis in March of 1808 and set to the task of keeping the Osage Nation allied to The United States. His efforts did little to soothe the common white man's anxiety regarding his increasingly irritable native neighbors. After Meriwether Lewis blew his brains out along the Natchez Trail, the territory was leaderless and no one else seemed to want the job. The common people were by now in a near panic. News that Benjamin Howard of Kentucky had finally been appointed governor brought some reassurance. Howard was a hard-nails administrator with a military background; just the sort of fellow Missourians felt they needed. By then the Shawnee, the Winnebago, the Kickapoo and Sauks were all openly hostile. Bloodshed soon followed. In July, a band of Potawatomie stole several horses from a settlement. When four of the whites had the temerity to pursue them, the Indians killed them. The spring of 1811 brought more reports of Indian raids. Even the peacefully-inclined Osage were in a sour mood, having seen their lands dwindling and their people debouched by liquor. When Howard finally arrived, he found the entire region in a state of disorganized alarm. He set to work beefing up defenses and ordered the formation of more militia units.[12]

Late fall of that year brought portentous and welcome news. On November 11th, Harrison had delivered a demoralizing blow to the Shawnee at Tippecanoe, defeating and routing the Indian forces of Tecumseh and his brother The Prophet.

So, when it arrived, the War in 1812 came as no surprise to the frontier. In Missouri, it would be a typical Indian war of raids, counter strikes and skirmishes. After Kickapoo and Potawatomie warriors killed nine members of the Neal Family along the Salt River in February of 1812, Governor Howard authorized the formation of companies of mounted riflemen to act as rangers.[13] Nathan Boone, son of Daniel Boone, led one company christened the "Minute Men of the Frontier."[14] When the war broke out, there were only 250 regular U.S. soldiers in the entire region. Their ability to protect the general public was limited at best. After Indian parties attacked several settlements, folks realized they would have to provide their own defense rather than depend on their government for it. Farmers threw up rickety stockades and hunkered down in makeshift blockhouses, primed muskets in hand.

It was that fear and vulnerability that drove Missourians to agitate for upgrading Upper Louisiana to second-class territorial status, expecting it would accordingly upgrade the territory's troop strength. William Clark, was appointed governor. Howard remained in military command, but, to the dismay of the people, no vast influx of troops materialized. In the meantime, rumors abounded that the Winnebago, Kickapoo, Potowatomie, Shawnee and Miami had all declared war on the United States.[15] In hopes of bolstering the territory's defenses, Clark made overtures of friendship to the Osage and the Sauk. One of those to take up the offer was a Sauk fighter named Black Hawk, who would some twenty years later regret his early fraternization with Americans. However, Black Hawk's loyalties proved purely practical. He later defected to the British after discovering that they were offering better provisions.[16]

Although the year of 1812 departed in a shroud of anxiety and depression, the following year saw the American mood brighten considerably. Admiral Perry had whipped the British fleet on Lake Erie. Harrison's forces had forced the British forces to retreat, while at the same time crushing Tecumseh and his Shawnee forces. The Shawnee chief had figured large in the British war effort. It was through his efforts that the English had captured Detroit and Fort Dearborn early in the war. When the British decided to withdraw into Ontario in the face of Harrison's advance, Tecumseh objected. Displaying more honor than his British allies apparently possessed, he then marshaled his Indian forces to protect the Redcoats' retreat. His heroism got him killed. On October 5, 1813, Colonel Richard Johnson and his Kentucky mounted riflemen under Harrison's command charged the Shawnee line at the Thames River and shot the chief dead.[17]

On January 17th, 1814, Henry Dodge was appointed Brigadier General of the Militia for Missouri Territory. He had already been on continuous patrol of the frontier for better than a year. On the day Harrison defeated the Shawnee at Tippecanoe, Sheriff Henry Dodge had been appointed major of the territorial militia, having as early as September of 1812 organized a company of mounted riflemen to protect the settlements.[18] Apparently Dodge's wide-ranging reconnaissance had stirred up little action.[19] That would change when the Missouri Gazette reported that Indians had killed Johnathan Toold and Thomas Smith at Boone's Lick, two days ride west of Saint Louis.[20] In September, General Howard ordered Dodge and three company of militia to relieve Boone's Lick and Cooper's Fort. Dodge's force of 300 included companies from Saint Louis, Cape Girardeau and Ste. Genevieve and some four-dozen friendly Shawnee warriors.[21] Upon arrival at Boone's Lick, they were joined by Benjamin Cooper's local militia. Presently General Dodge's forces overtook a group of fleeing Miami families. Under a promise from Dodge that their lives would be "sacredly preserved", thirty one Miami warriors and better than one hundred women and children surrendered. While rummaging through the Miami belongings, Cooper's men discovered a musket they claimed had belonged to a murdered settler. Captain Cooper demanded the Miami surrender the killer for immediate execution and when they did not or could not comply, Cooper prepared to slaughter them all, right down to the last child. At this point General Dodge drew his sword. Pressing the point against Cooper's chest, he intoned that if indeed that was what Cooper intended to do; he could depend on being the first to pay the deadly consequences.[22] His bold act was less in defense of the lives of Indian than the inviolability of his own honor, having given his word. Cooper backed down. The act did make Dodge unpopular in the Boone's Lick area for years to come, but the incident didn't crimp his military career. He was later re-appointed Brigadier General of the Militia by Governor Clark. From that time on, irrespective of his official military rank, Dodge would habitually be known by the honorary title of General.[23]

The Treaty of Ghent, signed that December, ended war with the British, but not war with the Indians. The sudden armistice dismayed and confused the pro-British tribes, who had believed that England was in the fight for the long run, so some tribes continued fighting independently. As a result, the United States was obliged to treat peace with each hostile Indian nation separately, a long and frustrating process. The war had also been an economic disaster for the new territory. Markets were unstable. Prices fluctuated wildly as the routine of business was thrown into disarray. Specie, which had always been in very short supply out west, was almost impossible to come by. Lead mining in Missouri had all but ceased. Men who worked the mines were either serving in the militia or were hunkered down in some safe spot.[24]

But with the war's end, the bust turned into boom. Settlers, primarily from Kentucky, Tennessee, North Carolina and Virginia, flooded Missouri in immense numbers, nearly all settling in Howard County in the Boone's Lick area. It was a perfect inundation. The St. Louis Enquirer at one point boasted that thirty to fifty wagons or the equivalent of four to five hundred new settlers were arriving in Missouri daily.[25] Land prices skyrocketed and an epidemic of land speculation intoxicated the more astute senses of usually savvy financiers. In 1815 Congress passed a law allowing settlers to exchange up to 640 acres of damaged land for land elsewhere. Speculators bought up many claims, often fraudulently. Even William Clark was besmirched by the scandal. The land rush brought the Indians of Missouri the inevitable consequence. Eviction. Yankee settlers particularly coveted Indian country and frequently squatted on native lands illegally. All efforts by the government to drive them out were doomed at the start. After all, no white militia in the territory would march against its own people in favor of the savage.[26]

After the war, Dodge resumed his varied businesses and his political aspirations. He had been active in local and in territorial politics and, like his peers, had supported petitions to enhance Missouri's territorial status.[27] The act served to bare sectional jealousies. The perfect inundation of post-war immigrants, almost exclusively Southerners, posed a real threat of disinheriting the "traditionalist", the French Creole and their long time American allies who represented the old guard. Heated arguments frequently led to violence. After the future preeminent senator Thomas Hart Benton derided lawyer Charles Lucas as a "puppy", Lucas insisted on the typical remedy. The two duelists met on Bloody Island on the Mississippi, a popular staging area for duels. In this affair, Benton seriously wounded Lucas, but failed to kill him. Unsatisfied, Lucas agreed to a second duel. This time, Benton shot him dead.[28] When Missouri obtained third class territorial status in 1816, more blood was spilled. Auguste De Mun and William McArthur of Ste. Genevieve were enthusiastically competing for a seat as representative to the legislature. Accordingly, they exchanged insults and set a date for a duel, each doubtlessly hoping to narrow the running field. They met on either end of the exterior staircase of the Sainte Genevieve courthouse. Pistols drawn, the two men converged, De Mun heading upstairs and McArthur coming down. When the smoke cleared, De Mun was dead.[29]

By 1816 petitions for full Missouri statehood were already circulating, something the traditionalist opposed. They bitterly recalled that when Missouri achieved second-class status in 1812, not one Creole was elected to the territorial legislature. Their opposition was almost immediately eclipsed by a larger obstacle born in Washington. Congressman Tallmadge's amendment to the statehood bill required slaves born in Missouri to be freed once they reached the age of 25. Southerners, who overwhelmingly represented the population in Missouri, raised a hue and cry over the violation of what they perceived as their constitutional rights. By 1820, there were over ten thousand slaves in Missouri, a sixth of the population; a considerable amount of property.[30] When the House of Representatives approved the Missouri bill in February of 1819, the Senate promptly rejected it and sent it flying back. In response, the House refused to revise the bill. They simply returned it to the Senate and there it sat, good as dead.[31]

Missouri received the news with anguish and anger. Protest meetings sprang up. On August 2nd, 1819, Henry Dodge presided over one at Ste. Genevieve. Finally the Senate struck a compromise. Missouri would be admitted as a slave state and Maine as a free one. To appease the abolitionists, lawmakers restricted the spread of slavery by scribing a line through the old Louisiana Purchase east to west. Territories north of the line would prohibit slavery. Those to the south could approve or reject it. In deference to the South, the law recognized the right of slaveholders to recover escaped slaves from northern states.

On March 6, 1820, President Monroe signed the enabling act authorizing Missouri to make plans for entering the Union. Elections to select delegates to the Missouri constitutional convention were spirited. There were a total of 41 representatives elected. The County of Sainte Genevieve selected John D. Cook, John Scott, R. T. Brown and Henry Dodge. Curiously, John Rice Jones, who had faced down John Dodge in Kaskaskia, was elected delegate from Washington County. Most if not all the delegates were pro-slavery men. After five weeks of work, the convention produced the first Missouri state constitution. General elections were held that August. Dodge's old friend Scott was elected to Congress. John Rice Jones was elected as one of three Supreme Court judges. On the long list of victorious candidates, those with French surnames were conspicuously absent. Indeed, with the exception of John Scott, every traditionalist went down to defeat. They were simply outnumbered by energetic Americans.[32]

8

NON EST

Non Est: Latin: Abbreviated form of the legal term non est inventus referring to a person summoned by the court as being gone or unable to be located. See absconded.

The spring of 1825 brought a significant and poignant event for Henry Dodge and his 15 year-old-son Lafayette. The Marquis de Lafayette, then pushing seventy years of age, had returned to the nation that he had helped build. The Marquis was on a triumphant tour of the United States at the invitation of President Monroe. That April news arrived in Ste. Genevieve that the Marquis would arrive in Saint Louis at the end of the month. On the 29th, a large and affectionate throng gathered at the Saint Louis docks to welcome the old French revolutionary, among them old Israel Dodge's son, Henry. When the Marquis' steamboat docked, Lafayette emerged on deck amid cheers, appearing, in contrast to his bygone aristocratic days, respectably republican and decidedly paunchy. The crowd burst into cheers. Saint Louis gave Lafayette a welcome fit for a true Revolutionary hero. He was praised and feted in unending speeches and testimonials. That evening, a grand banquet and ball were given in his honor at Saint Louis' upscale Mansion House Hotel.[1]

The following day, the Marquis crossed the Mississippi to Kaskaskia as the citizens of Saint Louis bid him farewell amid "scenes of the wildest enthusiasm." None other than Henry Dodge himself escorted the Marquis across the river. It was a tremendous honor to both him and the memory of his father Israel. It is unknown if Dodge's teenaged son Lafayette was there. It would have been sublimely appropriate, and it is hard to imagine that, at the very least, Henry Dodge would have failed to mention the boy to the Marquis, if not actually introduce him. Upon his eventual return to Washington, Congress bid him a final adieu with a gift of two hundred thousand dollars and twenty four thousand acres of land in Florida. Lafayette the sailed back to France in the frigate *Brandywine*, christened to commemorate the battle in which he and a youthful Israel Dodge had been wounded in the cause of Liberty.[2]

For Henry Dodge, it had been a delectably nostalgic diversion. Things weren't going so well in the present. Initially, the economic upswing after the close of the War of 1812 had seemed to guarantee lucrative opportunities without end. One could make a killing in land sales—even if one didn't have the capital to buy it. Most didn't. The Bank of St. Louis seemed particularly keen to loan money for such speculation. The bank was founded in 1813 and primarily backed by, among others, Moses Austin, Auguste Chouteau and the successful fur trader Manuel Lisa. Austin and company expected the bank to stimulate the post war economy and provide the hard cash to get that economy going.[3] Granted, the bank's later policies of offering relatively unsecured large real estate loans was at best imprudent and several of the original founders, including Chouteau and Lisa, quit the bank. They started a new one in 1816, the Bank of Missouri. Although conceived to be fiscally conservative and responsible, the Bank of Missouri also proved unable to resist the seductive allure of large land profits.

For a time, prospects looked excellent. With the surge in Missouri's population, demands for goods and services rocketed. The lead mines were back at full steam, producing more lead than ever before. Aside from his interests in mining, Henry Dodge had resumed his business of salt making at the mouth of the Saline River. He was eager to provide the new Missourians with this one popular commodity in abundance and expanded his operation. The salt works boasted 100 to 150 rending kettles, each taking about 200 gallons of water to make 1 bushel of salt. A bushel of salt sold at $1.50. With Dodge's works churning out some ten to fourteen thousand bushels of salt yearly, he made a fair sum of money.[4] Dodge had also invested in real estate in and around Ste. Genevieve, often in the company of John Scott and Edward Hempstead. For financing, they depended heavily on generous loans from the Bank of Missouri.

By the time that Henry Lafayette was ten years of age, economic conditions in Missouri and for his family in particular were rapidly worsening. Over-speculation on western lands had ignited the Panic of 1819. As with other banks, the Bank of the United States had heavily invested in frontier lands in the hopes of windfall returns. When the bubble burst, the Bank severely restricted credit. As financial panic seized the nation, the Bank of the United States called in loans made to regional banks. The frontier was especially hard hit. As the United States Bank leaned on western banks, those institutions turned around and called in the notes of their debtors, who of course could not pay. The bountiful flood of immigration dwindled to a mere trickle. Crop surplus sales fell. Property values hit rock-bottom. Lead prices plummeted. The precipitous fall in the price of salt particularly hurt the Dodge family. Throughout Missouri and the nation, businesses went bust. The Panic of 1819 killed the Bank of St. Louis and wiped out Moses Austin. From that point, he set Missouri aside and cultivated his dream of colonizing Texas. The supposedly more conservative Bank of Missouri fared little better. It closed in 1821.[5] Things became so desperate that Missourians pleaded for government intervention. There was little the government could do.

By 1820, Henry Dodge found himself haunted by debt and hounded by creditors, most conspicuously the United States Bank, which had taken up Bank of Missouri notes. Even given the fact that specie was nearly unheard of during Missouri's early years, it had become nearly an unseen sight in the pockets of many an entrepreneur. In most parts of Missouri, commodities provided the measure of exchange: gunpowder, lead and furs. The few silver dollars that found their way into the territory were cut into four or eight bits. The more enterprising but decidedly less scrupulous money changers known as sharp shiners would cut a coin into five, rather than four pieces, and pass the bits off as quarter-pieces.[6] Augustus Caesar Dodge, the second son, would recall late in his life:

> "I have frequently seen my father go to a blacksmith shop with a bag of silver dollars, and then cut them up into halves, quarters, and eighths, for small change. My mother made buckskin pockets in his clothes to carry this fractional currency."[7]

The Ste. Genevieve County Books of Conveyances testify to the slump in the Dodge fortune. In October of 1821, to extricate himself and his business partner John Scott out of difficulties with the State of Missouri Loan Office, Dodge sold his two story brick home on the public square. Shortly afterward, he formally purchased from John Scott the home at St. Laurent, in which he and his family had already been living, for ten dollars.[8] Within a few days of that, Dodge mortgaged to the State of Missouri the double two story frame house on the south side of town that he had earlier purchased from John McArthur, along with 2 ½ arpents of land, the old French equivalent of roughly two acres, as collateral for a $1000 loan and interest.[9]

From 1822 through 1825, Dodge unloaded more real estate, including the home and orchard of his late father Israel Dodge, as well as sections of his father's 1000 arpent tract at Prairie Gautier.[10] The year of 1826 proved critical for the Dodge family fortune. In order to cover over two thousand dollars in debts from notes, Dodge mortgaged his St. Laurent house and saline tracts. For a time, the Dodge family continued to reside at the home, but when forced to default in 1827, even that would be taken and sold at public auction for the measly sum of sixty dollars.[11]

It was unlikely that the Dodges would have been thrown out on the street.

Henry was a resourceful man, even if he were a broke one. One thing was certain. It was time to go. Over the years Ste. Genevieve had lost its influence in lead production, anyway. Herculaneum's docks some sixty miles to the north had stolen the old French town's glory. Herculaneum had distinct advantages over Ste. Genevieve. It was closer to the mining country and gave better access to the Mississippi. It also had a modern shot tower that facilitated the processing and shipping of the metal. Although Ste. Genevieve retained its importance as an agricultural and commercial center, Henry Dodge may have begun to feel that he and the place, with its French colonial airs, was being bypassed by Yankee industriousness blossoming upriver.

For some time, Missouri mining had been feeling the pinch of new and vigorous competition along the Mississippi, in Illinois and in Michigan territory. Prospecting and mining in the Fever River region was generating not only excitement, but profits. The northern mines boasted better river transportation, as the country was cut with large rivers. The surrounding country was better for farming, an indispensable part of keeping the mines going. By 1827 the upper Mississippi lead diggings were out-producing those of its southern neighbor. Many a citizen had already abandoned Missouri and cast their lots with the new El Dorado to the north. There was money to be made there, if not in mining then in businesses that supported mining. Land was plentiful there. Unlike Missouri, farm, timber and mineral lands were uninhabited and begging to be taken. All one had do was get rid of the Indians.

Henry realized he was forty-five years old and saddled with debt, a large family and few prospects. Things in Missouri weren't improving much, economically or politically. There was even talk of abolishing slavery. He spent a considerable time preparing for the move, methodically settling business in Ste. Genevieve and arranging a place for the family to stay once they arrived in Illinois. By June of 1827, he had booked passage upriver for his family. They would depart Saint Louis on the steamboat *Indiana*. The trip would be made up river, against the current. His wife Christiana, now forty-two years old, had eight children. There were six girls. The two oldest, Nancy and Louisiana were married and had their own families. The two boys were both in their teens. Henry Lafayette had just turned seventeen the previous April. Augustus Caesar was fifteen. The older boys looked after the younger siblings, all sisters: Elizabeth age 13, Mary age 11, Salina, age 9 and Christiana the tender age of six. With them came their Negro slave family, including Leah, who Augustus remembered fondly as the family mammy. Added to this throng was their accumulated baggage.[12] On the day they departed, the *Indiana* was crammed with passengers. Henry Dodge himself remained behind to tie up lingering details. Many years later, his daughter Salina recalled that he and a company of slaves he'd inherited from Israel made the trip up on horseback from Missouri and through the entire length of Illinois woodland, driving his remaining livestock towards their new promised land.

Dodge had promised the slaves their freedom, once they'd reached their new home. The law of the land as defined by the Missouri Compromise required him to do so. He also promised each of them forty acres of land, a yoke of oxen and a horse. Family legend asserts that he did free them upon arriving in Michigan territory, but the 1830 Census appears to dispute that. Henry Dodge's household was described as having 4 slaves and 4 free colored, ranging from ages under ten to over 55. He was not alone. Other prominent men also held slaves in free territory.

The steamboat *Indiana* had run the route up the Mississippi several times. As early as February 1, 1827, her captain John Newman advertised the *Indiana* as the first steamboat headed for the lead mines of the upper Mississippi. As if to demonstrate the riches awaiting hopeful immigrants to mining country, the *Indiana* arrived at St. Louis that April burdened low in the water with lead. Its first scheduled departure for the mines was on June 7th, with weekly departures following every Sunday morning.[13] In addition to taking on miners and settlers, the Indiana served as a troop transport. In July of 1827, the *Indiana* took U. S. troops from Jefferson Barracks outside of St. Louis to Michigan country to intimidate the Winnebago, who were taking exception to all the miners and settlers squatting on their lands.

How long the trip took depended wholly on the capriciousness of Mother Nature and the Mississippi and on the condition of the steamboat. A bit of good luck didn't hurt, either. Steamboats on the Mississippi were still a relatively new and somewhat distrusted form of transportation. It had been but ten years since the first paddle wheeler, the Zebulon M. Pike, had docked at Saint Louis. They could be cramped, dissonant, sweltering and stinky. Their maneuverability at times rivaled that of a recalcitrant mule. Sarcastic passengers were soon referring to steamboats as "floating bath houses" or "barracks." They were, essentially, a floating pallet of wood with a furnace on it. They caught fire with alarming regularity or blasted to bits by exploding boilers. The year before the Pike's arrival at St. Louis, a boiler explosion had converted the steamboat *Washington*, near Marietta, Ohio, into toothpicks.[14] The Mississippi River was unimpressed by the smoke-spewing, chugging innovation, habitually exasperating the best steamboat captains with fickle currents and a host of unseen but potentially fatal obstacles. Snags and sandbars were a formidable adversary to the steamboat, particularly when the river level dropped. In low water, a trip that might usually take six days upriver could take better than two weeks.

The Dodge family's destination was Galena in northern Illinois. As its name might indicate, Galena had become the center of lead mining for the entire northern Mississippi. Considering how thoroughly unpleasant a trip the Old Muddy might whip up—rough waters, floating trees and withering heat and humidity during the summer, not to mention the swarms of gnats, flies and fever-laden mosquitoes, Christiana and the children's voyage passed comfortably enough . . . until the *Indiana* reached the Des Moines Rapids, just south of present day Keokuk. There the steamboat was stymied by water too shallow to navigate the rapids. It could go no further. Galena still lay 160 miles upriver.

Fortunately, the owners of the *Indiana* had arranged for a flotilla of keelboats to take the travelers onward.[15] Christiana and her nanny, with Lafayette and Augustus shepherding the smaller children along, trundled into a claustrophobic and dank keelboat. The keelboat was actually a covered freighter, up to 70 feet in length and bearing a three to four foot deep hold, and had all the comfort of a boxcar. The cargo cabin had been divided into two sections—one for the men and another for the women and children. Passengers did their best to wedge themselves in among a clutter of mining equipment and personal baggage.

The keelboat's progress upstream depended solely on the strength of the forty French oarsmen making up her crew. When the keelboat passed over relatively shallow water, the crew used their poles to urge her forward. When water grew too deep or the river bottom too muddy, the boatmen stowed the poles and resorted to the cordelle, a stout rope up to 1000 feet long, tied to the top of the keelboat's mast. Unlimbering the cordelle, the crew put ashore, took up the rope in their arms and began to pull the boat upriver. More often than not they were fortified by whiskey. Reeling drunk and swearing blasphemously, the keelboat men coaxed the boat along against the current. They were as course and scandalous a crew as any refined lady and mother might dare apprehend.

The crew made their treacherous, plodding way along the bank, cursing and swearing, slogging through mud and brush and stumbling over fallen trees and rocks. Occasionally the crew had to "bushwhack," or grab trunks and branches to pull themselves forward.[16] When the Mississippi's current proved too strong to pull the boat upriver, the oarsmen were forced to employ "warping." The crew first extended the cordelle and tied it to a stout tree. This precaution prevented the boat with its passengers and cargo from floating back unhindered in the general direction of Saint Louis. With the other end secured to the keelboat mast, the cordelle became the "warp", a horizontal pull-rope stretching from the deck to the bank up stream. Each crewman took his position in a line along the keelboat deck. In unison the oarsmen grabbed the warp and walked in line from the bow to the stern of the boat, pulling on the warp as they walked. As each man in turn reached the stern, he would "break off" and run to the bow for a new grip. This inch-by-inch process of moving the craft went on until they reached the trunk where the keelboat had originally been tied off. Needless to say, it was excruciatingly slow and tedious traveling.[17] If that failed, the oarsmen had to resort to actually rowing the damned thing upstream. At times of extreme good fortune, favorable winds filled the keelboat's sail and glided the craft upstream, but that was a rare event.[18]

Yet on they went. Christiana, Lafayette and the family endured twenty days of confinement in the creaking and groaning keelboat cabin, perhaps in a small way coming to appreciate their forbearer Tristram Dodge's experience on the *Lion's Whelp*. There were no berths or bunks or beds. Christiana and the children slept on one another's shoulders or on the floor. The quality of their meals on this voyage was consistent with the cabin accommodations.

> "During the warm June days passengers as well as the perspiring oarsmen were without ice, vegetables, fruit, milk or cream. Salted meat, sailors' biscuits, hard tack, and black coffee were served for breakfast, dinner and supper. Now and then a band of Indians with venison or game would be spied on the bank of the river and the boat would be pulled ashore to enable the passengers to "swap" beads, trinkets, and salt pork for the appetizing fresh meat."[19]

The voyage continued at less than nine miles a day. Fort Madison just north of the rapids provided the only facsimile of a settlement along the entire route and it offered no accommodations. Each evening the boat tied up along the banks and bluffs of the Mississippi. In good weather, many chose to sleep on deck or on the edge of the forest wilderness. Lafayette and Augustus probably took any excuse to escape the cabin and go up on deck, where the sun still shone, the blue sky arched overhead and the air was not fouled, save by the raw language and odor emanating from the crewmembers.

Several days into the voyage, the Mississippi shifted its course almost due eastward and passed Rock Island. If Lafayette were on deck, the vision he beheld would have mesmerized any impressionable young fellow. On Rock Island stood the mighty Sauk and Fox nation. There were at least a hundred lodges, and hundreds more ponies grazing in the pastures beyond. The Indians themselves must have excited the boy's imagination, decked out in their colorful clothing, head ornaments and wampum. Nine-year-old Salina Dodge remembered the scene quite vividly as the keelboat docked at Rock Island to take on supplies. During the voyage, Christiana and the other passengers had feared "attacks from Indians and torture and horrible death at the hands of the savages" as one contemporary put it.[20] Truthfully, stopping in the midst of the butchering barbarians absolutely terrified them. Little Salina wasn't intimidated, apparently. She remembered seeing Black Hawk himself and may have actually spoken with him. Had she known, her mother Christiana might well have had a stroke.

What seventeen-year-old Henry Lafayette and Augustus thought of the spectacle is untold, but it was fated that they would meet Black Hawk and the Sauk again and sooner than they themselves probably imagined. After departing Rock Island, it would be two more weeks before the Dodge family's voyage would mercifully end. On July 4th, their reeking keelboat crept into the lead port of Fever River and into yet another crisis—the Winnebago Excitement.

Dodge had abandoned Missouri, but he was not forgotten. Despite his absence, the Bank of Missouri continued to press the legal system for some $13,000 dollars they claimed Dodge yet owed them, an astronomic amount by those days' standards. The bank would remain unsatisfied. Warrants were issued to Henry Dodge commanding his appearance in court. With each attempt to deliver it, the document invariably returned to the judge with the Latin notation, "non est" scrawled across it. Dodge was nowhere to be found. He wasn't only one to take refuge from financial woe in Michigan Territory. Several friends and business partners, including Charles L. Hempstead and John Scott took the same remedy for debt relief.[21]

9

FEVER RIVER

Extending from the Rock River in northwest Illinois up to the Wisconsin River in what was then the Territory of Michigan, the Fever River area had been long known for its lead mining potential. As early as 1690 the French soldier Nicholas Perrot was digging around a bit at the invitation of some Miami Indians. Nearly a century later, Julien Dubuque got permission from the Fox Indians to mine lead on the west side of the Mississippi. Little came of these endeavors, however. Contrary to the romantic image of the noble savage, the Indians themselves did considerable lead mining. By 1810 the Fox Indians were extracting some 400,000 pounds of lead out of the area. Apparently they had made the lead trade at Fever River profitable enough to justify having some twenty primitive furnaces in operation. In 1810 Henry Miller Shreve was the first American to take a boatload of lead out of the area. A few years afterwards, George Davenport sent the first boatload of lead to Saint Louis, exciting the interest of savvy Missouri businessmen. By 1821, Saint Louis was receiving modest but regular lead shipments from Fever River country.

The first serious migrations to the area began during the Panic, but the true rush for riches began in 1823 when the United States began granting mining leases in the area. Nine leases were granted in 1823, although there was probably ten fold of that number working illegally. By posting a $5,000 bond, the grantee received 160 acres to mine for three years, provided he paid the United States a tenth of the ore he extracted.[1] It was not unknown for these immigrant miners to bring in their slaves to work the claims.[2] Though not in the spirit of the Missouri Compromise, the existence of slave labor at Fever River may have encouraged immigration from the South. The trickle of miners from Tennessee, Kentucky, Missouri and Southern Illinois began to swell. Between the years of 1825 and 1826 the white population quadrupled, from less than 100 miners to a total of 453, merely a hint of the flood to come.[3] New mining operations sprung up across the prairie like weeds: Hardscrabble, Council Hill, New Diggings, Gratiot's Grove, Wiota, Sinsinawa Mound, Platteville and Mineral Point were but a few of the more notable.[4]

The founding of Galena itself is credited to the arrival of the Meeker immigrants from Cincinnati in 1823. Lead by Moses Meeker, they found conditions there abysmally primitive. There were less than 100 miners and traders and "only one white woman."[5] Prospective miners were leery of moving their families to a place associated with the term 'fever.' Actually, the name Fever River was a corruption of the French term *Riviere aux Feves*, or Bean River. The remedy for this unfortunate misinterpretation was simple. Change the name. In 1827, the settlement suddenly became known as Galena, taking its name from the subterranean commodity that would first make and then break her.[6] It apparently worked. In the spring of that very year, the stampede began. Thousands left from the docks at St. Louis, hoping for a chance at turning their financial fortunes. Galena mushroomed. By 1829, it had a population of around a thousand. The number of white miners in the surrounding area was probably tenfold.

There remained, however, some doubt as to whether the Fever River would live up to its prospectus. During this time, John Atchinson, a lead miner and steamboat man wagered "a suit of Cloaths for Head to foot" with William Hamilton, the son of the slain founding father Alexander Hamilton, that the Fever River mines would produce an excess of 6 million pounds of lead that year. As it turned out, the region produced better than five times that amount and Mr. Atchinson most likely paraded steamboat decks in a new suit at Mr. Hamilton's expense.[7]

Once the hopeful fortune seekers arrived at the lead fields, they lost little time in getting underway with the digs. Miners first staked claims in areas that had been mined earlier by Indians. Some miners searched for the "Masonic weed" to select a claim. Folks claimed the bush was so attracted to lead ore that it could send its roots as far as fifty feet beneath the surface to get to it. Others hunted for evidence of mineral lying on the open ground or on hills that had an unusual feature or shape. Once the claim was staked, the prospector dismissed everything else, such as housing, as of minor importance. Some miners tossed together the rudest homes out of logs, sod or rock. Others contented themselves with dwelling in a hole burrowed on the side of a slope. All energy was spent on the diggings. Primitive tools and methods hampered their efforts, as did the inherent dangers of cave-ins or flooding. Miners seldom burrowed very far into the earth, perhaps a maximum of fifty to sixty feet. Once they reached a vein, the miner used a windlass to descend into the mine, riding in the ore bucket as his partners slowly lowered it. A simple candle lit his descent into the murky and damp depths. Much of this freelance subterranean mining was done horizontally on the belly, hacking away at the ore in a tunnel barely the diameter of the miner's own body.

Yet the mines produced handsomely. The ore a miner painstaking extracted was smelted to produce seventy-pound pigs of lead to be shipped to Saint Louis. Smelting demanded brick furnaces and the furnaces demanded a steady supply of timber. If the miner were lucky enough to have a stream or creek running through his claim, he'd erect a water wheel to run the furnace bellows. Relentlessly, the land was torn up into slag heaps, the water muddied and polluted and the hills and prairies denuded of forest. The pristine countryside rapidly appeared having been stripped clean by ants. It was the sacrifice required to earn a living.

There certainly was money to be made and not just in lead. The U. S. government discouraged farming in lead country, not wanting agriculture endeavors to interfere with the more lucrative mining operations. Therefore, the food the miners and their families required had to be shipped up from the south. Many an enterprising grocer made good profits catering to lead country. When the Fever River mines were struck with extreme shortages during the winter of 1827-1828, grocers extracted up to thirty dollars a barrel for even the poorest grade of flour. Every other commodity in demand, from miner's lamps to mineral spirits, commanded exorbitant prices.

The immigrants flooding into the Fever River that summer of 1827 had graver concerns than merely high prices. When Henry Dodge arrived to join his family at Galena, he found the entire town in pandemonium. The long simmering feud between the Winnebago and the settlers usurping their lands had finally boiled over.

The land so coveted by profit-eager lead miners was, of course, Indian land. Admittedly, individual Winnebago leaders had previously leased sections of land to miners. When Henry and J.B. P. Gratiot began digging ore at the settlement they founded, Gratiot Grove, they paid some Winnebago $500 in supplies. It is doubtful Gratiot ever questioned whether the particular enterprising Winnebago fellow he'd struck a deal with had any tribal authority to do so. The Chippewa, Ottawa, Potawatomi and Winnebago all had claims to the territory between the Wisconsin River in the north and the Rock River to the south. Of them all, it was the Winnebago that seemed to historically have the most damning luck holding their own.[8]

The Winnebago were a sedentary Northeastern Prairie tribe hailing originally from central Wisconsin and had a protracted reputation for being less than friendly.[9] In 1620 the French, in hopes of convincing the Winnebago to join them in the fur trade, sent a party of Ottawa to deliver the invitation. Singularly unimpressed with the French or their messengers, they rejected the proposal in the clearest terms imaginable. According to the French accounts, the Winnebago "ate the Ottawa envoys."

It was most certainly an exaggeration. Even so, killing the envoys ignited a long war with the Ottawa and their allies. As violent competition between the French and British for the fur trade pushed Indian groups westward, the Winnebago clashed with those tribes as well. European-introduced diseases and starvation also reaped a ghastly harvest, purportedly so decimating the Winnebago that a charitable band of Illinois Indians offered to feed them. For all their kindness, the Illinois were repaid with cold-blooded treachery. Some time after feasting, the Winnebago secretly cut all the Illinois men's bowstrings, then slaughtered their hosts. Knowing that the Illinois didn't use canoes, the Winnebago paddled to a lake island for protection. Vengeance, however, is patient. Eventually winter froze the lake and the Illinois crossed over to the island. The Winnebago had fled, but not soon enough, and the Illinois overtook their ungrateful guests, killing and capturing as many as they could get their hands on.

The Winnebago, now near extinction, were finally compelled to make peace and intermarry with their enemies, notably with the Potawatomi, Menominee, and the Sauk and Fox. By the dawn of the 18th century, the revitalized Winnebago had joined the French fur industry and moved westward toward the new trading areas at Portage and Prairie du Chien on the Mississippi. By 1820 they were living in some forty dispersed settlements throughout lead territory. Although they had regained their previous strength, their luck remained abysmal. As most Old Northwest tribes during the 18th century, the Winnebago had first sided with the French against the hated English and paid for that defeat, then allied with the English against the upstart colonists, and consequently paid again. Predictably, they allied with Tecumseh and the Shawnee during the War of 1812 and shared his eventual trouncing. In 1816 Winnebago finally signed a treaty of peace with the United States in St. Louis, but as it turned out, the wages of peace would eventually cost them dearly more than those of war.[10]

The Winnebago well understood the land that white miners were squatting upon had value. The Indians were mining the lead themselves and selling it to white traders for provisions, an endeavor the United States, through their Indian agents, actively discouraged. Uncle Sam wanted the mineral lands and knew the Winnebago would never consent to give them up once they learned the full potential for profits.[11] The tribe's troubles steadily multiplied. With the sponsorship of the United States, in 1821 a group of Oneidas asked the Menominee tribe if they might settle along the lower Fox River on land that was traditionally Winnebago. The Oneida were clearly a long way from their homelands in New York. The American had paid them for their loyalty during the Revolutionary War by evicting them. The Menominee requested this favor from the Winnebago and the Winnebago agreed. The following year, the United States requested more land for the Oneida. This time, the Winnebago balked. Rather than negotiate an agreement, the Americans simply cut them out and secured permission from the Menominee. Further intrusions came in 1825, when the government treated with the Winnebago and several other tribes at Prairie du Chien. The purpose was to "secure" Indian homelands by creating boundaries for tribal territories.

Of course, the true intent and real effect was to divest the Indians of land. Any real estate falling outside those boundaries reverted to public domain, which rapidly filled with white settlers.[12] Homesteaders then squatted on reservation land. Tensions grew to the point of detonation. In 1826, a small group of Winnebago ambushed the Methode family while they were collecting maple sugar at Painted

Rock, north of Prairie du Chien. One can only wonder at the motivation for such a heinous act, but the Winnebago were certainly thorough in their work. The men slaughtered them all—Methode, his wife, their five children and their pet dog. The alleged murderers were soon caught, shackled and transported up river to Fort Snelling near Saint Paul. Believing in their innocence, the Winnebago threatened to attack the settlements if the men were not released. Troops were hastily dispatched from Fort Snelling to reinforce tiny Fort Crawford at Prairie du Chien and the settlers held their breaths. A year passed. The Winnebago men remained incarcerated at Fort Snelling. Nothing happened.

In June of 1827, just as the edgy pioneers were daring to relax, two incidents one right after the other rekindled their fears. The first involved the Winnebago chief, Red Bird, long reputed among whites as the most amicable and trustworthy of Indians. Not surprisingly he had become increasingly resentful of the usurpation of his lands. More specifically he had been outraged by a rumor the Winnebago had heard from a party of Sioux, who claimed soldiers at Fort Snelling had sadistically hacked two of the Winnebago prisoners "into pieces no bigger than the spots in a bead garter."[13]

The story was a blatant lie. Nevertheless, the enraged Winnebago determined to take revenge on the settlers. Whether Red Bird, who was about forty years old at the time, was actually delegated or volunteered to lead the raid is unknown. At the least, he seemed reluctant. After passing up several opportunities to attack various homesteads, he and three men finally struck a French cabin near Prairie du Chien. Some claim they were under the influence of liquor at the time, having been seen earlier leaving Jean Brunet's tavern at Prairie du Chien with a jug of whiskey. Killed outright were Registre Gagnier and Solomon Lipcap. Gagnier's baby daughter was seriously injured. Gagnier's wife and son escaped and fled terror-stricken to Prairie du Chien.[14]

Two days after that attack, came the second incident. A group of Winnebago had fired on the keelboat *Oliver Perry* near the confluence of the Bad Axe and Mississippi Rivers, killing two oarsmen and wounding others. It is agreed that the keelboats supplying Fort Snelling came under attack, but there are various spins on the actual event. One maintains that the two keelboats under the command of Capt. Allen Lindsey were attacked without provocation. When several hostile Winnebago paddled out and attempted to board his boat, Lindsey replied with musketry. The Winnebago then "bequeathed their canoes to him in return and became bait for the fish of the Mississippi."[15] Another version holds that the two keelboats had stopped at a Winnebago village above Prairie du Chien for the evening. The crewmembers feasted and drank rum with their Indian hosts. Sufficiently lubricated, the men either persuaded or coerced seven Winnebago women onto their boats. They quickly pushed off from shore and once on the river raped the women. When the Winnebago men discovered the abduction, they gave pursuit. When the Indians attempted to board the keelboats, a fight ensued and several men on both sides were killed. The women were able to make their escape.[16]

Irrespective of which version was accurate, when the keelboats reached Galena, Lindsey's harrowing tale . . . doubtlessly edited for content . . . spread throughout the town.[17] The response was immediate. The entire population of lead country flew into a white-faced panic. They abandoned their diggings and cascaded into Galena. Mrs. Adele P. Gratiot, a Galena resident and eyewitness to the mayhem, remembered that the wide prairie between the bluffs and the Mississippi was covered with the wagons and camps of refugee families. Men were throwing up blockhouses on the hills. Militias had suddenly sprung to life, companies forming and drilling to the incessant roll of drums.[18] Daniel Parkinson, a recent émigré from Tennessee and later close friend of Henry Dodge, described a scene of complete panic.

> "The roads were lined in all directions with frantic and fleeing men, women and children, expecting every moment to be overtaken, tomahawked and scalped by the Indians. It was said, and I presume with truth, that the encampment of fugitives, at the head of Apple River, on the first night of the alarm, was four miles in extent, and numbered three thousand persons."[19]

Settlers demanded the government send troops for their protection. Michigan Territorial Governor Lewis Cass rushed to St. Louis to plead their case and five hundred federal soldiers under the command of General Henry Atkinson were speedily dispatched on the *Indiana* from nearby Jefferson Barracks. They would not arrive in lead country until July 29th.

In the midst of it all, Henry Dodge stepped up to assert command. He organized a company of 100 mounted volunteers to patrol and protect the mining homesteads. Included in his newly formed mounted militia were his two teenage sons, Lafayette and Augustus. John Rice Jones' son George W. Jones also volunteered. A relieved Mrs. Gratiot noted, "General Dodge was busily engaged in organizing troops and creating order and confidence out of terror and confusion."[20] Dodge's decisive actions were driven by necessity. He too had a family and property at stake.

By this time, apparently Dodge had a claim northeast of Galena at what later was known as Dodge's Diggings, where he'd already assumed a bristling defense. Morgan Martin, in the company of Judge James Duane Doty, stopped by Dodge's Diggings during the height of the crisis.

> "We found his cabins surrounded by a formidable stockade, and the miners liberally supplied with ammunition . . . Dodge entertained us at his cabin, the walls of which were well covered with guns. He said that he had a man for every gun and would not leave the country unless the Indians were stronger than he."[21]

Knowing that Atkinson was in route up the Mississippi, Dodge nevertheless undertook his own expeditionary force into Michigan territory, taking Lafayette and Augustus with him. It was Lafayette's first taste of Indian fighting. General Dodge moved his men up either side of the Wisconsin River just below Prairie du Chien, driving the alarmed and desperate Winnebago ahead of him. At this time Dodge purportedly saved the life of the fifteen year old son of the Winnebago chief Winneshiek, who was very nearly mowed down because he refused to surrender.[22] The general's merciful act may have been motivated by opportunity. Dodge retained the boy as a hostage and had him delivered as captive to Galena, where he was held for two weeks.[23]

For young Lafayette and Augustus, the campaign with their father was brief but exhilarating. Many years later, after time had fermented memories, George Wallace Jones nostalgically reminisced of those days. He was twenty-three years old then and full of youthful manhood.

> "[Augustus] could have told you of his own services when under fifteen years of age, in the Winnebago War of 1827, with his only brother Henry L. Dodge; how he and I campaigned together in the regiment led by his gallant father; of how we slept and sweetly, too, o'er nights, with our saddles for pillows, and resting upon the under saddle blanket, with no other cover than the upper saddle blanket, save the starry heavens; of how frequently we swam rivers together, drawing over them the hastily constructed rafts, laden with men who could not swim; and when at one time for several days our only rations were fresh beef killed and butchered upon the ground, the hard cooked and burnt part being used as bread, we having none of the staff of life, and being without flour to make it."[24]

Salina Dodge's later recollections of that time fairly corroborate George Jones' remembrances. She was but a young girl during the Winnebago crisis. The Dodge family lived in a small log blockhouse complete with gun ports and surrounded by a log stockade and gates heavily barred and always locked. The women and children depended on a handful of "white men and negroes" for their protection. According to her, Augustus was a mere lad nearly unable to hoist a musket. Undeterred, he unrelentingly begged his father to let him join the expedition. Henry finally gave in. Presenting the boy with a small shotgun, he intoned, "Shoot well, my boy." Salina recalled that he fought gallantly in every battle. She also recalled that victory wasn't won before "the women and children in the little stockade had been subjected to many days and nights of terror. The prairies were covered with the redskins and they afterward threatened the stockade and the lives of those entrenched behind its walls."[25]

Salina's tale of savage war and harsh privations were an exaggeration fueled by family lore. There were no battles or hordes of hostiles. Henry Lafayette and Augustus saw many miles of riding with their father's command but saw no fighting. As a war the Winnebago conflict proved a complete disappointment. Red Bird and his followers fled inland up the Wisconsin River, pursued by the combined forces of Atkinson, Cass, General Samuel Whiteside and Dodge's militia. Red Bird's retreat was finally cut off at the Wisconsin portage by federal troops under Major Whistler, who had come up the Fox River from Fort Howard at Green Bay.[26] Hoping to avoid the unbridled slaughter of his people by the whites, Red Bird surrendered. On September 2nd, 1827, he came into Whistler's camp, a white flag in one hand and a calumet of peace in the other. He fully expected to be executed. Lafayette's first sight of Red Bird would have impressed if not awed him outright, for it did most everyone else there. Witnesses described Red Bird's noble physique and his regal clothing in admiration. He wore Yankton suit of white elk skin, fringed and decorated in blue beads. About his neck, a collar of blue and white wampum, with wildcat claws forming the collar rim.

> "As he stood in princely grandeur before the military tribunal, with features as immobile as stone, his direst enemies could not conceal the admiration they secretly felt for him."[27]

For the first time during the entire campaign Henry Lafayette had seen a human face on the enemy. That day he observed two lessons about native justice that would resound through his later years—the law of exacting blood vengeance and the custom of paying of blood money. Red Bird admitted he and his men had killed Gagnier and Lipcap. They had done it in retaliation for the murders of his men at Fort Snelling. He also admitted he had later learned the Sioux had lied. Yet Red Bird adamantly insisted that he had done no wrong.

> "When word came to us that Wamangoosgaraha was slain, I went forth and took meat. I did not know it was false; so I did no wrong. I fulfilled the law of the Winnebago. I am not ashamed. I would not be ashamed. I have come because the white men are too strong and I do not wish my people to suffer. Now I am ready. Take me."[28]

Although the idea of blood vengeance and blood money was deeply imbedded in their Judeo-Christian consciousness, the Americans found the act both reprehensible and incomprehensible. To most Indian nations it was logical. Each tribe held the absolute right to exact vengeance on any member of an offending nation who had the misfortune of being in the wrong place at the wrong time. They equally expected that any tribe they had so injured would exact the same of them. Such convention could spark wars of endless retaliation, and the Indians knew it. A Winnebago thought twice about killing an Illinois if he knew they would retaliate in kind. And retaliate, they would. Failure to exact revenge was an utter humiliation, a sign of tribal weakness and an invitation to be run over roughshod by the enemy. As a result, the fear of blood vengeance encouraged nations to adjust their disagreements without bloodshed.

To avoid a retaliatory killing, the offending tribe might opt to preserve peace by offering a traditional payment of blood money. Red Bird himself admitted that, if he had indeed done wrong, he was willing to pay for it with "horses or my life." A Winnebago leader interceding for Red Bird asked Whistler to favor the prisoners who had given themselves up voluntarily by not shackling them. He also offered blood money payment of twenty horses for the murders of Gagnier and Lipcap. The Americans almost always rejected such an offer outright, to the undying bewilderment of the Indians. They never understood the white man's insistence on hanging someone for a killing, irrespective of the price offered. To them, the Americans were incurably afflicted with bloodlust. True to form, the white men rejected the Winnebago offer of reparations. After brief lecture by Major Whistler regarding the Indians' misbehavior, Red Bird stepped forward. He did not fear great sacrifice, but dreaded confinement and in its place preferred death.

"I do not wish to be put in irons; let me be free. I have given away my life; it is gone." Bending and taking a pinch of dust between his fingers, he blew it away, repeating as he eyed the vanishing dust—"Like that; I would not take it back; it is gone."[29]

He then gave a damning indictment of the Americans. He didn't understand the white's laws, in which there were two versions—one for the white and one for the red. The Americans had promised the Winnebago would retain their lead country, but instead the troops at Fort Crawford had idly stood by as settlers seized it. He noted wryly that if an Indian had seized white property, the soldiers would have showed up lickity-split.

"We have seen the ancient burial grounds plowed over. We have seen our braves shot down like dogs for stealing corn. We have seen our women mocked and raped. We have seen the white men steal our lands, our quarries, our forests, our waterways, by lying to us and cheating us and making us drunk enough to put marks on papers without knowing what we were doing."[30]

Red Bird and his accomplices, We-Kaw and Chic-hon-ic, were tried before Judge James. D. Doty in Prairie du Chien that spring and sentenced to hang on December 28th.[31] Rather than being hanged on the given day, the chief languished for months in his cell at Fort Crawford. Still incarcerated, Red Bird died on February 17, 1828. For her husband's killing, the Widow Gagnier was paid two sections of land and $50 a year for fifteen years, the money paid out of the Winnebago treaty annuity. Thus, blood money was paid . . . in the form of a fine.

So ended Red Bird and the small but tragic Winnebago War. The chief's reputation, at first reviled as a scalp-lifting savage by the pioneers of southwest Wisconsin, would experience among whites a transformation common for vanquished Indian leaders; Red Bird was enshrined in stories, paintings and stage plays.[32]

By the end of September, peace had returned to the mining region. Having been assured of good intentions by the Winnebago, Atkinson dismissed Dodge and his volunteers. They returned to their homes, families and diggings, many of them, including Henry Dodge and family, still residing illegally on Winnebago lands. In July and August of 1829, United States officials would met with the Chippewa, Ottawa, Potowatomie and Winnebago nations to secure further land cessions.

The government promise to pay for the lands gave the sordid transaction some respectability of sorts.[33] Three years later the United States would liquidate the last of the Winnebago lands and send the tribe over the Mississippi into present day Iowa. Ironically, it was land already claimed by the Sauk, who promptly declared war on the hapless refugees. It must be at least conceded that, however bad the Winnebago fortune, it was excruciatingly consistent.

10

CAPTAIN OF AN AGGRESSIVE CIVILIZATION

Rather than discourage immigration into the lead country, the Winnebago affair actually stimulated it. Militiamen in pursuit of hostile Indians discovered along the Wisconsin River a heretofore unknown and attractive country vastly rich in lead. The rush into the area began immediately after Red Bird's surrender. The entire region, as one observer noted, had a "hurly-burly business aspect."[1] In the early fall of 1827, Henry Dodge, his family and a small following of miners relocated some 40 miles northeast of Galena in what would later become Iowa County, Wisconsin. The miners who accompanied him were most likely volunteers who had served with him during the Winnebago affair. In a matter of weeks, other groups threw up sod shanties and log stockades in the vicinity—Daniel Moore and James McRaney and partners, Jesse W. Shull, the brothers Jaff and Louis Van Matre, George Medary, Charles Gaines and company—all staked their hopes in the new lead El Dorado.[2]

It was a beautiful country of mildly undulating prairie land, well watered by springs and streams at every turn and lush in trees and grass. A few miles north of Dodge's claim, the country gradually rose into forested ridges and hills. To the northeast, Blue Mounds emerged from the emerald landscape like an ancient, forest-shrouded pyramid. The lead country was dotted with similar geologic landmarks, most notably the Platte and Sinsinawa Mounds. Stretching from east to west behind Blue Mounds rose the long escarpment later named Military Road Ridge and beyond that flowed the meandering Wisconsin River. The massive glaciers that had previously obliterated the upper Midwest 50,000 years before had spared flattening the Wisconsin River uplands. The prairies rolled gently along, curling up into ridges and hills or unexpectedly dropping off into wooded gullies and draws. Natural springs and fountains seeping from the hidden ravines provided settlers with a dependable source of water. These sudden crevices offered another fortunate attribute. Chunks of mineral ore occasionally peeked out from the cliff face, hinting at tantalizing subterranean veins that lay below. So it was that geological quirk that brought the miners, who would later be dubbed "badgers" for their habit of frenetic burrowing, to settle there.

Henry Dodge's first task was to cement a clear claim to the land he'd selected. There was a slight complication, however. Several months before, Ezra Lamb and two partners, one Mr. Putnam and Mr. Morehead, had staked claims in the area. For Dodge it was a trifling inconvenience. When Morehead angrily challenged Dodge's claim, the unfortunate fellow was summarily ejected by Dodge's gang of miners. Having thusly substantiated their claim, Dodge's followers staked off lots and hastily threw up dug-out log cabins along the hillside. The rude homes were enclosed by a log palisade to discourage Indians and any further interlopers. To further insure their safety, the miners built a blockhouse on a nearby hill to defiantly proclaim their stake over the wild prairie.

It was a prudent precaution. There was no scarcity of Indians in the area—indeed they outnumbered the whites ten to one. It was after all still their country. Understandably, the Indians wanted to know what Dodge was doing there. Martin Van Sickle, a transient trader familiar with the Winnebago, told the Indians that Dodge was quite the important leader among the whites. The Indians must have believed him, for when Henry Dodge approached them one day, the Winnebago seized their muskets and formed a line facing him. It must have been a moment of some consternation for Dodge, facing as it were a potential firing squad. Instead the Winnebago fired a volley into the air as a salute. The following day, Dodge ambled down to the Winnebago encampment along Jenkins Branch where the Indians were smelting lead and making shot. Dodge proposed that his miners and the Indians live together in peace. The Winnebago, he assured them, would benefit materially from that relationship. According to the story the local Winnebago leader Bear struck a deal with Dodge in return for supplies and merchandise. Whether he had authority to do so is doubtful.[3]

The deal materially benefitted Dodge almost immediately. The site around his stockade gave all the promise of supporting a lucrative mining operation. The abundance of ore was obvious and there was a good supply of oak to fire the smelting furnaces. Unsupported by law, he held what miners of the time referred to as "a buckshot claim." The barrel of a gun was all the authority needed to legitimize his claim.[4] The complement of men at the Dodge diggings grew and Dodge rapidly became recognized as a person of substance and influence. By January of 1828 the Dodge enterprise had already taken out three thousand dollars worth of lead and were extracting roughly two thousand pounds a day.[5]

Legally the land yet belonged to the Winnebago and Dodge probably used a combination of bribery and intimidation to insure continued Winnebago willingness to grant him the rights to particular parcels. Concurrently, he sold portions of those parcels to other miners. Business dealings aside, Dodge's relationship with the Indians was tense at best. Salina recalled him regularly plying the local Indian leaders with presents—barrels of flour and sides of pork and such—but their uneasy coexistence was fraught with suspicion and hostility. In one anxious moment, one of his boys, either Lafayette or Augustus, had to intervene to prevent their enraged father from bringing the wrath of the Winnebago down on their heads.

> "I remember one time when a warrior, a tremendous fellow, over six feet tall, came to the house and made resolute demands. Father told him to go away, but the Indian became more persistent and insolent, and Father knocked him down with a three-legged stool. Father lost his temper and was about to kill the Indian, but my brother interfered and prevented this, and it is well that he did so, for if the savage had been killed the men of his tribe would have massacred our whole family."

In another incident, a group of Indians appeared at Dodge's door one cold day demanding food and drink. Henry Dodge's response must have riled them, for they angrily demanded that he leave or be killed. Salina recalled that as emotions escalated, Augustus drew out a sword and pressed the point against the Indian leader's throat. The boy ordered him to leave or die. The group left. The accuracy of Salina's story, told to a newspaper reporter almost fifty years after the fact, might be questioned. As the reporter noted, her story was interesting but hampered by "her memory somewhat dimmed by the flight of years." Salina apparently had no fondness for her red brethren. From her telling the whole family lived in constant fear of being massacred.

> "The prairies were covered with the redskins and they afterward threatened the stockade and the lives of those entrenched behind its walls. Unscrupulous white men would sell whisky to non-combatant Indians, who

hung about the settlements and they would become obstreperous and threaten the lives of the whites."[6]

Of course, any thought of acquiescing to the Winnebago request to leave never entered Dodge's mind. The mines were making him money. He still had sizeable debts in Missouri that even the forced sale of all his property in Ste. Genevieve could not repay. He needed every resource. In his biography of Augustus Dodge, Louis Pelzer noted that Augustus "was earnest and untiring in his efforts to aid his father in the support and education of a large family and in extricating himself from the heavy debts which he had contracted while at Ste. Genevieve." The same might be presumed of his older brother Lafayette.[7] As late as 1831 the Bank of Missouri was filing writs in court to draw some eight thousand dollars from Dodge for his debts.[8] Dodge could ill afford to quit and move on and there was absolutely no way he'd be pushed off by any authority, Indian or white.

The Winnebago had regularly complained to government officials about the miners' encroachments. Winnebago chief Carumna aired his grievances to Joseph Street, their agent in Prairie du Chien, reminding Street that the Winnebago had honored their agreement not to molest the miners at the Fever River. Yet the whites' thirst for lead seemed unquenchable. They had since moved deep into Winnebago land. Exasperated, Carumna wondered aloud why when the Indian ventured onto the white men's land they were promptly driven off, but when the white men usurped Winnebago land, nothing happened. He warned Street that trouble was sure to follow.[9]

Joseph Street responded that, if the Winnebago remained at peace, he would move against the squatters. As one of his first acts, Street resolved to evict Henry Dodge from his diggings. In January of 1828, he sent subagent John Marsh to inform Dodge that he was trespassing on Winnebago lands.

Upon arriving at the Dodge Diggings, Marsh discovered the extent to which the modest settlement had grown. The once lonely stockade was surrounded by twenty or more log homes, with more a short distance away. About one hundred and thirty heavily armed miners were working the site. Dodge's smelting furnaces were in operation day and night. Stacks of lead pigs and unprocessed ore testified to the success of his business. Dodge was also buying off a local band of Winnebago with provisions and dry goods. Perhaps with some trepidation, Marsh dutifully delivered Street's message, which ordered Dodge to abandon Winnebago land, unless he preferred being forced off by federal troops. Henry Dodge wouldn't be intimidated by anyone—not the Indians—not Marsh or Street and certainly not by the troops at piddley Fort Crawford. Dodge replied that he would leave the country as soon as it was "convenient", in other words—never.[10] He then proclaimed, "Let them march, sir. With my miners, I can whip all the old sore-shinned regulars that are stationed at Prairie du Chien!"[11]

Both Joseph Street and Henry Dodge knew that Fort Crawford's garrison would be sorely insufficient to force an eviction and nothing more was done. Meanwhile, the United States pressed ahead to buy Indian lands. In 1829 the Winnebago were coerced into surrendering their final claims to the lead country for a payment of $18,000 dollars and some trade goods. Henry Dodge, who had everything to gain, was one of the treaty signatories. The tribe actually received little of the money. Traders and other whites in the region demanded payment for voluminous debts they claim the Indians owed them. Those claims, fraudulent or not, were consequently deducted from the Winnebago's settlement.[12] With the Indians out of the way, settlements popped up like toadstools; Mineral Point, Ridgeway, Linden, Blue River. Diamond Grove and Helena on the banks of the Wisconsin River.

Helena was laid out by Dodge in partnership with others and settled by miners from Mineral Point and Dodgeville with the view of transporting lead by flatboat.[13] In 1829, he sent a portion of his lead from there eastward to Green Bay. Huge oxcarts lugged the lead from Dodgeville to the Wisconsin River, where it was shipped in flatboats to the recently erected Fort Winnebago. From there it was hauled overland to the Fox River, reloaded onto boats and shipped to Green Bay.[14]

By 1829 no fewer than eighteen smelting furnaces were devouring the forests and befouling the air of southwest Wisconsin.[15] The town of Dodgeville proper, named for Henry Dodge, sprung up a short distance from his compound. It was known as the Patch Diggings when Dodge and his cohorts had the township site drawn up. Conditions in the small village were primitive. In 1828 W. Davidson passed through Dodgeville Diggings, as they were then known and found but five or six cabins in the town. Of them, three sold rotgut whiskey and poor tobacco.[16] In the spring of 1828 the first general merchandise store opened there. Shortly after that the partnership of Chatsy and Manlove opened a black smith shop. Mr. Manlove was reputed to be able to "bruise a piece of iron or the best man in camp with almost equal readiness and celerity."[17] That year two taverns to cater to thirsty miners were opened by a Mr. Wentworth and a Mr. Chapman.

During those early years Dodge's Diggings remained the larger of the two settlements. Dodgeville had one store. Dodge's Diggings had three, all doing brisk business with the surrounding settlements. By 1831, Henry Lafayette was managing one of them, a dry goods outfit, for his father. For a time, his partner was young Charles S. Hertich, son of the old schoolmaster Joseph Hertich of Ste. Genevieve. Charles didn't stay long and soon returned home to help his father run The Asylum.[18]

As for a social life, Lafayette's was probably like everyone else's in mining country—hard to come by. For entertainment, homesteaders might be resigned to partake of the talents of the "quack doctor and fiddler named Prevat" or the itinerant concert singer Ben Higby. The mail was always appreciated, though service was spotty. The government mail carrier, a half-Indian named Joseph Cleary, occasionally stopped with deliveries enroute to Prairie du Chien from Green Bay.[19] A more common past time in the lead field settlements could be found at the tavern. After a hard day's grubbing at the mines, the men were eager for distraction. Card games, not surprisingly, were common and could last for days. Faro, poker, euchre and seven-up: all were popular vehicles for gambling. There were a few other ways to lose money as well.

> "There someone might happen along with a pair of wolves and a good fight would be staged. Or perhaps a wolf and a few dogs would be matched. Watching horse races also occupied the leisure hours. Most taverns had bowling alleys, where a wooden ball about a foot in diameter was rolled at ten large pins."[20]

One historian observed that the "fatigues of the day were usually supplemented in the evening by revelry and indulgence ... of course the principal ingredient necessary to a royally good time was the enthusing ardent."[21] In other words, they got snot-slinging drunk. Fights were a regular occurrence and the combatants heavily beat on. A winner was usually proclaimed once his foe had suffered some trifling injury such as an eye gouging or a broken arm. However, miners avoided getting into serious trouble, although not for any fear of the law. The legal arm of the territory was distant to be sure. Any court issues waited on Judge Doty's arrival on his regular circuit from Green Bay. The local folks enforced what they perceived as the common good and they usually kept troublemakers in line. The most serious punishment an offender might get would be a thorough thrashing. If caught, a petty thief could expect his fellow miners to lay the skin on his back open with the whip. Claim jumpers were a concern but any miner who felt threatened could hire bodyguards to beat off the interlopers.[22]

Dodge's first year on his claim was profitable beyond his expectations, but the following year brought a sudden reversal of fortune. In 1829, the price of lead dropped from 5 cents a pound to about a measly one cent. Even with abysmal prices, production didn't slow. Miners simply couldn't afford to let it. They were digging a lot more for a lot less just to survive. The United States government's demand for rent payments on public mineral lands compounded the economic crisis. Those who refused or were unable to pay deserted their diggings. The cost of the most basic commodities became exorbitant. A miner would have to dig four to five thousand pounds of lead ore to make enough money to buy a barrel of flour at eighteen dollars or of pork, then selling for as much as thirty dollars.[23] Many a Badger gave up mining and turned to farming, although federal policy frowned on it. Lead had become nearly worthless. In comparison, food was like gold.[24] Those who chose not to farm left. Those who remained braved disease and a crippling winter as well as poverty. By 1832, Dodgeville and Dodge's Diggings, once the economic center of the country, were quite nearly turned to ghost towns. General Dodge himself abandoned the place. He moved his family a few miles south and built a new and somewhat more commodious home later known simply as Dodge's Place.[25]

Through flush times and famine, as the lead district population expanded, so too did the reputation of the Dodge clan. Henry Dodge regularly championed the interests of lead, miners and homesteaders and lobbied the government for the sale of federal lands to settlers. He defended the rights of squatters and endorsed the principle of preemption, which recognized the right of squatters to keep their homestead rather than having it yanked out from under them at a government land sale. For all that, he basked in the settlers' admiration. Dodge's growing influence over the regional politics was not lost on the government. In 1829, Michigan Territorial Governor Cass commissioned Henry Dodge for a four-year term as the Chief Justice of newly created Iowa County. That same year, Cass appointed him Colonel of the Michigan Territorial Militia.[26]

All in all, Henry Dodge was the perfect representative for the mining country. Most of the first settlers were his personal friends and acquaintances. Self educated, honest yet domineering, arrogant and tough, he had the definite swagger of confidence. One contemporary described him as "tall, straight and rather pompous and most familiar to his fellow townsmen when clothed in his miner's buckskins with immense horse pistols resting in his holsters."[27] Although a rough and tumble chap, he was also the astute politician. To those in lead country who aspired to employment as a civil servant, Dodge's support was essential. His supporters even proclaimed their devotion to him in song, sung roughly to the tune of Auld Lang Syne.

Should savage warfare be forgot,
And ne'er again appear
With hands upon our bosoms put,
We'll say Dodge shall live here!²⁸

The man had become a hero.

In 1831, Henry Dodge was elected as councilman for the Iowa County legislature and sat in the Michigan Territorial legislature. At about this time, a movement to form a territory separate from Michigan began to gain steam and Dodge played no small part in the effort. By 1830, both Henry Lafayette and Augustus had begun to show some interest in family politics. Augustus and his father signed petitions to Congress for establishing a new territorial government. Lafayette's signature was not to be found among those agitating for territorial recognition. However, that same year his signature, in company with his father's and brother's, appears on a petition to Congress requesting that Helena be laid out in town lots and permit those lots to be sold.²⁹

At last the depression of 1829 slowly began to turn around. The gloom and doom years of 1830 and 1831, when so much had been lost, gradually gave way to the light of economic revival. The markets slowly came back to life and immigrants returned to the mine district. By1832 miners and merchants were back in the black.³⁰ Although Dodgeville proper was slow to recover, many towns, most notably Mineral Point ten miles to the south, experienced a boom rivaling the one of 1827. The Lead District was speeding down the path to recovery once more... completely oblivious to the abrupt hair pin curve in the road just ahead.

11

A NASTIER LITTLE WAR

During winter of 1833-1834, the journalist Charles Fenno Hoffman made an extended visit to the northwestern frontier country and regularly sent correspondence highlighting his adventures back east to be published in the *New York American Magazine*. In one such letter he noted a paradoxical characteristic among the frontiersmen he felt his readers would find incredulous, but one he insisted was "a fact as notorious as the open day."

> ". . . that there have been and are men on the frontiers whose dealings with civilized society, whose general humanity, whose exact attendance even to their religious duties, are such as to ensure them respect, if not to give them weight, in any well-ordered community—and that with these very men the rights and privileges, the property, the life of an Indian, do not weigh a feather."[1]

The truth of his observation would be brutally substantiated in the next Indian conflict to hit the Northwest, the Black Hawk War of 1832.

The Black Hawk War was a murderous affair of sporadic slaughter on one side and wholesale butchery on the other. The war resulted from a serious miscalculation on the part of the Sauk war chief Makataimeshekiakiak, or The Black Sparrow Hawk, who hoped to reclaim from the whites traditional Sauk lands. Given his long experience with Americans, Black Hawk's underestimation of white hatred for Indians was baffling. It also proved to be lethal. Moreover, had General Atkinson moved decisively in the beginning, the entire crisis might have been regulated to a minor footnote in history. Instead, Atkinson dithered. The result was a three-month conflagration that climaxed in a bloodbath.

For Henry Lafayette Dodge, the Black Hawk War gave him his first real experience in a frontier Indian fracas. It would stand in stark contrast to his fleeting experience in the Winnebago distraction five years previously. During the Black Hawk War, Lafayette would endure scores of excruciating days in the saddle, one moment broiling under unrelenting sun and the next shivering under a pounding rain. He endured long nights lying on the sodden ground under the sparse cover of his saddle blanket, curled and cramped against the evening cold and damps. His rations were at best meager and at times nonexistent, where the luxury of even a sip of water could not be taken for granted. His ragged clothes reeked of sweat and horse lather. Grime and acrid camp smoke matted his brown hair and smudged the blush of youth on his cheeks. Henry Lafayette came to know the enemy at close range. For the first time he beheld the Indians' terrifying assault and heard the shrill scream of their battle cry. For the first time, he would shoot to kill and in turn be shot at. Lafayette would behold the emaciated Indian dead—Sauk men, women, and children—strewn along the trail and would help his comrades collect and bury the remnants of butchered settlers.

The Sauk referred to themselves as the Asakiwaki and they were a horticultural people. During the winter the Sauk dispersed into family hunting camps, but with the advent of the planting season, the nation again congregated at Rock Island on the Mississippi in their beloved capital, Saukenak. Above the immense cornfields spread out along the river bottom stood a thriving town of a hundred bark and wood longhouses neatly arranged along streets. With a summer population of two to three thousand, Saukenak easily rivaled any white frontier settlement of the time.

Like many of their Indian neighbors, the Asakiwaki had earlier allied with the ill-fated French. After being ejected from their Michigan homelands, the Sauk moved west and merged with the Fox Indians. In 1766 they migrated westward to the Wisconsin River. The Chippewa took exception to their presence and drove them southward to the Mississippi, where they eventually settled. By the American Revolution, Sauk enthusiasm for making alliances had cooled. They initially supported neither the colonists nor the crown. This would change. In 1780, acting on a rumor that the Sauk had helped the British attack St. Louis and Cahokia, an American militia torched the Sauk villages at Rock Island; villages that had actually been sympathetic to the colonists. That willful act snuffed out any lingering sympathy for Americans. When the colonists finally won their independence and made peace with several tribes, the Asakiwaki refused. William H. Harrison's notorious Treaty of 1804, which divested the Sauk of all their lands east of the Mississippi, infuriated the main body of Sauk and Fox people, no one more so than Makataimeshekiakiak, and guaranteed continued hostilities.[2]

A perpetual state of war now existed between the Sauk Nation and the United States. The Asakiwaki laid siege to Fort Madison twice, in 1808 and 1811 and fought at Tecumseh's side with the British in 1812. Following the end of that war, Black Hawk's forces continued the fight, at one point assaulting Fort Howard at Green Bay and killing fifteen soldiers before being compelled to make peace in 1816.[3] The Americans required the Sauk leaders, including Black Hawk and his longtime rival chief Keokuk, to reaffirm the hated provisions of the Treaty of 1804. Believing he was taking the more practical side, Chief Keokuk steadfastly professed friendship and cooperation with the Americans. Many Sauk endorsed Keokuk as most adept at placating the Americans' incessant demands. Conversely, Black Hawk's followers dismissed Keokuk as an American puppet. They believed Makataimeshekiakiak was the one Sauk leader who could forcefully defend their lands.[4] Predictably, the United

States appointed the more malleable Keokuk head chief of the Sauk nation. Black Hawk rejected American gestures of friendship outright. He and his supporters, the so-called British Band, steadfastly clung to their alliance to England; a fact boldly proclaimed by the Union Jack habitually fluttering in the breeze over their camps.

By 1829, white squatters had begun settling at and around Saukenak. While the Sauk were absent for the winter hunt, settlers destroyed Indian lodges and confiscated Indian farmland. The United States expected the Indians to abide by the provisions of the Treaty of 1804 and leave. The new Illinois state governor, John Reynolds, was particularly anxious to oust the Indians, whipping up passions in the state assembly with horror stories of Indian thievery, vandalism, treachery and even rape. It had the desired effect. There arose such a clamor to drive all the Indians from northern Illinois that Reynolds called up 700 eager militiamen to do the job.

Alarmed at Reynolds' audacity and fearing an Indian war, General Edmund P. Gaines brought federal forces to Rock Island on June 4 of 1831 to persuade the Indians to abandon Saukenak and join Keokuk's Sauk in Iowa. In response, Black Hawk asserted that he would prefer to fight and die among the bones of his ancestors. Gaines then summarily ordered the Sauk to leave or he would oblige Black Hawk's request. To drive home the point, Gaines had Saukenak shelled and assaulted. On June 30th Black Hawk and twenty-four Sauk chiefs approached Gaines under a white flag and agreed to move across the river and submit to Keokuk's authority. Black Hawk reserved the final word, however. When it came his turn to sign the treaty, he seized the ink quill and marked "a large bold cross with a force which rendered that pen forever unfit for further use."[5]

Although the British Band had moved onto the Iowa side, the sixty-six year old Black Hawk remained belligerent. He vowed that one day he would lead the Asakiwaki triumphantly back over the Mississippi and drive the whites from Saukenak. They would regain their lodges, their farmlands, their burial grounds, their prosperity and their dignity. He had many supporters, including Neopope and a Winnebago medicine man by the name of White Cloud, also known as the Winnebago Prophet, who had long preached against the whites and was building sympathy for Black Hawk among the Winnebago and Potowatomie.[6]

The Sauk's exile on the west bank began poorly and degenerated from desperate to catastrophic. Deprived of their east bank farms, now claimed and defended by white settlers, the Asakiwaki faced starvation. Before long, famine, depression and desperation soon inflamed old tribal animosities. In late summer of 1831, a Fox war party killed 25 Menominee near Prairie du Chien. Fearing that Indians might make similar attacks against whites, the now Secretary of War Lewis

Cass ordered General Henry Atkinson and Indian Superintendent William Clark to apprehend the perpetrators.[7] Clark and Atkinson, who was known by the Indians as White Beaver, met the Sauk at Fort Armstrong, on the western tip of Rock Island, on September 5th, 1831. They soon discovered the murderers had vanished. Still, given that disappointment, the Sauk hadn't actually demonstrated any overt hostility. Indeed, White Beaver believed, the Sauk and Fox sincerely desired peace. Reassured albeit empty-handed, Atkinson and Clark returned to Saint Louis. Atkinson's confidence was little consolation to the jittery homesteaders. The vision of a thousand-warrior horde of savages was enough to send a bolt of terror through northern Illinois. Settlers fled their farms in masse. Once more, Reynolds called out the militia.

White Beaver had seriously misinterpreted Black Hawk's intentions. As early as 1830, the chief had been sending out emissaries to various potential Indian allies, notably to the Cherokee, the Creek and the Osage, to gauge their willingness to fight the whites. He had been in sporadic contact with the English as well and had of late received encouraging news. Neopope, who had just returned from Canada, informed Black Hawk that the British had encouraged him to take back Asakiwaki lands and would assist him. The Ottawa, Chippewa, Potawatomi and Winnebago were also encouraging the British Band to strike and confirmed that the British would supply the guns and ammunition. All Makataimeshekiakiak needed to do was move against the Americans.

On April 5th, 1832 Black Hawk and his followers assembled on the western banks of the Mississippi. They stood, as it were, on the very precipice of history. None there could have failed to appreciate that crossing the river was a fateful decision. They would have never attempted it but for the conviction of their inevitable victory over the whites. Perhaps Black Hawk and his leaders believed a militant demonstration would cow the Americans more than old Keokuk's concessions. Black Hawk was confident he could eventually forge an army of allied Indians nations and he likewise believed that British aid would guarantee a victory. To remain in Iowa was to die, anyway. So across they went on that April day, some two thousand Sauk and Fox and a handful of Kickapoo, embarking on a quixotic quest for their homeland. In their ranks were roughly 650 mounted fighting men. The majority, thirteen hundred of them, was the common folk; the elderly and infirm borne on litters, the nervously excited wives and mothers, the scampering, playful children and the infants warmly bundled in their cradleboards. In a matter of four months, most of them would be dead.

Once across, Black Hawk avoided returning to Saukenak and prematurely precipitating a fight. His aim was to guide his people up the Rock River to a new homeland along the Kishwaukee River in north central Illinois, gathering up allies along the way. White Cloud the Winnebago Prophet reassured Black Hawk that Atkinson and the soldiers wouldn't assault his people as long as they were peacefully disposed. Once they had forged a powerful confederacy, the Prophet proclaimed, it wouldn't matter. Black Hawk would be able to hurl back any assault by American regulars or by the Illinois militia. Significantly, Atkinson hadn't made a move against them, although he could have. This hesitancy doubtlessly reassured the Sauk leaders. They started up the Rock River towards the Prophet's village, the warriors mounted on horseback moving on either side of the river banks while their families paddled upstream in canoes. Still half-expecting an attack by Army steamboats from Fort Armstrong, Black Hawk instructed his men to begin singing and beating drums "to show the Americans that we were not afraid."[8]

General Atkinson learned of the news five days after Black Hawk's crossing, while steaming up the river for Fort Armstrong with six companies of the 6th Regiment.[9] He first stopped to assure Keokuk that he would crush Black Hawk's British band like a dirt clod and appealed for the friendly chief's help in persuading them to return to the reservation.[10] Privately, the general hoped he could end Black Hawk's infraction peacefully, but rather than use troops to block the British Band from ascending the Rock River, he sent two Sauk messengers to urge them to turn back. Black Hawk promptly rebuffed them. White Beaver then sent two threatening dispatches by express. Makataimeshekiakiak remained defiant, replying that if Atkinson "wished to fight us, he might come on!" His own efforts frustrated, Atkinson wrote Henry Gratiot, the Winnebago Indian agent, on April 16th, instructing him to enlist the aid of the Winnebago chiefs to convince Makataimeshekiakiak to return.

Three days later, Atkinson informed the citizens of the lead country that Black Hawk and the Sauk had invaded Illinois.[11] Immediately the call to arms resounded through Iowa County and all of western Michigan territory. Henry Dodge called an emergency meeting of citizens at Mineral Point, which sent Daniel Parkinson galloping off to trader John Dixon at Dixon's Ferry on the Rock River and to Henry Gratiot at Gratiot's Grove for more intelligence. Both men were well acquainted with the Sauk and Fox. Dodge wanted to know Black Hawk's strength, his direction of movement and his intentions.

The results of Parkinson's errand, other than completely exhausting him, were minimal. It is doubtful he caught up with Gratiot, who was already among the Winnebago. On the 23rd, Gratiot and two dozen Winnebago leaders, including White Crow, Whirling Thunder and Little Priest, appeared before Black Hawk at the Prophet's Village. The meeting proved unproductive. Black Hawk reiterated that he would fight the Americans rather than rejoin Keokuk on the west bank. He then allowed Gratiot to depart. Gratiot returned to Fort Armstrong on the 27th and confirmed that the Sauk posed a significant threat.[12]

Bravado aside, Black Hawk realized that his plans were beginning to go awry. The Potawatomie and Winnebago had refused to join his crusade and many of his own people spoke of abandoning their quest. Still, Makataimeshekiakiak urged them onward. Shortly after departing the Prophet's Village for the Kishwaukee River, Black Hawk received another demoralizing revelation. Contrary to Neopope's glowing claims, there would be no help from the British. Without allies, abandoned again by the British, with no place to seek refuge and his people nearly destitute, Makataimeshekiakiak was left with one option. If White Beaver Atkinson pursued them, he and his people would surrender.[13]

Meanwhile, General Atkinson arrived in lead country to review frontier defenses. At Galena, he conferred with Henry Dodge regarding the best way to secure the settlements. Atkinson yet hoped to end the crisis promptly, but as a precaution, he authorized General Dodge to draw enough muskets from Fort Crawford to arm an efficient militia. On April 24th and with no word from Gratiot, Atkinson instructed Dodge to raise a force of mounted volunteers. In short order, General Dodge assembled the Iowa County Regiment of Michigan Volunteers, an undisciplined cavalry of local miners, roughnecks and rowdies.[14] As a historian later described them, they were "a dare-devil adventurous set of men gathered from the fields and mines. They knew no manual of arms but were spurred on by a deep hatred of the red race."[15]

For the life of an Indian did not weigh a feather.

On May 1st, 1832, General Dodge's eldest son, Henry Lafayette, enlisted in his father's cavalry. He signed up at Mineral Point with Captain James H. Gentry's company C. The young Dodge was 22 years of age and probably shared the redskin-hating sentiments of his fellow militiamen. He was a stout young fellow, an Army musket cradled in the crook of an arm, five foot nine or ten with penetrating blue-gray eyes, dark hair and of a dark complexion with the prematurely rough exterior of a miner. As with nearly all volunteers, he had to provide his own horse and accoutrements. Lafayette was appointed a lieutenant of Company C. His brother Augustus, all of twenty years, enlisted as well and served as a sergeant in Captain Gehon's company.[16]

On May 8th, General Atkinson mustered 600 mounted volunteers and 200 volunteer infantry into service at Fort Armstrong. Colonel Zachary Taylor would command the 340 regular infantry while General Samuel Whiteside commanded the Illinois mounted volunteers. It was Whiteside's task to pursue the British Band up the banks of the Rock while Atkinson's federals and volunteers ascended the river by boat. The men were outfitted with twenty-five days of provisions, surely more than adequate for a campaign that would be over well before the Illinois volunteers' terms of service expired.[17]

The same day that Atkinson mustered his forces, General Dodge wrote Governor Reynolds commanding the Illinois militia. He reasoned that if Reynolds' force prematurely routed Black Hawk, the British Band would be forced to retreat northward into Michigan lead country, exposing the settlements to grave danger, as most of the miners would be away serving in the militia. Dodge suggested that Reynolds assign a company to patrol the west bank of the Rock River to protect the mining settlements should the Indians cross the river.[18] As it turned out, Dodge had reason to worry.

On the day he wrote the governor, General Dodge and Lafayette, with a party of Michigan Volunteers, struck out on the southern trail to rendezvous with Atkinson's army on the Rock River. Everyone's boldness was tempered by a case of the jitters, knowing they were leaving their wives and families behind under the dubious protection of a Sucker patrol. Six days into their march, an express rider overtook them with alarming news. The Indians had indeed massed to slaughter their undefended women and children. The panicked volunteers promptly wheeled their horses about and thundered back home. They arrived to a scene of pandemonium as terrified families feverously worked to fortify their homes. A quick reconnaissance, however, revealed it had all been a false alarm. The only murderous hatchet swinging Indians to be found in the region were in the agitated imaginations of the whites. Once more the volunteers, their ranks swelled by three new companies, turned their horses southward towards Atkinson.[19]

In the meantime, Whiteside's force had arrived at Dixon's Ferry on the Rock. With only two days of rations remaining and the British Band still some twenty-five miles up the river, Whiteside was compelled to forgo pursuit and wait for Atkinson's supply boats. Governor Reynolds, in command there with his Illinois militia, was in no mood for delay. He ordered Major David Baily to scout the south of the Rock River, and then dispatched a second column under Major Isaiah Stillman in pursuit of Black Hawk, thus leaving the mining district completely unprotected. On May 13th, Stillman's boisterous warriors tramped off through the woodlands and prairies in high spirits, their courage and patriotic fervor substantially fortified by whiskey. They would find the foe far more quickly than even Reynolds might have hoped.

12

A SOFT SHELLED BREED

On May 15th, two days after Stillman disappeared into the Illinois brush, a tattered express rider met Dodge's Michigan Volunteers along the Galena road. Pulling alongside of General Dodge, he handed him a dispatch from Governor Reynolds. From the grim expression on Dodge's face as he read it, the volunteers knew it contained singularly bad news.

> "General Dodge, This night at 1 o'clock we received intelligence that Major Stillman's troops have been **defeated** on Sycamore creek, by the Sacks. I cannot inform you of the number of the **slain** but enough to be a serious Disaster. I apprize you of this, as you will return with your troops to the protection of the settlements. The frontier of the mining country is in danger, and they ought to Fort or secure themselves from the Indians."

Dodge's fears had come to pass with a vengeance. As the hours passed, rumors trickled in detailing the extent of the disaster. Of Stillman's force of 275, fifty men at least had purportedly been slaughtered and probably more. The entire militia had been utterly routed, while Black Hawk and two thousand Sauk warriors were allegedly sweeping down onto Illinois in an apocalyptic scourge. General Dodge may not have believed half of the information, but he knew two things were certain. Rather than sweep into Illinois, the Sauk would move away from Atkinson's army and retreat northward into Michigan. He also knew news of a Sauk victory would ignite Indian attacks throughout the lead region. The General rode for Dodgeville. On May 16th, he paused long enough at Gratiot's Grove to write Atkinson.

> "The people of the Mining Country are badly prepared to receive so great a shock as a Defeat of the Illinois Militia is calculated to produce. I will endeavor to Draw the settlements in immediately and if possible get the inhabitants to fort themselves the mounted men I may be able to bring to the field will act as an immediate cover to the settlements."[1]

True to form, the first reports were far worse than the facts. Essentially, Stillman's Suckers had been routed by their own fear. Early in the evening of May 14th, the well-liquored Illinois volunteers had just set camp along Sycamore Creek twenty-five miles northeast of Dixon's Ferry when they were stunned to see three Indians approaching, carrying a white flag. It was a Sauk peace party. Black Hawk had instructed the emissaries to offer his surrender to Stillman and was waiting in camp beyond a rise of trees several hundred yards away. To learn what might transpire, he sent a party of mounted scouts out into a clearing to watch the proceedings.

Stillman's troops, in a state of intoxicated anxiety, reacted in the worst possible way. Ineradicably suspicious of the Red Man even when sober, they unleashed a volley on the emissaries, killing one and seizing the remaining two. It was then when someone spotted Black Hawk's scouts on the wooded rise and a cry went up among the woozy militiamen, "Every man draw his rations of Sauks!"

Captain Eads and his company thundered towards the rise, overtaking the Indian lookouts and killing two of them. Onward Eads' men came, plunging blindly into the trees and unknowingly towards the all but unprotected Sauk camp. Most of Black Hawk's men were out foraging for food, leaving Makataimeshekiakiak with less than forty warriors. The chief hastily ordered his men into the brush and, concealed, they waited. When Ead's company was nearly on top of them, the Sauk let loose a hail of fire. The astonished whites staggered back and the Indians, shrieking like demons, charged at them from out of the growing darkness. The Illinois men ran, as Black Hawk remembered, in "utmost confusion and consternation before my little but brave band of warriors." When Ead's terrified volunteers suddenly tumbled back out of the twilight into Stillman's camp, sheer pandemonium erupted and Stillman's Sucker militia, down to the last man, fled panic-stricken across the prairie and into the night. The first of them stumbled into Dixon's Ferry at 1 am, babbling tales of massacre that defied belief. Of course, as clearer heads there deduced and an investigation later proved, the yarns were terror-inspired exaggerations. Stillman had lost a total of eleven men, some of who had probably been shot in the darkness by their own trigger-happy comrades. The total Sauk casualties: an emissary and two scouts.

The greatest Sauk casualty, of course, was the opportunity to end the war. The Stillman incident convinced Black Hawk the whites were determined to murder them all, down to the last child, and he dismissed any further thought of surrender.[2]

However, at that time none in the mining district were privy to the facts of Stillman's disgrace. Alarm again seized the countryside. Miners threw up ramshackle stockades. Fifteen odd blockhouses were tossed together in short order, complete with crude motes dug around their perimeter. They were christened by a variety of brave names: Fort Jackson at Mineral Point, Fort Hamilton at W. S. Hamilton's Diggings, Fort Napoleon, Fort Defiance, Blue Mound Fort and Fort Gratiot. Every tiny settlement and mine had its own equally tiny fort. Weapons from Fort Crawford were distributed at Mineral Point. General Dodge initially received forty stands of musket and four hundred cartridges for the protection of Dodgeville.[3] Dodge himself headquartered at his smelting works, newly christened as Fort Union. He assigned Augustus as lieutenant of volunteers for home protection there, while Lafayette remained in the field with Gentry's company, an arrangement that may have chaffed the younger brother a bit. According to family lore, Mrs. Dodge and her girls busied themselves providing mess for the men, molding lead bullets, hauling water to fill the supply barrels in the fort and endlessly fretting over the threat of prowling savages.[4] In a newspaper interview many years later, Salina Dodge's description of the times, although fantastic, left no doubt as to the mind-set of the whites.

> " . . . for two months the fiendish savages reveled in a carnival of blood. Old men and women and children, as well as the young and strong of the whites, were cruelly butchered . . . The Indians killed their victims in the most brutal manner and often ate their flesh and drank their blood."[5]

Christiana McDonald Dodge, of old family Kentucky stock, would not be easily intimidated, however. In later years George W. Jones recalled that when friends advised Mrs. Dodge to leave Fort Union and take the girls to the relative safety of Galena, she simply replied, "My husband and sons are between me and the Indians. I am safe so long as they live."[6]

And so they were . . . literally . . . between her and the Indians. The defense of the entire Michigan territory had fallen irrevocably on the shoulders of Dodge and his volunteers.

In the meantime, Atkinson's progress had ground to a halt at Dixon's Ferry. Stillman's debacle was just one more setback. White Beaver's own force, now better than a month into campaign, was rapidly evaporating. The Illinois volunteers' 30 day enlistment period had expired and they were going home en masse. In short order, his fighting force was cleaved in half, from 1700 men to 640. Exasperated, he asked Reynolds to provide two thousand more volunteers. It may have comforted the beleaguered Atkinson had he known that Black Hawk was suffering more serious problems. The British Band had retreated northward into Michigan territory, nursing hopes that the Winnebago would guide them to safety at Four Lakes, near what would become Madison, Wisconsin. Makataimeshekiakiak and his band were buoyed by their unexpected victory against the hated Illinois militia but it did little to soothe their growing hunger and exhaustion, or diffuse the specter of pursuing white angels of death. Just over a month and a half had passed since Black Hawk's people had crossed the Mississippi into Illinois. It must have seemed more like an eternity.

True to Dodge's prediction, Stillman's defeat had emboldened groups of revenge-hungry Potawatomie, Winnebago and Kickapoo raiders, who struck the frontier in a series of attacks. On May 19th, a Winnebago war party killed William Durley, an express man carrying dispatches from Galena to General Atkinson.[7] Three days later forty-odd Potawatomie fighters struck the William Davis farm on Indian Creek, some six miles north of Ottawa, Illinois. In the bloody mêlée, the raiders killed fifteen men, women and children and kidnapped two teenage girls, Sylvia and Rachel Hall. On May 23rd, thirty Winnebago waylaid seven men who were out to bury Durley's remains, killing four of them. One of the victims was the Fox Indian Agent Felix St. Vrain, who Atkinson had just appointed as the new express man in Durley's place.[8] The Winnebago boasted of their successes to Black Hawk, displaying scalps and booty as proof, prodding Makataimeshekiakiak's pride. When the Sauk arrived at Four Lakes on May 25th, Black Hawk immediately dispatched raiding parties to take meat, to avenge the deaths they'd suffered in the Stillman fight.[9]

During this time, General Dodge and his son Henry Lafayette were patrolling the Four Lakes area with two companies under James Gentry and John Roundtree. They'd originally been reconnoitering the Apple River area, but when they came across the Sauk trail at the Kishwaukee River, Dodge followed it northward. He had no intention of actually engaging Black Hawk with his small force. The Winnebago agent Henry Gratiot was with him and Dodge's goal was to persuade or coerce White Crow and his Rock River Winnebago to remain at peace before Black Hawk could enlist them. On May 25th; the same day the British Band had arrived in the Four Lakes vicinity, Dodge and Gratiot met with the Winnebago at Lake Mendota and extracted a promise of neutrality. Content with that, Dodge and his volunteers eagerly headed home, completely oblivious to Black Hawk's proximity.

On May 27th, Henry Gratiot received an urgent dispatch from Atkinson, detailing the kidnapping of the Hall girls during the Davies Farm raid. Rumors had it that the girls were being held by the Sauk at Black Hawk's camp. He instructed Gratiot to enlist the Winnebago to procure their release and to offer up to a thousand dollars reward for each sister.[10] Gratiot met with White Crow on the 29th and authorized him to rescue the girls by force if need be.[11] On June 2nd, a mere four days later, White Crow returned to Blue Mound stockade with Sylvia and

Rachel in tow, having ransomed them from the Sauk for some horses, corn and some wampum.[12] Indeed, Black Hawk later insisted that the Sauk had actually saved the girls from Potawatomie vengeance by bringing them into his camp.

In the meantime, Lafayette was encamped with his father's command at Kirker's Place on the Apple River just over the border in Illinois. For two weeks, news from the frontier had been uniformly bad, first with the Stillman debacle and the disintegration of the Illinois army, then the Davis farm massacre, the abduction of the Hall girls, and the murders of Durley, St. Vrain and others. Morale must have been rock bottom. Now reports had it that hostile Winnebago bands were gathering for an attack on Blue Mound. Determined to stir his men's spirits, Dodge solemnly addressed the volunteers, essentially telling them that they were the sole salvation of their homes and families, by God, whether they liked it or not. The enemy had drawn the tomahawk and scalping knife over the heads of their defenseless wives and children, and the only remedy was an unrelenting attack on the "faithless banditti of savages."[13] There would be no quarter.

Having stoked their fire with patriotic zeal and a craving for revenge, Dodge ordered his volunteers forward and off they rumbled towards Blue Mound. They arrived thirsty for action on the afternoon of June 3rd, right after White Crow had delivered the Hall girls to Gratiot. Initially, Dodge praised White Crow's success, but it was an appreciation not shared by his men, who would have enthusiastically slaughtered the Winnebago had they the chance. Instead, Dodge had a cow butchered for White Crow's party, secured cabins for them to sleep in that night and posted several guards around them. Whether he placed them there to prevent Indian treachery or to protect them from the blood lust of his militiamen is a matter of speculation. Either way, the precaution paid off. That evening, White Crow mentioned to an officer that Black Hawk had sworn to kill Old Hairy Face, as they called Dodge, and all his men. Furthermore, he claimed the Sauk chief had characterized the whites as nothing more than "a soft-shelled breed, that when the spear was put to them they would quack like ducks" just as they did at Stillman's Run.[14]

When Dodge learned of the insult, he angrily proclaimed, "Be not alarmed . . . Let them come; we will show them, Sir, that *we are not* of the soft-shelled breed . . ." General Dodge then took White Crow and his men hostage. To further illustrate the hardness of his shell, he spent the night in the cabin with them, sleeping unarmed by their side.[15] Conversely, Henry Gratiot was dismayed at such a display, that White Crow and his redeemers of the Hall girls should have been so shabbily treated.[16]

The next morning, Gratiot, Dodge and his militia departed Blue Mounds for Morrison's Grove, fifteen miles to the west, taking White Crow and his men along. White Crow assured Dodge that he was a sincere friend and a loyal ally, as his past actions had repeatedly proven. In reply, Henry Dodge announced he would hold in arrest Whirling Thunder, Spotted Arm, and Little Priest to insure White Crow adhered to his loyalty. He then bade White Crow farewell and moved off down the road to Gratiot's Grove. For White Crow it must have seemed the epitome of duplicity. The following day a group of Winnebago ambushed two members of the Blue Mound garrison, Jefferson Smith and William Aubrey, who had ventured out to fetch water. Smith managed his escape. Aubrey did not. Was it merely a coincidence or had Dodge's actions inadvertently gotten Aubrey murdered? Coincidence or not, treachery had been repaid in kind. [17]

On June 6th, while Dodge's company was camped at Gratiot Grove, Lafayette observed a company of horse approaching. It was Captain James Stephenson and the Galena militia, searching for the bodies of Felix St. Vrain and his slain companions. Riding with them in buckskin hunting shirt and an arsenal of weapons tucked in his Kentucky jean pantaloons was George Wallace Jones of Sinsinawa Mound. St. Vrain had been Jones' brother-in-law. He'd ridden out of Galena alone to find the body when he overtook Stephenson's company. Since Dodge's company was headed into Illinois to find Atkinson, Stephenson and Jones opted to join them.

On the 8th, as the Dodge's force moved down the Galena road, two militia officers, Captain Elijah Iles and General James Henry, appeared on the trail. Atkinson had sent them out from Dixon's Ferry with a fifty-man detachment to bury the St. Vrain party and secure the express route to Galena. Initially they believed Dodge's men had been an Indian force of five hundred. Relieved, they turned the burial task over to Stephenson and Dodge and moved on towards Apple Fort. Dodge's men found St. Vrain's remains two days later. Fifty-seven years later, George Jones described the nightmarish scene with a clarity and horror as if it had occurred but the day before.

> "His head, feet and hands had been cut off and with his heart and the most of the flesh of his body had been taken off by the Indians as trophies of war, and as food, he being a pretty fat man. We were directed to his corpse by the turkey buzzards which we saw flying and circling around at a considerable distance. I knew him from the color of his black hair, some of which was strewn around as the Indians scalped him, his blue dress coat, swallow-tailed through the large collar of which, then the style, the bullet which had broken his neck." [18]

They buried what was left of St. Vrain near Kirker's Place. George Jones and Stephenson's company departed for Galena that afternoon while Dodge's men encamped, believing there were no Indians in the vicinity.

The following morning they discovered their mistake. A Sauk party had stolen five of their horses. Dodge detailed Captain Gentry's company to retrieve them. As lieutenant to Gentry, Lafayette was most likely among them. They were on horseback for the greater part of the next day, finally rejoining General Dodge late that evening at Hickory Point. Lieutenant Lafayette and his comrades had enjoyed more success than they'd expected, having managed to retrieve greater number of horses than they had actually lost. When the Indians realized they were being pursued, they abandoned the miners' horses and a handful of others taken from the settlements earlier.[19]

Dodge reached Dixon's Ferry on the 12th of June. Leaving his command staged there, he forded the Rock River and rode off with an escort toward Ottowa to confer with Atkinson about the campaign's heretofore-infuriating lack of progress and the general's future strategy. Dodge found the general enrolling Reynolds' new militia volunteers and waiting for the arrival of federal troops from Chicago. He informed General Dodge that until he had reconstructed his army, there was maddeningly little that could be done. Black Hawk and his people had taken refuge in the Trembling County north of Lake Koshkonong, a nearly inaccessible morass of swampy forests and thicket and White Beaver hadn't the troops or supplies to drive them out.

General Dodge subsequently rejoined his men at Dixon's Ferry and moved them back towards Gratiot's Grove. For Lafayette, it had been a quick, arduous but relatively mundane march. There had been a few tense moments, but they had all been more worried more about saddle sores and filling their stomachs than falling victim to the tomahawk. R. H. Magoon, who served in Dodge's militia, recalled that during the march, the column came across a deserted home. The famished men searched in and around the premises for anything edible. After finding a rusty cooking kettle in the field, the desperately hungry volunteers cleaned it out and boiled up some mustard greens. Their effort was so repugnant that the boys opted to stay hungry and the much-anticipated supper ended up dumped in the grass.[20]

The men reached Gratiot's Grove late on the 13th of June. With provisions exhausted and Atkinson's campaign stalemated, General Dodge ordered his men back to their homes. The horses were nearly all broken down, as were the miners. On the home front, the war had nearly destroyed the lead country. The commerce of mining country had collapsed. Houses stood empty. Farm, smelter and mine were abandoned. Business had suffocated. All mail delivery had stopped. At the same time food supplies in the stockades were running out. Livestock, the main source of food, had strayed from the settlements and were ranging wild on the prairie. People were too frightened to venture out of the stockade and bring them in. Nothing less than the shroud of famine itself was hovering over the empty pantries and kitchens of Iowa County.[21]

13

ARMY OF THE FRONTIER

For the remainder of June, whites and Indians skirmished on a daily basis, keeping everyone in a state of fear. On June 14th Lieutenant Lafayette Dodge parted company with Captain Gentry's disbanded company at Gratiot's Grove and rode home with his father to Fort Union. Exhausted, father and son had hardly time to unsaddle their horses when an express came tearing up to them from Fort Defiance, a few miles south of Mineral Point, bearing an urgent dispatch from Captain Hoard at Hamilton Fort. Indians had killed four men at Spafford and Spencer's farm some six miles southeast of William S. Hamilton's diggings and Hoard urgently needed reinforcements.

"We are not to have peace with this bandit collection of Indians until they are killed up in their dens!" an exasperated Dodge proclaimed and sent out the call to arms. General Dodge then galloped off towards Fort Hamilton well ahead of any mustering militia.[1] Although Captain Gentry and his lieutenants Porter and Paschal Bequette were among those to meet General Dodge at Hamilton, Lieutenant H. L. Dodge apparently wasn't with them, thereby missing out on an exhilarating victory and the lasting fame that attended surviving it . . . provided one survived, for some did not.

Upon General Dodge's arrival, he immediately organized a small force of 29 men and sallied forth in pursuit of the Indians. On June 16th, they overtook thirteen Kickapoo warriors at the Pecatonica River.[2] At Dodge's approach, the Indians let loose a volley from a line of brush along the banks. Three militia men dropped from their saddles. Unruffled, Old Hairy Face rallied his men, his exhortations, according to adjutant Charles Bracken, liberally punctuated by profanity.

> "Charge them, God damn them, every man sword in hand! There's an Indian, kill him! There, by God! I've killed him myself!"[3]

A heroic cry, certainly, but the fact was that General Dodge was the only man with a sword that day. The engagement later known as the Battle of Horseshoe Bend was over in a matter of a few minutes. As skirmishes generally go, it had been a small affair. Nevertheless the miners had managed to kill the entire group of Kickapoo, earning the first real victory for the Americans and one that General Dodge reported with great satisfaction to General Atkinson.[4]

All the same, reports of Indian thefts and attacks continued. The day after the Pecatonica fight, the Sauk stole ten horses from farmers near Apple River Fort. Captain Stephenson and twenty-one men pursued, only to be bushwhacked on the 18th near Kellogg's Grove. Stephenson lost three men that day.[5] On the 20th the Sauk killed two men at Blue Mound. Messengers reported the incident to General Dodge that same day and he immediately took Lafayette and Gentry's company to reinforce the stockade. For some unexplained reason, they did not arrive at Blue Mound, a mere 20 miles from Dodgeville, until the 24th, a knuckle-gnawing delay of four days.

They found no Indians but did find a stockade filled with terrorized defenders who had minute by minute been watching for Dodge's arrival. It seemed that Lieutenant George Force and Private Emerson Green had left the fort on the 20th to reconnoiter the Sauk's position. After crossing the prairie they came up to a stand of trees, where the Indians ambushed them. Force was killed instantly. Green fled for the stockade but the warriors soon overtook and dispatched him as well. All this had transpired within sight of the horrified guards on the stockade walls. Ebenezer Brigham, who was present that day, recorded the events of the moment in his diary.

> "June 21. Emerson Green and George Force both killed and scalped. Force horribly mangled, his head cut off, a gold watch taken, a sum of money and two horses. Force is lying on the prairie unburied. It is dangerous to go out of sight of the fort. The General (Dodge) has not performed agreeable to promise; seems to neglect us; appears to bear malice against us for no cause; our situation is a delicate one. I expect an attack from the Indians; we cannot stand a siege."[6]

Brigham's comments about General Dodge's antipathy further cast suspicion on what motivated the tardiness. By the time Dodge's company arrived, a member of the fort garrison, Edward Beouchard, had recovered and buried Green's body. Force's butchered remains still lay at the fringe of the forest. That had been no accident. When the Indians had killed a fort defender, one James Aubrey on June 4th, Beouchard had asked Lieutenant George Force to help him get Aubrey's remains. Force refused and Beouchard told him straight out that if he "got killed and was only six feet off, I would not go for his body." When his comrades asked if he were so cold as to hold a grudge against the dead, Edward Beouchard simply replied he kept his word, whether a man lived or died.[7]

Gentry's company was able to track the Indian trail along the Sugar River for some distance until the Sauk footprints scattered in all directions, making pursuit impossible. The company then turned back towards Dodgeville, pausing long enough for Lafayette and his companions to help bury the scraps that had been Lieutenant George Force. Force's gold watch would be discovered a year later in a field near Four Lakes, glinting in the summer sun through the bleaching bones of a Sauk warrior.[8]

While Gentry's company was relieving Blue Mound Fort, Black Hawk and two hundred fighters had assaulted the Apple River stockade outright, killing five whites and making off with much needed provisions, horses and cattle.[9] A day later they ambushed the pursuing Illinois militia under Captain John Dement, who would later wed Lafayette's sister Mary Louise. Black Hawk himself expressed admiration of Dement's courage and bravery for holding his ground while the bulk of his militia fled in terror.[10]

At Dixon's Ferry, White Beaver had finally resurrected his expeditionary force. General Hugh Brady's 1st Division of regulars and General Alexander's three volunteer brigades led by Henry and Posey and Dodge brought his complete fighting force to about four thousand men.[11] Atkinson grandly christened his great host the Army of the Frontier. On June 28th, they took the field. Atkinson and Brady's regulars, braced by Henry's brigade, formed the right and would move up the east bank of the Rock River. Moving up the west bank, General Alexander's brigade comprised the center. Posey was to be the left, the northernmost arm of the three-pronged assault on Black Hawk. They were to move resolutely towards the Four Lakes region and frustrate any attempt by Black Hawk to escape Atkinson's columns by moving westward. The three branches of the Army of the Frontier were to converge at his proposed field headquarters at Lake Koshkonong, some 40 miles southeast of present-day Madison, where Atkinson supposed he'd find the British Band.

The general instructed Henry Dodge and his volunteers to rendezvous with General Alexander Posey's Illinois militia at Fort Hamilton. Before departing, General Dodge sent Lieutenant Lafayette Dodge and his adjutant, Lieutenant W. W. Woodbridge, to Sinsinawa Mound. The General had been impressed with 28 year old George Wallace Jones, who lived there just north of Galena, and wanted him on his staff. Arriving at the Jones' stone fort, Lafayette and Woodbridge encouraged him to accept an appointment in the General's militia as his aide-de-camp. George Jones later confided that he was overwhelmed by the opportunity to serve with Dodge, "him whom I had loved from my childhood," and he accompanied Lafayette to Fort Union. General Dodge, clad in his familiar buckskin hunting shirt and jeans, warmly embraced the man and declared he had utmost faith in Jones' friendship and honor and praised his bravery in searching for Felix St. Vrain's body by himself.[12]

General Dodge, Henry Lafayette, George Jones and about two hundred volunteers arrived at Fort Hamilton to find Posey's Illinois brigade encamped on the prairie. Atkinson apparently intended Dodge to take command of Posy's troops as well as his own, but the General declined the honor unless the Illinois volunteers actually elected him. John Dement, a member of Posey's Spy Battalion and an Illinois man himself, campaigned for Dodge, announcing that he would "lead us to victory." Nevertheless, the bulk of the Illinois volunteers voted for Posey. George Jones later claimed that the Suckers, the term the Michigan volunteers frequently and disparagingly applied to Illinois men, supposedly confessed to him they had voted to retain Posey because they believed Dodge would put them up front and in the direct line of fire.[13]

Under direct orders from Atkinson to meet him and the main army at Koshkonong, Posey and Dodge immediately decamped. Dodge's command consisted of five mounted companies under the command of Captains Clark, Gentry, Dickson, Parkinson and Jones. Riding with Gentry's company, Lafayette experienced the tribulations and setbacks that afflict a battalion on the march. The first night's camp was made at East Pecatonica, where the forces had to swim their horses and raft their equipment across the river. At Sugar River on the second night, thirty Winnebago warriors under White Crow and some eighty men under Capt. Stephenson joined Dodge's force. Stephenson's men had brought some grim news. A few days earlier Indians had killed two men near Jones' fort at Sinsinawa Mound. Upon hearing the news, George Jones departed immediately to check up on his workers and his home before rejoining the Michigan volunteers.[14] Col. W. S. "Billy" Hamilton of Hamilton's Diggings also joined the expedition that night, leading twenty Menominee warriors and about a dozen scouts.[15]

White Crow and his Winnebago proposed to lead the miners directly to

Black Hawk's camp via Four Lakes. General Dodge eagerly took up their offer. After several days trudging through impassible swamps and fording the Rock River, with suspicions of Winnebago trickery growing by the hour, Dodge's volunteers approached the mouth of White Water Creek, where White Crow insisted Black Hawk's people were concealed. Just as Dodge's excitement peaked, it was doused by the arrival of an express. Atkinson had ordered Dodge to abandon the pursuit and proceed without delay to his headquarters on the Bark River a few miles northeast of Koshkonong. The order infuriated Dodge, but he complied.[16] He joined Atkinson on July 6th, having completed his march without serious incident other than having formed the opinion that Posey's Illinois men were a rabble of insubordinate bastards. Whether this had anything to do with being rejected by them in the election at Fort Hamilton, no one knows. Dodge did request Atkinson to have Posey's command exchanged for Alexander's, a request White Beaver granted.[17]

Up to that point, Atkinson's pursuit of Black Hawk had been wholly unsuccessful. He had arrived on the south shores of Lake Koshkonong on July 2nd, encouraged by the reports of his Winnebago scouts. Although he found abundant evidence of recent Indian camps there, Black Hawk remained as elusive as ever. White Beaver encamped and sent patrols out to scour both shores of the lake for any sign of hostiles. On July 4th, the scouts returned with an old Sauk man. Half starved, blind and exhausted, the frail fellow was gaunt testament to the deteriorating state of the British Band. Atkinson promised he would be released unharmed if he would divulge Black Hawk's plans. The old Sauk informed White Beaver that Makataimeshekiakiak's band had skirted Koshkonong's left shore and were headed northward towards the head of the Rock River. On that information, Atkinson sent scouts to search the area, but they returned without finding a trace of Black Hawk. In the end, the old Sauk's cooperation was for naught. A group of militiamen soon murdered him and lifted his scalp.[18]

Atkinson was becoming more frustrated with each passing day. From July 7th through July 9th, Lafayette and comrades in arms struggled lost through thicket, swamps and bog holes, losing both supplies and horses to the sucking morass, searching for a trace of the Sauk. The Winnebago and Pottawatomie guides proved either ignorant or purposely misleading; though no white man could discern which. After a "perplexing march" of several miles north of White Water, Atkinson's men met friendly Indians who informed them that they were headed into a complete and impassible wilderness. Quite perturbed, White Beaver returned to Koshkonong, where Lafayette, Augustus and their companions would endure two more days of mud, hunger and vicious hordes of mosquitoes.

Things were in a wretched state of repair for the Army of the Frontier. Two weeks in the field and Atkinson hadn't a clue where Black Hawk was. He had also learned that President Andrew Jackson had dispatched Winfield Scott to replace him. Governor Reynolds and his staff were in a depressed funk. No small number of Sucker volunteers was laid low with the dysentery. Those who weren't ill proved insubordinate and incorrigible, while Dodge had openly refused to have his Michigan volunteers build White Beaver a stockade. Incredibly, the general discovered the army's generous provisions were already exhausted. Unlike the regular troops, the volunteers had been overly liberal devouring rations. Without resupply, the expedition was doomed to fail. It looked to be a complete debacle.

To head off such an unthinkable calamity, Atkinson sent a good number of the ill-disciplined Illinois militia home. He then ordered Posey's men back to Fort Hamilton to await his orders. Governor Reynolds subsequently abandoned the expedition, convinced that Black Hawk would never be cornered, and departed on July 10th.[19] On that day, White Beaver directed Dodge, Henry and Alexander's brigades to march to Fort Winnebago on the Wisconsin River to get supplies for their men and admonished them to return promptly.[20] Fort Winnebago lay fifty miles or so to the northwest, and Dodge and his miners soon outdistanced Henry and Alexander. Lafayette endured a rugged, exhausting ride through seemingly impenetrable wilderness before arriving at the fort on July 11th. To everyone's disappointment, Dodge could get nothing better than some bread for his men, whose hunger quickly consumed that and what little remained of their morale as well. The Michigan miners flatly informed General Dodge that if they had to return to Atkinson the same way they'd come, they'd up and go home instead. It was nothing short of mutiny. Noting his father's intense, seething expression Lafayette Dodge braced himself for the predictable detonation.

It never came. At the critical moment John Kinzie, the subagent for the Winnebago at Portage, presented to Dodge his veritable salvation . . . the tracker Pierre Pacquette. Pacquette was a long time employee of the American Fur Company, a guide and half Indian who spoke Winnebago. In turn, Pacquette introduced a group of Winnebago bearing some interesting news. Black Hawk was presently camped at the Rock River Rapids, they claimed, thirty-five miles or so northeast of Koshkonong and was planning to avoid Atkinson by moving his band westward to the Mississippi, where he would cross to safety.[21] A flush of excitement coursed through General Dodge. Atkinson had thwarted him once. He was not about to let him do it again, even if it meant disobeying a direct order.

On July 12th, Alexander and Henry's militia joined Dodge, who urged them to join him in pursuing Black Hawk. Henry was hot to get after the Indians, but Alexander was hesitant. He pointed out that Atkinson had ordered them to return immediately. True, Dodge mused, but Atkinson hadn't specified any particular route to take back. The Rock River Rapids were out of line with a direct return to Koshkonong, but wouldn't it be prudent to take the route most advantageous to the war effort, even if it took a bit longer? Alexander remained unconvinced, but Dodge would not be dissuaded. His pursuit of Black Hawk would begin with the morning light.

The initial omens for Dodge's foray weren't reassuring. That night the entire militia horse herd stampeded, as one soldier said, "running through our encampment with a noise equal to thunder . . . scattering the Suckers like dry leaves in a gale." A good number of the mounts streaked off along the most direct route back to Atkinson and it took the men two days to round them up. Ninety horses were never found. The Winnebago were blamed, of course. Whether they were culpable or not, they couldn't have failed to have been heartily entertained by the spectacle.[22]

On July 15th, Alexander turned back toward Koshkonong and General Atkinson. Guided by Paquette and the Winnebago, General Dodge, General James D. Henry and six to seven hundred mounted men headed for the Rapids of the Rock. Three days of hard riding brought them to a Sauk camp. It was deserted. The volunteers' spirits dropped. The British Band had fled.[23] There were a number of trails, at best several days old. A group of Winnebago camped nearby told the militia that Black Hawk had dodged, in a sense, Old Hairy Face's approach and was camped near Cranberry Lakes, a mere twenty miles north of them. Dodge glanced up at the afternoon sun. It was still early, about 2 pm. Determined to pursue, he sent adjutants Woodbridge and Merryman with the Winnebago guide Little Thunder off to update Atkinson on their movements. To Dodge's surprise, a few hours later Little Thunder galloped back and announced that he had just come across Black Hawk's fresh trail, heading directly west-southwest. Little Thunder had tried to tell Woodbridge and Merryman, but neither of them understood Winnebago, forcing the guide to abruptly turn about and race back to where they'd left Dodge, followed by the perplexed adjutants.[24]

It was superb news. The following morning dawned dreary and overcast, yet the men were so eager to start after the Sauk that many of them abandoned their camp equipment. The pursuit was grueling, leading the miners through thickets and muddy swamps under an unrelenting and punishing rain. Yet the men struggled onward, fueled by eager anticipation. Evidence of the Sauk's dire condition began to appear. Along the trail, the famished Indians had stripped the bark off the oaks for food. The ground was dotted with holes where the desperate had searched for edible roots. Occasionally, the column would pass the body of a woman or a child who had starved to death. Such macabre sights cheered the militia considerably. General Dodge, Lafayette and indeed the entire command believed they were but days from snuffing out Black Hawk's misguided aspirations. Night finally demanded an end to the hunt. Nothing, not water-soaked firewood, hunger cramped stomachs, neither soggy blankets nor bone-tired fatigue, could dampen the militiamen's fervor.[25]

On July 19th, a Winnebago captive informed Dodge that Black Hawk was close at hand. Mustering into battle array, the Americans forged on until dusk, bearing the scorching sauna of a 90-degree heat steaming the countryside. That night they encamped on the east shore of Lake Monona. Early the following morning, the volunteers choked down raw bacon and dough for breakfast and mounted up once more. Capt. Gentry and fourteen men headed out ahead of the main force to scout out the Sauk positions. Whether Lafayette accompanied them or not is unknown. Two miles out they discovered an Indian man at the lake edge, sitting on his wife's recently arranged grave. Doubtlessly the man knew of the whites approach, but turned his back on them in resigned indifference. Mourning her death from exposure and hunger, he seemed to await the inevitable fatal volley. As he partially turned toward them, Gentry's men obliged him, blowing off the back of his head and tearing away his scalp. Moving roughly along the west bank of Lake Mendota, Gentry's men took fire from a Sauk sniper hidden behind a tree. It was poor cover. The militia shot him dead. The scouting party then rejoined General Dodge's advance.[26]

After crossing the Catfish River, Dodge's and Henry's troops took up the march in two columns, with Henry's Illinois brigade in the lead. Dodge's Badgers soon became irritated with what they considered the leisurely pace Henry's Suckers were taking and they clamored for General Dodge to take the lead. Acknowledging his men and his own impatience, Dodge brought his command around as the commander of Henry's lead column cussed them heartily. Ahead there was a faint but electrifying rattle of musketry. Dodge's skirmishers had found Neopope and twenty warriors covering Black Hawk's retreat.

At that critical point the horses began to give out. The Michigan militia would lose forty horses that day and forty mounted volunteers suddenly would find themselves demoted to the infantry. Unable to carry the heavier equipment, they tossed it aside. A clutter of camp junk collected along the trail already marked by the refuse of the desperately retreating Sauk; kettles, mats, bags and par fleches, a variety of domestic knickknacks, occasionally an exhausted old man or a starving women, all dispassionately murdered and harvested by the militia for grotesque keepsakes.[27]

The rain again began to fall, further hampering Dodge's slogging progress down the valley toward the Wisconsin River. At long last they reached the Wisconsin bottom.

It was the first time the British Band and Dodge's men would clash and it was Lieutenant Lafayette Dodge's first baptism by fire. While Makataimeshekiakiak hastily drew up lines of defense, a mile away the Sauk were frantically ferrying their families out to an island in the middle of the river. Neopope's rear guard was now making near suicidal attacks, anything to impede the whites' advance.

The order to dismount was given. It was late afternoon of July 21st. Dodge was within a mile and a half from the river, some thirty miles below Fort Winnebago.[28] Just as Lafayette and his comrades swung down from their mounts, Captain Joseph Dickson and a party of Dodge's spies came racing back through the brush.

"Here they come," Dickson bellowed, "Thick as bees!"

Shrieking Sauk warriors were right behind him. Old Hairy Face ordered his men forward to a rise. His phalanx of volunteers parted long enough to admit Dickson's men and then closed to face the Sauk attack. Squatting down in the grass, they raised their rifles. The Indians were no more than thirty yards from them when Dodge ordered a volley. The roar of rifle fire and white musketry smoke seemed to obliterate the oncoming hostiles. The sheer audacity of their charge must have saved the Indians, for when the smoke cleared, only one Sauk had fallen. The Indians quickly retreated and took cover into a ravine of tall grass. From the bluffs overhead, Sauk snipers poured shot down on Dodge and his men. The firefight lasted thirty minutes. For Lafayette, it must have been hot going. The militia was taking more punishment than they could mete out.

Rather than retreat, Dodge ordered a charge. Under the sound of crackling muskets, Lafayette lunged ahead with Gentry's men, driving the Sauk warriors out of the ravine and onto the bluff. Fearing that the Americans would flank them and attack their families, the Sauk snipers suddenly abandoned their position and dashed down towards the Wisconsin River. The miners sent a storm of lead after them, perhaps killing as many as six warriors.[29] One scout later recalled that during the fight an "Indian of noble form" stood on a tall rock, directing his men. Guns drew a bead on him and discharged, but with no effect. At length the leader retreated with his forces. It was presumed that the man was Black Hawk himself.[30] Americans estimated Sauk losses might have been as high as seventy warriors. Based on the number of scalps Paquette and his Winnebago guides took that day, Dodge estimated thirty to forty Indians killed. Black Hawk's count was substantially lower: six. Nightfall and heavy rain finally extinguished the fighting and Dodge ordered a stand-down. Henry's Illinois squadron had lost one killed and several injured, while the Michigan volunteers suffered but one wounded. The flintlocks were soaked, as were the exhausted men. The Sauk wouldn't be going anywhere. They would assault Black Hawk's stronghold on Wisconsin Heights tomorrow.[31]

The next morning, Lieutenant H. L. Dodge awoke to the news that the British Band had vanished. The Sauk had fashioned crude rafts and canoes from whatever they could scrounge and had crossed to the north bank under the cover of darkness. General Dodge chose not to pursue. He faced more pressing issues. His men were exhausted and nearly destitute of supplies. They needed to dry out and recollect their gear. Hence, Lafayette spent the day of the 22nd in camp with the men, reorganizing equipment and rehashing their victory. General Dodge wrote out the report of his march and the battle to Atkinson and concluded by praising his men for their valor and coolness under fire, having "done honor to their state & themselves." The day ended uneventfully. Bivouac fires twinkled through the damp mists and heavy shadows as dusk flowed into the valley.

The cloak of night brought little rest to the weary men. In the pit of their convulsing guts, Lafayette and his companions apprehended a surprise attack by the treacherous Black Hawk. So they lay in the clammy dew-sodden grass, their eyes wide to the dark stillness, their arms cradling the security of their muskets. With rattling regularity a sentry's alarm shattered the silence and jolted them all to their feet. About an hour before sunrise, through the calm of the predawn haze, a distant but clear voice abruptly echoed through camp, launching into a long oratory. The orator was no sentry and the words were not English. The volunteers bolted up in a panic, believing their worst fears realized. Certain eyewitnesses with clearly Michigan loyalties claimed Dodge's men reacted to the crisis calmly, while Henry had to pump up his Illinois boys' courage with patriotic harangue, invoking "the name of their Sucker mothers, to vindicate the valor of the Suckers and the Sucker State" and in general made "a great Sucker speech."[32] It was obvious to all the men in camp, Badgers and Suckers alike, that the Indians were taunting them before launching a vicious predawn assault. Some of the militia might have recognized the language as Winnebago, but there were no Winnebagos in camp with the whites that night. Paquette and his faithful scouts had already departed. Finally, just before dawn, the voice faded away.

The instrument for such wholesale terror had been Neopope. Unbeknownst to the whites, he had just spent better than an hour complementing Dodge and his men on their victory and attempting to arrange the capitulation of the British Band and their peaceful return to the reservation. They would surrender completely, under the sole condition that their women and children would be protected. Neither General

Dodge nor General Henry nor anyone of their jittery command had comprehended a single word. Another attempt at ending the war was lost. Dispirited, Neopope abandoned the British Band and struck out on his own while his companions reported the bad news to Black Hawk.[33] Guided on by Winnebago friends, Black Hawk and his followers continued across the foreign countryside in the fading hope of reaching the Mississippi, leaving in their wake the dead and dying.

The next morning Dodge's column marched some twenty miles from Wisconsin Heights to Blue Mound Fort, where they found Atkinson. He'd arrived the day before. While Dodge had been chasing Black Hawk, Atkinson's force had been resupplied. On July 16th, White Beaver had received two messages, the first informing him about Dodge's pursuit and the second from General Winfield Scott, apprising him a change of fortune. Scott's entire army was in Chicago, immobilized by the cholera and he advised Atkinson to carry on without him. Rather than terrible news, for Atkinson it was, perhaps, a chance for redemption. Five days after that, Atkinson and his regulars departed for Blue Mound in hopes of seeing the action that had so annoyingly eluded them.

Exhausted but heartened by the news that Black Hawk's band was in dire straits, Atkinson hastily drew up a final campaign. With 1,300 men and only eight days of rations, he hoped make quick time in pursuit. To ferry his army across the Wisconsin, Atkinson had rafts built from the logs of the now abandoned town of Helena. That alone took two days. At last, on July 28th the Army of the Frontier stood on the north side of the river and in completely unknown territory.[34] Dodge's command took the advance and came across the Sauk trail almost immediately. They continued at a brisk pace, the prairie giving way to rugged ravine-cut ridge country of thick forest and tangling undergrowth, so foreign that even the Winnebago scouts had difficulty recognizing the lay of the land. Still Atkinson was unrelenting. When the army's progress was slowed by sluggish medical supply wagons, Atkinson ordered them left behind. For three days the army lurched forward along a trail increasingly well marked by the emaciated corpses of the starving Sauk.[35]

14

KILL THE NITS, THEN YOU'LL HAVE NO LICE

As the day of August 1st dawned, Makataimeshekiakiak's demoralized refugees straggled down steep forested bluffs and onto the east bank of the meandering Mississippi River. They were twenty-odd miles above Prairie du Chien and two miles below the mouth of the Bad Axe River. For almost five months they had been afflicted, starved and endlessly pursued, their families decimated. The sight of the great river gave the Sauk a sudden rush of hope. Safety and shelter lay on the opposite bank. All they need do was cross over. Constructing enough rafts and boats to do so would take precious time, time Black Hawk knew they didn't have. In vain he tried to dissuade them. He had always depended on Neopope and his scouts to keep him informed as to Atkinson's position and progress, but they had not rejoined him. Consequently Makataimeshekiakiak had no idea where White Beaver's army was. Although he believed they still had a five-day advantage, there was still a real danger of being overtaken. He urged his people to go northward where they could take refuge among the Chippewa, but the vision of salvation set so closely on the far bank over ruled his advice. Men, women and children set themselves to throwing together crude rafts.

Black Hawk's fears shortly materialized on the misty Mississippi upstream. A steamboat appeared around the bend, a hellacious 100-foot ogre belching black smoke. Black Hawk recognized it. It was the steamboat *Warrior*, piloted by Captain Joseph Throckmorton, carrying an officer, fifteen regular soldiers, six volunteers, and a handful of Winnebago guides. They were returning from up river after having warned the Sioux, inveterate enemies of the Sauk, that Black Hawk was headed in their direction.[1]

Makataimeshekiakiak had forbidden his warriors to shoot as the steamboat approached. Fluttering a small white cloth in the air, he hoped to coax the steamboat towards shore. The chief intended to board the *Warrior*, surrender himself as a hostage and insure the safety of his women and children. He knew Captain Throckmorton and believed him to be a fair and just man. Throckmorton captained the boat that day, but the officer, Lieutenant James Kingsbury, commanded the steamboat. Forever suspicious of the Indians he ordered Throckmorton heave to at a discretionary distance, then ordered the leader of the Indians to send the white flag up to him. Hoisting up a larger white surrender flag onto a pole, a Sauk warrior waded into the water. As he approached the *Warrior*, those on board demanded to know if Black Hawk's people were Winnebago or Sauk. He replied that they were Sauk and they wished to surrender. There was a long and tense silence. Abruptly a Winnebago on deck blurted out a warning. Run! The soldiers were going to shoot! Immediately Kingsbury's men loosed a volley at the Indians. Taking cover among the thickets and driftwood, the Sauk returned fire.[2]

Lieutenant Kingsbury unleashed three volleys of canister into the Indians from his deck cannon with savage effect, but the wicked toll failed to route the Sauk fighters. The firefight continued for two hours and ended only when the *Warrior* ran short of wood to fuel the boilers. Almost nonchalantly its guns fell silent and it floated off downriver towards Prairie du Chien. It was late afternoon. In the relative calm, Black Hawk surveyed the casualties. Two-dozen people lay dead. A large number were wounded. The day was by then growing short. Knowing the boat would return Black Hawk once more pleaded with his people to leave their pitiful rafts and accompany him northward. It was useless. By then their initial hope had been replaced by desperation. Reluctantly, Makataimeshekiakiak, the Winnebago Prophet and some fifty men, women and children left the obstinate survivors to their fate. They moved upstream in hopes of doubling back towards the Dells of the Wisconsin, where they might at last find refuge.[3]

The return of the *Warrior* would be the least of the Sauk troubles. Neither Black Hawk nor those struggling to get across the river realized that Atkinson's Army of the Frontier was nearly on top of them, coming on hard just beyond the bluffs. After crossing the Wisconsin on the 28th, Atkinson had rapidly moved west-northwest along the Pine River Valley. The Sauk trail turned west, forded Mill Creek, then angled northwest again into the Ocooch Mountains. Marching with the army, Lafayette beheld an absolute wilderness. The terrain became increasingly rugged and jumbled. On July 30th, volunteers discovered a recent Sauk camp and telling evidence of their desperation: fresh skeletons of dead horses stripped of meat. The Sauk were eating their ponies. They also came across a crippled and wasted Sauk warrior, who revealed that his people were planning to cross the Mississippi. The militia then killed him.

The march took on a greater sense of urgency. Forward Atkinson's Army of the Frontier lurched, scaling steep hills, plunging through bramble and thicket, forest and swamp. On July 31st, they forded the Kickapoo River, and then paused to allow the horses to graze. The signs that they were catching up to Black Hawk's band were unmistakable. Indian kettles and traps, mats and blankets cluttered the route. The militia counted at least a dozen Sauk corpses along the way that day, primarily women who had starved to death. At 8 o'clock that evening, Atkinson reluctantly ordered a halt. The men must have heaved a sigh of relief. Fatigued, parched and hungry, Lafayette set his horse out to graze, but kept a guarded watch on the animal. His father had cautioned the volunteers to keep their mounts close at hand, suspecting that their rest would be brief. Gradually cooking fires sputtered to life in the gathering gloom as the volunteers prepared a hasty and meager meal.[4]

Lieutenant Lafayette Dodge had just settled into his blanket when an order rippled through the darkness. Mount up. It was two o'clock in the morning. A thick fog had crept in. Henry and Alexander's Illinois volunteers were still searching for their horses in the gloom when Gentry's command swung into the saddle. General Dodge had no intention of delaying for Suckers or sore-shinned regulars. Old Hairy Face's 147-man company slipped stealthily out of camp and into the eerie murkiness. Under General Dodge was Major R. H. Kirkpatrick. Under him were five captains; J. Craig and B. B. Craig of Illinois, Duncan, Hoard and James H. Gentry and with Gentry came his first lieutenant, Henry Lafayette Dodge.[5] The sun rose reluctantly through the low lying mists, casting the clear sky directly overhead in a rosy glow. Dodge pressed on as Dickson's spy company took the lead. When they emerged from the glade and into the open, Lafayette gazed down. Below them stretched the grand ravine of the Mississippi. A bank of clouds obscured the riverbanks below. General Dodge's men halted and dismounted. Grimly and methodically they shed all their knapsacks and baggage and picketed their pack animals. Then they coolly checked their weapons. It was about eight o'clock.

While Dodge's men were closing in on the British Band at Bad Axe, some distance north of there a Sauk runner entered Black Hawk's camp. He informed the chief that although several Sauk families had successfully crossed the Mississippi to the west bank, the American army would soon fall upon those thronging the east shore. At that news, Black Hawk immediately turned back to organize a resistance. If the Americans were to slaughter the remnants of his people, Makataimeshekiakiak wished to die with them fighting.[6]

Dodge's men began to advance through thick timber toward the edge of the bluffs. Somewhere ahead of them and to the north, the popping of musketry confirmed Sauk fighters had initiated the battle. War cries echoed through the woodlands, raising the hairs on Lafayette's neck. In reality the Sauk attack had been a ruse to draw the soldiers' fire and lead them northward, away from the Sauk women and children at the Mississippi. It had worked brilliantly. Colonel Zachary Taylor's regulars swung hard right towards the firing. Posey's and Alexander's Illinois brigades promptly followed Taylor. As a result, Henry's Sucker brigade, assigned by

Atkinson to bring up the rear with the pack train suddenly found itself at the front. Neither Henry nor Dodge realized the main body of Sauk was straight ahead. They would be apprised of the fact shortly.[7]

Lafayette heard another burst of musketry, this time directly in front of him. Dickson's spy company had flushed out a line of Sauk snipers forming a rear guard. At once General Dodge realized the British Band was directly ahead. That revelation wasn't lost on Atkinson, either. He ordered Dodge and Henry to hold their positions and await reinforcement. General Dodge refused. To the raucous cheering of the men, he ordered his men forward at the quick step. They crested the heights and descended pell-mell down toward the river, where they came across Dickson, lying on the ground seriously wounded by a Sauk bullet. At that moment, the bushes ahead erupted in a frantic fusillade. The volunteers staggered back, replied with a volley of their own, then reformed and advanced. The Sauk retreated down the bluffs, bounding along ravines, through fallen timbers and undergrowth, hoping to reach the brush-choked river bottom where they could make another stand. Right behind them came Dodge's miners.[8]

In tandem, Henry's militia came crashing through the willows and swept across the river bottom, hitting the main body of the British Band like a tidal wave. Men, women, and children alike fell in bloody heaps as the families scrambled for whatever cover they could find. Some Sauk threw themselves into the river only to drown or be shot. Others scrambled up trees, cowered under logs or buried themselves in sand. Black Hawk described Henry and Dodge's assault as simply unfettered butchery.

> "Early in the morning a party of whites, being in advance of the army, came upon our people . . . They tried to give themselves up—the whites paid no attention to their entreaties—but commenced slaughtering them! In a little while the whole army arrived. Our brave, but few in number, found that the enemy paid no regard to age or sex, and seeing that they were murdering helpless women and little children, determined to fight until they were all killed . . ."

Atkinson later referred to it as an assault "where much execution was done."[9]

The carnage was now at its height. It was at this chaotic, apocalyptic moment that General Dodge's eldest son, according to family lore, did something extraordinary. Considering the temperament of the times, the nature of the men and the place, it was inconceivable. Most professional officers and soldiers of the United States viewed the killing of Indian women and children as a misfortune of war, regrettable but easily dismissed. Atkinson's aide-de-camp Lieutenant Albert Sidney Johnston noted that the federal soldiers "much deplored" the slaughter of the Sauk women and children trying to cross the Mississippi that day. On the other hand the volunteers were unfettered by such sympathies. They didn't give a damn for the Indian and had no qualms about lifting Indian scalps, lopping off their fingers and ears as keepsakes, or slicing off strips of skin from the backs of the dead for razor straps.

Man, woman, child or babe, it didn't matter. One battle-dazed Michigan volunteer spotted a cowering Sauk woman with a baby strapped to her back. He raised his musket, drew a bead on her and fired. The bullet shattered the baby's arm before plunging into its mother's back. Another volunteer known as Big Tooth John House dispassionately murdered a Sauk baby after the battle, explaining to his comrades that if one kills "the nits then you'll have no lice." Members of Alexander's brigade, piqued at having lost their chance for glory to Henry and Dodge's men, made up for it when they discovered a group of Sauk women concealed under a sand bank. The women had buried themselves so completely that only their nostrils showed. The miners made light of their muffled cries as they shot and bayoneted them, one by one.[10]

It would then seem utterly out of the question that, given the sensibilities of the times, Lieutenant Henry Lafayette Dodge, the son of an Indian fighter and miner, with his thoughts fired in adrenaline, could have resisted that lust for Indian blood. Yet people do strange things at the height of danger... unexplainable things. Pressing ahead across the river bottom, bullets whizzing past him, Lafayette spotted an Indian mother and her toddler pinned down by volunteer fire. The two had but moments before being shot to pieces. At that moment, Lafayette apparently dropped his musket, dashed ahead, seized the woman and her child, and dragged them to safety. It was an act of absolute insanity, one that must have confounded and perhaps outraged his comrades. General Dodge, some family members later claimed, subsequently accused his son of cowardice and was so angry that he never again spoke to him. Was this tale of mercy merely an endearing fabrication spun years later from family nostalgia? Perhaps. If not, it would have been a rare and sublime act of compassion.[11]

As if to administer the coup de grace, the steamboat *Warrior* reappeared down river. Replenished with fuel and ammunition, the crewmen brought their cannon to bear on the scattering Sauk. The few that had managed to swim out to an island were raked by the *Warrior's* cannon shot or picked off by sharpshooters.[12] Most of those few who were able to reach the Mississippi's west bank were dispatched by the Sioux. By the time the Battle of Bad Axe ended, the Sauk dead was estimated at a upwards of three hundred. There were all of thirty-nine prisoners taken, mostly women and children.[13] During the Black Hawk War, of the entire British Band of over one thousand souls perhaps as few as 150 survived. Of the American forces, eleven soldiers were killed and sixteen wounded that day.[14] Lafayette and his fellow miners in Gentry's company came out of the fight generally unscathed. Dodge's entire command, having been in the thick of the assault on Black Hawk, suffered no fatalities, but six wounded, three of which who would die from their wounds.[15] In his memoirs, George Jones claimed to have served in that battle and noted that Dodge's "brave sons Henry Lewis and Augustus Caesar, as well as his son-in-law Paschal Bequette . . . acted bravely their parts . . . "[16] It is curious that Jones failed to get Lafayette's name right, though he knew him well.

Makataimeshekiakiak's late arrival at the battle denied him the noble death he later claimed to have wanted. After fleeing to the Winnebago at Prairie La Crosse, the aged and weary Black Hawk determined to give himself up. On August 27th, three weeks after the battle, Black Hawk, the Winnebago Prophet and Neopope surrendered to Agent Joseph Street at Prairie du Chien. They were sent downriver to St. Louis under the guard of a young officer from moldy tumble down Fort Crawford, Lieutenant Jefferson Davis. The old chief and his cohorts spent the winter imprisoned at Jefferson Barracks in ball and chain. In April of 1833, Black Hawk became the most famous and infamous member of an Indian delegation sent to Washington, DC. Makataimeshekiakiak visited President Jackson and toured New York and Baltimore, where curious whites received him with the warmth of a celebrity.[17] Paradoxically, the old chief seemed to hold no enmity toward the Americans. He did vigorously protest newspaper claims that he had "murdered women and children among the whites," something he had never done.[18]

Blackhawk would return to prison and dictate his autobiography to Sauk interpreter Antoine LeClair. He dedicated it to his nemesis and conqueror, General Atkinson. The book, published in 1833, outraged Michigan and Illinois veterans of the war, portraying as it did Black Hawk as a human being with human sentiments. Makataimeshekiakiak was at last released to Keokuk's supervision. He lived for five more years, residing near the Iowa River in a lodge of bark, watching the inevitable erosion of Keokuk's power and the slow evaporation of Sauk land.

The United States considered the Black Hawk War justification for taking what little land the Sauk and Fox nation still had on the east side of the Mississippi as well as a fifty-mile strip on the west bank. The Americans blamed the entire Sauk nation for the fracas, though most of them had peacefully resided in Iowa for the duration of the conflict. The treaty of 1832 penned at Fort Armstrong in September also stripped the Winnebago of vast tracts of real estate, disregarding the consideration that friendly members of the tribe had been indispensable to Atkinson during his campaign. Appropriately, General Dodge was a signatory to the treaty. In 1833, the Chippewa, Ottawa and Pottawatomie lost their lands in Michigan Territory. In 1836, the Americans coerced the Menominee, proven allies of the whites, to sell four million acres of their country. That same year the Sauk surrendered the last of their Iowa lands and were shipped first to Kansas and later to Oklahoma. By 1842, not one acre of Indian land remained in Wisconsin.[19]

After the Battle of Bad Axe, General Atkinson and his forces retired to Prairie du Chien to arrange the capture of Black Hawk, and then removed to Rock Island. On August 20th, Major General Winfield Scott and his sickened army finally arrived at Rock Island, having fired not one shot. With them marched an unwelcome companion: Cholera. Six days later, an epidemic was doing far more damage to the Americans than Black Hawk could have ever hoped.[20] It is another point of irony that Atkinson was more highly regarded as a warrior by Black Hawk than by his own superiors. President Andrew Jackson suspected Atkinson lacked rigor and consequently appointed Scott as supreme commander of U. S. forces. In December of 1832, Zachary Taylor asserted that if Atkinson had immediately brought federal forces against the Sauk before they had moved up the Rock River, there would have been no Indian war at all.[21] In hindsight, it was probably true. In his own defense, White Beaver stated that his forces hadn't been in position to prevent Black Hawk from going up the Rock. Nevertheless, fear of criticism had kept Atkinson under a great amount of pressure and the end of the war brought tremendous relief. According to George Jones, when Atkinson met General Dodge at Prairie du Chien after the Battle of Bad Axe, he rushed up to him, threw his arms around Dodge in intimate embrace and exclaimed, "Dodge, you have saved me, you have dragged me on to victory!"

Although Atkinson officially praised both General Dodge and General Henry for their actions during the battle, his pique over Dodge's infuriating refusal to obey his order to wait for reinforcements, coupled with a well-earned revulsion for Badger and Sucker militias in general, makes Jones' tale of effusive gratitude suspect at best.[22]

15

POLITICS AGAIN

James Duane Doty, the judge who had prosecuted Red Bird, was leisurely strolling the streets of Galena one fall day in 1833 when a young gentleman in his early twenties walked up, his face flushed scarlet in fury. Stopping directly in Doty's path, he launched into a unruly verbal assault. The judge had sullied his family's name with lies and innuendo, the firebrand announced, raising his voice to amused pedestrians gathering around.

"The name of Dodge shall never be slandered by such a damned scoundrel!" he proclaimed and then challenged Judge Doty to a duel.

"Stand back, young man. I know you not." Doty coolly replied and turned away.

The young man wasn't so easily discouraged. He continued his harangue from the middle of the street as Doty, somewhat taken aback, ignored him. The judge had just made his acquaintance with Henry Dodge's eldest son, Henry Lafayette, who had taken offense to Doty's perceived insinuations about his father. After Doty failed to answer his demand for gentlemanly satisfaction, Lafayette slapped up notices around Galena trumpeting that he'd "shaken his whip" over the judge's head and Doty had skulked off chastised like the cowardly mongrel he was.[1]

It had been one more shot in the long feud between Judge James D. Doty and Lafayette's father, General Henry Dodge. Dodge shrank from no confrontation, whether he was bashing an Indian with a footstool, calling offending rivals onto the field of honor, or intimidating Eastern toadies like Judge Doty. As to be expected, his sons Lafayette and Augustus defended their father's ambitions and reputation with equal zeal. Political rivalries were a rough pastime in mining country, engaged in with such unrestrained fervor that they were regularly marred by intimidation, scandal, duels and bloodshed. Animosities were forged that lasted a lifetime. Such was the Doty-Dodge feud. The overwhelming majority of folks residing in the mining district, at least those who knew what was good for them, were staunch Democrats and loyal supporters of General Dodge. They were Democrats with strong Missouri ties and cherished in their hearts a singular Southern sentiment. Many yet held slaves. The citizens residing at Green Bay and along Lake Michigan held no such affections. Still relatively few in numbers, they shared little in common with their western colleagues. Democrats or Whigs, they were generally Yankees with Yankee values. Doty was just that. He was a New Yorker. Although he was quite familiar with mining country and was a Democrat as well, he held the northern sentiments of Green Bay . . . provided they did not conflict with his own. Well educated and well dressed, he strode the streets of Galena with a studied air of sophistication. Dodge and his miners found him a snobbish and arrogant elitist. In return, Doty saw Dodge as a grime-besmirched despot whose lack of erudition left him no recourse other than intimidation to get his way. In that assessment Doty seriously erred. Dodge's undeniable penchant for intimidation was equaled by his acute political savvy, as the judge would discover to his constant consternation.

Yet personal differences alone couldn't explain the depth of enmity that Dodge and Doty cultivated for one another. Some claimed it all began in 1836 when Doty managed to sabotage Dodge's choice for the capital city of the newly created Wisconsin Territory, but the fact that Henry Lafayette publicly lambasted Doty in the streets of Galena three years earlier refutes that account. Some years before, after the close of the Black Hawk War, the judge had the gall to stick his nose into Indian affairs; always a dangerous thing when one sympathizes with the wrong side—in this case, the Indians. Henry Dodge made no secret that he wanted the last of the Winnebago evicted. Doty apparently disagreed, quite critically and quite publicly, to Dodge's intense indignation. In a letter to his old boss Governor Lewis Cass of Michigan, James Doty's comments about Dodge were reminiscent of similar complaints lodged against John Dodge of Kaskaskia so long ago by Father Gibault.

> "The officers of Justice seem to be intimidated by the swaggering of Genl. Dodge and his band who can as readily procure a conviction as they have a bill [of indictment]. You are perhaps aware that my own life is threatened by the Genl. and subalterns, in consequence of my attempt to rescue these Indians from the effects of this excitement."[2]

Rather than acting as a friend of the Indian, Doty's actions were motivated more by a desire to settle scores. In 1823, President Monroe had appointed Doty circuit judge for Northern Michigan Territory. It was a dauntingly vast area, particularly since Judge Doty and his young family lived at Green Bay. In November of 1832, after nine years on the job, Doty resigned. It was true that the position subjected him to the hardships of travel and the long absences from his family. It's more likely Doty resigned upon learning that Henry Dodge had requested President Jackson, as one good Democrat to another, to do him the favor of firing the man. That was probably payback for an earlier Doty transgression. Years before, General Dodge had appeared at Doty's court in Prairie du Chien. He had an interest in the outcome of the proceedings that day and intended to see them concluded in his favor. Daunting he was as he swaggered into the courtroom like a buccaneer, his belt jammed with bowie knives and pistols. Judge Doty was outraged. He publicly rebuked Dodge for his impudence and had him ejected from the courtroom. It was likely that this fairly minor insult by the young judge ignited their life-long grudge.[3]

On October 9th, 1832, Henry Lafayette mustered out of service in the Black Hawk War after five months of service and returned to his father's diggings and smelting furnace.[4] Once again, war had thrown the entire region into stagnation. It was rough going for a time, but gradually the mines and farms once more began producing. Mail service was restored. Businesses reopened and the economy prospered. During this time, Henry Dodge and his sons built a new and more spacious home a few miles outside of Dodgeville and named it "The Grove." It was a two-story frame house, with the luxury of a white coat of paint and dormer windows. Behind the main house they erected a summer washhouse, the cookhouses, a springhouse and smoke house. There was also a cluster of small cabins for either the Dodge slaves, or the Dodge free servants, depending on who was doing the asking. Three blacks resided there: Joshua and his wife Phoebe and another fellow named Toby. Toby had originally belonged to Israel Dodge and was particularly conspicuous for a set of ghastly scars on his head. When the Dodge youngsters asked how he got them, he always claimed that "the Injuns" had got his scalp. Apparently a wild cat had actually jumped him while he was out riding in the woods one day.

Predictably, The Grove became a center of activity. Visitors were nearly always on hand. There were Indians—groups of Winnebago who came to feast on Hairy Face's celebrated generosity, provided they avoided Hairy Face's legendary hair-trigger temper. There was a stream of sycophants and favor seekers, political chums and old friends, speculators and even a few young soldiers from Fort Crawford. And in parlor and kitchen, on porch and in hallway, the Dodge home constantly hummed with the ardor of political argument.[5]

In 1834, Henry Lafayette built a hewn log store in Dodgeville, where he lived. Through the years it would serve a multitude of functions: post office, livery stable, and general store. Lafayette would call Dodgeville home for the next ten years and his life would be comparable to that of the other mildly illustrious citizens of Iowa County. He sat on a variety of juries and boards; served as an election judge and as a school representative.[6] Although he dabbled in politics, his younger brother

Augustus had shown a real flair for the game. Perhaps he had fewer responsibilities than his older brother and a more natural predilection for affairs of state. Possibly Lafayette lacked the seriousness expected of him by his father and was distracted by the other, frivolous pleasures of life. At any rate, General Dodge recognized Augustus' potential and in 1833 arranged for him to return to Ste. Genevieve and polish his qualities up a bit at Hertich's Asylum. Four years later, Augustus would marry his 18-year-old grammar tutor, Clara Ann, who was, incidentally, Professor Hertich's daughter.[7]

Still, Henry Dodge would depend on Lafayette to oversee his business operations while a new responsibility kept him away. On March 4th, 1833, President Andrew Jackson gave command of the First Regiment of United States Dragoons to Moses Henry Dodge. He held the rank of colonel.[8] Dodge would be absent from home for the better part of three years, stationed with the 1st Regiment at Jefferson Barracks, Missouri and then Fort Gibson in present day Oklahoma. It would prove to be a unpleasant tour of duty. Troubles plagued Dodge from the get go. The men of the 1st Dragoons were underfed, under educated, undisciplined, ill mannered and nearly devoid uniforms. Generally the men were armed with rattletrap muskets that had been pulled from the fort arsenal where they had lain since the War of 1812. Desertion was a persistent problem and the guardhouse was usually jammed full with troopers guilty of some infraction. Morale was abysmal.

Henry Dodge could bear all that, but he could not endure the infuriating insubordination of his snooty subordinates. His officers saw themselves as polished and professional soldiers and a list of them read like a who's who of American military figures. Among them were Lieutenant Colonel Stephen Watts Kearny, who would lead the Army of the West into Santa Fe, Captain Edwin V. Sumner, later to command the Department of New Mexico, and of course Dodge's post adjutant, the contentious 25 year old Lt. Jefferson Davis. With the sole exception of Kearny, they held their unrefined frontier-forged commanding officer in contempt.

> "Col. Dodge . . . a man about say fifty, thick set, somewhat gray, a thorough backwoodsman, very fond of talking over his own exploits . . . on the whole a clever man, but not much of a soldier."[9]

Lt. Jefferson Davis absolutely loathed Dodge. He disguised his antipathy as inspired by professional, soldierly concerns but it almost certainly arose from a painfully personal affront. Davis had been stationed at Fort Crawford during the years of the Black Hawk conflict. To break the doldrums, he and a group of young soldiers made regular trips to Dodgeville for entertainment. Invariably, they stopped by the Dodge residence to pay their respects and enjoy a drink and a meal or two. During one visit, Davis was smitten by General Dodge's sixteen-year-old daughter Mary Louise and a discreet romance soon blossomed. Whenever Davis could escape Fort Crawford, he visited Mary. The young lovers strolled on the prairies, plucking the bright spring flowers of hope and devotion. Alas, it was not to be. After a long duty-related absence, the hopeful lieutenant returned to ask Henry Dodge for Mary's hand in marriage. It wasn't clear whether Dodge disapproved of Davis, if Mary had changed her mind, or had been betrothed to another, but in 1836 she wed the brave Captain John Dement of Illinois instead.[10]

Whatever the reason for their enmity, by August of 1834 Dodge and Davis were quarreling openly. It infuriated him that he couldn't just take Davis and the other whiners onto the field of honor and dispatch them one by one, if only they would agree to give him the satisfaction. But more significantly, Henry Dodge felt isolated from important events occurring in western Michigan. There had been a proposal to cleave a new territory from Michigan, the Territory of Wisconsin. Dodge hoped to be its first governor but the distractions of military command were inevitably strangling his political aspirations. Still, all was not bad. On May 14th, 1834, General Dodge learned that George Wallace Jones had been able to defeat James Doty for the nomination as Congressional delegate for the new territory. As a result, so much the better were Dodge's chances.[11]

Two years later, his aspirations were realized. In 1836, Wisconsin officially became a separate territory and President Jackson appointed Henry Dodge to a three year term as its first Governor and Superintendent of Indian Affairs. General Dodge took the oath of office on July 4th, 1836 at Mineral Point and with palpable relief bid the United States 1st Regiment of Dragoons farewell.[12] The new territory of Wisconsin was huge, encompassing modern Wisconsin, Iowa and Minnesota. Of the original four counties that made up the new territory, Iowa County boasted five thousand souls, roughly the same number contained in Crawford, Brown and Milwaukee Counties combined. Iowa County thus had a political significance few could fail to appreciate.[13] For Governor Dodge, the foremost citizen of the county, it amounted to a political sledgehammer. He had every intention of using it.

The year 1836 brought significant changes to Henry Lafayette's life as well. He was to be married. The bride was Adele Bequette, the daughter of old Dodge family friends Jean Baptiste and Marie Louise Misplais Bequette of Ste. Genevieve. It is unknown when Henry Lafayette and Adele met and the circumstances of the marriage, but married they were, on June 2, 1836, with Henry Lafayette's mother as witness and signatory. Henry was 26 years old. Adele was 23. The matrimonial document was penned entirely in French.[14] The Dodges claimed to be Episcopalian, but it was no particular surprise that Henry would marry a Catholic French Creole from the old hometown in a Catholic ceremony. Over the years personal and business interests had linked the Bequettes and the Dodges. Adele's brother Paschal Bequette, a close Dodge ally, had relocated to Wisconsin during the 20s, built a lucrative lead furnace and founded the town of Diamond Grove, just west of Mineral Point. Four years before Lafayette and Adele's marriage, Paschal had married Henry Lafayette's older sister, Elizabeth Piety Dodge.

The newlyweds soon returned to Wisconsin. The Michigan Territorial Census of 1836 lists both Henry Lafayette and Augustus as residing in Iowa County. H. L. Dodge was counted as the head of his household of three, although he and Adele had yet to have their first child. The household of Augustus, who was yet unmarried, numbered twelve. James Gentry himself had a household count of fifty souls. A phrase scribbled in the margin of the enumeration sheet explained "Probably lead-mine employees." Lafayette built a log furnace a few miles north northeast of Dodgeville, at Cox Hollow during the year of 1832, but his operation there only lasted a year and no employees appeared in his household census save one. The odd person was probably Michael Bennett, his clerk in the general store.[15]

As governor, one of Dodge's first intentions was to see that the territorial capitol be established at Belmont, a stone's throw from Dodgeville. The little hamlet of Belmont was filled with wild excitement at the prospect. Luxurious hotels, mansions, a grand capitol edifice; all were planned to grace their fair village. It was said that town lots were selling for the exorbitant price of $500.[16] Irrespective of the grandiose visions, when the first Wisconsin legislative assembly convened there October 25th, 1836, they found accommodations miserable. Time and again during deliberations, the representatives turned back to their most pressing issue: a decent location for the Wisconsin capitol.[17] Exasperated, Dodge at last exclaimed that he would agree with any town that the legislature chose, if they would just choose one. He'd soon regret his words. Representative James D. Doty stepped forward with a slightly different proposal. Rather than selecting an existing town, why not build a new capitol more befitting the glorious birth of the new territory? The Four Lakes area fifty miles northeast of Belmont would be perfect and, Doty added as he drew out a detailed map of the site, the city was already platted out.[18] It would be named Madison.

Of course, it was Doty who had the site platted. During the Black Hawk War, he'd seen the region and realized its potential in land sales. When Wisconsin's creation had appeared certain, he bought 1,000 acres around Four Lakes for as little as $1.25 an acre. For its own merits, Four Lakes was an attractive site, but Doty left nothing to chance. He secured his fellow lawmakers' support with such things as free Madison town lots and buffalo robes. Strangely enough, friends and family of Governor Dodge were no exception. In 1837 both Augustus Dodge and George Jones received gifts of Madison town lots, courtesy of James Duane Doty. In an acrimonious vote of fifteen to eleven the legislature approved the Madison site on November 28th, 1836 and appointed Doty as one of three commissioners to oversee the construction of the government buildings.[19]

That contentious November did bring Henry Dodge some good news. Jackson's handpicked heir, Secretary of State Martin Van Buren, was elected President. Van Buren was a Jacksonian Democrat but also a savvy New Yorker who was so skilled at political string pulling and persuasion his enemies referred to him as "The Magician." The new and seriously inept Whig Party had fielded not one but four candidates, including William Harrison and Daniel Webster. Van Buren's election gave every indication that Democrats high and low would continue enjoying favor for some time to come. After taking office in 1837, Van Buren reappointed Henry Dodge governor of Wisconsin, his second term to begin on March 9, 1839.

Those years were prosperous ones for Henry Lafayette Dodge, to some extent courtesy of the political nepotism and intrigues that followed Van Buren's election. In the spring of 1837, he received permission from Federal Receiver John Sheldon of the Mineral Point Land Office to buy four 80-acre lots around Dodgeville. In July Lafayette purchased an acre of land adjoining his Dodgeville store from William Crawford Young, no doubt in hopes of expanding that enterprise. In 1838 he also opened a "sort of stopping place," as one contemporary described it, in a row of long and low cabins near his store. The enterprise was probably a rude inn and grog house. That same year Lafayette landed a job as commissioner to establish a road from Mineral Point via Dodgeville to Helena on the Wisconsin River. Concurrently, his father commissioned him as captain of riflemen for the Iowa County Militia. In September of 1838, Lafayette was appointed postmaster at Dodgeville and served in that capacity until September 30th of 1843, keeping the post office in his own store for seven years.[20] At the same time, his brother-in-law Paschal Bequette was appointed postmaster at Diamond Grove.

From all indications, Henry and Adele enjoyed a fortuitous start to their marriage. On April 5th, 1837, four days after her husband's birthday, Adele gave birth to their first son. They named the baby George Wallace Jones Dodge in honor of their close family friend who was serving as the Wisconsin territorial delegate to Congress.

On August 1st, 1838, Henry L. Dodge handed Adele a new family bible. It was a token of his undying love, dedicated in his own hand as "Mms. Adele Dodge's Book presented by her affectionate husband."[21] Ten months after that, on May 7, 1839, Adele gave birth to a daughter, Marie Therésé. In April of 1839, the Dodgeville Mining Company was incorporated by the territorial legislature and approved by Governor Dodge. His son Henry L. Dodge, son-in-law William I. Madden who had married his daughter Louisiana, and George W. Jones led the company.[22] Madden stood to lose much in the endeavor. His mineral lands were offered up as a substantial basis for the company's capital stock. How well the company did is unclear. Although it was a serious commitment, one gets the impression Henry was a restless spirit. Business, politics and family occasionally made for a hectic life.

Wedged between business, politics and a growing family, Henry Lafayette managed to find time to support Democratic causes, chronicled by the local paper, the Mineral Point Miner's Free Press. Typically of most papers of the time, it was a four to eight page collection of curiosities embracing local events and hot issues as well as diverse items of interest. Poetry and prose, the mysteries of the Egyptian pyramids, news of the Seminole War of 1837, announcements of lawsuits and sheriff sales, advertisements for local attorneys and storekeepers, the bizarre customs of the Chinese; all graced the pages of the Free Press. As with most papers of the period, the Miner's Free Press and its editor Henry B. Welsh were vehemently partisan. Any candidate who was a Democrat allied with the Dodge clan was sure to receive a warm endorsement.

In the August 28th, 1838 issue, The Free Press noted Henry L. Dodge, Esquire served as an Iowa County delegate to Wisconsin's Internal Improvement Convention held at Madison in June of 1838. The purpose of the meeting was to lobby for a variety of territorial improvements, including a railroad line to run from Milwaukee through Madison to the Mississippi. Henry L. Dodge served as one of the two convention vice-presidents, convening and adjourning the sessions. As luck would have it, in a closing resolution Lafayette moved that the convention recognize the city of Madison as ready to accommodate the upcoming legislative session, a delectable irony for Doty, no doubt.[23]

In November of 1838, Henry L. Dodge, in company with John Sheldon, Cromwell Lloyd and others, announced in the Free Press that there would be a meeting in Mineral Point to discuss establishing a territorial bank. The purpose was to wrest control from the highly speculative private banks and put it in the hands of the common people, who theoretically would have the good of the territory more in mind. At the same time, the bank would allow the honest citizen to free themselves from "the incubus which the sharks commonly called financiers, have cast upon them." The Free Press later reported the meeting was well attended.[24] There was considerable alarm over the banks, primarily due to the Panic of 1837. Doty, who had substantial real estate holdings and a large volume of stock in the Mineral Point Bank, was nearly wiped out. On the national level, hardship and worry abounded, with no remedy on the horizon. Jackson's philosophy of minimal government had become dysfunctional, hamstringing Van Buren's efforts to end the financial crisis. Even those in The Magician's own party began to view him as weak and vacillating.[25]

Things would only grow worse for the Democrats. Governor Dodge received an early hint of the troubles lying ahead when George Jones, who had skillfully steered all of Dodge's initiatives through Congress, was defeated in a bid for re-election as territorial delegate. To a great extent, Jones was undone by the notorious Cilley-Graves duel outside of Washington, in which Kentucky representative William Graves shot and killed the highly respected representative of Maine, Jonathan Cilley. Jones had served as Cilley's second. General outrage drove Congress to enact anti-dueling laws and formally censor Jones for his role in the affair.[26] To add insult to injury, the man chosen to complete Jones' term was none other than James Duane Doty.

As for politics back home, Governor Dodge undertook the task of serving his second term as governor. During his tenure, he steadfastly supported the interests of Wisconsin miners and homesteaders. He fought for federal recognition of the settlers' right of preemption and labored to have more lands released into the public domain.[27] Central to that cause was Dodge's relentless efforts to eject the Winnebago still remaining in the territory, threatening to raise a militia and do it himself if need be. He also urged for the speedy removal of the Chippewa, the Menominee, Oneida, Munsee and Stockbridge Iroquois from Wisconsin, as "these Indians were few in number, civilized, and desirous of obtaining the rights of citizenship." It was advised that they be relocated to free them from the evil influences of white civilization, most notably alcohol. In the end it didn't matter whether the Indians were civilized or not. They were removed.[28]

With Van Buren's problems multiplying, the Whigs saw in the upcoming national election of 1840 a splendid opportunity such as they'd not seen before. They unleashed a barrage of attacks on the Democrats through the Whig newspapers. In Wisconsin, the Milwaukee Sentinel routinely lambasted Dodge and his cronies for a variety of improprieties, from misconduct to his incendiary message on Winnebago removal. The Sentinel did not fail to note the scandalous fact that Governor Dodge was a slaveholder. In April of 1838, Dodge formally granted his servants their freedom, doubtlessly a result of that blistering Whig criticism. The paper particularly relished attacking Dodge for one of his most appalling habits, his habit of carrying an arsenal of weapons irrespective of whether he was strolling among desperados or debutantes. One incident hit the Whig papers in which it was related that during Dodge's stay at a Milwaukee hotel, the cleaning maid actually discovered a bowie knife hidden under his pillow.[29]

But the gravest accusations that arose were claims that the governor and his family were involved in fraudulent land sales. In 1834, land offices were opened at Mineral Point and Green Bay to sell conquered Indian lands. Federal law specifically forbade registers of Land Offices from selling any parcels that had evidence of valuable timber and ore.[30] If a settler wished to buy a parcel, he had to demonstrate that it was practically worthless. The temptation to defraud the United States was often irresistible. One early settler, Theodore Rodolf, stated he had heard of cases where witnesses were blindfolded and led across the desired parcel, thereby being honestly able to swear that they had not seen any mineral deposits.[31]

It was inevitable that Henry L. Dodge, through his close relationship with the registrar of the Mineral Point Land Office John P. Sheldon, would be drawn into the scandal. In 1836, Sheldon, an ardent Democrat, was accused of concealing mineral riches on lands to allow Governor Dodge, his family members and allies to buy them. The politician responsible for exposing Sheldon's malfeasance was, of course, James D. Doty.[32] A deposition taken on June 26, 1837 from one Isaac Martin implicated Lafayette Dodge by name. Martin claimed that he had applied to purchase a particular plot of land. After determining that the parcel held no valuable timber or mineral, he went to the Land Office to enter it. John Sheldon refused him and stated "very bluntly" that the parcel was reserved for mining. Nevertheless, Martin asserted that a month after his application was refused, "Mr. H. L. Dodge [son of the noble Governor] entered the above land without any difficulty from Mr. Sheldon himself, so stated Mr. H. L. Dodge." In March of 1839 the Milwaukee Sentinel reported that Lafayette had gotten land in 1836 through 'fraudulent nepotism' on John P. Sheldon's part.[33] In the Dodge defense, the Mineral Point Miner's Free Press conceded that many of Dodge's friends and relatives held valuable mineral lands and lucrative political appointments, but protested that, "because men happen to be sons or sons-in-laws to Henry Dodge . . . their rights and privileges be taken away—must their mouths be closed—and must they be the serfs and vassals of others?"[34]

A feeble defense, at best. Van Buren was compelled to dismiss Sheldon.

16

THE DEVIL'S FOOTHOLD

The election of 1840 would be the most serious challenge the dysfunctional Whigs would pose to the Democrats. The contest pitted the incumbent Martin Van Buren, an Easterner, against a candidate from the West, someone cut from the same cloth as the revered Jackson himself. He was the old Indiana frontiersman and war hero, 69-year-old William Henry Harrison, known affectionately as Old Tip, as in "Tippecanoe and Tyler, Too." This time Harrison was the sole Whig candidate and had the backing of both Daniel Webster and Henry Clay. The Whigs were confident that Van Buren had supped up the last of Jackson's well of popularity and the sentiments of the nation had shifted to their favor. Accordingly, the Whig papers pressed ahead with assaults on the Democrats. In Wisconsin, the Milwaukee Sentinel continued its editorial assaults on Dodge and his clan.

Governor Dodge was under no illusions as to the danger the upcoming election presented. Victorious candidates for public office had always handed out choice plums to their supporters, but during his term President Jackson had turned the spoils system into a national institution. Accordingly Henry Dodge, his family, friends, and supporters had benefited handsomely. In 1838, young Augustus and his wife Clara moved to Burlington after he received an appointment as Registrar of Public Lands for the new territory of Iowa. When a border dispute between Iowa and Missouri threatened to become violent, Iowa Territorial Governor Lucas, a loyal Democrat, appointed the young Dodge a brigadier general in the militia. Within a year after that, Augustus would be elected as Iowa's delegate to Congress. Although one Whig journal labeled him "a power-loving, place-hunting demagogue", Augustus' spectacular rise continued unabated.[1] The governor's son-in-law Paschal Bequette secured a position as Receiver of Public Monies at the land office in Mineral Point, a highly sought public office. Henry Lafayette Dodge, who had endorsed Paschal's bond of fifty thousand dollars, fed at the same trough as well, never finding himself wanting for a steady government job. He participated in local politics: signing petitions, judging elections, attending Democratic dinners and protest meetings, and playing a role in party conventions. It paid to be a Democrat.[2]

Now all that was threatened. In Wisconsin, the indefatigable James Duane Doty was posturing for George W. Jones' spot as territorial delegate. Democrats across the territory mobilized to fight off the challenge. Nowhere was the fight more contentious than in Iowa County and Henry Lafayette Dodge was in the middle of it. On April 16th, 1839 he attended a meeting of the Democratic Citizens of Iowa County at the Mineral Point courthouse, helping draft resolutions exhorting Democrats to unite and beat off the Whig federalist encroachments on liberty. The meeting also appointed H. L. Dodge to the County Committee of Correspondence, which then appointed Committees of Vigilance to oversee voting in the Iowa County precincts. He also served as an election judge for Dodgeville that year.[3]

In June of 1839 Henry Lafayette Dodge served as a delegate to the territorial Democratic convention in Madison. He sat on the three-man committee that examined and approved the delegates' credentials, including his own and those of his brothers-in-law Paschal Bequette and William I. Madden.[4] On June 19th, the convention took up the crucial task of selecting a candidate for territorial delegate to Congress. Someone relatively clean was required but, more importantly, someone who could defeat Doty in a close race. Lafayette made the motion to call for nominees. There were four: George W. Jones, Morgan Martin of Green Bay, John P. Sheldon and Byron Kilbourne. Both Jones and Sheldon were favorites, but they were seriously tainted politically. In the end, the convention selected Kilbourne over Martin. Originally from Connecticut, the 38 year-old Kilbourne had grown up in Ohio before moving to the Milwaukee area in 1834. There he secured a federal land grant to construct the Milwaukee-Rock River Canal in support of the southwest Wisconsin lead industry. That alone seemed to prove he was a fast friend of the Dodge faction.[5] Lafayette Dodge moved that the convention chair appoint a three-man committee to inform Mr. Kilbourne, who was absent at the time, that he had been elected. The chairman assigned Lafayette Dodge, John Sheldon, and a Mr. Haney to do the honors. After exhorting all Democrats to vote the party line, the convention adjourned. Kilbourne graciously accepted the nomination, promising "fixed determination and laborious perseverance will ensure success in this glorious cause."[6]

Following Kilbourne's letter of acceptance, the Free Press praised him as honest, upright and well qualified, and then launched a scathing broadside against James P. Doty. During the traditional toasts given to heroes of American liberty for the 4th of July, Henry L. Dodge toasted Kilbourne as "the able and efficient friend of Internal Improvement, may he reap a rich harvest in the August fields of Wisconsin."[7] From Prairie du Chien to Lake Michigan, the Miner's Free Press regularly reported glowing prospects for Kilbourne's chances to whip Doty.

Kilbourne had become the prince of the Dodge clique and the western Wisconsin Democrats, but his coronation was seriously in doubt. A good number of Wisconsin Democrats believed the Iowa County-dominated convention had railroaded Kilbourne's candidacy through and they were more than peeved about it. Subsequently on June 29th, a member of the Wisconsin Territorial Council, the Democrat Thomas P. Burnett, also announced his candidacy. Paradoxically enough, he was a local chap from Mt. Hope, only thirty odd miles west of Dodgeville. Although a Democrat, he urged voters from both parties to support him over Kilbourne and Doty as the only true friend of the territory. No one underestimated the gravity of his announcement, which must have delighted Doty. In what was already a close race, Burnett's candidacy would split the Democratic vote—fatally. The Mineral Point Miner's Free Press opened up on Burnett with both barrels, maligning his credentials and sincerity and accusing him of being Doty's lackey. On August 6th, while territorial election results were still being reported, Henry L. Dodge, Free Press editor Henry B. Welsh and other local Democrat leaders ran a card in the paper, answering the charge by the Wisconsin Democrat that Iowa County had rigged Kilbourne's nomination and that many delegates who had voted for him had switched to Burnett. Henry L. Dodge and company didn't mince words.

> " . . . your informant, if there was one, is *a Liar and a base Poltroon*, and that we believe from your inconsistency and various false charges that have appeared in your paper—that the whole was a statement concocted by yourself for political effect, and is *as false as you are base and contemptible.*"[8]

In the end Kilbourne and Burnett split the Democratic vote, but in perverse consolation, it wouldn't have mattered anyway. Taken together, the ballots cast for both Democratic candidates fell two hundred short of Doty's total. Hardly bothering to disguise his bile, Welsh bitterly conceded the disaster in an editorial in the Free Press.

> "The people of Wisconsin have saw fit to re-elect James D. Doty, notwithstanding the many sins he has committed . . . so unworthy of confidence and who stands convicted of being morally and politically corrupt. We unhesitatingly say what we believe to be true, that Judge Doty is the most corrupt man in the Territory of Wisconsin . . . "[9]

It was a stinging defeat for Dodge and the Democrats. Still, the national election was a little more than a year away, yet enough time to turn back the Whig tide. In June of 1840, Lafayette attended a Dodgeville meeting of Democratic citizens and in the same month was present at the Iowa County Democratic Convention in Belmont. He was nominated among a host of others to serve as candidate to the Wisconsin legislature, but apparently he was not selected.[10] On July 4th of 1840, with the presidential election but four months away, Henry L. Dodge raised another Independence Day toast, this time in honor of Richard M. Johnson of Kentucky.

Richard M. Johnson had been Van Buren's vice president. That fact alone was sufficient to warrant a salute from Lafayette, but he embellished by solemnly proclaiming Johnson as a patriot, statesman and as "the justly celebrated hero of the Thames."[11] The toast was actually a stinging criticism of presidential candidate Henry Harrison, who had commanded American forces at the Battle of the Thames in 1813. The Whigs were touting Harrison as the hero who, in the thick of action, had whipped Tecumseh. For Democrats, it was insulting and infuriating, and they liberally heaped abuse on Old Tip's head. It was not Harrison, the Democrats stridently claimed, but Colonel Richard Mentor Johnson and the Kentucky militia who had won the day at the Battle of the Thames. It was Richard Johnson who had actually killed Tecumseh. Harrison, dithering far to the rear, hadn't been anywhere near the action.

> "Colonel Johnson received five balls thro' his body and limbs. His clothes and accoutrements were perforated and cut from head to foot with balls... How was it, then, if Gen. Harrison was "in the heat of the battle and in every part of it, " that he came off without the smell of powder on his garments. His escape must have been as miraculous as the escape of Daniel from the den of hungry lions... "[12]

Nevertheless, that November Van Buren and Johnson went down to defeat. The popular vote had been close, but the electoral vote was a landslide for Harrison and his vice-president, John Tyler of Virginia. As he perused the election results, Governor Henry Dodge contemplated the unthinkable, that Wisconsin would soon have a new territorial governor and it would be, of all people, James Duane Doty.

After the disappointments of the fall elections, Henry Lafayette continued for a time participating in local politics. In February of 1841, he again served as delegate for Iowa County at the Democratic convention held in Madison. Much of the business encompassed resolutions and speeches attacking Harrison and the Whigs as inveterate enemies of America. Old Tip himself would live but a month after being sworn in. Whether it was the chill of Inaugural day or the Democratic invective that killed him, it was all the same and he died of pneumonia on April 4th. Vice President John Tyler, his "Accidency," as the Democrats dubbed him, was suddenly President. Tyler was a conservative Virginian, a slave-holder, avid state-rightist and held little enthusiasm for Old Tip's platform. The Whigs, of course, were utterly horrified.

Shortly after Tyler took office, Democratic heads began to roll, including many a Dodge supporter. The most notable was Governor Dodge himself, removed by President Tyler on May 4th, succeeded by Wisconsin's newest congressional delegate, James Duane Doty. Doty's selection was no coincidence. Even before winning the delegate election, he aspired to being appointed governor. He had ingratiated himself with both Henry Clay and Daniel Webster, having shared a boarding house room in Washington City with Clay, and financially advised Webster, who was speculating heavily in Wisconsin lands.[13] Among a host of others getting the sack, George Jones was removed as Surveyor General of Wisconsin and Pasqual Bequette as Receiver of the Wisconsin Public Lands.[14] That June Lafayette, who had retained his position as postmaster, attended the local Iowa County convention. This time he was not a nominee for local political office or for delegate, apparently served on no committees and made no motions. Before concluding, the convention damned Governor Dodge's removal and swore to unflaggingly campaign to get the Old Roman, as they affectionately called him, elected as delegate to Congress.[15]

During the period between 1836 and 1846, Wisconsin's population increased twelve fold, from roughly 11,683 souls to over 155,000. As the population swelled and diversified so did the economy. As a result, the disproportionate influence previously exercised by the lead industry of southwest Wisconsin steadily dwindled. Although lead production has increased steadily through the early 1840s it subsequently fell into steep decline. Many miners cashed in their operations and moved to northern Wisconsin and Michigan for the copper. Some mining communities seemed to absolutely empty out. In 1844 the Reverend John Lewis noted that the community of New Diggings had only about one third the population it had had two years earlier.[16] Immigrants soon filled the void. In 1845, southwest Wisconsin saw an influx of foreigners, the bulk of them being Irish or British. English from Cornwall and Wales, or the "Cousin Jacks", as they were called, began arriving between 1835 and 1845 and were able to make an acceptable profit by raking through old mines for remnants of ore, or working as domestics in the homes of the more well-to-do citizens.[17]

By 1841 Henry Lafayette was entering middle age. He was thirty-one years old, a husband and father of two children, George at four years and Mary still a toddler. Adele had given birth to another son on December 19th, 1840. They named the boy Henry Paschal, after his grandfather and Adele's brother, but a month later the child died. It was their first tragic loss. Their next child was to be a girl, Christiana, born on March 4, 1843. She was named for Henry's mother, but was later known simply and lovingly as Kitty.

Business occasionally gave Henry L. Dodge an escape from routine of domestic life. Most moderately successful men of the times were perpetually distracted with a variety of enterprises and as a result spent little time at home and less time with household concerns and children. Lafayette was probably no different. Some Dodge descendents would later claim that his mother-in-law, Marie Louise Mesplait Bequette, who occasionally lived with them, provided Henry an irresistible excuse to avoid home. Adele's father Jean Baptiste had died in 1825 and her mother apparently never remarried. Instead she came to the Wisconsin mining districts with her son Paschal in 1827. It was rumored that she could be very irritating and demanding and that she despised the coarse Welsh maids waiting on her in Paschal's home. If true, it was not surprising that Paschal would hand Mother off to his sister Adele whenever he could, and that after the requisite time, Henry Lafayette would just as enthusiastically send her packing back. Whatever the case, Henry L. Dodge readily embraced an adventure. A business trip during the dead of winter in 1842 provided just such an excuse.

The miners of southwest Wisconsin had always transported their lead down the Mississippi by freighter from nearby Galena, which held a solid monopoly on shipping. H. L. Dodge hoped to break up that monopoly and had arranged to meet with two affluent businessmen and brothers, Joseph and Lindsey Ward in Milwaukee. Lafayette planned to freight lead from the southwest Wisconsin mines to Milwaukee in ore wagons, and then ship it across the Great Lakes to the east. The Wards would finance the scheme and take consignment of the lead. When Henry Lafayette Dodge and neighbor Theodore Rodolf departed for Milwaukee that winter in a horse-drawn sleigh, the snow was two to three feet deep and the temperature hovered close to forty below. Rodolf described the five-day journey as long and tedious, noting with some ridicule that once past Waukesha, they "tasted the sweet comforts of traveling over the corduroy roads through the so-called Milwaukee woods."[18] Dodge was apparently able to get the Wards to put up the money, but shipping the lead in wagons proved too expensive and the scheme died. All was not for naught, however. Joseph Ward married Henry Lafayette's older sister Nancy later that year.[19]

Henry and Adele's last child was a boy; Louis Fields Linn, born on September 27th, 1844.[20] Little Linn was named after Henry Lafayette Dodge's step uncle, the late Senator Lewis Fields Linn. It was Lewis Linn who had ushered Augustus and his father around during a visit to Washington, pressing the flesh with various politicians and enthralling his nephew with the machinery of national politics. Linn, who was extolled by friends as "a model of manly beauty, the handsomest man of his day, possessed of great intellectual gifts and polite manners" had tremendous potential and the Dodges adored him. Tragically, the illustrious flower is as easily plucked by the grim reaper as any other. In 1843, after a severe illness worsened by the lingering effects of the cholera, Lewis Fields Linn died. He was 48 years old.[21] True to his namesake little Lewis Linn Dodge was a darling lad, the baby of the family and Adele's cherished favorite.

However respectable Lafayette might have appeared, he also had a propensity for getting involved in legal troubles. This wasn't particularly unusual, particularly in mining country. The court dockets were flooded with suits for bills and loans unpaid. Most often Lafayette was being sued for debts or trespass on promises and initially the amounts he owed were negligible, but as time passed the sums appeared to increase. In April of 1840, Bradley Sherman sued him for $150. Four months later, John and Henry Morrison sued him for one hundred dollars plus court costs. James H. Gentry, his ex-commanding officer and then sheriff of Iowa County, served Lafayette the summons. On May 10th, 1842, one Gustavus P. Billon and the courts wrung a promise out of Dodge to pay $1329.23 by September 1st of that year, quite a substantial amount of cash.[22] From all appearances, Gustavus still hadn't his money by the time September 1st had come and gone. On August 11, 1843, Mr. George W. Fay brought suit against Dodge for $500 in damages, due to Dodge's failure to make good $528.40 payable in lead delivered to Milwaukee, money he'd promised Fay the previous January.[23]

In most instances, the amounts owed appear to have come from day to day business concerns. Concomitantly, Henry Lafayette Dodge may have been a little lax on his financial management skills. That would bring further difficulties. In February of 1839, the Iowa County Board of Supervisors brought suit against H. L. Dodge for failing to secure a proper license for his store and tavern for the year 1838, but that, too, was not uncommon. Prying the ten dollars out of the various drinking establishments for a liquor license was like drawing an eyetooth.[24] For every suit brought against him, Henry L. Dodge reciprocated in kind, suing various people for debts.[25]

H. L. Dodge was repeatedly called into court for assault and battery, as well. On December 16, 1837, the Honorable Judge Charles Dunn of Mineral Point ordered the sheriff to extract court fines from Lafayette for assaulting Richard G. Ridgeby and, if that failed, to "take the body of the said Henry L. Dodge and him convey and deliver to the keeper of the common prison of said county who is hereby commanded to keep the said Henry L. Dodge until the aforesaid sums and all legal expenses be paid . . ." There's no evidence they jailed him, so he probably paid the fine and court costs, which totaled $14.18 ¾. Two days later, on December 18th, the judge fined Dodge five dollars for assault and battery on John D. Ansley, a copper miner, speculator and dry goods storeowner in Mineral Point. Again, charges of assault and battery were fairly common for the time, given that many disputes were adjudicated by fisticuffs, thrashings and shootings, even fatal ones, all of which seldom ruined a reputation.[26]

In Madison, the new governor James Doty was finding it was one thing to secure an appointment but another to actually serve. After Dodge's removal, the Democrats successfully elected Henry Dodge as territorial delegate to Congress. Indeed, he had nearly been elected by acclamation. Governor Doty thus found himself under attack on two fronts, from the Democrat-dominated Wisconsin legislature and from Dodge in Washington, DC. Judge Doty had few friends in Madison and his tenure proved to be fraught with frustration and conflict. The legislature endlessly feuded with him over nearly every issue no matter how miniscule, including the proper spelling of the territory's name. Doty favored "Wiskonsan" over "Wisconsin" and was ridiculed by the Democratic papers for it. The legislature, by joint resolution, finally corrected the governor's errant spelling.[27] In very little time, the lawmakers were simply ignoring the man. In December of 1842, when the 4th Legislative Assembly convened, Doty branded it an illegal meeting and refused to attend. The assembly then sent a heated memorial to Tyler accusing Doty of despotism.

In Congress, Henry Dodge and his allies faithfully thwarted Doty's initiatives and lobbied to have him removed as governor, claiming he was forging " . . . an absolute tyranny over the people of Wisconsin." Dodge wrote to George Jones with barely concealed delight.

> "You will perceive from the Documents I have enclosed You lately that I have been *Nailing Doty* You will See from My remarks in the House that I treated *his Excy* with great Courtesy at the same time. I shall keep a good Look Out while I am here and will make *D y.* a heavy weight for *Tyler to Carry before I am done with him.*"[28]

Dodge's efforts to get him sacked eventually failed, but Doty needed no crystal ball to divine his future as governor. Old Hairy Face's re-election as Congressional delegate prophesized continued harassment and frustration in Washington. One term was enough. As he did in 1832, Doty simply stepped aside rather than endure the humiliation of being sacked. His successor Senator Nathaniel Tallmadge of New York lasted but a short time. In the presidential election of 1844, the Democrats regained power under James K. Polk of Tennessee. The Party of Jackson was once more at the helm and Henry Dodge once again behind the Wisconsin governor's desk.[29] The Old Roman began his second term in May of 1845, his victory celebrated wildly in Mineral Point with speechifying and grand balls and toasts at Abe Nichol's Mansion House, all marshaled by George Wallace Jones in the pleasurable company of "thirteen of the handsomest girls in town."[30]

In the midst of this heady political furor, Henry L. Dodge, Adele and the children moved from Dodgeville to Mineral Point, some eight miles to the south. Years later, Adele would state the move had been made around 1840, but insomuch as her husband remained Postmaster at Dodgeville during that time, it is possible she was mistaken. His tenure with the post office expired in 1843, the year Henry L. was nominated for and elected as Sheriff of Iowa County.

> "Elections in the southwest in the spring of 1843 revealed an unshaken solidarity in Dodge's ranks. In Iowa County, Henry L. Dodge, the same young man who had issued the challenge to Doty a decade before, was elected sheriff by a substantial majority..."[31]

A different chronicler more succinctly observed that, once more, "the Devil had a firm foothold" in Mineral Point.[32]

17

MINERAL POINT

Mineral Point was named for a high piece of land that gradually sloped downward to a point carved by converging tributaries of the Pecatonica River. As a result the town site bore a steep and hilly, ravine-run aspect. Its modest beginning was a rude cabin built by a Calvinistic Baptist preacher in that pivotal year of 1827. The following year Nat Morris and two other prospectors discovered lead there.[1] With the Indians run out and the miners flooding in, the place rapidly became the center of mining activity in southwestern Wisconsin, with its predictable complement of gambling houses, taverns and "groceries", as groggeries were referred to in those days. As with other settlements in the area, drinking was more or less a universal habit.[2]

By 1829 the settlement's population had swelled to about one thousand souls, almost exclusively men. Lead mining became so intense that ore wagons lugging lead to Galena turned the primitive roads to nearly impassable morasses.[3] Due to the lack of women there in the early years, the miners were compelled to take turns cooking for their comrades. When dinner was ready, the designated cook hoisted a rag to signal those in the diggings. Fittingly, the settlement was nicknamed Shake Rag, or Shake Rag Under the Hill. It made a good story, anyway. Some claim that old Colonel Abner Nichols conjured up this tale, perhaps to entertain his guests at the Mansion House. In spite of its refined name, Uncle Ab's Mansion House was actually a rough collection of cabins joined by passageways, but, as Strange M. Palmer described it during a visit there, a veritable paradise of "at all hours, music, dancing, singing, drinking and gambling of every description..."[4] Other than Ab's establishment, there wasn't much more in Mineral Point in 1829, a haphazard scattering of log huts and crude shacks—not that the miners required anything else for entertainment.

"The miners were in the habit of assembling there on Saturday nights, to drink, gamble and frolic until Monday morning.... The bar room, in which we were sitting, contained a large bar, well supplied with all kinds of liquors. In one corner of the room, was a Faro Bank... in another corner a Roulette; and in another, sat a party engaged in playing at cards. One man sat back in a corner, playing a fiddle, to whose music two others were dancing in the middle of the room. Hundreds of dollars were lying upon the tables; and among the crowd were the principal men of the Territory . . . "[5]

In 1830 Mineral Point was designated the seat of Iowa County, requiring a certain amount of polishing and refinement, if that were possible, and the Iowa County Board initiated some civilizing influences. There was a court to try criminals and a jail to house lawbreakers and any drunks who became too cantankerous, but the first efforts at upholding the law were amateur ones.[6] George W. Featherstone, an English traveler, wrote a wry description of court proceedings.

"It was but a sorry exhibition of a court of justice, dark, and filled with filthy-looking men, spitting about in every direction . . . The prosecuting attorney, who summed up, exceeded all the pleaders I ever listened to for absurdity of language and bad grammar."[7]

When Palmer visited the town, he found the jail or the 'pen', as he described it, a comically primitive affair. The hoosegow was built of rough logs, both walls and roof, with a dirt floor and a ceiling so low as to give any occupant a permanent stoop. Its only security was a thick wooden door padlocked with a chain, a minor obstacle when any determined inmate could escape by prying up one corner of the pen and slipping out beneath the wall. Once or twice a convict was hanged, drawing everyone within a day's travel into Mineral Point for the sensational event. No traveling circus or county fair ever drew an equally large and enthusiastic crowd.[8]

In addition to the usual brawls and gouging, there were occasional duels. One well-known instance occurred in 1840 between Henry B. Welsh, editor of the Miner's Free Press and the notorious Major Charles Bracken. All in all Bracken was a contrary chap with a penchant for aggression. Although he had served Dodge as his adjutant during the Black Hawk War, in later years he became quite the General's antagonist. The Miner's Free Press had embraced an editorial policy of humiliating Charles Bracken by referring to him by the diminutive "Charley" and sarcastically nicknaming him the "Knight of the Double Barreled Gun" and the "Hero of Walnut Grove" for the previous times he had threatened Welsh and his staff.

One version of the shooting held that Charley called out Welsh after the Free Press had branded him a "LIAR, SCOUNDREL AND COWARD" in the November 24th, 1840 edition of the paper.[9] A second version held that Welsh had accidentally come across Bracken on the outskirts of the town. Harsh words escalated into a fistfight on horseback, during which the editor mortified the Hero of Walnut Grove by pulling him off his mount. In either instance the Knight of the Double Barrel came galloping into Mineral Point the following morning, a brace of irons tucked in his pants. Spying Welsh in the street, he advanced and drew a horse pistol from his belt. Rather than doing the prudent thing and taking cover, Welsh called out for a weapon, fully intending to duel Bracken. As Old Ab' Nichols was handing Welsh a pistol, Bracken fired. The ball struck Welsh in the neck. His honor satisfied, Charley then turned and rode calmly out of town. Bracken's own brother, the deputy marshal at the time, arrested him at home and brought him in. Welsh's wound was bloody, but not mortal and he eventually recovered to spar with Bracken again. Apparently the Hero of Walnut Grove suffered no legal repercussions and nothing more came of the incident other than good sensationalistic press.[10]

In 1834 the Federal Land Office under John P. Sheldon opened in Mineral Point. When settlers rushed in to have their lands confirmed, Shake Rag suddenly became a boomtown. Taverns were jammed full and revelers flowed out onto the streets, already thronged with land speculators and gamblers. It was fine for business, but became a bit too larcenous for the more correct citizenry.[11] Once Doty became governor, he attempted to move the land office to the township of Muscoda, located some forty miles northward on a sandy flat along the Wisconsin River. The Mineral Point Free Press gleefully lampooned the move, asking if someone would tell them "as the whereabouts of "Muskoday" . . . Is it one of Judge Doty's paper towns?"[12] The answer to that question was, of course, yes. There was no actual town. The land where Muscoda theoretically existed was owned and had been platted out by his Excellency James Duane Doty.[13]

By 1836 Mineral Point boasted over 2,000 residents. Mining had devoured the land so that there was nary a stick of timber left in the area. A handful of profitable mines and a dozen furnaces around the town were in continual operation. Some seriously suggested Mineral Point should become the new territorial capitol and the town residents fully expected it would happen. After all, Governor Dodge had taken his oath of office there. Others were less enthusiastic. In response to the idea, one elderly skeptic exclaimed sarcastically, "That is rich! Shake Rag, indeed!"[14]

Still, by 1840, the town had shrugged off much of its uncouth beginnings and taken on a more metropolitan air. There were several large stone buildings constructed of native rock. Lumber was prohibitively expensive to purchase and to ship, and frame buildings were rare.[15] There were seven dry goods stores, four groceries, two tailors, two blacksmiths and two carpenters, a cabinet-maker and a brewery.[16] There were both public and private schools in the town and five churches, including the Episcopalians, whose services Governor Dodge's family attended.[17] The three hotels in town, the Mansion House, the Franklin House, and the Central, regularly hosted parties and balls and socials for the younger folks, inviting residents near and far to attend, provided their behavior was acceptable. The temperance movement had built up a good head of steam in Mineral Point by then, but it had little effect other than raising the cost of licenses to run the groggeries. Concurrent with that groundswell of Christian respectability, civic leaders enacted laws against hooliganism and its related behaviors.

> "Sec. 6. Any person hallowing, shouting, bawling, screaming, profane or obscene language, fighting, dancing, singing, whooping, quarrelling, or making an unusual noise or sounds, in any house or in any part of this corporation, in such a manner as to disturb the good people of the neighborhood, or those passing through the streets, he, she, or they, so offending, shall be fined twenty dollars for the first offence."[18]

Selling spirituous liquids on Sunday drew a fine. Chucking garbage into the public streets drew a fine. The owners of any swine found running loose and rooting in the garbage illegally chucked into the street would be fined fifty cents for each offending hog.[19] All dogs were required to be licensed at one to two dollars a head. Many an old timer must have been thoroughly disgusted. Busy bodies, bible-thumpers and do-gooders were suffocating the place with a lethal dose of civilization. The laws may not have altogether had the desired effect. The miners were not to be easily subdued and used a variety of methods to defend their interests, some legal and some not. Rodolf noted that, due to the many disputes arising regarding land claims and mining, there were a good number of lawyers in the place, who never wanted for work. There was "endless litigation, presenting a fruitful field for the exercise of the talents of the lawyer."[20]

Into that tumultuous scene entered Henry L. Dodge, Iowa County Sheriff, his wife Adele and the children. Lafayette succeeded his old superior officer from the Black Hawk conflict, James Gentry, as sheriff and posted a bond of four thousand dollars. Having won a resounding endorsement in his election, it is therefore strange that Henry only served a year and a half, from July of 1843 through December of 1844. In that time he became a familiar face at the county courthouse, as did the ex-territorial delegate George W. Jones, who had been appointed Clerk of the Iowa County Courts and Paschal Bequette, reappointed to the Mineral Point Land Office.[21]

Henry L. Dodge's job was generally uneventful. He opened and closed meetings of the Iowa County Board of Supervisor sessions, acted as assessor and issued licenses for a variety of taverns, groceries, inns and other businesses. He delivered summons and warrants and directed the public sale of lands and property for payment of court fines, fees and debts. He was required to submit his expenses to the court for remuneration and perform a myriad of other trivial jobs. Invariably, the court sessions minutes began with liturgy "the Court duly opened by Henry L. Dodge Esquire, Sheriff." If he ever participated in the excitement of a fugitive round up, a barroom brawl or a public hanging, it wasn't anything of particular historical note. His last noted public sale was for December 10, 1844. Henry's own legal difficulties apparently interfered with his duties from time to time and may have been the reason for his relatively short tenure. When in August of 1843 Judge Charles Dunn summoned Henry L. Dodge to appear in court to answer to George Fay's suit for money owed, he had to have the coroner, Cromwell Lloyd, serve it rather than the sheriff . . . for obvious reasons. Nevertheless, whatever the circumstances were, by January of 1845, Timothy Burns had taken Dodge's place as sheriff.

As Mineral Point was preparing for a grand celebration of the elder Dodge's reappointment as governor, the Whig papers of Green Bay and Milwaukee renewed attacks on Dodge nepotism, accusing the newly re-elevated governor of doling out lucrative positions to his closest relatives, specifically naming Augustus, Paschal Bequette, William Dement, George W. Jones and " . . . Henry Dodge, Jr., son, Clerk of the Iowa Court." [22] In the following week's edition, squeezed into the column between an account of Governor Dodge's honorary banquet and Professor McLeake's lecture on the Edinburgh system of Phrenology, appeared a brief announcement.

> "Henry L. Dodge Esq. has been appointed by his Honor Judge Dunn Clerk of the U. S. Dist. Court of Iowa County, in place of George W. Jones Esq. Resigned. We are informed that Mr. Dodge was recommended for the above appointment by Democrats and Whigs generally."[23]

In the wake of the 1844 elections, Jones had been reappointed surveyor general of Iowa and Wisconsin and had moved to Dubuque. Lafayette's family affiliation had again secured him a job, albeit a dull job, consumed with paperwork—something Henry L. Dodge most likely loathed. There were endless issuing of writs of attachment or posting of public announcements ordering some estranged wife to a divorce hearing, signing and sealing marriage licenses or affidavits of Welsh immigrants seeking citizenship and overseeing the lengthy criminal docket:

"The United States vs. Abraham Hathaway and Alice Alcott. Indictment for Adultery."
"The United States vs. Allen Phillips On charge of Larceny"
"The United States vs. McMichael and Henry Fagan. Indictment for Gambling."[24]

And so it went. The ennui must have very nearly killed him. During this time Henry had an announcement repeatedly run in the Mineral Point Democrat notifying his creditors that all notes and accounts due Henry L. Dodge were under the care of his lawyers, Dunn, Jones & Crawford of Mineral Point and should be settled up before May of 1845.[25] What that signified remains a mystery, but it conjures a suspicion that he was in debt. Henry's participation in local politics through 1845 appeared lukewarm. He was briefly involved in a movement to improve education, appearing as one of the signatories of a proposal to hold a meeting regarding improving the common schools in Wisconsin, held at the Mineral Point Courthouse on the 16th of October, 1845. George Jones, Paschal Bequette and Uncle Ab Nichols also penned their endorsement to the meeting.[26] The Mineral Point Democrat listed H. L. Dodge as one of fifteen organizers of a meeting of the Democratic citizens of Iowa County, held on April 25, 1845 in Mineral Point, to prepare for the territorial party convention in Madison. The meeting came off as scheduled, the paper reporting that John Sheldon was prominent in the affair as was the ex-editor of the Mineral Point Free Press, Henry Welsh. Henry Lafayette was not mentioned.[27] In contrast, his brother Augustus' successes were as luminous as Lafayette's were lackluster, having just won re-election as Congressional Delegate for Iowa.

The fact that Henry L. Dodge had been sheriff and was serving as clerk of the county courts did not make him immune to his own legal difficulties. The issue over suits brought against him for money continued. Whether these suits were related to his businesses in Dodgeville or to his land purchases around the town is not clear. He may have been caught up, as his father had before him in Missouri, in unsecured loans for land speculation. The engine driving this land rush was the Bank of Wisconsin, which had a branch at Mineral Point, where H. L. Dodge held accounts. The charter provided that stock in the bank had to be paid for in hard cash. The bank then would issue bank notes at a ratio of three dollars for every one dollar of specie, then lend the notes at an interest rate of up to seven percent. Engaged as it was in wildcat banking, the Bank of Mineral Point issued huge amounts of bank notes and suffered heavy losses as a result. The bank failed in 1841 and its officers arrested and charged with fraud. As a result, miners and most everyone else in the region refused to accept paper currency, derisively known as "shinplasters" or "yellow dogs" and demanded silver or gold. In the end, the bank had to lean on its debtors to pay its $100,000 liabilities, which only covered half the amount, and left thousands of dollars of worthless notes in circulation.[28]

In 1844 the United States cited Henry L. Dodge and his partner John Lindsey for failing to vacate public lands. Lindsey had served under Lafayette in the Iowa County Riflemen, Company C, Henry Lafayette as a Captain and John as 1st Lieutenant.[29] Apparently their plot of land, contrary to regulations, turned out to contain mineral resources. No surprise that. Nor was it surprising to find the Dodge and Lindsey names in a long list of others similarly favored.[30] These legal proceedings were of little consequence and many thought them ludicrous and petty. The following year Henry faced a more serious challenge. On August 29th, 1845, U. S. Treasury auditor P. G. Washington instructed U. S. District Attorney William P. Lynde to bring suit against H. L. Dodge and his sureties Abner Nichols and Cromwell Lloyd for the balance of his account owed as postmaster of Dodgeville. An audit of H. L. Dodge's accounts for 1838 through 1843 had uncovered a serious deficit.

> "United States vs. Henry L. Dodge Abner Nichols Cromwell Lloyd} District Court of the United States for Iowa County in the Territory of Wisconsin. Please issue a summons in this cause in a "plea that they the said Defendants render unto the said Plaintiff the sum of Three Hundred dollars which they owe to and unjustly detain from" them returnable at next Term of this Court. Yours &c. Wm P. Lynde, U. S. Atty. To Henry L. Dodge Esq. Clerk I C 8th Sept. 1845."[31]

The request for summons was addressed to the Clerk of the Court, Iowa County who, of course, was Henry L. Dodge Esquire. It must have been awkward presiding over one's own suit. U. S. Marshal John Rockwell summoned Clerk Dodge to appear in court that October. Henry L. Dodge attested to his own summons as well and served as clerk while the charges against him were read. Dodge, through his attorneys, Dunn, Jones & Crawford, denied the charge.[32] The case was pursued through March of 1846 but the outcome is a mystery. Lynde noted that one of Dodge's sureties, Cromwell Lloyd, was broke. He may have concluded that his chances of getting payment from H. L. Dodge and old Uncle Ab' Nichols was equivalent to that of squeezing water from a rock. As for the $300 bookkeeping discrepancy, Henry may have simply acquired the bad habit of failing to submit proper expense forms. R. J. Walker, Secretary of the Treasury, on April 20th, 1846, denied Dodge his expense claim because he did not file his returns at the proper time. This was not the only occasion for such oversight.[33] Of course, there is also the chance that the government's three hundred bucks ended up on the losing end of a gambling table.

In the midst of the legal falderal, on the surface Henry's family life appeared relatively normal, even given the presence of Adele's mother. Henry and Adele's children eight-year-old George and six-year-old Mary attended the Mineral Point public school, while the toddler Kitty at two and Louis Linn just under a year stayed at home.[34] They appeared to lead respectable middle class lives, as far as the times defined a respectable middle class, and had accumulated a good amount of stout household furniture—a large dresser with fine glass handles, upon the back of which was inscribed Adele Dodge's name, a set of hardwood chairs, a table and a bed—things that would have been previously considered luxuries. Yet beneath the domestic surface there seemed to be disquiet.

During 1845, the Mineral Point Democrat began reporting on events of potentially significant and serious consequence. As the United States pushed its claims ever westward across the continent, it was increasingly clear there would be a war, probably a major war at that, with either Great Britain over Oregon or with Mexico over Texas and California. It was even reported that England was preparing to seize California from Mexico. Meanwhile the Republic of Mexico steadfastly refused to sell California to the Americans, outraged over the United States' annexation of Texas. Of the two circumstances, the Mexican issue consumed the most newspaper print and through the spring, summer and fall of 1845 there were repeated rumors that Mexico had declared war on the United States. In most minds, particularly those of the Polk administration, war was inevitable. It was but a matter of time and happenstance. What would transpire later on a fateful April day in 1846 along the Rio Grande would affect Henry Lafayette Dodge profoundly, though he little appreciated it at the time. He had bigger worries closer to home.

On June 8th, 1846, Secretary of the Treasury Walker penned a letter to Henry Lafayette Dodge Esquire, Clerk of the U. S. District Court for Iowa County, Wisconsin Territory.

"Treasury Dept. June 8, 1846.
> Sir: Your report of fees & emoluments for the months of June 1845, and for the half year ending 31st Dec. last has been received.
> I am Very Respectfully etc.
> R. Walker, Secy of the Treasury."[35]

This type of correspondence was usually good news for Henry, having been accused of both mismanagement and fraud in the post office, but Henry L. Dodge never saw it. The letter had arrived at the Iowa County Court House in a timely manner, which was more than could be said about the court clerk himself, for Henry Lafayette Dodge had suddenly disappeared—vanished. He was never again to be seen loitering on the steps of the county court house, strolling the steep hillside streets of Mineral Point, nor to be hailed at the taverns and card tables. The passing years would inexorably wipe the memory of his face from everyone he knew; Adele his wife and the three children, his brother Augustus, his stern father and his dear mother Christiana—just as surely as the lingering prairie mists evaporate before a warm Wisconsin summer.

18

ABSQUATULATED

To absquatulate: American frontier slang, loosely meaning to pull up stakes and settle at another locale, from the term "squat" as in a squatter or homesteader. See abscond.

On August 28th, 1846, Colonel Stephen Watts Kearny, subjugator of New Mexico and conqueror of Santa Fe, set to work creating a provisional government for the newly seized province before setting off for the real fighting in California. It had been four short months since the United States had declared war on the Republic of Mexico, almost two months since Kearny and his army had departed Fort Leavenworth and a mere ten days since he'd occupied Santa Fe. Under Kearny, the recently vanquished civil servants of the Mexican government would not necessarily be removed from office. Judiciously, he made most of his civil appointments from among local officials. A practical and efficient officer, Kearny understood the need to keep what functioning government there was intact, at least until the Americans consolidated control over the province.

In that spirit, he appointed Tomás Rivera as Collector of Santa Fe, responsible for extracting newly established fees from the businesses of the city. Wagons of trade were charged four dollars, pleasure carriages at two dollars. Private wagons and carriages passing into the public plaza would be charged twenty-five cents. Failure to pay the fee in advance would quadruple the cost and land the proprietor in jail until he coughed up the money. Kearny instructed Rivera to collect and deliver these fees to the Treasurer of Santa Fe, who would keep the books and be held "strictly responsible" for the money collected. Kearny had intended to reappoint Francisco Ortiz as Treasurer of Santa Fe, but an illness had rendered the man unable to serve. In his place, Kearny made an unlikely choice, a recently arrived American.

"Henry L. Dodge is appointed Treasurer of Santa Fe, New Mexico, in the place of Francisco Ortis, who, in consequence of sickness, is unable to perform the duties. Mr. Ortis will turn over to his successor, any public funds, books, or property pertaining to his office, which he may have in his possession. Santa Fe, New Mexico, August 28th, 1846. S. W. Kearny, Brig Gen USA."[1]

The most pressing mystery was not whether Henry Lafayette Dodge could be trusted with such sums of money. That was a real concern, for he'd had issues before. Kearny may have been simply unaware of Henry's difficulties, although a reputation such as that usually precedes the man. The mystery was what the 36 year-old Dodge was doing in Santa Fe, New Mexico in the first place, when he should have been twelve hundred miles away behind his clerk's desk at the Iowa County Courthouse in Mineral Point on the emerald Wisconsin prairies. Yet there he was, slouching under the August heat, joshing and jostling with Kearny's soldiers on a dusty adobe plaza in a distant, arid and cinnamon hued land.

Henry Lafayette Dodge's extraordinary appearance in New Mexico would not only be a source of consternation for his family, his business partners and those suing him in court, but a cause of confusion for later historians. Richard Van Valkenburgh, a student of Navajo history, suggested Dodge had first appeared in Santa Fe in 1849. Of course, Kearny's appointment of Dodge proves that suggestion wrong. Some claimed that Henry had arrived as much as a year before Kearny, and that he was practicing law in Santa Fe.[2] Ruth Underhill, a renowned Navajo ethnologist, stated H. L. Dodge had been a soldier and caravan guard along the Santa Fe Trail.[3] Iowa County court documents at that time, bearing Henry's signature, clearly refute both those assertions.

Indeed for a time the skilled researcher and writer Frank McNitt contemplated that the Henry *Linn* Dodge of New Mexico notoriety and the Wisconsin governor's son Henry *Lafayette* Dodge weren't the same person at all. He based his concern on a slight incongruity in Henry's age as listed on an 1849 muster roll and a reference to the middle name *Linn* by Indian Agent James Calhoun, who later served as New Mexico Territorial Governor. Calhoun assumed that Henry's middle initial stood for the surname of his late uncle, the well-known deceased senator, Lewis Fields Linn. Consequently, in his reports he referred to Henry as Henry Linn Dodge. If Henry had learned of the error, he probably wouldn't have corrected Calhoun. He'd never thought much of the name *Lafayette* and without fail diminished it to the initial *L*.

Yet, however amazing it might seem, it is a verifiable fact. In May of 1846, Henry Lafayette Dodge was in Wisconsin, serving as Clerk of the District Court for Iowa County. Three months later, on August 28th of 1846, he was in New Mexico, appointed Treasurer of the City of Santa Fe by General Kearny.

Why did he abruptly leave? Such a decision was no small matter, even for Henry Dodge, who was probably more easy-going than his father approved, for the consequences were as devastating as they were irreversible. He'd abandoned pretty much everything he had ever had: his wife Adele, his four small children, his family and friends, his home, his business and career, his prospects and reputation.

He was in fact ruined. And his wife and children were ruined. For years after Henry's disappearance, Adele would struggle on the edge of poverty, depending on the financial help of Governor Dodge and her brother Paschal to augment the meager income she got from taking in boarders. Aside from her four children, she had her aging mother Marie Louise Mesplait Bequette and her spinster sister Euphrenia living with them. As for Henry's children, they would never see their father again. The oldest boy, George, was nine years old when Henry left—hardly old enough to be the man of the family. His little sister Kitty was a toddling three-year-old and baby Linn had hardly begun to walk. The youngest two would have no recollection of their father whatsoever.

On the other hand seven-year-old Marie Therese would never forget, and never quite recover, from her father's disappearance. She was the very image of Henry; those gray eyes, wavy brown hair and high color. Marie was hardly old enough to comprehend his desertion but as she matured she felt the lingering ache of his absence. Sheridan Spearman, her granddaughter, later told Frank McNitt that her grandmother "always, all her life, had a feeling of sadness and longing where her father was concerned."[4]

The circumstances that forced Henry L. Dodge to abscond must have been dire, indeed. It was true that he had faced a number scandals, but assault and battery, land fraud, breach of promises, misuse of funds, even murder, could be and were forgiven, as many a prominent Wisconsin citizen could testify. Even if Henry had been vilified for those offenses, it wouldn't have been enough to drive him into exile. The mere fact that Henry was the eldest son of Governor Dodge would have diluted any repercussions. Neil Giffey, a prominent Dodge family historian, proposed that Lafayette was too much of a free spirit to accept the restraints of responsible citizenship and that many of the accusations against him may have simply been attempts by political rivals to get him into hot water.[5] Certainly Henry may have lacked the upstanding qualities expected by the upper crust of Mineral Point, but being a free spirit in the midst of an entire region of free-spirited, hard drinking miners would have insured him a host of loyal friends, in spite of the tepid temperance movement in town.

Eugene Beckett, genealogist and direct descendant of the Missouri Bequettes, proposed that Lafayette had become an embarrassment to the Dodge family, having made some bad business decisions and challenged several gentlemen to duels.[6] That explanation seems to fall short. As far as bad business deals, Henry was small pickings and the amounts for which he was sued were comparatively miniscule. It would have taken much more than that to justify Henry Lafayette Dodge's sudden and complete exile. Dueling may have brought censure but would have hardly been a sin worthy of expulsion. Even killing an opponent outright would not have done lasting damage to someone well-connected. Furthermore, there is no record that Henry Dodge ever dueled or killed anyone.

Clearly Henry L. Dodge's departure from Wisconsin was as deliberate as it was sudden. Indeed, Eugene Beckett believed that Governor Dodge had facilitated his son's exit. That assertion was probably correct. In the years following his disappearance Henry L. Dodge received many favors, the kinds that are habitually bestowed by a prominent politician. Was it coincidence that Henry arrived in Santa Fe at the same time as General Kearny and the army? Why had the general chosen H. L. Dodge, of all people, Treasurer of Santa Fe, a position for which his qualifications were few to none? Of course, Kearny had known the Dodge family since 1828, when he commanded Fort Crawford at Prairie du Chien. He had served with Governor Dodge in the First Dragoons and, although the two could have hardly been more dissimilar, they had preserved a mutual respect and personal friendship.

It seems certain that although Henry L. Dodge never actually enlisted in the Army, he had accompanied Kearny to Santa Fe, either with the troops or with an accompanying caravan of Santa Fe merchants. It is a short leap of faith to imagine

Henry, upon arriving at Fort Leavenworth, handing Kearny a surreptitious letter from Governor Dodge, a request for a special favor or two—from one old comrade in arms to another, all off the record, of course.[7]

No. If Governor Dodge facilitated his son's departure as it appears he did, the source of Henry's problem must have lay more closely to home. Sheridan Spearman postulated that Lafayette's mother-in-law must have made life hell for him. She saw herself as high French Creole and therefore could be "a problem," expecting to be waited upon by her servants in Mineral Point with the same alacrity of her slaves when she lived in Missouri.[8] Is it possible that Henry may have drank and gambled to excess, to the growing exasperation of both Adele and her mother, and that precipitated his departure? Doubtful.

There is, however, evidence that he had family problems. On May 21st, 1846, Andrew J. Hewett gave a sworn deposition to William T. Henry, who had been appointed court clerk after Henry L. Dodge's sudden departure. Hewett had sued Dodge for an unpaid debt of $124. In his deposition, he divulged some tantalizing information. He knew for a fact that Henry L. Dodge had left Wisconsin and that "he has had very grave and serious family difficulties" and that Adele had "separated from him." He also flatly stated that Dodge had left his home "at a late hour of the night taking his clothing with him" and had not been heard from since.[9]

Hewett did not elaborate further. He didn't need to. Any lasciviously fertile mind could fill in the blanks. Tatters and scraps of the record certainly invite such salacious speculation. One such scrap emerged nearly a century and a half after Henry's departure and it came in the form of a non-assuming little old lady. During the mid 1980s, the Dodge family descendents had gathered at Dodgeville to dedicate a monument to the Old Roman when they learned of a previously unknown Dodge descendant. She was Mary Gibson from Sun Prairie, Wisconsin. Mary Gibson had been born on April 10, 1903, and was the daughter of Henry Oliver and Luella Stam. Curiously, a few years before her birth, Henry Stam had attended a dedication commemorating Belmont as the first capitol of Wisconsin. He was not only warmly received as an honored guest by the Dodge family, but embraced as a family member, for Henry Oliver Stam had been the son of John and Mary Josephine Stam. John Stam had died in 1877 when Henry Oliver was still a youngster, but his mother Mary lived another forty-seven years, dying in 1924 at the age of 78. Mary had lived nearly her entire life in Belmont, on the old farm she had inherited from her parents.

Mary's parents were Oliver and Johanna Holtshouser. Oliver Holtshouser was originally from Kentucky but, like so many others, he settled in the mining district in 1829, engaged as a lead miner and later farmer and blacksmith.[10] Perhaps his one contribution to local folklore was in 1839, when he went hunting and managed to kill six deer in a mere fifteen minutes, or so reported the Miner's Free Press.[11] He proved to be a good, solid and steady citizen, the very kind of person history rubs out. Holtshouser had known Governor Dodge personally for years, admired him, and counted him as a close friend. He had served under Dodge in James Gentry's company during the Black Hawk War and doubtlessly knew Lafayette well. Apparently Governor Dodge held Oliver in equally high esteem.

Oliver Holtshouser married Johanna Ludlam of Ohio on April 11, 1838. Oliver was thirty-one years old. It was a late start, but like younger couples Oliver and Johanna wanted children and quickly, but after eight years of trying, they remained childless. They were devastated. Yet, paradoxically, when the enumerator for the Wisconsin census arrived at the Holtshouser home on September 6th, 1850, he counted not two, but three residents. There was John age 42, his wife Johanna age 42 and their daughter, a petite four-year-old girl named Mary Josephine born sometime in 1846.

Her last name was not Holtshouser however. It was Dodge.

Knowing Oliver and Johanna longed for children, Governor Dodge had given them the baby girl as early as 1847. Of course Mary Josephine was not the governor's child, but the daughter of his son, Henry Lafayette Dodge. Nonetheless, John and Johanna adored her as their own.[12] There is also evidence that Mary hadn't been the only Dodge child given up for adoption. A rough genealogy chart in the Mineral Point Room archives lists another nameless baby—a boy—purportedly given to a Thompson family.[13] In one version of the story, family descendants claimed that Governor Dodge arranged for their adoption because, with his son suddenly gone, Adele couldn't afford two more children along with those she had. In order to get by with the help of her brother and father-in-law, Adele may have indeed acquiesced to adopting out her two small children. Mary Gibson herself said as much in a newspaper interview in 1964, stating that "Henry's youngest children were given out for adoption..."[14]

An Iowa County historian, Gerald Fieldhouse, once speculated that Lafayette had been compelled to leave because he had committed some kind of religious transgression.[15] That conjecture may have originated from a second version of the story, that Mary had been given up for adoption because Henry L. Dodge had married "outside the family faith" and was disowned. The belief that Henry had committed the unacceptable sin of marrying a Catholic is unsupported by the facts. The Dodges, Episcopalians, had had a long, close relationship with the Bequettes and other notoriously Catholic residents of Ste. Genevieve. Both

Henry and Christiana allowed their daughter Elizabeth to wed a Catholic, Paschal Bequette, and Christiana herself witnessed Lafayette's very Catholic marriage to Adele in 1835. So it seems inconceivable that Henry L. Dodge was stigmatized because he married a Catholic girl.

What is conceivable is that the phrase "married outside the family faith" had been misinterpreted, that it had actually been a euphemism for a sin seldom discussed openly and never, ever written about. Political infighting, duels and pummelings, debts and deceptions and fraud; all those peccadilloes were discussed openly in Wisconsin, most of it voiced loudly and written about voraciously, but in the personal letters and in the press one subject was never addressed directly and only alluded to with the most circumspect similes. That was the subject of sex and extra-marital sex. If Henry had been caught in adultery, would it have been enough to eject him from his home and family?

Perhaps. Given the tenor of the times, what could have possibly been a worse scandal?

Indeed. It would be remarkable that the Dodges, one of the most influential and affluent families in Wisconsin, could not or would not accommodate two more small children. As sons of the frontier, the Dodges were dead serious about the family history and legacy. Adele received considerable help from her relatives and in-laws through the years. Paschal sold her a home in Dodgeville—a respectable two-story frame house, accepting in payment nothing more than love and affection, and she took in boarders to make money. Governor Dodge occasionally augmented her income and helped with raising her children. Marie Therese recalled being raised as much by her grandfather in his home as by her own mother.[16] Why then would the Old Roman not accept the two smallest of his errant son's children?

Or, for that matter, even fail recognize them? Yet Beverly Finlay, a granddaughter of Marie Therese, confessed she found it curious that her grandmother had never mentioned Mary Josephine, "this person who would have been her aunt."[17] The Holtshousers had lived in Belmont, a short buggy ride from Dodgeville and Mary must have grown up seeing and knowing the Dodge clan just down the road and her Dodge parentage would have been common knowledge. Although Oliver Stam was honored as a Dodge at the turn of the century, it appears that for whatever reason the family failed to acknowledge his mother Mary.

The 1850 census indicated that both Mary Josephine's father and mother were born in Missouri, completely consistent with Henry and Adele being her birth parents. Henry and Adele's children were regularly born a year and a half to two years apart. After Adele lost her son Henry Paschal at one month, it was two years before she gave birth to Kitty. Louis Linn had been born on schedule eighteen months afterwards, in September of 1844. So it is conceivable but unlikely that Adele could have had Mary in the second half of 1845. She had most likely been born in the first half of 1846. The second child given up to the Thompson family then presents a problem. It would have been unusual, though not impossible, to conceive another of Henry's children before her husband bolted the territory in early May.

What then indeed could have possibly been a worse disgrace? Were Mary Josephine and the Thompson boy illegitimate, their mother obscured and lost to time? That might account for the omission of Mary in the family lore. On the other hand, if Mary had been illegitimate would the Dodges have christened her with the family names Mary and Josephine? Whichever circumstance might seem most plausible, one can imagine the resulting scene in the Dodge household. Upon discovering the affair, Adele probably left Henry and went to her brother's house, taking her mother and the kids with her. That would have been the least of Henry L. Dodge's worries. The resulting scandal would wreak great damage on the reputation of the entire family, something Governor Dodge would avoid by any means short of murder. The year 1846 had been a rewarding year for him. He had been officially reappointed as territorial governor in February and was anxious to pick up where he'd left off. There was also a push underway to launch Wisconsin into statehood with Dodge at the helm. There was much to lose and the last thing he needed was a sordid sex scandal in the family. If it meant cajoling or buying the silence of the mistress, concealing the children by declaring them as Lafayette and Adele's and adopting them out, then arranging for his son's quick departure, then so be it.

It is all simply conjecture. The mists spread by the family's conspiracy of silence, though dissipated by some tantalizing coincidences and speculations, obscure the truth to this day. Excised from the family legacy in Wisconsin, Henry L. Dodge would start again in New Mexico, embrace a new life, start at least one new family, change history a bit and along the way establish a legacy in his own right ... and all for the good.

19

ARMY OF THE WEST

In crossing the Santa Fe Trail in search of adventure during the summer of 1838, the young and perilously frail Matt Field scratched out a melancholy eulogy to their cook Bernardo, who had suddenly contracted a mysterious fever and died.

> "Oh! Poor Bernardo! Thy lone grave
> Is by the swift "Arkansas" wave.
> No friendly tear can bless the spot
> Where thou are slumbering forgot,
> None but the wolves shall visit thee,
> Their howl thy requiem shall be.
> And not unlike, some ripped up bone
> Shall be thy brief recording stone."[1]

They buried him near Chouteau's Island near the crossing of the upper Arkansas and moved on.

The election of 1844 was hardly a ringing endorsement of Democratic policies, but James K. Polk's narrow victory was an affirmation of the American conviction that they were destined sweep over the continent. A treaty with Britain had already delivered upper Oregon Territory. The only remaining impediment to complete domination was an intractable Mexico. The United States' 1845 annexation of Texas, which Mexico still considered a province in rebellion, had infuriated the Mexican government. Threatening war, Mexico severed relations with Washington and flatly refused to negotiate the purchase of California. In 1846, Polk ordered General Zachary Taylor and four thousand soldiers into disputed territory between the Nueces and the Rio Grande rivers in the dearest hope of provoking a war. It did. On April 26th, Mexican lancers attacked an American patrol, killing eleven dragoons.[2] When the news reached Washington two weeks later, an outraged Congress, swept by patriotic fervor over the supposed shedding of American blood on American soil, declared war. America's first national war of conquest would be fought on three fronts. In Texas, Zachary Taylor would invade Mexico from Matamoras. Winfield Scott's forces would stage an amphibious assault on Vera Cruz and lay siege to

Mexico City. A third column under Colonel Stephen Watts Kearny was to take New Mexico and then seize California.

Colonel Kearny, in command at Fort Leavenworth, feverishly undertook assembling an invasion force. The logistics of arranging troops and supplies for a summer plains crossing was staggering. Rations, weapons, tents, uniforms, and wagons in which to haul them; all had to be hastily procured. Prodding the preparations along, the Missouri papers regularly published alarming rumors. Governor Manuel Armijo of New Mexico had an army of up to five thousand men, its ranks swelling with patriotic Mexican citizens every day—General Urrea and three to five thousand men were already marching from Sonora to reinforce Santa Fe—Mexican troops had occupied William Bent's trading post on the Arkansas and were poised to seize the Santa Fe Trail itself.[3] As for enthusiastic volunteers, there was a flood of them. By June 27th, a force of better than 1500 men had collected at Leavenworth, the bulk of them Missouri volunteers. Colonel Alexander Doniphan's eight mounted companies and an additional two known as the Laclede Rangers accounted for some 800 of the men. These combined with two light artillery companies, two companies of infantry, and some four hundred dragoons, made up Kearny's Army of the West.[4]

In the meantime, the quartermaster department scraped together the hardware needed to support the troops and stockpiled a mountain of provisions along the banks of the Missouri River. Many of the wagons arriving from St. Louis were in rattletrap shape, but Kearny had them packed with supplies and sent off at the rate of twenty to thirty wagons a day to forge a reliable chain of provisions for his men as they crossed the Plains.[5] The invasion force would follow the Mountain Route of the Santa Fe Trail as far as Bent's Fort on the Arkansas River where, hopefully, sufficient rations would be stockpiled. The Army of the West would then proceed south through Raton Pass and take Santa Fe.

One of Kearny's first concerns was the trader caravans already headed to Santa Fe, some of which carried materials that could support the Mexican war effort. On June 5th, he ordered Capt. Benjamin Moore and two companies of dragoons to overtake and stop them until the Army of the West had marched by. Moore wouldn't be able overtake them all. Wagons had been departing Independence for Santa Fe since early May. On May 9th, trains belonging to George Doan, James J. Webb, W. S. McKnight, Colburn and Turley left. Pruet, Peacock, Charles Blumner, Norris and others followed them on May 15th. Speyer's train of 22 wagons, including the two packed with armaments, had lumbered off on May 22nd. Moore's detachment was able to detain the more recent departures at Pawnee Fork.[6] These and any subsequent trains were compelled to follow Kearny's invasion force.

The Army of the West actually departed Leavenworth in stages. On June 12th, fifty men of Company I First Dragoons, tasked with reinforcing Moore's detachment, were the first to leave. During the final week of June, the Missouri Volunteer companies left, while Kearny himself departed Leavenworth on June 30th. It was during these initial departures that Henry Lafayette Dodge probably attached himself to the expedition. If he had departed Wisconsin shortly before Hewett had given his deposition in mid May, he would have had ample time to reach Leavenworth, whether he traveled by steamboat or by horseback.

Henry's place in Kearny's command, if he had one at all, remains a mystery. He most likely had not enlisted, at least under his own name, for there is no sign of him in the military records for Kearny's expedition. Furthermore, serving in the Army would have disqualified him for Kearny's selection as interim treasurer of Santa Fe. Had Henry been a civilian teamster? The crumbling, yellowed quartermaster records of Mexican War wagon masters, drivers, ferriers and mule handlers fail to reveal Dodge's presence. Hundreds of civilians were hired by the government during the war and Army was notoriously meticulous about documenting them. So it seems that if Henry were attached to Kearny's command, he was more than likely admitted in some unofficial capacity. Conversely, it is possible that Dodge left for Santa Fe in a trade caravan, one that departed ahead of Kearny or one that directly followed him. Regardless, by June 30th the entire Army of the West was enroute to New Mexico and most likely with them in some unfathomed capacity was Henry L. Dodge.

Proposing to advance an army along the Santa Fe Trail was one thing. Doing it was another. The trail could be as cruel and callous as it was alluring and glamorous. There were hostile Indians and Texan bandits to contend with, true, but the greatest challenge to travelers were the natural elements: heat, wind, drought, lightning and thunderstorms. At times the forces of sky and earth could combine to shatter even the best-planned expedition. Nevertheless, for some twenty years the trail had bustled with wagon trains carrying goods to and from New Mexico enroute to Chihuahua. The distances alone were daunting. The average time for making the Independence to Santa Fe trek was about a month, though a caravan heavily loaded with merchandise could take substantially longer. A relatively fast trip was one that took 28 days.[7] It was well worth the effort. Those engaged in the Santa Fe-Chihuahua trade routinely recouped tremendous earnings. In May of 1841, James Magoffin, Giddings and Chávez arrived in Independence carrying about $200,000 in hard currency. On the eve of war with Mexico the St. Louis Republican reported one group of traders had arrived at Independence with about $350,000.[8]

However profitable the trade had been for Mexico, it had some unforeseen results that would later prove deleterious. As relationships developed between the businessmen of Santa Fe and St. Louis, the northernmost Mexican province became increasingly oriented towards the United States materially, economically and to some extent culturally. American traders married New Mexican belles. Hispanic businessmen traveled to St. Louis and points east to observe American culture and mercantilism. Several prominent New Mexican citizens had their children schooled in the United States. Twenty-two years of unencumbered fraternization and profit served to dilute the national loyalties residing in the hearts of many a native New Mexican entrepreneur.

Novices first striking out for New Mexico on the Santa Fe Trail invariably praised the experience. Folks claimed it good for the body and soul, erasing the poisoning effects on a person's health of the humid and heavy air of the East, believed to be contaminated by the vapors of rotting humus. An enthusiastic Private Frank Edwards, on the march with Kearny, proclaimed the virtues of the trail in gushing terms.

> "But, oh, the breath of the prairies! When the breeze, which always rises at sundown, fans your cheek after hot day's ride, you sink quietly to sleep, feeling that that soft delicious air is bringing health and strength to your weary body. How much I felt this can only be known to myself. -One of my reasons for going on this expedition was, to obtain the restoration of my health, which had been, for some time, very much impaired; and when I bade adieu to St. Louis, I hardly expected to get across the prairies alive. But I had not been a week upon them before I felt that my whole being was changed, and ere I reached the settlements, I was one of the most robust of the whole company."[9]

It was precisely for health that the very young and very pregnant Susan Magoffin had accompanied her husband, the trader Samuel Magoffin, on a return trip to Santa Fe. They departed on June 21st, 1846 in loose company with Kearny's invasion force. Magoffin's train was a respectable one; fourteen ox-drawn freight wagons, a baggage wagon and even a carriage for the comfort of Susan and her maid.[10] Five nights out under the stars, an enraptured Susan purred that she had never felt such independence, breathed such pristine air and experienced such purity and peace of mind.[11]

She'd soon have her mind changed. As the trail miles lurched along beneath her carriage, Susan's tone gradually sunk into gloom and despair. The trail loped off into a vast yucca studded desert extending to a blank horizon and an equally vast and empty sky. Driving wind and drenching rainstorms, lightning and thunder exploding as if to cleave the very earth, the bone-rattling roads and bone-chilling nights, the blazing July sun and putrid waterholes; all eroded Susan's gallant appreciation. There were the swarms of mosquitoes, clouds of black gnats, tangles of rattlesnakes, howling wolves and coyotes. As if to administer the coup de grace, the Santa Fe Trail overturned her carriage as they crossed a dry wash, tossing her out into the dirt like a rag doll. Convalescing bedridden at Bent's Fort, she expressed deep regret.

> "I never should have consented to take the trip on the plains had it not been with that view and a hope that it would prove beneficial; but so far my hopes have been blasted, for I am rather going down hill than up, and it is so bad to be sick and under a physician all the time." [12]

Eight days later she had a miscarriage. It could have been worse. At least she survived. Lieutenant James W. Abert, the topographical engineer with Kearny's command, later described the fate of one tuberculosis-afflicted traveler.

> "Last night a Mr. Phelps, who had left his home to try the health restoring climate of the Rocky Mountains, died. . . . he had hoped that the pure air of the prairie might ameliorate his disease . . . yet the exposure under the thin canvas walls of a tent; the long journeys during the days of heat and cold; the deleterious effects of the deprivation of the various conveniences of civilized life; the necessity of traveling daily, whether the patient be sick or well, more than cancel the good influences of the healthful climate."[13]

Ironically, young Abert himself fell victim to the trail. While in transit along the Arkansas, he became so ill that he was forced to delay at Bent's Fort as Kearny's expedition continued their march to Santa Fe.[14]

Predictably, the expedition was plagued at the outset by a variety of problems and Henry L. Dodge would endure them along with Kearny and his men. The trail leading from Leavenworth to the Santa Fe Trail was poorly marked and shortly after leaving Leavenworth, entire companies became lost. The Missouri infantry under Captain W. Z. Angney ended up traipsing along the Oregon rather than the Santa Fe Trail for some ten miles before realizing their mistake.[15] Following in the army's footsteps, Susan Magoffin noted one night a soldier came into camp to "inquire the way." She suspected he was inquiring the way to "a bottle grog, though he said to the next camping place."[16]

The supply trains and their overseers were ill prepared for the rigors of the trip. Wagons fell apart or got stuck in the soft prairie ground. Many of the teamsters had only signed on to the trains because they had arrived too late to join the Army. They proved woefully ignorant, having no clue as how to repair a wheel or axle. When wagons overturned or broke down, they were often abandoned, supplies and all. At regular intervals, travelers following the Army of the West were subjected to the pungent stench of dead, rotting mules and oxen that had keeled over in their harnesses. One fellow observed that after Kearny's passing, the trail from Leavenworth to Santa Fe was clearly marked with about five million dollars worth of abandoned government equipment.[17]

In spite of all their troubles, the trains had still managed a superior head start on Kearny's forces, so much so that his troops were unable to replenish their supplies when rations ran low. More often than not their provisions were days ahead of them. As a result, the soldiers were ordered onto half rations. Several units hovered just above starvation. The soldiers endured dysentery and measles, foot rot, low rations, dying horses, bad water or no water, thunderstorms and the ever-present simmering heat of July that seemed to glare up at them from the ground or, as Frank Edwards noted, assault them in searing gusts.

> "While on our march along the banks of the river a singular phenomenon occurred. Towards the middle of the day, while no breeze was stirring, we were met by successive blasts of heated air, so hot as to scorch the skin and make it exceedingly painful to breathe; and these continued upwards of two hours. The sky, at the time, was entirely cloudless; but these gusts bore no resemblance to an ordinary current of wind, but rather to a blast from a furnace."[18]

Through it all Kearny kept up the quick step, fighting off the fever himself and driving his men ahead at thirty miles a day, a phenomenal rate for an army on the march. They forged across Kansas, passing the remnants of Indian nations that the United States had vanquished in 1832 with the assistance of Henry L. Dodge's father: the Sauk and Fox, still under Keokuk's leadership, the Potawatomie and Kickapoo. By July 7th, the army had reached Council Grove. Beyond that, the gentle hills of Kansas gradually unrolled into flatness. By the 17th, the entire army had crossed the Arkansas River at Pawnee Fork, where the country became excruciatingly mundane and arid.

On July 21st, after three weeks on the march, Kearny's men caught their first glimpse of the Rocky Mountains. On July 29th, the vanguard of Colonel Kearny's invasion force arrived at Bent's Fort on the north banks of the Arkansas. The men encamped a few miles downriver, among the cool cottonwoods and the trade caravans that were now a reluctant part of the expedition.[19] They'd been on the trail for more than a month and they were still 300 miles from Santa Fe.

Bent's Fort was, thankfully, unoccupied by Mexican troops. The proprietors of the fort were the brothers Charles and William Bent, natives of Virginia and raised in St. Louis. They had built it in 1833 as a trading center for fur trappers and Indians and, with Ceran St. Vrain, had created an enterprise that influenced not only the Great Plains, but Taos and Santa Fe and the greater Southwest. Some years afterwards, Charles had moved to Taos, leaving William in charge. The trading post itself appeared more of a fortress than a store. In anticipation of possible Indian troubles, it was built of stout adobe, roughly in the shape of a closed rectangle. On the inside, the adjoining rooms formed an interior plaza. On the outside, they presented an intimidating defense of solid, ten-foot high, two-foot thick walls. On opposite corners of the fort two adobe turrets, each boasting a small cannon piece, stood guard. The front entrance, barred by a pair of heavy pine doors, was just high and wide enough to admit a wagon. On the gate wall stood a small guardhouse equipped with a spyglass. Inside these formidable redoubts the weary traveler found a comfortable, compact and self-sufficient community. There was a store, a carpenter and blacksmith shop, storehouses, a kitchen, dining room and pantry, and private rooms for guests.

Such extravagant defensive precautions were seldom necessary. In all the years of operation, there had been only one minor incident with the Comanche. Invariably, those who came, the Indians, fur trappers, Mexicans and Americans, came to do business. Enemies who in any other instance would have gladly cut one another's throats, whether Pawnee or Sioux, Comanche or Cheyenne, Ute or occasionally Navajo, observed a truce when visiting the fort.[20]

Although the army had made it to Bent's in one piece, food supplies remained dangerously low. The situation become more serious after Colonel Kearny discovered that a good number of the supply train teamsters were refusing to drive their wagons any further. The quartermaster had only contracted them to take Army provisions as far as Bent's Fort, the drivers indignantly insisted, not all the way to Santa Fe. As it turned out, they were right. When it came to getting paid, Manifest

Destiny took second shrift, so the wagons remained at Bent's Fort as the Army of the West resumed the march.[21]

The expedition crossed the south bank of the Arkansas, for the first time entering Mexico proper. The column then angled off towards the southwest across a bleak and parched plain, the tentative supplies of food and water trickling away with each step. Mirages danced ahead of the column, teasing many a parched soldier. Men would occasionally wander off in search of a spring or basin. On August 4th, just two days out of Bent's, Kearny's chief topographical engineer officer W. H. Emory noted the troops were nearly mad from thirst.[22] At a brackish pond in Timpas Creek, desperate soldiers had to shut their eyes and hold their noses before they could bear sucking up the reeking black but life-preserving liquid.

To the west, the Rockies commanded the western horizon. Directly ahead, the column met the Purgatoire River, a shallow but refreshing clear stream meandering along an impressive line of mesas concealing rugged Raton Pass. As Kearny's men followed the Purgatoire southward, the mountains and forests gradually closed in on them and they began the ascent of Raton Pass. The climb proved relatively easy. The subsequent descent proved hellacious. From the summit, the road dwindled to little better than a footpath and boulders transformed it into a jumbled obstacle course, shattering wheels and splitting axles. With dismaying frequency, the men had to use ropes to jack the wagons around especially tight turns and down precipitous drops. The troops only made a half a mile that day. Passing through Raton Pass a short time after Kearny's army had, Susan Magoffin summed up the sentiments of the troops.

> "Worse and worse the road! They are even taking the mules from the carriages this P.M. and a half dozen men by bodily exertions are pulling them down the hills. And it takes a dozen men to steady a wagon with all its wheels locked—and for one who is some distance off to hear the crash it makes over the stones, is truly alarming. Till I rode ahead and understood the business, I supposed that every wagon had fallen over a precipice. We came to camp about half an hour after dusk, having accomplished the great travel of *six or eight hundred yards during the day.*"[23]

After descending into the broad Canadian River valley, the column came across a Mr. Towle, an American trader from Taos. Towle sold them some much-needed flour and warned Kearny that Governor Manuel Armijo and the New Mexicans were determined to fight the invasion. There had been a conference of the New Mexican leaders in Santa Fe and, although Armijo had opposed resisting the Americans, the more patriotic citizens had overruled him. The Governor General of New Mexico was gathering a force of two thousand Mexicans and Pueblo Indians to hurl back the gringos; this in addition to 300 crack Mexican dragoons said to be in Santa Fe at the moment and another 1200 more expected any day. As for the people of New Mexico, they had been thrown into an uproar over the approach of the heathen Americans.

> "Expresses had been sent out in every direction by the Governor and private citizens . . . the whole country is in a state of alarm—Farmers adjoining Santa Fe are driving their stock into the mountains, securing their possessions, and putting themselves in a position that they can be out of harm's way in a moment's warning. . . ."[24]

Priests, so claimed the trader, had been terrorizing the people with predictions of blasphemous desecrations of the Holy Catholic Church and the banning of the religion, that the women would be subjected to "misuse" by American soldiers and then branded on the cheek like a lowly mule.[25]

Yet all of Kearny's intelligence still indicated that Armijo would take flight rather than fight, that the troops at Armijo's disposal numbered no more than 300 and were miserably clad and armed, and that the common folks hadn't the spirit to resist the Americans. Indeed, the St. Louis Republican claimed that the Mexican were anxiously awaiting Kearny's arrival, thinking "it would furnish them a harvest in the way of trade, and protection from the troublesome Indians in their vicinity . . . that the ladies of Santa Fe were making extensive preparations for the reception of United States troops . . . making for fandango dances and other sports."[26]

Kearny shrugged off Towle's warnings and moved on. On August 11th the army encamped at the Ocate River crossing, where fresh grass and clear water greeted them. On August 14th, four Mexican lancers under a flag of truce appeared on the southern horizon, carrying a message for Kearny from General Armijo. Would Kearny meet him at the settlement of Las Vegas and negotiate a peace? Kearny demurred, politely responding that he would be meeting Armijo soon enough and hoped that their meeting would be an amicable one. The Army of the West then occupied Las Vegas. Kearny proclaimed to the people that they were under United States jurisdiction. He then administered loyalty oaths to the local alcalde and his assistants, who seemed willing enough. The adobe buildings, all single story, were laid out around a central plaza, typical of the times. To one American, the town appeared as "a great pile of unbaked brick," a disparaging description that many a New Mexican town would come to suffer. Apparently the people welcomed Kearny, if not with outright acclamation then at worst with curiosity. During the pause at Las Vegas, Chief Quartermaster Thomas Swords arrived from Leavenworth with the mail and a commission dated June 30th promoting Colonel Kearny to brigadier general.[27]

The town rightly conquered and pacified, the newly promoted commander led his expedition southward into the Santa Fe Mountains, the advance uncontested other than by rumors of Mexican surprise attacks that never materialized. Presently, Kearny was informed that Governor Armijo and an army of six hundred men had occupied the pass in Apache Canyon, just east of Santa Fe. Apache Pass was a narrow and deep three-mile defile, through which the Santa Fe Trail passed. It was the only route into Santa Fe. Rugged piñon-forested hills and cliffs increasingly encroached on the road. At its narrowest point, where the track was just wide enough to accommodate a single wagon, towering cliffs loomed overhead. It was the perfect place to make a defense. General Kearny grimly understood that a determined force positioned there could forestall his invasion indefinitely. On the night of August 17th, the Army of the West encamped near San Miguel, some twenty miles from Apache Pass, and in the gathering gloom pondered what fortune the following day's fight might bring.

It was raining as Kearny's columns approached Armijo's position the next morning. Curiously, as skirmishers advanced through the storm to draw the Mexicans' fire, there was absolutely no resistance. Scouts soon informed Kearny they had discovered on the heights some small fortifications concealing nine antiquated cannon, but that the fortifications themselves were entirely abandoned. The drama that had transpired from atop Apache Pass had already played out long before the appearance of the Americans. While Kearny took Las Vegas, Governor Armijo, his dragoons and a volunteer militia had occupied the site. Nevertheless, Armijo apparently believed that any resistance to the Americans would not only be futile, but jeopardize lives and property in Santa Fe. Accordingly, he announced he was disbanding the militia and forbidding the regular troops from resisting Kearny's advance. Manuel Antonio Chávez, Diego Archuleta and several of the younger leaders cajoled and implored him to stand and fight, but the governor was unwavering. Once Armijo and his dragoons had departed towards Albuquerque, remaining resistance crumbled and the volunteers returned to Santa Fe.[28]

The collapse of the resistance threw the citizens of Santa Fe into pandemonium. Stories raced through the capitol that Armijo had been assassinated, that rogue Mexican soldiers were coming to murder all the American traders they could find and loot the town. Believing that the gringo soldiers were on the verge of rape and pillage and converting their sacred churches into stables, some citizens conspired to destroy the shrines themselves rather than allow Americans to desecrate them. Several influential American businessmen assured the people that the soldiers would not commit any such outrages. All the same, several prominent families fled Santa Fe with their property and their daughters. Juan Bautista Vigil y Alarid assumed the governorship and, on August 18th, met General Kearny on the outskirts of the capital to negotiate a surrender.[29] Kearny's ensuing procession into Santa Fe was reminiscent of those given a conquering hero. That evening New Mexican officials feted the general and his officers with a banquet at the Palace of the Governor on the Plaza. It was a sublime moment for Kearny. His Army of the West had taken Santa Fe without firing a shot and not a moment too soon. Kearny's famished soldiers were down to their last scraps of food.

20

MONTEZUMA'S FIRE

On the evening of August 17th, with the Army of the West encamped near San Miguel, private Frank Edwards and several of his comrades decided to tour the nearby ruins of Pecos Pueblo. Centuries before, the pueblo had been a vibrant community of about 2500 souls, a trade center and a crossroads of cultures. Local tradition claimed that during its glory days Pecos had been the home of the great Aztec king Montezuma, and that when he departed for Mexico, he had promised to come back some day and free Pecos from Spanish oppression. Montezuma then kindled a sacred kiva fire and instructed his people to keep it burning until he returned. He never did. Standing then beneath the eroded walls of the old Pecos mission church, Edwards was inspired.

"The fire was kept alive for more than three hundred years, when, having, by some accident, been allowed to go out . . . There are many traditions connected with this old church, one of which is that it was built by a race of giants fifteen feet in height, but these dying off, they were succeeded by dwarfs with red head, who, being in their turn exterminated, were followed by the Aztecs. But a singular part of the story is that both the large and the small men were white. The bones which have been dug from the floor of the church are, certainly, of gigantic size. A thigh bone that I saw could never have belonged to a man less than ten feet high."[1]

The story of Montezuma and his sacred fire would capture the imagination of even the most skeptical Americans. Susan Magoffin doubted the story's truth from the start but, like so many of her traveling companions, felt compelled to tell it anyway. It was, after all, a mesmerizing saga, a tale that epitomized the romantic and mystical mirage that was Enchanted Cibola.

New Mexico was unlike anything that Henry L. Dodge or any of Kearny's Missouri farm boys had ever seen. The most overwhelming aspect of the landscape was not the land itself, but the immense azure sky plunging down onto a horizon seemingly etched in granite. The crystalline air and the piercing sunlight worked a strange sorcery on the eye, where distant peaks and mesas appeared but a short jaunt away. Gently rolling plains would abruptly vault into towering vermillion cliffs and colossal ridges of volcanic rock. Evergreen mantled mountains thrust up from blistering deserts, then tumbled away into convoluted canyons or badlands. Invariably, every locale held some enigmatic, mystical significance. Every mesa and butte concealed a legend; every grove of cottonwoods a wandering apparition, every canyon phantoms of exotic races.

Winters in New Mexico could be deceptively cold and the summers utterly scorching. The snows were deeper, the rains heavier, the winds more violent and the sandstorms more unmerciful. Nevertheless, old trail guides praised New Mexico for its robust healing properties. Cibola was marvelously dry. Bilious and yellow fevers were unheard of. Miasma and malaria were unknown. Even the dreaded cholera, that scourge of the East, was exiled. In New Mexico, erudite men insisted, vegetable matter and flesh would not rot. One new arrival, W. W. H. Davis, made the somewhat silly assertion that "if you kill your dog and lay his body on your doorstep, you will not smell him; he dries up and blows away."[2] Josiah Gregg observed that the dryness extended life itself, that some New Mexicans attained such great age that they appeared "withered almost to mummies"[3]

The nature and mannerisms of the people proved just as striking as the climate. Burros, adobe, tortillas and chilies, the *reboso, aguardiente*, the chicken-pulls and the *fandangos*—all were an infinite source of fascination for the newly arrived Americans. Indians the Americans knew ... or believed they did. Indians were to be fought, defeated and removed. The conquest of New Mexico was an entirely new experience. Having proclaimed the Mexican province and all its citizens under United States' jurisdiction, one could not simply remove them, though some later suggested it. For the first time the United States was not only ruling a conquered people conspicuously different in ethnicity, language and custom, but serving, protecting and extending to them the rights of American citizenship.

And different the culture was. Hispanic New Mexico was a culture of antiquity, essentially unchanged over the centuries. The majority of the settlements were strung in clusters along the Rio Grande, collections of single-story adobe homes roughly arranged around the main plaza, where stood the Catholic Church, for the people were exclusively Catholic. Surrounding the villages were the farms, watered from the Rio Grande by a system of acequias. Hoes and spades were universally used. To the unprepared American traveler, it was as if he'd suddenly dropped through a hole in the modern world and landed with a thud on the outskirts of biblical Jerusalem. W. W. H. Davis noted that the standard wooden plow was more primitive than that of the Romans. Burros and mules were the usual transportation, whether moving produce or people. More bulky loads were loaded onto the *carreta*, a rough-hewn oxen-drawn cart with two solid cottonwood wheels, which made an utterly supernatural sound as it creaked through the streets. New Mexicans raised considerable amounts of livestock: horses, cattle and sheep—particularly sheep and goats. Herds of rugged *churro* sheep sometimes numbering in the thousands grazed throughout the countryside.[4]

Santa Fe was the provincial hub of New Mexican culture, commerce and government. Founded in 1607, there were no other communities north of Chihuahua that could claim to be as large or as cosmopolitan. Even so, the newly arrived Gringos were immediately swept with an overwhelming sense of foreignness. It was a smallish looking place, single storied, built almost entirely of adobe. Although Americans tended to denigrate it, the adobe was ideally suited to New Mexico. Cool in the summer and cozy in the winter, tough, resilient, and easily repairable, it could withstand almost any assault by the elements. The adobe's greatest adversary was the rain. Occasionally, summer monsoons would crash through the earthen roof and send a cascade of mud and debris down onto the unfortunate occupants below. The homes were nearly always alike, with adjoining windowless rooms, earthen floor and walls white-washed with gypsum, surrounding an enclosed central patio. The largest room of the home, the parlor or *sala*, was often furnished with a course wool carpet, with the walls lined chest-high with calico to prevent the gypsum from rubbing off on one's clothes. The type of heavy oak furniture that Henry and Adele had been accustomed to back home in Wisconsin was conspicuously absent in the typical New

Mexican household. Family members sat on, slept under and ate around quilts and soft mattresses, while a couple of trunks and chests served as an armoire.[5]

The Plaza of Santa Fe was the city's center of entertainment and commerce. The Governor's palace, also built of adobe, squatted on the north side of the Plaza. Stores occupied the remaining three sides and had displayed evidence of Yankee commerce years before Kearny had arrived. The Spiegelbergs, the Staabs, the brothers Joseph and Henry Mercure: all had businesses there, as well as the New Mexicans Felipe Delgado and Francisco Ortiz. Charles L. Spencer ran a jewelry shop. Hugh N. Smith and Richard H. Weightman were the local lawyers. Frank Green and Thomas Bowler would soon open up The Exchange Hotel, also known as *La Fonda Americana*, on the Plaza's southeast corner. It boasted the finest that New Mexico hospitality could offer, including waiters, bartenders, a harpist and Pancho's musical band, all brought from Chihuahua for the comforts of the Southwest traveler. Yet at every turn, antiquity dominated. Just off the Plaza to the west was the Church *La Iglesia de Paroquia*. On the south side stood the sagging walls of the old church, the marble image of Nuestra Senora de la Luz staring mournfully down at passers by.[6]

Crossing the Plaza could be a daunting task on market day. There were lines of burros bending under kegs of Taos whiskey and immense carreta loads of melons and grapes. Vendors barked out their wares amid the cackling chickens and braying donkeys, the laughter of playing urchins, the haggling of picky buyers and the pleading of beggars, the excited cries or vehement swearing over a cockfight and through all the noise, the chiming of the church bells. Groups of uniformed American soldiers swaggered their way through the crowds, bedecked in epaulets and shoulder straps, swords swinging in their scabbards. Lines of mutton swung on lines from one portal post to another; corn, beans, milk, onions, peaches and grapes, melons, cheese and breads were spread out on mats or planks, as well as wild fruits and venison, all sold by the rural folk in the Plaza. The typical family meal tended to be a modest fare of wheat or cornmeal breads, combined with onions, red peppers, beans and infrequently a bit of meat. The more well-to-do families had coffee, sugar and chocolate. Gastronomically timid Americans were particularly captivated by the role hot peppers played in the meal, frequently describing the New Mexican entrée as volcanic or cauterizing.[7]

Down a narrow side street from the Plaza was a booming business in fodder, hay and firewood. Santa Fe's ravenous appetite for these essentials insured an unending line of beleaguered burros, so weighted down as to be swallowed by their loads. At a discreet distance off the Plaza, a huddled group of dejected Indian prisoners, Navajo, Ute, Apache and Paiute women and children, waited to be sold as servants at prices ranging from 100 to 400 American dollars each, particularly for children. Slave raiding had long been a limited but seductively lucrative enterprise in New Mexico.

Peonage, or indentured servitude, was also common. Rural New Mexicans generally had few possessions and to Americans they appeared desperately poor. A significant number of the poorest, the *pelados*, or roughly "the skinned ones" were peons. James Abert noted among the large New Mexican herds, the indentured shepherds who guarded the animals were ". . . miserably clad in tattered blankets and armed with bows and arrows."[8] On occasion it was not uncommon for New Mexicans to sell their servant as one would a slave. Susan Magoffin came across a young orphaned lad in such circumstances during a trip to El Paso. His name was Francisco, Susan recalled, and he politely asked if her husband Samuel would buy him. Francisco explained he'd been held as a servant by the Apache for three years before escaping. The old man who subsequently adopted him was so poverty-stricken that Susan suspected the astute lad was engineering yet another escape by being "bought with the sum of $7.00 which he owes the man for his protection." Samuel obliged Francisco, who upon payment became their servant.[9]

The arrival of Kearny's army had sparked an economic boom by infusing more hard cash into Santa Fe than at any time before. The gambling, grog and whorehouses catering to soldiers did smashing business, of course, but the big money was in Army contracts. The United States hired labor and bought materials for constructing Fort Marcy just north of the Plaza and anyone who wished to work was guaranteed a job and steady pay. The quartermaster's office bought tons of grain and fodder for cavalry horses and army livestock. The Commissary bought copious amounts of food and supplies of every description.[10] With a certain amount of cunning and application, almost anyone could make a good living off of Uncle Sam. With money relatively plentiful and the demand for goods up, prices skyrocketed. Santa Fe became, if not the exclusive place, then quite the expensive place to live.

There were more debonair entertainments than cards and liquor to be had in Santa Fe. There were dinner parties and military balls, chorales and concerts. Soldiers formed thespian groups and presented plays. Richard Smith Elliot, newspaper correspondent for the *Reveille*, rounded up some St. Louis boys to put up a modest theatre in the Palace of the Governors, where they played *Pizzaro* and the *Virginia Minstrels*, complete with blackface actors. In addition, there were traditional New Mexican diversions, many of which involved the reluctant participation of some animal. One might take in the *Correr el Gallo* or, as Davis coined it, testing the stretching qualities of chicken necks. Usually celebrated on San Juan Feast Day, a chicken was greased with lard, bound by the feet and hung from a tree branch or post in the Plaza. A mounted contestant would gallop by in an attempt to grab the bird. If successful, his equally mounted opponents rushed forward in a frenzied attempt to snatch his prize. Usually the hapless chicken was torn to shreds. If not, the rider presented the bloodied trophy to his fair lady. For variation the bird was occasionally buried up to its neck in the ground.

El Coleo or "The Tailing" pitted riders against a more formidable opponent. The object was pursue at full gallop a wild steer, then bend down and throw the animal to the ground by giving its tail a rough yank. As often as not, it was the brave caballero and his trusty steed suddenly airborne ass-over-teakettle, the rider being "fortunate if he is not mashed into a jelly." One could always take in a round of cock fighting, which was very popular at the time. Sunday was the favorite day for the sport and the crowd of aficionados ranged from pelados to wealthy ricos.[11]

For those less inclined towards the agrarian pastimes, there were always parties and dances. Formal celebrations and *bailes* were generally given by the well-to-do and respectable. Abert drolly observed one occasion.

> "The Mexican ladies ... were clothed much after the manner of our own females. Stuffs most rich, and skirts of monstrous width or fullness. While sitting down they were wrapped in splendid shawls. These were generally thrown over the head like the reboza. They gazed round the room with great complaisance as they smoked their cigarritos. Waltzing forms the chief part of all their dances. The principal ones are the 'cumbe', and the 'Italiano'."[12]

On the other hand, the common folk attended the *fandangos*, dance-hall revelry as it were. By 19th century American standards, fandangos were scandalous scenes of vivacious abandon. There wasn't much to the orchestra, perhaps a lone violin and guitar. Rather it was the dancers who infused the party with energy and they did so with gusto. Twenty-eight year old Josiah Webb, a Santa Fe trader and Connecticut Yankee, extolled fandangos as having "a wildness and novelty truly enchanting to such young enthusiasts as we were."[13] Conversely, Frank Edwards labeled them as a rather inferior diversion. The singing was as "dreary and monotonous as a dead march" accompanied by a dissonant duet of squeaking fiddles.[14] Even Josiah Webb could be somewhat condescending.

"I have witnessed some most ludicrous scenes at these *fandangos*. It was not anything uncommon or surprising to see the most elaborately dressed and aristocratic woman at the ball dancing with a peon dressed only in his shirt and trousers open from the hip down, with very wide and full drawers underneath, and frequently barefoot, but usually with moccasins. And such a disparity of ages! On one occasion I saw at a ball given by Governor Armijo an old man of eighty or over dancing with a child not over eight or ten. I could not help the reflection that it was a dance of the cradle to the grave."[15]

At the invitation of an officer, Susan Magoffin reluctantly decided to take in the "menagerie" one evening. The ballroom was filled with dancers in antiquated costume, she wrote, the ladies and maids dressed in silk and satin and gingham and covered in an avalanche of jewelry. She noted Gertrudes "La Tules" Barcelo, the notorious monte-bank keeper and premier madam of Santa Fe, was there in scandalous company with the senior priest of the city. Army officers were there, too, including Major Swords and Colonel Alexander Doniphan and Captain Moore of the 1st Dragoons. In the corner a dark-eyed belle caught her gaze, seated as she was on the bent back of her kneeling servant. Over the entire scene hung a heavy pall of cigarette smoke.[16]

Men, women, children, rich and poor—everyone seemed to smoke. It was considered courteous for the lady of the house to offer visitors a smoke in the same manner as a Missouri farmer offered up a jolt of whiskey, and she would immediately roll up a pinch of tobacco in a small corn husk, light it and hand it to her guest.[17] Private Josiah Rice wrote that even small children ask their mothers for a *cigarito*, then "sit down quietly and smoke with the most ludicrous gravity."[18] The finest ladies of Santa Fe could be seen smoking while waltzing, dining, or reclining in bed. During a grand ball given at the Governor's Palace celebrating the American occupation, clouds of cigarette smoke so sickened General Kearny that he had to go to bed.[19]

Private James Bennett noted that one fandango he had attended degenerated into a free-for all. It was after midnight and a group of women suddenly erupted into a fight. They attacked one another furiously; "pulled each other's hair, scratched each other's faces, tore each other's dresses" until they were finally pulled away by their friends.[20] Such altercations appeared to be uncommon, however. Josiah Webb stated that, even with such unrestrained freedom, the people seldom quarreled. In the rare case when there was an argument, he found it was often started by "some imprudent conduct of the Americans themselves." As for a lapse of etiquette, Webb flatly stated that he had never seen any lady at a fandango behave in any way other than that showing virtue, decorum and self respect.[21]

Despite such diversions, among the soldiers nothing surpassed the popularity of gambling and drinking. Though Henry Lafayette probably took in many of the local diversions, he almost certainly preferred the card games. There was plenty of opportunity to indulge. An outraged Elliot lamented the fact that Santa Fe seemed infested with, as he termed them, gambling "hells" and grog shops, open 24 hours a day, every day, including the Sabbath. Soldiers ran many of the shops, with soldier barkeeps and soldier waiters and soldier attendants, supervised by officers who ran the gambling tables.[22]

Gambling was a long-standing tradition of the country and many of the principal citizens could be found in gambling dens; in that sense New Mexico differed little from the Missouri or Wisconsin of Henry L. Dodge's youth. Even children played cards for a pittance, their faces reflecting all the seriousness of a professional card shark. Of all the card games played, none was played more avidly than *monte*. Indeed, Abert stated that "word *monte* is one of the first a stranger learns. In the market place, by the road side, nay, almost everywhere, you will see the *villanos* seated around, in little groups, deeply absorbed in their games."[23] There were monte parlors and halls, monte tables set up at fandangos, an entire block just off the Plaza devoted to monte run by "La Tules" Barcelo with adjacent taverns to lubricate the betting.

The game itself relied little on skill. The dealer dealt four cards from a deck of forty. The object was to bet on a card that would be paired. The players wagered on the cards they believed lucky and the dealer would then deal the remaining cards until he paired one. The monte tables were usually rowdy until the dealer was actually dealing, at which time an intense silence descended.[24] One historian lamented that the "mysteries of the game could be learned only by losing it."[25] What was not a mystery was just how much money was regularly won and lost. Francisco Perea, son of an influential trader, recalled that by 1849 the amount of money being wagered at any particular table could be astronomical. At one game, $40,000 was lost, while wagers of $10,000 were hardly worthy of mention.[26]

Yet however intrigued or enthralled Americans may have seemed by Santa Fe and old New Mexico, the descriptions in their letters, journals and reports often started with a disclaimer; that the use of lofty terms such as "beautiful" or "verdant" or "inspiring" to describe New Mexico was only relative, for nothing about New Mexico ever compared favorably to back home. Nothing. After all, the authors reasoned, New Mexico was overwhelmingly arid and desolate and nearly everything was brown. The streets were brown, the buildings were brown, the hills and the valleys were brown, the river was brown, and when the wind roared each spring, the air—even the air was brown.

And the people ... the people were brown. Americans believed the Anglo-Saxon overwhelmingly superior—in color, manner and appearance, intelligence, morality and civilization—to all other races bar none, a notion so thoroughly and deeply embedded that few ever thought to reflect upon it. It was a conviction that stained much of their commentary. The cavalryman James Bennett described the ladies of Santa Fe as "very dirty, which does not add to the attractiveness of their ugly dark countenances."[27] In describing Las Vegas, he found everything about the town was filthy; the buildings, the streets and the people "... men, women, children of all ages, sizes, and color; all ragged, squalid, poverty-stricken, undressed or half dressed, bare-footed, and bareheaded. If they were dressed at all it was in the most outlandish styles.[28] His viewpoint was typical.

Americans were generally appalled at what they considered the people's dreadful immorality and lack of modesty. Davis commented more than once that there was no other civilized place on earth where vice was more prevalent than in New Mexico. The women were of the lowest moral standard. Cohabitation was nearly "a universal practice." Prostitution was rampant.[29] Susan Shelby Magoffin often lamented how mortifying it could be to travel through the Mexican settlements.

> "The women slap about with their arms and necks bare, perhaps their bosoms exposed (and they are none of the prettiest or whitest) if they are about to cross the little creek that is near all the villages, regardless of those about them, they pull their dresses, which in the first place but little more than cover their calves-up above their knees and paddle through the water like ducks, sloshing and spattering every thing about them.... And it is repulsive to see the children running about perfectly naked, or if they have on a chimese it is in such ribbands it had better be off at once. I am constrained to keep my veil drawn closely over my face all the time to protect my blushes."[30]

In a similar vein, an amused Richard Elliot described a group of small boys he witnessed playing soldier at San Miguel.

> "As our boys do at home, a little juvenile had elected himself Captain of a company of miniature soldiers, whom he was marching through

the plaza of the town, to the infinite diversion of a crowd of men, women, and children, who were looking on. I thought he intended to represent the entrance of the American army in August last; but if so, he failed in some important particulars. The juvenile Captain was, I suppose, some seven or eight years old, and he was dressed in a costume which you folks in St. Louis would consider, no doubt, extremely interesting and attractive . . . The costume of the little company, as they marched along and faced to the front before the crowd of spectators, corresponded entirely, almost, with that of the Captain, and was, besides a perfect uniform. The Captain was dressed in a pair of bright yellow shoes, laced round the ankle, and a string of beads round his neck. The costume of the little soldiers was the same, *all but the shoes and beads.*"[31]

The lads, of course, were stark naked. Elliot may have completely missed the significance of the villagers' delight. Naked children were common, but the notion of American soldiers prancing *au naturel* into Santa Fe must have been wickedly comical.

Immodesty was not the only moral deficit Americans tended to discern. Mexicans were conniving and untrustworthy. In a letter to his family back East, homesick private John Rice lamented that he was "no less than thirteen hundred miles from the white features of the civilized race, except the mingled race of Mexicans, who are entirely much treacherous, although half-savage themselves," and that if one took refuge in a Mexican settlement and happened to have a good suit of clothes "a Mexican will surely have the price of your life" in exchange.[32]

It was said Mexicans loathed work and when they did work, they didn't treat it with the seriousness that work deserved. One day while visiting a ranch outside of Albuquerque, Lieutenant William Emory observed several families crushing corn stalks in a press to extract the juice. After boiling, the stalks were dumped into a hollowed out cottonwood trunk. The press was a block of wood attached midway along a long pole. At the foreman's signal, men, women and children clambered onto either side of the pole and began ". . . see-sawing in the highest glee." Emory watched soberly for a while, then suggested to the foreman that it would be more efficient a press if they moved everyone to one end. The foreman replied, "No! No! If I do that, the fun of see-sawing will be over and I can't get anybody to work!"[33]

Although contempt for the Mexican, rooted deeply in the conviction of Anglo-American Protestant superiority, was widely held by a broad swath of Americans, the prejudice percolating through their New Mexican letters home also served to reaffirm those values for the benefit of friends and family. Doubtlessly, there were many Americans who envied the comparatively passionate and extroverted New Mexicans . . . but dared not confess it. An Army officer in Santa Fe may have sincerely adored a girl whose "bosom was not the prettiest nor the whitest," but God forbid he'd ever admit it to family back in Boston. There were other reasons to indulge in such racist hyperbole. Part of the reason Private Rice scribbled his harrowing descriptions was to convince his father to get him out of the Army altogether.[34] To what extent the more mature and congenial Henry L. Dodge shared those bigotries is unclear, but if his subsequent activities are any indication, he probably didn't.

True, Americans were not universally damning of the country and its people. Susan Magoffin noticed how quick and inquisitive the people were, though she couldn't restrain herself from noting their curiosity over having never seen "a white woman" before. She very nearly purred about the genteel deportment of one small child.

> "This morning I have rather taken a little protégé, a little market girl . . . Just to see the true politeness and ease displayed by that child is truly amazing, 'twould put many a mother in the U.S. to the blush. And she is so graceful too, her rabozo was thrown to one side and a nice white napkin of pease set down from off her head with quite as much grace as some ladies display in a minuet."[35]

William Watts Hart Davis noted that New Mexicans were generally an amiable folk, very seldom given to drunkenness and generous to a fault.

> "The Mexicans are distinguished for their politeness and suavity, and the lepero, covered with abominations, often exhibits a refinement of manners and address that would well become a prince . . . In their houses they are particularly courteous, and in appearance even outdo the most refined code of politeness. It is customary for them to assure you that you are in your own house the moment you cross their threshold, or to place themselves entirely at your disposal. If you admire an article, the owner immediately says to you, "*Tómele Ud., Señor, es suyo.*" (Take it, sir, it is yours)"[36]

Abert found the New Mexicans equally courteous, with fine singing voices and a deep love for music, adding that they wouldn't think of lighting a cigarette without asking permission.

Conversely but not surprisingly, many New Mexicans grew increasingly offended by what they considered boorish American behavior. Richard Elliot perceived a deep resentment towards Americans among both the Hispanic rich and poor.[37] On one occasion Abert overheard men commenting in irritated bewilderment on his countrymen, exclaiming *"¡No tienen vergüenza!*—They have no shame!"[38] Many Hispanics viewed Americans as lecherous drunkards. Indeed, Americans who did not drink copiously were an anomaly. When Abert and his party refused a neighbor's offering of *aguardiente*, the potent liquor distilled from the root of the agave, the astounded New Mexican replied, *"¡Usted no quiere aguardiente! ¡Usted ciertamente no es Americano!"* "You don't want *aguardiente*! You certainly aren't an American!"[39] The ladies of Santa Fe ceased taking customary evening walks in the Plaza; so humiliated were they by the lewd stares and comments of the *Americanos*. Susan Magoffin related that her acquaintance, Doña Julienne, was admiring her cape one day and announced she wanted one like it because it concealed the neck and she detested going into the plaza with her neck exposed to the stares of so many idle American soldiers.[40]

Unfortunately the behavior of idle American soldiers regularly surpassed bad manners. In its November 20th, 1846 issue, The *Missouri Republican* reported that drunkenness and violence ran rampant among both soldiers and officers and it was common for gangs of Americans to roam the streets of Santa Fe, beating up on New Mexicans and ominously noted, "Men forget the object for which they are here, and forget the position which they occupy. We have seen some of the consequences fairly before us now at Santa Fe-for I do not exaggerate at all, when I say, that not a day passes, but what some outrage, some crime is committed . . . whose victims usually are Mexicans."[41] Signs of mounting aggravation by the Hispanic citizens were so worrisome that Charles Bent, appointed Governor of New Mexico by Kearny, implored Colonel Alexander Doniphan to restrain his men's abusive conduct and compel them to respect New Mexican rights, warning that "these outrages are becoming so frequent, that I apprehend serious consequences must result sooner or later, if measures are not taken to prevent them."[42]

He could not have been more accurate.

21

REBELLION

On August 19th, the day after occupying Santa Fe, Kearny proclaimed the United States' annexation of New Mexico to an assembly of local officials and citizens in the Plaza. To punctuate the fact, he administered oaths of allegiance to Juan Bautista Vigil y Alarid, Donaciano Vigil and other acquiescent officials and ordered a hundred foot flagpole to be erected on the Plaza. In a second proclamation three days later, he promised the United States would respect the people's religion, their persons and property, defend them from marauding Indians, and grant them the right of self-government sometime in the future. He encouraged New Mexicans who had fled Santa Fe to return for their own good lest they be labeled as hostile. His declaration had absolved all the inhabitants of allegiance to Mexico—whether they wished it or not—and twice stated that anyone found fomenting revolt would be treated as a traitor, regardless. He signed it as the Governor of New Mexico, and hosted a grand ball of celebration at the Governor's Palace on the 27th.[1]

Decreeing the annexation of New Mexico was simple, but insuring it would stick occupied much of Kearny's efforts in Santa Fe. He sincerely believed he could earn the peoples' loyalty but, failing that, he would guarantee their cooperation through intimidation. Accordingly, Kearny began construction of Fort Marcy, named in honor of the Secretary of War, barely a stone's throw from the Plaza. Local masons were paid fifty cents to one dollar a day wages to erect it.[2] In the meantime rumors and alarms of a Mexican reconquest continually bubbled up, rumors that Kearny couldn't afford to simply dismiss. On September 2nd, after hearing that a force under Manuel Armijo and General Ugarte was coming up the Rio Grande Valley, General Kearny led 700 soldiers south out of Santa Fe to blunt the purported invasion. They followed the Rio Grande southward some ninety miles before determining the rumors were false.

Kearny constructed the provisional government for New Mexico almost single-handedly, having the laws and regulations translated into Spanish, and promulgated them by proclamation on September 22nd. He later received criticism from Congress for this action and rightfully so. If a military officer could so circumvent the legislative and judicial branches of the United States to create his own regime, he was nothing less than a dictator. Nonetheless, the general unilaterally appointed

Charles Bent as governor, Donaciano Vigil, the brother of Juan Bautista Vigil y Alarid as secretary of the territory, Francis P. Blair as district attorney, and Joab Houghton, Antonio José Otero and Charles Beaubien as judges of the superior court and, of course, as interim Treasurer of Santa Fe, Henry L. Dodge.[3]

Satisfied with his efforts and anxious to continue on to California, General Kearny and a force of three hundred cavalry departed Santa Fe on September 24th. He left Colonel Alexander Doniphan of the Missouri Volunteers in command, assuring him that the majority of New Mexicans had sincerely accepted American rule and that there was little chance lingering malcontents could inspire any organized resistance.[4] Upon reaching Socorro, Kearny's column was met by Christopher "Kit" Carson, just returning from California. He carried dispatches from Fremont and Stockton detailing their success in defeating the Californian and Mexican forces. Believing the bulk of his force would not then be needed, Kearny sent three companies back to Doniphan and, with a mere 100 dragoons, continued on towards California, conscripting the trail-worn and unenthusiastic Carson as a guide.[5]

Kearny's assurances did little to soothe American anxieties as tales continued to circulate about an imminent Mexican offensive or a New Mexican rebellion. At El Paso Susan Magoffin wrote that she'd learned General Ampudia and an army from Chihuahua, having supposedly defeated General Taylor, was poised to invade the province. If true, the anxious young wife expected then she and her husband Samuel, and presumably Francisco their young peon servant, would have to flee up the Rio Grande to Santa Fe for safety, "for 'twill inspire this fickle people with such confidence . . . that en mass they will rise on our heads and murder us without regard."[6]

Yet as the October frosts descended on the mountains and November settled in, the dreaded invasion and insurrection failed to materialize. Meanwhile, Colonel Doniphan was beset by more urgent problems. Quartermaster McKissack reported that sickness and death among the troops was becoming epidemic, so much so that they were breaking apart wagons to make coffins.[7] Richard Elliot noted the prevailing illnesses were chronic diarrhea, typhoid and scurvy, which he believed were complicated by eating the flour issued by the commissary, which "operates constantly on the bowels of many . . ."[8] In late January of 1847, Jacob Hall wrote a mournful letter home detailing his own agonizing illness.

> "All the medicine the doctor gave me for two weeks had no effect in checking it. I became mainly senseless—he then began pouring heavy doses of calornel into me as the last alternative—this soon produced

favorable results.... About one in ten of those who are attacked with the same fever ever recover—nearly 100 of the troops have died with it since I came to Santa Fe—Boswell died last Tuesday—they bury from one to four nearly every day..."[9]

It was an epidemic, the result of crowding soldiers together in close quarters. It the midst of that crisis, Colonel Doniphan was struggling to get his men ready to join General Wool's army in Chihuahua. Their replacements, the Second Missouri Volunteers and the Mormon Battalion commanded by Colonel Sterling Price had arrived from Fort Leavenworth on October 3rd. Shortly after that, Doniphan received orders from Kearny, ten days enroute to California, to delay his departure and pacify Ute and Navajo Indians harassing the settlements. As a result, it wasn't until mid-December, nearly two months after Price's arrival, that Colonel Doniphan and his nine hundred men were finally Mexico bound.

With Doniphan gone, Price was assaulted by several alarming problems that were growing with each passing week. For two months Santa Fe had been a perfect inundation of soldiers, which, as one observer understated, "operates rather disadvantageously for all purposes of peace and order." In reality, discipline had all but collapsed. Insubordination was rampant. Gangs of soldiers roamed the town, terrorizing the populace, and the more affluent citizens were said to be leaving Santa Fe in droves. Sickness was rife and those soldiers who weren't sick were irate. Most hadn't been paid and those who had were paid by check of dubious value. What little hard cash the paymasters had was apparently reserved for the officers. Meanwhile, the dissatisfaction simmering among the New Mexicans was beginning to roil.[10]

To resolve some these problems, Colonel Price determined to get as many soldiers out of Santa Fe as possible. Reducing the number of soldiers in the capitol would reduce the tensions between soldier and citizen, lower the rate of disease, keep idle soldiers busy building new posts and thereby re-establishing some order and discipline. Troops were assigned to erecting posts as far flung as Cebolleta west of Albuquerque, and Mora near Las Vegas. They were definitely a step-down from hurly-burly Santa Fe, each garrison being little more than a clump of adobe homes, outbuildings and a corral or two, all of which the Army rented from local land owner for a preposterous sum. Even with redeployments, the majority of soldiers remained garrisoned in the capitol. For them the Colonel sternly tightened the thumbscrews of discipline.

In December, apprehensions over an insurrection suddenly intensified, for the first time driven not by rumor but by hard evidence. Several prominent New Mexicans were implicated in an alleged plot, among them the brother of the vicar of Santa Fe, Don Tomás Ortiz, a former military officer, Don Diego Archuleta, and Manuel Antonio Chávez, cousin to ex-governor Manuel Armijo and a decorated officer himself. As early as October, the insurgents had notified the Mexican government they intended to overthrow the Americans and create an interim regime ruled by Ortiz as governor and Archuleta as military commander.[11]

According to one account, the rebellion was to begin on December 19th at the ever-fateful hour of midnight. To insure complete secrecy, the conspirators vowed not to divulge their plans to any woman, the assumption being that females were loose tongued, perhaps. The conspirators would seize the seat of government and then fan out over the territory to whip local enthusiasm into a general insurrection. A second account held that the revolutionaries would butcher the Americans during the Christmas holiday celebrations, while they were all besotted. As the tale had it, a woman predictably spilled the beans—the illustrious Gertrudes Las Tules Barcelo, no less—who warned Donaciano Vigil after overhearing the plans. A variant of this *femme fatale* motif asserted that a "mulatto girl", the wife of one of the conspirators, tipped off Colonel Price, while another claimed that Barcelo actually learned of the plot through her servant, a "mulatto girl." Where history ends, mythology begins.[12]

Nevertheless, clearly something was afoot. Informed of the plot on December 17th, Governor Bent immediately began gathering information as to the identity of the conspirators, convinced that the conspiracy was "confined to the four northern counties of the Territory."[13] Upon his arrest, Don Diego Archuleta implicated several co-conspirators and the plot was thwarted. Curiously, the hypothetical reason behind the conspiracy was not the American oppression of the common citizen, but an American breach of promise. Archuleta had supposedly participated in secret negotiations held in August between Governor Armijo and Kearny's emissary Don Santiago Magoffin, during which Magoffin presumably told Archuleta if he cooperated, Kearny would only seize the east bank of the Rio Grande and he would retain control over the west side. Given that Archuleta had strongly urged Armijo to stand and fight at Apache Pass, the story is suspect.[14]

The verification of the conspiracy stunned Americans in the capital. Lieutenant Abert described a tense scene when he arrived two days before Christmas.

> "About midday I reached Santa Fe and found all the Americans there talking about an intended insurrection which had fortunately been discovered. Sentinels had been placed in every direction, all the field pieces

and heavy guns had been parked in the plaza, everything was in a state of preparation and everybody in a state of vigilance."[15]

The heightened paranoia was encouraged by fanciful tales of a Comanche-Mexican alliance forming that would close the Santa Fe Trail and rob Army paymasters and supply trains, or that the village of San Miguel was already in open revolt. It appeared to the Americans that the whole territory was suddenly clamoring for "any hellish scheme to tear down the Stars and Stripes." Artillery that Price was preparing to send Doniphan in Mexico were abruptly appropriated to preserve American control in Santa Fe.[16]

Price's caution was judicious. Late in the day of January 20th, 1847, shocking news arrived in Santa Fe. As Bent had prophesized, the Northern provinces had arisen in armed rebellion. There had been fighting at Mora, northwest of Las Vegas, during which a group of American traders had been killed by an estimated two hundred fighters under the command of Manuel Cortez. More disastrous events had transpired at Taos. Early in the morning of the 19th, a group of insurgents under the joint leadership of the Taos Indian leader Tomas Romero and the prominent New Mexican Pablo Montoya entered the village of Don Fernando de Taos. As luck would have it, Governor Bent and his family were at home there. Donaciano Vigil had earlier beseeched Bent not to go up to Taos, at least not without a military escort, but the governor had brushed aside his qualms. After all, Taos had been his home for ten pleasant years. He had married Maria Ignacia Jaramillo, a local, affluent widow. He was a profitable trader, a friend of Manuel Armijo, had many friends and business associates there, and was active in community affairs. Bent believed he had little to fear. He was wrong.

Accounts of the attack vary in all but one aspect: it was sudden and it was bloody. Bent's brother-in-law Pablo Jaramillo, the circuit judge Charles Beaubien's son Narciso, the sheriff Stephen Lee, Judge Cornelio Vigil and attorney J. W. Leal were all killed. Trying to force their way into Bent's home, the insurgents let loose a fusillade through the main door, hitting the governor in the stomach and chin. They then broke the door down and finished him off with arrows, "three of which the prostrate governor pulled from his face before he was killed."[17] After reportedly mutilating his body, scalping him and lopping off his head, the rebels rampaged through the town, destroying Yankee homes and businesses and killing several other Americans unfortunate enough to be in the area. Bent's fate was doubly incomprehensible considering how influential he had been in the region, the fatal flaw possibly being that he had come to symbolize American tyranny.[18]

Upon receiving the news, Colonel Sterling Price called up the dragoons from Albuquerque to reinforce the capital and prepared a battalion to face the insurgency. The population of Santa Fe was all but hysterical. Donaciano Vigil, now the acting governor, issued a proclamation to calm the people, urging them to keep quiet and go about business. On January 23rd, Sterling Price led 350 men and four cannon northward towards Taos, some seventy miles away through deep snow and bitter temperatures. Included in the column were elements of the 2nd Missouri Volunteers, Captain Angney's battalion of Missouri infantry, and Captain Ceran St. Vrain's mounted company of Santa Fe volunteers, composed of French-Canadian and American mountain men, traders and trappers, teamsters and miners. It would seem likely, considering subsequent events, that Henry L. Dodge would have joined St. Vrain's company, but if he was among them, the evidence has yet to be discovered.[19]

Twice on the march, Price's force met the insurgent army estimated at nearly two thousand men, once at La Cañada on January 24th and again five days later at Embudo, both times driving them from the heights commanding the trail. It was a full two weeks before he and his troops trundled into Taos Pueblo which, with over two thousand inhabitants, was the largest settlement in the region. The rebels had erected defenses in the fortified Catholic mission church on the west end of Taos Pueblo. At two o'clock on the afternoon of February 3rd, Price ordered Lieutenant Hassendaubel's artillery to open up on the church. His barrage had little effect. The stout adobe walls merely absorbed the cannon balls. Frustrated, Price had his forces retire for the night. The following morning Price sent St. Vrain's company to the east side of the pueblo to block any rebel attempt to escape, and then ordered the artillery to hammer away at the church once more. In a succession of dull thuds, the adobe walls once again swallowed the ordnance.

At midday Price ordered his troops to storm the church. The soldiers desperately tried forcing entry by burrowing into the west wall with axes. They put up a ladder and set the roof afire. Captain Burgwin and several of his men attempted to force the massive front doors and was mortally wounded for the effort. Finally the soldiers hand lit cannon balls and lobbed them, grenade-style, through holes they'd punched in the church walls. The explosions tore the resistance to shreds. When the church was finally taken that late afternoon, the surviving rebels ran for the mountains and into St. Vrain's waiting regiment. Most of them were killed or captured. On February 5th Romero and Montoya surrendered.

The Americans lost a total of 7 dead, though many of those 45 soldiers horribly wounded in the fight would later die. The rebel dead were estimated by Price at about 150. Montoya and fourteen other conspirators were quickly tried and hung for treason. Judge Charles Beaubien, whose son Narcisco had been murdered, did not excuse himself from presiding over the trials. Associate Judge Joab Houghton later summed up the prevalent attitude of the Americans at the sentencing of Antonio María Trujillo, that he "be taken hence to the place of execution, and there be hanged by the neck till you are Dead! Dead! Dead!"[20] Taos leader Tomas Romero didn't fare quite so well. Upon his capture, a dragoon by the name of Fitzgerald dispensed with the legal formalities and shot him dead. Secretary of War William L. Marcy later acknowledged that insurgents who had not taken an oath of allegiance to the United States could not be lawfully executed for treason. Although Trujillo was subsequently pardoned, the decision came too late to spare Montoya and several others from the hangman's noose.[21]

During the fracas, Henry L. Dodge probably remained in Santa Fe participating in home defense preparations. His tenure as the city treasurer had apparently expired and it isn't clear if Henry took another occupation. One thing was certain. He definitely needed one. Beginning in November of 1846 and running through January of 1847, Dodge ran up a hefty debt with the Army post sutler, A. G. Wilson. His purchases were mundane and personal domestic items such as sugar, whiskey, coffee and calico, soap, matches and candles. A pair of boots cost him the inflated price of $5.50, a shirt and a pair of pants for $3.00 each; a tin cup—nineteen cents. Affording himself a luxury, he picked up some peach jelly on December 10th at the exorbitant cost of $3.00 and a silk handkerchief at $4.50. His purchase of several decks of cards on January 11th appears to imply that, if he wasn't running a store, he was running a monte table. Of course, Dodge didn't need hard cash buy $138.82 of merchandise. He took it on account, as did most in that specie-starved region. Interestingly, Lieutenants Adams and Ingalls, E. W. Pomeroy of the company Rich & Pomeroy, and the quartermaster Captain McKissack paid the bulk of Dodge's debt, either with hard cash or promissory note. For what services they had owed him is a mystery. It is tempting to surmise that these gentlemen had lost money to Mr. Dodge in card games, but that is mere conjecture. During the spring of 1847, Henry Dodge served as a lawyer for at least one case, representing himself as William Williamson's attorney, in which he wrote and signed a complaint of breach of promise against one James Powell. Powell owed Williamson $17.50.[22]

The uprisings at Taos and Mora had been crushed, but sporadic fighting continued. Manuel Cortez, who had survived the destruction of Mora on January 24th by Captain Jesse Morin's Missouri volunteers, was leading a guerrilla band of up to 300 Indians and Mexicans in attacks on American grazing camps. Price called for volunteers to meet the threat. Dodge, who may have been motivated by either a sense of patriotism or the promise of extra cash, decided to sign up, enlisting in Major Robert Walker's newly formed Santa Fe Battalion of Mounted Volunteers. He was mustered into service as a private at Santa Fe on July 15th and assigned to Capt. Hassendaubel's Company A of Light Artillery, a company of five officers and 98 men. Henry L. Dodge was five foot nine inches in height, with a florid complexion, gray eyes and dark hair. The enrolling officer listed Henry as being thirty years old, although he was actually thirty-seven, and as having the occupation of lawyer, for which he'd never been trained. He had brought his own mount, valued at $75, as well as his own tack.[23]

Initially Dodge was fortunate enough to be stationed in and around Santa Fe. Despite the worries over insurrection, the town's entertainment industry was booming. It had its first newspaper, the *Santa Fe Republican*, edited by two Americans, Hovey & Davies, published in Spanish on one side and English on the other, under the slogan "We Die but Never Surrender!" The Beck & Redman's Hotel, the German Hotel and a host of boarding houses had opened for business. Henry could stop at the Hilliard Saloon in Nabel and Pino's Missouri House, which boasted of "good music, good wine and pretty girls." The Santa Fe House on the Plaza, owned by John C. Ronald advertised the "best of liquors" and—incredibly—oysters. Francis X. Aubrey did a brisk business selling "Gin Brandy and Port Wine." Colonel Price's disapproval notwithstanding, fandangos continued providing excitement, with an American soldier occasionally shooting another, while one danced the "Coonie", which was described as a country dance changing into an Indian swing and finally ending in a waltz. There was even a billiard hall and a ten-pin alley. True, scarlet fever had come to town and that Doctor Wirtz at the general hospital reported the place was jammed with typhoid cases, but over all there were plenty of sunny distractions to offset the negative.[24]

On September 2nd, 1847 Major Walker's Santa Fe Battalion departed the city pleasures and marched for Navajo country to chastise the Indians for stealing stock and harassing citizens. A good number of his men were as drunk as skunks. Details of the expedition's history are scanty at best. Walker did take a portion of Hassendaubel's artillery, but that apparently did not include Henry L. Dodge. If so, it was fortunate for him. In mid October, Walker's expedition returned in a wretched condition, their rations exhausted and the men so starved they had first eaten their pack mules and then subsisted on meat from stray dogs they'd killed.

With Sterling Price promoted to brigadier general and temporarily reassigned, Colonel Edward W. B. Newby inherited command of the department. To keep the number of soldiers down in Santa Fe, he ordered Walker's company and others to southern posts. Although Walker was sent south, Hassendaubel's redeployment was delayed and Dodge was on hand in Santa Fe when his company fired a lunch time howitzer salute to General Winfield Scott's victories in Mexico. Hassendaubel's artillery may not have ever been redeployed. On Christmas of 1847 the Santa Fe Republican reported that Walker's command was returning to the capital for the winter.[25]

In early 1848 Dodge found himself in that hot-bed of insurrection, San Fernando de Taos, where Hassendaubel's company was temporarily attached to Major B. L. Beall's command.[26] A stout contingency of U.S. troops had remained in Taos after the revolt to expedite the hanging of convicted revolutionaries and to guard an uneasy peace. Major W. W. Reynolds commanded three companies of Missouri Volunteers there, whose greatest contribution was to regularly insult and persecute the locals, further embittering both Indians and Hispanics.[27] Dodge's tenure with Beall's command in Taos was at best brief. Whether he ever saw any action is unknown. He was discharged on August 28th, 1848 at the expiration of his term of service at camp near Mora.[28] Henry Dodge had spent just over a year in the Army. He would see service again in 1849, but at an appreciably higher rank.[29] As a volunteer, Dodge was eligible for a bounty in land or cash. O n the day of his discharge he scratched out a letter to the Commissioner of Pensions in Washington City, requesting:

> "... my claim to Bounty Land, under the 9th Section of the Act of the 11th February 1847 ... may be examined; and if I am entitled to Land, I wish to relinquish, and do hereby relinquish my right thereto, and in lieu thereof to receive ...One Hundred Dollars. I am respectfully, your obt Svt. Henry L. Dodge."

His request was granted and a draft, number 1773 issued November 21st, 1848, made payable for $100 to Henry L. Dodge.[30]

Dodge afterward returned to Santa Fe and within two months had found employment, once more courtesy of the Army. In November of that year, Colonel John Washington, who had been appointed military governor of the territory, appointed him Notary Public for Santa Fe.[31] On November 28th, the Santa Fe Republican listed Henry Dodge among the civil officers of New Mexico Territory.[32] Surprisingly, Henry served as an *alcalde*—what credentials Henry had for the position is a mystery. The alcalde was an old Hispanic civil office, similar to a judge and justice of the peace. Under the American administration, the alcalde had jurisdiction over minor bonds and contracts, as well as cases of injury and trespass for less than $100. They also issued summons and warrants for arrest.[33] As alcalde, Henry was paid on average eleven dollars a month for his services, sometimes less, beginning around November of 1848 through at least April of 1849.[34]

There is little doubt that during this period Henry L. Dodge received news from home, although to what depth is unclear. He certainly knew of his brother Augustus and family friend George Jones having become senators of the new State of Iowa and that his father, who had been vital in bringing Wisconsin into the Union, had also become a senator for the new Badger state. Once in Washington, the Old Roman was touted as a candidate for vice president on Van Buren's Free Soil ticket, but graciously declined. The news, although somewhat delayed in transit, had been in the papers from Missouri. Less known to him perhaps was the condition of his family in Dodgeville, struggling to make ends meet. Adele had inherited legal problems regarding Henry's business dealings and the courts had garnished her absent husband's property to satisfy debtors. A few months after that she'd been presented with a subpoena to answer an accusation that Henry had illegally sold land to one Mr. Read.[35]

On the national stage, the Mexican War had been a glorious success, and that success had intensified the conflict over slavery in Congress. Most on both sides of the issue believed California and Oregon territories would remain free territories. New Mexico's status was less clear. The population was against institutionalized slavery, but Texas had claimed all New Mexico's territory east of the Rio Grande, and annexation of it would represent an expansion of servitude. Democrats and Whigs had become divided not only along party lines, but along the Mason Dixon line, giving rise to a fervently inflexible sectionalism. The three-way election of 1850 gutted the Democrats' prospects for the presidency when they split between Lewis Cass and Martin Van Buren. As a result, the Whigs would take the White House. Ironically, the Whig candidate was a Louisiana sugar cane plantation and slave owner, someone it would seem would be wholly opposed to cherished Whig principles. Yet another incongruity—he had prosecuted a war that the Whigs had vehemently opposed. Never mind. General Zachary Taylor had what counted among voters. He was a national hero, The Hero of Buena Vista.

In the meantime Europe, racked by crisis and revolution, would send a multitude of her people fleeing for American shores and eventually to the far West.

22

INDIANS

One thing that could be said with certainty about New Mexico was that it was as fundamentally Indian as Hispanic. Indians had lived in the region for better than a millennium and evidence of their long vanished civilizations was inescapable. Each step a traveler took revealed some ancient revelation . . . pieces of chipped flint, a scattering of glistening pot shards, a misplaced grinding stone, a remnant of a wall or a collapsed ceremonial kiva, mysterious etchings covering a canyon wall and ancient towers seemingly carved from the face of sandstone cliffs, defying both the ages and the elements. Henry L. Dodge had long been familiar with a variety of woodland tribes: the Shawnee, the Winnebago, the Sauk and the Fox and most likely had passing familiarity with prairie and plains groups such as the Osage and Pawnee, but the diversity of contrasting cultures among the tribes of New Mexico must have been for him remarkable.

Kearny's conquest had seized a territory stretching from the eastern plains of Texas to the banks of the desert-bound Colorado River, embracing the present day states of New Mexico and Arizona, as well as swaths of Nevada, Utah, and Colorado. Within this colossal topography existed better than three dozen distinct Indian groups, speaking as many dialects. From the Gulf of California northward along the Colorado River were communities of Cocopa, Yuma, Chemehuevi, and Mohave. Maricopa, Papago, Pima, Yaqui and the Yavapai villages clustered along the Gila, Salt, Verde and San Pedro rivers, all tributaries of the Colorado. In the north, the Walapai, Havasupai, and Paiute lived within the convoluted plateau refuge carved through the ages by that immense stream. Below the great bend where the San Juan River descends to meet the Colorado, the ancient Hopi and the more recent Navajo lived. South from there, several mysterious Western Apache groups roamed the mountains and canyons of the Mogollon Rim country. Along the foothills of the Rockies, among the San Juan and Sangre de Cristo mountains, lived bands of Ute and Jicarilla Apache. Groups of Chiricahua and Mescalero Apache claimed the southern Chihuahua deserts straddling Mexico, while the Comanche, Kiowa and Kiowa Apache ranged over the eastern plains and into Texas.

The Pueblo Indian peoples alone represented more than twenty distinct communities speaking dialects from four language families. Languages of the Keresan family were spoken in the pueblos of Cochiti, San Felipe, Santo Domingo, Zia, Acoma and Laguna. Three varieties of the Tanoan-Kiowa family—Towa, Tewa and Tewa—were represented by twelve separate communities, including Towa speakers of Jemez, Tewa speakers of San Ildefonso and Santa Clara, and Tiwa speakers of Taos. Perhaps somewhat incongruously, the sedentary and peaceful Hopi spoke a language related to warrior peoples, the Uto-Aztecan. The enigmatic Zuni spoke a language that has yet to be proven related to any Pueblo tongue, or to any other tongue on earth, for that matter.

It was a mind-numbing mix of languages and cultures made all the more complex by the cultural and political pressures brought by three hundred years of Spanish influence. For simplicity's sake, Hispanics and their American successors routinely grouped the Indians into two simple categories—the civilized and the savage. The sedentary and agricultural Pueblo were the civilized branch of the race, while their nomadic brethren were judged as wild and savage and probably unredeemable.

In terms of territory and population distribution, Indians held the lion's share of the Southwest. In 1846, with the exception of a few settlements in the west and skirting the eastern plains, Hispanic settlements congregated along the Rio Grande, often near older Pueblo communities. Tiny San Francisco de Albuquerque founded in 1706 clung to the east banks of the Rio Grande just north of Isleta Pueblo. The village of Bernalillo abutted the Sandia Pueblo lands, while the cotton patches of Algodones hinged on the Indian towns of San Felipe and Santa Ana. As far north as La Bajada, the massive volcanic escarpment where the Chihuahua trail climbed out of the valley for Santa Fe, Pueblo communities lined the river valley: Santo Domingo, Cochiti, San Ildefonso, Santa Clara, San Juan, Pojoaque, Nambe, Pircuris, Tesuque and Taos. Northwest of Bernalillo along the Jemez River stood the pueblos of Zia and Santa Ana and, wedged in its own remote canyon fastness, the Pueblo of Jemez. Two days ride due west from Albuquerque were the Pueblos of Laguna and lofty Acoma. Nearby one would find the edge of the frontier and the miniscule towns of Cebolleta and Cubero. A few days' ride from Acoma brought the traveler to the sprawling Pueblo of Zuni. In another week and with a good amount of luck, one might survive passing through untamed Navajo country to reach the Hopi villages secluded atop desert mesas. Beyond that one would have to walk to California to get to the next dusty point of civilization. Across that expanse, with the exception of an occasional landmark or river, maps were emblazoned with the ominous word *Unexplored.*

In 1846 Americans generally viewed the Pueblo Indians as the decayed remnants of Montezuma's great Aztec culture, overlooking the fact that, with the exception of Santa Fe and Las Vegas, the largest and best-organized cities in New Mexico were pueblo communities. Not only were these adobe cities more populous but they were without rival the tallest. When Santa Fe had but a handful of two-story structures, Zuni and Taos boasted three or four stories. Each pueblo was a complete and complicated society, with closely intertwined social, religious, economic and political institutions. Villages might be related to one another through language, as were the Laguna and Acoma, but that alone did not guarantee harmonious coexistence. Each pueblo was autonomous and never hesitant to defend their rights against an interloper, related or not.

The fact that Pueblo peoples spoke several mutually unintelligible languages did not preclude them from living in close proximity to one another and forming alliances, even against their own linguistic relatives. Generally thought of as semi-civilized and peace loving, the various Pueblos were quite capable of waging an effective war. This lesson the Spaniards had learned the hard way in 1680 when the Pueblos united and, without the promised assistance of Montezuma, drove the oppressive Spaniards completely out of New Mexico. After De Vargas retook the province ten years later, the Spanish administration sagaciously softened their repressive policies, giving the Pueblo a measure of respect and enlisting them as allies to blunt the increasingly bold depredations of the wild and savage tribes.

Ironically, it was the Spaniards who had made the so-called savage Indians such efficient fighters, courtesy of the horse. Not only did the horse transform the Comanche, Apache, and Ute into swift adversaries but it also revolutionized their way of life. Entire tepee villages and all the domestic paraphernalia that came with them were transported by horses, wealth and prestige was counted in horses, religious ceremonies revolved around horses. It was as if an earthbound culture had been bestowed wings, and by the early 18th century the wild and mounted tribes had become a formidable force.

Although often characterized as antagonistic, relations between Hispanics and nomadic Indians fluctuated between cooperation and conflict. During times of relative peace, Navajo, Apache, Ute, Jicarilla, Comanche, Pueblo and New Mexican would visit one another's settlements to trade in a variety of commodities, horses and captives being the principle and most desirable items of exchange. Certain places became associated with trade: Pecos Pueblo, Anton Chico, Dona Ana, Jemez and Bent's Fort, among others. Invariably these relationships went sour for one reason or another, bringing a period of conflict, characterized by sudden raids and reprisals, in which groups that had previously been bitter enemies, such as the Navajo and Ute, might ally to attack a third. New Mexicans warring with the Navajo might enlist the help of a heretofore-bitter antagonist, the Comanche.

Whether at war or at peace, the relationship was edgy at best. To the north, various nomadic Ute bands occupied the broken mesa lands and craggy peaks and plains of the southern Rockies, occasionally harassing encroaching New Mexican settlements along the northern Rio Grande, the Trinchera and Huerfano in present-day southern Colorado. On the immense plains of the east the Comanche and Jicarilla Apache jealously guarded their territory, periodically threatening New Mexican towns and travelers along the Santa Fe Trail. The Mescalero and Chiricahua Apache, bitter enemies of the Mexicans, ranged from the Capitan and Sacramento mountains of southern New Mexico, westward to the rushing Gila River of the Mogollon range and deep into Old Mexico. Yet even with that brutal hostility, there were periods of peace and even mutual cooperation.

American feelings towards the Indian were inevitably shaped by attitudes oozing from that "dark and bloody ground" of the 18th century Indian wars. That the Redman was a doomed race was generally accepted and there was serious doubt the missionaries could save the wild Indian from hell in this life or the next, or if the government could or should civilize him. Apache Agent John Cremony once pronounced that any attempt at rehabilitation was doomed to failure, for however impressed the wild Indian might be by American cities and farms and tools, he refused to surrender his life in the fastness of his benighted wilderness.[1]

Some early accounts portrayed the Indians as dullards, a conjecture that was soon proved wrong. As early as August 19th, 1846, when Pueblo chiefs and other Indian leaders came to visit Kearny and confirm or disprove the rumors regarding the American conquest, Lieutenant Emory wrote that, aside from being naked and thin, the savages, "... ate, drank, and slept all the time, noticing nothing but a little cinnamon-colored naked brat that was playing in the court..."[2] It had been Emory who had suffered from a lack of perception. As many an American soon learned, Indian emissaries ate, drank, slept and unfailingly noticed everything. They were astute observers, savvy politicians and cagey negotiators, as Henry Smith Turner discovered during Kearny's march through the country of the Chiricahua chief Mangas Coloradas.

> "Some 30 Apaches came into our camp just before we left. A few good mules were obtained from them, with much difficulty—they exhibit much more shrewdness in trade than we expected, and have the same provoking way of asking more when you offer what is first demanded."[3]

Officers and common soldiers, civil servants and traders could be downright magnanimous in their opinions of Indians—usually in the context of denigrating Hispanics. In such cases, Americans viewed the Indians as industrious, thrifty, generous, shrewd and noble. Even the Apache, rumored to be the most cruel and barbaric savage, earned a bit of respect from Emory.

> "There was amongst them a poor deformed woman, with legs and arms no longer than an infant's. I could not learn her history, but she had a melancholy cast of countenance. She was well mounted, and the gallant manner in which some of the plumed Apaches waited on her, for she was perfectly helpless when dismounted, made it hard for me to believe the tales of blood and vice told of these people. She asked for water, and one or two were at her side; one handed it to her in a tin wash basin, which, from its size, was the favorite drinking cup."[4]

To laud the noble savage was fine enough philosophically, but many felt dealing with the harsh realities of New Mexico required a more cynical, frontiersman view of wild Indians. For many settlers, the killing of an Apache or Navajo attended no more concern than the killing of a rabid dog. For years there had been instances of shocking carnage between *El Indio Salvaje*, the Savage Indian, and the New Mexican, and American soldiers found themselves incessantly stamping out brush fires sparked by some senseless butchery. Although the military frequently found citizens responsible for the outrage, there was never a doubt who the Americans would support once an Indian war started. The historic remedy usually adopted by the United States for even relatively minor Indian effronteries had been mass retribution against entire tribes, and so it became in New Mexico. Even that was rarely satisfactory for the majority of New Mexicans, who preferred the offending tribes, whether Ute, Jicarilla, Comanche or Apache, utterly pulverized and swept away.

Then there was the Navajo.

They were known as the *Los Duenos de la Tierra*, Lords of the Earth, the scourge of the settlements, an arrogant Indian nation capable of putting more warriors to horse than all the other wild tribes combined, and as deeply feared as they were hated. The Navajo were the largest and wealthiest of the Southwestern nomadic tribes, if tribe it could be called. At best they were a collection of widespread groups sharing a common language and culture. They had a national identity of sorts, but with only tenuous social, economic and political interdependence. In decisions of war and of peace, each Navajo band was autonomous. Any agreement made by the headmen of one group was binding on the others only with their consent.

Linguists and ethnologists believe the Navajo and Apache were related hunting and gathering Nadene speakers originating from Canada, and had arrived in the Southwest relatively late, probably shortly before Columbus had stumbled onto the New World. Although their skeptical Pueblo neighbors kept them at arm's length, the proximity of the Navajo to the Pueblo eventually changed Navajo society into something uniquely distinct from their Apache cousins. Of all the changes, the most extraordinary came after 1598, in the wake of Juan de Oñate and his colonists, when the Navajo obtained Spanish horses and livestock. This in itself is not particularly notable. The Apache, Ute and Comanche also obtained horses and were soon relieving colonists of their livestock, which was usually butchered and consumed shortly after the raid. But the Navajo took to driving the cattle and sheep home and raising them, having great success with the hardy churro sheep and goats. Within a single generation the Navajo became a pastoral people, their original wandering as hunters largely restricted to moving their vast flocks of sheep and huge herds of horses ... sometimes in the thousands ... from summer to winter grazing lands and back again with the seasons.

While scientists dissect the minutia scratched from ancient Navajo home sites to divine when and how the Navajo arrived in Cibola, the Navajo, who refer to themselves as *Dineh*, or The People, know precisely from whence they sprang. They and all their animal cousins arrived by ascending into four successive worlds, the Black World, the Blue World, the Yellow World where Brother Coyote had cheated Water Monster out of his children, and then up into the Glittering World through a magic reed, thereby escaping the flood the infuriated Water Monster had sent after them. They emerged from a hole in the ground in northwest New Mexico, not far from the present day Jicarilla town of Dulce. The *Dineh* understood it was not an ending, but the beginning of their saga, and their claim to the land where they emerged, given to them by the holy being Changing Woman, was indisputable. All the *Dineh* need do to answer the skeptic was point out the landmarks she had laid down, the four sacred rivers and the four sacred mountains marking the horizons of their country—Mount Blanca Peak to the east in the Sangre de Cristo range in Colorado, in the south Mount Taylor, to the west in Arizona, the San Francisco Peaks, and to the north, again in Colorado, Mount Hesperus. And so it is to the present day.

When the Americans arrived, the Navajo claimed an area from the Little Colorado in Arizona to the west banks of the Puerco River just west of Albuquerque, and from as far south as Zuni to the great arc of the San Juan River. From the *Dineh* point of view, it was their land and only at their convenience did these Lords of the Earth willingly grant the Hopi, the Zuni, the Acoma, Laguna and Jemez and, of course, the New Mexicans, a bit of elbowroom. Not surprisingly, the other inhabitants of Cibola rejected the Navajo point of view, which inevitably led to conflict. For two centuries, there had been relative parity between the Navajo and their neighbors, but it was a parity regularly tested by war. When planned carefully, war proved profitable—a business strategy that enriched many a Navajo leader and his band. When planned badly, it proved catastrophic.

Greeted with that state of affairs in August of 1846, General Kearny promised the New Mexicans that the United States would do something that, up to that point, had been impossible to do—pacify the Navajo. It was a promise more easily made than kept. As for the Navajo themselves, the leaders were at once perplexed and intrigued by the Americans. The Navajo sent representatives to confer with Kearny and to gather intelligence regarding the *Bilagáana*, the Navajo spin on the Spanish word *Americano*. Susan Magoffin noted that the Navajo "deem the General something superhuman since he has walked in so quietly and taken possession of the palace of the Great Armijo, their former fear."[5] The accuracy of that assessment was doubtful. What truly impressed the *Dineh* was the strength and weaponry of Kearny's force, heretofore unseen in the province. A good musket or functioning cannon had been a rare commodity in New Mexico. New Mexican and Indian were often equally matched in arms, as the local militias were as likely as the Indians to depend on bows and arrows and lances to take the day.

The revelation that the United States had defeated Mexico was warmly received by several wild tribes. The Chiricahua Apache chief Mangas Coloradas was so pleased that he guided Kearny and his dragoons through the rugged country of the Gila River to facilitate their attack on Mexicans in California. The Navajo were likewise contented, but having fought with the New Mexicans for decades, could not comprehend why Kearny now insisted they stop. The concept of one force conquering another was utterly foreign to the *Dineh*. For them, the war continued as it always had.

Anticipating trouble, in early September Kearny had positioned troops to protect settlements along the Navajo and Ute frontiers, with little effect. While on reconnaissance, he was beleaguered by reports of Navajo raids. Navajo had killed several New Mexican herders and stolen some two thousand sheep just south of Albuquerque. Forty Navajo had been seen fording the Rio Grande nearby, and Kearny was cautioned to watch out for his own animals. One hundred Navajo had run off all the livestock in the town of Polvadera, a mere twelve miles downriver from Kearny's camp. Hoping to make some gesture of defense, Kearny sent a squad of dragoons after them, only to find the village looted of their stock and the Navajo raiders gone. With gnawing exasperation, on October 5th Kearny formally authorized all inhabitants of the Rio Abajo to "form War Parties" and attack the Navajo to recover their losses. It was, essentially, a confession that for the time being the citizens of Rio Abajo would have to rely on themselves for protection.[6]

Nevertheless, Kearny remained confident that an American military expedition could subjugate the Navajo into a lasting peace. Fourteen companies of Second Missouri Regiment under Colonel Price had just arrived in the capital, hauling along with them a good amount of heavy artillery.[7] On October 26th, 1846 three weeks after receiving Kearny's order to pacify the Lords of the Earth, Colonel Doniphan and his force left for Navajo country. Before their departure Assistant Quartermaster McKissack in Santa Fe confided in a report to Adjutant General Thomas S. Jesup that the Navajos had raided the New Mexicans for eons and doubtlessly it would require a severe flogging before they would be induced to stop. He had no doubt that the Navajos would treat with Doniphan, but that once troops left their vicinity, the raids would commence again, resulting in "another Florida War if the Indians desire to protract it; as they live in the mountains impracticable for roads & can only be pursued slowly with pack mules for transporting stores, etc."[8]

Almost prophetically, a few days before the expedition's departure, a Navajo war party struck the settlements below Albuquerque, killing several citizens and running off five thousand head of sheep.[9]

The expedition comprised two columns. The first, under Doniphan, proceeded south out of Santa Fe, then due west across the Rio Grande from Albuquerque over strikingly arid table land. They passed Laguna Pueblo, Cebolleta, and scruffy Cubero, then entered the broad Wingate Valley. A second column under Major Gilpin moved north and west from Abiquiu in the Rio Arriba country, ranging westward along the San Juan before turning south into the Chuska Mountains, the heart of Navajo county, and rendezvousing with Doniphan's troops.

Doniphan met with several senior Navajo headmen, most notably Narbona and Zarcillos Largos, at Ojo de Oso, or Bear Springs near present-day Gallup, New Mexico on November 23rd. In presenting his case for peace, the colonel emphasized that New Mexicans had become citizens of the United States and therefore were under American protection and that all war between the Navajo and the New Mexicans must cease. In response, Zarcillos Largos criticized what he saw as meddling by the *Bilagáana*.

"Americans! You have a strange cause of war against the Navajos. We have waged war against New Mexicans for several years. We have plundered their villages and killed many of their people, and made many prisoners. We had just cause for all this. You have lately commenced a war against the same people. You are powerful. You have great guns and many brave soldiers. You have therefore conquered them, the very thing we have been attempting to do for so many years. You now turn upon us for attempting to do what you have done yourselves. We cannot see why you have cause of quarrel with us for fighting the New Mexicans on the west, while you do the same thing on the east. Look how matters stand. This is our war. We have more right to complain of you interfering in our war, than you have to quarrel with us for continuing a war we had begun long before you got here. If you will act justly, you will allow us to settle our own differences."[10]

Zarcillos Largo's words may have been inflammatory, but his people had already demonstrated friendship by warmly embracing Doniphan's advance troops, feasting and trading with them and caring for their horses. In a reconciliatory tone, *Naat'áanii Náádleel* conceded that, if the Americans had indeed usurped all of New Mexico, then he would endorse peace, not wishing to war with a nation of such power. The Navajo leadership knew full well the strength of the U. S. military in Santa Fe.

Thus America's first treaty with the Navajo Nation was consummated. The reporter Richard Smith Elliot, who had accompanied Doniphan's expedition, described the exchange of some presents, in particular three hand woven wool blankets "of rare workmanship" the Navajo had given Colonel Doniphan. The treaty itself was less well-crafted, containing wording that would become a distressingly familiar litany to succeeding Navajo leaders. It provided for a lasting peace between the Navajo Nation and the Americans, free trade and access to one another's territory, and the mutual restitution of all property and captives. Elliot and most Americans there were under little illusion that the treaty would actually hold, that the Navajo would eventually have to be chastised, but as the loquacious reporter observed ". . .unfortunately, like the Seminoles or Comanches, they are not easily caught, and, for that reason, are difficult to whip."[11]

Elliot was right. In the end neither side honored the treaty's provisions. New Mexican raiders continued to raid the Navajo with relative impunity. Army dragoons were spread thin and would have been hard pressed to intercede on behalf of the Navajo, had they the inclination to do so, which of course they didn't. Even as Doniphan met with Narbona and Zarcillos Largos, Navajo warriors struck a variety of locales, driving off flocks of sheep from the very doorstep of Santa Fe. Soldiers under Captain Grier pursued the Indians, recapturing the sheep and shooting two of the raiders. As quickly as the troops departed, the Navajos reappeared and seized the flock again, this time making good their escape. Doniphan, who had a reputation of being skilled in the use of profanity, must have been cussing like a Missouri teamster. On November 26th, Navajos attacked a herd of five hundred sheep meant for American troops, killing two soldiers, Privates James Stewart and Robert Spears, mangling the bodies and bashing out their brains with rocks. The Navajo would continue their strikes along the Rio Grande Valley long after Doniphan had marched for Mexico.[12]

Events proceeded with perfect predictability into the following year. On March 12th 1847, the Navajo ran off a herd of sheep from Manuel Pino. Three days later, nine animals from Polvadera were stolen, and then on March 18th thirty head of stock were seized from Salvador Candalaria. On April 12, 1847, so claimed Santiago Gonzales of Valencia County, the Navajos made off with nine more of his animals, after previously having absconded with the bulk of his stock and three shepherd boys.[13]

The Navajo, who were as frequently victims of raids as the citizens they preyed upon, continued to express confusion over the new relationship the Americans professed with their old enemies. Richard Elliot noted that a delegation of Navajo leaders had come in at Colonel Price's request on March 9th, 1847 to answer for the recent depredations on the settlements. The headmen promised to get the stolen livestock back, but according to Elliot expressed consternation that "in their own country, that they cannot understand the conduct of the Americans, who came here to *fight* the Mexicans and are now so friendly that they *protect* them!" Even so, the Navajo claimed they were ready to join with the soldiers "at any time, against the Mexicans." At the same time Elliot noted that some disaffected New Mexican conspirators had recently slain four to eight Navajo and made off with several prisoners, then blamed the Americans in hopes of inciting "a rupture between the Indians and ourselves."[14]

There were certainly those in New Mexico who wanted war, whether for blood or booty and they took every opportunity to incite it. The fact that the sides in the conflict were hardly well defined further complicated the situation. It was seldom simply Navajo against New Mexican. One group of Navajo living in the San Mateo Mountains, known by the majority of Navajo as the *Diné Anaa'í* or The

Enemy Navajo, had a tentative but long-standing friendship with New Mexicans in the nearby settlements of Cubero and Cebolleta. If they weren't actively aiding New Mexican raiders from those towns, they were themselves taking captives and livestock from the more remote groups of Navajos. When Abert and a detachment of soldiers paused in the village of Moquino north of Laguna one October day in 1846, the local folks were amazed to hear that they'd safely come over the *"camino diabolo"* or Devil's Road. A war party of fifty or so Navajos had crossed that road a few hours before. Hadn't the Americans seen their tracks? Abert confessed that, yes, they had but hadn't realized their significance. After recovering from a wave of intense relief, he thought to ask the townsfolk why the Navajo war party hadn't bothered them. They replied simply because at that particular moment "they were good friends to the Navajoes."[15]

The Navajo problem, initially thought as being so easily resolved, would plague the American administration for the next twenty years.

23

EXPEDITION

It was precisely because of the Navajo problem that Henry L. Dodge found himself seated with quill and ink at a table in the Plaza of Santa Fe on March 21st, 1849, scratching out the names of local men enrolling in a volunteer infantry company that he would personally command as captain. They were nearly all names long known in New Mexico, among them *Torres, Arias, Gallegos* and *Baca*... sixty rough, largely illiterate but determined men, seeking employment more than a chance to fight Indians. Dodge appointed Lorenzo Torres first lieutenant and Thomas Seacon as second. Three of the four company sergeants were Americans as well: John Smith, D. L. Rood and Henry Tucker. The fourth was Ysidro Torres. The remainder of Dodge's company, including three corporals, and two buglers, was exclusively Hispanic. Felipe García, Miguel Corrales, Santiago Gallego, Jesus Leyba, Anastacio Montoya, Miguel Naranjo: the list went on more than three score. Although Dodge and his men had mustered in for six months paid service, they wouldn't receive a penny of it while on duty.[1]

Captain H. L. Dodge dubbed his ragtag band the "Eutaw Rangers", not in recognition of the Ute they might fight, but as a pun on the Eutaw House, a St. Louis hotel where several companies had been formed at the beginning of the Mexican War. It doubtlessly meant little more to the recruits than a moniker under which they might strike a mortal blow against the Indians and get paid at the same time. The Eutaw Rangers, officially known as Dodge's Company of New Mexico Volunteers, were mustered in by Lieutenant John Dickerson in Santa Fe two days later, on March 23rd. The purpose of Dodge's company was to compliment units of a grand expedition being organized by the most recent officer to command the territory, Brevet Lt. Colonel John Macrae Washington. He had arrived in Santa Fe to assume the military governorship of the territory in the fall of 1848, having marched from Monterey, California with his company. Nearly fifty years old, Washington was a stern, ramrod straight graduate of West Point, a proud Virginian and a skilled artillerist who had fought the Creek in 1833 and later the Seminole in 1836. Washington had a manner as cold as a Calvinist deacon and a resolve to match. During his tenure in New Mexico, he would earn the reputation of being strict and unyielding to a fault.[2]

The four volunteer companies were raised that March to punish not the Navajo, but hostile Ute and Jicarilla. Accordingly, a company of mounted volunteers under Captain John Chapman was sent to Abiquiu on the Ute frontier, while companies commanded by Captains Valdez and Papin remained in reserve at Santa Fe, doubtlessly to the men's utter delight.[3] Why Colonel Washington chose Henry L. Dodge to lead the fourth company is uncertain. He may have known of Dodge's influential relations back in the States, or had been recommended to him by someone who did. Whatever the circumstance, Dodge and his men saw no immediate opportunity for gallantry. They were sent to Don Fernando de Taos and attached to Major Beall's forces at Cantonment Burgwin.

On April 2nd, Colonel Washington sent Dodge to a makeshift post at Jemez Pueblo. He also gave the captain the chore of adjudicating a thorny land dispute between the pueblos of Laguna and Acoma.[4] The two pueblos located some seventy-odd miles due west of Albuquerque were actually one people who had been separated during Spanish times. They had shared farmlands along a stream named the Gallo for years, and had bickered for about as long over who owned what land and how much water. Captain Henry L. Dodge gave it his best effort.

"Know all to whom it may conserne that I Henry L Dodge Capt Commanding the Eutaw Rangers by and under the direction of J. M. Washington Governor of the Territory of New Mexico have made this

22nd day of April AD 1849 a division of the lands in dispute between the Puabalons of Lagona and Aquama in the following manner..."

Dodge meticulously noted the landmarks and laid the lines dividing Acoma from Laguna lands, running from a hill forming a canyon and along the highlands bracing the valley, and so on, to a plot of land "upon which the said Purbelo of Lagona" had constructed fourteen homes. The agreement was witnessed by Juan Ortiz, the alcalde of Cubero, and Dodge's subaltern Lieutenant Seacon. Three representatives for the Pueblo of Laguna signed. A representative from the Pueblo of Acoma was conspicuously absent. As a result, the agreement failed.[5] Several others would try, with equal results, including the Baptist missionary Samuel Gorman, a special agent Spruce M. Baird and Dodge's own future business partner, John R. Tullis, who noted in a letter to Governor Calhoun in 1851 that the squabbling between Laguna and Acoma had been going on for decades.[6]

The Army post of Jemez was situated just outside of the Pueblo of Jemez, nestled along Vallecito Creek beneath the breast of the Nacimiento Mountains. Jemez was typical of most pueblos of that time, possessing up to five hundred souls living in one and two story adobe homes along a few parallel streets. The post itself was among a scattering of New Mexican adobes, replete with goat pens, gardens of corn, melons and squash and the ever-present peach and apricot orchards. It was a modest affair at best, composed of patched up buildings rented from the locals. Dodge's post had no formal mess or officer's quarters to speak of. There was no infirmary. A sprawling parade ground and grand flagstaff were certainly out of the question. During high winds, the ceilings cascaded sand down on everything and everyone below and, during heavy downpours, leaked like colanders.

Not that Dodge, his officers and the volunteers had many possessions to sully. Furniture was nearly non-existent. There were no bunks—only bedrolls spread across a clay floor. Dodge's volunteers had to provide most of their own equipment and clothing. They were an infantry unit, so horses and tack weren't a concern. Most of the men didn't own them, anyway. They may have brought a few weapons to augment the old muskets issued them by the Army. The volunteer made due with his own attire—usually the bare minimum: a plain cotton shirt, a pair of pantaloons and, on exceptional occasion, a pair of shoes. Standard uniforms, often scarce or out of date among even the regular soldiers in New Mexico, were nonexistent for the volunteer. Although conditions were rugged, the men appear to have been fairly healthy. One volunteer was listed as having succumbed to illness, José Duran, who died on July 9th. Surprisingly, Dodge's men weren't prone to desertion. On May

30th, Simon García, Disideria García and Gregorio Feliz jumped ship, but the others hung in there. They weren't completely isolated. There were opportunities to go into Jemez and hobnob with the villagers, who were probably selling the Eutaw Rangers a variety of foodstuffs and supplies. Henry L. Dodge became familiar with most of the Jemez leaders, most notably Hosta, the Governor of Jemez.

Dodge commanded the post through that summer, but apparently had little inclination to submit the required reports. On June 11th, Lieutenant Dickerson wrote H. L. Dodge Commanding at Jemez, New Mexico stating in the most polite terms that his Post Return was late, thereby delaying the entire Department Return, and that he needed to be more punctual with his reports.[7] Through the years, nearly all of Henry Dodge's frustrated superiors would make the same request . . . repeatedly.

By summer of 1849, Colonel Washington had turned his gunsights on the Navajo. From the moment the American conquerors had entered Cibola, the New Mexicans had lodged a liturgy of complaints against the tribe. Andres Lucero of Bernalillo claimed Navajos had driven off a mule and fourteen oxen in April of 1847. In July of that year, Manuel Jaramillo blamed Navajos for murdering one of his herders, then making off with a horse and nine mules. There were numerous other claims for that year and again in 1848 and during the first half of 1849. Initial attempts by the United States to discourage Navajo attacks had little effect.[8] After the Doniphan and Walker campaigns, there was a brief lull in hostilities, but the familiar pattern of raid and retaliation resumed the following spring of 1848. Colonel Edward W. B. Newby, the commander of the 9th Military Department at the time, did note the renewed attacks may have been touched off by New Mexican raiders previously running off large numbers of Navajo stock. All the same, Newby was determined to punish the Navajo. The Santa Fe Republican applauded the move, hoping the soldiers would "give them a good flogging."[9]

The subsequent expedition of May 1848 hardly qualified as a complete intimidation of the Navajo. Once in the field, Newby quickly realized that any attempt at chasing and overtaking the Navajo was futile, since the "difference between the speed of their animals and *ours* infinitely surpassed my expectations." Upon reaching the Tunicha Mountains, Newby sent a column under Captain Stockton ahead to track down and arrest the Navajo raiders. An incomprehensible sight greeted the colonel when he found Stockton later that day.

"I was astonished to find that the Prisoners were mounted, well armed, and running at large through the encampment. I was still further surprised to find that there was a number of Indians in the hills around at a very short distance from the command, and that the men were scattered around, the greater number of them without their guns."

It looked more like a church picnic than a military operation. Newby was livid. He ordered Stockton to strip the Navajos of their weapons and take them into proper custody. The Navajo understandably made a dash for the hills, and Newby sent several dozen rounds of musket ball after them, killing four. In spite of that provocation, a peace delegation of headmen later appeared in the colonel's camp. Among these were the most influential and richest Navajos; José Largo, Narbona, and Zarcillos Largos, all of whom had been at Doniphan's meeting a year and a half earlier. Newby and the Navajo made second treaty of peace that day, once more promising a cessation of all hostilities, rights of mutual trade and visitation, and the mutual surrender of all captured prisoners and property. Newby also required the Navajos to pay for the cost of the campaign by surrendering three hundred sheep and one hundred mules.[10]

For a brief time, Newby's treaty appeared to have done the trick, for that summer an encouraging event occurred in Santa Fe. The Navajo and New Mexican actually exchanged prisoners, an unprecedented act. The Anglo-Saxon editors of the Santa Fe Republican perfectly oozed sentimentality when reporting "the Navijos manifested great parental affection on meeting with their children and wives, which had been taken prisoners by the Mexicans . . ." then adding in their own indubitable Anglo-Saxon style, ". . . We have every reason now to believe that . . . all hostilities will cease unless the Mexicans are the first to transgress."[11]

Their optimism was premature. Following a particularly severe winter of 1848-1849, a Navajo party ran off several thousand sheep from the Rio Puerco, due west of Albuquerque. In July Navajos bushwhacked a herder by the name of Vicente García near Jemez Pueblo, under the very nose of Dodge's garrison, killing him and driving off all his livestock. The local citizens captured several Navajos to hold as hostages in Jemez but failed to catch the actual killers. Soon afterward Colonel Washington ordered Major William Grier and twenty dragoons to Dodge's post, instructing the major to take command of the Eutaw Rangers, await reinforcement by Captain Valdez's company at Taos, and then take aggressive measures to bring García's murderers to justice.

On July 12th, withering under the apex of summer heat and the day's grueling march, Grier and his tiny detachment of dragoons arrived at Dodge's post. Grier immediately began to plan an expedition. Washington instructed the major to demand the Indians surrender the culprits and to hold the Navajo hostages in

Jemez "until your demands have been complied with."[12] For five days an anxious Grier and Dodge waited in vain for Valdez and the reinforcements to arrive. Writing headquarters in Santa Fe on July 17th, Major Grier confessed with some impatience that all was quiet around Jemez and that he had no intelligence whatsoever regarding the Navajos, but he'd wait for Valdez's unit until the following Sunday, then reluctantly push on without him. Clearly his initial enthusiasm was fading. If Major Grier was unimpressed with the Jemez post, he was less impressed with Dodge's foot soldiers.

>"Captain Dodge will have about sixty men available for the march- to this force I can only add the twenty Dragoons I brought with me when I left Santa Fe-A small force with which to enter the Country of the Navajoes, who will probably be hostile-the "Materiel" of the Infantry Company stationed here is not of the best."[13]

In the end, there was no expedition. The threat of Ute hostilities had stranded Valdez at Taos. In the meantime the Navajo had again struck along the Rio Grande near Albuquerque, killing a herder and driving off his sheep.[14] On July 19th Washington ordered Grier back to Santa Fe, where he would take Company F and reinforce Albuquerque. Henry Dodge and the Eutaw Rangers remained at Jemez.[15] Thus ended a brief chance for, if not battle glory, at least a break in the grinding tedium. The Eutaw Rangers would get another chance soon enough.

On August 14th, 1849, with plans for an expedition against the Navajo completed, Colonel John Washington ordered a force of about five hundred men to assemble at Jemez by August 19th in preparation for the invasion. Two days later, four companies of the 3d Infantry, two companies of Major Henry Lane Kendrick's 2nd Artillery hauling one six-pounder gun and three mountain howitzers, Captain Croghan Ker's Company K of the 2nd Dragoons, and Capt. John Chapman's company of mounted volunteers prepared to depart for Dodge's post.[16] Immediately there were complications. The day after issuing his order, Washington had to suddenly divert Ker and Chapman's companies to Abiquiu to meet the Ute threat and instructed them to rejoin him in the Navajo stronghold of Canyon de Chelly as soon as circumstances allowed.[17] Washington and his own force arrived at Jemez late on August 18th. The trip hadn't afforded the exhausted soldiers a drop of water, while Washington's own command wagon had to be abandoned after becoming hopelessly stuck in the sand. Deprived of tents and camp furniture, the Colonel and his staff were obliged to "bivouac" for the night.[18]

Henry L. Dodge doubtlessly knew most of the colonel's staff, but it would be three newcomers who would be his closest companions on the expedition. Thirty-six year-old West Point graduate Lt. James H. Simpson of the Topographical Engineers had been assigned to do an initial survey of Navajo land.[19] In his eventual report on the expedition to the 31st Congress, Simpson would thank Henry L. Dodge and his lieutenant Lorenzo Torres for their invaluable assistance during the trip, particularly in regards to the Spanish language. On Simpson's coattails were his assistants, the young brothers Edward and Richard Kern. They were both artists and would serve him as topographers and cartographers.[20]

Also making his appearance on this expedition was a middle-aged Carolinian by the name of James S. Calhoun, a successful politician and businessman late of Georgia, who had arrived in Santa Fe on July 22nd. President Taylor had appointed him Indian agent for New Mexico in April of 1849, doubtlessly by virtue of the fact that he was a fervent Whig. On the surface Calhoun's assignment was to negotiate a Navajo treaty of peace, but reasons for his arrival in New Mexico went deeper than pacifying the natives. Texans had been agitating to annex New Mexico territory and President Zachary Taylor was determined to frustrate them. It was Calhoun's assignment to discreetly encourage New Mexicans to form their own state government in opposition to Texan ambitions. Henry L. Dodge may have been cool towards any acquaintance with the infidel Whig, but there is no evidence that their passing relationship was anything but respectful. Indeed, Calhoun later reserved special praise for Captain Dodge's role on Washington's expedition.[21]

Colonel Washington remained at Jemez for four days, waiting for New Mexican and Pueblo reinforcements. In the meantime, the assistant quartermaster busied himself loading all the expedition's equipment out of the wagons and onto the backs of pack mules. Dodge, Simpson and the Kern brothers were able to fill this delay with some diversion. On the day reinforcements were to arrive, Jemez Pueblo held a green corn dance, which Simpson described with an academic coolness, finishing with the note that the "movements in the dance differed but slightly from those of Indians in general." That evening brought terrifying entertainment, courtesy of Mother Nature, in a breathtaking downpour, respite with teeth-rattling thunder and blazing lightning.

The following day Dodge, Simpson and the Kern boys, in company with the Jemez lieutenant governor and Major Kendrick, explored the *Ojos Calientes*, a series of hot springs some twelve miles above Jemez. On the 21st Henry L. Dodge prevailed on Hosta to guide Simpson and the Kerns through the pueblo and the Catholic mission church. The church was the largest structure in the village, but failed to impress Lieutenant Simpson as little more than a shadow of its previous glory. Hosta then led them into the the two kivas of Jemez, which caught Simpson's interest.

> "Both are one story high and, like the one noticed at Santo Domingo, have no doors or windows laterally, and are only accessible from above, through the flat roof.... On the walls were representations of plants, birds, and animals-the turkey, the deer, the wolf, the fox, and the dog [coyote], being plainly depicted..."

Their scientific fancy engaged, the Kerns set to sketching the images in the obscure kiva light while Hosta entertained them with a lengthy explanation of Montezuma worship among the Jemez people. It wasn't accurate in the least, but being the good host, Hosta humored his American guests while preserving the secrets of the true ceremonies. Moved to praise, Simpson noted, "Hosta is one of the finest looking and most intelligent Pueblo Indians I have seen, and on account of his vivacity and offhand graciousness, is quite a favorite among us." Before leaving Jemez, Richard Kern took time to sketch a flattering portrait of their sociable host himself.[22]

On the morning of August 24th, Washington's assault of Navajo country began in earnest. The troops made very modest progress that first day, marching south by southwest a mere six miles before pitching camp at the tiny Hispanic hamlet of San Ysidro, Simpson observing, "it having been deemed prudent, on the first day's trial with the packs, to go but a short distance." The following morning, Carravahal, a skilled Mexican tracker of the village joined the expedition as guide. Heading out north of west, the column was soon braced on either side by striated mesas and jagged ashen-hued ridges. The men marched steadily up the gradual ascent, finally coming out to overlook a vast plain and valley spread westward.

Immediately they noted Cabezon Peak rising in the distance to the south. A sheer-walled butte with deeply eroded arroyos flowing from the base like tresses of hair, it eerily resembled its name sake—a human head gazing sightlessly skyward. The Navajo asserted it was indeed the head of *Ye'iitso* the fearsome giant who had long ago been slain by the Navajo Warrior Twins.[23] It was a sobering gateway to the emptiness stretching ahead, miles of barren plain, naked hillocks and arroyos dotted with sage and juniper. Sixteen odd miles of rough going later, rugged enough to break the limber on Kendrick's six pounder, the expedition encamped in a valley with good grass and wood. Later that evening, Captain John Chapman's troop of eighty-three mounted riflemen came rattling into camp, bringing Washington's command to over four hundred. That night it rained and the next morning, seven of Chapman's volunteers had disappeared.

The men's march that day was uneventful, other than coming across the ruins of a thirty foot wide stone corral—perhaps the first evidence of Navajo habitation—and having to grade down the steep sides of the Rio Puerco so the mules could pack the dismantled cannon across. The episode gave Simpson a moment of unexpected amusement.

> "A mule, with one of the howitzers packed on his back ... lost his footing and capsized—the howitzer, on account of its great weight, naturally seeking the lowest place, and the legs of the poor animal correspondingly tending upwards. The sight, it may well be conceived, partook both of the painful and the ludicrous."[24]

The water was distinctly uninviting—scattered pools of sickeningly green, brackish ponds. By now exhausted as well as thirsty, the soldiers camped at the Arroyo Piedra Lumbre that night, with the pasturage "being but tolerable" and the water "barely endurable." They covered just over thirteen miles that day. Once again, dawn illuminated the fact that three more of Chapman's men had vanished. Dodge, meanwhile, had not lost a single member of his company.

Early that day, the expedition emerged from hillock and arroyo onto a more prairie-like, rolling landscape. Water became rare and so imbued with clay it was undrinkable. Colonel Washington sent Carravahal ahead to scout for a dependable spring. When the guide failed to return promptly, the colonel ordered camp set on a parched clearing of scant grass and a few struggling cottonwoods. The nights had turned surprising cold for August and in the morning the dew lay heavy around them.

On August 26th, Washington's column crossed the Continental Divide. It was hardly noticeable until the soldiers turned to see the tremendous distances that stretched out behind them. Moving ahead along Chaco Wash, Anasazi pueblo ruins began emerging from the terrain, at first modest and then growing increasingly impressive. Fascinated, Simpson and the Kern brothers left the expedition and descended into Chaco Canyon, marveling at the expanse of pueblo ruins while the column continued on. They spent considerable ink and the better part of three days exploring, writing and drawing descriptions of them while Hosta and Sandoval regaled them with stories of Montezuma's travels.

"Sandoval, a very intelligent Navaho chief, also says they were built by Montezuma, but further states that the Navahos and all the other Indians were once but one people and lived in the vicinity of the Silver Mountain; that this mountain is about one hundred miles north of the Chaco ruins; that the Pueblo Indians separated from them (the Navahos) and built towns on the Rio Grande and its tributaries . . . "[25]

Sandoval was the principal headman of the Navajo who inhabited an area around the mountain they knew as *Tsoodzil*, the sacred Navajo mountain of the east, or among the New Mexicans as old Mount San Mateo. Being in proximity to the settlements, the San Mateo Navajo often bore the brunt of retaliation for raids executed by more distant Navajo bands. It was a dicey predicament that required of Sandoval shrewd diplomacy. While professing allegiance to the main body of Navajo, the headman likewise placated his Hispanic neighbors. Knowing every fastness of Navajo canyon, mesa and mountain, he served both Mexican military expeditions and New Mexican vigilante raiders as an advisor and guide, and at the same time enriched himself with his own share of Navajo captives and livestock. Thus, the majority of Navajo referred to Sandoval's people as *Diné Anaa'í*, the Enemy People and, understandably, would have willingly spent a musket ball to send the headman into the spirit world. Conversely, cooperation with the New Mexicans and the Americans earned Sandoval very few accolades. Both groups had a pervasive distrust of him for the mere fact he was Indian. Being Navajo and in apparent close contact with hostile Navajo bands simply intensified their suspicions.

Meanwhile, a full fourth of Chapman's command had deserted, while Dodge's Eutaw Rangers had not suffered a single loss. On August 27th, Washington's men marched nearly fifteen miles. The next day they forged an amazing twenty-five miles, the best distance yet made, and a gnawing anticipation grew that they'd soon encounter the enemy. That night the expedition camped near a rain-fed pond, upon a ground strewn with petrified wood. The subsequent day's march covered fifteen more miles through country that had become utterly devoid of vegetation; as Simpson described it, an ashen panorama of broken hills and arid plains "a most singular profusion and confusion of deep, rugged ravines and high sandstone rocks of almost every shape and character imaginable . . ." When at last they came to a patch of ragged Navajo corn fields, the expedition pitched camp.

That afternoon, after Colonel Washington sent the cavalry horses to feed on the Indian cornfields, several Navajo men and women came into his camp. In a disarmingly matter-of-fact way, they divulged that their homes were nearby and apologized for not expecting him to arrive so soon. In addition, the Navajo professed they were completely willing to abide by the Newby treaty and, as evidence of their sincerity, presented Colonel Washington with some fifteen horses and mules and a herd of sheep. Richard Kern later learned through his interpreter that the Navajo distrusted Colonel Washington. If the Americans truly wanted peace with the Navajo, why had they come as vandals, turning their horses out to destroy cornfields while their hosts were powerless to prevent it?

On August 30th, the expedition moved off towards the northwest, approaching the lofty Tunicha Mountains. Seven miles into the march, a band of mounted Navajos suddenly appeared no more than a mile ahead of the column. With whoops of excitement, the Pueblo auxiliaries suddenly charged them in a boisterous display of prowess. The Navajo and Pueblo merged, making according to Simpson "an interesting and formidable group." Here then was Henry L. Dodge's first close look at Navajos of the parched west, the near naked, painted warriors, many crowned with leather helmet caps adorned in a crown of eagle feathers swirling in impetuous agitation around him, a startling contrast to the Winnebago and Sauk back home.

With the Navajo men were their wives, riding bareback as a man would, and with as much grace and skill, their homespun knee length wool dresses hitched up as they straddled their mounts, one mother suckling a babe in cradleboard. Simpson noted that one warrior resembled a redheaded white man while another elderly Navajo gentleman had a strong resemblance to General George Washington. The majority of the Navajo warriors were dressed for battle—a light shirt, breechcloth, leggings and moccasins. One ferocious looking fellow was completely unclothed ".. . excepting his breechcloth, his whole person at the same time looking ghastly on account of a kind of whitewash with which it was covered."[26]

It was an exhilarating scene, one of camaraderie and salutation most contrary to what one expected of the enemy. It must have perturbed Colonel Washington to no end. He commanded Sandoval to order the entire body of Indians ahead. Off they raced, Pueblo and Navajo alike, leading the American forces down the valley towards the Tunichas. Washington and his retinue advanced—the Kern brothers and Simpson, Agent James Calhoun and the interpreters James Collins and James Conklin. Behind came the Army—the pack train first, followed by Alexander's 3rd Infantry and Henry Lane Kendrick's two companies of 2nd Artillery. Loping along was what remained of Chapman's mounted volunteers and Henry L. Dodge with his Eutaw Rangers. The lofty peaks of the Ojos Calientes rose off to their right as they passed through extensive and lush cornfields. Ahead heavy thunderheads hurled forks of lightning over the mountain peaks and sent thunder rumbling ominously through the forested canyon slopes, as if to deride the military display below.

Washington's force moved some fifteen miles up the valley before coming to a hill, upon which the Colonel ordered Kendrick to station his artillery at the ready. Moving ahead a few more miles, he called a halt. The expedition pitched camp on a wide prominence near Big Tree Wash, roughly a mile from Two Grey Hills. Wood and water was sufficient and dependable, but forage for the horses was not. Therefore, Washington sent a detachment of men into those luxuriant Navajo cornfields to cut fodder for Alexander's horses.[27] Knowing the Navajos might resist, he assigned Henry Dodge and his command to protect the foragers. Dodge organized a detail and oversaw the destruction of a good swath of Navajo corn. It is doubtful Colonel Washington authorized any compensation for that tremendous imposition on Navajo livelihood. Nevertheless, Dodge's men apparently encountered no resistance.

Colonel Washington and Calhoun then met with several Navajo leaders. In no uncertain terms Washington demanded that the principal men of the Navajo nation meet with him the following day for a grand council to air grievances and plan a treaty meeting in Canyon de Chelly. The American expectations were clear. The Navajo must adhere to the Newby Treaty, surrender all captives, hand over to justice any Navajo accused of murdering New Mexican citizens and to turn over all livestock stolen since 1846. It was an impossible set of demands, yet clearly the alternative would be a full-scale invasion of Navajo lands and the destruction of their farms and livestock at a time when harvest was upon them. Before departing, the Navajo agreed to deliver Washington's message to the principal men of the Navajo Nation and that they would return the following day at noon for council.[28]

24

INTO DE CHELLY

The morning of August 31st dawned with some anticipation. At noon, Colonel Washington intended to iron out details for the actual treaty council to be held in Canyon de Chelly, at which leaders of the entire Navajo Nation would be present—or so he hoped. Knowing little or nothing of the route to Canyon de Chelly, the colonel assigned Henry L. Dodge and Major H. L. Kendrick to reconnoiter a route through the Tunicha Mountains. Dodge and Kendrick left shortly after dawn, accompanied by several of the Eutaw Rangers, Hosta and a squad of Pueblo auxiliaries, the guide Carravahal and one of Sandoval's Navajo trackers. The ascent started easily enough, through rocky hills scattered with sage and yucca and expanses of buff sandstone bedrock, eventually giving way to piñon and juniper, mulberry and Mormon tea.

Some distance up the mountain slopes, they entered the pines. A glance back afforded a superlative panorama of the badlands the expedition had recently crossed. Relentlessly the sun climbed, passing from morning to afternoon, as the group labored upward. The narrow ruggedness of the pass looming over them, with its vaulted gray cliffs and maze of boulders, gave Dodge and Kendrick some concern for the safety of the troops who would pass that way, but what they momentarily heard echoing up to them through the pines was absolutely unsettling. It was the faint rattle of musketry, soon followed by the pop of artillery. Perhaps the Indians were putting on a show, riding about and shooting and, in response, Washington had ordered an artillery volley to awe the Navajo. Reassuringly, the popping soon faded away and the detachment continued upward.

Towards evening, the scouting party was brought up short when, out of nowhere, a Navajo suddenly appeared through the thicket and called out to Sandoval's Navajo tracker. The two conversed briefly in their native tongue but apparently not about anything particularly significant. That fact alone was enough raise Kendrick and Dodge's suspicions. Sandoval's tracker explained that one of the Navajo's kinsmen had cornered a bear and he wanted the soldiers to help kill it. It was a peculiar request to say the least. Kendrick flatly refused and he ordered the scouting party ahead. After some time, the guide again insisted that they follow him and administer the coup de grace to the mysterious bear. Kendrick again refused. They continued on, picking their way through the narrowing passage through the cliffs.

As they rounded a corner, Kendrick and Dodge discovered their Navajo guide had suddenly vanished. A queasy touch of apprehension rose in Dodge's stomach. Something had definitely gone awry and he became acutely away of how vulnerable they were, perched alone on the side of a mountain in clear view of any hostiles. The rapidly fading sun seared the sky in fiery orange and cast the distant plains in the rusty glow of dusk as darkness swept across the forested mountain slopes and poured into the canyons below. Reasonably certain that Washington's column could get through the narrow pass above them, Kendrick and Dodge lead their exhausted patrol back down the mountain and into the gathering gloom.

In time, the Pueblo horses started to give out and Hosta's men quickly fell to the rear. Kendrick, Carravahal and Dodge forged ahead, stumbling their way down through the darkness, their anxious ears analyzing every sound emerging from the night. When they finally broke out of the pines, above where Washington's camp should have been, Kendrick and Dodge abruptly realized the camp was gone. It soon occurred to them that the colonel's entire command had inexplicably moved a short distance up the valley. Their campfires were just visible through the thicket, no more than a few miles away. Particularly odd—such a short march. As the weary scouting party emerged from the wooded slopes, the horses sensed the ground leveling off beneath them and picked up pace. Washington's camp was then but a few hundred yards off.

The flash of muskets suddenly sent Dodge reeling and, in a horrifying instant, he realized he was under fire. There was another flash as a second volley came whistling at them out of the dark. One soldier was thrown from his panicked horse. A ball tore through Carravahal's shirtsleeve and gashed his arm. Dodge's horse reared, catapulting Henry into the air as a musket ball hissed past his ear, and he hit the ground with a resounding thud. Given all the action he'd seen in the Black Hawk War, he had never come as close to death as at that very moment, death not at the hands of the Indian but from Washington's own sentries. Dodge and Kendrick's men let out a howl of protest and the sentries ceased fire and rushed up. The greatest damage done to the scouting party, fortunately, was to their sense of pride. Dodge later learned that one of his own edgy Eutaw Rangers had fired the shot that had nearly killed him.[1]

The reason for the guards' hair trigger soon became clear. As expected, the Navajo headmen had arrived at Colonel Washington's camp at noon. Things got off to a splendid start. As a gesture of cooperation and good faith, the headmen gave the colonel one hundred-thirty sheep and several horses and mules. The noteworthy Navajo leaders were all there, led by the principle headman, 80 year old Narbona. For an octogenarian he was surprisingly agile and imposing, fully a head taller than most in camp that day. Later, Richard Kern would describe him as a "wise and great warrior." Two other prominent men accompanied him, José Largo, bearing some seventy-odd years and Archuleta of the San Juan Navajo. As for their retinue, there was a score of minor headmen and literally hundreds of mounted Navajo warriors. As the curious warriors crowded around, Colonel Washington, James Calhoun and the headmen sat in council. Washington went lock-step down the list of points he wished to make, commanding the Navajos to consummate a treaty at Canyon de Chelly meant to bring peace and justice to all aggrieved parties, to recognize the indivisible and irrevocable jurisdiction of the United States over Navajo affairs, and to agree to allow free trade, travel, and military posts on Navajo land. For this, the colonel promised that the "United States will, from time to time, make them presents, such as axes, hoes, and other farming utensils, blankets, &c." According to the interpreter, all the headmen expressed their complete satisfaction. Still, Narbona and José Largo stated that, due to their age, they could not make the trip to de Chelly, but granted authority to two younger headmen, Armijo and Pedro José, to make agreements for them.

At that juncture, for some mystifying and ill-conceived reason, Sandoval began haranguing the crowd of two to three hundred mounted Navajo pressing around the council grounds for their failure to renounce their raiding ways. He was less than popular to start with and when he began lecturing them, his hostile audience was absolutely fuming, noting sarcastically that Sandoval himself had raided, stole and slaughtered. Even Lieutenant Simpson perceived an ominous mood descending on the gathering.

> "Sandoval himself habited in his gorgeously-colored dress, and all the Navahos as gorgeously decked in red, blue, and white, with rifle erect in hand, the spectacle was very imposing. But soon I perceived there was likely to be some more serious work than mere talking."[2]

Whether he knew it at the time or merely in retrospect, Simpson was right. Shortly after Sandoval's tongue lashing, a commotion erupted. One of Dodge's rangers claimed he'd seen a Navajo in the crowd riding a horse that had been stolen from him some time ago. The accusation was promptly reported to Colonel Washington. In a moment of diplomatic indiscretion painfully typical of American haughtiness, Washington decided to make the horse a test of Navajo sincerity. He demanded it be returned unconditionally. An anxious silence descended on the council. Growing impatient, Washington strode out of the meeting and announced that he'd open fire on the crowd, by God, if it weren't given up. When this demand was translated, a wave of tension rippled through the mounted warriors. In an effort to diffuse the situation, Narbona attempted to calm the crowd and told the colonel that the horse couldn't be surrendered because the guilty man had already run off. Washington turned to Dodge's second in command, Lieutenant Lorenzo Torres and ordered him as officer of the guard to seize a horse, any horse, in reprisal. When Torres made a move towards a pony of interest, its rider snapped his mount around and streaked off.

In reply, Washington ordered a volley. The soldiers seized their muskets and the Navajo warriors as one wheeled about and tore off up the wide ravine leading from the camp. A deadly hail of lead followed them. Washington then ordered the artillery to send a couple of rounds of cannon ball into the hills "much to their terror, when they were afar off and thought they could with safety relax their flight."[3]

Accounts told by the witnesses of that unfortunate event differ in the minor details. Indian Agent Calhoun stated the animal had belonged to a Pueblo Indian, while Richard Kern stated that the horse had actually belonged to Lieutenant Torres. The result was the same. The sanguine prospects for a lasting peace had been mortally wounded over a single horse. Narbona and six of his people were killed outright—Narbona shot, according to Richard Kern, in "four or five places and scalped." He had been the most influential and persuasive advocate of peace, first with the Spanish and Mexican, then more recently with the American. Apparently the Kern brothers' only regret regarding the incident was that they didn't think to hack off the old man's head to deliver to a scientist friend at the Philadelphia Academy of Natural Sciences.[4]

Even with such a provocation, the Navajos were either unable or unwilling to launch a serious reprisal. They killed a few American horses and mules that had scattered in the fracas and made unsuccessful attempts to cut off and ambush the small parties of soldiers pursuing them. Nearing five o'clock in the afternoon, Colonel Washington abruptly ordered his men to break camp. He may have felt his position vulnerable there. It is more likely he wanted to position his force for the next day's long and difficult ascent of the Tunichas. They'd hardly tramped a mile through the lengthening afternoon shadows when a Navajo man appeared in their path. He stood before the column in tears, protesting peace and pleading with the soldiers to allow him to take his mother to safety among relatives living with Sandoval's people. Washington encouraged him to do so and sent him on his way. The column then marched another three miles, halted and set camp for the evening.[5]

It was there where Kendrick and Dodge found them that evening of August 31st. Fearing the Navajo may have waylaid the reconnoitering party, Washington had sent out Sandoval and a squad of Mexican volunteers to find the patrol, but they had yet to return. Everyone in camp slept fitfully that night, as much from the guards who raised the alarm twice as from a deep anxiety over an Indian counter attack. At dawn, the expedition prepared to march. There was still no sign of Sandoval's search party and Hosta's Pueblo trackers. Colonel Washington angled his advance on the pass back to the southwest. As they edged up the slopes, Kendrick's description of the dominating cliffs above weighed heavily on the colonel. Flankers were out and moving ahead to flush out any Navajo skirmishers, but he expected that if the Navajos made a stand, they would make it above the narrow pass, among the boulders and on the heights.

At roughly ten o'clock in the morning, there was an outburst of applause among the men in the rear. Sandoval, Hosta and their entire party had returned no worse for their experience in the mountains. The relief among the troops was nearly universal.

> "They were received with cheers and Hosta—the handsome, magnanimous Hosta . . . was greeted with a most cordial welcome. They reported that three of their mules had been stolen by the enemy, but no attack had been made upon them."

The Navajo clearly had the numbers, the opportunity and the motivation to fight, but for some reason had chosen not to. They could have easily chewed up Hosta or Sandoval's men and given Dodge and Kendrick's detachment the devil. Instead, they seemed to behave more like a bewildered and alarmed people, which in truth they were. Despite the tragedy of the previous day, the Navajo remained anxious to make peace.

Almost immediately after Sandoval and Hosta's men arrived, Navajo voices were heard echoing down from the heights. A glance up the slope revealed two Indian men signaling the column. Although they were a great distance away their words carried with amazing clarity. They wanted to parley with Sandoval. Cautiously, Sandoval and James Collins moved up to meet them. After a brief conversation, the Navajo men expressed not anger but regret; that "for so trifling a thing as a horse, so much damage had been done; that by it they had lost one of their greatest warriors." Indeed, one of the men stated that a relative of his had been shot in the fight and would probably die. Even so, the Navajo insisted they wished peace and as proof promised that if the expedition stop, their people would come into the soldiers' camp that very day to arrange it.

Colonel Washington remained unmoved and simply gave the order to advance. The column continued up the boulder-strewn slopes; for the first time spotting Navajo homes, the conical earth-covered hogan. Washington surveyed the pass above them, which Simpson characterized as "extraordinarily formidable." It was dominated by perpendicular walls hundreds of feet tall, while the narrowness of the defile would require his army to laboriously squeeze through. A Navajo force of nearly any size, positioned on those heights, would be able to make it hot going for his men. Washington gave the command to encamp. The expedition would remain there for the night and surmount the pass tomorrow. Once more an uneasy sleep was broken in the dead of the night by a gunshot. An amused but skeptical Simpson wrote that a guard had fired "at an Indian, as he says, prowling about the camp on horseback."

The following morning, September 2nd, the troops resumed the ascent. After a steady climb of four miles Washington ordered a halt along a small stream cascading down from the pass. He had the cannons unlimbered and set up to cover their passage as his men prepared to file through the gorge. The colonel wanted the heights secured beforehand and he assigned a party of forty Pueblo auxiliaries under their elected leader Owtewa to climb the cliffs and seize them. Henry L. Dodge promptly offered to lead the party. No one knew what opposition Dodge and the Pueblos might encounter, but, as Simpson observed, there was reason to worry.

> "I had noticed with my reconnoitering glass several of the enemy upon the heights to the left of the defile, and it was not at all improbable that they were strongly posted on the still more commanding heights on the right..."[6]

The group moved up to the base of the cliffs, where the Pueblo men paused to pray, blessing and spiritually emboldening themselves and their weapons. Then they proceeded to grapple their way up the cliff face through the brush and jagged boulders and soon vanished into the undergrowth. There was a long and quiet period of anxiety among the troops below. Eventually Dodge and his detachment emerged at the summit. The cliff top was unoccupied. If there had been any potential Navajo resistance there, it had vanished. Henry fired off a rifle to signal the all clear and the soldiers advanced. The gorge was every bit as daunting as Kendrick had said, particularly for the artillery. The worst part of the pass was some three hundred yards long and at its widest point no more than fifty feet across. The entire entourage was better than three hours passing through. Colonel Washington proclaimed the passage to be the worst he'd ever experienced but once they got through, they were rewarded with an almost idyllic scene.

> "The narrow portion of the pass got through, it immediately expands into one of about a quarter of a mile in breadth and which, for this country, is of extraordinary beauty. The soil here is of a very rich quality. The pines are tall and large, the grass luxuriant, and the surface of the ground, which is sweetly undulating, is covered with a profusion of the most beautiful and delicate flowers... a stream of pure, wholesome water, trickling along through this scene, westward, adds its beauty to the picture."[7]

Without a doubt, it was the most luxuriant and welcoming country any of them had beheld since leaving Jemez. Here, after a tedious march of only six miles, the expedition again camped, oblivious to the Navajo scouts secretly skirting their column and marking their progress. In honor of their conquest of the pass, Simpson christened it *Pass Washington*.[8]

The following day's march brought further tribulations as they passed through yet another wooded canyon, straggling along the invitingly clear Crystal Wash, spoken of by Simpson as the *Rio Negro*. The magnificence of the alpine surroundings enchanted the men, the lofty mountains layered with pine and fir, oak and aspen, and the banks and valley of Crystal Wash adorned in willow thicket and a profusion of wild flowers. Indeed it appeared a land so rich as to illicit praise from Simpson as "a thing I have not seen since I left the confines of the United States." They made twelve miles that day and camped along the Crystal in the midst of verdant sagebrush meadows. Since entering the Tunicha Mountains, the days had been pleasantly warm and the nights refreshingly cool. Least the Americans become too cavalier about their present environs, Carravahal reminded them that it was in that very pass where the Navajo had ambushed and completely routed a Mexican military expedition fourteen years earlier. Undeniably there was evidence of a Navajo presence all around them. Stock trails strung out on either side of the route and the watering areas and meadows revealed an abundance of sheep and horse manure. Still, not a single hostile Indian had been spotted since they'd come through Pass Washington.[9]

The morning of September 4th would change that. Four Navajos appeared outside the camp to speak with Sandoval regarding the Americans' intentions. Presently they were joined by four more. Apparently nothing of substance came from the talks and they soon left. Meandering more or less northwest, Washington's force forded Whiskey and Wheatfield Creeks on their approach to Canyon de Chelly. Simpson noted fine fields of wheat some five feet tall and "a great deal of horse ordure lying about." Still, they had seen nearly nothing of the enemy or their immense animal herds. After camp had been set that afternoon, yet another delegation of Navajos approached the sentinel lines. Unassuming and appeasing, they merely requested to speak with Sandoval again. Again, they expressed their desire for peace. Sandoval informed Washington that they had been unimportant fellows. The colonel dismissed them, resolving then to continue on to De Chelly, rendezvous with Captain Ker's company supposedly in route to join the expedition, and compel the Navajo leaders to submit to a treaty.[10]

The morning of September 5th brought the expedition to the edge of that fabled Navajo stronghold. The first view of the canyon was a sight worthy of wonder. The piñon dotted landscape suddenly fell away into an immense canyon, it's towering sandstone cliffs like crimson ramparts of Valhalla stretching westward away to the horizon and diving vertically in breathtaking depths to the valley floor below. Winding through the canyon valley was a river, its size so diminished from above that it seemed little more than a ribbon of quicksilver. It was a sight that awed them all, from Colonel Washington and his staff down to the rudest private, a vision that Henry L. Dodge, who had had his share of traipsing across dramatic scenery in Wisconsin, had never beheld.

Washington had actually brought his force to the edge of the northern tributary of De Chelly, *Cañon Del Muerto* or Canyon of the Dead. After setting camp along the canyon's north rim, Washington dispatched twenty-five of the Mexican militia under Carravahal to reconnoiter the creek. No sooner had they left camp than "seeing three or four of the enemy, their hearts failed them and they returned to camp." Dodge's first officer, Lieutenant Torres then took command of the party and after adding a few Pueblo strong hearts to their group went back out. They returned at sunset, reporting that good terrain lay along their route to the west.

The trail the following day appeared to be a major thoroughfare for Navajos of the area. It initially ran along the northern rim of Canyon del Muerto through an open, rolling country of cedar and piñon, but before long the expedition's progress would be regularly delayed by deep arroyos cutting across their road before dropping into the main canyon. Lieutenant Simpson confessed that Kendrick and his artillery "have been obliged to work harder than they have done any day since they started on the expedition."[11]

A reminder of how closely the Navajo were shadowing the column came when one of the pack mules managed to fall behind. The soldier in charge of the mule dropped back to bring it up, but stopped short when he saw a Navajo rummaging through the stray animal's pack. Believing others were about, he sensibly retreated, leaving the animal and the pack to the enemy. As it happened, Lieutenant Dickerson arrived with the New Mexican cavalry. Dickerson pulled off four or five revolver shots at the man. He didn't hit him, but it was enough to make him abandon his prize and flee.

The day passed and the canyon's depth steadily decreased as Washington's column moved southwest along the north rim. In the widening valley ahead the men spotted plumes of acrid smoke springing up in the late afternoon haze. The Navajos were abandoning their camps and firing their homes to deny the Americans even the modest comfort they might afford. As dusk gathered around them, the column straggled down a sand dune and onto a wide flat. After a grueling march of 27 miles, they had reached the western end of Canyon de Chelly. Parched, dust-covered and done-in, they camped along the banks of Chinle Wash, in Navajo *Ch'ínílí* or Water Flows Out. Dodge and his thirsty men, along with the rest of the command, would have to forgo their evening coffee. There was no potable water to be found. So utterly exposed were they that even the comfort of a campfire was forbidden. The weary troops bedded down in the sand and brush, beneath the gaze of the cold night stars, their ears turned irresistibly toward any sound from the legion of Navajo that they all believed were surrounding them and waited anxiously for sunrise.

September 7th brought early developments. Sandoval appeared, leading two Navajo leaders, Mariano Martinez and his assistant, a brother of the slain Narbona. Obviously a man of some importance, Mariano had dressed solemnly in a fashion he hoped would impress the Americans. He arrived wearing a sky blue greatcoat, which Simpson noted was very much like his own and sporting "a tarpaulin hat of rather narrow brim and semi-spherical crown." His buckskin leggings, bow and quiver slung over a shoulder, and a leather pouch and knife on his belt completed the outfit. In spite of his eclectic dress, Simpson appreciated his noble bearing.

> " . . . possessing a somber cast of countenance which seemed to indicate energy and perseverance combined—appeared like a man who had naturally risen up by virtue of the energy of his character . . ."[12]

In the style of Hispanic New Mexico, Mariano and his aide boldly embraced Colonel Washington and James Calhoun. Through an interpreter, Washington informed Mariano of his demands and wanted to know the headman's intentions. Mariano expressed a serious desire for peace, was anxious to comply with the Newby Treaty, and was willing to bring in whatever property the Americans demanded. The colonel then produced a list of stock purportedly stolen by the Navajos: roughly 1,000 head of sheep, 34 mules, 19 horses and 78 cows. Mariano mildly protested the demand for cattle, stating he knew nothing of them. Perhaps, he suggested, the Apaches were responsible. Nevertheless, in the spirit of cooperation and friendship, he promised that, if he could not find the 78 head of cattle, he would substitute others in their place. Washington seemed pleased with the results of the impromptu meeting, but admonished that if the Navajo failed to remain true to the Newby treaty, their complete destruction would result. Once more, Mariano and Narbona's brother gave the colonel a hearty hug and departed.[13]

The following morning Washington detailed Lieutenant Simpson and the Kerns to reconnoiter the canyon. Major Henry Kendrick and Captain Henry L. Dodge were assigned to escort them with a combined force of sixty men. As they huddled to plan their route, a Navajo man roughly thirty years old entered camp. This was no man of great influence, but in truth a captive Mexican by the name of Juan Anaya. James Calhoun described him, Josea Ignacio Anañe, as being one of four captives that Mariano had agreed to surrender. While just a lad, Anaya had been whisked away by Navajo raiders while he was herding sheep near the town of Tecalote, just south of Las Vegas. Standing before Calhoun, he appeared every bit as Navajo in his dress, speech and mannerisms as Mariano himself. Anaya told Calhoun that although he believed his original parents were residing in Santa Fe, he preferred remaining with his present family and the Navajo.

> "He is the fortunate possessor of two wives and three children, living at Mecina Gorda (Big Oak) north of Cheille two and a half days travel. He was originally sold to an Indian named Waro, to whom he yet belongs. I do not think he is under many restraints, for he prefers most decidedly to remain with the Navajos..."[14]

That day Dodge may not have paid Juan Anaya much notice, but he would eventually come to trust and depend on him implicitly.

The exploring party trotted out of camp and headed east through the Navajo cornfields and through the broad entrance of Canyon De Chelly. They hoped to find the Navajo fortress that, according to southwestern lore, lay in the heart of the canyon recesses. The canyon floor was broad and the deep sand made for some tedious going. De Chelly was at that point less than impressive, almost undeserving of comment, but as they rode the walls steadily resumed their astonishing height.

> "Proceeding up the canyon, the walls gradually attain a higher altitude till, at about three miles from the mouth, they begin to assume a stupendous appearance. Almost perfectly vertical they look as if they had been chiseled by the hand of art..."

The detachment traipsed along the canyon floor, craning their necks at the brilliant red sandstone ramparts looming hundreds of feet overhead. Through the millennia winter snows and ice had carved deep clefts along the parapets and the winds had etched out eerie pinnacles and vast alcoves sheltering ancient and silent

Anasazi ruins. Sediments washed from the cliff tops by generations of rain painted the crimson cliffs in alternating black stripes of desert varnish. The sound of the men's voices echoed off the walls from a dozen places. At intervals along the canyon floor there were Navajo cornfields and peach orchards and one or two occupied Navajo hogans. The Navajos they met all greeted them with endearing cordiality and brought out blankets full of peaches for their refreshment. Mariano Martinez himself presently joined them as host and guide. As they rode along, a truly amazing spectacle played out along the canyon walls overhead.

> " . . . several Navahos high above us on the verge of the north wall, shouting and gesticulating as if they were glad to see us, what was our astonishment when they commenced tripping down the almost vertical wall before them as nimbly and dexterously as minuet-dancers! Indeed, the force of gravity and their descent upon a steep inclined plane made such a kind of performance absolutely necessary to insure their equilibrium. All seemed to allow that this was one of the most wonderful feats they had ever witnessed."[15]

The party had progressed up Canyon de Chelly some nine miles with each mile more impressive than the previous. They paused to admire White House Ruin. Simpson seemed disappointed to still see Navajo families living in "the conical pole, brush and mud lodge." He expected perhaps a Navajo upper class further in the canyon would be living in Anasazi style buildings, or at the very least an actual village rather than merely scattered homesteads. A New Mexican of the command who had himself been a Navajo prisoner explained that the Navajo lived in hogans or simple shades of willow and cottonwood, tended their fields and followed their stock season after season. They had no need to seek security in large, fortified villages. The very ruggedness and remoteness of their land protected them. With no sign of the Navajo fort and the day drawing to a close, the explorers reluctantly returned to camp, completely delighted with their fieldtrip.[16]

On September 9th, true to his promise, Mariano and Chapitone, the headman of the northern San Juan Navajos, arrived at Washington's camp. They brought 104 sheep, a handful of mules and horses and four Mexican captives to certify their desire for peace. Juan Anaya, the oldest captive, had wanted to remain with the Navajos. Calhoun noted that two of the captives, Anto Josea and Teodosia Gonzales, young boys of ten and twelve, were healthy and had been treated well. The third captive, eighteen year old Marceito, had been among the Navajo so long that he no longer spoke Spanish. Nevertheless, Calhoun got the impression that, "the novelty of a home, as explained to him, seemed to excite him somewhat." Mariano explained that the bulk of their required payment would have to be brought in later, due to the distances involved in rounding up the livestock. Washington consented, giving the headmen thirty days to deliver the balance due at Jemez.[17]

The treaty meeting then got underway in earnest. The primary participants were, of course, John M. Washington acting as governor of New Mexico Territory as well as commander of the troops presently occupying the territory, James S. Calhoun, the appointed Indian Agent, Mariano Martinez as head chief and Chapitone as second in command of the Navajo Nation. Significantly, Zarcillos Largos, José Largo, Archuleta and other principal men who had signed the Doniphan and Newby treaties were absent, as were their designated representatives Armijo and Pedro José, certainly a direct result of the killing of Narbona and his men at Two Grey Hills. It was a preposterous assumption on the part of Washington that these two headmen could make an agreement that would bind all Navajo groups . . . but never mind. He was there to make a treaty and he would have it.

It is doubly doubtful that Martinez and Chapitone had the authority to make such an agreement, even if they understood all the provisions once the tediousness of going through two translators was done, English to Spanish and Spanish to Navajo, but never mind. If it would speed the pesky *Bilagáana* exit from Navajo land . . . so much the better.

The provisions of the treaty were more comprehensive than the previous two. The Navajos agreed to end hostilities with and recognize the absolute authority of the United States Government. They promised not to aid tribes hostile to the Americans and agreed that the United States would settle disputes the Navajo had with other Indian tribes or with the citizens of New Mexico. Citizens of the United States were to be allowed to travel through Navajo country freely and safely. Should any citizen harm the Navajo, the United States would be arrest that citizen. The Navajo were specifically required to deliver up the killers of Vicente García at Santa Fe and to surrender all stolen livestock and captives at Jemez by October 9th.

In signing the treaty, Mariano and Chapitone also agreed to accept fixed boundaries to Navajo land and to allow the federal government to establish forts, agencies and trading houses as well as other unspecified structures and roads. In return, the United States would pass laws to benefit the tribe and as a reward for good behavior would grant "such donations, presents, and implements, and adopt such other liberal and humane measures, as said Government may deem meet and proper." Twenty-one men affixed their hand and seal to the document as either signatories or witnesses, including Henry L. Dodge and his lieutenant, Lorenzo Torres and Hosta, as the Governor of Jemez Pueblo. Washington and Calhoun both scribed their names, as did Collins and James Conklin, Kendrick, Simpson, Richard Kern, the surgeon Hammond, Calhoun's son-in-law W. E. Love.

There were only three Navajo signatories: Mariano, Chapitone and, oddly, Sandoval. Lieutenant James Simpson conceded that the Navajo might fail to adhere to the treaty's terms, but such a failure would give the United States with ample justification to attack them, however small the provocation.

> "... whether they comply or not, the fact still remains the same, that a treaty covering the whole ground of their fealty ... as well in the general as the particular, was necessary in order to satisfy the public mind, as well as testify to the whole world that should any future coercion become necessary, it would be but a just retribution and, in a manner, their own act."[18]

The United States Senate ratified the treaty a year later, to the day, but for all practical purposes, from the moment it was signed, the Navajo Treaty of 1849 was irrelevant.

25

EL MORRO

With the formalities of treaty making completed to the complete satisfaction of Mariano and Chapitone, at least according to Calhoun's account, an air of amicability seemed to pervade the camp as a hundred armed Navajos came into to trade for small incidentals that the soldiers had, such as tobacco, pen knives and the brass buttons so in demand among the Indians. They bartered dressed buckskins, peaches and other curiosities, but the most highly prized item was the hand-woven Navajo blanket. Simpson expressed amazement that "a nation living in such miserably constructed mud lodges should, at the same time, be capable of making, probably, the best blankets in the world!"

> "The blankets ... were sold in some instances for the most trifling article of ornament or clothing—it being their manner, if they saw anything about your dress which they fancied and wanted to buy, to point to it and then to the article for which they were willing to barter it."[1]

While complementing themselves on their own shrewdness in getting such a fine item for trinkets, the Americans probably failed to appreciate the more sophisticated Navajo purpose for such transactions. Trading was used to establish a relationship of trust and mutual cooperation. One was less likely to quarrel with a trading partner, particularly if that partner hadn't yet reciprocated with a trade of equal value. In just such a gesture, Mariano presented Colonel Washington with a mule and, according to Simpson, a particularly fine one at that. Keener on the rules of propriety than on the merits of good manners, Washington refused the gift, in effect insulting Mariano infront of his own people. At very least, it must have caused the headman deep discomfiture but, after all, Americans were a bizarre and erratic set of creatures. Perhaps he simply shrugged it off.

Or perhaps he did not. Shortly after that humiliation, Chapitone approached Colonel Washington with some troubling news. He had been reliably informed that Apaches had attacked the peaceful pueblo of Zuni to the south, killing a score of people. The colonel was immediately energized. At first light the next morning, the expedition trundled off to Zuni's rescue, the warm Navajo embraces of farewell no doubt motivated more by relief than affection. They traveled southward along the broad and barren Chinle Valley twenty dusty miles that day and, after ascending a gap into the mesas, camped without water. They began again at a quarter past six the next morning, gradually climbing a trail into the mountain pines and covering another twenty-five miles.

The night of September 11th, the column camped at the head of Quartzite Canyon, overlooking the broad Cañoncito Bonito, a wide pastured valley framed by red and white sandstone cliffs, a site Henry L. Dodge would come to know well. Their camp that night was unusually pleasant, replete with a meadow of thick grass and a clear pond thronging with ducks. The next day the expedition descended southward into the narrow recesses of Quartzite Canyon, crossed Cañoncito Bonito proper, and then followed the clear and meandering waters of Black Creek. Immediately ahead of them rose a massive volcanic dyke, resembling the runied parapets and turrets of some dark medieval castle. A deer, the first one spotted on their long trip, provided brief target practice for several rounds of musket ball until it was finally brought down. The troops continued on a southern tack, refreshed by the amenities of fine water, fair weather, a welcoming road and the mysterious and wild beauty around them. They made another twenty-three miles that day and settled in for the evening along Black Creek.

It rained heavily that night and it took everyone a good amount of time the next day dragging themselves out of their soaked blankets, wringing out their clothes and drying their weapons. The column finally left camp at noon, eventually veering away from the creek and moving southeast through a narrow valley buttressed by vermilion cliffs. However soggy the men were, their journey and the following night's camp impressed upon them the stunning beauty of the Navajo country.

> "Our encampment tonight appears peculiarly beautiful. The heavens are deeply blue; the stars shine resplendently bright; the bivouac fires mark well the form and extent of the camp; and peacefully ascending can be seen the blue smoke—the whole forming, in combination with the general cheerfulness which pervades all nature, both animate and inanimate, a most pleasant picture. Indeed, this cheerfulness has been a general characteristic of our encampments ever since we began the march."[2]

If Henry Dodge had been enchanted by Navajo country that evening, the next day's march would disenthrall him a bit. September 14th brought oppressive heat, so punishing that the column only made twelve miles that day. All agreed it had been the expedition's most exhausting march yet. On the 15th Washington's men finally began to see signs they were approaching Zuni. They passed extensive fields of corn and stubbled fields of harvested wheat and, about mid day, they caught their first sight of the pueblo three miles away, appearing like a treeless ridge of angular boulders. Almost at the same moment they spotted a large delegation of Indians heading towards them. It was led by the governor and his assistant, the alcalde of Zuni, outfitted in a manner appropriate for welcoming his Excellency Colonel Washington, Governor of New Mexico.

> "After proceeding in company about a mile, we were unexpectedly saluted . . . with an exhibition of a sham fight, in which men, young and old, and boys entered with great spirit. Guns were fired, dust was thrown in the air, men on foot and on horseback could be seen running hurry-skurry hither and thither, the war-whoop was yelled, and altogether quite an exciting scene was exhibited."[3]

Zuni itself was a typical pueblo of about 2000 people, set along the river in a broad valley dominated by massive Corn Mesa. As Dodge and his men moved along they morbidly noted the body of a dead Navajo man laid out on the ground, ravens perched about it, probing the rotting flesh. The Zuni had earlier killed him when he and his raiding compatriots tried to drive off a flock of their sheep. Later that evening Edward Kern, in the interest of science and recalling his failure to snatch off Narbona's skull, "rode out like Perseus, brought back the head ... "[4]

When at last they entered Zuni, every man, young and old, insisted on shaking hands with Washington. The village then held a feast for the governor and his entourage, at which time Washington inquired about the recent Apache raids. The bewildered reaction of his hosts told him the truth before their tongues could; that there had been no attack and that Chapitone's warning had been either a rumor or a ruse. Zuni leaders did complain that they had been badly treated by a group of California emigrants who, a week earlier, coerced them out of food, horses and mules, in the name of the United States government. There was little Washington could do but apologize for his errant countrymen.[5]

That afternoon two Navajos from the Tunicha arrived in the American camp to surrender a Mexican captive, a boy of some fourteen years. Calhoun noted that the boy, Manuel Lucero, had been flogged and abused by the Navajos and apparently sold several times. Such abuse was more the exception than the rule ... he must have been a particularly recalcitrant peon.[6]

Washington's expedition departed Zuni on September 16th, proceeding nearly due east along a pleasantly sloping valley girdled by mesas and more distant, pine covered uplands. They followed the Rio Pescado, a modest tributary of the Rio Zuni, and found the trail strewn with ruins and potshards, the flotsam of millennia of Pueblo occupation. The Americans made nearly fourteen miles and camped beside a tumble down ruin, among the rich Indian farmlands bordering the Rio Pescado. The following morning as Washington's column got underway, Simpson, his orderly Mr. Bird and Richard Kern left the expedition to explore the valley further. They were guided by a Mr. Lewis, who had for several years traded among the Navajo and was familiar with the country. Simpson's purpose was to investigate a towering butte Lewis claimed to be resplendent with inscriptions of not only ancient Pueblo but also early Spanish origin. Though Simpson does not specifically mention others with his tiny expedition, there is no doubt Henry Dodge and Carravahal accompanied them. Armed with little more than their side arms and a trusty mule stacked with provisions, the group struck out across the sandy, sage and cedar dotted valley as

Washington's column marched away through a canyon portal and into the Zuni Mountains. The tiny expedition continued along another seven or so miles until, directly to their southeast, a weathered, tan sandstone pinnacle appeared like a massive bowsprit at the end of a low mesa. It was El Morro, or simply The Bluff.

Whether Indian, Spaniard or Mexican, El Morro had been a favorite resting spot for travelers along the sparse and lonely trail between Acoma and Zuni for uncounted years. The site was fairly denuded of pinyon and juniper, but it did have a dependable source of water. A deep pool lay in a cool and dark rock recess at the base of the bluff, fed in summer by runoff from thunderstorms and in winter by the snows. As with travelers everywhere, those resting in El Morro's shadows and drinking of her waters felt the urge to leave some evidence of their passing, a fact Simpson's party discovered when Lewis rushed up a sand dune skirting the base El Morro. With a hallo, he beckoned them to come up for a look.

> "We immediately went up, and, sure enough, here were inscriptions, and some of them very beautiful...here were indeed inscriptions of interest, if not of value, one of them dating as far back as 1606, all of them very ancient, and several of them very deeply as well as beautifully engraven."[7]

The smooth sandstone walls proved an irresistible tablet upon which visitors of the ages scrawled their names and dates and occasionally a boast or two about their great achievements. While Mr. Bird whipped up some lunch for the group, Simpson and Kern immediately set to work documenting the most notable engravings. Henry Dodge strolled the length of the bluff, examining the inscriptions. Many of the ancient, weather-eroded Pueblo petroglyphs were barely visible in the rock face and were occasionally marked over with the scratchings of more recent visitors.

> *Passed by here the Governor don Juan de Oñate from the discovery of the Sea of the South on the 16th of April, 1605*

Juan de Oñate had led the first Spanish colony into New Mexico a mere seven years prior to his inscription and had already earned a reputation among both his own men and the Indians for his unbending ruthlessness. In response to a revolt at Acoma in the winter of 1599 he had the pueblo utterly obliterated and its people enslaved or scattered.[8] Seventy-five years afterward he had scratched his mark, the Pueblos of New Mexico would unite and hurl the insidious Spaniards back to Mexico. Evidence of how fleeting that victory had been soon appeared.

> Here was the General Don Diego de Vargas, who conquered for our Holy Faith, and for the Royal Crown, all of New Mexico at his own expense, year of 1692

Nobleman Don Diego de Vargas Zapata y Luján Ponce de León of Castile had been appointed governor by the king of Spain and instructed to retake the entire province following the Pueblo Revolt of 1680. When he made his mark, he was returning from Zuni, where he had persuaded the Indians to return to their homes and live peaceably under Spanish authority.

With each step Dodge found more engravings, some mysterious and undecipherable; others were merely mundane.

> O. R., March 19, 1836

It was written in English—the only inscription written in English. The identity of O.R. remains unknown. Perhaps less lofty visitors such as O. R. were intimidated by the well-engraved etchings of history spread before them.

> In the year 1716, upon the 26th day of August, passed by this place Don Feliz Martinez, Governor and Captain General of this kingdom for the purpose of reducing and uniting Moqui.

The Moqui were later known as the Hopi, a name roughly translating as the Peaceful People. They proved to be a harder nut to crack than their pacifist name indicated. In 1701, after the Spaniards persuaded one Hopi village, Awatovi to accept Franciscan missionaries, the other Hopi villages utterly destroyed the place, killing all the men and scattering the women and children among the other Hopi villages. From that day hence, Awatovi laid in ruins. It was never again inhabited.

Kern and Simpson labored from noon until near sunset meticulously setting down the inscriptions in pen and ink. Finally they set the work aside to explore ruins that Lewis indicated were on top of El Morro Mesa. Moving along the southeast wall of El Morro, the group passed the pond, noting other inscriptions, all nearly head-high, then made a precipitous scramble up a steep cleft in the mesa wall. The landscape that greeted them was magnificent. From the mesa top, a panorama lay before them in the evening glow—the Zuni Mountains defining the north and the distant peaks of the Gila region marking the south. To west, a more broken country of mesas and mysterious valleys, the distant Zuni Plateau brooding in the copper dusk. The men then turned their attention to the ruins. Twilight finally convinced them to end their investigations and they made the perilous climb back down the mesa in darkness.

The morning of the 18th dawned early, around three o'clock according to Simpson's figuring. They grabbed breakfast in the darkness and continued their transcriptions at first light. Simpson and Kern worked feverishly. When they finished copying the inscriptions, they carved one of their own, though it was somewhat less than perfect, having managed to leave out the "c" in the word "inscription" before adding it later.

>   *Lt. J. H. Simpson, U. S. A. & R. H. Kern, artist, visited and copied these ins^criptions, September 17th, 18th, 1849*

Simpson's orderly made the modest addition of "W. Bird, 1849" in the cliff face. Even Dodge succumbed to the temptation. A short distance from the Simpson-Kern engraving, and somewhat higher up on the narrow face of El Morro, in bold upper case letters, a style most certainly consistent with his personality, Henry wrote . . .

>   *H. L. DODGE, 1849*

It would not be his last inscription there.

By eight o'clock that morning Simpson's group had left El Morro, hoping to overtake Washington's force by that evening. Moving along the valley, they climbed their way through the pines and sandy slopes of the mesas, suddenly cresting the summit where Simpson noted "bearing north of east, some thirty miles off, we caught sight, for the first time, of one of the finest mountain peaks I have seen in this country. This peak I have, in honor of the President of the United States, called Mount Taylor"[9] Simpson had indeed seen the mountain before, during the opening days of the expedition after they'd climbed out of Jemez, though it certainly appeared less imposing then. It was *Tsoodzil*, or old San Mateo Peak.

The party eventually came onto the Ojo de Gallinas, where fires of Washington's previous night's camp still smoldered. They proceeded on through a hilly and more barren terrain until finally joining Washington's camp at Ojo de Gallo at dusk, having trekked over thirty-two miles. The next morning, the soldiers began the last leg of their journey. Following the Rio de San José due east, the expedition skirted the south side of massive Mount Taylor. As the broad valley gradually narrowed, a sea of rock appeared at their flanks formed in a series of black, petrified waves. It was the Malpais, or Bad Lands, the spew of primordial volcanic violence that had uplifted and tore the land apart. Across the inhospitable badlands, the pleasant banks of the Rio de San José beckoned. A stream of cold and clear water flowed through a narrow pass, crowded by the San Mateo Mountains on the north and buff colored mesas on the south, choked with brush and a tangled profusion of grape vines. When the men emerged, the valley again broadened. Here and there along the way were the pueblo farms, expansive fields of corn and melons and wheat and a flock of some two thousand sheep grazing along the route. Ahead of them was Laguna. The expedition at last camped near a shallow lake guarded by a detachment of cranes. The day's twenty eight mile march had been grueling. Earlier the artillery horses had given out, preventing Kendrick and his men from getting in to camp until sometime after sunset.

Once the troops had settled, the amicable alcalde of Laguna Pueblo came to pay his respects to Colonel Washington and offer whatever assistance the soldiers might require. The true purpose of his visit, however, came to light the next morning when he returned to lodge a complaint. A week earlier, he related, a party of American emigrants had come to Laguna. They had perfunctorily seized eight mules, claiming they needed them for their trip. They then demanded sheep. The alcalde explained that he'd gladly give them but the flocks were out and couldn't be provided immediately. In response the Americans tied him up and threatened to lynch him there in the pueblo plaza. Having thoroughly terrorized the people, the emigrants departed for Zuni taking the bound and trussed alcalde with them as hostage before releasing him along the trail. Colonel Washington condemned the acts and urged the alcalde to defend Laguna property with force if need be. To ward off any future such embarrassments, he wrote a proclamation commanding all citizens to respect the rights of the Laguna people and handed it to the governor. Simpson confessed a certain amount of mortification over the bad behavior.

> "They, like the Zunis, regard us with considerable reserve; but how could it be otherwise, when they have been so shamefully treated as they have been recently by persons bearing the name of Americans, like ourselves?"[10]

The expedition continued along the Rio San José, the road generally good but the trip uneventful. Fifteen miles east of Laguna they camped along a shallow and uninviting stream of bright red water. Washington discharged what remained of Chapman's mounted militia that evening. The next day the distant Sandia Mountains peeked over the eastern rise, marking the town of Albuquerque, the first town of any appreciable size they'd seen in over a month. With the men nearly desperate from thirst, the Colonel sent an express ahead to the commander of the Albuquerque post, Major Marshall Howe, instructing him to send out water. After traversing a series of broad, sandy basins and crossing the Rio Puerco, the column descended into the Rio Grande Valley. As requested, a detail of Howe's Second Dragoon met them on the west side of the Rio Grande with a wagon loaded with water barrels. The parched men drank eagerly, ignoring the fact that the water was brown with mud and infused with sand. At dusk they settled into camp at Atrisco, just across from Albuquerque.[11] The men's well-earned rest was interrupted by some bad news—the first of its kind associated with the entire expedition. Navajos had killed the mail carrier Charles Malone and his New Mexican guide fifteen days earlier somewhere west of Chaco Mesa. They had been enroute to deliver the mail to Washington's troops at Tunicha. The mail, so anxiously anticipated by the homesick soldiers, had been, as Calhoun put it, "distributed to suit the fancy of the Indians" and lost. There was little consolation to the rumor that Malone and his guide had killed eight of the attackers before going under.[12]

Of all the soldiers, the news inflicted the most melancholy on Captain Dodge and his Eutaw Rangers. Malone's guide had been one of his volunteers, 23-year-old private Juan Baca, who had signed on with the rest of them the previous March. Malone and Baca's murders were certainly a Navajo act of retribution for Narbona's slaying.[13] The men moved on the following day, fording the river and turning north out of Albuquerque. The final camp of the expedition as a whole was pitched at Algodones, just north of Albuquerque. Bit by bit, the separate units broke off and headed back to Santa Fe at their own pace, passing the familiar chain of Mexican towns and pueblos situated up and down the Rio Grande, then up the Bajada to Santa Fe.

To a certain extent Washington's expedition had impressed the Navajo with the military might of the United States and the ruthlessness with which the United States would use it, but fell well short of awing them. A mere day after Dodge's unit was disbanded Navajos attacked a flock of sheep and killed five Mexicans near Sandia. On October 5th Navajos attacked and kill two men near Cebolleta and carried off a woman. Similar attacks soon followed at Santo Domingo and San Ildefonso Pueblos. As for Henry Dodge, he had gotten his first close and comprehensive look at a land and people he would come to know intimately. James S. Calhoun, who would soon be appointed New Mexico's next civil governor, did not overlook Dodge's service in the Expedition of 1849 or the fact he was the son of an influential Wisconsin politician. In writing to Commissioner of Indian Affairs Medill, Calhoun singled out Henry for praise. Indeed, Dodge was the only American Calhoun commended by name.

> "In this connection, I may be pardoned, I trust, for commending, in terms of decided praise, *Henry Linn Dodge*, Captain commanding a Volunteer Company, also, with us in the late Navajo expedition. He was at all times, efficient and prompt, and commanded the admiration of Governor Washington, as well as others. If I mistake not, Capt. Dodge has a father and brother now Senators in Congress."[14]

It was a pretty magnanimous gesture for a Whig. Although he got Henry's middle name wrong, James Calhoun had certainly not mistaken his connections. Politicians and government sycophants take every advantage to enhance their careers. Calhoun was no different. Such recognition would serve Henry very well and very soon. Calhoun's career, on the other hand, would not fare nearly as well.

At the close of the expedition, Dodge and his men were sent first to Santa Fe, then eastward to Las Vegas. Henry was mustered out and paid for his service on September 23rd, 1849. For the next two and a half months, Dodge's activities and whereabouts are unknown and apparently were of little note. In the meantime, his old post at Jemez was relocated to the nearby New Mexican settlement of San Ysidro. On November 14th Navajos brazenly struck several ranches in that vicinity.

It was soon painfully clear to the New Mexicans that the few remaining salutary effects of Washington's expedition were rapidly evaporating. Believing rumors that the Americans intended to slaughter every member of his tribe, Navajo headman Chapitone sent word that he would skip the meeting with Washington and Calhoun at Jemez as previously agreed. In the meantime, Navajo forays against the settlements forced Colonel Washington take further steps to blunt the raids. He was no less exasperated than agent James Calhoun, who saw the Navajos' power and potential, but condemned their lust for war.

> "The Navajoes commit their wrongs from a pure love of rapine and plunder. They have extensive fields of Corn & Wheat-fine Peach orchards, and grow quantities of Melons, Squashes, Beans, and Peas, and have immense flocks of sheep, a great number of mules and horses of a superior breed . . . They derive their title to the country over which they roam, from

mere possession, not knowing from whence they came, or how they were planted upon its soil . . . I respectfully suggest, these people should have their limits circumscribed . . . These Indians are hardy, and intelligent, and it is as natural for them to war against all men, and to take the property of others as it is for the sun to give light by day."[15]

In his October 1st report to the Commissioner of Indian Affairs Medill, Calhoun suggested a firm policy of subjugation by establishing a permanent military outpost at Laguna, Jemez and Zuni, and then erecting forts in the heart of Navajo land in the Tunicha Mountains and even perhaps in Canyon de Chelly itself. At the end of the month the exasperated agent begged Medill to allow him personally to lead four companies of dragoons and a force of Pueblo Indians, promising that he would "so tame the Navajoes and Utahs that you will scarcely hear of them again." It was a request Medill was both reluctant and unable to grant him.[16]

Neither Calhoun nor Washington could ignore the growing outcry of the beleaguered New Mexican citizenry. On September 24th a convention in Santa Fe circulated a petition demanded the Army throw up a military post deep in Navajo country.[17] Washington doubtlessly though it was an excellent idea, but he knew a permanent army presence in Navajo land would have to wait. The Army was already stretched thin in New Mexico, understaffed and undersupplied, wedged between disturbing fears of Indian raids east and west, the ever present paranoia of another Hispanic uprising and undying suspicions of a planned invasion by Mexican troops from Chihuahua.

Given the restraints, he conceded that a post closer to the Rio Grande settlements was feasible, one that straddled the well-worn Navajo raiding trails meandering out of western New Mexico. Accordingly, on September 29th Washington dispatched Lieutenant Simpson to do a quick survey of potential locations around Laguna. Simpson found a promising site near the miniscule community of Cebolleta. There was a meager source of dependable water, wood and grass there, the site was accessible by wagon and the roads were generally in good shape. In addition, the cost of erecting quarters would be minimal. The Army could simply rent various adobes from local prominent citizens and then throw up whatever other structures were needed.[18]

Colonel Washington would not long remain in the territory. On October 23rd, 1849, military command and the governorship of New Mexico was transfered to Brevet Colonel John Monroe, a granite-headed 53-year-old Scotsman.

26

CEBOLLETA

In late November of 1849, Henry Dodge received a letter from Army Quartermaster A. W. Reynolds in Santa Fe. Colonel John Munroe had ordered Captain Croghan Ker and his company of the 2nd Dragoons to immediately occupy Cebolleta on the Navajo frontier. Invariably the new army post would require a handful of civilian workers: blacksmiths, ferriers and wagon masters, and an agent to procure supplies and fodder for the dragoon horses and post livestock, and to receive and issue commissary stores.[1]

> "Captain,
> You are hereby appointed an Agent in the Quarter Masters Department at Ciboletta, New Mexico, subject to the approval of the Senr. Quarter Master of this Department. You will proceed to Cibolletta and take charge of the Quarter Masters Department at that place. You will make all expenditures that may be necessary for the Post, such as the purchase of Corn, hiring Men to herd Animals &c.—The live Animals which you take with you are sent to the region about Cibolletta to graze, and it is understood that they are not to be used by any one except for the benefit of the Department without authority from this office. Please make a Monthly Summary Statement of disbursements and expenditures.
> A.W. Reynolds, Capt. A.Q.M."[2]

Henry would be paid a salary of forty dollars a month. Other than being a personal acquaintance of Reynold's, the reason for Dodge's nomination was a mystery. Had he been appointed for his service, or his connections? Colonel Washington had earlier appointed Henry Dodge notary public for Santa Fe and subsequently had been impressed with his service during the Campaign of 1849. Conversely, Colonel John Munroe probably knew little of Dodge or his family connections and, in truth, it may not have mattered to him in the least. Munroe was a stern, seasoned West Point graduate, with granite-like Scot resistance to the panderings of political nepotism.[3]

Dodge left Santa Fe for Cebolleta on December 14th, supervising a herd of commissary stock. As expected, circumstances at the windswept and isolated post were rigorously austere. Compared to the settlements along the Rio Grande, Cebolleta was a fairly new village. Initially, Spanish priests had established a mission in the area in the mid 1700s to concentrate, settle and convert the Navajo, but the effort eventually failed and the mission abandoned. That failure did not discourage attempts to settle the area. During an uneasy twenty-year truce with the Navajo, Spanish authorities doled out land grants along the Rio Puerco and around Mount Taylor to prominent citizens, but when hostilities erupted, the settlers fled for the safety of the Rio Grande.[4]

In March of 1801, Governor Fernando Chacon issued a land grant to thirty families from Albuquerque who had expressed a desire to settle at San Mateo.[5] Cebolleta proved a fairly attractive spot, but resources were limited. Water souces were tentative. To the north, a stream flowed from deep canyon cut into Mount Taylor's flank, but it ran intermittently. There was wood, but it was distant and grass grew, but sparsely. A view from Cebolleta westward certainly provided an awesome vista of rough mesas chisled in basaltic cliffs, the black parapets occasionally cleaved by gorges. Behind loomed the cool, pine-studded peak of Mount Taylor. Stretching eastward from the mountain, the land opened into a vast panorama of arid emptiness as it imperceptibly dipped towards the Rio Grande and the Sandia Mountains. That panorama was broken by two landmarks: a massive volcanic plug known as *Cerro Negro*, or Black Hill, and a butte called *Cerro de la Celosa*, Jealous Woman Hill where, according to an old folktale, a Navajo woman spurned by her husband for another, had supposedly leaped from the heights to her death.[6]

Although Cebolleta was conceived as a farming and ranching community, Chacon's intention was to plop the new settlement square in the path of Navajo raiders then ranging eastward out of the San Mateos. If the colonists had any qualms about being made a stumbling block to Navajo war parties, their trepidation wasn't immediately apparent. They took possession of the site with symbolic enthusiasm on March 16th, 1801, throwing stones in the air, pulling weeds and shouting 'God Save the King' three times. They then set to work building a compact and fortified hamlet. Huddled insecurely below San Mateo, the tiny village resembled more a fort than a community. The entire place occupied a space no larger than the typical town plaza, with individual adobe homes joining one another in a high walled enclosure, unbroken by windows or doors. There were only two narrow entrances, one facing south towards Laguna and the other set to the east towards distant Albuquerque, each barred by a massive door of twelve inch pine and crowned with a circular guard tower. There were out-buildings of course, to support ranching and farming, readily abandoned for the fortifications at the first hint of danger.[7]

Danger there was. The Navajo took immediate offense to the settlement and more so the subsequent increase of New Mexican slave raids. Spanish law prohibited taking slaves, but it could be circumvented by a somewhat skewed and clearly self-serving excuse. Rather than enslavement, New Mexican raiders characterized kidnapping as their Christian duty to rescue Navajo children from a fate of heathen darkness and savagery . . . and they truly believed it. If they happened to make money on the side, so much the better. A descendant of one raider, Armando Chávez, recalled that when captured Navajo children were brought into Cebolleta, the raiders took them to the priest to be baptized and given a Christian name.

> "They would naturally take your name and as they grew up they would consider you and your wife as their parents. If you did not have the pluck to go after Indian children yourself you could buy one for five hundred."

The argument held that the children were not really *peones* but *criados*, or servants apprenticing in the skills of Christian progress.

In time the settlers of Cebolleta, being on the edge of the Navajo frontier, became infamous slave raiders, and were referred to in that vein as the *Cebolletanos*. Should the daughter of a wealthy man be betrothed, her father would commission the Cebolletanos to capture a Navajo boy or girl as a wedding gift. Grooms not of affluent families, desperate to impress their bride and more importantly her family, would go out themselves to capture a child. Armando Chávez admitted it was dangerous work "that many parties that went after servants never returned. The Indians killed them all."[8]

In September of 1804, Navajo forces finally laid siege to little Cebolleta. It was hand-to-hand butchery, the Navajo and Cebolletano battling one another with the lance and knife, the bow and arrow. Navajos once attempted to burn the settlers out by throwing lighted pine pitch into the village. In one attack, a woman, Antonia Romero, climbed onto the fort rooftop to check for Indians and was horrified to see a Navajo inside the compound, lifting the bar that secured the village gate. She supposedly smashed the man's skull with a stone metate. In the same fight, it was said that Don Domingo Baca was skewered with lances no less than seven times. With his bowels bulging out into his shirt, he managed to tie a pillow around them and went on fighting. When the Navajos finally retreated, he stuffed his guts back into his abdomen, stitched up the wound and, amazingly, survived it all.[9]

In the end, the Cebolletanos could have claimed victory, but they were thoroughly demoralized. They packed up their belongings and retreated to the protection of the Spanish dragoons at Laguna. The governor subsequently cajoled them for their cowardice and promised them military protection if they'd go back. Reluctantly they consented.[10] Predictably, in 1805 the Navajos attacked Cebolleta again, and again failed to destroy the town. The following three decades were marked by sporadic hit-and-run skirmishing. By 1846, the San Mateo Navajo had resigned themselves to enduring settlements in their country and had ceased raiding them. The same couldn't be said for the western Navajos, who carried on an intermittent raiding. Such was the state of affairs when Ker and Company K of the 2nd Dragoons arrived on December 1st of 1849.

From Spanish *Cebolla* translated into English as onion and *Cebolleta* as chive or small wild onion. The Army post was actually a mile or two south of Cebolleta proper at *Cebolletita*, or Little Small Wild Onion, along a creek appropriately named *Rio Cebolletita*.

Right from the get-go, the garrison was beset with irritating inconveniences, most of which the frenetic Captain Ker proved consummately unable to handle. The country was sparse, the supplies short and the costs exorbitant. Prices the local entrepreneurs exacted for the simplest things, from dried peaches to firewood, bordered on the obscene, but Ker had little choice but to pay them. The recruits on post had barely adequate clothing—they were promised that uniforms would be sent, but when precisely no soul could divine. The officers were short on side arms— no Colt pistols were available. Not a single building was erected or owned outright by the government and although the rented quarters were crumbling and the roofs leaking wind and rain, Captain Ker was not allowed to employ civilians to repair them.[11]

In an effort to preserve the meager grass for his dragoon horses, Ker forbade the locals from cutting and hauling away forage from around his post, drawing a protest from Alcalde Sarricino, who consequently complained to Colonel Munroe. On December 15th, Munroe sent a dispatch commanding Ker to rescind the restriction, the dispatch probably handed to the captain personally by his new commissary agent, Henry L. Dodge.

It must have been truly maddening. And Ker's troubles were just beginning. As with most post commanders, he was anxious to get his men out to see some action. Daily routine during idle days in camp kept the soldiers' minds on their duties and away from drinking, carousing and desertion, though the first two options weren't available unless a soldier considered the third and deserted for Cubero and the tavern. Still, a commander could only keep his men intermittently busy and with the major tasks to erecting a post done, the excruciating boredom that descended could drive a despondent recruit to contemplate suicide.

There was a heart palpitating promise of action on December 24th when Colonel Munroe told Ker he'd authorized Major Howe in Albuquerque to enlist Cebolleta troops to pursue raiding Apaches. Exhilarated at the prospect, Ker and his crusaders saddled their steeds and thundered forth. Alas, Howe sent word that he didn't need them after all and ordered them to return untested to Cebolleta. Whether Ker held that indignity against the major, or harbored earlier resentments, he soon earned an acrimonious hatred for Howe.[12]

Before long, another opportunity arose. Although it was illegal for New Mexican traders to do business among hostile tribes, Cebolleta was a common jumping off spot for such trading expeditions among the Navajo and Ker knew it. On December 28th, he informed Munroe that several unlawful traders had recently left Cebolleta to trade with the Indians. He offered to intercept the traders, prudently requesting a copy of the laws relative to Indian trade to flash in their faces when he caught them.[13] No authorization to pursue ever came from headquarters, so the chance for action was lost.

A week after that, news arrived that Navajos had raided Zuni and carried off horses, mules and two women. This time Captain Croghan Ker's lust for action would not be delayed by following standard military protocol. So early on January 8th, the company bugler called the men to horse and Company K Second Dragoons thundered out southward into the snowfall, leaving the garrison in the hands of commissary agent Henry L. Dodge, the young 22-year-old post surgeon William Hammond and a skeleton garrison. In his enthusiasm, Ker managed to mistakenly arrest a group of peaceful Mount Taylor Navajos and impound their stock. On the 12th, approaching the Tunicha Mountains under a lingering snow, they sighted a wary group of Navajo in the distance. Ker attempted to arrange a council but, to his consternation, the headmen refused to come within gunshot range. The following morning a group of Navajos charged the dragoon camp. The captain ordered a pursuit, but a heavy snowstorm extinguished any hope of overtaking the Indians. Reluctantly, Ker ordered his detachment back to Cebolleta. His unauthorized foray had taken fourteen days.

From all indications, Henry L. Dodge managed well enough in the unusually hushed post during Ker's absence. He had already spent better than $1600 of the Army's money for sundry supplies and services: Supporting an army post was expensive. He'd bought 874 bags of feed corn, one hundred carts of fodder and six wagons of grass, three cows, and three leather bags ordered specially by Captain Ker at three and a half dollars apiece. From José Salas Henry purchased seventy-five fanegas or roughly 300 bushels by American measure, of feed corn for $225.00, an astronomical sum but not significantly worse than what businessmen were gouging out of Monroe and his command in Santa Fe.[14]

While Ker was out chasing Navajos, a letter from Colonel Munroe arrived at the post, specifically addressed to Henry Dodge.

> "I wish to see you here without delay on special business. As the purpose for which I desire to employ you may interfere with your return to Cebolleta I have asked Capt. Ker to furnish you with a memorandum receipt for such public property as you are responsible, so that in the event of your having a successor in your present duties, regular receipts may be passed (Capt Ker's receipt returned to him) without its becoming necessary for you to revisit that post."[15]

Few clues clear the mystery of Munroe's cryptic request. Was it political? The colonel would soon become quite active in manipulating an infant statehood movement in the territory and may have configured some role that Dodge might have played in his schemes. Was Dodge to be reassigned? On January 29th Ker wrote to Munroe's assistant adjutant Lt. Lafayette McLaws inquiring about a rumor of establishing a permanent post south of Albuquerque, along the western slopes of the Manzanos Mountains. Along that tack, Ker offer his own suggestions on the best way to protect the citizens of New Mexico.

> "In a conversation with Capt. Dodge I think I perceive a desire on the part of the Governor to establish a post at or near the Manzanas, for the purpose of protecting the inhabitants of New Mexico from the encroaches of the Apache Indians. the only obstacle in the way being the want of Troops. If I might be permitted to suggest a way to remove this obstacle, I would advise that Captain Dodge or some other person of inteligence & energy be authorized by the Governor to raise a Company of 100 Pueblo Indians to be stationed in the vicinity of Savoyetta, this Compy. (and the Pueblo Indians & Mexicans who would join them at any moment the Commander wished to make an expedition against the Navajoe Indians), would be more than sufficient to protect this Frontier . . . "

Ker impudently announced that once Cebolleta had been secured, he and his 2nd Dragoons could garrison the new Manzanos post at the drop of a hat provided that he was not placed under Major Howe's command. Why Munroe would take Henry Dodge, a civilian with apparently no civil or military credentials into his confidence is not clear. Perhaps the colonel was considering enlisting his assistance in putting up the new post. In the end, nothing came of it.

February and early March of 1850 apparently passed quietly for the Cebolleta garrison. Navajo raids had dropped sharply—there were few alarms to raise the blood pressure as monotony settled onto the thawing, snow-muddied post grounds. Commissary Agent Dodge opened accounts with local traders to loan money and supplies for post operations and requested $160 and $260 from Reynolds to reimburse them.[16] The end of March brought a dramatic turn of events.

On March 28th, instead of heeding headquarter's order to send in his monthly reports, Captain Croghan Ker and twenty-two of his cavalry abruptly rode out of Cebolleta towards Navajo country, leaving Hammond and Dodge in charge and, for all intents, simply vanished.[17] March passed into April and Ker's column had still not returned to post. Dodge conducted business as usual, buying fresh beef at seven cents a pound and made several payments to traders and teamsters. On May 1st, he purchased beef from Manuel Sena for about $89, then on the 7th requested Reynolds pay the trader Nolan $60 for corn he provided Ker's horses at Zuni during Company K's earlier jaunt that previous December. April 30th found Henry in Santa Fe, arranging an Army payment of $660 to the prominent trading firm of Messervy & Webb for goods rendered. Weeks passed. Ker and his men were still unaccounted for.[18]

On May 4th, to the amazement of Hammond, Dodge and the undermanned garrison, Ker and his dragoons suddenly reappeared at the post. They had been gone for over a month and from the haggard looks of horse and rider it had been a difficult trek. Ker unraveled his saga of what had become a quixotic quest across the wilds of New Mexico, a tale he'd later represent as the complete truth in his official report to headquarters. Ker had left post in response to rumors of Navajo depredations. Around April 2nd, some five days out towards Zuni his column came across a trail of what Ker interpreted as an Indian raiding party driving a herd of sheep he believed had been stolen from the Rio Grande. The fact the tracks were old convinced Ker to move on to Zuni, where the governor told him that a more recent Indian raiding party had been spotted headed towards Socorro.

Away Ker and his men thundered to overtake the Indians. At some length they came to a river in flood stage and were forced to turn back, at which time they came across a party led by the well-known trader Mr. Noland of Santa Fe. According to Ker, Noland beseeched him to escort the traders through treacherous Apache country. After several days of hard travel, they ended up in a Gila Apache camp. Ker claimed that during their stay the Apaches told him a group of Americans had come in recently, shot up the camp, killed a few of their people, then carried their chief off for several days as hostage before setting him free—a story suspiciously reminiscent of what had happened to the Laguna governor. Ker took credit for smoothing the Apache's ruffled feathers, single handedly, as the captain later claimed, making a significant contribution to peace between the Apache and the whites.[19] At about that time, it apparently occurred to the captain that, as far as he knew, no one at headquarters had actually been informed of his expedition. Perhaps it was time to be getting back to Cebolleta.

It was a particularly entertaining melodrama, Dodge had to admit, but based on the recent and ominous rumblings from Munroe it wouldn't play in Santa Fe. The captain had left his command and post without orders. He hadn't even bothered to notify headquarters or send timely reports. He had been absent for a month, leaving his post and the entire region unprotected. In truth, Monroe was furious.

Ker must have sensed the gathering maelstrom and as the day passed anxiety insidiously gnawed away at his stomach. By that evening, his temper was on a hair trigger, and it would be the unfortunate Sergeant A. L. Kittloss who would set it off. Kittloss was a dependable and conscientious career soldier with fourteen faithful years in the service. That evening of the 4th Captain Ker ordered Kittloss to form a detail of ten men. When Kittloss respectfully replied that he didn't have ten men available for the detail, Ker exploded. He tore into Kittloss, shoving him into the horse corral and beating him in the manure until Dr. Hammond's wife pulled him off. Ker then had the sergeant shackled, confined, reduced to ranks. As a coup de grace he ordered the sergeant's head shaved.[20]

Having spent his rage on Kittloss, a real angst over his own impending doom swept over him. On May 9th, rather than waiting like a school boy for a switching, Captain Ker decided to take the initiative, something that had never failed to get him into trouble. Accordingly, he rode off alone for Santa Fe at a good clip to explain his valuable reconnaissance to Munroe in person and, if need be, apologize profusely.

It was too late for apologies. Four days earlier, an exasperated Colonel Munroe, infuriated over what he saw as blatant desertion, had ordered Major Howe to take command of Ker's garrison, investigate the whereabouts of the missing Company K 2nd Dragoons and their errant captain, and for heaven's sake to stay in touch. He admonished Howe that upon "the arrival of Captain Ker, you will place him in arrest."²¹ Of course Major Howe was delighted to render the service. Howe arrived in Cebolleta on the 10th, the day after Ker had galloped off for headquarters. Dodge and Hammond filled Howe in on events since Ker's return and in particular Ker's thrashing of Sergeant Kittloss.²²

Meanwhile, as soon as Ker arrived at headquarters, he was summarily arrested and ordered confined to quarters at Cebolleta to await court martial. In the end, given the choice between a court-martial and a quiet resignation, Captain Croghan Ker wisely chose the latter. Ker's Company K's stay at Cebolleta didn't outlast the month. On May 22nd Munroe ordered them to reinforce Las Vegas after Jicarilla and Ute warriors had slaughtered a mail party at Wagon Mound.²³

Captain Croghan Ker's successor was an easily offended, opinionated, 24-year-young 2nd Lieutenant John Buford of Company J, 2nd Dragoons. From the moment he took command on May 25th, it was clear he despised the place and the people. Buford hadn't been there but a week before he was whining to Munroe about the crumbling cramped quarters infested with bed bugs and the fact that he was stuck in the middle of a bunch of Mexicans, though he admit they were not as contaminated as "our greaser countrymen" of the more populated areas. Then there was the matter of one Henry L. Dodge.

> "I arrived here on the 25th ultimo and relieved Lt. Adams 1st Drags in command of the Post. I found in the Commissary Dept provisions enough for 15 or 18 days and in the Qr Mr's Dept nothing save a soar backed mule and a man pretending to be agent without being responsible for any public property."

> "Capt Dodge is Commissary agent here and pretends to be an agent for the Qr Mr's Dept without being at all responsible for any public property. The reason of this I believe is the Qr Mr is afraid to trust him. His character I have understood would not withstand investigation. I should like some responsible person sent here who would be responsible for all public property and be under my supervision. I want a man too that has no store at Cebolleta to supply the wants of the Qr Mr's Dept that owned no houses to rent to Government And one that had no private property such [as] Mexican families, mules and horses to be supported by Uncle Sam."

Buford suspected Dodge of impropriety at the best and outright theft of government property at the worst, his personal habits outrageous, and he wanted him fired. As blatantly critical as youth is given to be, so too is it idealistic and brash. Buford seemed irritated by sordid, miniscule details and, like Ker, itched for the chance to be after the savages, declaring the horses "are fat, my men are healthy and extremely anxious to be in the Indian Country." He wanted to be in the saddle and comfortable knowing that while he was gone "some responsible person" would be watching after the post's property rather than having to detail part of his command to guard it.[24]

The young lieutenant would have little luck accomplishing either endeavor. Buford's acerbic letter was ill advised, as Munroe thought well of Dodge. His sarcastic reference to Henry Dodge's reputation indicated he believed the man a scoundrel, but if the young man knew anything substantial it never came to light. In 1834 when John was but a tadpole his family had moved to Rock Island, Illinois. His father had supposedly served as a colonel of the Illinois Militia in the Black Hawk War two years earlier. If so, there is no doubt the Bufords had known of the Dodges but, outside of the rivalry between Badgers and Suckers, there is no verification of any antagonism. It was even less likely John Buford knew the circumstances of H. L. Dodge's departure. Whatever it was, the young officer had made public the kind of innuendos that usually invited a bullet from a dueling pistol.

Fortunately for him, Henry had mellowed considerably from the days he had shaken the whip over James D. Doty's head. Certainly, Dodge's record keeping was spotty at best, raising some suspicion in the 3rd Auditor's office of the Treasury struggling to keep the books straight. It is likely that some of Henry's government time and perhaps expenses may have been spent featherbedding his own financial position. Having run a store for some time in Wisconsin and seeing the lucrative trade the locals were doing with the Army, he probably concluded he'd be a fool to ignore such opportunity. Perhaps as early as January of 1850, Henry started his own store near Cebolleta, partnering with 25 year old John R. Tullis of Santa Fe.[25] By that summer the firm of Tullis & Dodge was doing good business with local Hispanics and Indians alike. But when it came to paying in hard coin, none excelled Uncle Sam.

Buford's invective revealed a personal side of Henry Dodge not disclosed by official reports. Although Dodge had quarters at the post, he kept a separate home. According to the 1850 federal census for "Sevoyetta, New Mexico" enumerated by John Tullis himself, Henry was living in Cebolleta. Tullis noted Henry Dodge was 35 years old rather than his true age of 40, a merchant from Wisconsin and living in a home he probably rented from Ramon Baca, for forty dollars a month.[26] There were three others in his household: the two young sisters, 20 year old Tomasa Gallegos and 18 year old Placeda Gallegos, and a two-year-old toddler named James Robbins.

It was an improbable circumstance, to be sure, but Tullis would have known. He lived at the next home listed with three other gentlemen: his clerk, his cook and his handyman.[27]

Immediately, Dodge's relationship to the two local girls commands interest. He could have been living with one or the other conjugally, but both of them? And who was the strange boy? James Robbins remains a mystery and after 1850 vanishes from the record completely.

If Buford had any proof that Dodge was using his commissary agent account to support his budding business and his "Mexican" family, the lieutenant either failed to submit it to headquarters or the evidence was ignored. Dodge retained the confidence of Colonel Monroe and remained on the job. In April and May, he spent just under $2700 for a variety of Army expenses, most of it rent due for the post quarters, all of which were leased from Cebolletanos: $150 rent to José Vallejos for the company quarters, $220 to Manuel Jaramillo for Captain Ker's quarters, and $75.00 to Rafael Jarvis for Henry's own post quarters. It was all leased; the company hospital, the corn storage houses, Dr. Hammond's home and even the guardhouse.

There were incidental expenses by the score. Dodge paid the express men at the rate of one dollar a day, while the lowly packmen ranked at fifty cents. Then there was the grass cut and corn shucked by private citizens to keep the broken down dragoon horses alive—no small expense certainly. Even Sr. Montanello, the local priest, had sold 251 bags of corn feed at roughly six bits each for a total of $376.00. Of course, there was the twenty bucks for hiring José Aragon to baby-sit the government mules, and six bucks for whitewashing Company H's quarters.[28] Small wonder why the locals howled when an army post was closed.

Buford continued to harp on Henry Dodge's lack of attentiveness and efficiency and openly impugned his honesty in doing Army business. Damn it, the lieutenant grumbled, the man had been continuously absent and probably using Army money and properties to bankroll his own interests.

"Since my arrival at this Post Capt H L Dodge Qr. Mr's and Com' Agent has been present and attending to his duties only some 5 or 6 days. From the 1st to the 15th of June he was absent from the Post for the purpose of transacting some business with Qr Mr. at Santa Fe. This I believe terminated satisfactorily for himself but not for his Dept. here. Since the 16th of June he has been absent without any authority from me and his duties as Qr Mr & Com Agent have been entirely neglected. Under these circumstances I respectfully recommend that his situation be filled by some suitable person whose private interests are not paramount to those he is paid to protect. I consider some change necessary for the public service."[29]

Munroe brushed off Buford's complaints. In a communiqué regarding illegal traders, he enclosed a separate letter expressing to the lieutenant his own confidence in Henry's work.

> "Mr. Dodge was engaged to perform the duties of Qr. Master & Commissary Agent at Cibolletta being of course under the entire control of the Commanding Officer of the Post. If you do not like the Quarters in which your company are placed, or if there are any irregularities committed by the Government Agents it is for you as Commanding Officer to make such corrections & changes as will remedy the evils; from Mr. Dodge's reputation for zeal & activity & from his knowledge of the people & the country there is no doubt but that he will act according as you direct & give satisfaction. Your duty which is entirely military in its character is to guard and protect the frontier on which you are stationed from the depredatory of all marauding Bands of Indians or otherwise, pursuing & endeavoring to capture or destroy them . . . "[30]

Henry probably viewed Buford's indignant airs with mild irritation, like a particularly pesky horsefly. True, Dodge had been doing a variety of business in Santa Fe that summer, with the civil and military authorities. Outside of his dealings with Reynolds in the quartermaster's department, he'd spent a considerable amount of time assisting James Calhoun, who was earnestly entreating with a dozen or so Pueblo villages in Santa Fe to guarantee their rights would be protected by the United States. Between July 9th and July 12th Dodge was a witness to Calhoun's treaties with Jemez, San Ildefonso and San Felipe, where the signature page listed him as an adjutant quartermaster of the Santa Fe Battalion of Volunteers.[31]

Concurrently, the summer months beheld a steady increase in Navajo forays. Navajo raiders struck a ranch near Jemez, killed the herdsman and stole two-dozen animals. An Acoma man was murdered on June 8th and his stock run off down a trail into Navajo land. That same day the Navajos struck at La Cañada de los Corrales near Abiquiu, taking horses, mules and two New Mexican shepherds.[32] Navajos later ran off two flocks of sheep from Corrales north of Albuquerque. Antonio Sandoval, always eager to prove his trustworthiness and importance to Munroe, informed Buford at Cebolleta that the Navajos were making plans for yet more raids. Primed for a fight, Buford would experience only frustration. Plans for a scouting party had to be canceled due to a lack of flour at the post, something the lieutenant probably blamed on Dodge. Buford did arrest a party of illegal traders headed for Apache country in mid June, seizing powder, lead, a variety of domestic gewgaws and all their animals. Among the 54 individuals he arrested were Manuel Chávez and Manuel Antonio Romero, both prominent men of the territory.[33] Munroe warmly congratulated Buford for his zeal and alacrity, but it was small consolation. He'd yet to meet the savage foe in battle.[34]

New opportunities for glory arose, but proved instead to be embarrassments. When a sizeable Navajo raiding party had driven off several thousand sheep from along the Rio Puerco, Buford ordered an immediate pursuit. On June 22nd his dragoons came across the Navajo trail and a band of New Mexicans pursuing the Indians as well. Buford ordered them to return home, assuring them his cavalry would make a quick end to the Indians' thieving career, and continued along the trail. Shortly thereafter, his men began to run out of water and there was none to be found. Deflated, Lieutenant Buford ordered the dragoons back to Cebolleta. Much to his aggravation, Buford later learned the New Mexicans he'd so off-handedly dismissed had continued after the Indians, at last overtaking them. They launched a valiant charge. The Navajo promptly counter charged, routing them. Stuck behind his desk, the lieutenant groused that several of the New Mexicans "were wounded with arrows in the back but I am sorry to say, none mortally. All this occurred within five miles of my command without its even hearing a sound."[35]

On July 15th, an express galloped into the post carrying urgent news from Albuquerque that Navajos had just killed a herder and driven 2000 sheep from Corrales. They were headed for the Puerco. Could Buford intercept them? Once more, Buford and fifteen dragoons sallied forth into the wilderness. They made 30 miles that day without seeing a single Navajo. In the evening, Buford left the dragoon camp along the Puerco with his guide to continue searching the darkness for some telltale track. When Buford got back to camp at eight the next morning, his sergeant told him a herder had come through camp saying a New Mexican party had already recovered the stolen animals. Buford refused to believe it, keeping his men on the trail until it became clear the herder had spoken true. Dejected and more than a little irritated, Buford turned his column back to Cebolleta, an incessant rain pounding them the entire way.

And so the maddening summer went. One promising moment came when Lieutenant Buford had got Munroe's permission to organize an August expedition against the Navajo, but he never got the chance to launch it. Just a few days after reporting his abortive pursuit along the Puerco, Buford was transferred to Las Vegas with Company H 2nd Dragoons, where perhaps he'd have better luck fighting the Jicarilla and Comanche.[36]

27

AN EXTREMELY VIOLENT CONTEST

In Wisconsin, a thousand miles away from Cebolleta, the year of 1850 had been a difficult one for Adele Dodge. She was a weary thirty-four year old mother of four, unemployed and perpetually teetering on the edge of poverty. After Henry had run off four years earlier, she and the children moved back to Dodgeville, compelled to depend on her brother Paschal and her father-in-law Governor Dodge for support. Paschal provided Adele with a two-story frame house there, accepting as payment nothing more than love and affection and she made a small income keeping boarders. Governor Dodge took a paternal interest in the children, providing shelter, meals and an education. Years later years Mary Therese Dodge admitted that they all came to feel The Grove as much their home as their gruff but doting grandfather's. In addition, over time Governor Dodge would give Adele four thousand-seven hundred dollars in assistance.[1]

1850 had also brought a scythe of sickness. In February Louis Linn fell critically ill with what folks called the lung fever. It was pneumonia. In Washington D. C., the boy's grandmother Christiana feared her grandson's impending death.

> "We hear often from home. Last night Henry Becquette received a letter from his father. He says his two youngest daughters had the whooping cough very bad and he was afraid the babe would not survive it & that Linn Dodge had the Lung Fever very badly. He almost despaired of his life. This makes me feel very much for them. Poor Adele, if she looses her young son she loses her most interesting child I think, but not too much so to go to heaven to be the companion of little children for of such our Savior says is the Kingdom of heaven."[2]

252

Little Linn survived and, mercifully, avoided the onslaught of other killers: whooping cough, influenza, yellow fever and the dreaded cholera. That summer the Asiatic strain of cholera felled folks up and down the Mississippi, and when the plague surfaced in Dodgeville, panicked residents fled their homes for the open prairie. Nevertheless, of the nine hundred people in Dodgeville, the cholera killed better than one out of ten. Those losses were typical.[3]

Although Adele and her children survived, one of the Dodge daughters did not. Christiana Helen and her busband, the ex-governor of Iowa Territory, James Clarke, succumbed to cholera, along with one of their small sons.

It is uncertain that Henry L. Dodge knew of Adele's troubles. If he and his family ever exchanged occasional letters, none apparently survived. As for his sister, Henry may have learned of her death from no other source than the newspapers. Missouri papers were widely circulated in Santa Fe and cholera epidemics were big news. He probably followed his father and brother's careers in the papers as well, though one wonders how, as the ne'er-do-well eldest son, the news of their achievements affected him. Augustus continued his rapid political ascent. Iowa had been admitted to the Union in 1846 and both Augustus Dodge and George Wallace Jones became the state's first senators, the love-spurned Senator Jefferson Davis himself presenting A. C. Dodges' credentials to the Congress.[4] Dodge the father had fared equally well. In 1848 he was chosen Senator for the new state of Wisconsin and consequently was seated in the same chambers as his son. Two years later the Old Roman was re-elected to a full six-year senate term in delectable triumph over his old nemisis, James Duane Doty.[5] Having turned down a nomination as a vice-presidential candidate to Van Buren in 1848, Dodge was seriously being considered by Democrats as their presidential candidate for 1852.[6]

Then there was Henry Lafayette, whose political successes might be seen as tepid when compared to those of his brother and father. Be that as it may, one item of business that had drawn Henry L. Dodge into Santa Fe early in July, 1850 was strictly political. He carried in his coat a carefully worded but brief letter addressed to the acting governor of the newly created State of New Mexico, Manuel Alvarez.

"Santa Fe, July 8, 1850
　　　　　To His Excellency Manuel Alvarez, Acting Gov. of the State of New Mexico
Sir: I herewith resign the seat that I have had the Honour of holding in the Legislature of this state.

Very Respectfully,
Your Most Obdt. Sevt.
Henry L. Dodge"[7]

Dodge's decision to abruptly resign from the New Mexico State legislature is intriguing. Had the demands of his store in Cebolleta precluded doing government business in Santa Fe? His partner John Tullis had been elected to a seat, but also chose to resign at around the same time.[8]

What proves more intriguing still was the fact that Dodge had been elected to an assembly seat for the State—not the Territory—of New Mexico, a state that technically, despite fervent campaigning and a divisive election, did not exist. The years have all but consumed any record of that anomaly—a mere handful of handwritten ballots for the election of 1850 survive. All the same, in June of 1850, in open defiance of the Congress of the United States of America, the citizens of fabled Cibola overwhelmingly induced the birth of the State of New Mexico . . . and it was a breach birth at best.

Up to that point, New Mexico had endured a fate unique to all other U. S. territories. Rather than enjoying the basic rights and freedoms of self-government guaranteed all citizens by the Constitution, for five years New Mexico had been arbitrarily ruled by an autocratic military dictatorship. It was not supposed to have happened that way. In September of 1846, General Kearny had promised New Mexicans eventual self-rule, but until that day arrived, he recognized some government was necessary to insure security, tranquility and American control over the recently conquered province. Consequently and almost single-handedly, Kearny created one, known later as the Kearny Codes, and draped it over the political system of prefects and alcaldes he had found upon his arrival.

In design it resembled the classic representative government, but in practice there was little very democratic about it. Alexander Doniphan wrote the laws and Stephen Watts Kearny personally appointed all the major officials, carefully inserting Americans in the critical positions. The United States Marshal, the United States District Attorney, the Treasurer and Territorial Auditor; all were Americans.[9] Almost immediately, both New Mexico and Washington DC were in confusion over the legal and practical status of Kearny's government. It was most distressing that a military officer had essentially usurped the U. S. Constitution and the Congress by not only bestowing American citizenship on foreign combatants, but proclaiming a civil government. It was an abomination, and the anti-war Whigs in Washington had a political field day with it. Though it failed to become the scandal Whigs had hoped, the Democrats were nonetheless mortified, not the least of whom was President James Polk. He disapproved Kearny's audacity but hesitatingly endorsed the interim government as a regrettable necessity during war. The people of New Mexico would be allowed their civil government, but the true authority would remain firmly in the hands of the Army and its new commander in Santa Fe, Colonel Sterling Price.

New Mexicans soon realized that the civil government for what it was—a sham. Everything it did had to pass Colonel Price's muster. It was with his blessing and his blessing alone that the people of New Mexico held their first legislative election in the fall of 1847 and convened the new legislature on December 6th of that year. Price peremptorily appointed forty-five year old Donaciano Vigil to succeed murdered Charles Bent. In his address to the new legislature, Vigil stressed the grave responsibility of the legislators to nurture their fledgling democracy. The irony of his words could not have gone unappreciated. None knew when they'd actually get to see that democracy, for it was Colonel Price who validated elections, appointed or endorsed civil officers, unilaterally approved or rejected legislative acts, enforced the civil laws, arrested and jailed civilians, and arbitrarily levied taxes on the people without the sanction or input of those being taxed. He did so without malice, of course, believing his actions were in the best interests of the people of New Mexico. His was a benevolent tyranny, but a tyranny nonetheless.[10]

In February of 1848, the Treaty of Guadalupe Hidalgo ended the Mexican War, again throwing the status of New Mexico's peculiar government into question. The war was over. With peace, New Mexicans became citizens of the United States, with the right to self-government. All they need do was petition Congress to grant that right by admitting New Mexico into the Union as an organized territory. Unfortunately that event, barring some divine intercession, was about as likely to happen as Montezuma's return to Pecos.

In the history of the westward movement to that time, Americans had invariably moved into unsettled regions already claimed or soon to be claimed by the United States. Vast territories were eventually carved into smaller ones. Iowa and Missouri had been sliced from Louisiana Territory, Wisconsin cleaved from Michigan Territory, Minnesota from Iowa and so on.

New Mexico provided startling contrast. It was a conquered province of a foreign country, with a large and distinctly foreign population, speaking a foreign tongue; a population that possessed a society with a government and code of laws a hundred years older than the first English colonies. However, these proved minor considerations compared to New Mexican attitudes regarding organized slavery. They were resolutely opposed to it and, as long as Congress remained hamstrung over slavery's expansion, New Mexico's admission was rendered utterly impossible. The old Kearny government was defunct, and the admission of New Mexico blocked. President Taylor's administration chose the easiest solution to the conundrum. They did nothing. Kearny's civil government would be allowed to continue under tight military control until Congress decided to act . . . if ever.

It was no solution at all and New Mexicans—Hispanic and American—detested it. Even before Sterling Price had taken command, they had been clamoring for popular sovereignty. As early as October of 1847, the Santa Fe Republican ran editorials endorsing a civil government, and public protests against military rule were held in parlors and lobbies, in the streets and in front of the Governor's Palace. With the end of the Mexican War, a debate ignited over whether the people of New Mexico would actually choose to join the United States. Several influential Hispanic leaders loathed the idea of annexation, preferring to rejoin Mexico or go it on their own. Many others, most notably the Americans and their mouthpiece, the *Santa Fe Republican*, lobbied passionately in favor of annexation.

> "We see in the present war, the steady advance of that astonishing, yes almost incomprehensible enterprise and activity of the Anglo-Saxon blood . . . in fact wherever it has come in contact with any other than its own kind, all obstacles have melted away like the April snow. The Frenchman, the Spaniard, the Hollander, and the Portuguese have all felt its power and been compelled to acknowledge its irresistible superiority."

Early in January of 1848, New Mexicans elected a convention to address the issue. The results were less than a resounding endorsement for joining the United States. When Bernalillo County selected anti-annexation delegates José Chavez and José C. Armijo, the pro-annexation editors of the Republican accused the Catholic clergy of rigging the election. The Church regularly served as handy whipping boy for New Mexico's ills and was vilified early and often by Americans as the corrupt and licentious enemy of progress.

Gradually, opponents of annexation sullenly accepted the obvious. In the midst of wild rumors that Mexico was preparing to invade the territory, or rescue it, depending on one's point of view, it was clear that whatever the delegates decided would in the end be irrelevant. Annexation to the United States was already a fact as plain as the Army cannon poised on the Plaza, and nothing would reverse that fact, as Sterling Price himself reminded the convention delegates.

"The Territory of New Mexico, by the movement of armies and military occupation, has become permanently subject to the government of the United States. The acts of your Convention cannot in that particular, change the destiny of New Mexico..."

Oliver P. Hovey, the editor of the *Republican*, was more succinct. It was an absolute waste of time to discuss the matter further simply because "the antagonistic character of the Anglo Saxon" would not and could not be suppressed.[11]

The point of debate then turned to the type of government the citizens of New Mexico were to have when the inevitable came. Would it be one of arbitrary and absolute military rule or a robust republican one elected and empowered by the people? The citizens' preference was clear but once more immaterial. Colonel Sterling Price remained in charge and the situation remained unchanged. Price eventually passed his authority to Colonel Edward Newby and Newby to Major Benjamin Lloyd Beall, who finally transferred the scepter to Colonel John Washington in the fall of 1848. Colonel Washington became the first commander to officially hold the title Military Governor of New Mexico. There was no sign of a loosening of Army rule. Quite the contrary, its grip on power was as tenacious as ever.

As John Washington was getting settled in Santa Fe that October, Donaciano Vigil issued a call for delegates to a convention to agitate for self-government. Delegates met in Santa Fe on October 10th and elected the purportedly anti-American Taos priest Antonio José Martinez as president. Although the proceedings were apparently fraught with ethnic strife, a committee composed of Governor Vigil, Francisco Sarracino, James Quinn and Juan Perea did draft a memorial, unanimously endorsed by the delegates, urging Congress to act on New Mexico's behalf.[12] The memorial had included a declaration against slavery. However commendable, the provision was the practical equivalent poking oneself in the eye. Southern senators angrily condemned it as inflammatory and insolent.[13] Meanwhile Colonel Washington formally replaced Governor Vigil as the chief executive of New Mexico. As a nod to Donaciano Vigil's long experience in administration, for John Macrae Washington had none, the Colonel retained Vigil as secretary to the territory.

The people's doggedness for self-rule was also motivated by the fear that New Mexico was about to be gutted. For better than a decade Texas had claimed all lands east of the Rio Grande. Both the United States and Mexico acknowledged that the Rio Grande Valley and the eastern New Mexican plains had been a part of the province of Nuevo México since before the war, but that mattered not to the Texans. They had Polk's tacit support to annex the region and they were determined to press their claim. After officially proclaiming New Mexico a part of the Lone Star State, the Texas legislators created counties and judicial districts, appointed officials and arranged municipal elections for the annexed territory. They did so without the support of their recently naturalized brethren. The New Mexican position was clearly articulated in their ill-fated memorial to Congress.

> "We respectfully, but firmly, protest against the dismemberment of our territory in favor of Texas for any cause."[14]

Texas remained undeterred. When Texas agent Judge Spruce M. Baird showed up in Santa Fe in November of 1848 to take his appointed position as judge of the new Texas 11th Judicial District, the Santa Fe Republican noted with amusement that Baird wasn't at fault for "such an expedition of folly" because he was only obeying orders.

> ". . . we therefore trust that he will receive that attention and respect due to his character as a gentleman, however we may laugh at his pretensions as Judge of the County of Santa Fe; so that on his return to his country, he may be able to say in honor of New Mexico that it knows what is due to a gentleman, as well as it knows how to defend its rights against all aggression or interference."[15]

Predictably, the judge received no assistance from either the citizens of Santa Fe or the military governor Colonel John M. Washington, who received the judge with a noticeable lack of warmth.

Washington gave an equally cool reception to the incessant New Mexican clamoring for civil rights, but he was practical enough to realize he needed to mollify the activists before things got out of hand. Hence before departing on his month-long Navajo expedition in 1849, Washington authorized the acting commander Benjamin Beall to allow the citizens to elect delegates to develop a blueprint for a civil government . . . a blueprint and no more than that. The delegates met on the 24th of September and immediately went beyond Colonel Washington's restrictions. On the 26th a committee issued not one but two proposals for a New Mexican government. The majority proposal endorsed the traditional pursuit of territorial status through Congress. In shocking contrast, the minority report seized a radical stance. They held that since Congress had failed to extend the basic right of self-determination to the people, then the people had the right to seize it themselves.

The report urged rejection of the tedious territorial process and a proclamation of full and immediate statehood.[16]

The two factions did agree on one count. They wanted representation in Congress, promptly electing Hugh N. Smith as their congressional delegate and sent him off to Washington, DC. In the end, the bold move failed. Colonel Washington refused to recognize the acts of the convention and when Hugh N. Smith reached Washington, DC with a memorial supporting territorial status tucked in his vest, he was barred from Congress. The furor for civil rule reached such a crescendo that Colonel Washington deemed it a threat to security and ordered citizens to stop attending seditious meetings on pain of arrest.[17]

The convention of 1849 had exposed a rift that would divide the territory for the next two years. The radical statehood faction was lead by Manuel Alvarez, a long-time resident and prominent political leader. Those who endorsed the Alvarez Party's position included such men as Army officers Captain William Z. Angney, Richard Weightman and trader William Messervy.[18] Furthermore, the Alvarez Party had received plenty of encouragement. As early as 1848, Senator Thomas H. Benton had urged both New Mexico and California to create their own government. No less than the President of the United States, Zachary Taylor, had made it known he supported New Mexican statehood and had sent James S. Calhoun and Colonel George A. McCall to New Mexico, expecting both to covertly aid the movement. Officially McCall was sent to New Mexico on a fact-finding mission, but was instructed to thwart attempts by Texas to seize the territory and bolster the resolve of Colonel Washington's successor John Munroe to use military force againt Texas, if need be.[19]

Supporters of territorial annexation, on the other hand, were more often than not officers of Kearny's civil government. They claimed, perhaps rightly, that their position was more the practical, but in fact they had enjoyed influence and prosperity during the Army's administration, and expected it to continue under a territorial administration. An Alvarez victory would upset their cart and toss them all out. Richard Weightman, an Alvarez supporter, later recounted that those who signed a petition against statehood at the end of December 1849 included "all the judges and the circuit courts, the prefects, the sheriffs, the alcaldes and, in fact, the great body of the officers of the civil government."

On April 20th of 1850, the citizens petitioned Colonel Munroe to call for a constitutional convention. Munroe doubtlessly had mixed feelings but, with McCall's encouragement, he set May 6th for the election of delegates. The election went off as planned. The delegates met on May 15th and drafted a state constitution, including an article which outlawed slavery.[20] Munroe then issued a proclamation for a popular election to endorse or reject the constitution and elect officers, to be held on June 20th, 1850. Apparently both John R. Tullis and Henry L. Dodge were put up as candidates for the Territorial Party. Dodge's practical resume was the same as any number of pro-territorial civil officers and his allegiance probably lay with the civil government, for what it was worth. The same could be said without hesitation for John R. Tullis who had been elected to the first senate under the Kearny government in 1847 and later proved to be a loyal and loud ally to the old guard.

Monroe's actions did not represent an endorsement of statehood. Quite the contrary. In authorizing the election, the Colonel sternly warned that if a state government was adopted, it would have no immediate jurisdiction over the territory. He would retain the position and power as civil and military governor, while the officials presently serving in the Kearny government would remain the acting administration until "by the action of Congress another shall be substituted."

In essence, Monroe wished to emasculate the mandate. The state government would be legitimate only on paper, regulated to a feeble exercise in preparing for self-determination.

Munroe's warning didn't seem to damper the people's excitement. During the intervening month before the election, bitter fighting between the statehood and territorial factions enflamed the country. Calhoun described the contest as "extremely violent."[21] A heated dispute erupted over the printing of ballots. The only printing press in the district was housed in Santa Fe, and the territorial party controlled it. Strangely, the press had been shipped to Santa Fe in 1846, several weeks ahead of the American invasion, by the order of Stephen Watts Kearny himself, and was used to print Army sheet and the Republican newspaper. Alvarez's faction therefore requested their party ballots be printed on the government press. The editors of the Santa Fe Republican, strong territorialists, flatly refused. As a result, the ballots had to be scribbled out by hand ... twenty thousand of them. For this and other reasons, Alvarez and his supporters vilified the Army quartermaster's department for influencing a popular election. It was an accurate accusation. A. W. Reynolds, the assistant quartermaster for the department and a pro-territory supporter, had been active in local politics, lately aspiring to become the future Congressional delegate for the Territory of New Mexico.

As assistant quartermaster, if he was not actually Henry Dodge's boss, he was certainly someone whose favors Dodge depended upon, so it was not surprising to find Dodge in Santa Fe at the height of these excitements. On Election Day, both he and John Tullis were elected to the State legislature, despite their territorialist leanings, and found themselves in the minority. Generally, the election had been an unequivocal call for statehood. The people overwhelmingly endorsed the state constitution, elected a state governor, the well-known and popular trader Henry Connelly, who was also pro-territory. Despite these anomilies, statehood candidates swept the remaining positions, including the race for lieutenant governor, where Manuel Alvarez defeated the illustrious Ceran St. Vrain.[22]

When Connelly took an extended leave of absence to travel back east, Alvarez assumed all the powers, real or imagined, of the governor of the State of New Mexico. The extent of those powers rapidly became a point of contention. Munroe asserted the governor-elect had no powers; nor did the state judicial or legislative branches. Alvarez viewed the matter differently. The people of New Mexico deserved self-rule and they had elected him to provide it. It was their right to seize the initiative without suffering to wait for paternalistic approval from either a military despot or a distant and deadlocked Congress.

Predictably, this peeved Munroe—those pesky citizens had again overstepped their authority, ignoring him and insulting Congress by first creating a state and then having the temerity to demand admission retroactively.[23] Thus began, as James Calhoun characterized it, a frequent and "unpleasant correspondence" between Colonel Munroe and Lieutenant Governor Alvarez that went on for months. Meanwhile, the state legislature wrote and passed laws, created Socorro County, and elected Francis Cunningham and Richard Weightman as state senators to Congress; and all swatted down by the stern and fatherly hand of Colonel Munroe.

Dodge resigned as a member of the legislature on July 8th, thus avoiding the feud between Alvarez, governor-civil, and Munroe, governor-military. John R. Tullis retained his seat for a time and helped flame the rancorous infighting in the legislature, for tensions had swelled in the wake of the election.[24] Munroe thwarted the state government at every opportunity, while the Territorial Party busily undermined the Alvarez faction by stirring up public anxieties about the future. In the meantime, Texas continued its efforts to organize its own county governments. On July 20th Alvarez called for county elections for New Mexico state officials. On that same date, Spruce M. Baird announced general elections for similar positions for the state of Texas. Anticipating serious troubles ahead, Colonel Munroe abruptly pulled American forces from the more outlying posts and posted them in strategic positions along the Rio Grande Valley. During that sudden shift, the garrison at Cebolleta suddenly found itself posted to Albuquerque. The outside chance that Texas might attempt to take New Mexico by force was a legitimate concern, but served more as a convenient excuse. Munroe's redeployment was probably intended to bully Alvarez's government rather than discourage a Lone Star invasion.[25]

Undaunted by the squabbling, Senator-designate Richard Weightman departed Santa Fe enroute to Washington, DC to take his seat in Congress. That year had been a particularly nasty one for the 31st Congress. The atmosphere in the Senate was absolutely poisonous. There had been fist fights and lawmakers had taken to carrying weapons. In April Thomas H. Benton of Missouri had been involved in a shouting match on the floor with one Senator Henry Foote of Mississippi. When Benton, a large, intimdating man, advanced on Foote from across the aisle, the senator from Mississippi coolly pulled a pistol from his waistcoat. Somehow, Senator Henry Dodge got between them, restraining his bombastic friend while bullish Benton bellowed, "I have no pistols!" "Let him fire" "Stand out of the way." "I have no pistols." "I disdain to carry arms!"[26]

President Taylor had been anything but a calming influence. Although elected to the presidency in 1848 as a Whig, Old Rough and Ready was a Kentuckian, a southerner in spirit, and held slaves himself. Those facts initially gave southerners some comfort he'd be sympathetic to the cause of Dixie, but they soon discovered their error. The Hero of Buena Vista was at best unsupportive of Southerners, who perceived quite correctly that Taylor was conspiring to restrict slavery's expansion. When some aggravated Southern representatives threatened to secede from the Union, Old Rough and Ready swore in so many words he'd send the Army in and have them hanged. Between abolitionists and fire-eaters in Congress and the intractable President, any hope of a compromise over New Mexico's status or, for that matter, any other issue of gravity, was dead.

Then, on July 4th, the hand of fate intervened. After attending Independence Day celebrations on a torrid and stiflingly afternoon typical of a Washington, DC summer, Zachary Taylor became suddenly and violently ill. In less than a week he was dead. Admittedly it was a tragic event but, by killing The Hero of Buena Vista, the Asiatic cholera had granted the 31st Congress and the country salvation. Into Taylor's boots stepped his mild-mannered vice president, Millard Fillmore, whose calming approach cooled Congressional tempers. In short order, Congress hammered out what would be called the Compromise of 1850. Both Senators Augustus Dodge and his father Henry Dodge were in the thick of the debate over the wide spectrum of its provisions. Neither man was thrilled with the bill and both were suspicious of Northern motives, particularly of the abolitionists, but they voted for it. Thus, the Union was preserved.

When Richard Weightman finally arrived in Washington, DC he discovered that his seat in the Senate had evaporated. As a provision of the compromise,

Congress had at last created the Territory of New Mexico, assuaging Texan pride with ten million dollars to settle claims to the Rio Grande. When Millard Fillmore signed the bill on September 9th, he in effect signed the death warrant for the hard-fought, short-lived State of New Mexico. Sixty odd years would pass before New Mexico would see another.

28

CHUPADERO

After his resignation, Henry Dodge returned to his store in Cebolleta and to his job as commissary agent for the Army, issuing John Tullis a voucher for $300 worth of supplies on behalf of the Quartermaster's office and making several other purchases.[1] In mid August, Dodge again journeyed to Santa Fe to buy an impressive amount of merchandise from the firms of Messervy & Webb and St. Vrain & McCarty. He bought everything one might imagine a general store could offer, from clothing to tobacco. There were cotton prints, manta, cambric and corduroy, bundles of handkerchiefs, a dozen children's shoes, paper tacks and umbrellas, ivory combs and hawks bells, sugar and soap, tin cups and matches, rings, thimbles, needles and thread, buttons and silver beads, gun flints and caps . . . and a 37-gallon barrel of whiskey. Dodge's diverse choice of clothing was perhaps eccentric for a store located in such a backwater spot, but practical items were well represented: buck gloves and suspenders, vests, great coats and wool hats, but also the more incongruent, such as gray, brown and black satin pants.[2]

Going over the list of goods, one can imagine much of it being popular among the troops at Cebolleta—particularly the whiskey, but clearly Dodge was buying for three distinct groups: the soldier, the New Mexican and the Indian. He probably did a fair amount of regular business from Acoma and Laguna Pueblo, while members of Sandoval's Mount Taylor Navajo doubtlessly frequented the store. The Indians favored the hawk bells, silver beads, handkerchiefs and the ever-indispensable smoking tobacco and cornhusks, but generally shunned conventional clothing, particularly shoes. Indian children not only went perpetually barefoot, but during temperate weather were perpetually bare—as naked as spring sunlight and an irksome affront to any American reverend who might be passing by.

Dodge had been charging the fort sutler's account from May through September for various items bought by several teamsters posted at Cebolleta.[3] Some of Dodge's purchases, bought with a draft on the quartermaster's department in Santa Fe, appear suspiciously non-military. The soldiers at Cebolleta were often compelled to buy what the Army should have provided. Hence they were a rather tattered assembly and found the prices for clothing were exorbitantly priced by the sutler, another reason to frequent Dodge's store. The 3rd Auditor of the United States Treasury did note some irregularities in Dodge's accounts that year, but that was nothing out of the ordinary—chalk it up to shoddy paper work. Henry collected his salary for nine month's work, a total of $360 in Santa Fe on September 30th.[4]

By the beginning of 1851, the County of Valencia listed Dodge as holding a merchant's license at Cebolleta, with a sworn invoice amount of three thousand dollars, of which the county took $37.50 in taxes. Henry was doing well enough to employ a clerk, an Irish fellow by the last name of Mulligan.[5] Around this time, Dodge and Tullis decided to relocate their business, located in the town north of the actual post, to a more advantageous location. A first glance of the spot makes one wonder if they hadn't been inebriated when they chose it. It was only a mile or so west of the garrison, true, but it appeared to be anything but convenient. The place was perched half way up a rocky canyon gouged into the craggy mesa cliffs bracing Mount Taylor. The boulder-strewn ascent through twisted cedar and piñon was punishing enough to challenge the most skilled wagon master. On arrival, an overwhelming sense of windblown isolation swept in—a most peculiar place for doing mercantile transactions. Yet wedged in against the immense sandstone parapets, there lay a pleasant meadow fed by a faithful spring, guarded by a scattering of adobe buildings. It afforded a breathtaking view of the vast, arid Puerco River watershed falling away eastward toward the Sandia Mountains and Albuquerque. The site also stood along a major trail that skirted the mountain and decended into Cubero. If Tullis and Dodge had intended to compete with the infamous Cubero grog houses for the enlisted man's drinking coin, the place would have been perfect, a short jaunt from the fort but obscured from the disapproving gaze of company officers, excluding those who were already faithful customers. The place was called *Chupadero*, or in Spanish "The Seep." Coincidentally, the term also implied drunkard.

However much the store might have interrupted his prompt attention to Army business, Dodge continued to enjoy Colonel Munroe's unequivocal favor. Furthermore, the most recent commander at Cebolleta apparently took to Henry as well. He was Brevet Lieutenant Colonel David T. Chandler of the 3rd Infantry. Chandler arrived on September 3rd from Albuquerque, bring with him Company I of the 3rd Infantry and Company H of the 2nd Dragoons under the command of Captain William H. Saunders, all in all a force of roughly 70 men. It was a diverse body of soldiers, typical of the Army of that day, and perfect prospective customers for any convenient grog shop, however rude.

They were generally young European immigrants, in their twenties and early thirties, and their skills in English were suspect at best. There were a few Scots and a handful of Englishmen, a chap from Canada and one from Wales, a Prussian and a Bavarian. There was even a Frenchman. However, the majority were German and Irish. A complement of civilian workers accompanied them, including a dozen teamsters, a wood cutter and several laundresses, some married to soldiers and a handful of them, married or not, with young children. Lieutenant Joseph Whistler and Lieutenant William Duncan Smith had brought their wives. The young post surgeon, twenty-year-old William Hammond's wife Helen had returned with their infant daughter and a thirteen-year-old boy Jesús, who was probably Helen's personal valet.[6]

On his arrival Chandler wrote Munroe requesting that he make "Dodge, late agent, or some other person as forage master and interpreter."[7] The colonel had been horrified by conditions at the post. The horses were broken down. Grasshoppers had destroyed the corn crop and the price charged for forage was not much short of extortion. The quarters were cramped and crumbling, hardly better than hovels. The men were ill and Dr. Hammond's list of sick recruits was growing daily. There weren't enough rations. Clothing was scarce and what was to be had was in miserable condition. The men were borrowing jackets from one another just to pass Sunday guard inspections.[8]

Chandler's biggest irritation, though, would be one he'd brought with him, the commander of Company H, Captain William Saunders. Sneaking off without leave or merely deserting outright was a tempting remedy for post melancholy, and some did, although the punishment for getting caught could be severe. For the less daring, liquor could bring more temporary relief, but was not without its own share of unpleasant consequences. Saunders in particular had a real penchant for drinking. He hadn't been in Cebolleta a month when Colonel Chandler had him arrested and relieved of duty for drunkenness. He ordered the captain to pen out his letter of resignation from the service, then to write a solemn promise to abstain from strong spirits. Chandler vowed the next time he discovered Captain Saunders was drunk, he'd have that resignation processed.[9]

The captain also had a penchant for writing letters, and he began making lengthy and unending complaints to headquarters about the condition of the Cebolleta post, strongly implying that all of it was Chandler's fault. Army regulations required such correspondence to pass across Chandler's desk before being forwarded. Saunders simply ignored that technicality.

There was no denying the garrison was in roughshod shape. First the post was seriously undermanned. When Chandler asked Munroe for permission to take his men to Zuni to aid in putting down depredations by the Navajos, Munroe told him his force wasn't big enough to do the job. Chandler proposed enlisting and arming the local New Mexicans to beef up the garrison's strength. Munroe dismissed the idea, choosing to arm the Zunis with surplus muskets instead.[10] Even if Munroe had allowed Chandler's force to take the field, they couldn't have sustained a long march. According to Saunders, only nine of the forty-three dragoon horses were fit for service and would be easily outdistanced by the fleet Indian ponies. The situation was so bad that Colonel Chandler contemplated buying and mounting his own men on Indian ponies.[11]

November proved a particularly awkward month for Chandler. After Navajo warriors ran off ten cows and two thousand sheep from the locals, the Prefect of Valencia County, Ramón Luna, asked Chandler to support a retaliatory expedition.[12] Colonel Chandler regretfully explained that the dragoon horses were "in a wild state" and unfit for action. Undaunted, Luna returned to Cubero and gathered a force of fifty-five men, among them the illustrious Chato Aragon and his Cebolletanos, and rode off for Navajo country. Luna's expediton proved impressively successful, capturing upward of 5000 Navajo sheep, 150 horses, eleven oxen, and fifty-two Navajo captives.[13] It was a resounding victory of which any Army field commander would be proud. Chandler must have been somewhat mortified.

Despite the descent of winter on New Mexico, Navajo raiders remained active. On December 4th, a Mexican herder appeared at the Cebolleta post to announce that a band of Navajos had driven off four to five thousand of his livestock. Chandler sent a small scouting party out to investigate but they returned that evening suffering from frostbite, claiming drifting snows had obliterated any trace of the trail.[14]

On January 12th a story surfaced that Navajos had bushwhacked Chato Aragon and his Cebolletanos in the mountains. While returning from Navajo country with Luna's expedition, they had split from the main force to take the short cut home over Mount Taylor, and they were days overdue. The rumor was soon reported to Captain Saunders, who was commanding the post in Chandler's absence. The citizens of Cebolleta requested the captain send out a rescue party. Saunders refused. The snow was deep, the trails impassable and the details of the story were confused and conflicting. The fact he spoke no Spanish and had to depend on the interpreter Mr. Tolin to translate probably didn't help clarity, either.[15] Once more, the citizens had to take matters into their own hands. Fifteen of them braved the cold to search for Chato's band but found the sierra trails completely snow-bound. Eventually the worst was confirmed. Chato and his men were found dead in the snow drifts of San Mateo. The Navajo had rushed their camp at night, disarmed them and then chased the desperate men until they caught and killed them.[16]

Winter tightened its grip on Chandler's little outpost. The heavens turned dark and bitterly cold, casting the whole country in a depressing gray. The thermometer regularly plunged below zero. Heavy blankets of snow fell in rapid succession, piling up in the canyons and blocking trails. The bone-chilling winter must have been especially challenging for Henry L. Dodge, tasked to provide basic forage and supplies to the garrison and if anyone could appreciate the extent of the deepening crisis at Cebolleta it was Dodge. This fact was not lost on Captain Saunders, who was contemplating yet another letter to headquarters. In December, the captain asked Henry his opinion about the situation at the post. Dodge apparently gave it to him, and Saunders departed to scrawl out another essay to Munroe's adjutant, Captain Lafayette McLaws, detailing the scope of the crisis.

The dragoon horses were nearly starved, Saunders wrote, and so beaten up that, should the savages sweep down on the local Mexicans, the cavalry forty-seven miles away in Albuquerque would be able to respond faster than Saunders' own troops. To remain at Cebolleta for the duration of the winter would be catastrophic. The garrison was already on half rations and the post unsupportable. Commissary Agent Dodge himself had assured him of the fact, making it imperative to move the dragoons to a more hospitable site ... Cubero for example ... and that Agent Dodge, a knowledgeable and intelligent fellow, unhesitatingly supported his assessment. Captain Saunders sent the letter off by courier, who doubtlessly galloped past Chandler's office on his way to Santa Fe.[17]

Chandler knew nothing of that letter until around December 24th, when McLaws peremptorily sent it to him with a note criticizing Saunders' failure to follow the chain of command. Chandler was livid. He confronted Saunders with the letter and then called for Henry Dodge. Chandler trusted H. L. Dodge's judgment, yet the statements Saunders represented as his were glaringly contrary to what Dodge had personally told Chandler. When Henry arrived, Chandler read Saunders' allegations aloud, with Lieutenants Joseph Whistler and John Alley 3rd Infantry in the room as witnesses, and demanded Dodge account for the discrepancies as to his opinion of the post. Henry unequivocally stated that he'd never made the statements Saunders had claimed. Quite to the contrary, he felt Cebolleta was clearly more advantageous than Cubero, particularly given the harsh winter. Colonel Chandler required that in writing and Dodge obliged.[18]

> "Sir: Being called upon by you to make a brief statement of my views as to the practicability of supplying this Post with Forage for the present year and whether the public service would be benefited by a removal of the troops from this post to the Town of Cubero. I beg leave to submit the following facts derived from personal observation & knowledge of the country and its resources during a residence of three years one year of which time I have been in the employ of the U. S. in the purchase of forage. I have no hesitation in saying that either place can be supplied with corn sufficient but that long forage cannot be had at either in sufficient quantity unless the necessary arrangements are made before the commencement of winter. Cubero can barely furnish its present inhabitants with water and wood quarters for troops are not to be had but by constructing and as to their relative position as regards to the great pass to the Navajo Country Cebolleta has the advantage by twelve miles. I am Respectfully your Obdt Servt H. L. Dodge."[19]

In truth Dodge may have well told Saunders what he wanted to hear, as gregarious chaps are prone to do, but that mattered not. It was another official nail in the coffin of the cantankerous complaint-scribbling captain. Smugly, Chandler sent Dodge's account up to Munroe. Nonetheless, Saunders inexplicably refused to let the matter lay. In an act of career suicide he sent a long epistle on the post's problems to no less than Adjutant General Jones in Washington, DC.[20] Blame it on the weather. Winter doldrums had a way of dissolving common sense and sanity.

With the advent of spring, conditions at the post began to improve. By mid March, rations of forage were back to full strength and twenty-nine of the forty-seven broken down dragoon horses were being fattened in the hay fields of Albuquerque. The arrival of new recruits lifted spirits as well, although Saunders sullenly observed that several were liars and thieves and "totally irreclaimable and incorrigibly worthless" and recommended sacking them.[21] It was Captain Saunders, however, whose days of service were numbered. On April 28th, Chandler found his dragoon captain in "a state of gross intoxication." Saunders was not only intoxicated, but he was gravely ill. Rather than being drunk, he protested that his stupor had been a side effect of the medicines Dr. Hammond had prescribed to him. Hammond denied the claim.

That was that. Chandler sent Saunders' letter of resignation and specifications of charges to Munroe, who forwarded them to the Adjutant General in Washington.[22] A short time after that, Saunders' health crumbled. On June 20th Chandler wrote to headquarters, observing that the captain was "in a most lamentable condition and is not expected to survive if entirely deprived of liquor . . . the medical office thinks he would die in a very short time..." Saunders did die in a very short time, there at the post, two weeks after Chandler's observations.[23]

With the spring thaw, Dodge was anxious to be out and about. Early in March, he grabbed the chance to accompany a Baptist missionary, the Reverend Hiram W. Read of Santa Fe, on a brief visit to the Cebolleta area. Henry planned to be in Albuquerque about the time Read was to come down, so he offered to escort him as far as the post. The Missionary Society had originally assigned Hiram and his wife to preach the Word in the sin-soaked gold fields of California, but they ended up in Santa Fe where the Reverend founded a Baptist primary school and served as the Fort Marcy chaplain. More significantly, prior to coming to New Mexico Hiram had been chaplain to the Wisconsin State Senate. He had known Governor Henry Dodge and the Dodge family. Henry L. Dodge may not have known Read personally, but it is likely he knew of him.[24]

Dodge was in Albuquerque on March 7th when Read and his escort arrived from Santa Fe. His first sight of the man that morning must have taken him somewhat aback. The Reverend resembled more the adventurous mercenary than the messenger of Christian love, clad as he was in boots and buckskin britches, a wide brimmed white hat that nearly swallowed his head and an intimidating brace of pistols slung around his hips. The trip down had been difficult. The early spring snow and resulting mud had made the roads into quagmires. At least Albuquerque was temperate, dry and dusty. They tarried not, but after an exchange of niceties continued on across the Rio Grande early the following morning.

> "Saturday 8th, resumed our journey at 8 A.M. Forded the river, and started toward Cibolletta. But before leaving the river filled our water casks and canteens, as we shall probably find no water for the next two days. As this is a more dangerous part of the journey our escort is doubled. We have a baggage wagon and a carriage or ambulance. Capt. Dodge, son of Gen. Dodge, of Wisconsin, whom we met at this place [Albuquerque] accompanied us . . ."

They camped across the Rio Puerco that evening among a small copse of cedar trees—hardly more than bushes—a dozen or so miles west of Albuquerque and slept the entire night under a military sentry. In Navajo country, no amount of caution was deemed excessive and despite his intimidating outfit, Reverend Read slept fitfully that night, frequently startled awake by an icy breeze and the somber cry of coyotes. After crossing the Rio San José the next day, they passed Laguna, Paguate and Moquino.

The party arrived in Cebolleta post at dusk, where the Reverend enjoyed as much Army hospitality as Chandler's humble post could afford. The Reverend wasn't impressed with Cebolleta itself. Why, he sniffed, it wasn't worth the money it cost the Army to protect it for a month. The people were "ignorant and indolent in the extreme" and, he added, so degenerate that when an Army mule died they gathered round the carcass like so many buzzards and stripped the carcass of meat. At least that was what Colonel Chandler had told him. On Tuesday the 11th while under a pall of extreme boredom, Read noted that the "half-tamed'" Navajo chief Sandoval appeared in Cebolleta and sold an eighteen year old Indian man for thirty dollars, one of several Navajo captives his raiders captured on his last foray into western Navajo country.[25]

Read's successors, all of them Baptists, would share the Reverend's ineffaceable attitude towards New Mexicans. Initially they would bask in the warm welcome of their host community, who displayed all the enthusiasm and encouragement a budding mission might desire, only later to discover that despite their unceasing efforts they seldom succeeded converting souls. That came as no surprise to anyone but the missionaries themselves. Indians and New Mexicans alike saw them as overbearing, impudent and meddling; an irritant to be grudgingly but silently endured lest one offend the Americans. The Baptists usually blamed Satan in the form of conspiring Roman priests for subverting their every effort and turning the simple-minded people against them. Predictably, Read didn't tarry at Cebolleta any longer than he had to, but returned to the Rio Grande Valley for a better class of hosts, getting the opportunity to dine with the ex-Mexican governor Manuel Armijo himself, whose "furniture of the table was massive silver."[26]

Spring invariably stimulated renewed Navajo-New Mexican warfare. News arrived of Navajo raids at New Placer and Chilili. James Calhoun, who had just been appointed the first Territorial Governor of New Mexico, issued a proclamation authorizing local communities to raise militias in defense of their homes and property.[27] Both Calhoun and Major Munroe were itching to get at the Navajos, though they hadn't the slightest predisposition for cooperating with one another. The rumor going around had it that Munroe was planning to strike the Navajo at the first possible moment. Calhoun was impatient, apparently more enthusiastic about attacking and less so on checking the veracity of the information he was getting. An Army investigation subsequently determined the report of a Navajo raid at Chilili had been concocted by New Mexicans to precipitate conflict.

Governor Calhoun was undeterred. At the end of March, he asked Munroe to provide muskets to Hosta, the governor of Jemez, to beat back Navajo attacks. Munroe coolly demurred, stating that Hosta had just been in to see him with the Navajo chief Archuleta and all indications were that "the intercourse between the Pueblos of Jemez and the Navajos was not beyond suspicion." He'd send no arms without "a very evident necessity."

Monroe soon came to regard Calhoun in the same standoffish way he'd regarded Alvarez, as an alarmist, and disapproved of Calhoun's meddling in what the colonel considered military affairs. He was indeed planning an expedition for that spring. On March 16th, Munroe ordered Chandler to assist in setting up a supply depot at Laguna to support the expedition.[28] He had John G. Parker, senior top engineer, write up and submit a detailed map of trails into Navajo county, noting sites possessing all the necessary accommodations: grass, wood and water.[29] On April 1st, Munroe formally proposed his expedition against the Navajos to Adjutant General Jones in Washington, "Should the peaceable state of our relations with the adjacent Indian tribes authorize the movement."[30]

Word of the impending expedition spread quickly. There was no lack of interested parties wanting a share of the spoils of war. Having unloaded his latest cache of captives from a previous foray into Navajo land, Sandoval appeared before Calhoun in mid April, asking to volunteer for the expedition. Calhoun sent him on to Munroe.[31] As McLaws later explained to Chandler, Colonel Munroe told Sandoval he'd consider his request, but that he'd best go back and confer with Chandler at Cebolleta. After determining what role the Mount Taylor Navajo headman might take, Chandler was told to write headquarters a letter of reference on Sandoval's behalf.

> "Sandoval may be ostensibly at War with the one portion of his Tribe but at peace & in communication with the other & by giving information of our movements to the last, it will be communicated to the whole."[32]

And that was precisely what happened. On April 14th the Quartermaster's

Department directed Henry L. Dodge to ride to Zuni and secure a large supply of feed corn in preparation for the movement of troops. The task would take him the better part of the month. The Zuni were quite enthusiastic over the prospect of thrashing the Navajos while at the same time making a nifty profit supplying Munroe's troops. Dodge successfully negotiated for better than one thousand bags of corn and found to his satisfaction that he could get more, much more, if needed. Their business was suddenly interrupted when, out across the flat, six Navajos had appeared. Dodge described the event in his report of May 12th. He was convinced the Navajo desired peace.[33]

> "...I proceeded to Zuni on the 14th of last month and accomplished the object for which I went-I purchased one thousand bags of corn in twenty days and am having it shelled-twenty fanegas per day-and can purchase a thousand bags more at the same cost. I left a trusty American in charge, and he is superintending the shelling of it.
>
> "The Navajos a few days previous to my arrival wounded a man and stole four horses from the immediate vicinity of the village. Some ten days afterwards, six Navajos came within sight of the town, and made demonstrations of a peaceful nature. On my approaching them with forty of the inhabitants of Zuni they fled and would not permit proximity sufficiently near to hold with them a conversation. They might if they had so chosen . . . The Zunians say that they learn from the inhabitants of seven pueblos of Moque that the Navajoes are planting intensively in the Cañon of Chey: that many of them are living to the west of the Cañon of Chey near a mountain called the Calculasa and that the rich have retired with their flocks and herds to the Rio St. Juan."

It was uncanny. The far-flung and secluded western Navajos had learned of the expedition nearly as quickly as the citizens hobnobbing in the Santa Fe plaza. Dodge continued.

> "I had a conversation with the Moques themselves and they stated to me that the Navajos came daily to their pueblos traded them mules horses and sheep-for corn bread and flannel indigo &c The Moques have a large number of government mules purchased by them from the Navajos. I observed two of those mules in Zuni and have delivered them here to the Quarter Master and I can with ten Dragoons go to Moque and get some fifty

or sixty more with the aid of the Zunians and some Mexicans whom I have in my employ by paying the Moques ten dollars a piece . . ." [34]

Munroe later agreed purchasing the mules was a good idea, but the proposition of crossing hostile country with a mere ten dragoons was at best indiscreet, particularly since the Hopi were presently rumored to be on good terms with the enemy. It was out of the question. Dodge's suggestion would have to wait.[35]

Delegations of Navajos seeking peace abruptly began appearing along the frontier settlements.[36] Chandler himself reported to headquarters that two Navajos had come in to the post to discuss a truce and were succinct in their request. All the Navajo wished peace. Their headmen wished to meet with the Army but feared coming into the settlements. For that reason, the men explained, the headmen had sent them, "because we are very poor men. Sandoval in his last campaign against us, stole everything we had, our horses, wives, children, & even the sheep skins we slept on, and if we are killed it will not be much loss to the tribe." They had learned of the expedition from some American traders almost two weeks previously, a fact that must have irked Chandler as he sat and listened. The two Navajo understood Chandler would hold one of them hostage and and allow the other to return with regarding a parley, but they cautioned the commander that, if one did not return within a week, the headmen would believe them dead and disperse their people into the wilderness north of the San Juan River.[37]

Chandler sent the second Navajo back with word that he wished to meet with the Navajo leaders on April 29th, but he was at a loss as to what to do if the meeting came off. Treat with them? Send them on to Munroe in Santa Fe? Rebuke them and refuse to talk peace until they'd been thoroughly roughed up by the Army? He wrote headquarters for instructions. Presently those instructions came back. Munroe and Calhoun were as one in their belief that any peace made prior to punishing the Navajos would last only so long as was convenient to the savages. Therefore, no new treaty would be undertaken. To the Americans, the issue was simple. If the Navajos wanted peace, they need only to adhere, without exception, to that treaty signed in Canyon de Chelly in 1849. Otherwise the American Army would inflict upon the Navajo people, peaceful and hostile alike, utter destruction.

29

FORT DEFIANCE

It was one thing to threaten the Navajo with annihilation . . . quite another to exact it. Clearly American military might had impressed the Navajo, but they were also impressed by the fact Americans seemed completely unable to follow through on threats. The Navajos certainly desired peace, but at the same time were confident in their own fighting prowess as well. They were not a people to be trifled with, as Lieutenant Colonel George A. McCall observed in his report to Secretary of War Crawford in 1850. The Apache and Navajo were the territory's most formidable Indian enemies, he explained, raiding the settlements with impunity, boldly murdering citizens and driving off livestock, even within earshot of nearby military posts. Of the two, he felt the Navajo presented the greatest threat.

The scattered Apache bands were small and, although noted for their ferocity, only stole what sheep they planned to eat in the immediate future. In contrast, McCall noted the Navajo as the larger and more "civilized" tribe, estimated at ten to twelve thousand, all of who had a decidedly entrepreneurial approach to war. They raided not to satisfy immediate necessity, but to increase their herds at home. McCall described the Navajo horse herds as enormous and their sheep rumored to be "numerous beyond calculation." The Navajo were well-organized, well-armed and resided deep in a country bristling with natural fortifications.

> ". . . Although they have no permanent villages, they cultivate the soil to a considerable extent, making periodical visits to their fields at planting and harvesting times. In this way they make a sufficiency of grain for all their wants, besides a few vegetables and fruits. They are said to be intelligent and industrious, and their manufactures (blankets and coarse cloths) in their neatness and finish, go far to prove this . . . For some years past they are believed to have steadily increased in numbers, and to count now about eighteen hundred lodges . . . "[1]

The Navajo likewise viewed Americans with a bit of denigrating humor. They referred American soldiers as *Bijaa' yee njahi* or "those who sleep on their ears" or *Bigod dook'ali*, "the ones who scorch their kneecaps," observing them from afar as they bedded down or huddled ridiculously close to their campfires.[2]

Both McCall and Colonel Munroe were unamused. They understood that any American expedition that fell short of completely crushing the Navajo would simply reinforce the perception of impotence. Munroe planned to unleash a scythe of destruction on the Navajo, a consummate, humiliating defeat and an enduring lesson for generations of Navajo to come. He hoped to launch his expedition in May, but the month came and went as he waded through conflicting intelligence regarding where most of the Navajos might actually be found. Then the Army tossed a wrench into the machinery by reassigning Monroe to duty back East. The expedition would have to wait upon the arrival of the new commander for the 9th Military District, the cantankerous Edwin Vose Sumner.

In the meantime, the richer bands of Navajos, most of whom had nothing to gain from raiding the settlements and everything to lose in a protracted war, continued efforts to broker a peace. Navajo emissaries appeared regularly in the settlements while the headmen labored to restrain the war-like propensities of the young firebrands and the poorer classes. Some Navajo had even expressed a willingness to avoid war by joining Sandoval's band. All the peace overtures notwithstanding, the Navajo leaders discreetly began moving their people, livestock and possessions northward toward the relative safety of the San Juan River and Ute country.[3]

There were fears in Santa Fe that the Navajo overtures were merely a ruse, and that the Indians fully intended to fight. The sporadic raiding along the frontier, as well as rumors circulating that the Navajos and Ute on the San Juan were trading with Utah Mormons for new rifles, seemed to confirm that. Early in July Major Graham, commanding at Abiquiu, detained ten New Mexican traders for swapping ammunition to the San Juan Navajos for "some fifteen or twenty of the finest animals that I have seen in the country."[4] That summer tension over a serious Indian war grew like a painful abcess. It would burst in, of all places, Cebolleta.

On June 15th, Henry Dodge's store clerk, the Irish fellow Mulligan, staggered into Chandler's post, beaten and bloody. The hapless fellow managed to relate that eight Navajos had attacked him earlier that day near a spring on the Rio Puerco. Both he and his mule had been wounded, but he managed to pull off three pistol shots at his attackers and they broke off their attack. He thought he'd hit one. Chandler soon received word that the same band had attacked a citizen on the Albuquerque road, albeit unsuccessfully. That was followed by more ominous news.

Chapitone, the Navajo headman, peace proponent and signatory of Colonel Washington's 1849 treaty, had been killed a mere five miles from Cebolleta. He and a handful of assistants had been coming in to discuss peace with Chandler when they were stopped by a group of Mount Taylor Navajos and Cebolletanos. Feigning friendship, the Cebolletanos said that if Chapitone and his men truly desired peace they should surrender their weapons. Chapitone's party complied, whereupon the Cebolletanos beat them to death with rocks and clubs. Amazingly, one of the Navajo escaped and carried the news of the massacre back to Tunicha. Munroe later commented that he believed the brutal attack was designed to goad the Navajos into war. If so, it worked. Navajo raiders promptly struck Isleta Pueblo, south of Albuquerque and then attacked a hay camp at Valle Grande, northwest of Santa Fe.[5]

Despite Chapitone's murder, the Navajo never fully retaliated and by late June Chandler was able to report that Navajo incursions in his area had ceased entirely. Still, following Munroe's instructions, he continued buying up all the local corn to support the coming campaign and suggested to headquarters that Dodge go to Zuni to purchase more. Chandler also mentioned that he had established a hay camp at Ojo de Gallo, or Rooster Spring, a good two days ride southwest of the garrison. It was known as Owenby's Camp, after the trader James Owenby who had contracted with the Army . . . a lovely spot of wide meadows and good water, lying within the cool shadows of the Zuni Mountains. Chandler had sent a number of broken down horses to recover there under the care of an overseer named Fitzgerald and several civilians.[6] The distance of the camp from Cebolleta gave little concern. Navajo raids had dropped off and by the first week of July, the only wild Indians in the area were three hundred mounted and heavily armed Comanche warriors.

Usually that would have thrown the entire territory into a screaming panic, but this particular Comanche expedition was welcomed, although hesitantly. They had actually been allowed to cross through New Mexico with the full knowledge and tacit encouragement of Colonel Munroe. The Comanche leaders had informed headquarters they planned to raid the Tunicha Navajo. It was potentially fortuitous news for the Americans, who were revving up their own military expedition, and the Comanche expedition was allowed to go towards Albuquerque unmolested. At some point, a hundred of them split from the main body and headed towards Cebolleta. They approached Chandler's garrison on July 4th and dispatched messengers to the post asking permission to continue through into Navajo country. Chandler sent word to come on through, but oddly enough, the Comache war party never appeared.

Nine days later, on July 13th, grave news reached Cebolleta. An enormous party of Indians had attacked Owenby's Camp. Camp overseer Fitzgerald survived the assault and related the horrifying details. Before dawn, he explained, one of his men had got up to kindle a fire and boil up some coffee. Everyone else was asleep.

"Shortly after, hearing a very loud Indian yell, I arose and saw we were completely surrounded by about three hundred Indians...immediately commenced firing upon us before we had time to put on an article of clothing. The majority of our party was soon wounded, and believing their situation to be hopeless, they took to flight, but rallied and then fled again. [Parker] was soon brought to the ground and [Smith] in attempting to fight through was also brought down. I found my way through, got two more wounds, and crossed the creek where I hid. It was then day and I saw them mutilate and scalp Parker, and, apparently, go through the same operation with B. Smith—after which, taking everything transportable which was about, they burnt the wagon body &c and fired several shots, and left the place."

Late that morning, a Cebolleta post patrol commanded by Lieutenant William Duncan Smith learned of the massacre and rushed to Cubero where survivors had begun to gather. Four wounded men pierced through with arrows were there, and several more were straggling in. Others remained missing. After commandeering a lumbering ox cart to draw in potential casualties, Smith his men struck out for Ojo de Gallo in the waning daylight. Under the pall of dusk, they moved westward ten miles through the Canyon Rio Azul, where they found Fitzgerald, pierced at least four or five times by arrows. Cautiously, Lt. Smith sent a scouting patrol ahead to survey the hay camps. When the scouts returned they brought in yet another wounded man and reported two men at the campsite dead, scalped and mutilated.[7]

The Comanche were immediate suspects. After failing to show, had they turned back again and swept over the hay camp? Chandler seemed to think so. The description of the number and dress of the Indians—feathers, war paint and buckskin "a costume unusual with the Navajoes on stealing expeditions & reserved solely for war parties" was credible evidence. The fact that the men had been scalped and mutilated was also highly unusual for Navajo warfare, and Chandler knew that such a large Navajo war party could not have slipped into the region without being detected.[8] Dressed like Comanches, fighting like Comanches and in numbers equivalent to that of the Comanche war party, the conclusion was inescapable.

Nevertheless, there were some who insisted it had been the Navajo. During Lieutenant Smith's investigation, Sandoval claimed that the night before the attack, one of his men oveheard a hostile Navajo bragging that the Tunicha Navajos were soon to launch a massive three-pronged assault on the settlements. Of course, it was in Sandoval's complete interest to make such an assertion. The Mount Taylor headman had conspired to precipitate and then participate in war with his estranged brethren before, so it was quite likely the story was concocted to compel the Americans to declare all out war. True or not, Munroe took the path of caution. On July 19th, McLaws sent a dispatch to Major Howe at Albuquerque, ordering him to reinforce Cebolleta, the very day Colonel Munroe was relieved of command by Colonel Sumner.[9]

Edwin Vose Sumner was a fifty-five year old New England officer: hardheaded and testy, caustic and patently uncooperative with any civilian he viewed as meddling in military matters, so it was unsurprising that he and James S. Calhoun would soon come to loathe one another. Subordinate officers referred to him as "Bullhead Sumner" as a result of earlier having a musket ball bounced off his noggin. He had been a life long soldier, an original member of Colonel Dodge's First Dragoons and veteran of the Mexican War. The War Department had sent him to New Mexico with a mandate to cut costs, remove troops from their lives of sloth in the settlements and get them out onto the frontier facing down the savage Indian. One of Sumner's first intentions was to get U. S. troops out of Santa Fe, that stinking cesspool of vice and extravagance, and cared very little as to who he offended or enraged in the process.[10]

Shortly after coming into the territory, Sumner ordered up a new fort to serve as his headquarters and main military depot. He established it in the middle of nowhere, skirting the Santa Fe Trail on the isolated eastern plains just north of Las Vegas.[11] Having already broken up the posts at Rayado and Las Vegas, he informed his superiors he would do the same with Albuquerque, Abiquiu, Taos, Socorro and Cebolleta. Encamped in that windblown and forlorn site that was to become Fort Union, Colonel Sumner devoted his first month in New Mexico planning the fort's layout and fine-tuning his plans for a severe chastising of the Navajos. By mid August, Sumner's grand campaign was coming together. He would march into Navajo country on August 15th or thereabouts, taking four company of cavalry, three infantry and one artillery company.[12] His was a majestic vision of a war against the savage in which no quarter would be given. Once the trouncing was complete, the colonel would erect a fort in the heart of Navajo country from which the Army might flog the Indians whenever deemed necessary. There would be no treating or parley—only unconditional submission and humiliation would suffice. Sumner instructed Chandler at Cebolleta to hire as many scouts as needed to track the Indians' movements, to suppress Navajo raids while the main expedition was in Navajo land and, in all instances, to pursue the Navajos without mercy.[13] At the same time, Sumner initiated the Cebolleta post breakup, to the dismay of the local businessmen. Military equipment and supplies were cached in an impromptu and scantily guarded warehouse ten miles south at Laguna.

On August 17th, 1851 Colonel Sumner and his expedition of 350 soldiers, fifty wagons and a large herd of livestock got underway. They followed the Rio Grande as far as Albuquerque, then crossed to the west side and marched for Laguna. Henry L. Dodge may have joined the expedition there as sutler, responsible for the drovers, mules and other livestock earmarked for the new fort Sumner intended to plant in the heart of Navajo country. He apparently brought a herd of his own pack mules as well. Richard Kern, who accompanied the expedition, noted in his diary that when the expedition departed Laguna for Zuni, "Capt Dodge prevailed on the Col. to go over the Mountain", thereby making a more direct route.[14]

With the exception of one other entry by Kern, Dodge's activities during the march are unknown. There are three known records of Sumner's campaign, none of which directly mention Dodge: Sumner's official report, which was brief and lackluster, and the diaries of James Bennett of Company I, First Dragoons and Josiah M. Rice of the artillery, both of which were unreliable in their own peculiar ways. Richard Kern, known for his thoroughness and accuracy during Washington's campaign of 1849, only chronicled Chandler's march as far as Zuni, where he remained to join the Sitgreaves exploratory expedition of the Colorado River.

The two remaining accounts provide historians a valuable lesson in the virtues of skepticism. Bennett's work, published as *Forts and Forays: James A. Bennett, a Dragoon in New Mexico, 1850-1856*, was written from recollection long after events had transpired and proves erratic in relation to dates. Josiah M. Rice's journal, published under the title *A Cannoneer in Navajo Country, 1851* appeared at first blush to be an exquisite historical treasure. Unfortunately, Rice was a blatant plagiarist. He pilfered entire paragraphs from soldier Frank S. Edwards' *A Campaign in New Mexico with Colonel Doniphan*, published four years earlier. It is beyond doubt that Rice was present for Sumner's 1851 campaign, but almost everything he said that was unsubstantiated by Bennett's account deserves the utmost scrutiny.[15]

There is one other piece of evidence that Henry Dodge accompanied the expedition, and it is written in stone . . . literally. On the face of Inscription Rock, directly to the right of the first etching Dodge did on the Washington Expedition, *H. L. Dodge 1849*, appears in the same rude scrawl the etching *1851*.

Colonel Sumner's grand invasion hadn't gone far before it had its first hostile action. It would take them completely by surprise and provide Henry Dodge, who had taken his pack mule herd with the expedition, with his share of headaches. On Friday August 29th, just west of El Morro, Sumner's force camped where his predecessor Colonel Washington had two years earlier, in the meadows fringed by the small but crystalline Rio Pescado. Dodge, Kern and other companions probably spent the following Saturday hiking El Morro Rock, a few miles east of Sumner's command. That evening, moods turned sour when the head mule driver meekly approached Sumner to report that, somehow, Navajos had stealthily managed to run off all but two of the Army pack animals and all of Henry Dodge's mules. In his diary, Richard Kern related that Old Bullhead went ballistic. He ordered everyone up on high alert and had the expedition's livestock and mounts picketed near their camp. The following morning Kern noted that their loss was greater than first suspected.

> "Sunday 31. Awoke with a dark sky and gloomy prospect in the way of mule flesh staring us in the face—Capt. Dodge the Sutler had also lost all his mulada—Col. Sumner on being applied to for aid-Sent a command out under Lt. Field, who proceeded about two miles and said he could see nothing of the trail— "

As it happened, they found most of the missing animals an hour or two later. Forty five of them were located peacefully grazing in a nearby canyon. "Old Bull" as Kern referred to Sumner, decided to take up the march, despite the fact Henry's entire herd was still unaccounted for. Certain now that Navajos had not been responsible for running off the animals, Dodge sent a handful of men out to search for his mules. They found them without incident and brought them in after the expedition had arrived at Zuni.[16] Private Josiah Rice asserted that the hostiles had been wolves rather than Navajos, which seems to make sense insomuch as no signs of the Navajo had been seen. Nevertheless, it served as a cautionary lesson on the pitfalls of overconfidence. It wouldn't be Sumner's last pitfall.

The column reached Zuni the following day, September 1st. Rather than set camp at the pueblo, Colonel Sumner directed his men to encamp six miles or so east of the pueblo, near some natural water tanks.[17] Conceivably it could have been a near fatal decision. Keen on their own defense and unbeknownst to Sumner, the Zunis had booby trapped the trail to Navajo country with several concealed pits set with sharpened poles to discourage marauding Navajos. Whether or not Sumner's order to encamp away from the pueblo prevented him from learning of these booby traps is immaterial, the result was the same. The following morning, he confidently started off astride his steed at the head of the column. Rice bore witness to what happened next.

"Our Colonel . . . rode into one, and nigh killed his horse, and also, at the same time, our herder drove his flock of sheep into another, just below and killed three sheep, and caused us much trouble to get the remainder out."[18]

Sumner managed to extract himself. Reasserting his position in the saddle, he shook off the dust and resolutely led the column onward over rolling and sandy terrain. The troops reached the Rio Puerco of the West some 22 miles southwest of present day Gallup, New Mexico on September 2nd. From there, they proceeded due north into the juniper and pinyon forested mesas. On September 4th, they struck Black Creek, back tracking the route Washington's expedition had followed to Zuni in 1849.

As with most large expeditions encumbered by artillery, wagons and livestock, Colonel Sumner's lumbering columns preceded at a snail's pace. Not surprisingly, they did not encounter a single Navajo and saw no sign that the enemy was even in the area. The Indians were there, of course. Navajo sentinels watched the American's plodding progress from a dozen hidden positions.

At last Sumner came into the valley of Cañoncito Bonito. To the Navajos it was known as *Tsehootsoi*, Meadow of the Rock, a prized grazing and watering area. There was good water, wood and grass—a perfect place for a fort. Strangely, Sumner's final selection of the site, the mouth of a canyon cut into a low mesa, was clearly vulnerable. Once the fort was constructed, it would be open to fire from the canyon cliffs behind and from a rocky ridge top directly to the east. A determined and entrenched Navajo force would be able hold the high ground and rain lead down onto the parade ground as easily as a toddler pitching pennies into a cistern.

That fact apparently failed to disturb Sumner. With all due ceremony, the spot was christened Fort Defiance. It would soon be known to the troops serving there by a less flattering name . . . Hell's Gate. Major Electus Backus was given command and the arduous task of laying out and assembling the log and adobe fort buildings. On the 8th Bullhead Sumner left Backus, the infantry, the wagon train and a unit of artillery at the fort site and proceeded due north with his cavalry and two mountain howitzers.[19]

Presently a group of soldiers escorted a Navajo man—one of the first Navajos they'd seen—up to the Colonel. Sumner demanded an explanation as to his presence there. Was he a spy, then? Clearly, he'd been sent in to negotiate. Through the interpreter, the fellow explained he'd merely been watching the column pass when the soldiers spotted him and forced him to come into camp. Sumner demanded that three of his leaders come in immediately and they would have a talk, then sent the man back to his people. Predictably the headmen failed to appear, Sumner grimly declared "in pursuance of the instructions from the War Department," all Navajos would be treated as combatants, to be hunted and shot "whenever they were seen hovering about."[20]

The following day Sumner led his column northward, tracing the route that Henry Dodge had followed in 1849. Near Cienega Grande, they spied a group of Navajo men on a rocky prominence overlooking the trail. The Colonel, shouting up at them through the interpreter, asked what they wanted. Some bread and meat came the reply. According to Rice, Sumner retorted that if they didn't make tracks quickly, he'd deliver them bread and meat all right, from the barrel of a gun. Before disappearing the Navajos smugly replied that they'd give him plenty of the same once he and his Scorched-Kneecap Men entered Canyon de Chelly. Meanwhile, Sumner's dragoon horses and pack mules, already shockingly dilapidated from their journey to Navajo country, were beginning to keel over. As the expedition skirted the canyon ledge westward, animals collapsed and died at an alarming rate. Sumner ordered the rear guard to kill the lame and fallen mounts, lest the Navajos get hold of them. What animals fatigue failed to dispatch, the treachery of the trail did.

> "On leading down our pack mules, which had died with the exception of two, being very heavily loaded, and on making a slight stumble [one] went headlong down the rocks, dashing itself into a slapjack and leaving our rations in a manner that did not look over pleasing in our minds, being very scant, and the few left with blood and dough, it was a horrible sight."[21]

On September 14th, short of water, rations, pack mules and horses, Sumner's men finally descended into the mouth of Canyon de Chelly and camped along Chinle Wash. On the morning of September 15th, following a brief review and inspection, Bullhead moved his men up the canyon, intent on whipping the savages. Some eight miles in it became increasingly clear that it was the Americans who were the likely candidates for a whipping. From the clifftops overhead, Navajos began pouring musketry and arrows down on them, so much so that Sumner felt compelled to call his flankers in and out of range. In the relative safety of the middle of the canyon, the troopers stopped for a picnic.

> ". . . After traveling about two miles we came to a fine cornfield and a nice watermelon patch where we feasted sumptuously, with only an

occasional ball passing by. We destroyed the cornfield and the melon patch. A little farther forward we found a large and flourishing peach orchard. Here we regaled ourselves and filled our pockets and sacks but the lead balls began to fall thickly and we had no way to retaliate. Prospects look bad ahead with no visible outlet. We concluded as we found a shelter of rocks to remain there for the day."[22]

If Bennett's description can be relied upon, he and his comrades apparently expected to be massacred there in the canyon. Such scenario soon appeared likely. Four miles in, with the red cliffs towering over them like a supernatural castle keep, a shower of arrows, rocks and a scattering of musket balls again rained down on them. The frustrated soldiers could clearly see the Navajos overhead, infuriatingly beyond musket range. The fire got thicker as the Navajo warriors boldly harangued and derided them from the cliff tops. Suddenly from the rear, "ordering us to retreat back from under the crash, was heard the coarse, grim voice of the Col." and the men staggered back.[23] Sumner ordered a few rounds of howitzer shot toward the cliff tops to drive the combatants off. The booming cannon may have impressed and even terrified the Navajo, but it wrought no other damage than chipping the sandstone ramparts. The Americans continued up the canyon a total of some fourteen miles before making camp, all the while under the taunts and withering fire of the agile warriors on the precipices above.

The expedition finally came to a halt and encamped at a wide sandy area of the canyon. In the gathering gloom Sumner and his officers began to have doubts as to the sagacity of remaining there. Hunkered down in the dirt, they were in complete darkness, having no wood for campfires or even compunction for starting one, as it would transform the camp into a conveniently illuminated target. The Navajo were still sending potshots in through the darkness. Along the canyon parapets above, like an emerging cloud of glimmering fireflies, Indian campfires flickered to life, conjuring the ghastly specter of a vast, savage horde preparing to sweep down over them and tear the scalps from their heads.

Few Americans there were able to sleep, with perhaps the exception of Henry Dodge. Unlike the young and frightened recruits, he had a gritty, hand-to-hand familiarity with Indians warfare and tactics. The evening was spookily reminiscent of the tense night after the Battle of Wisconsin Heights nearly twenty years earlier, when Neopope's strange harangue had thrown the Suckers into panic. Dodge had a pretty good idea of what would probably transpire. Chances of an attack on the column were slim, provided they all stayed close. It would be the stragglers who'd get it. If Dodge shared that expertise with Sumner that night, it apparently didn't assuage the colonel's anxieties. The colonel called a brief conference of his officers. Their position was obviously untenable. Sumner then ordered a strategic redeployment of his men, one to be done in extreme silence.

> "Night came. Over our heads and around us were to be seen at least 1000 little fires. The dark forms of the savages were seen moving about them. A council of our officers was called. All concluded 'twas best for us to retrace our steps as no one knew the country and the Indians by far outnumbered us. Saddled our horses about 10 o'clock and started back through the darkness."[24]

Rather than retreat, the soldiers advanced intending to slip out through the canyon's broad western entrance. One contemporary observer dryly noted that Sumner's maneuver was "thought by some [done] rather hurriedly." Josiah Rice described the late night move in less than heroic terms.

> "We slowly marched down the winding Cañon for three or four miles when I espied in the rocks, about four hundred feet from the ground, live embers of fire. I immediately whispered to the Lieut., "See that fire?" "Yes." "Do you see it, Col.?" "Where? No, I don't see it. Hurry up a little faster, Mr. Griffin." It seemed the Col. had changed his mind materially as we were marching in. It was "Take your time, Mr. Griffin," but now it was, "Hurry up a little faster, Mr. Griffin."[25]

They were all scared stiff. During the retreat, Rice claimed to have had a ball pass just over his head, while the company's musician took an arrow in the left arm. In his official report, Sumner's explanation made for less exciting reading. He state that as the road was getting worse and his outnumbered force completely defenseless, "I thought it prudent and proper to leave the canyon, which I did the same evening and happily without loss." He also mentions his orderly was shot the following day, in camp at the mouth of Canyon de Chelly, and wounded slightly.[26]

Frustrated, Old Bullhead ordered his force out of the canyon altogether and struck the trail south along Chinle Valley towards Fort Defiance. The troops moved through the valley for four days. On the evening of September 19th, Private Rice and his comrades gathered at the campfire to attempt to have a meager cup of coffee and softened hardtack. Lieutenant Griffin volunteered to give it a taste. Raising the cup to his lips, he took a sip, smacked his lips and, in three words effectively summed up not only the coffee but possibly the entire campaign.

"Shit, by God," he intoned, "Shit."

According to Rice, shortly thereafter the flash of musket lit the camp and a thicket of Navajo arrows sailed in, pin cushioning Sumner's tent and wounding his orderly. Although Sumner later claimed in his report that during the entire campaign his troops had killed and wounded several Indians, the only confirmable enemy casualty came that evening. Both Bennett and Rice mention the incident. A Navajo warrior had slipped in among the picketed dragoon horses in hopes of lassoing one, apparently oblivious to the three privates and dragoon Sergeant Good of K Company concealed behind a scrub oak thicket nearby.

> "The Sergeant, being the only one awake, fired his carbine, which the ball passed through the pit of his chest. At this, the Indian resisted, to stick the Sergeant, when he drew his horse pistol from his waist belt, and shot him again through the brain. At this, the Indian fell to the ground but strove to get up again. At this, the Sergeant took the Indian's knife and cut his throat, which, in deep groans, he died. . . . His scalp was taken off and his war cap was given to Capt. Dodds, a Volunteer Officer, who took it to Fort Defiance, and his bow and arrows given to 1st Lieut. Whistler of I Company, 3rd Infantry . . ."[27]

The warrior's corpse was cut up to a fair-thee-well by the troopers. As for the mysterious Captain Dodds, the man may have been Henry Dodge, who had been a volunteer captain and yet held the honorific rank. The following day, Sumner led his column back to Fort Defiance. They marched on foot, leading what remained of their exhausted animals, fervently wishing that upon reaching the fort, they'd fall deathly ill and thereby have the luxury of being able to ride home in the wagons.

Thus ended Sumner's first and only expedition against the Navajo. Its effects fell far short of what he had hoped, a regret he confessed in his official report.

> "This expedition was not as decisive as I could wish, but I believe it was as much so, as I ought to have expected. It was hardly possible to close an Indian war of many years standing by one expedition."[28]

Sumner's foray into the canyon to wage destruction had been a failure. His grand vision, in that sense, had actually been delusion. One salient lesson he'd learned was that American cavalry horses were incapable of surviving a march into Navajo terrain and were no match for the Indian ponies, advising that the next expedition be composed of infantry. Sumner remained confident, however, that five well-supplied companies at Fort Defiance could harass and punish the Indians until they embraced peace. Keeping those companies supplied would be no small task. Defiance was at that time the most remote American garrison in the West, nearly two hundred miles distant from the point of re-supply, Albuquerque. The nearest reliable source of food was through seventy miles of hostile country south to Zuni. Should Fort Defiance fail to subdue the Navajo, Sumner concluded nothing less than a war of complete extermination would be required.[29]

30

WILD AS HAWKS

Sumner's abrupt break up of the Cebolleta garrison in the late summer of 1851 came as a double blow to Henry Dodge. The loss of his government job was distressing enough, but Dodge and Tullis also witnessed the near vaporization of business at their Chupadero store. Indeed, the entire Cebolleta area felt the pangs of being so unceremoniously dumped by the Army, a pain they shared with businessmen up and down the Rio Grande. The esteemed business leaders in Santa Fe, heretofore well heeled by Uncle Sam's greenbacks, were absolutely howling. The loss of Army security was worrisome enough, but the denial of Army specie was intolerable. True to form however, Sumner was neither moved nor cowed by the protest.

It appears the Dodge & Tullis Company was able to stay in business for a time, but the end was inevitable. Dodge himself claimed residence at either Cebolleta or Laguna during the fall and in late October was still stocking his inventory by buying over one thousand dollars worth of merchandise, primarily clothing and cloth from traders Simon Delgado and Henry Connelly, the ex-governor of the ex-State of New Mexico.[1] Although he frequently teetered on the precipice of poverty, Henry had always avoided falling in by trolling for any opportunity to make a buck. A particularly enticing prospect appears of have hooked him in early 1852, and the lure was gold.

Gold fever was an epidemic apparently without cure and it had swept the nation. The gold strikes in California in '49 drew many to the west, including scores of would-be millionaires from Dodge's old stomping grounds at Dodgeville and Mineral Point. So many Badgers deserted the fields of lead for those of gold that the economy of southwest Wisconsin crumbled into recession. Henry's own sister and brother in law, Elizabeth and Paschal Bequette and their seven children, made the three month wagon journey to Sacramento via Salt Lake City. Paschal had no intention of grubbing in the mines. Having been appointed U. S. Lands Receiver for California by President Pierce, he had a dependable and decidedly cleaner employment. It was nice to have friends in high places.[2]

Without a doubt, the desertion rate among the troops in New Mexico was fueled by the allure of California gold. For those New Mexican citizens more reluctant to cut ties and make such an arduous journey, there were hopes that El Dorado might be found somewhere closer to home—such as the headwaters of the Gila River in southwest New Mexico, rumored to abound in undiscovered wealth. When John Russell Bartlett visited the area with the United States/Mexican Boundary Commission in 1850, he did much to fuel that speculation.

> "Gold is said to have been found here when the mines were worked; and many stories are told of large quantities that were buried when the place was abandoned. About four miles distant, a deep shaft had been sunk, where it was said a skin containing more than five thousand dollars worth of gold had been buried. Several men took their discharge here for the purpose of clearing out the shaft and getting the buried treasure. After several weeks labor, they reached the bottom, and even dug some feet below; but their search was not rewarded with success."[3]

Bartlett's protégé, John Cremony, reinforced the story by claiming gold had actually been discovered a stone's throw from their encampment at Santa Rita del Cobre or, as the Americans knew it, The Copper Mines. The claim peaked interests in Santa Fe and in 1851, Hezekiah Johnston, the editor of Albuquerque's Rio Abajo News, led a group of hopefuls to scope out the possibilities.[4] Four-dozen American and Hispanic men, including Henry L. Dodge and James Calhoun's son-in-law William E. Love, joined Johnston's expedition for the hazardous fifteen-day trip into the Gila. Mindful of Apaches, Love approached Colonel Sumner and suggested that since Sumner was going to garrison a fort there anyway, could he please detail a dozen dragoons and two howitzers to accompany the expedition? Predictably,

Sumner refused. Johnston, Love, Dodge & Company would have to go it alone.[5]

The country southward from Albuquerque rapidly degenerated into a parched and desolate region, the road plagued with a fiery sun, deep sand and stinging dust storms. Even the once inviting mountains to the east seemed to desiccate into jagged rubble as the expedition passed the dust-covered adobe hamlets clinging to life along the Rio Grande: Tome, Socorro, San Pedro, and San Diego. Somewhere below Las Palomas, the party abruptly turned west away from the river and climbed into the Black Mountain range, a challenging labyrinth of steep, convoluted ridges bristling with parched pine. Eventually, they descended and forded the cool, clear and soothing Mimbres River, then continued westward, skirting the Pinos Altos Range to the north. Several miles further, a lofty red stone pinnacle emerged ahead of them. It was said that the column was possessed by the condemned soul of a Jesuit convent nun who in eons past had been executed for some odious and unnatural act. The rock eventually became known as the Kneeling Nun, though it would also be called the Kneeling Virgin and the Kneeling Jesus, possibly by those pious souls offended by the more titillating version of the telling.

Upon arriving at the Copper Mines, any dream Dodge or the others may have nurtured for a quick fortune were dashed. The gold, if it even existed, proved elusive . . . too much so for the impatient prospectors.

> "That expedition was attended with no beneficial results, not because gold did not exist, but for want of industry in a majority of its seekers."[6]

The failure and quick return of Johnston's expedition to Santa Fe may have resulted as much from the uncomfortable proximity of the Gila Apache as from indolence. At any rate, a good number of the "Gila Boys" probably decided California was the better option after all.[7] However, Dodge apparently wasn't deterred. He saw opportunity at Santa Rita. Gold may have existed there in minute amounts, certainly . . . but should it remain undiscovered there were other ores from which to extract a living and, if that failed, the proximity of a new Army post and bands of Indians there guaranteed more dependable and less arduous business opportunities.

The region was already famous for copper, a metal less alluring than gold, but for decades paying enough to induce Mexican prospectors to brave isolation and the hazards of the indignant Chiricahua Apaches, upon whose land they burrowed and to whom they paid trade goods for the favor. As early as 1798, Spanish explorers touted the exceptional quality of Santa Rita's copper ore. Two years later, mining had begun in earnest. Roughly two years after that, Don Francisco Manuel Elguea erected a small presidio in the valley.[8] As Bartlett noted, it was small but extraordinarily stout, a "triangular form, each side presenting a front of about 200 feet, with circular towers on the corners." The walls were at least three feet thick, breached only once by a narrow gate opening to the east.[9] By 1804 mining the Valle de Santa Rita de Cobre supported up to six hundred miners and their families. Arable land was almost nonexistent in that jagged landscape, so all supplies had to be freighted in from the distant valleys of San Miguel and Casa Grandes to the south. The mined ore was loaded on ox carts and hauled down to central Mexico, where it brought a good enough price to make the effort worthwhile.[10]

Staying in good standing with the Indians was paramount. The nearest military post was at Janos, Sonora, one hundred and fifty miles hard ride, so the survival of the mines hinged precariously on the cooperativeness of the Chiricahua Apache, a people dismissed lightly only at the peril of one's life. Their fame as legendary raiders was well-earned, and they were dreaded by the settlements of Chihuahua, Sonora and New Mexico. Variously referred to in the journals and correspondence as the Gila Apache, the Mimbres Apache, the Copper Mine Apaches, among other names, it was with the Eastern Chiricahua that Henry Dodge would become familiar, if not intimate.[11]

When Mexico earned its independence from Spain, the garrison at Janos abruptly shrank to a mere twenty soldiers. As a result, the number of prospectors at Santa Rita dwindled. Robert McKnight, an American, began working the mines around 1826. With careful planning and edgy diplomacy he was able to keep the Apache satisfied and make a good living as well. However, that ten-year collaboration abruptly ended in 1837, shortly after a party headed by an Englishman named Johnson appeared at McKnight's diggings. Johnson was there on business, but it wasn't mining. With McKnight's concurrence, he arranged a feast for the local Chiricahua leaders and their kin, notably Juan José and a young Mangas Coloradas. The British gentleman intended to serve up more than victuals to his guests. The Mexican government was offering large bounties on Apache scalps and Johnson intended to harvest some. When niceties had been disposed of and the Apache settled down to eat, Johnson and his conspirators produced a cannon rather than a banquet, and loosed a scythe of grape shot directly into the Indians. They then opened up on the survivors with pistol and musket ball, killing Juan José and slaughtering scores of his people. With his belt draped in fresh scalps, Johnson departed Santa Rita, leaving McKnight and the other miners to shoulder the repercussions of his murderous enterprise.

Miraculously, Mangas Coloradas managed to escape the slaughter and flee into the mountains. His people promptly regrouped and dispatched war parties, severing the supply lines to Janos and forcing McKnight to abandon the mines. Legend tells that from that bloody year on, Mangas Coloradas waged an unyielding war of vengeance, repeatedly exercising his right to bear the ghoulish Spanish name given him, Red Sleeves, for his practice of dipping his shirt in the blood of his victims.

When the U. S. Boundary Commission and their escort of some 250 men arrived in January 1851 to survey America's newly conquered territory, the mines, the settlement and the presidio were deserted. The Commission renamed the presidio Cantonment Dawson, although within a year it would become Fort Webster under the command of Colonel Craig and one company of Second Dragoons.[12] Not surprisingly, Mangas Coloradas initially had applauded Kearny's victory over the Mexican and considered himself an ally of the United States. It was Mangas' captain, Cuchillo Negro, who had led Bartlett's party to the mine site with assurances that the Apache desired peace.

Promises and abrazos not withstanding, Bartlett and associates found their hosts wary at best. Conversely, the Americans' view of the Chiricahua was tinged with contempt and suspicion. John Cremony recounted his first view of the fabled Apache, a group of unarmed Chiricahua who had come in for a visit, shortly after pitching camp. He described them as "the most villainous looking Apaches it is possible to conceive," noting that while snow lay a half foot deep everywhere and the weather was bitingly cold, the warriors "were wholly nude, with the exception of a diminutive breechcloth . . ."[13]

And thus the American-Chiricahua relationship remained, fraught with uneasiness and mistrust. While the Americans saw the Apache as unprincipled savages, Mangas Coloradas and his people considered the whites stubborn and basically unfriendly nature. On one friendly Apache visit to Bartlett's camp, two captive Mexican boys bolted from their Apache owners and ducked into Cremony's tent in hopes of escape. Cremony immediately resolved to save the boys from a life of savagery and refused to surrender them. Mangas Coloradas lodged a protest.

> "You came to our country. You were well received. Your lives, your property, your animals were safe. You passed by ones, by twos, by threes through our country. You went and came in peace. Your strayed animals were always brought home to you again. Our wives, our women and children came here and visited your houses. We were friends-we were brothers! Believing this, we came among you and brought our captives, relying on it that we were brothers and that you would feel as we feel?"[14]

When Cremony remained adamant, the headman Delgadito brokered a face-saving exchange. Cremony could have the boys for the price of twenty horses. The obstinate Americans summarily rejected that offer and several others as well before prudently reconsidering their own tenuous position in the Apache stronghold. In the interest of peace, Bartlett offered to buy off the owner with a payment of dry goods. It was an insult, but reluctantly, the perturbed Apache accepted. The deal was struck and the boys freed, but the incident had poisoned the well of friendship. By that summer the Chiricahua were regularly raiding Bartlett's party, at one point in July running off scores of Commission mules and, in August stampeding Fort Webster's livestock, as well as those eighteen hardy mules that Captain John Buford, late of Cebolleta, used to pull the garrison's supply wagons from Doña Ana on the Rio Grande. Shortly after that, Bartlett and the Commission left for the Rio San Pedro and Tucson, doubtlessly relieved to be done with their tenure in Apache Country.[15]

The Commission was gone, but the conflict lived on. The Army was less than enthusiastic on keeping peace with the Apache and on more than one occasion selected hot lead as their tool of diplomacy. In January, when a group of Chiricahua envoys led by Delgadito arrived at Fort Webster, three officers of the post, Major Richardson, Lieutenant O'Bannon and Doctor Hammond chose to parley with pistols. O'Bannon's gun failed to fire, but the good surgeon Hammond was able to wing Delgadito in the back as the Indians ran for their lives, so the encounter was seen as not a total loss.[16] The immediate result of Hammond's pot shot was an end to Apache peace overtures and an escalation of Apache raids. Colonel Sumner ordered the cantankerous Major Howe and his men to give the Gila Apaches a thorough flogging and teach them an enduring lesson. The campaign produced little result—depending on whom one asked—and was generally seen as an ill-planned fiasco.[17] The enduring lesson learned by the Chiricahua was that the Americans could do little to really harm them.

Henry Dodge probably made his appearance at Santa Rita in March of 1852 on the heels of Howe's abortive campaign, so security at the Copper Mines remained in chaos. Apaches had been hostile all winter and the presence of Fort Webster had failed to stymie Apache raids. Dodge had come to prospect and it is unknown if he had come alone. Circumstances at the mines undoubtedly hampered Henry's labors. The lives and livestock of the miners were in daily peril from Chiricahua raids, and merely traveling in the region demanded the protection of hefty and heavily armed bodyguards. Frustrated miners were eager to get at the Apache, and Dodge shared their sentiment. In a scathing report to Colonel Sumner over Howe's failed expedition, the commander at Fort Webster, Major Gouverneir Morris, 3rd Infantry, stated that if the colonel wouldn't give Major Morris a command to properly chastise the Apache, at least allow him to muster a company of fervent miners that had suddenly appeared pounding at his office door.

> "Capt Dodge who was formerly in the Service under Col Washington, W. Love Postmaster of Santa Fe and W. King of Socorro are here with a party of over sixty-men, who are willing to be enrolled for this duty, and from the efficient and known character of the individuals composing this party, I feel confident they would render the State some service."[18]

On April 1st, Sumner turned down Morris' request. There had been jitters in Santa Fe over rumors of another Taos style insurrection. The Hispanic population of New Mexico once more was seething—not a good time to be sending troops out into the wilderness. Sumner also nixed mustering the miners but instructed Morris to do what was "prudent & beneficial." He specifically asked Morris to have Mangas Coloradas persuade the Apache leaders to come in to Santa Fe for a peace meeting.[19]

By the end of May, most of the miners had moved on or gone home, as much for a lack of productive prospecting as from the Apache inroads. Once more, the mines at Santa Rita lay neglected. Major Morris proposed moving Fort Webster to a better location. The original purpose of garrisoning the old presidio was to protect the prospectors at the Copper Mines, who had subsequently left.[20] Sumner agreed and Fort Webster was relocated fourteen miles east of the Copper Mines, along the banks of the Mimbres River. There was water, wood and grass aplenty, but from its inception the new Fort Webster was a rough affair of mud and logs and tents, lots of tents. Furthermore, it was no closer to a supply depot than it was at Santa Rita, with provisions coming through either Fort Fillmore 135 miles distant or through Fort Conrad, 150 miles away.[21] Yes, it was closer to the California trail loping across the desert to the south and theoretically could provide protection to emigrant trains, but in practical application, the new site was an insignificant improvement and a little over a year later, it was abandoned in favor of Fort Thorn on the Rio Grande.[22]

Through it all, Henry Dodge kept his interests in the Gila region alive, dividing his time between enterprises at Laguna and at the Copper Mines. Among his various ventures, Henry made a living selling ponies and mules to Sumner's horse-starved army posts. Although there is no record of his official licensure as an Indian trader or of having such a contract with the Army, there is evidence he had come to know Mangas Coloradas and had finagled a trading relationship with the Chiricahua. From whence these fine steeds came didn't appear to bother Henry. The fact that he sold a mule bearing upon its rump the bold brand "US" to an Army teamster, Henry Carpenter, indicated at least some of animals were filched in raids.[23] That raised a good bit of soldierly outrage over the idea of Dodge dealing in stolen U.S. property and all. Certain officers even demanded Sumner hold Dodge accountable for conspiring with and giving comfort to the enemy.[24]

Nothing ever came of it. If the mule had been taken in war, whether by Navajo or Apache, it could be seen as acquired through the well-accepted but unwritten conventions of war as spoils. Sumner perhaps shrugged it off as a minor embarrassment. After all, he had contracted with Dodge to provide sturdy ponies. Henry continued to provide horses to the Army through May of 1852, delivering eight mounts to the post at Albuquerque for $40 a head, which the suspicious commander Major Rucker accepted only after being assured by Lieutenant Robertson that Dodge indeed had a contract with the Army.[25]

Henry Dodge's relationship with Mangas Coloradas and the Chiricahua put him in a unique position as an intermediary of sorts. He seemed to have a knack for that kind of thing. Dodge had mediated, albeit unsuccessfully, a boundary dispute between the incessantly quarreling pueblos of Acoma and Laguna three years before. The reputation of the Apache as dangerous and formidable enemies made Dodge's latest role that much more remarkable, though he himself might have just shrugged it off. Mangas must have trusted Dodge enough to hold him in some confidence. So while in Santa Fe, Dodge met with territorial secretary John Greiner on May 31st, to discuss peace with the Apache.

By coincidence, Greiner had that day officially become the interim Governor and Superintendent of Indian Affairs. His superior James Calhoun had been seriously sick for sometime, but when his health plummeted that spring, he decided to try and reach his family in Georgia before he died. Prostrate in the back of a lurching ambulance, James Calhoun had departed the capital earlier that day, so certain he'd not survive the trip that he had his own coffin built and loaded in an accompanying wagon. Even Sumner was moved by the sight. The governor's prophecy proved accurate. On July 2nd, Calhoun died on the Santa Fe Trail, still hundreds of miles from his beloved Georgia. His son in law William Love buried him in the little town of Kansas, Missouri, to allow Calhoun's corpse to decompose "sufficiently to enable his friends to take him home and place him along side of his wife and daughter."[26] His bones never made it home and to this day rest beneath the sod of Union Cemetery in modern day Kansas City.

Calhoun and Greiner had worked diligently to arrange for a Chiricahua treaty meeting and Dodge may have been instrumental in setting up a preliminary conference at Acoma to dispel Apache apprehensions. Henry assured Greiner that the Apache were quiet, well behaved and most fervently desirous of peace. It was encouraging news. The following day, Dodge accompanied Greiner to Acoma.

"Wed. June 2d, 1852, Mr. Greiner left this morning towards Acoma in company with Mr. Dodge of Laguna, and an Indian from the Pueblo of Jemez in order to meet the Apaches . . . having themselves sent in word to this superintendency that they wished for some person authorized and invested with powers to talk and treat with them, being a matter of great importance, Mr. Greiner thought advisable to comply with their request by going out to see them, and finding out if possible their true wishes and design towards making peace"[27]

Dodge followed up this meeting with a letter to Greiner early in June, indicating that the Chiricahua had agreed to meet with the acting governor on June 15th, but cautioned not to pin his hopes on it.

"Messenger from Santo Domingo, brought letter from Capt. Dodge at Laguna that the Gila Apaches would probably be in about the 15" inst, They have been told that a trap was laid for them, to get them in here and kill them off, probably will prevent them from coming in, he also states that the governor of Acoma sent out ten men to the Gila Apaches, probably be in about the 15" inst. Genl Baird was expected the day after the letter was written and he would see to it."[28]

Judge Spruce M. Baird, having severed his ties with Texas, was the newly appointed Indian Agent for New Mexico and was living in Albuquerque. It was Baird's responsibility to work with Dodge to bring Mangas and his people to the treaty table.[29]

On June 14th, Agent Baird informed Greiner that Dodge had made all the arrangements necessary with the Apache, though he had doubts as well as to whether they'd actually show up.[30] At roughly the same time, Major Morris at Fort Webster confirmed with Sumner what Dodge had been telling Greiner. He'd met with Cuchillo Negro at Fort Webster, who promised to encourage Mangas, Delgadito and other principal Chiricahua men to come in to Santa Fe.[31] Clearly the Apache desired peace and were willing to meet as a nation at Acoma Pueblo. It was a neutral ground and the people of Acoma were known to be on good terms with the Chiricahua. The crucial question then was would Colonel Sumner of the Army, in the interest of territorial tranquility and harmony, bring himself to make peace with John Greiner of the Indian Service. Given the colonel's previous track record, the prognosis was grim.

On July 1st, 1852 Mangas Coloradas and a delegation of Chiricahua headmen appeared at the Governor's Palace in Santa Fe to endorse a preliminary agreement for a treaty of peace with Colonel E. V. Sumner, John Greiner and Spruce M. Baird representing the Americans. Sumner had usurped the role of acting governor of New Mexico, regulating John Greiner to acting territorial superintendent of Indian Affairs. Spruce M. Baird signed the document as witness to Mangas' signature.[32] The delegates agreed that the Chiricahua and Americans would meet again at Acoma in ten days to consummate the treaty in the presence of the Apache nation.

Even with that spirit of hope and reconciliation, relations between Sumner and Calhoun's loyal secretary John Greiner were strained. Both men had planned to meet independently with Mangas and his Chiricahua at Acoma, and each man jealously claimed to be the sole representative empowered to execute a treaty. When Greiner requested a military escort to the meeting, Sumner promptly refused. He replied rather imperiously that since he himself was planning to meet at the same time with the Chiricahua at Acoma, he'd let Greiner come along for the ride, should he choose to do so. Greiner replied with scorn. He agreed to "accompany" the troops, but proclaimed that Sumner's audacious seizure of civil authority wouldn't stop him, the dedicated civil servant, from doing his job.

In spite of the animosity, on the appointed day Sumner, Greiner, Agent Baird, together with a column of soldiers, approached Acoma in high anticipation. Henry Dodge met them along the trail near Laguna, in the course of conversation mentioning that the Navajos in the area were peaceful. The entire affair must have gripped John Greiner's imagination, for he kept copious and detailed notes along the way.

> "Sunday, July 11" 1852. Acoma, great rocky pillars, sundry roads, houses built of adobes and stones, steep ascent to the town by a foot path, fine view from the town, church 100 feet long, 40 feet high-they have fine flocks of sheep and goats, made arrangement with Navajos not to steal their stock, Mexican traders will have to be stop soon-they have to carry their wood and water up the hill, population about 150 men in arms, Laguna about 200-Navajos about here very kind-Apaches are to be in at noon . . ."

The company arrived at Acoma, only to find that Mangas Coloradas and his people had failed to appear. Discouragement set in as Greiner and Sumner fretted that the carefully crafted meeting would fail before even getting under way. They were encouraged to learn the Apache had camped some distance outside the pueblo, hesitating with understandable suspicion as to the Americans' intentions. A group of friendly Navajo suggested that Greiner entice the Chiricahua to come up into Acoma with a gift for Mangas and a promise of a feast. Having nothing to give, Greiner turned to Baird, pried twenty dollars out of him and sent it out to the Chiricahua chief. Mangas accepted Greiner's gesture and the Apache entered Acoma.

Greiner need not have worried. It was in Mangas Coloradas' complete interest to nail down a peace agreement with the Americans. His people had escalated their long battle with Mexico's northern settlements and couldn't accommodate fighting the Americans at the same time. Mangas was an imposing man, both in stature and posture. Greiner referred to him as "a magnificent looking Indian . . . the master spirit of his tribe." He strutted into Sumner's tent, sat down and told the colonel that they should immediately undertake negotiations. Although Mangas protested the Americans' insistence that he cease his war across the border with Mexico, he and his delegation of headmen promptly approved the treaty.[33] Meanwhile the Chiricahua feasted; consuming no less than forty-two sheep. There seemed to be a seldom seen spirit of cooperation and hope wafting in the air.

> "Monday July 12" 1852. Made treaty with Mangas Coloradas, yesterday Apaches wild as hawks, afraid to come in, Mangas is however their chief captain and councilor and can speak for all his people, he promises fair for them, Navajos and Pueblos they all appear satisfied and contented . . ."[34]

The road to peace with the Chiricahua remained relatively smooth following the treaty at Acoma, with the exception of a few bumps. There were some Apache depredations in September; Fort Webster cattle had been run off, several U. S. mules had vanished; James Owenby had lost his mule—a small loss compared to the one he suffered at the Cebolleta garrison hay camp the year before.[35] By December the new Apache Indian Agent Edward Wingfield stationed three quarters miles from Fort Webster on the Mimbres noted the Chiricahua had run off 26 head of stock from a local citizen, one Mr. Duvall. He also mentioned that as he was coming across to Webster from Fort Conrad on the Rio Grande, well within U. S. territory, his party came across one hundred Mexican dragoons pursing Apaches. Clearly Mangas

Coloradas' war with Mexico was yet raging.[36] Nevertheless that was a violation that the Americans would address with nothing more than a little lip service.

31

HEARTH AND HOME

"Once the game is over, the king and the pawn go back in the same box."
Italian Proverb

Time has a distressing way of erasing people.

With few exceptions individuals celebrated and admired—people so prominent that simply asking who they might be would elicit an astonished stare—all end up forgotten. Famous or unremarkable, they die and ultimately the memory of them dies, as well. Frequently, the evidence vouching for the fact they'd even lived disappears. Town halls, county courthouses and libraries are destroyed by flood or fire or war, and the archives go with them: land conveyances, tax rolls, the crumbling probate files, the parched dry newspapers and yellowing correspondence. The United States Federal Census for 1890 was nearly completely destroyed in 1921 when a fire swept the Commerce Department in Washington, DC. It seems there had only been a single copy of that census. In moments, the only testament to the existence of tens of thousands of people was obliterated.

For the great majority of those souls whose historical records did survive, their names stare up from the crumbling parchment completely mute, made anonymous by the sorcery of time. The United States Army hired hundreds of American civilians to serve as teamsters during the Mexican War. Their names are painstakingly listed in the National Archives, found to this day in folded, brittle paper packets, still carefully tied with red ribbon a century old. There are names inside to be read if one is willing to risk shattering the document by opening it, but the reward proves disappointing. The names are there, but are as empty and anonymous as the faded pen strokes that made them.

To an extent, Henry L. Dodge narrowly avoided such anonymity. He wrote no private correspondence, kept no journal, and saved no personal finances. The scant historical records remaining from that period only hint at how Henry divided his time between Chupadero and the Copper Mines in 1852. It appears that he spent a greater amount of time around the Cebolleta area as summer drifted into autumn, attending to business matters. He was a moderately influential person, again demonstrating that influence by mediating a spat between the aggravated people of Laguna Pueblo and one fervent Baptist preacher from Ohio. Still, Dodge's impact proved, in the end, short-lived. In four years he'd be gone. In five or six years his name might come up in idle conversation; in a decade the mention of Henry L. Dodge might spark a vague memory at best. At Chupadero tucked among the canyon mesas, along Cebolleta's wind-swept streets, on the plaza of Albuquerque and in the monte parlors of Santa Fe, nothing of him would remain to testify that, among the familiar New Mexican names of Sandoval, Chavez, Candelaria or Baca, the peculiar sounding moniker of Dodge had ever been heard.

It is therefore particularly startling that, more than a century later, in an isolated cemetery on the outskirts of a New Mexican town Henry Dodge had never known, in a canyon he'd never seen, his own name would resurface, carried by someone that he could have only conjured up in a moment of self-indulgent fantasy.

It was a solemn scene, one more melancholic than sentimental. In a tumbledown graveyard perched on a sandy incline skirting a canyon wall, a funeral procession halted among the slightly awry tombstones. New Mexico was unkind to monuments of remembrance. Wind and rain quickly effaced names and dates on sandstone markers and wooden crosses alike, and what remained the sands finally consumed. An intense stillness descended over the Campo Santo, broken only by the sound of the breeze furtively whisking through the sage and the measured intonations of the parish priest. In the valley below, the banks of the Rio Pecos had blossomed in thatches of spring alfalfa and fresh cottonwood leaves, and peering through the trees, the solitary Church of Nuestra Señora del Refugio bore witness as the casket was lowered into the earth. Presently a gloomy cadence echoed along the cliffs—the thump, thump, thumping of dirt raining down on the casket—then gradually faded as the grave filled.

The poor fellow hadn't been particularly old . . . only sixty four . . . but dead nevertheless. A miniscule tin-styled marker from the Lucas-Wooten Mortuary in Santa Rosa was placed one end of the flower-strewn mound.

HENRY DODGE—JULY 18, 1901 - MAY 23, 1966

It was a pathetic memorial, but there would be time to get a decent headstone . . . someday.

Santa Rosa sat on the vast *Llano Estacado* of New Mexico, situated some 120 miles due east of Albuquerque. Over the centuries a string of Hispanic farming towns had sprung up along the Pecos River rolling southward out of the Santa Fe Mountains; Pecos of Montezuma's fire, San Miguel, Villanueva and Anton Chico of Comanche fame. Much later, towns bearing Anglo American names and sensibilities followed the river as it meandered three hundred miles into Texas; past infamous Fort Sumner, Roswell, Carlsbad, past Rio Pecos and Sheffield, Texas, then struggling another 200 miles through the parched west Texas desert before surrendering as a mere trickle to the Rio Grande.

By New Mexico standards, Santa Rosa was a new town. It was only first settled in 1865 and was known as *Agua Negra Chiquita*, or Small Black Spring. It was renamed Santa Rosa in 1890, after the chapel built there by Don Celso Baca in honor of his mother and the saint, Santa Rosa de Lima. With the arrival of the railroad, Santa Rosa was transformed from a backwater village to a town of some importance—important enough to be designated the seat of Guadalupe County. Santa Rosa boasted of having a railroad, a huge natural artesian well called the Big Blue Hole and being featured in the railroad scene from the movie *Grapes of Wrath*. It also had a newspaper, the Santa Rosa News. Late in May of 1966, the paper ran an obituary.

> "Henry Dodge, 64, former long time resident of Santa Rosa and Guadalupe County, died in an Albuquerque Hospital Monday afternoon following an illness of about one month..."

Henry had spent most of his life within a hundred-fifty mile radius of Santa Rosa, living for a time in Clovis, where he'd worked for the Santa Fe Railroad. He'd lost his wife, Dominga Madrid Dodge in 1936, when he was still a young man and remained a widower for the next 24 years. After retiring in 1960, he married the widow Adela Gallegos. They had lived the following five years in Albuquerque before Henry fell fatally ill. Adela survived him, as did four sons, three daughters and two older brothers, Herman and Andres Dodge.[1]

Certainly there was no shortage of Dodges in the region, in or out of cemeteries. That in itself was not particularly surprising. Dodge was a common Protestant Anglo Saxon surname found throughout the United States. What was notable was that the Dodges of Santa Rosa were not of Anglo Saxon stock at all, but were as deeply Hispanic as old New Mexico itself. Henry... some would say Enrique... had been born at a time when Spanish names and the Spanish tongue were nearly universal. Nevertheless, among the overwhelming flood of Spanish names of the children listed by the 1910 Federal Census, that strapping nine-year-old boy's name was written clearly in English. Not Enrique, but Henry. Let the name not deceive, for in all aspects of appearance, language and habit, Henry was an Enrique.[2]

Henry's parents were Román and Cayetana Dodge and, by the standards of the times, they had had a moderately sized family. In order there had been Mártin born in 1880, then the boys Bernabí and Esteván. A series of girls followed beginning with María Juana in 1886, then Predicanda, Martina, and Marcelina, followed up by the boy Andrés and the girl Anastacia. Henry came in 1901 and the baby Román Junior in 1903. Typical of the times, Román and Cayetana lost five of their twelve children before adulthood: Mártin, Esteván, María Juana, Marcelina and an unknown infant. The loss of any child was tragic, but losing María Juana might have been particularly poignant. She had been named for Román's mother, Juana Sandoval, who had the honor of witnessing the girl's baptism as her *madrina*, or godmother.[3]

The Dodges lived in the small hamlet of Puerto de Luna, ten miles south of Santa Rosa. Although there is no evidence of it today, Puerto de Luna had been the seat of Guadalupe County before surrendering the honor to Santa Rosa. It was founded in 1863, after the close of the Indian wars, and if its history was relatively shallow, its folklore ran deep. It earned its poetic name from Coronado's conquistadors who had camped there in 1641. They had been so inspired by the beauty of the moon rising through a cleft in the bluffs they named the site *Refuge of the Moon*. It was a lovely spot indeed, a wide sandstone canyon embracing broad and fertile farm land, watered by cliff side springs and the gentle Pecos—an oasis where one could lounge for hours under the cottonwoods and feel no guilt whatsoever over being blissfully idle.

Henry's father Román hadn't been born and raised at Puerto de Luna, but he had spent his entire adult life there. He was known as a generous community member and influential local leader. Unfortunately, Henry never had a chance to really know his father. Román died in 1903 at the age of fifty, when Henry was only two. He was the first of many Dodges to be buried in the Nuestra Señora del Refugio Cemetery, appropriately enough, for he himself had donated the cemetery land to the church. As for Henry's mother, Cayetana, she would outlive her husband by more than two decades.[4]

Román and Cayetana were married July 12, 1876, he twenty-three and she a tender fourteen. Their marriage was duly recorded in Spanish in the La Iglesia de San José marriage book in Anton Chico.

"Julio 12 de 1876. De Puerto de Luna, case a Roman Deuch, solter, hijo legitimo de Enrique Deuch, ya difunto, y de Juana Sandoval, con Cayetana Sylva, soltera, hija legitima de Jesús María Sylva y de Anastacia Martinez. Testigos: Juan Sylva y Dolores Ramires."[5]

The priest had a bit of trouble spelling the names. Roman Deuch, bachelor and legitimate son of Enrique Deuch now deceased and of Juana Sandoval, wed Cayetana Sylva the legitimate daughter of Jesús María Sylva and Anastacia Martinez. It was not unusual to find names misspelled in the church records, particularly those with unusual pronunciations. The priest took his best shot and spelled "Dodge" as he heard it, "Deuch." Census takers were likewise susceptible to error. Although he was literate in both Spanish and English, the trader and politician Lorenzo Labadie listed that young married couple in the 1880 census as "Doch."[6] As late as 1930, Henry's older brother Andrés Dodge and his family were listed as "Dutch."[7] "Deuch", "Doch" or "Dutch"—it didn't matter. They were all Dodges and, so too were Román's Dodge's parents, Enrique and Juana.

When taking the census, an enumerator was required to ask each head of household a variety of intrusive questions. Were they employed? Could they read and write? Was anyone blind? Were the children in school? Were there any idiots in the home? People were often hesitant and suspicious, but they answered them, truthfully or not. Of all the questions, folks generally answered two of them without hesitation. Where had their mother been born? Where had their father been born? Overwhelmingly, the reply was New Mexico. When Lorenzo Labadie arrived at the Dodge home, Román stated that his mother had been born in New Mexico, but when Lorenzo departed, the space in the census record for Román's father remained blank. Apparently he didn't know.

Six years before his marriage to Cayetana, Román was living with his 48 year-old mother, Juana Sandoval, at Puerto de Luna, where she appears in the 1870 census as Juana Marraquín, the wife of Juan Marraquín, a 53 year old farm laborer. Interestingly, eighteen year old Román was listed not as Román Deuch, but as Juan Dodge.[8] The enumerator may have simply got it wrong. Nevertheless, the young fellow was doubtlessly Román Dodge. Through the years, the Dodges and the Marraquíns would remain very close.[9]

The census provided yet another intrigue. There was another Dodge living next door. María Dodge, age 16, was residing with one Jesús María Gonzales age 24. María was Román's little sister and she was not the only sibling in the family. There had been at least two older ones: Juana named for her mother, who at that time would have been 22 years old, and Gabriél, who would have been 20. Román had been the third known child and María the fourth. Although the two oldest children were no longer with the family in 1870, the 1860 census taker Jesús M. Sena y Baca had found them together under the surname Sandoval ten years earlier, in a village two hundred miles due west of Puerto de Luna. Juana was the sole adult in the home, unemployed and illiterate. She had four children: twelve year old Juana, ten year old Gabriél, seven year old Román, and little María, age four. The village where she lived was known as "Sevoyetta" or Cebolleta.[10]

After Román and Cayetana were wed in 1876, the number of Dodges in New Mexico expanded exponentially. Yet prior to 1876, the number of Dodges in New Mexico could be counted on the fingers of a single hand, even with a missing digit or two. There were absolutely no Dodges recorded in the 1860 New Mexico Territorial Census, while the 1850 census listed only one: Henry L. Dodge, living next door to his business partner, John Tullis, in the town of Cebolleta.

Román Sandoval Dodge had been born in June of 1853.[11] The boy may not have known where his father came from, and certainly did not know his father well, but he did know his father's identity, Enrique Duech. The American Henry Lafayette Dodge.

Henry L. Dodge had been in the right place, at the right time, and with the right set of propensities. It was he that Captain John Buford had sanctimoniously accused of supporting a "Mexican family" with Army property. It appears that having a family back in Dodgeville hadn't deterred Dodge from embracing another in New Mexico. That comes as no surprise, given his reputation, and there are indications that it wouldn't be the last he'd make, either. Given the times, the distance and circumstances, it would be difficult to condemn the man by the gauge of modern sensibilities. On the other hand, one could hardly criticize Adele and Juana if, at the mention of Henry's name, they assessed his manhood in most shockingly unladylike language.

And so it appears to have been. Autumn of 1852 found Henry Dodge at Cebolleta, perhaps actually living with Juana and her two older children, running a store, raising livestock and providing his habitual sutler services to the troops temporarily posted at Laguna. It is fairly assured that Henry barely knew his two children, constantly traveling about on business with the care of little children left exclusively to the mother. Hence, any memories little Román and María had of their father rapidly faded.

For someone without any official capacity, Dodge exercised a surprising amount of influence and seemed to have a warm hearted empathy for preachers in particular, a rather incongruous sentiment considering his own scurrilous past. Still, that sentiment earned him the profuse gratitude, respect and friendship of one cantankerous Baptist missionary who found himself close to starvation at Laguna.

Reverend Samuel Gorman, his wife Catharine and their two very young children, Mary and James, arrived in Laguna Pueblo on October 5, 1852. They had come out of Dayton, Ohio, where Gorman had ministered a church through the cholera epidemic. He was thirty-six years old when the Baptist Home Mission Society appointed him missionary to New Mexico territory. Their description of the passage over the Santa Fe Trail was a typical one... threatened by wolves, rattlers and heathen savages on every side, the trip further marred when Catharine fell dangerously ill. All and all, the task of bringing the corrupted, idol worshipping people of Laguna to the Protestant Jesus would prove the more daunting adventure. In the coming six years, through poverty, rejection, neglect and frustration, he would make only four converts.[12]

It was tough from the get-go. The Gormans had arrived nearly destitute. Of the hundred bucks Samuel had borrowed in Santa Fe, they had eleven dollars left. They had planned to buy supplies and firewood from the Laguna people, the idea being to support the Indians' economy and thereby earn their loyalty, but found the prices absurdly astronomical.

> "They want 30 to 40 cents a dozen for eggs, 12 cents for a quart of milk; 12 cents for an armful of wood ... My wife went from house to house this morning, trying to get some ground [corn], or rather rubbed, on their hand stones, which every family keeps, till tired out she came home, and these were the prices the asked. ... I have tried now for five weeks to get a cartload of wood and have failed. I sold one shirt for 2 'barro' loads of wood ($1.50). ... All the rest of my wood I had to get from house to house by the armful ... Now I am out of money except $1 with which, I hope to get a little wood."[13]

Inevitably, the Gormans were reduced to begging. It was at this crucial juncture that Samuel Gorman met Henry L. Dodge. After hearing of Gorman's troubles, he promised to arrange to have Samuel formally accepted by the Pueblo of Laguna. Dodge also introduced the Reverend and his family to José Sanon, the man who became Gorman's closest friend in Laguna. Dodge unhesitatingly vouched for his honesty and his ability to read a bit, a rare skill for anyone in the territory, particularly the Indian.[14]

As fall lengthened into winter, Gorman depended on Dodge's generosity. In November Henry provisioned the Gorman family with beef, flour and firewood, accepting only a promise for payment. When the Gormans proposed to start a school for the Indian children, Henry got them a small crumbling adobe house in the pueblo for a classroom. It lacked a roof and was little better than a ruin, but he informed Gorman he could have it rent free if he repaired the roof and re-plastered the walls. Initially, the actual owner of the place proved recalcitrant, knowing that once the missionary fixed it up, he'd never get it back. Only the intercession of the pueblo governor, probably solicited by Dodge, persuaded the reluctant landlord to change his mind.

Dodge also tipped off the Gormans when opportunities to get food arose, though such often brought more trouble than reward, as Samuel discovered one wintry day after Henry told him about an available beef cow.

> "I learned from Captain D. [Dodge] that a good beef cow could be bought on time, and some ground wheat unbolted . . . I engaged a horse of the Governor to go and obtain them. But when the horse was brought, it had neither saddle nor bridle, and being an Indian horse I dare not venture to ride it. I was told it was but about five miles. The day was very cold. I set out with an Indian who served as guide on foot, through villages, and over mountains."

The guide soon lost the trail in the heavy and wet snow. After he found it again, Gorman's scout mentioned matter-of-factly that the cow would cost the missionary thirty dollars up front, not on time. With the pang of hunger prodding him on, Gorman urged his guide onward. He would make the owner a reasonable enough offer. After a day long trek through deep snow, they never did find the animal. Diminishing light and the snow finally forced them to turn back.

> "We reached home at 10 o'clock. The 'about five miles,' I found to be very fair ten miles. . . . I shall make arrangements with Capt. D. [Dodge] to get me some flour of the Mexicans in the future."[15]

Lesson learned and no hard feelings apparently, but by the end of November, Gorman was starting to panic. He looked daily to the arrival of fellow missionary John Shaw, the new post chaplain at distant Fort Defiance, to stop by during his return from Albuquerque with a provender of flour and money.

"We have been compelled to sell, or I might say, almost to give away, our own clothes to get the necessaries of life ... But I have succeeded in getting a cart load of wood from Capt. D. [Dodge], and some unbolted flour. I also got some rice of the soldiers. Capt. D. [Dodge] hired two cows for us till June, gives $6 paid in advance."

Dodge had promised to have Gorman and his family adopted into the pueblo, but the mere promise hardly gave Gorman the right to demand favors. The reverend's attempts to persuade, cajole or bribe the Indians to help repair his house invariably brought the evasive response "mañana." Needless to say, tomorrow never came. Once more he turned to Dodge. Henry hired two men and two women to work for two days at fifty cents a day for the men, thirty-seven cents for the women. Gorman complained that they worked barely ten hours for those two days and very slowly at that, finally leaving the job unfinished. Predictably, the Reverend was unable to get anyone else to complete the repairs.[16]

In the meantime, Henry Dodge's promise to get Gorman adopted into the pueblo went unfulfilled. Samuel heard nothing from Dodge about it for the remainder of 1852 and half way through 1853. He later stated that Dodge's delay "for nine months caused the greatest uncertainty that I ever knew." What Dodge was up to during that time is pure speculation. Accounts paid by Henry totaling $1156 at the end of the year 1852 indicated he was still in the merchandise and livestock business, purchasing corn, sheep, and mules, a forty gallon barrel of whiskey and paying handymen and herders around Cebolleta, Laguna, Albuquerque and Zuni.[17] After that, there is a record vacuum stretching from January to the beginning of May, 1853. Business may have been slow and perhaps Dodge was laying low for the winter. Conversely, it is possible that he may have left New Mexico for the States ... to Dubuque, Iowa specifically, where a letter addressed to him waited in the care of George Wallace Jones. It was an important letter, on official government letterhead, with the official wax seal of the fledgling Department of the Interior ... a letter that would change Henry's life.

Meanwhile, the Reverend Gorman and his family did as best they could. Ignorant of both Laguna language and customs, Samuel was essentially helpless. He couldn't make a living, couldn't make friends and couldn't get converts. Most troubling, Samuel and Catharine noted that the children Mary and James were learning Laguna language and customs, and who knew what other debasing heathen habits. After Bishop Jean-Baptiste Lamy of Santa Fe barred Gorman from using the Laguna church for sermons on Sunday, the Baptist preacher was compelled to preach out of his own house. On more than one Sunday, proper worship of the Lord was interrupted by the infuriating propensity of the Indians to purse their profane traditions, in one case a rabbit hunt.

> "The whole town was in an uproar. Horses neighing, Indians whooping, dogs barking, chickens cackling . . . It looked like anything else than the calmness of the day of rest. The red, streaked, and spotted faces of the painted natives, with bows, arrows, clubs and guns, running to and fro, presented quite a warlike appearance."[18]

His dependence on José Sanon's tedious translation for communicating anything and everything to the Indians was exasperating, even if he did get a few Indians to attend church. At every turn he expected a conspiracy of Catholic priests to drive him and his family out of town.[19]

Catherine's school for the Laguna children essentially failed after the pueblo governor voiced his disapproval; an act Samuel blamed on papist meddling.[20] By June of 1853, an asphyxiating cloud of hostility seemed to hang over the mission. The people of the pueblo, if not openly hostile, treated them with a chilly indifference. Since their arrival in Laguna, Samuel and his family had never felt so utterly alienated and abandoned. The money was gone and even hope had become a dear commodity. So Samuel Gorman waited, fussed and suffered through his intolerable situation at Laguna, praying Henry Dodge would intervene, and soon.

32

NAVAJO AGENT

On November 11th, 1852 the newly arrived Governor for the Territory of New Mexico, William Carr Lane, penned a letter of recommendation to Wisconsin Senator Henry M. Dodge on behalf of one Lt. Colonel Horace Brooks, who was heading back to Washington City. In an attached note, Governor Lane casually added:

> "I have had the pleasure to see Capt. Dodge... He was in excellent health. The first opportunity [that may] offer will be eagerly embraced to [be of] service."[1]

That was more than the new governor could have said for himself. He had entered Santa Fe two months earlier, abysmally sick and depressed, and still hadn't recovered.

William Carr Lane was an experienced but somewhat unrefined 52-year-old politician. Essentially he was a civilian duplicate of his military counterpart in New Mexico, Colonel Edwin Sumner, with the one exception; Lane had a sentimental side to him. Originally from Pennsylvania, he had served as the first mayor of the city of Saint Louis and eventually held that office nine times. He doubtlessly knew the elder Dodge from those early days and, as mayor of Saint Louis, had probably been with him on the docks when the Marquis de Lafayette arrived in 1825. Elected to the Missouri House of Representatives, Lane was a staunch Democrat until his party chose Thomas Hart Benton over him for a Congressional seat. Piqued, he joined the Whig party, yet even that blasphemy didn't sour the camaraderie he shared with Henry and Augustus Dodge and George Jones.[2] Indeed, those three had been primarily responsible for his appointment as Governor for the Territory of New Mexico.

Lane appreciated that chance for political advancement, but his wife and children in Saint Louis were utterly horrified. They worried about the hazardous journey, the demands of the job, and they fretted over Father's advancing age. Indeed, his wife Mary had collapsed in a flood of tears, inconsolable, as his carriage rumbled off for Santa Fe that previous July.[3]

The journey had started well enough, but after a month on the trail, Lane's bucolic enthusiasm for fresh air, vast views and starry nights evaporated as he became increasingly ill. It started on August 25th with a queasy stomach, then a round of nausea and vomiting. Medicated on opiates and chloroform, he passed the hours jolting along, prostrate and delirious. His caravan mercifully spent a few days at Fort Union to allow him some recuperation before going on to Santa Fe. On September 9th, John Greiner and some hastily assembled dignitaries escorted the governor into the city. Upon arriving at the Plaza, a battery of Colonel Brook's cannon punctuated his dismal condition with a thunderous volley, and Lane promptly took to his bed. He spent the next three days struggling to build up enough strength to appear at his inauguration. On September 13th, he joined a handful of other celebrities on a rickety platform in front of the Governor's Palace. As the ceremony began, the platform supports suddenly gave way and the entire contraption dropped some eighteen inches, jolting Lane and the entire delegation. Putting on a smile, he brushed it off, simply commenting that perhaps a bad beginning might make for a good ending.[4]

He may not have believed it himself, for he was not only ill but abysmally homesick, as he later confessed in a letter to his wife.

> "I had the blues dreadfully, at first, and would have made an immediate retreat, if I could have done it with honor; but I am becoming more reconciled. Your agony, when we parted, still wrings my heart. What would I not give to have my six little ones here. At church today, the missionary prayed for my family, and it was fortunate for me that my face was to the wall, for I could not help shedding tears."[5]

There was little time to contemplate family and very little inkling of a good ending ahead with the legion of troubles rising before him. First, Lane's introduction to Colonel Edwin Vose Sumner proved less than amiable. On shaking hands, Sumner displayed all the warmth of rattlesnake. He had already tongue-lashed Colonel Brooks for giving Lane an artillery salute, and made it clear he disapproved of such violations of the separation of the military and civil government. In reality, his scathing criticism of Brooks was probably inspired by his own recent humiliation. After Governor James S. Calhoun departed for the States the previous spring, Sumner had pushed Greiner aside and peremptorily assumed the governorship. When that news reached Washington, both Army command and Congress were furious. Secretary of War Conrad himself censured Sumner, ordering him to cooperate with, rather than frustrate, the civilian government. Hence, Colonel Sumner relinquished the office to Lane in the manner of a petulant schoolboy, withdrawing the Army from Santa Fe and even absconding with the flag that Stephen Watts Kearney had raised over the capital in 1846. When Lane requested another flag, Sumner politely told him no, that he didn't have authorization to issue civilians Army property. Thoroughly livid, Lane sent several indignant letters to both Secretary Sumner and his superiors in Washington.[6]

Relations between the civil and military in New Mexico were right back to normal—venomous.

As Governor of the Territory of New Mexico, William Carr Lane was duty-bound to advance the interests of the citizens, particularly regarding the "Indian issue." Most of the New Mexican citizens were in agreement on that, calling for the extermination, or at very least the removal of the wild tribes. Yet, at the same time, Lane was New Mexico's Superintendent of Indian Affairs, therefore required to represent the welfare of the Indians, sedentary or wild. It was an impossible situation, and Lane himself must have realized his chances of succeeding were slim—less than slim, actually, for his success depended in a large part on the cooperation of a man he'd come to detest: Edwin Vose Sumner. True to expectations, as long as Sumner commanded the 9th Military District, Lane would not get an iota of cooperation.

It must be noted that Governor Lane was in a situation typical of the Indian Service. The Office of Indian Affairs had its origins in the British tradition of accommodating Indian tribes, but it was born in 1774, when the Continental Congress created Indian districts to insure that, if tribes did not actually support the colonists' revolution, they'd remain neutral. Patriots of no less stature than Patrick Henry and Benjamin Franklin served among the first Indian Affairs commissioners. As with the British, the infant United States treated tribes as sovereign nations, albeit savage ones. Hoping to insure peace by making the Indians dependant on American goods, the United States established trade factories, or trading posts, on Indian lands. These factories distributed supplies and gifts to the Indian so long as they did Uncle Sam's bidding. Once they did not, the trade factories were closed.

The Indian Office was officially created in 1824 by Secretary of War John C. Calhoun and placed under the Department of War. It was headed by Thomas McKenney, who had run the government's trade factory policy. With the stingy allocation of two clerks, Commissioner McKenney managed treaty negotiations, the Indian trade system and general relations with the tribes, Indian appropriations, expenditures and correspondence. The task was overwhelming. The responsibilities of the Indian Bureau changed as the nature of the white-Indian relationship changed. By the 1830s, the era of accommodating Indians as sovereign peoples was over. President Jackson and his administration viewed Indian nations as hindrances, like tree stumps to be torn from a farm field. Consequently, in the next two decades of American expansion, the Shawnee, Delaware, Piankeshaw, Winnebago, Sauk and Fox, the Choctaw, Chickasaw, Cherokee and scores other tribes, would be uprooted and relocated across the Mississippi.

In 1849, the Indian Office was attached to the newly-created Department of the Interior. By then Indian tribes were viewed as conquered, dependant peoples, and the Bureau undertook the task of civilizing them. In return for surrendering their lands, submitting to American law and cooperating with the federal government, tribes received yearly allotments and annuities, agricultural seed and tools, a Christian education for their children and vocational training for the adults. Of course, there was never any expectation that the red man would actually assimilate into American society. Their ultimate destiny was total extinction and it was the job of the Office of Indian Affairs to teach the Indians the rudimentary of civilization and to keep them quiet until that day came.

The Indian Bureau was in Washington City, a vast distance from the several hundred distinct native groups under its jurisdiction. An efficient and highly organized bureaucracy was clearly required. Unfortunately, the Bureau fell short of that benchmark. Beneath the Commissioner, the next level of Indian Affairs administration consisted of the territorial governors, who Congress had authorized to serve as superintendents for their respective territories, and for the most part they had little interest in the welfare of their charges. Predictably, the arrangement proved disastrous for the Indian. No governor was compelled to represent Indian interests over those of whites, and any governor who did risked political suicide. So many governors, including the illustrious Governor Dodge of Wisconsin, used their position to confiscate Indian lands for appreciative homesteading constituents, and never lost a moment of sleep.

The first governor of New Mexico, the ill-fated Charles Bent, recognized the magnitude of the job when he wrote to Missouri's Thomas Benton in 1846. The territory was huge and the number of Indians in the thousands. No less than four agents would be needed to deal with the natives.[7] Bent's calculations were seriously deficient. James Calhoun later struggled to make the New Mexico Superintendency at least somewhat effective, although it was critically under-staffed, under-supplied and under-funded. There were no agency houses, no storage facilities, no mules, no wagons and but a few tools. Initially Calhoun claimed it would take at least ten thousand dollars to provide for the superintendency in Santa Fe alone.[8] The following year, he requested not ten, but one hundred thousand dollars.

Clearly four agents for the entire territory would not even approximate the need. Nevertheless, that was the number that stuck in the minds of the policy makers in Washington City, so four agents it would be. William Carr Lane and his predecessors could suggest candidates for the position of agent, but had no power to appoint them. Candidates were appointed back in Washington, and the appointments were in high demand. The job paid relatively well and could serve as a springboard for future advancement in the civil service, so eager candidates curled up at their Congressman's office door to vie for the coveted bone. Concern for the welfare of the Indian was not a job requirement. Obsequiousness towards congressmen was. It was Congress that approved each and every appointment submitted by the President, who in turn had received them from influential politicians. Given the circumstances, it is no shock to find that a sympathetic, dedicated or competent Indian agent was a rare commodity in the Service.

New Mexico had already seen a smattering of agents. There had been Calhoun in 1849, Abraham Woolley, Richard Weightman, John Greiner and a collection of temporary, subagents including Charles Overman and Edward Wingfield, who had died of disease while among the Apache, and the less than proficient agent to the Navajo, Judge Spruce M. Baird. By act of Congress, three official agents were assigned to New Mexico in 1853: Edmund A. Graves for the Ute and Jicarilla, James M. Smith for the Apache, and Henry L. Dodge for the Navajo, Zuni, Jemez and Hopi.

The announcement of Henry Dodge's appointment appeared in the papers back east. The April 22nd edition of the Missouri Liberty Tribune had it sandwiched between stories of the frigate Macedonian departing for Japan, Santa Anna regaining the presidency of Mexico, California gold miners massacuring a group of Indians, and an advertisement urging heartburn sufferers to buy Dr. J. S. Houghton's Pepsin, a sure cure for dyspepsia.

> "W. L. Dodge of Iowa has been appointed Indian Agent for New Mexico, in place of John Greiner, the present very excellent agent, who has been removed."[9]

Aside from butchering his name and ex-place of residence, the Tribune failed to note that Dodge had replaced Baird, not Greiner. Dodge's official letter of commission had been sent in May of 1853 by the Commissioner of Indian Affairs, who had a name that positively oozed parsimony, the Honorable George W. Manypenny.

> "Dodge, Esq. Henry L.
> Care of Hon. Geo. W. Jones
> Dubuque, Iowa
> Sir:
>   You have been appointed by the President one of the Agents for the Indians in New Mexico, and I, herewith, endorse your commission.
>   You will take the oath of Office and execute the enclosed bond in the penal sum of Five Thousand Dollars, with two or more securities whose sufficiency must be certified by a U. S. Judge or District Attorney; and when executed, you will file the bond and oath of Office with the Governor of New Mexico, at Santa Fe, to whom you will report for instructions in the discharge of your official duties, and thro' whom all your official

correspondence with this office will be conducted. He will be instructed to assign you to duty and to direct the present incumbent, of the place which you shall take, to turn over to you all public moneys and other property, belonging to the agency, taking your receipt for the same.

Your compensation will be at the rate of $1550 per annum, to commence from the day on which you shall relieve the present incumbent."[10]

Although a gap in the record as to Dodge's whereabouts for the first half of 1853 might indicate he'd traveled to Jones' home to receive the appointment, evidence that he did remains elusive.

At the time of his appointment, Dodge had just turned 43 years old—not a particularly young man. HIs agency included not only the far-flung Navajos, but the pueblos of Zuni, Laguna, Acoma and the isolated Hopi as well. His father Senator Dodge had probably arranged his appointment and had posted his bond.[11] Although H. L. Dodge had been officially appointed agent on May 7th, 1853, he wouldn't assume his duties until his commission arrived in June. Like Christopher Kit Carson, who would later serve as agent to the Ute, Henry Dodge had a certain Indian expertise lacking in most other agents. He hadn't been a trapper, guide or Indian fighter like Carson, but he had survival skills old Kit sorely lacked. For one, he could read and write. More importantly Dodge was savvy to a realm that completely mystified Kit, that baffling universe of bureaucratic paper work and rigmarole.

Dodge had no rose-colored illusions regarding the job. It would be a demanding one, working among a wild and impetuous people who had repeatedly displayed a serious indifference to American wishes, and he got an early reminder of that fact from Edwin Vose Sumner. On May 29th, 1853, while preparing for a three month vacation in the States, Sumner sent Dodge a warm letter congratulating him on his appointment as Indian agent. The colonel's tone then abruptly turned serious.

" . . . As I suppose you will be assigned to the Navajos, I wish to give you some information about the late doings of some of that tribe. A party of five killed a Mexican recently and took away his two boys and several animals; the boys and animals have been returned but they said to the Governor they could not get the murderers. He has given them till the 1st of July to bring them in, or take them to Fort Defiance, and has offered a reward for them. I think the time given is rather too short.

"There is also a rumor that Dr. Connelly's flock of sheep has been driven off from near Zunia and some pastors killed. If there is any truth in the report, I would by all means impress it upon all the principal men that both these crimes must be atoned for, by giving up the criminals. If they will not do this, we shall march a large command into their country early next fall, and impel them to do it, or to see their whole country laid waste. From your knowledge of these Indians, and their knowledge of you, I feel quite sure that these difficulties will be settled without obliging us to make war upon them..."[12]

Immediately after Sumner's expedition and the founding of Fort Defiance in the fall of 1851, the Navajo launched a series of attacks on the settlements. With the Army seemingly powerless to stop them, the citizens scrambled to take up arms. Up to five hundred residents of Taos and the Rio Arriba alone were begging the government for weapons.[13] Governor Calhoun subsequently authorized the formation of militias and formally requested firearms from Colonel Sumner. Sumner agreed in principle to arm the volunteer companies but sternly admonished that they could only use those weapons in support of Army troops. Of course, that requirement fairly well emasculated Calhoun's citizen militia.[14]

During this time Dodge had kept Calhoun informed of Navajo war parties ranging the Cebolleta area, information that Calhoun used on at least one occasion to needle Sumner.

"... You are aware, I suppose, for, I regard Capt Dodge as reliable authority, that many animals have been driven from the neighbourhood of Cibolletta during the last two months..."[15]

As for tiny Fort Defiance, which was to have restrained such attacks, Major Backus' men were hurrying to complete rough-hewn log cabins before winter set in. The local Navajo had watched their work with concerned fascination but had never demonstrated any hostility. Indeed, Zarcillos Largos, *Naat'áanii Náádleel* of the Bear Springs meeting of 1846, professed cooperation and friendship with the Americans at the fort. The headman's amicable stance eventually allowed Backus to broker a peace agreement between Zarcillos Largos' Navajo and the people of Zuni and Hopi.[16] The major's unauthorized initiative subsequently persuaded both Sumner and Calhoun to meet with the Navajo at Jemez on October 26th, 1851. The two men agreed on very little. Calhoun was appeasing; Sumner intimidating. Calhoun planned to encourage the Navajo delegates with gifts. Sumner disapproved, believing it base bribery. Once the gifts were gone, so too would be the peace. Bull Head favored the incentive of a "rod of iron over their heads." In the end, Calhoun ignored him and distributed some three thousand dollars worth of merchandise to a crowd of two thousand or so Navajo that had gathered at the pueblo.[17]

Then, seemingly overnight, the Navajo nation settled into an undeclared and prolonged truce that lasted for more than a year. Even more striking, it was a truce imbued with amicability, diplomacy and cooperation unknown in the region since Kearny's arrival seven years earlier. In January, the Navajo headmen Armijo, Aguila Negra, and Barboncito surrendered three captive Hispanic boys to John Greiner in Santa Fe as evidence of their desire for peace.[18] Greiner thanked them, and then noted that the citizens of the Rio Abajo had recently been complaining of Navajo thefts. Armijo promptly denied the accusation.

> "My people are all crying in the same way. Three of our chiefs now sitting before you mourn for their children . . . more than two hundred of our children have been carried off and we know not where they are. The Mexicans have lost but a few children in comparison to what they have stolen from us . . . Eleven times we have given up our captives—only once have they given us ours. My people are yet crying for the children they have lost. Is it American justice that we must give up everything and receive nothing?"

Greiner later confessed that Armijo's eloquence had left him all but speechless. All he could do was assure the headmen that justice would be done someday. The meeting ended in a most affectionate manner and peace prevailed. Even Sumner allowed himself a bit of guarded optimism that the Navajo would "continue perfectly quiet" and concentrate on planting extensively that spring.[19]

Such extraordinary and effective efforts by Navajos to preserve the peace had been a God-send for Calhoun. The winter of 1852 brought renewed rumors of yet another general uprising among the New Mexicans, in which an alliance of Pueblos and the savage tribes would join in the slaughter of Americans. Once again, paranoia swept the capital. Sumner returned his troops to Santa Fe in April of 1852, where he found the place consumed in "a state of anarchy." The Army helped bring Santa Fe back to some semblance of order and discouraged, as Sumner put it, "the abandoned and restless spirits at work to bring about revolution."[20]

The one pimple on the visage of peace appeared in October of 1852, when a Navajo man, for unknown reasons, superficially wounded the civilian farmer at Fort Defiance, Mr. Jonathan Wyatt, with an arrow. At that time, Colonel Sumner happened to be at Defiance assessing the state of Navajo affairs. He demanded surrender of the perpetrator, but Backus' successor, the astute Henry Lane Kendrick of the 2nd Artillery, politely suggested Sumner drop the issue rather than spark a war. Wyatt was only slightly injured and the Navajo perpetrator, one Ish-kit-sa-ne, was a known miscreant. Although it was true the Navajo were at peace, they remained highly suspicious of American motives. Before Sumner had arrived at Defiance, a story had circulated that the colonel planned to have all Navajo leaders visiting the fort hogtied and their throats cut. It was a lie purportedly spread by Antonio Sandoval. A misstep would simply shatter the truce. Sumner wisely never pressed the matter.[21]

Among those who could claim to have helped forge the peace, the least of them was the Navajo agent himself, Spruce M. Baird. At best, Baird had been distant and aloof. His superior, William Carr Lane, viewed him as a shirker. When Lane arrived in New Mexico, he had wasted little time in letting his agents know what he expected of them. On November 2nd, 1852, he issued a circular. First, in his superintendency there would be no more honorary positions that were paid but required no work. Second, the sole dedication of agents was to advance the public interest, not their own. Tending to private business on government pay and spending Indian Service funds on private interests was forbidden. The agent was expected to live with their tribe. Agency reports containing phrases such as "I can't, I couldn't, or I don't know" were expressly forbidden.[22]

On each count it seemed Lane might have had Judge Baird specifically in mind. Calhoun appeared to have similar concerns over the judge. In February of 1852, perhaps under some pressure to perform, Baird informed then Superintendent Calhoun that he was contemplating a trip to Navajo country "if considered safe and prudent" but insomuch as the Navajos were all out on hunting trips, he preferred going in March.[23] The agent much preferred conducting agency business from his home in Albuquerque, from his law practice in Santa Fe, or if absolutely necessary, from Jemez, the location of the agency itself.

In June of 1852, Baird did manage to get out to Navajo land where he glowingly predicted that hostilities with Indians throughout the territory would soon cease. In March of 1853, Baird again appeared at Fort Defiance to distribute annuity goods to the Navajos, optimistically reporting to then Commissioner Luke Lea that the prospects for civilizing the Navajo were very good and that only a small appropriation of the agency was necessary "to hold this tribe in a state of dependence." Governor Lane had to concur, stating that the Navajos were "at profound peace & with due attention within wants, may soon be made an agricultural & pastoral people..."[24]

In late April of 1853 an event on a remote, juniper covered mesa near Abiquiu would change his assessment. Five Navajo men, all related, rode into Capote Ute country north of the San Juan River to avenge an earlier raid led by the Ute war leader Tamouche on Celedona Valdez's Navajos. The Ute had taken a mule and a paint pony and the Navajo boys intended to make an accounting. Despite their enthusiasm, they failed to locate the Capote camp and finally had to turn back towards home, seething in frustration. After learning that Tamouche's band had been seen near Abiquiu, the Navajo raiders turned southward in renewed anticipation, through the fractured country of the Rio Chama, towards the small village of Vallecito.

Late in the afternoon of May 3, while crossing Vallecito Mesa, they spotted a makeshift sheep camp in the piñon and junipers. Don Ramon Martín, his sons José María, José Claudio and a nephew José Leonicio, in company with three shepherd boys, had just pitched camp and were penning their sheep in an improvised corral for the night. The Navajo men likely saw the improbable concidence as a gift of redemption. For Don Ramon, it would prove fatal.

As the sun gradually dipped behind the mesas and twilight crept over the camp, a musket shot rang out. The ball passed through Ramon Martín's coat and into his chest, killing him immediately. Martín's son José leaped up as two arrows whisked past his ears, and ran for his life. Cautiously the Navajos entered the camp where they found the remaining five boys, petrified with fear, cowering among the sheep in the corral. They seized the boys and in Spanish asked the lads if they knew where any Ute or Jicarilla Apache were. The boys swore they knew nothing.[25] After ransacking the camp, the marauders left the sheep in the corral, took up the boys, three horses and a mule and set their path westward for home. After passing about a quarter mile, the Navajos paused at a watering hole. Taking the three herders boys aside, the Navajos told them that if the Ute returned the paint and the mule to them, they would free José Claudio and José Leonicio and return the horses and mule they'd taken from Martín's camp. Then they set herder boys free.[26]

When the news reached Santa Fe, Governor Lane reacted with considerable indignation. There had already been a claim that Navajos had run off some 400 sheep belonging to Thomas Baca the previous March. Now there had been a killing. The governor deputized Donaciano Vigil to investigate the Baca and Martín incidents and find out what Navajo Agent Baird intended to do about them. If Baird failed to demand from the Navajo the return of the stock and captives and the surrender of Don Martín's murderers, Lane authorized Vigil to do it himself.[27]

It was an ultimatum. There would be no negotiations. If the Navajos did not restore the captives and livestock and surrender Don Martín's killers, a state of war would exist. He confirmed as much in a letter to Sumner, urging upon him "the propriety—nay absolute necessity—of inflicting . . . severe chastisement."[28] Lane backed up his position by promising to raise volunteer companies to assist the regular troops.

Sumner's reply of May 12th was surprisingly mild and contemplative. The colonel counseled discretion and suggested sending Baird to Fort Defiance to work with the Navajo leaders in resolving the crisis.[29] Lane, on the other hand, had considerably less confidence in the Navajo or for that matter in Agent Baird, who was apparently too busy to attend to the crisis. The next logical choice, Baird's interpreter William Keithly, was dreadfully ill and incapacitated. Keithly urged Vigil to take George Carter the agency blacksmith with him to Navajo country. Carter was experienced and competent in Indian matters. So, a week after Lane's ultimatum, Vigil, Carter, Samuel Ellison and the Jemez leader Hosta met with Navajo leaders Armijo, Aguila Negra and 300 of their people at Tunicha. The leaders understood the gravity of the situation and promptly surrendered the two boys Claudio and Leonicio, the horses and the mule. The men responsible for the raid were among the crowd that day, Jesús—reputed to be the actual triggerman, Amarillo, Chiquito, Palo de Cochillo and Asha. In way of apology they explained through an interpreter that they hadn't intended to kill Ramon Martín but to just scare him a bit.[30] It was a tragic mistake, but they offered to pay indemnity for Martín's life. Vigil returned to Governor Lane on May 24th with the boys and animals in tow. Lane summarily rejected the Navajo offer of indemnity and posted rewards for the murderers' apprehension, dead or alive.

> ". . . I have given the Navajoes until the next full Moon, say 1st of July, to surrender these villains & have consented that they may be surrendered to the officer in command at Fort Defiance . . . the Navajoes were assured again & again that either a neglect or refusal on their part to surrender these well-known murderers would be followed by an invasion of their country." [31]

It was under that gathering storm that Henry L. Dodge inherited the Navajo agency.

33

ON THE BRINK

From the outset, Henry Dodge looked to be a good candidate for Indian agent. He had acquired a practical and personal knowledge of the Navajo that Baird not only lacked, but disdained. Henry had cultivated a close relationship with the Indians who frequented his store at Chupadero. He knew their tastes and eccentricities and their opinions on issues greater than simple curios and bobbles. He also had taken his business directly to the Navajo, venturing as far as the Tunicha and Canyon de Chelly on trading expeditions. Additionally, Dodge wasn't a pretentious politician or a haughty lawyer. He'd dabbled in both law and politics, but favored a life more akin to his Indian clients. He was agreeable and easy going, yet tempered and tough, with leather reins resting more comfortably in his hand than a quill pen. He knew the nature and challenges of the New Mexican landscape as intimately as he had come to know the Navajo. Lastly, he had no business in Santa Fe that would monopolize his time, a circumstance Governor Lane likely appreciated. Lane had been so incensed over Judge Baird's inaction during the latest crisis he informed the agent that he had paid Donaciano Vigil nearly all of the agent's quarterly salary, "... for the services of himself & party in performing your duty ... when your services were not available to the Dept."[1]

Although Henry wouldn't formally assume his new job until June 30th, circumstances demanded he act as agent in every sense save official. He seemed to take up task with enthusiasm. He had been at Fort Defiance preparing a trading expedition among the Navajos when news of Don Ramon Martín's killing arrived. There was a new commander at Fort Defiance—a West Point fellow—Brevet Major Henry Lane Kendrick. Dodge and Kendrick had served together during John Washington's Navajo expedition of 1849 and nearly shared the same fate when they were fired on through the gloom by nervous pickets. Brevet Major Kendrick had assumed command of Fort Defiance on September 8, 1852.[2] While Backus had been a good commander, Kendrick would be better. He was highly educated, yet neither high-handed nor aloof: an efficient, demanding but practical administrator. Kendrick and Dodge probably could not have been more dissimilar; Kendrick, the stern visage of propriety, discipline and dedication, and Dodge the spontaneous, congenial aficionado of the nonchalant life. It seemed a recipe for disaster. Certainly

H. L. Kendrick and H. L. Dodge would thoroughly exasperate one another—with Kendrick usually the more afflicted party, but together they would form a team unrivaled in its skill handling volatile Navajo-American relations.

Major Kendrick arrived on the scene deeply suspicious of the real motives behind the Navajo exhortations for friendship. He was, after all, an Army officer on the Indian frontier. By the first of May his suspicions were reinforced. It seemed two fort horses sent out to graze had vanished. Kendrick believed the Navajo had taken them. Knowing Dodge was preparing to go into Navajo country, he asked him to make a few inquiries about them while he was among the Indians. Dodge said he would. It proved to be unnecessary. Kendrick later discovered both horses had simply wandered off the fort grazing fields and into a nearby canyon.[3]

At first Kendrick may have been skeptical as to Dodge's qualifications. On the surface the man seemed to care little for either duty or responsibility and appeared almost cavalier about his safety while traversing Indian country. Still, he clearly knew his way around and had a subtle skill with the Indians. At the same time, the Navajo remained amiable. On a daily basis they strolled the grounds of Defiance as if they were at a county fair. So when the fort chaplain John Milton Shaw asked to go along on Dodge's trading expedition, Kendrick approved. Dodge heartily welcomed yet another preacher into his confidences.

As the fort chaplain, the Baptist Reverend Shaw of New York enjoyed a cushier position than Samuel Gorman did at Laguna. It paid better, for one. Even so, he had started in much the same circumstances. Shaw had been all of thirty years old when he received his appointment to New Mexico. His wife Harriett Bidwell had been twenty-seven. Their melodramatic tales of crossing the plains could have compared favorably in drama with the Gormans', having survived wild grass fires, freezing weather and wolves. After arriving in Santa Fe in November of 1851, they began mission work in Albuquerque and, much like the Gormans, scraped by on a few dollars and a lot of prayer. Their first child, George, was born in Albuquerque in August of 1852. On February 1st, 1853 Shaw was appointed chaplain at Fort Defiance. True, the small family was even more isolated from the rude veneer of civilization they'd known in Albuquerque. It was also true that Harriett constantly fussed over little George's health and her own; they were both frequently ill. She obsessed about the cleanliness of their quarters, particularly when the winds howled and red sand drifted down from the ceiling and sifted through the walls. She devoted nearly as much time worrying about little George's moral upbringing, as he was surrounded by what she considered the heathen attitudes, dubious motives, and filthy habits of the wild Indian, not to mention that unutterable, guttural language of theirs.

319

Nevertheless, Milton's position was secure, so she took some comfort in knowing they'd not teeter on starvation like their less fortunate friends in Laguna.[4]

Shaw endeavored to meet the spiritual needs of the Indians as well as those of the soldiers. Of the two, he'd have better luck with the enlisted men, most of whom were émigrés from Europe. While Mrs. Shaw tutored two Mexican servants and the girls of the officers' families, Mr. Shaw taught evening class for the soldiers—a large class of about eighty who were "mostly foreigners." He was assured good attendance. Fort Defiance presented the bored soldier with few opportunities for nocturnal entertainment and it was too far from anywhere to simply jump ship. So under the approving gaze of the officers, they came. Shaw planned to start a school for the Navajo children as well, to convert and civilize them and clothe them as "they are now nearly naked." He also required an interpreter and an increasing supply of gifts and handouts going to the Navajo, who were appearing at his door with alarming regularity. All that took money, and he hoped to solicit donations in letters back home to the Baptist Home Mission Society, even if it meant dramatizing the seriousness of his situation a tad.

John Shaw had asked for Spruce M. Baird's help starting a school during the agent's visit to Defiance. Baird raised the subject during a meeting with the Navajo leadership and several of the headmen voiced enthusiasm for the idea. That early zeal for education failed to bear fruit. Unlike the hapless soldier, the Navajo child was not as easily corralled. In the meantime, the family was inundated with good Indian relations. The Shaws had offered potential converts the hospitality of their home and it seemed the Navajo were not reticent in accepting.

> "Our house is overrun with them [Navajos], and they manifest a great curiosity and interest in visiting us, as the most of them never saw a white woman or child, till we came among them. But it requires much patience and self-denial to get along with them. A much larger number of women and children are now in than I have before seen, and, from morning till night, one company goes and another comes. Could some of our more civilized friends in the States be placed here this evening, they might not sleep very soundly, for, look in either direction and nothing is to be seen but the camp fires of Indians, a blazing amid the surrounding darkness, forming an enclosure around us with a wall of fire; and the hideous noises of the natives, as they sing and dance, imparts a feeling of native wildness which bring thoughts of cruelty and revenge lurking within the breasts of many, perhaps, which are camped around."

With each visit the Navajo headmen urged Shaw to come visit their homes and enjoy their generosity, and to bring Harriet and little white baby as well, for he and his family would be perfectly safe. The idea intrigued Shaw but he viewed taking Harriett and George out into that wilderness as ill-advised. Shaw politely acknowledged the invitation and let it lay until mid May, when he saddled up with Henry L. Dodge.[5]

On May 16th they struck out into Navajo country. Dodge confidently headed north along the Tunicha range, angling toward Red Lake. Shaw perhaps felt less confident, but he believed he was adequately protected, armed with a pistol, musket and his faithful dog trotting alongside. At every turn, the reverend marveled at the awesome majesty of the striped sandstone bluffs and crimson pinnacles rising around him.

> "Proceeding some two or three miles farther, we struck a beautiful sheet of water called, "Laguna Negra" (Black Lake) covered with ducks and water hens, and surrounded with droves of sheep and horses, from which we were assured that we were near the Indian camp.[6]

Dodge shouted a greeting to the headman Gordo and his band of some fifteen families. Gordo was brother to the headman Zarcillos Largos. Shaw described him as clever in appearance, a very fat and well-disposed old patriarch blessed with four wives.[7] Shaw noted that the Indians were living in light and cool brush summer shelters and assumed incorrectly the Indians had no permanent lodges, but he did notice quite correctly that Navajo women owned the sheep and wove the famous Navajo blankets. Dodge and Shaw spent the night, dined on goat milk and bread, which the reverend described as "a very comfortable supper" and slept wrapped in blankets beneath the star-strewn sky.

Henry Dodge and John Shaw passed the following day visiting around camp. Each successive family insisted the two men stay and eat ... to try this food and that dish: dried peaches, corn gruel, boiled and roasted mutton. They sat in a tight circle on a blanket spread across the sand, dipping first one hand then another into the communal wooden dishes set before them.

> "They also make corn-bread of meal and water, baked in the ashes, which to a hungry man relishes very well; in fact I have thought it better than the best cake I ever ate in the East; and a piece of mutton roasted in the fire was really a luxury ..."

Although his writing was tinged with hints of distaste, Shaw kept meticulous notes on all he saw around him: the way Navajos slept, the use of a cradleboard to carry infants, their earthen cooking pots with the peculiar pointed bottoms, designed to be set upright in holes dug in the ground, and their willow jugs, woven so tightly as to be nearly water tight. The Reverend also noticed the two dozen children in camp, perhaps future students for his school.[8]

Despite his prejudices, he was fascinated with the Navajo, seeing them as he had never seen them before. The people were so energetic and seemingly filled with mirth and laughter that he regretted being completely ignorant of their language. He hoped to get Dodge to teach him something of the Indians' wants and condition, and a little of their language, if possible. Henry Dodge must have spoken a passable amount of Navajo, though in his journal Shaw never directly mentioned it or for that matter the kinds of merchandise that Dodge was trading with the Navajos. They were doubtlessly articles that could be easily packed in. Iron pots and pans, knives, honing stones, hoes and shovels were always popular, as were bolts of cloth, matches and scarves, beads, bells and trifling gewgaws. Shoes were not.

The following day, Dodge and Shaw continued their journey northward, escorted by several armed Navajo men from Gordo's camp. Crossing a large valley of sparse grass, they climbed up a mountain ridge. Reaching the summit, they crossed by a stone altar strewn with sprigs of evergreen, offerings to the spirits. To traverse Navajo country was to journey through the realm of numerous spirits who were acknowledged and placated with small offerings. Descending the ridge, Dodge's troupe came to a spring. A group of Navajos had paused there on the first leg of their journey to make salt at the distant Laguna Salado, a brackish salt impregnated lake two days travel south of Zuni. They would take the Zuni Salt Trail, recognized as sacred and mutually respected by the Apache, Navajo and Pueblo. Before departing, the Navajos welcomed Dodge and Shaw cordially and presented them with gifts of corn bread.

In time the trading entourage emerged from the pine trees and descended into a lush valley cut by the Cienega Juanico, a large, clear stream. On either side of the stream, the valley seemed carpeted with sheep and horses, a breathtaking testament to the power and wealth of the Navajo. The headmen and their families appeared and hailed the trading expedition.

". . . On seeing us approach, they came to meet us and made us welcome to their homes. Most of them had been at our house. One was the family to whom Mrs. Shaw gave some medicine for inflamed eyes, which had cured them, and attached them to us very strongly; and they said they were now willing to let their children live with us, and as soon as the big dance is over they will bring them ..."

It was the beginning of the summer season of religious healing ceremonies, predominantly the Enemy Way Ceremony, the *Anaa'jí*. With a little more knowledge, Shaw would realize he'd not soon see his Indian students at study. The ceremonial season usually lasted all summer.

The Navajo immediately invited Dodge and Shaw to eat, again reassuring the missionary that he need not fear coming into their country, as long as he had a guide and an interpreter. They further promised that once he'd learned to speak the Navajo language well enough to be understood, it would be completely safe traveling alone. Shaw also got his first look at the tepee shaped earth covered Navajo lodge, the *hooghan*. The term embodied more than simply "a house." It meant a place of sanctuary, peace and calm contemplation; the embodiment of *hózhó*, or harmony itself, the fundamental precept of Navajo life. He confessed he did not find the "wigwam" very welcoming. Subsequently he spent the night outside, his dog at his side, beneath the sky's sparkling meteor splendors and slept like a baby.[9]

They spent the following day, May 19th, hobnobbing among the locals and again they were showered with goodwill. Every turn brought such a convincingly genuine embrace that John believed the Navajo sincerely liked him. They asked John about the health of his wife and his little son, and again encouraged them to all come out and visit soon. As Dodge and Shaw moved from one lodge to another, they were escorted by a band of excited, dusty, disheveled kids.

> "The children were very glad to see me, and some little presents soon collected them around me, and were delighted to speak English words; and I find I can learn the language faster from the children than the parents, and thus, while amusing them, securing my own purposes. The boys seem to be active and quick of comprehension, and with proper training might be made good, and industrious, and honest men."

Dodge and the Reverend left camp on the following day with yet another escort of Navajos, traveling until sunset and spending the evening in the same manner as the previous nights. In the course of conversation, one of the Navajo mentioned that an Apache had some time ago killed a relative of his and he was anxious to take vengeance. Shaw made a note of that remarkable trait of Navajo character. A kindness was never forgotten and an injury always repaid in full.

Dodge and Shaw returned to Fort Defiance on Saturday the 21st to allow the Reverend to attend to his Sabbath duties. Shaw's experience with Dodge among the Navajo must have been exhilarating and encouraging, but the positive aspects of his adventure failed to surface in his missives to the Baptist Home Mission.

> "To travel and sleep in the wilderness, where no human habitation meets the eye, and no social circle to cheer the toil-worn missionary after the day's labors are over, save a group of half-clad, dirty savages, as they hover around their camp fire ... And instead of the sweet sounding music of the piano or guitar to induce sweet repose, is the hideous howling of wolves and other wild beasts of prey, mingled with no less disagreeable yells and wild songs of the Indians...."[10]

Such theatric embellishment did stimulate generous donations, so perhaps Shaw's penchant for hyperbole could be forgiven.

In the meantime, the potential ramifications of the murder at Vallecito continued to boil ominously. On May 25th, Kendrick reported to Colonel Sumner that Zarcillos Largos and other headmen had come in and were cooperating to resolve a variety of issues. Upon his return to Defiance, Henry Dodge briefed the major fully on his trip and the state of affairs among the Navajo, stating that the herd of sheep purportedly stolen by the Navajo, had actually run off by a band of "pelados", or poor New Mexicans, knowing the Indians would take the blame.

> "Mr. Dodge who gives me some of these items has just returned from a trading expedition among the Navajoes, some 30 or 35 miles north of this place. He found the Navajoes very friendly; he returns among them and will bring me additional information."

Kendrick well appreciated the fact that Dodge's apparent ease among the Navajo would provide crucial intelligence. Kendrick also got excellent information from his fort interpreter, Juan Anaya, the captive New Mexican who had been so reluctant to be "redeemed" from his captors by Calhoun in 1849. The major appreciated the need for prompt resolution of the crisis, and urged Sumner to tell Lane to get Spruce Baird or some other agent from the Indian Office out to Fort Defiance, to work with him and the Navajo and to keep him abreast of any new developments in the Martin incident.[11] Of course, Baird wouldn't be showing up.

As the weeks moved steadily toward Lane's deadline date, the Navajo professed confusion over what the Americans expected them to do. Dodge and Anaya both told Kendrick that the Indians believed Donaciano Vigil had accepted their offer of blood money, to reimburse Ramon Martin's family with ten good horses. Incorrectly, they thought that settled the issue.[12] It wasn't with Colonel Sumner. He had backed Lane's demands and had given the Navajos until July 1st to surrender the five killers at Fort Defiance. If they failed to do so, the American Army would sweep over Navajo land two days later, on July 3rd. Another event soon aggravated the crisis further. On May 22nd, Anastacio García had 5,600 sheep run off from the slopes of the Zuni Mountains. He identified the thieves as Navajo. When confronted with the accusation, Zarcillos Largos insisted that Antonio Sandoval's Enemy Navajo had been responsible. It didn't matter. Kendrick bluntly told him that if the sheep were not returned, war was inevitable. The major had put *Naat'áanii Náádleel* in an impossible position, but he promised to do his best to rectify the loss.

The outlook for peace had become so grim that Sumner, who had already relinquished his command in anticipation of returning to the States, reluctantly reassumed it.[13] As May passed into June, the mood in the territory clouded over. None believed the Navajo would comply with Lane's demands, and nearly all thought there would be a general war. Each day brought another pessimistic revelation. News arrived in Santa Fe that Navajos had brazenly murdered the Reverend John Shaw and Henry L. Dodge along the road to Fort Defiance. It was a disturbing report, and one that couldn't be easily dismissed, but Governor Lane expressed his doubts in a letter to Sumner. There was another rumor that hostile Navajo bands were allying with the Ute for all-out war. Lane was skeptical about that one as well, but he sent Agent Michael Steck northward to investigate.[14]

With the deadline of July 1st looming and no hint of willingness by the Navajo to surrender Ramon Martin's murderers, Colonel Sumner realized his troops wouldn't be ready to strike the Navajo by July 3rd. He then did something he always abhorred. He moved his absolute deadline back a week, to July 6th, and informed Lane if that deadline passed, the troops would be in Navajo country by July 8th. It is hard to understand why a mere six days would have made a significant difference. However much Old Bull Head was girding for a fight, he seemed to like it about as much as a school boy steeling himself for a shot of castor oil. Nevertheless, Sumner sent Major Kendrick a list of preparations to be made for war. Fort Defiance would be the staging area for six to seven hundred soldiers. Keep the fort cattle and stock well guarded and near. They would be essential to the campaign. Bring in all the hay and wood cutting parties—keep them close and secure. Meet with all the principle chiefs and explain carefully and in depth what was expected of them. If the Colonel did not receive a letter from Kendrick by July 6th stating he'd received the murderers, Sumner would unleash a scythe of destruction.

> "... I shall put to death every man that I can catch. I shall destroy every field of grain, and at the time when it will be too late to plant again for this year-and I shall take all the flocks that I can find. Say to Sarcio Largo and the other chiefs, to some of whom I am personally known, that it will give me great pain to destroy their crops and to leave their women and children to starve..."

That was about as sentimental as Old Bull Head got. He also cautioned Kendrick to secure Juan Anaya's services as interpreter. Anaya's cooperation would be crucial and "... if there is the least doubt about his remaining with you, increase his pay till you are sure of him."[15] Sumner then instructed the storekeeper at Fort Union to send the expected shipment of new Sharps rifles directly to Santa Fe and to set aside thirty rockets for use against the Navajo.[16]

By June 8th, Governor Lane's initial resolve was slipping. He knew Aguila Negra's people wouldn't surrender the murderers. The Navajo would rather endure a war. He also knew he couldn't afford to back down. It was yet another untenable position, made all the harder by the realization that the destruction of Navajo land was certain to "shed innocent blood or to destroy the property of unoffending Indians..." What to do? Lane hadn't the heart to move forward but he couldn't take a step back. He pondered and fretted possible options. Perhaps Sumner could simply attack Aguila Negra's band. They were, after all, harboring the killers. Conversely, an awesome show of Army power in the heart of Navajo country might be enough to get the headmen themselves to surrender the killers.

It was a desperate delusion and William Carr Lane knew it. It was damned exasperating. He wrote to Sumner and confessed his growing reluctance.[17] Lane was perhaps surprised to learn that the Colonel shared his hesitancy. Sumner acknowledged that war might teach the Indians a lesson in the short run, but to leave the entire Navajo nation destitute would turn all the Navajo into thieves; they'd have to steal or starve. The resulting epidemic of Navajo raids on the settlements might very well embolden the other wild tribes. Certainly the cost to the government would be astronomical.

Yet how could they avoid war and still preserve honor? They needed an excuse, an easy door out. Sumner tentatively suggested one. He admitted to Lane that he had always nursed a suspicion of the Mount Taylor headman, Antonio

Sandoval. That man, the colonel groused, was doubtlessly agitating all the present problems the Americans were having with the Navajo.

> "I think we should take the matter into serious consideration, from what Maj. Kendrick says about Sandoval, I have suspected this fellow for a long time, with his half Pueblo half Navajo band, and I have no doubt but he has had something to do with getting up these difficulties. He is an unprincipled scoundrel and it is plain that he has everything to gain by a war between the Navajos and whites, for he can steal from both sides."[18]

It was a curious and completely unexpected line of thought for Sumner, bolstered more by expediency than substance. Major Kendrick had clearly indicated to Sumner that Sandoval and his men would one of the most effective scourges that could be used against the Navajo, for the tribe's greatest dread was to be enslaved by Sandoval or the Mexicans. Never mind. Sumner and Lane were trying to convince themselves more than one another that there was a way out.

At Fort Defiance, gloom over the impending war had blown in with one of those infamous spring dust storms. On June 11th, Harriett Bidwell Shaw glumly noted its ferocity while imprisoned inside her rude adobe home.

> "For a few days past we have had weather warm enough to have our doors open without a fire, and I put on a thin dress. But with this weather I caught a severe cold, and we are today housed up with a good fire while the cold wind without is blowing a perfect hurricane and sand and dust so thick that at times we can see only a short distance from our window, while you, no doubt, are enjoying all the loveliness of spring..."

How she longed for Vermont! She was sick and depressed and predicted all their missionary efforts among the friendly Navajos would be blasted by a few evil miscreants. A body of dragoons had come into the fort a few days previously to find Defiance under a high state of vigilance. Guards were posted at every point around the garrison, their calls and replies booming through the night every fifteen minutes—that and the howling and barking of coyotes and the thundering, wailing gale. A few days later an express arrived bearing grave news. War was inevitable. Harriet rushed to finish another letter home. There would be no further mail delivery, in or out, in the next few weeks. Headquarters had ordered all personnel to remain close to the garrison. The one bit of good news was that her husband and Agent

Dodge had returned safely and had not been killed by the Indians as the rumor had it. Harriet had actually received several expressions of sympathy for her loss from the citizens of the Rio Grande Valley.[19]

At this critical moment Kendrick and Dodge were working to find a glint of hope for resolving the whole mess, for they had come to the same conclusion as their respective superiors in Santa Fe. At the time Mrs. Shaw penned her letter, the Major and Dodge with an escort of U. S. dragoons under Captain Ewell had ridden out into Navajo country for another congress with the Indian leaders. They left on June 7th, moving northward towards the Cienega Grande, then ascending eastward over the Chuska Mountains just north of Washington Pass before turning southward along the Tunicha. Dodge and Kendrick discovered that Navajos along the western slopes of the Chuska Mountains were without exception desirous of peace.

> "Every thing convinced us that all on this side, or to the west of the mountains, are quite adverse to war, the natural effect of this Post, and that the Acts of which we complain have been committed by a few bad and irresponsible men living near the mesa of Chacra, the Oso, and in the vicinity of Chuska. Col. Sumner will remember that the division between the Navajoes on the east and those on the west of this range is very discernable; a fact which complicates the questions, in as much as the western Navajoes have done no wrong and disclaim all power of intermeddling with those living on the east side of the mountains."

Kendrick believed them. Still, at each stop where they met large groups of Navajos, Kendrick and Dodge grimly warned them of the inevitable outcome of war. The Navajos protested that but one man was guilty of the actual murder. Kendrick insisted the lone killer be surrendered and García's stolen stock be returned. It was an impossible request and the Indians explained that very clearly to Kendrick and Dodge. The two returned to Defiance on the 13th, driving in a few hundred sheep and fourteen horses surrendered by the Navajo as a payment and bond for promises to attempt apprehension of the killers. The Navajo had also allowed a Mexican captive, José Pablo Montoya, to escape to the Kendrick's camp. His Navajo owner, by Montoya's own admission, had paid eleven horses for him yet did nothing to stop his escape.

In a meeting at the fort a few days later, Zarcillos Largos and the young headman Manuelito informed Kendrick that Martin's killer had crossed the San Juan River and taken refuge among the Ute.[20] Again *Naat'áanii Náádleel* and Manuelito insisted that they could not deliver up the man, that it would precipitate a civil war among them, but they promised to make all the restitution necessary to satisfy the Americans. Kendrick told them he would deliver their words to Colonel Sumner. Although he made no guarantee that it would turn aside American wrath, Kendrick did intimate that it just might be enough.

> "They protested their inability to deliver up the murderer, but made the same promises as we received on our route, to which we could only say that if they complied with <u>those</u> promises the matter would be referred to Col. Sumner without our being able to say that he would grant them peace, while on <u>his</u> terms they certainly could have it."

Upon returning to Fort Defiance Dodge and Kendrick had learned that the supply train had arrived during their absence. The rations it had brought in preparation for the invasion, by Kendrick's estimation, would fall well short of supplying Defiance in a war with the Indians.

> "Under these circumstances I have thought proper to direct Lt. Long to purchase of Mr. Dodge and a Mexican some 650 sheep of which we have now on hand about 600. Some of them are small but they have been bought at a very good bargain. In case of a war sheep will be better than cattle to take with troops..."[21]

In his report, Kendrick essentially confirmed what both Colonel Sumner and Governor Lane had concluded. The Navajo leaders could not, before or after a devastating campaign, deliver up the guilty parties. They would rather run the risk of a war with the Americans than civil war with bands of the surrendered killer. Kendrick then respectfully made a suggestion to Sumner. Would it not be perhaps prudent for the Colonel Commanding to hold off his campaign for a bit?

> "...should Col. Sumner find it proper to adjourn the campaign until the first of August, starting from this Post, it might be well for Capt Ewell to come out with 50 or 60 mounted men with whom Mr. Dodge and myself would go to such points as we might judge best, with a view of getting the murderers and collecting the sheep. We should at least see the country and be better prepared to <u>see it again</u>..."

It would also give them time to reconnoiter the San Juan River area for a suitable site for a new fort that could cow the eastern Navajo and the Ute in the same way that Fort Defiance had intimidated the western bands.[22] With that, Kendrick handed his report to Captain Ewell. Ewell, Dodge and an escort immediately departed for Sumner's headquarters in Albuquerque.[23] They arrived on June 19th and delivered Kendrick's report. As it turned out, Colonel Sumner had already embraced the major's suggestion. On the very day that Kendrick had written him, Sumner sent the Fort Union supply officer orders to get a horse team ready for his personal use. He'd be leaving for the States on July 1st. He'd decided to postpone the Navajo campaign indefinitely. The Navajo were almost to the man desirous of peace and "if we move against them now, and lay waste to their country, we shall make robbers of the whole of them . . . "[24]

Sumner sent Dodge and Ewell on to Santa Fe with a letter to Governor Lane, confirming his abrupt decision.[25] Dodge and Ewell arrived in Santa Fe on June 21st and briefed the Governor. Lane's secretary John Ward was under the impression that Ewell and Dodge had stated the Navajos would deliver up not only stolen property but Ramon Martin's murderer as well. If indeed Dodge said so, he must have known it would never happen. Perhaps Ward had heard him wrong. It didn't matter. The southern mails had just arrived with confirmation that Sumner was to be permanently relieved by General John Garland and, as Sumner reasoned, if ". . . Garland should come out, he will have to conduct the affair, it would therefore, seem right that he should have the decision of this question."[26]

Colonel Edwin Vose Sumner's sigh of relief must have been deep and gratifying. He was off the hook. There would be no war and he would be going home. As it turned out, Governor Lane would be going home, too, but under less pleasurable circumstances.

34

UNFIT FOR CIVILIZED MAN

During the early months of 1853, William Carr Lane decided to assess the general situation in the southern part of New Mexico. He was specifically interested in the Mesilla valley north of El Paso, disputed by both the United States and Mexico. In a move described at best as misguided, Lane completed his survey, peremptorily dismissed Mexico's claim and publicly proclaimed the Mesilla valley annexed to the United States. He would soon regret his act.

Upon returning to the Governor's Palace on the Plaza, Lane's feelings of achievement were deflated a bit when he discovered that, in his absence, his home had been burglarized. Not much was missing—just one Indian medal—but the fact that no less than the governor's mansion itself could be robbed with impunity confirmed in him a conviction held by many Americans, that no proper gentleman could reside safely in the wilderness of New Mexico.[1]

Indeed, it was a rare American who arrived in New Mexico without carrying in his heart a burning desire to leave. Travelers from the States believed the territory was a desiccated wasteland offering no promise of industry or agriculture, inhabited by races abysmally inferior to the Anglo American. American civil and military officials generally shared those beliefs, but up to then had usually kept them tactfully concealed. That was about to change.

On May 27, 1852 Colonel Edwin Vose Sumner sent Secretary of War Conrad an unsolicited dissertation, for the Secretary's edification at "some leisure moment," on the nature of and prospects for the territory of New Mexico. Sumner concluded that New Mexico was clearly a waste of American effort and money. The "class of our people" would never want to live there. The country was so lawless that only a military dictatorship could suppress the chaos. The colonel suggested pulling out altogether and giving the territory back to the Mexicans, leaving them enough weapons to fight off the wild Indians. He furthermore assured Conrad that New Mexican citizens themselves would applaud such a decision.[2] Secretary Conrad was apparently pursuaded. That December he openly endorsed abandoning New Mexico and ruminated over a scheme to bribe the better classes of citizens to relocate, as New Mexico was essentially "a country that seems hardly fit for the inhabitation of civilized man." Coincidentally, at that time an additional proposal was circulating in Washington. Why not turn New Mexico into an Indian reservation? It was already filled with wild Indians and it would be a convenient place to relocate some 40,000 California natives . . . for their own good, of course.

The citizens of New Mexico reacted to such proposals with unabashed fury. The Santa Fe Gazette lambasted Conrad's statements as ignorant, absurd and foolish, worthy of the derision of every true New Mexican high or low. In a memorial to Congress, the prominent men of Santa Fe contemptuously rejected any plan to turn New Mexico into a reservation and petitioned against plans to move thousands of California Indians into Cíbola. The petition had no less than twenty pages of signatures.[3] William Carr Lane did not endorse abandoning the entire territory, but he did propose making all lands west of the Rio Grande into one vast Indian reserve.

Such a suggestion could get Lane hanged in effigy on the Plaza, but he soon had bigger worries, confirmed when Lane's secretary, John Ward, opened the day's mail on June 26th, 1853.

"Mail from Independence arrived this morning and by the news brought by it we learn that Mr. Meriwether is the new Gov. and also that Capt. Dodge has been appointed Ind. Agent in place of S. M. Baird . . ."

Henry L. Dodge had been officially hired, William Carr Lane officially sacked. Governor Lane's proclamation annexing the Mesilla Valley had so angered the Mexican government that they had fired off a furious protest to President Franklin Pierce, threatening war. Already Mexican troops were rumored to be on the move in northern Chihuahua. Given the alarming disintegration of relations with Mexico, Pierce could ill afford to keep Lane in office. He gave him a choice—resign or be removed. Lane had been governor for ten months. Short of political suicide, he had little choice but to resign, asserting he had only done so to pursue a seat in Congress as the Territory of New Mexico's delegate.[4]

Predictably, Lane's successor was a good Democrat, David Meriwether from Louisville, Kentucky, and, as his successor, he inherited Lane's copious problems. On the eve of his departure, Commissioner George Manypenny informed Meriwether that of the ten thousand dollars originally appropriated by Congress for running the New Mexico superintendency in 1853, only four thousand remained on the books and that was probably all gone as well. In other words, the superintendency was broke. All Manypenny could spare Meriwether was $500.[5]

Meriwether would not arrive in Santa Fe until August 8th. In the interim, Governor Lane carried on, sending Henry L. Dodge's oath of office and executed bond to Manypenny in Washington. He expected Dodge's agency to be established at or near Fort Defiance, probably at Kendrick's suggestion. As agent, Dodge would have jurisdiction over the Navajo, Zuni, Laguna, Acoma and Hopi tribes, covering an area of about 79,000 square miles. Given the immense size, it was a jurisdiction of the imagination at best.[6] Dodge was in Santa Fe the day his appointment arrived on Lane's desk. He spent the day infront of Justice of the Peace J. M. Mink, applying for the bounty land due him for his military service as captain of the Eutaw Rangers in 1849.[7] Henry requested the Commissioner of Pensions to forward his warrant to his agent in Santa Fe, the trader S. I. Speigelberg. Two days later Henry issued a credit voucher to the traders Messervy and Webb for $315.00 to cover the cost of presents for the Navajos. The items were all quite practical and, looking at the list, one might think Henry was restocking his store. The one notable exception was a pair of holster pistols, no doubt purchased for his own protection in his new job.[8]

Dodge's initial plan was to establish his agency at Chupadero, a site somewhat more removed from Navajo country than either Lane or Kendrick might have preferred. In his pocket he had what little remained of the five hundred dollars Lane had given him for agency supplies. Agent Dodge used thirty of that to pay James Sullivan to haul the Indian goods down to Albuquerque.[9] Henry also carried a circular from the Indian Affairs Office, admonishing all agents to back up all travel and agency expenses with receipts or at the very least a reasonable written explanation. Through his correspondence to Meriwether, Commissioner Manypenny had explicitly required Dodge to account for all travel expenses to Santa Fe "with receipts & explanations of why expenses were incurred." It was hardly a vote of confidence.[10]

Henry certainly wasn't shy about spending money. The previous June, Dodge had bought over $400 in provisions for the Navajo from John Weber, the Fort Defiance sutler, all to be distributed to the Indians: Fifty shirts at a dollar each, saddle leather and butchering knives, coats, pants, straw hats, one hundred plugs of tobacco and one pair of pants, one shirt, one hat and a pair of shoes for the recently escaped Pablo Montoya, in Dodge's own hand:

> "... to clothe Perblo Montoller who ran way from the Navijos and came to our camp naked."

It was a worthwhile expense. Kendrick would later employ Pablo Montoya as the fort interpreter. Weber signed an affidavit stating that he sold those items to "Mr. Henry L. Dodge, acting as Indian Agent, under the direction of Major H. L. Kendrick commanding officer of that post . . . that the goods so purchased were distributed by him among the Navajo Indians and a Mexican captive."[11]

One last item in Dodge's pocket was a letter to Major Henry L. Kendrick from Lieutenant Colonel Dixon Stansbury Miles, late commander at Fort Fillmore and, until the arrival of General John Garland, the acting commander of the entire 9th Military District. Knowing Dodge would be going to Fort Defiance, the colonel asked him to deliver it. Unknown to him, the letter contained orders that would keep both Kendrick and Dodge busy in the saddle of public service for better than a week.

Agent Dodge departed for Chupadero on Thursday, June 30th. With him was George Carter, the savvy Jemez Agency blacksmith Keithly had recommended to Donaciano Vigil. As with Vigil, Carter would prove to be a valuable asset to Dodge.

His salary was $480 a year as the agency smithy, with an extra $120 thrown in for providing his own tools and saving the government the expense. Ironically, the Indian Service refused Carter the eighteen dollars he spent having those tools hauled to Chupadero.[12] Dodge's request to be reimbursed for renting a pony for a month would later be suspended as well. The auditors simply didn't believe it was possible spend that amount of time in the saddle.[13]

By July 3rd, Dodge was in Albuquerque, paying Jose Aramillo thirty bucks to freight the Indian goods out to Cebolleta.[14] Two days after that Dodge and Carter arrived at Chupadero to assemble the agency. It would be a rushed, preliminary effort since Henry had to move on to Fort Defiance to deliver Miles' letter. In the midst of this suddenly hectic schedule, Dodge decided to pop in on the Gormans at Laguna Pueblo. He discovered things hadn't gone well. The Reverend and his family had become outcasts, unable to get the Indians to work even for good wages and were "continually subjected to various petty annoyances from them and their children." It was Saturday when Dodge discovered Samuel's troubles. The next day was a Sunday, and all of that changed.

> " . . . Capt. Dodge, the Indian agent . . . in a large meeting of their principal men, made a most touching address, after which there ensued a spirited strain of remarks, and a vote was taken by the Governor which settled the question of my final settlement in the place. Then followed some singular ceremonies. The Cacique or chief and two of his associates in office rose up, and first the chief embraced me in his arms, and repeated words of about three or four minutes. Then he took both my hand, and, placing the palms together inside his own, he raised them in front of my face, and gently blew in my face over his hands. He then laid one hand on each of my shoulders, and passed them gently down my arms. Then each one of his associates did the same. Their conversation continued through all parts of the ceremony. It was in the Indian Language, and I could only understand an occasional word. But the ceremonies were subsequently explained to me by Lewis Sarocino in Spanish, and Capt. Dodge in English. It was a ceremony of <u>adoption</u>, by which the chief received me and my family, to be his children, and to live in a state of brotherhood with his people . . ."

It was a miracle. One moment the Gormans had been lepers and in the next moment cleansed and glorified. The Reverend found himself embraced by the governor, with his officers actually toadying to Gorman's needs. They urged him and his family to live among them, to select a home site in the community and to build upon that site a permanent mission house.[15]

Dodge also advised Gorman to open a store and make the Indians dependant on him. It would benefit the people of Laguna substantially, bolster Gorman's value in the community and insure him a steady income. Henry also suggested the Reverend arrange to donate clothes to the Laguna children, who were perpetually running through the pueblo jaybird-naked. To get him started, Henry probably offered to bankroll the enterprise. Gorman wisely took his advice and the little store was an immediate hit with the Indians. More importantly, Samuel's missionary zeal had been restored. Now when Gorman preached in the plaza, throngs of Indians attended.[16]

Be that as it may, success where it really counted continued to elude him. The Laguna people would listen well enough, but they just wouldn't convert. John Cremony, who became very familiar with the Apache, could have given Gorman a lesson regarding Christian civilization.

> "I admit that these are very persuasive and forcible argument; but, reverend sir, the red man absolutely refuses to come. He disdains to take my hand; he flouts my offered sympathy, and feels indignant at my presumption in proffering him my aid to improve his condition. He conceives himself not only my equal, but decidedly my superior."[17]

Gorman never forgot Dodge's help. In a brief note written in June of 1855, Gorman forgave him an expense of $12.18 3/4.

> "This I receipt to you as paid on account of the very valuable services you rendered me in my adoption into this community. That act of yours was a good one for the Indians. Were it not that I was adopted as a Son of the Pueblo no doubt I would be routed. I hope you will continue to aid us in every way... we have no other object in view other than the good of the Pueblos."[18]

Dodge would. The missionary secretly must have smarted over Dodge allowing him to suffer for so long and then magically getting him adopted with little more effort than it took to wink an eye. So be it. A bad beginning had made for a good end.

Upon his arrival at Defiance, Dodge learned from the dispatch in his rucksack that Colonel Miles had ordered a reconnaissance. Captain Ewell and fifty men of the

1st Dragoons were to march to Fort Defiance. Upon their arrival, Kendrick was to use Ewell's men and part of his own command to form an expedition to the San Juan and rendezvous there with Second Lieutenant Robert Ransom's 40 dragoons dispatched from Abiquiu. Their task was to impress the Navajos along the river with a show of force, remind them of their treaty responsibilities and to survey the countryside for future contingencies. Miles might have had the reputation of being bombastic and irritating—Lane thoroughly despised the man—but his message to the Navajo was both reasonable and upbeat.

> "I desire you to make known to the Navajos that I as the new Commander of the troops, have witnessed with great satisfaction their desire for peace, that the efforts they have made and are making to return the property which few of their evil minded persons stole from the people of New Mexico, and also their disposition to deliver up these bad men, has given me confidence in them. I fully rely upon the good men among them to do right, so that the treaty between the U.S. and them be not broken."

Miles believed neither Lane nor Sumner had given the Indians enough time to surrender the killers and he essentially told Kendrick to convey that to the Indians. He stressed that all stolen property must be returned or promptly reimbursed by the Indians and, if they did, he would never "disturb them by the invasion of their country ... so long as they show so evident a disposition to preserve peace." As for getting the killers of Don Ramon Martin, Miles gave Kendrick wide latitude, but warned that, under no circumstances, should that issue disrupt the reigning spirit of peace and cooperation.[19] In orders to Lieutenant Ransom, Miles cautioned him to tell the Navajo why he had come, but to do nothing until Kendrick's arrival other than keep a strong guard at camp and a sharp eye on the dragoon horses.[20]

On July 6th, Colonel Miles sent Kendrick a copy of Ransom's orders. He also informed Kendrick that it was urgent to get Ewell and his troops back to Los Lunas by August 10th at the latest. A war with Mexico over the Mesilla Valley was looming, with Mexican General Trias and 1500 Mexican regulars rumored to be bivouacked across from El Paso. With that he wished them every success.[21]

Kendrick's response on July 12th, the day Ransom's detachment departed Abiquiu for the San Juan, was both pessimistic and obliquely critical of Miles' policies towards the Navajos. He firmly believed setting aside Sumner's August deadline was both a mistake and a dangerous precedent. He reasoned the threat had kept the Navajo in a state of perpetual excitement and fear, a useful state for coercing them into cooperation. The Navajo were already coming to the conclusion that there would be no war even if the so-called criminals of Aguila Negra's band remained at large. To not follow through with Sumner's threatened invasion would be interpreted by the Indians as a lack of American resolve, thereby emboldening them. It would be better to embrace war, preferably a big war, rather display signs of weakness and hesitation.[22]

Meanwhile, Ransom and his forty dragoons had entered the valley of the San Juan. On the evening of July 17th, they encamped just west of the confluence of the San Juan and La Plata Rivers, on the south bank near present day Farmington, New Mexico. Here they had their first visit from the Navajos. A small band of men entered camp and explained that their people, at seeing the troops approach, had fled across the river. Ransom penned out a dispatch to Kendrick, updating him on their progress and sent it off to Fort Defiance in the hands of one of the Navajo warriors.[23]

Kendrick, Ewell and the dragoons departed Fort Defiance before the dispatch from Ransom arrived. Kendrick persuaded Dodge to accompany the expedition. Their group consisted of Ewell's 50 dragoons, some 25 fort infantry and artillerymen, and Antonio Sandoval with his own band of warriors. Dodge knew Sandoval well from his Cebolleta days and had hired him as principal guide, at a rate of forty dollars a month. He'd later pay Sandoval $120 for three months' service. Kendrick perhaps thought Sandoval's presence would intimidate the San Juan Navajos and offset what he considered Miles' watery message to the Indians. Kendrick allowed Dodge to draw mutton rations from the Army to feed Sandoval and his men while they were in the field.[24] Reverend Shaw joined in for the tour, leaving Harriet at the fort to fret over the impending war alone.

They rode out on July 19th. Passing through Red Lake and Zarcillos Largos' country, the column crossed over the Chuska Mountains beneath the peaks of the Ojo Calientes before again turning north and descending into the Cañon Blanco towards the San Juan. With the east slopes of the Chuskas on their left, Kendrick's trail gradually dropped into an increasingly barren and hot country. It was midsummer and the stifling heat shimmering from the naked landscape must have been at times intense. Towards the sunset, a singularly enormous butte loomed silhouetted over the desert horizon, like a colossal, jagged tooth. It was *Tsé Bit'ah*, or Winged Rock. Navajos believed it to be the fossilized body of one of many monsters slain by the Warrior Twins. Americans later saw in it the billowing sails of a great ship and named it Shiprock. In the dusk the brooding colossus seemed to hover along with the column, keeping a guarded eye on the soldiers.

Kendrick and Dodge reached the San Juan on the morning of July 23rd. It had taken the better part of five days to make the hundred-mile trip. There, where the Chaco Wash met the broad and surging San Juan, they found Ransom's men encamped, fishing for catfish. Later, Henry Dodge described the river in a letter that appeared in the September 1st edition of the Santa Fe Gazette.

"The Rio San Juan is a bold mountain stream about one hundred yards in general width, affording nearly as much water as the Rio del Norte. The Indians represent it as exceedingly difficult to cross on account of the rapidity and power of the current, and that it is frequently attended with the loss of life and property. The rapidity of the current of this stream is much greater than that of the Missouri or the Rio Grande del Norte.

"The bottoms are wide and the soil rich, of a mixed loam and sandy formation very similar to that of the Rio Grande and equally susceptible to irrigation. Some of the bottoms are heavily timbered with cottonwood, in many places forming dense forests, under grown with currant bushes that grow to a height of ten feet, bearing a most delicious fruit on which our party feasted most bountifully.[25]

While the soldiers snacked on currant berries, Ransom briefed Kendrick and Dodge. There had been some tense moments. After the initial group of Navajo had come into Ransom's camp on July 17th, the lieutenant resolved to keep his men moving, perhaps anticipating an attack. The following day they marched fifteen miles westward down river, noting Indian farms along the way. After settling into camp that evening, an even larger group of Navajo appeared, led by the headmen Cayetano and Archuletta. The Indians expressed a desire for peace and promised they would surrender Ramon Martín's killers as soon as they could find them. The heavily armed Navajo remained in camp that night and Ransom noted that among them were twenty Ute warriors. None in camp that night slept easily.

Ransom continued down river the next morning despite Navajo attempts to dissuade him. Presently his column came across a substantial number of sheep tracks, as if the animals had been driven northward across the river to safety. Ransom decided not to pursue the matter so they pitched camp to await Kendrick's arrival. That evening the Navajos again arrived, bringing the Americans several butchered sheep and in every way demonstrating their friendship. Indians and Americans feasted and the evening passed pleasantly enough. On the 20th, Ransom's command backtracked up river some distance and again encamped. Aguila Negra, Miguelito and Archuletta returned to request a council. Ransom agreed. During the course of the discussions, during which the lieutenant demanded the murderers and stolen livestock, they had, as Ransom mysteriously described it in his final report, a slight disturbance. He did not elaborate, but the seemingly ever-present James A. Bennett, who was assigned to Ransom's command, did.

Bennett related that talks were going well when another headman unexpectedly arrived to join the council. Ransom had set several items in the center of the council circle to give to the headmen as gifts. In a grand gesture, the lieutenant offered the newcomer a present, a sack of flour. Apparently that infuriated Archuletta, who felt snubbed because Ransom had not yet given him, a headman of greater status, a gift of equal worth.

> "He sprang to his feet, seized the flour sack by the bottom corners, and giving it a swing, scattered the flour to the four winds. Those seated in the circle were given the appearance of an assemblage of millers."

In retrospect it was an act worthy of vaudeville, but through the settling cloud of flour dust emerged a scene perilously familiar. Ransom and his men were up, their weapons in their hands. When the Navajo responded in kind, the lieutenant seized Archuletta and threatened to kill him then and there. According to Bennett, after an edgy standoff, Ransom finally told the Indians he'd release their headman if they would bring in five or six sheep for his men.

> "In fifteen minutes time a round dozen of the largest and fattest sheep I have ever seen in any country were brought to us."

As with his earlier description of events under Sumner in Canyon de Chelly, Bennett's story is certainly worthy of skepticism. It is a rather peculiar one but not altogether incredible. Ransom eventually released Archuletta, who protested that the whole squabble had been a misunderstanding. He agreed to return to council the next day, and then departed. Not surprisingly, he didn't show. On the 22nd, the lieutenant moved his men back down river to the mouth of the Chaco, where Kendrick found him the following day.[26]

It was clear that Ransom had alienated the Navajo. Kendrick and Dodge probably did not expect to see them again soon. The major judged Ransom's command to then be "unnecessary" and the next day ordered him and his column to explore along the Animas River if practicable. It was not. Ransom's men couldn't get across the San Juan. Low on provisions, suffering from heat and broken down horses, Ransom turned his dragoons towards Abiquiu. Since chances of meeting with the San Juan Navajos had been blasted, Major Kendrick decided to explore down river, keeping in mind a suitable spot for a new military post, "contrary to the efforts of the Navajoes" who he believed attempted to deter him. With Sandoval and his men as guides, Kendrick, Dodge and the column followed the course of the San Juan moving from west to northwest along its southern banks. As the days passed, the pleasant wideness of the arid river valley had gradually crept in on them and the banks bracing the river rose. On July 28th, just as the river began to swing due west again, the San Juan flowed into a convoluted chasm known later as the Goosenecks. Henry described the yawning switch back canyons that seemed to devour the river just above present day Mexican Hat, Utah.

> "We traveled down the San Juan six days to where it runs into a deep canon. This canon, the Indians informed me, extends to the Rio Colorado, about one hundred miles from where we struck it, and rises in many places to the height of several hundred feet..."[27]

Sandoval informed Kendrick and Dodge that the river remained entrenched for ten to fifteen days of marching. Any further exploration would be useless. Major Kendrick turned his command southward where the Rio de Cheille, or Chinle Wash, met the San Juan. They were seven days march from Fort Defiance. Chinle Wash itself provided little better road. It meandered its way southward through the sandstone cliffs, sweeping past ancient Indian ruins and switch backing around petrified dunes. Neither Dodge nor Kendrick mentioned these notable sites—the column may have left the Chinle early and made their way up over the rolling country of Nokaito Bench. As they entered the expansive Chinle Valley south of Rock Point and Round Rock, Henry again began to see evidence of Navajo habitation.

> "After leaving the San Juan we returned to the valley of the Chella, which we found to be a wide rich valley, extensively cultivated in corn and some wheat. The wheat grows finely and ripens in June and much of the Indian corn we found well matured and ready for the harvesting the latter end of July. The Navajoes have cultivated much more extensively this year than in any former year, owing perhaps to the supply of hoes and spades furnished them by the government. The plow is now used by them. Their

crop consists of wheat, Indian corn, beans, pumpkins and melons. They have also fine peaches that grow abundantly and of a superior quality. The corn crop from the best estimate that I was able to make exceeds two thousand acres and much of it must give an abundant yield and will doubtless give them a large surplus, which it is my intention to induce them to sell to the troops at Fort Defiance."[28]

To their west some twenty miles away was vast and foreboding Black Mesa, a Navajo refuge of juniper, piñon and pine. To the east, the uplands of Canyon de Chelly and the Defiance Plateau. As the Cheille turned to the east, so did Kendrick's column. They entered the canyon from the western portal, the first Americans known to have done so. The Navajos here were decidedly friendlier than their skittish cousins on the San Juan. A contingency of twenty Indians joined Kendrick's column. Somewhere in the canyon, Dodge noted that they met a headman he called "Fair-weather." The name was obviously a loose translation insomuch as the Navajo term *hózhóní* can imply pleasant climate or weather. Chief Fair Weather may have been *Hastiin Hózhó*, meaning roughly Man of Well Being, rather than weather. Historically, he was known by his Spanish name of Barboncito.

> "We were treated with great attention and kindness by the chief and all his people, who feasted us with green corn, melons, milk and cheese. Amagoso the principal war captain urged the Rev. Mr. Shaw very hard to pay him a visit when his peaches were ripe. Mr. Shaw is quite popular with the Indians, and has an extensive vocabulary with them, he has made a couple vocabularies of their language and speaks it sufficiently to make himself understood upon almost any subject. He is very kind and attentive to them, supplying their wants whenever it is in his power to do so."[29]

In the course of their trip and in previous outings, Dodge had helped Reverend Shaw learn basic Navajo customs and words. He was probably flattering Shaw a bit on his mastery of Navajo, which was as different from English as French from Vietnamese. After passing a pleasant time in Canyon de Chelly, Kendrick's men emerged from the east portal and turned their horses towards Fort Defiance. The expedition arrived at the fort on August 4th. As expeditions went, it had been inconclusive at best. Dodge had been unable to meet with any of the San Juan Navajo. Kendrick had not found a suitable site for a new fort. He had not affected any further surrender of stock and had not persuaded Aguila Negra and the San

Juan Navajo to surrender Don Martín's murderers. As a result, the major returned to Defiance firmly believing that another war with the Navajo was inevitable.

In addition, Kendrick suggested subtracting the cost of the stolen stock from the Navajo's annual Indian Service appropriation and thought it might be a good lesson if Dodge brought the Indians in to witness the effect it had on their much anticipated annuities and gifts. The major firmly believed that no agreement with the Navajo would be effective unless it was continually "guaranteed by their interests or their fears."[30]

35

BLESSINGS OF A CHRISTIAN CIVILIZATION

From the day Dodge succeeded Baird as Indian agent, the actual location of his agency was in the saddle. Having the Treasury Department suspend Voucher 17, the forty-six dollars he spent to rent a horse robust enough to accommodate the job, must have been irritating, but that was typical. The auditors had questioned his expenses before and they would again, such as the issue of the fifty dollars Lane claimed to have given Dodge on July 23rd for "making presents, &c" to the Navajos, money that was never accounted for. Had Dodge just neglected to get a receipt or had he used it to finance a quick game of *monte*? The date on the voucher was wrong, anyway. Rather than being in Santa Fe on July 23rd, as it indicated, Henry L. Dodge was with Kendrick and Ransom on the San Juan.[1]

As with so many Indian agents, Dodge was presented with nearly impossible duties. He was accountable for the many Navajo bands strewn across a huge territory, the seven isolated and secretive Hopi towns, as well as the Zuni, Acoma and Laguna pueblos, overseeing their welfare and making them "participants in all the advantages and blessings of a Christian civilization." The Navajo alone would be a handful, and would consume nearly all his time. Theoretically, Dodge was to represent the tribe's interests. In reality, agents were expected to serve American interests over those of the Indian, to persuade Indian leaders to comply with the wishes of the Great White Father, to make them malleable, and to act as the stern, disciplining parent when they were not. Given the impracticality of doing the entire job well, it was hardly surprising that many an agent opted to concentrate on what proved to be the most important duty—filing timely reports, accounting for every penny spent, and punctually executing all Indian Office directives.

Right off the bat Dodge had trouble with timely-reports and penny-counting. Commissioner of Indian Affairs George Manypenny himself had admonished the man to mind his paperwork. Henry frequently didn't respond to Bureau directives with the alacrity the Commissioner expected, either. Manypenny had sent all agents a circular dated August 3rd requiring them to reprimand licensed Indian traders who were retarding the civilization of the Indian by keeping their stores open on the Sabbath.

> "You will see that compliance with this direction is strictly enforced in your agency; a violation of it will be considered just cause for the revocation of the License of the offending Trader, and you are required to make report of such violation."[2]

Such orders delivered from on-high invariably spelled trouble for those in the field. The new Ute agent, E. A. Graves, who was not-so-coincidentally the son-in-law of Governor David Meriwether, noted that Sunday was the most important of business days. Enforcing the directive would put a lot of noses out of joint. Nevertheless, in his response to Manypenny, Graves gushingly proclaimed he would take great pleasure in carrying out the government's "Christian, philanthropic & humane policy." Graves wasn't stupid. He was kissing up to superiors, as did any obsequious subservient civil servant. What he actually did about it is another question. Dodge got a circular too, addressed to *Henry L. Dodge, Esquire, Agent etc. care of the Prefect of Santa Fe*. His reaction was probably less fervent than Graves', if indeed he reacted at all. Issuing a directive was always easier than getting it done, a fact the distant bureaucrats seemed unable to grasp. Dodge's directive likely served a useful purpose . . . kindling a fire for morning's first cup of coffee, perhaps.[3]

Upon returning to Defiance from the San Juan, Kendrick and Dodge decided it would be advantageous to have a Navajo delegation meet the newly arrived departmental commander, General John Garland, as well as the new governor, David Meriwether. Small groups of Navajo had gone in before, but Kendrick and Dodge intended a truly impressive showing. There would be at least a dozen principle Navajo leaders representing diverse Navajo bands, headed by Zarcillos Largos and

Barboncito, and their entourage would number over one hundred. On August 6th Kendrick departed for Santa Fe to confer with Garland, leaving Dodge at the fort to complete preparations. Two weeks later, the Navajo delegation departed, riding their best horses, clothed in their finest regalia and bristling with weaponry. That formidable Indian battalion must have inspired both awe and fear as it passed the scattered settlements along its way to Santa Fe. They arrived at Dodge's Chupadero Agency on August 22nd. Henry bought seven sheep and six sacks of corn for the Navajo from Francisco Sandoval at Cebolleta. After a day or two of rest, the delegation continued towards Albuquerque. On August 30th they arrived at Isleta Pueblo on the Rio Grande, where Dodge purchased forty-five dollars worth of supplies, including a cow.[4]

In Santa Fe, recently arrived Governor David Meriwether must have wondered how he would ever cover the cost of hosting the Navajo. He had already written Commissioner Manypenny stridently requesting more money. In a second letter, Meriwether wrote that he had been compelled raise money by holding the equivalent of a yard sale, disposing of various items of discarded Indian Service property including an old satchel stuffed with the late James Calhoun's belongings. Furthermore, his predecessor, William Carr Lane, had been of no assistance whatsoever. From the moment Meriwether planted his boots on New Mexican soil, he'd been squabbling with Lane. The superintendency had been left a shambles. There was a dearth of equipment and supplies, and what remained was in atrocious condition. The wagons were little better than scrap and Lane had repeatedly refused to return the one acceptable carriage, the superintendent's official ambulance. When he finally did, Meriwether discovered that it, too, was broken down. On top of that there were renewed Indian troubles. The Ute had become antagonistic and were threatening war, while Apache Agent Michael Steck had reported that the Mescalero were being quarrelsome, twice attacking John Tullis' trade caravan along the San Antonio road below Socorro.[5]

Yet David Meriwether was no stranger to adversity. A true Southern Democrat, the 53 year-old Kentuckian had been involved in the Missouri fur trade from the time he was eighteen, was briefly imprisoned in Santa Fe by the Spanish in 1819 for spying, and managed to survive Indian attacks, a bitter winter and near starvation before getting back to Kentucky. Upon his return, he farmed, studied law and entered politics.[6] Having survived those adventures, Meriwether returned to Kentucky. He farmed, studied law and served in the Kentucky statehouse. In 1852 he was appointed interim Senator for the deceased Henry Clay, but chose not run for election to the seat when Clay's term expired. Subsequently, President

Pierce appointed Meriwether governor and superintendent of Indian affairs for New Mexico and specifically instructed him to first soothe Mexican anger over Lane's Mesilla Valley gaff and then to crack down on Indian slave trafficking of Mexican captives.[7]

Meriwether's role in New Mexico as governor and superintendent of Indian affairs would follow the standard—he would be the striking flint of controversy. In contrast, his traveling companion to Santa Fe, the new commander of the 9th Military District, Brevet Brigadier General John Garland, appeared to be the very antithesis of controversy. He was no hothead and toted no axe to grind. Garland was a sixty-one year old native of Virginia, a career soldier who survived service in the War of 1812, the Black Hawk and Seminole Wars, and the hottest of action during the War with Mexico. He was a solid and efficient administrator—all business—with a low-key, accommodating posture, strikingly dissimilar to his predecessor Edwin V. Sumner.[8]

Dodge and the Navajo delegation met first with Garland at his Albuquerque headquarters on August 29th. Dodge later related that the General received the headmen with "great courtesy and kindness" and that his "mild and gentlemanly deportment made a favorable impression on the chiefs." After obtaining some salt and a cow from the garrison, the delegation headed for Santa Fe.[9] Meanwhile, Meriwether was scribbling out a report to Commissioner Manypenny, outlining his strategy for dealing with the troublesome wild tribes. There were daily robberies. Citizens, be they high or low, were afraid to travel the countryside without armed escort. Meriwether hesitatingly approved Lane's policies but, seeing himself as more knowledgeable of Indian character, proposed an innovative plan. First, he would systematically meet with each wild tribe and establish a lasting peace. To insure the tribes remained at peace, the Indian Service would grant them generous annuities. Once that was in place, Meriwether would then liquidate all tribal lands near the settlements and relocate the Indians to remote corners of the territory, removing them from the temptation to steal and drink liquor—for their own good, of course.[10] Innovative, it wasn't. It was essentially a policy as old as the United States itself. Remove the Indians for their own protection, usurp their lands and then make them dependent on the government.

Dodge and the Navajo entered Santa Fe on August 31st, in an unprecedented scene. The savage Navajo, the dreaded Lords of the Earth, the perpetual scourge of New Mexico, were camped on the outskirts of the territorial capital, housed and fed and feted by the government. As unique the experience was for the people of Santa Fe, who were doubtlessly unnerved by their proximity, it was equally unique for the Navajo leaders. Never had so many headmen of notoriety come to Santa Fe, a place where they knew they were viewed at best with animosity. At the head of the delegation were Zarcillos Largos, principal chief of the nation, Barboncito, Juan Lucero, Gordo de Pesqueso from Bear Springs; Cojo and the brother of Zarcillos Largo from Chuska; Colorado and Colas from San Juan; the brother of Many Mules from Ojos Calientes; Cobras Blancas from the mesas of Chaco; and Del Juanico from Cienega Grande, men who had for decades carried on intermittent war with New Mexicans.

On September 1st, the Navajo and Meriwether met, and they hit it off from the very start. Meriwether later characterized Zarcillos Largos and his group as a "fine and healthy looking people remarkably well clothed in fabrics of their own manufacture," stating that of all the Indians he'd seen, they looked to be the healthiest Indians west of the Arkansas River. Henry Dodge gave a glowing description of the Navajo condition, confirming what Kendrick had already told the governor. Dodge believed their population to be around ten thousand souls. The Indians had extensive herds of horse and sheep and vast, productive grain fields. He estimated that Navajo livestock numbered roughly 250,000 head, making many of the headmen among the wealthiest individuals in the entire territory, American, Hispanic or Indian.

It was an impressive gathering, but Meriwether noted the absence of the leaders of the Navajo bands he believed responsible for the Vallecito killing and other outrages, Archuleta foremost among them.

> "These bands have but little intercourse with our white settlements or with the band of Archuletta who I am inclined to think is guilty of most of the mischief attributed to the Navijos. This chief and his band together with a few other Navijos live nearer our settlements and on the border of the Utahs with whom they associate, and are a bad set of fellows in my opinion ..."

Meriwether's suspicions worked in his Navajo guests' favor. To what extent the governor distrusted the San Juan Navajo conversely made him amicable to the Navajo there before him. With the introductory formalities finished, the meeting adjourned until the following day, when Meriwether introduced more serious business to the delegation of chiefs. He started off by lecturing the Navajo that the "Great Father in Washington" had sent him to govern both his white and red children. Meriwether explained that he'd listen to white man complaints with one ear and red man complaints with the other, rattle them around in his skull a bit, and then a decision "would be given from my mouth." It would be curious to know what impact Meriwether's childish analogies, once translated from English to Spanish and then to Navajo, actually had on the headmen. Archuleta's flour slinging aside, the Navajo leaders conspicuously guarded their expressions and reactions, being at all times discreet and cautious, and their inner emotions remained nearly indiscernible. They listened patiently, thought carefully before responding and, when speaking, responded with circumspect and never offended unless that was the intent.

Zarcillos Largos replied that certainly there were criminals among the Navajo who respected no authority and could not be governed, but those men had fled out of reach across the San Juan. He assured Meriwether that no member of any of the Navajo bands there in council were guilty of hostile acts, that the Navajo leadership was determined to create a permanent peace. The headman then diplomatically reminded Meriwether of a disparity Americans had so often ignored. The Navajo had given up captives on several occasions, the New Mexicans not one. For years raiders had taken great numbers of Navajo women and children into slavery, but contrary to previous treaty promises, none of them had ever been redeemed.

Meriwether replied that he knew of no Navajos being held by New Mexicans but pledged that, if he discovered some, he would demand their immediate release. Perhaps as a mild parry to Zarcillos Largos' complaint, the governor noted that there were several Hispanics captives among the Navajo there. He suggested that, since those captives were familiar with the settlements, they could sleuth around a bit to locate Navajo captives and report their findings to him. However, Meriwether intoned, even if they did not find a single Navajo captive, it was absolutely incumbent upon the headmen to restore all New Mexican prisoners held by the Navajo. In his own unobtrusive but agile manner, Zarcillos Largos responded.

> " . . . there were two or three Mexicans with his people who had been made prisoners long since and had married Navijo wives and some such were then present and were at liberty to remain with their people if they chose to do so. . . . He then continued by saying that there were four other captives with his people who had no families and that they should be restored through our agent on his return."

The governor indeed discovered that, upon questioning, each of the Mexican prisoners "expressed a strong wish to return" with the Navajo. Meriwether was thus compelled to allow them to do so.[11]

At the conclusion of the meeting, Meriwether promised that, in the evening, each headman would receive a medal as a gift to commemorate their friendship. The council broke up with convincingly strong and sincere feelings of goodwill on both sides. That evening, Zarcillos Largos and five other headmen called on the governor. Meriwether was pleased to present the ribboned medals, but there were strings attached. Receiving a medal required each headman to be an agent of peace between the Navajos and the New Mexicans, each being individually responsible for the acts of their band members. Each would be required to surrender any offending members of their band to Agent Dodge for punishment, a requirement the Americans had heretofore been unable to enforce. If the Navajo were attacked or otherwise abused by New Mexicans, Meriwether instructed the headmen to seize the perpetrators and deliver them to Dodge for punishment rather than exacting their own retribution. If they couldn't seize the accused parties, they were required to report the incident to Agent Dodge and he would arrest the perpetrators.

Essentially, Meriwether had prohibited the Navajo from defending themselves. Still, the headmen agreed to the conditions, no doubt cognizant of the improbability of being able to fulfill any of those obligations, and "received their respective insignia of office with great apparent pride and satisfaction." Meriwether saved the most ornate medal for Zarcillos Largos. Draping it over his head, the governor appointed him the principle leader among the Navajo headmen there.

> ". . . I appointed him captain over all the others and would expect him to see that they obeyed my instructions and that he would be held responsible for their good conduct. To which he assented and received his Medal in great glee."

Zarcillos Largos received the gift with polite Navajo enthusiasm, secretly knowing Meriwether expected him to shoulder an impossible burden, given that dogged Navajo insistence on independence that seemed to drive *Bilagáana* leaders mad. The Navajo leadership had heard it all before with Doniphan, with Colonel Washington, Sumner, Calhoun and Lane. It was little more than rhetoric. Perhaps Zarcillos Largos believed Meriwether had implied that he would be a head councilor rather than the autocratic leader the Americans were looking for. If so, he was in grave error.

There were no meetings of significance the following day, September 3rd. Dodge spent time rounding up grub for his Navajo guests. He purchased fifty tin cups from Preston Beck, another forty-five cups from J. & H. Mecure and fourteen sheep from Juan Benavides. Dodge contracted with Messervy and Webb for almost ninety dollars worth of items from sugar to kettles to coffee. In bread alone the group would devour over 350 loaves during their stay, at a cost of $23.25.[12]

The evening brought feasting and a Navajo dance in the Plaza, a spectacle that few residents of Santa Fe had ever witnessed. Meriwether handed out two hundred and fifty dollars worth of merchandise and was thanked profusely at every turn. Contrary to his expectations, the governor was amazed that, during the entire stay in Santa Fe, that "sink hole of vice" as Sumner once described it, not one of the Navajo touched a drop of "spirits of any kind" and in all cases were orderly and peaceful. He was also greatly impressed by the quality of the woven Navajo blankets and other articles of their clothing.

On the 4th, Dodge and the Navajo delegation left for Navajo country. It is reasonable to conclude that the citizens of Santa Fe heaved a sweet sigh of relief at their departure. Meriwether was among them, as he confessed in a follow up report to Manypenny.

> "I am inclined to doubt the policy of bringing these Indians into our settlements for many reasons. In the first place it is expensive, then it brings them acquainted with our country its roads and settlements which would be a decided advantage in times of hostility. And last though not the least objection which I will mention is that I think it best for both races that they should have as little promiscuous intercourse as possible with each other.... It however has been the custom with the Indians of this Territory to send in delegations on the arrival of a new Governor to greet him and Agent Dodge has but conformed to this custom..."[13]

In a letter to the Santa Fe Gazette, Henry included some particulars from Meriwether's talk with the Navajo delegation that the governor himself did not include in his report to Manypenny. If accurate, Dodge's comments indicated that, irrespective of Garland's own stand on the issue of Ramon Martin, Meriwether was willing to forgive and forget.

> "Our excellent Governor, who by the way is an old Indian trader, well acquainted with the red man and his habits, gave them to understand very distinctly that he would expect them to comply with the conditions of the treaty made with them in 1849 by Col. Washington, and that any departure from its stipulations would bring down upon them the severest punishment.

"The Governor agreed to pass over all offenses committed before the 1st of September—to-day—and they on their part promised to deliver the murderer of Ramon Martin as soon as possible dead or alive. The council broke up in a friendly manner, the Indians agreeing to leave tomorrow morning for their own country. If they comply with the instructions of the Governor, and live in good faith, peace and quiet, prosperity must attend them, for they have all the elements within themselves to live independent and happy. But on the other hand, if they violate the promise made to the Governor, recommence their depredations; they are doomed to a desperate fate.

"I believe, Mr. Editor, you know me well enough to believe that nothing on my part will be left undone that I can accomplish to check the turbulent habits of these Indians, not only for their own benefit, but for the prosperity of the Territory, which depends so much upon the protection of our farmers from Indian robberies.

Yours truly
Henry L. Dodge, Agent"

From that moment on, the pursuit of justice over Ramon Martin's murder was all but dead. It was probably for the best. In his report to the adjutant general's office, General John Garland conceded with some personal embarrassment that Colonel Sumner, although an old friend and judged by all a gallant fighter, had left the department in a complete shambles. Specifically, he faulted Sumner for ordering a war against the Navajos that neither he nor Garland, to his own embarrassment, could sustain.[14]

Meriwether sent Henry Dodge a specific list of duties he was to undertake as Navajo agent. First and foremost, Meriwether instructed him to follow up on Zarcillos Largos' complaint. Dodge was to return captives to their Navajo families whenever he learned of them being held in the settlements, provided "such return is desired by such captive." He would also demand from the Navajos all captive New Mexicans and to return them to their families, "when desired by such captives," to mitigate disputes between the Navajos and other tribes within his agency, and to investigate and make "such decisions as justice and equity may require." Meriwether told Dodge to submit a complete report on the state of his agency and to include statistics on Navajo population and economy. Above all, the governor cautioned Henry to watch what he spent, to be stringently frugal, and if he found anyone hired without Indian Service authorization, to fire him.[15]

So, flush with optimism and satisfaction, Agent Dodge and the Navajo delegation headed home. Henry Dodge and Zarcillos Largos must have believed the entire conclave a complete success. The devil, of course, was in the details.

36

PASS WASHINGTON

The Navajo leaders had promised Meriwether they would restore stolen livestock and they proved committed to that promise. As a result, the early fall of 1853 found Henry L. Dodge weeks in the saddle, crossing Navajo country on horseback to herd donations of Navajo stock to Defiance and then back to the settlements.[1] He again hired Antonio Sandoval as his guide and interpreter at the lucrative rate of $40 a month. During this period, Dodge was instrumental in averting a nasty scrap between the Navajo and the Jicarilla Apache. A Navajo raiding party had stolen several horses from the Jicarilla, who threatened retaliation. Dodge managed to finagle the ponies' return before a war erupted between the two tribes. At the end of September, Dodge returned to Chupadero to tie up agency business for the 3rd quarter, paying Sandoval in full on September 30th, $120.00 for three months of work "in the recovery of sheep stolen by the Navijo Nation..." By his own tally, from July 1st to the end of the quarter, he ridden just over a thousand miles.[2]

Navajo-American relations remained so agreeable General Garland optimistically reported to headquarters that the tribe was rapidly becoming civilized. On the other hand, relations with the Ute and Jicarilla relations remained inhospitable at best.[3] Ute agent Graves kept up a steady stream of pessimistic correspondence with Meriwether and Manypenny, detailing Ute outrages. Chico Velasquez's band had been implicated in a robbery of some citizens and Graves fretted that a war was inevitable. Governor Meriwether was in agreement, stating the only lasting remedy was to completely exterminate Velasquez and his "daring band who has infested our borders for a long time..."[4]

On the other hand, Agent Henry L. Dodge seldom subjected Meriwether or Manypenny to rambling complaints. Just getting the man to put pen to paper on a regular basis was nigh impossible. The Navajo agent's reports were spotty at best. Extracting comprehensive and meticulous descriptions from him was like squeezing water from a stone; Dodge's first report to Manypenny consisted of a single sentence. The agent's explanation of expenses was often incomplete and his receipts wanting. Invariably the auditors would find him coming up short. In the tally of 3rd quarter expenses, Henry spent over three hundred dollars more on Indian business than he could rustle up in receipts. There was a voucher for $88.97 to Messervy and Webb for Navajo presents. No receipt. There was another one for $75.00 to pay herder Fernando Acuña for driving sheep during Dodge's tour of Navajo country. Again, no receipt. There were inappropriate expenses and unauthorized vouchers, notably the one he'd issued to himself for his travel expenses—$45.00—subsequently paid to José Francisco Aragon, and for Antonio Sandoval and George Carter, the agency blacksmith. Lane had not authorized them in writing, but Meriwether suggested Manypenny pay them both.

Then there was that matter of Dodge's rented horse, Voucher Number 17.

> "In view of the fact that the Agent had on hand 3 public animals (1 horse & 2 mules) the necessity for hiring this horse is not apparent. Moreover, as the Agent in his letter to this office of Sept. 30, 1853, reports that he was engaged in traveling almost the entire quarter, the question arises as to the propriety of charging for the use of this horse for every day of the quarter. Explanations as to these objections and the number of days the horse was in actual use, required."[5]

Suspended.

The General Accounting Office would also require a complete explanation of how the fifty bucks Lane had given him for Indian gifts had been spent. It was well and good that they might expect an explanation, but they wouldn't get one. There is little doubt Dodge actually spent the money.[6] In a separate letter to his first report to the Commissioner, Dodge instructed Manypenny to pay his 3rd quarter salary to the trader Henry Connelly, who held a draft for the same.

> "I have this day drawn on you a draft in favor of Henry Connelly for the sum of three hundred and eighty seven dollars and fifty cents being the amount of my salary for the Quarter ending the 30th day of September 1853; and which please honor at sight.
>
> "I certify, on honor, that I have preformed the duties of Indian

Agent from the 1st July to 30th Sept. 1853. Henry L. Dodge, Indian Agent for Navijos"[7]

A short time after filing his quarterly report, Dodge and Carter packed up their possessions and closed the Chupadero agency for good. Dodge wasn't retreating to a more comfortable locale; he was going forward. Relations with the gregarious Navajo had never been more affable . . . one might dare say affectionate. Navajo visitors regularly stopped by Fort Defiance and often spent the night, compelling Kendrick to assign them sleeping quarters on the north end of the post. The fort, initially meant to overawe the Indian, had become something of a bed and breakfast for them.[8]

Major Kendrick applauded Dodge's decision to establish the agency in Navajo country. Having the Navajo agency at Fort Defiance would be an important step towards preserving the peace. Dodge would be on hand and readily accessible to the Navajo and to Major Kendrick as well, to immediately address any crisis that might erupt . . . and it was only a matter of time, the major mused, until one did. However, to Kendrick's disapproval, Henry had no intention of hunkering down within the protection of Fort Defiance. He'd already picked out a site for the new agency, and it wasn't exactly a stone's throw from the garrison. It was some thirty miles northeast of the fort, deep in Navajo country, nestled on the slopes of the Chuska Mountains and, at best, a half-day's fast gallop back to Defiance.

Some claimed Dodge's act audacious, most others derided it as deluded and suicidal. Nevertheless, he chose a site near where he and Kendrick had reconnoitered the Tunicha heights together in 1849. The Navajo knew it as *Beeshlichíí Bigiizh*, Copper Pass. The Americans referred to it as Pass Washington, in honor of Colonel Washington, leader of the expedition. It was a site of inspirational beauty: a broad well-watered meadow fringed by rugged red sandstone spires and buttes set in glowing contrast to the deep green of surrounding pine forests. It was prime real estate by both Navajo and white standards, and was claimed by Zarcillos Largos and his people. Getting permission from him to put down stakes there would have been an absolute imperative, but it is more likely that Zarcillos Largos invited Dodge to come, offering him the valuable section to sweeten the deal. The old headman appreciated the potential contribution the middle-aged white man could make his people's well-being and prosperity and to the headman's own status.

Dodge paid Rafael Chávez eighty dollars to build two agency houses, good stout structures assembled of native sandstone and roofed with rafters of local pine.[9] Sturdy housing was crucial. The autumn months had portended an exceedingly cold and snowbound winter for Navajo country; the temperature at Defiance had already dipped nineteen degrees below zero—and it was still early in the season. By mid November, the agency was up and running with a staff of as many as seven men. H. L. Dodge occupied the agency house and George Carter the black smithy, along with an unnamed Hispanic silversmith employed to assist Carter. Juan Anaya, Kendrick's former interpreter, had come up from Defiance to serve as Henry's assistant and interpreter. Manuel Vallejos served as herder for the agency livestock, and another employee as a general servant.

In a letter to the editor in the Santa Fe Gazette dated November 16th, Dodge described the prospects for his agency's success. He paid Carter special tribute as "a man of sterling worth and every inch a soldier." The blacksmith shop had quickly became popular with the Navajo, who were fascinated with both the practical and artistic uses of metalworking; forging hoes, knives and plows as well as fashioning copper and silver into ornaments of personal adornment. The Indian men asked Carter and his Mexican silversmith to teach them the craft. Although Carter and his silversmith were both illiterate, they proved apt teachers, and the Navajo learned with amazing speed. Carter and his assistant probably hadn't an inkling of it at the time, but their lessons would permanently change the Navajo, for their most notable student, Herrero Delgadito, most likely started the distinctively-styled Navajo silverwork. Not coincidentally, his Spanish name translated as Thin Iron Worker and in Navajo as *Atsidí Sání*, Old Silversmith.[10]

David Meriwether understood that something as small as a smithy shop could be most effective in hammering out a durable peace, and he again approved George Carter's salary, stating to Manypenny that Agent Dodge was quite apprehensive that Carter's firing would "create dissatisfaction among the Navajos."[11] Unfortuntely, by early December, the money need to run such a program was nearly exhausted. Meriwether ordered Dodge to cut expenses. Meanwhile, the governor found himself reduced to begging Manypenny for money, blaming Lane for bankrupting the Indian Service by lavishing gifts on the Indians. Those Indians, now clamped in the teeth of a severe winter and near destitute, were expecting liberal handouts. Meriwether had nothing to give. Those hardships had already spawned "numerous thefts & robberies" by the Indian, and he feared the tribes would be forced to make bolder and more frequent attacks. The cure was money. He needed more money.[12]

Apparently Manypenny had none to give, reducing a much-irritated Meriwether to funding the superintendency out of his own wallet. He wasn't the only one. The five hundred dollars Dodge received to meet expenses for the 4th quarter ran out and he ended spending $121 of his own money.[13] His agency was scantily supplied, and to describe life there as sparse was an understatement. There were four mules and a few sheep, three camp kettles and various odds and ends. They didn't even have one of those broken down buckboards owned by the Indian Service, but, without a wagon road, it would have been a useless anyway. Every pound of food, tools and supplies Dodge brought had been packed in on his scar-backed mules.[14]

News of the general dire condition of the New Mexican Indian Superintendency eventually reached Washington and the desk of Senator Henry Dodge, who probably had his son's welfare in mind when he scribbled a pencil note to George W. Manypenny.

> "Being deeply impressed with the necessity of our having some sort of Agency Houses for our Indian Agencies in New Mexico I respectfully ask that you will furnish an estimate of the cost of such buildings to Hon. W. K. Sebastian as soon as possible & greatly oblige your friend."[15]

Isolated in the wilds of the Chuska, Dodge led an intrepid but vulnerable group. If things ever went sour between Dodge and the Navajo, their chances of survival would be roughly the same as those of a trussed sheep to slaughter. Dodge could expect no help from Defiance. The fort was too distant to count on for either defense or refuge, and there were those who expected the Indians to massacre Dodge and his men. Henry couldn't have helped but reflect on the possibility, but he gave it little weight, believing the Navajo friendship sincere and that they truly trusted him. He had promised to help the Navajo and had made good on that promise, the poverty of the Indian Service not withstanding. Indeed, both Dodge and Meriwether had undertaken the delicate task of locating any Navajo being held as a slave and returning them to their families. In January of 1854 Meriwether deputized José Castillo, alcalde of Cebolleta, to seize two Navajo captives taken and sold by the Mount Taylor headman Antonio Sandoval.

> "Sir: I am informed that there are two Navajo captives at this place, or in those environs and you are authorized and enforced to return them or cause to be returned to Captain Dodge, the Agent of the Navajoes, to return said captives to their parents. The captives were delivered to the Indian Sebolla to take care of and not to sell, but it seems they have been sold, one to Doña Marcelina, the widow of Don Juan Cháves, and it is not known who has the other, but I have faith in your efforts to return them to Sr. Dodge."[16]

Such an order put Castillo in a prickly situation, being a Cebolletano himself, and perhaps no less Meriwether, who must have calculated that the order would deflate his own popularity, but he was determined to preserve peace along the frontier, and redeeming stolen children would please and impress the Navajo. Dodge understood that as well. He had crossed Navajo country repeatedly, listening to the Indians' wants and concerns, and had earned the friendship and trust of Zarcillos Largos and several other leaders. When he asked of their troubles, it was always the same—they wanted their children.

At the close of 1853 Dodge journeyed to Santa Fe, where he cashed the voucher for his salary with Henry Connelly, who appeared to have acted as the agent's bank of convenience, and issued licenses to trade with the Navajo to Jarvis Nolan and James Conklin, both well-known New Mexican mercantilists. Apparently Dodge had kept Conklin waiting, not unlike Samuel Gorman.

> "Santa Fe, New Mexico, Dec. 31st, 1853. Henry L. Dodge Esq. Sir: I again make application for license to trade with the Nevijo Tribe of Indians and to reside in the Puebelo of Jemez with the privaledge of trading in said Pueblo. Respectfully Your Obdt Servt James Conklin."[17]

Dodge also made several purchases of agency supplies, Indian goods and "sundry presents" from Preston Beck's store.[18] It was a dear expenditure. Meriwether was down to his last thousand dollars and told Dodge the only purchases he'd approve would be for the care and feeding of agency animals. After perhaps catching a card game or two at the Exchange Hotel, possibly in company with Governor Meriwether and Agent Graves, both avid gamblers, he returned to Pass Washington. There on January 1st he scratched out a letter of introduction for Francisco Terrasino, a Navajo headman, who was headed into the settlements on business.

> "Know All to whom these presents shall come greeting that the bearer of this Francisco Terrasino has been recognized by his people the Navijo tribe as a good man and a man capable of promoting peace and good order among his people and after an acquaintance with him of two years I have found him a true friend to the United States of America and take pleasure in recommending him to the kind attention of all Americans. Given under my hand and Seal at Pass Washington Navijo Agency this first day of January A.D. one thousand eight hundred and fifty four."

Never one to let a moment of humor go to waste, Henry flippantly sketched a flowery symbol at the bottom and signed the letter "Henry L Dodge, Indian Agent for the Navijos . . . *a very fancy seal.*"[19]

Broke or not, Dodge knew he'd have to provide the Navajo relief from the bitter winter, so he went on buying provisions out of his own pocket and putting them on the Indian Services' books. On January 10th he bought 250 shirts and pairs of pants at a dollar or less a piece, fifty blankets and thirty-six buffalo robes, along with six dozen hoes and one hundred black silk handkerchiefs from G. A. J. Noel for a total of $849.50. Noel had packed the goods all the way in to snow-gripped Pass Washington. On February 1st, Dodge again issued a voucher for $31.00 to Fernandez Acuña for providing sheep and corn to feed Navajos visiting his agency. Major Kendrick had likewise been supporting the Navajo agency with military funds, completely contrary to policy. It may have been a wrenching resolution for such a stickler for regulation but, realizing the importance of Dodge's work, Kendrick exceeded his own authority to buy tobacco for the Indians.[20]

Despite the lack of funds and the severity of the winter, the Navajo hunkered down and bore the hardships without incident—with the single exception being a brief but nasty feud between the Navajo and Hopi. Sometime in early winter, a Hopi had killed a Navajo man, claiming he caught him stealing. The murdered man's relatives then retaliated by killing a Hopi. As emotions rose, the possibility of a tribal war grew, but apparently neither Kendrick nor Dodge expressed undue alarm. First, the quarrel posed no danger to the settlements or to the Navajo-American peace. Second, such squabbles between the Navajo and Hopi were to be expected. They'd intermittently fought for centuries. Lastly, The Navajo leaders had already expressed a desire to make up. Few doubted that soon it would all blow over.[21] At Fort Defiance, the Navajo-Hopi crisis was hardly noticeable—even Harriet Shaw's chronic apprehensions seemed to have evaporated. She and John had just had their second child, a girl they named Hattie. In writing home, she seemed light-heartedly dismissive of her relatives' anxieties, boasting that she could "laugh at your fears about us. Georgie has a spree with the Navajoes every day . . . the Navajos and Moquis are at war but it does not disturb us." As for the Navajo visiting their mission, they couldn't have been friendlier. They were even bringing in wild turkeys.[22]

A more ominous development soon arose. With the advent of spring, New Mexican herdsmen had begun grazing their vast herds along the Zuni Mountains, through the valley of El Moro and as far as westward of Zuni Pueblo. It was a blatant invasion of Zuni and Navajo territory, and at a time when American-Navajo relations couldn't have been better. A stockman who had lost 6000 sheep to the Navajos in the spring of 1853 had returned and moved his herds even further into Navajo land. Kendrick believed he'd only done so knowing that, if Navajos ran off his animals again, the government would eventually pay for them.[23]

Understandably, the Navajos and Zunis were livid. They had already roughed up a couple of herders, and it was only a matter of time before they'd resort to more severe remedies. Major Kendrick's assessment dispelled any doubt as to where his sympathies ultimately lay. In writing to Meriwether, he referred to the invasion not as criminal, per se, but as criminal recklessness, that the New Mexicans had boldly moved in before the United States was able to liquidate Indian possession and open the lands up. The fact that the Navajo had been grievously wronged by the act didn't bother him; rather it was regrettable that the stockmen had placed "an almost irresistible temptation to robbing before a people under whose exactions New Mexico has groaned for a third of a century."[24] Any desire Meriwether had to stop the encroachments was ultimately frustrated. The United States Territorial Court of New Mexico had ruled that, since there was no legally recognized Indian country in New Mexico, the governor had no legal jurisdiction to eject the New Mexican stockmen. Amazingly, even this outrage failed to torpedo good relations with the greater body of Navajos, to a great extent due to Henry Dodge's diligence.[25]

Dodge and Kendrick's success in preserving the Navajo peace was increasingly appreciated by both Governor Meriwether and General John Garland, as relations with the other Indian tribes, particularly the Chiricahua, Mescalero, Jicarilla and Ute, dramatically deteriorated. The previous November, and apparently for no other offense than his race, a New Mexican had murdered the prominent Chiricahua headman Cuentes Azules, who had come in to Doña Ana to trade. The miscreant splattered Azules' brains out on the ground with a club and then robbed him. The Chiricahua were outraged.[26] At about the same time, the Mescalero were harassing travelers along the southern branch of the California Trail, and Garland ordered Colonel Chandler to launch an expedition against them.[27] There were rumors of Indian depredations east of Santa Fe, near San Miguel. The Jicarilla, impoverished both by winter and the eradication of wild game by New Mexican hunters, were suspected of several robberies, as well as the brazen murder of two Americans hunting in the Santa Fe Mountains.[28] A subsequent investigation revealed that the killing had been the work of local scoundrels, later spotted in San Miguel trying to sell one of the victim's pants and boots.[29]

In early March the trader Auguste Lacombe appeared at Dodge's door with a letter from territorial secretary Messervy, shortly to assume the role of acting governor. Dodge knew him well and had done considerable business with his trading establishment over the years. Lacombe, Messervy wrote, had applied for a license to trade at Dodge's agency in the Chuska Mountains and along the San Juan River. Please to oblige him and sign the license, as Mr. Lacombe had already posted his bond and paid the ten-dollar fee, which Dodge could pick up when he came into Santa Fe. Lacombe presented the license to Dodge. It was addressed to "*Sr. D. Enrique L. Dodge, Ajente del Tribu Nabajos*" and executed completely in Spanish. Messervy requested Henry come in to Santa Fe before the end of March. Meriwether wanted to see him.

> The Gov. left to day for Taos. He will return on the 10th-and on the 22d he will start for the States to be absent for four or five months- so you see it is important that you come in before he starts that you may make suggestions as to what you want done in Washington I shall be left in charge of the Executive, and Indian Departments during his absence would like that you see the Gov. before he goes."[30]

David Meriwether departed New Mexico for the States on the 20th of March, 1854. On March 30th a Jicarilla and Ute force estimated at 250 fighters overwhelmed a company of sixty dragoons under the command of Lt. John Davidson thirty miles east of Taos. Two thirds of Davidson's men were casualties, twenty-two men dead, twenty-one men wounded. It was the worst defeat suffered by the Army since entering New Mexico in 1846.[31] Suddenly Messervy and Garland had a full-blown Indian war on their hands.

In contrast, the situation among the Navajo seemed idyllic. Agent Dodge, Major Kendrick and the Navajo leadership continued to express complete satisfaction with their mutual relationship. Silence from that quarter alone attested to that fact. During that otherwise turbulent time of petitions and dispatches cascading onto the governor's desk, there was almost no correspondence by either Dodge or Kendrick. There was really nothing to write about.[32]

Henry arrived in Santa Fe with a delegation of twelve Navajo headmen ten days afterward Meriwether's departure to collect the farm implements and other supplies promised them. William Messervy could only manage a token handful of tools for them, and wrote Manypenny on April 1st, stating that the superintendency was completely broke and that there were only two agents remaining in the entire territory, Carson and Dodge. The Apache agency having already claimed the lives of Wingfield and Smith, Agent Edmund Graves had decided against tempting fate and had left with his father-in-law Meriwether. Messervy also informed the commissioner that both he and Meriwether had been running the show with their own money, and that he for one was decidedly put out about it.[33]

Dodge gave Messervy his receipts and vouchers for the quarter expenses, and affidavit stating he had not been absent from his post or duties during the first quarter, so that he might be paid.[34] Once again the General Accounting Office would find the returns insufficient, particularly voucher 6 for sheep and corn he'd purchased without receipts, and voucher 3—for purchased stationary missing on his property report, noting that the "consumption of the stationery should be certified by disinterested persons . . ." On April 1st, the day Henry turned forty-four years old, he went shopping for his Navajo charges. He bought $129 worth of indigo dye and cloth, a dozen red sashes and curiously, "1 Hat for the son of Narbona," a young Navajo who had accompanied Henry to Santa Fe.[35] He then sauntered down the street to the establishment of Messervy and Webb, where he cashed in his salary and then bought a substantial stack of supplies, from blankets and bells to hoes and handkerchiefs and hatchets, yarn and strung coral.[36]

On the same day H. L. Dodge was in Santa Fe loading up goods and getting ready to return to Pass Washington, Major Kendrick wrote a terse note to Messervy. The major was in Albuquerque and had planned to attend to some business down the Rio Grande, but that would have to wait. He was returning in haste to Fort Defiance, fearing Davidson's shocking defeat near Taos, would entice the victorious Ute to "tamper with the Navajoes."

Oh, and by the way, where was Agent Dodge?

> "Should Capt. Dodge be in Santa Fe or elsewhere than in the Navajoes country, I deem it of great importance that he should return to his agency as soon as possible since he will hear of any intended outbreak sooner than we at the Fort will be made aware of it. Will you say to him that it will be well to send me information of his return to Tunicha in order that I may know what is going on & what to count upon in relation to him. In haste...
>
> P.S. It would be well if Capt. Dodge could take out with him some farming tools & tobacco for presents to the Indians. No effort should be spared to induce the Navajoes to remain friendly, in order that the more attention can be bestowed on the Utahs & Apaches-& to this end Capt. D. should be early on the ground & with presents if possible at least to some extent."[37]

Kendrick's exasperation would double as worries grew over the New Mexican seizures of Navajo grazing lands. With the Ute and Jicarilla already at war, and Dodge's influence with his charges suffering from neglect, Kendrick feared the Navajo would be unable to resist joining the plunder. There were already rumors of Navajo raids against Mexican flocks west of Jemez and around Laguna.

Where the hell was Dodge?

37

IN A HOUSE MADE OF DAWN

In the house made of the dawn,
In the house made of the evening twilight,
In the house made of the dark cloud,
Where the dark mist curtains the doorway,
The path to which is on the rainbow...
I have made your sacrifice.
I have prepared a smoke for you.
My feet restore for me.
My limbs restore for me.
My body restore for me.
Mt mind restore for me.
My voice restore for me...
In beauty I walk.
With beauty before me, I walk.
With beauty behind me, I walk.
With beauty below me, I walk.
With beauty above me, I walk.
With beauty all around me, I walk.
It is finished in beauty.

<small>Excerpts from the Navajo Nightway</small>

The purpose of Navajo ritual, almost without exception, was to cure sickness. Illnesses and problems in general were seen as a disruption of *hózhó*, harmony with the physical and spiritual world. The remedy was to restore the afflicted person to that natural state. It was the ultimate affirmation of a Navajo individual's importance to Navajo society. The concept of *hózhó* is central to Navajo religion and philosophy. Americans later mistranslated the word simply as "beauty." There was no English word capable of embracing the concept's depth and sophistication.

If the irritated tone of Major Kendrick's letter to Messervy is any indication, Henry Dodge had become so close to the Navajo that he'd become indispensible to preserving the peace. It is therefore all the more startling that Kendrick hadn't a clue as to the where Agent Dodge was. He'd seemingly vanished, without telling anyone where he'd gone. In the historical records, nearly two months would pass without the slightest reference to the man. For all Kendrick knew, Dodge could be dead, as some rumors had already claimed.

In truth, Dodge's relationship with the Navajo had become closer than either Kendrick or Messervy would have been comfortable detailing. On that aspect, the official records are silent, and there are no known personal accounts of his day-to-day dealings with the Navajo. From all evidence, Henry kept no letters or journals, and neither did anyone else at the agency, New Mexican or Navajo.

That is not to say the Navajo did not leave a record. Stories survived that were handed down orally as folklore, stories that, in the early 1930s, snagged the curiosity of a Bureau of Indian Affairs field worker named Richard Van Valkenburgh. Valkenburgh had an interest in Navajo culture and history, and an interest in Agent Dodge. Accordingly, he collected a few tales about the agent from an elderly Navajo man. Van Valkenburgh expressed complete confidence in the man's information and the claim he had first-hand knowledge of Captain Henry L. Dodge.[1]

In October of 1853, while preparing to move to Pass Washington, Henry purchased a bundle of goods from Messervy and Webb, including one red flannel shirt at the cost of a dollar and four bits. The Navajo soon were referring to him as *Bi'éé' Lichíí*, or Red Shirt, after his affection for red flannel.[2] Perhaps based on his informant, Van Valkenburgh believed Dodge entered Navajo land that year by skirting the San Juan River as far as Shiprock, then turning south along the eastern slopes of the Chuska Mountains. Crossing up and over Washington Pass, he continued on towards the head of Canyon de Chelly.

> "... When he reached the head of the canyon travel he was abruptly stopped by a series of waterfalls. Eventually finding a dangerous Navajo trail, he scaled down and came to the sandy bottom. Hemmed in by sheer walls of red, stained sandstone, he followed the small stream that flowed to

the northwest. After two days' travel the walls lowered and he came to the mouth of the canyon at Chinle. As far as is known, Captain Dodge was the first American to have traversed the entire length of the Canyon de Chelly."[3]

It would have certainly been a circuitous route, reminiscent of Dodge's trip to the San Juan with Kendrick, though badly skewed in location and direction, and seems somewhat far-fetched. Van Valkenburgh's old Navajo man recollected that once, while directing the distribution of gifts to the Navajo at Black Lake, Red Shirt allegedly did something remarkable.

> "After greeting Zarcillas Largo and the lesser chiefs, he amazed the Indians by pulling off his clothing and jumping into Laguna Negra, the lake that once filled the lower end of Todilto Park. The Navajos were spellbound as they watched him plunge into the water and start swimming. When he reached the middle of the lake, he turned and called back, 'Come on in!'
> "The Navajos muttered, 'No! One of the children of Toniholsodi, the water monster, lives in there. We are not fish or waterfowl. We would sink like stones.' The tribesmen were greatly impressed at this unheard of feat. The new agent's prestige grew."

It was always in the Indians' interest to indulge the white man, but they had no reason to take one into their lives, let alone trust one. The Navajo had a keen ability to detect deception, and they apparently detected none in Dodge. Of course, Zarcillos Largos and his people had accepted Red Shirt as a useful source of goods and services, but it seems that they had accepted him as a kinsman as well. Subsequently, Dodge spent more and more time among them, moving unrestrained through the fabric of their lives. Camaraderie aside, for Henry Dodge didn't seem a particularly sentimental fellow, there must have been a more substantial reason for him to go to the great trouble of relocating his agency to Pass Washington. Van Valkenburgh's loquacious informant provided an answer.

> "History fails to mention this, but the Navajos say that soon after the Washington Pass agency was built, Red Shirt acquired a Navajo belle for a wife. Her near relationship to the chief, Zarcillas Largo, without any doubt played an important part in her husband's congenial relationship with the tribe."[4]

Raymond Friday Locke later asserted Dodge had only moved his agency to Pass Washington because he had already married Zarcillos Largos' niece.[5] Such an arrangement would have benefited the Navajo considerably, as Zarcillos Largos would have certainly understood. Given Henry's repute, it isn't much of stretch to accept it as distinctly possible. Still, the tale smacks of the well-worn frontier cliché; the love-smitten white man and the nubile Indian princess, and could be easily dismissable but for some intriguing evidence.

During the winter of 1855, after Dodge had moved his agency to Fort Defiance, Brevet Major Henry L. Kendrick would ask permission from General Garland to direct the commissary to issue Agent Dodge supplies for "the use of his family, to be sold him at contract prices so long as he resides here."[6] To which family was Kendrick referring? There is no indication that Juana Sandoval and her children ever accompanied Henry to Navajo country, and it is unlikely that they did.

A second bit of evidence would surface thirty years later. In the mid 1880s, there worked for the Navajo Agency at Fort Defiance a Navajo man in his early thirties. Born on the fort grounds during the 1850s, he was named Chee, or *Kiilchii'* for Red Boy. Chee had been orphaned early in life. As a result, in 1868, the boy lived at Defiance with his aunt and her husband, the fort commissary clerk, Perry H. Williams, who not only taught the young boy English, but some business skills as well. In the early 1870s William Arny, the Navajo agent at the time, supposedly discovered Chee serving as a humble shepherd and was struck by the potential of the young man. He then took the boy in and had him schooled at Fort Defiance. It is safe to say that Arny's generosity was not as motivated by Christian charity as it was by believing Chee could very well have been the son of Henry Lafayette Dodge. In fact, the boy's full name was Henry Chee Dodge.

That information eventually reached one William Vandever, who had been appointed United States Indian Inspector by President Grant in 1873. Vandever, a long time lawyer at Dubuque, Iowa and former member of the U.S. House of Representatives, convayed that news to an old acquaintance he thought would be interested, the retired senator Augustus Dodge. August was, indeed, interested.

> "I learn from my old esteemed friend General Vandever... that my brother Capt. Henry L. Dodge, formerly Agent for the Navajos... left a son born of a Navajo woman. This boy now some 18 years of age is at, or near, Fort 'Defiance' within the Agency of Gov. W. F. M. Arny. He is represented to be a youth of more than ordinary promise in his condition and Genl.

Vandever mentions that the boy speaks the Navajo, Spanish, & English languages with fluency ..."⁷

In 1888 Ben Wittick, the well-known Southwest photographer, took a portrait of the young mustached Chee, then a man of roughly thirty years. He struck a confident pose, standing in a full-fringed buckskin suit, a cowboy hat rakishly cocked to one side of his head of curly black hair, and a rifle cradled in the crook of his arm. No image of H. L. Dodge is known to exist, but it is tempting to see in Chee's grayish eyes and high, furrowed brow the Dodge family features. Gifted and ambitious, Chee was one of the first to straddle the chasm between the Navajo and American worlds. He would later become an interpreter and mediator, the head of the Navajo police, a shrewd and wealthy businessman, the principal chief of the Navajo Nation and in 1921, the first Navajo Tribal Chairman. But was he Henry L. Dodge's son? Chee Dodge's descendants generally refute the idea. Chee Dodge himself, in his later years, insisted he was actually the son of Dodge's interpreter, Juan Casonisis—probably Juan Anaya—who named him in honor of Captain Dodge. Such a gesture was not uncommon among the Navajo.

Be that as it may, a much younger Chee stated quite the contrary in an affidavit he gave at Fort Defiance on March 10, 1888.

> "I am about 30 years old. I was born on *this Plaza* at Fort Defiance. My Father was a white Officer in the U S Army. My mother was a Navajo Woman..."⁸

The contradiction remains unresolved to this day.

So it was that in the Navajo month of *T'áá'tso*, May—the Month of Tall Corn, Henry Dodge left his agency to tour of Navajo country while, at Fort Defiance, Brevet Major Henry Kendrick fidgeted over Ute intrigues, believing the agent was neglecting his duty and malingering somewhere in Santa Fe or Albuquerque. On May 13th, Kendrick informed Messervy that Zarcillos Largos had reported a large theft of sheep west of Jemez and suggested that the Mexicans along the frontier draw their flocks back in as a precaution. Fort Defiance had fairly well cowed the Navajos on the west side of the Chuska, but the emboldened Ute could incite those Navajo on the east slopes.

> "It will be remembered that it was at this date last year that Garcías flock was run off, and it seems to be the season at which these Indians

are disposed to be troublesome, the very season when it is for our own interest to cause them to plant as much corn as possible. It is certainly to be regretted that at so critical a time, in our Navajoe relations, their agent should have gone to the settlements without the Navajoes knowing whether he is even coming back."

Kendrick asked Messervy to warn Agent Dodge that his influence among the Navajo was suffering. Stories were again circulating that Dodge had abandoned his agency out of fear, or that the Indians had chased him off, or that they had murdered him outright. Kendrick didn't buy any of it, but had no explanation of his own, and advised Messervy to inform Dodge about the gossip so he could put an end to it . . . that is, if he ever showed again.[9]

Ten days later, Kendrick was at Laguna, penning a report to General Garland about purported livestock thefts by the Navajo. He had learned he would find Dodge at the pueblo, but upon arrival found out the agent had already returned to Navajo country.

> "It may be proper for me to go to the Ojo Calientes, the range of Armijo (to whose band it is <u>said</u> the marauders belong) immediately after my return to my Post, for which I leave in the morning. I can place but little reliance, however, upon what he may say, & should I meet with the Navajoe agent it may not be necessary for me to go there at present, for I take it for granted that Capt. Dodge has fully informed these Indians, that reparation will be coerced from all marauding bands.

Kendrick had just missed him. It must have been maddening.

Zarcillos Largos had confirmed some Navajo had been culpable in the theft of the three hundred sheep, and that the headmen along the eastern slopes of the Chuska were collecting them to return to the settlements.[10] All the while, the Navajo leadership insisted they had no intention whatsoever of allying with the Ute, and there hadn't been anything to indicate the contrary. Even John Shaw, writing to the Home Mission Record with that theatrical flair he loved, stated that the Navajo were so congenial he had succumbed to their encouragement to visit and had gone galloping about the countryside alone to proselytize and exercise his Navajo language skills.

> "A few days since, while traveling over one hundred miles from home, I was surrounded by the most dangerous and hostile Indians I have

seen. I had no means of protection except my belt pistol and as they came up to me I felt somewhat alarmed, but I turned out my animals and appeared as calm as possible and sat down with them, and told them who I was and what I was. Very soon their wildness and reserve gave way to a familiar and common friendship that gave me perfect assurance of safety, and after a friendly smoke and shake of the hand, they left me to pursue my way unmolested."[11]

Meanwhile, Henry Dodge was deep in Navajo country, following the trail of sheep stolen from Rafael Mieres in early May. Juan Anaya and the agency herder Juan Vallejos accompanied him. The trace would lead them northward to the San Juan, and then back into the region Henry later referred to as "Cheyicito" before returning to Pass Washington.[12] Dodge and company relentlessly pushed on, visiting one Navajo camp after another. They had brought very few provisions with them, but they didn't need them. Dodge counted on the generosity of the Navajos for food and shelter, and was not disappointed. In the spring cool of the night, they may have been put up in a hogan or shade brush. The Navajo occasionally honored Dodge and his men with a meal of freshly butchered sheep. More frequently, they probably dined on dried venison, rabbit or prairie dog meat. A common dish of gruel made from parched corn, ground on the *mano* and *metate*, and flavored with cedar ash, might accompany the meal. Stews were made with bee weed and wild onions, carrots or potatoes, combined in the pot with chunks of meat or fat. Whatever was available was shared freely.

It was good manners to eat heartily and express one's satisfaction with a hefty belch, to make light discussion and perhaps show favors to the children. Red Shirt was acutely aware of the deep affection Navajo parents had for their children, and that they appreciated any kindness shown to their sons and daughters. The kind of discipline Henry had grown up with was unheard of among the Navajo. Parents almost never struck their children and seldom forced them to do anything. However Navajo children were not coddled. If a child was incorrigible, he was subject to thorough teasing and derision. In extreme cases, bad behavior could be adjusted by having his maternal uncle, the ultimate family disciplinarian, straighten him out. That threat alone was usually sufficient. Personal responsibility was taught through firm resolve and example and the young ones were taught to be tough and resilient. Their games were racing and riding and wrestling. During the winter, the older folks exhorted boys and girls alike to roll naked in the snow to toughen up and would toss the reluctant ones into a drift themselves. Navajo kids grew up quickly.

In the course of conversation, Dodge brought up the reason for his visit and asked where he might find the stolen livestock. The truthfulness of the answer probably depended on to what extent the hosts felt it was in their interest to cooperate. Stealing in itself was not a sin, but more of a skill. Lying was also not a serious transgression, but more a tool of convenience. Spinning a good lie was an art. The Navajo may have openly and easily misled Dodge about what they knew of the theft; it seems almost certain that they did. Yet patience and persistence eventually revealed the truth. The efforts of the headmen to gather up stolen stock eased Henry's job to a great extent, and if the results of his efforts are any indication, the Navajo dealt fairly with their agent.

It may have been through Henry Dodge's efforts that a New Mexican lad named Sisto, originally from Abiquiu, was redeemed from the Navajo. Navajo families often adopted captured children and treated them well, as in Juan Anaya's case, but there was no guarantee. The lot of a slave rested solely on the temperament of his master. A life of hard labor and abuse could easily be a captive's lot, to be bought, used, bartered and sold. He could be starved, beaten or killed. Should his master die, the slave might be executed and left at the graveside.[13] Sisto was a ragged apparition when he arrived at Fort Defiance, having been stolen first by the Ute and then sold to the Navajos. He had been badly abused for eight years and was terrified. Major Kendrick gave the lad some clothes, a few days' rations and a letter of introduction, then on June 22nd sent him off with a supply train returning to Albuquerque.[14]

On or around June 14th, Dodge, Anaya, Gallegos and forty-two Navajos drove some five hundred recaptured sheep into Santa Fe. It was a Sunday. On the following Wednesday the Santa Fe Gazette noted Dodge's arrival in the city and elaborated in the issue of the 24th.

> ". . . Until with the past year or two, the Navajoes, for the last thirty-five years, have been constantly committing depredations upon the Mexicans; and this change in their conduct can only be attributed to the action of Agent Dodge, in locating himself in the heart of their nation, which, thus far, has exercised the most beneficent influence over them. They seem to appreciate, highly, the course of their agent, in placing so much confidence in them, and we doubt not, will do more than all other causes to keep them quiet."[15]

For a paper often dedicated to the eradication of the Indian, it was praise indeed. The Tuesday after their arrival, Dodge and the Navajo met with Messervy. They remained in Santa Fe through June 24th, when Dodge issued a voucher to Webb and Kingsbury for $350.00 worth of presents for the Navajo. Messervy happily approved the purchase. From April 1st through June 30th, the New Mexico Superintendency had delivered to Dodge funds totaling around $1765 to meet agency expenses. Of that, Dodge paid out nearly six hundred dollars in salaries alone to Gallegos, Anaya, and himself, as well as $90.00 for expenses touring Navajo country to restore stolen livestock. Predictably, his account again fell victim to the insidious logic of accountants. They noted that on his previous trip to Navajo country, Dodge had charged the United States Government only $45.00, claiming he'd been able to subsist off of the Indians. They peevishly queried as to why Dodge hadn't done the same on his last expedition. Not only that, they criticized the policy of granting lump sum per diem amounts as irregular. Damned irregular.[16]

The Navajos most likely returned to their country shortly after the meeting with Messervy, while Dodge remained in Santa Fe. It was the end of the quarter and he had other business demanding his attention. On June 29th, he swore out a formal power of attorney in favor of his father, Senator Henry Dodge.

> "Know all men by these presents that I Henry L. Dodge of Santa Fe, Anna County, Territory of New Mexico, do nominate and appoint Henry Dodge of the County of Iowa, State of Wisconsin my true and lawful attorney for me and in my name to draw from the proper department of the government one thousand dollars of my salary as Indian Agent of said Territory of New Mexico, when the same shall become due, beginning on the first day of January A. D. 1855, in such sums and at such time as he my said attorney may think best, and for me and in my name to make and give all necessary vouchers, acquitrances; and receipts therefore hereby ratifying and confirming all my said attorney may lawfully do in the premises. In testimony whereof I have herewith set my hand & seal this 29th day of June A. D. 1854 [signed] Henry L. Dodge.[17]

The reason for allowing his father to draw on his salary wasn't altogether clear. Frank McNitt believed he'd borrowed the money to pay off his gambling debts, but there was no evidence supporting that conclusion other than Henry's reputation. It is more likely that the money in question stayed in Wisconsin. His wife Adele and their children were in a financial state reminiscent of New Mexico's Indian Superintendency—poor as church mice. Unpaid bills and unresolved legal fights over land claims that Henry had abandoned in 1846 may have required Senator Dodge's monetary and legal attention as well, something that a power of attorney could accomplish. On the other hand it may have been an arrangement for Henry to repay money his father may have loaned him rather than to see him destitute. If so, it is likely Henry L. spent it on himself, his agency and his habits—both good and bad— and on the Navajos. Augustus Dodge filed the power of attorney with Commissioner George Manypenny on January 22nd, 1855 and requested Manypenny to notify his brother of the fact. He also asked to have Henry's salary drawn and deposited with his father each quarter it became due.[18]

It appears that Henry Dodge remained in the general vicinity of Santa Fe for a considerable time. Two days after executing the power of attorney, Red Shirt wrote out a voucher for G. A. J. Noel for $435.00 to buy two hundred shirts, one hundred pairs of pants, 120 garden hoes and forty silk handkerchiefs for the Navajos. On July 3rd, Dodge made out a voucher for $284.00 to Webb & Kingsbury for supplies; beads, brass tacks and bells, tobacco and colored cloth, forty-eight butcher knives. He also purchased a dozen tin cups and six tin pans, two guns, a saddle—probably all for his own use and, of course, a red flannel shirt.[19]

Shortly after that, Henry Dodge headed into Navajo country to expedite the return of some stolen horses. On the tenth, probably enroute through Laguna, Dodge purchased some personal items from Simon Delgado—soap, files, a plug or two of tobacco on the Indian Agency account. Interestingly, among the items he purchased were several woman's and small girl's *rebozos*, the habitual headscarf worn by the New Mexican women of the country.[20] Dodge remained in Navajo country for some twenty days. Apparently neither Juan Anaya nor Manuel Vallejos accompanied him on this trip. Instead Henry later issued vouchers to G. F. Brown for services as his herder and to José Lopez as his interpreter.[21]

By the beginning of August, the financial situation of the New Mexico Superintendency was brightening. Meriwether was back from his leave of absence with news that Congress had at long last appropriated five thousand dollars for fulfilling the stipulations of the Navajo Treaty of 1849, nearly five years after the fact. That typical snail-paced rate of the white man's government would perpetually confound Indians who rightfully wondered why so much time had to pass before a promise made was fulfilled. Nevertheless, the money had been allocated. Manypenny also told Meriwether that $25,000 dollars had been set aside for general Superintendency expenses.[22] On August 15th Meriwether informed Dodge that he was cleared to draw up to one thousand dollars each quarter for Navajo purchases. He cautioned Dodge to fill out drafts "in strict accordance with regulations" and went so far as to send him examples done in his own hand.[23] The following day,

Meriwether wrote Henry again, telling him he was settling Noel's claims for goods he'd sold to Dodge, and enclosing a letter authorizing him to draw money from the superintendency and another from Henry's father the senator.[24]

Dodge was capable of some thriftiness. He had written Meriwether on August 5th from Defiance with a proposal sure to save Meriwether money. He suggested that half of the tobacco purchased for the Navajo be shipped to Fort Defiance. Kendrick would then have it to hand out to visiting Navajos, of which there was no lack. In return, Kendrick would ship Indian goods up to Dodge's agency in army wagons, free of charge, saving Meriwether the expense of wagons, horses and drivers.[25] It was probably as much Kendrick's idea as Dodge's. He'd sent his own letter to Meriwether out with Dodge's on August 19th, lauding the plan as practical as well as thrifty.

> "This Post is the most central point in the Navajoe Nation, being at the intersection of the trails from Zuni to the most favored Navajoe grazing grounds to the North & N. West of us, & on those from the Ojo del Oso to the Cañon of Chielle &c. Most if not all the Navajoes visit this Post, & much of our annoyance arises from the want of Tobacco to give them, & for which they always ask. They cannot be made to understand why I do not have it as formerly to give to them, especially as they see that our men have a plenty of it. From this I trust you will understand my anxiety on this subject & pardon me for troubling you at this time in relation to it.

In addition to offering to ship Indian goods in military transport, Kendrick also offered to assist in taking a general census of the tribe, something that could be "easily done by distributing the presents at some one point" on an appointed day.[26] Between them Kendrick and Dodge had stealthily managed to strike a harmonious note in the typically discordant din of civil and military squabbling. Hopefully it would grow.

38

STERN BUT NEEDFUL JUSTICE

The fall of 1854 arrived with a feeling of guarded optimism. Meriwether had abruptly returned to New Mexico from Washington upon hearing of the Jicarilla-Ute disturbance. After federal and volunteer troops crushed the uprising, the territory returned to a semblance of normality. In the meantime, to Meriwether's intense relief, Congress had finally funded his superintendency and authorized monies for Indian annuities. The law of July 1st provided a total of $30,000 for agricultural tools and supplies for the Navajo, Ute and Apache, as well as $10,000 for the Pueblo.[1] More amazing yet, relations between the civil and military departments of New Mexico had seemingly transformed from merely cooperative to almost affectionate.

Admittedly, the wild Indians did remain troublesome, but the Jicarilla and Mescalero Apache were suing for peace, the Ute were cowed and, according to Meriwether, the Chiricahua Apache had been of little nuisance primarily because they were busy plundering northern Mexico.[2] The Navajo, too, remained at peace, having resisted any temptation to join the Ute and Jicarilla in their ill-fated war. Meriwether spoke of the Navajo tribe in glowing terms as a nation of Indians that "can but challenge our admiration." They were self-sufficient and industrious, raising an abundance of corn and wheat, possessing herds of livestock numbering in the tens of thousands, and living "in a degree of comfort and plenty unknown to the other wild Indians of this Section of the Union."

Yet, the governor gravely cautioned, he anticipated troubles ahead. There were bad men in the tribe who the headmen could not control. One notoriously renegade band had gone so far as to separate the main tribe and ally with the Ute. That band had been linked to several thefts in the past. Doubtlessly they would continue to do so.

> "Such men pay but little regard to the Eighth commandment, which enjoins upon us not to steal, on the contrary they have heretofore often stolen the stock and cattle of their more civilized neighbors. But under the judicious management of Agent Dodge, who has taken up his abode among these Indians, we have had but little cause to complain of them during the present year."[3]

Late summer and early fall had given Henry Dodge very little in the way of excitement. Indeed, things were almost boring. With Meriwether's go ahead, he arranged to have part of the Navajo tobacco shipment sent to Defiance at Kendrick's request and made a purchases of goods at Pass Washington for the Indians from Auguste Lacombe.[4] There had been only one incident of concern. On August 14th Governor Meriwether informed Henry that a citizen, José Antonio Montoya, had complained some Navajo had stolen his gray mare and his good riding mule, "a fine go-er under the saddle without whip or spur." The animals had been spotted near Cañoncito Bonito within a half-day's ride from Dodge's agency. Would Dodge to look into the matter and to return the animals to Montoya if he indeed located them? It is unclear if Mr. Montoya ever got his "fine go-er" back. On August 31st, Dodge did pay Lorenzo Labadi $5.50 for recovering and keeping a horse reputedly stolen by the Navajo, but the owner of the animal remains a mystery.[5]

Other than that, there wasn't much news other than the customary stream of hogwash the Santa Fe gossip mills churned out. On August 20th, the Reverend Shaw at Laguna wrote traders Webb & Kingsbury and asked them to inform Governor Meriwether that Dodge had again definitely not been killed by his Indians.[6] The agent personally dispelled that rumor at the end of August, when he and a Navajo delegation entered Santa Fe to meet with Meriwether. While there, he bought supplies for the Navajo: mutton from Richard Owens, from Dolores García 522 loaves of bread, feed for the Indian ponies from Anastacio Romero and from J. & H. Mecure. Dodge's purchase from Webb and Kingsbury illustrated well how sanguine relations with the Navajo had become. At the top of Dodge's shopping list were ten guns; each one a gift to headmen of the Navajo delegation. It was a striking departure from previous policy that might have unsettled Meriwether, but Dodge had little fear the rifles would ever be turned against him or the New Mexican citizenry.[7]

While Dodge and the Navajo were in Santa Fe, they came under the scrutiny of one Brevet Major William Thomas Harbaugh Brooks, the commander of Fort Marcy. On August 28th, Brooks discovered among the Navajo horses a mule clearly branded "U.S." The major promptly approached Agent Dodge and demanded the Navajos surrender the animal. Henry wasn't one to be put back on his heels so easily.

" . . . On making claim to Capt Dodge their agent-he replied that this Mule was one taken by the Navajoes during Col Washington's Campaign against them; that Major Kendrick at Fort Defiance had seen a number of these public Mules, but had never made any claim for them, on the ground that they had been taken while we were at war with them, and that we have since made peace, and nothing was said about returning captured property-I therefore did not further urge a claim to this Mule..."

Nevertheless, Brooks reported his find to General Garland. He suspected Dodge was lying and he wanted an investigation.[8]

Garland turned to Kendrick for an explanation. The major admitted that on two occasions he'd seen Navajos with U.S. mules, and although he hadn't any information in relation to the particular public mule in question, it could have been just as Dodge had claimed. On the day that Washington's command shot Narbona and several others, the Navajo had indeed stolen several pack mules. The 1849 Treaty required the animals' return, but that requirement, which was never met, became moot when the treaty itself was never ratified. Furthermore, the previous summer Meriwether had told the Navajo he would forgive all their transgressions prior to the Ramon Martín incident. Kendrick was a by-the-book officer but, unlike Brooks, he was equally practical. He advised Garland to leave well enough alone. The practice of retaining the spoils of war had been a tradition in New Mexico "for time immemorial." It was not worth ransoming peace for the price of a mule.[9] Garland agreed and, with the exception of some grumbling by Brooks, the issue was fairly well buried. Major Brooks' sanctimonious inflexibility would surface again a few years later while he served as commandant of Fort Defiance... with predictably disastrous results.

Having brushed off Brooks' irksome meddling, Dodge lingered for a time in Santa Fe. On September 2nd he signed an affidavit stating he had bought Navajo goods from John Weber the Fort Defiance sutler in the summer of 1853, using $405.00 out of his own pockets and requested reimbursement.

> "I certify on honor that after receiving information of my appointment as Indian Agent for the Territory of New Mexico and before the receipt of my commission at the urgent request of Major H. L. Kendrick of the United States army I entered upon the duties of Said office. That I purchased the goods mentioned in the foregoing bill at the prices therein named and distributed the same as presents to the Navijo Indians that I paid the full amount of said bill out of my private funds and have never received any credit or reimbursement in any form whatever..."[10]

On September 10th, Henry Dodge wrote Governor Meriwether from Chupadero stating the prefect of Socorro County, Mr. Ramon Sanchez, was holding a ten-year-old Pima girl he had bought from her tribe. Sanchez was claiming her as his adopted daughter, a common rationale for holding Indian servants. Dodge also mentioned that Mr. Sanchez, as an ex-agent for Captain Ker, held a claim against the Navajo for the burning of a wagon in November of 1851 and he wanted compensation. When Dodge approached the Navajo, they denied having set it afire.[11] The fate of the Pima girl or Sanchez's claim remain unknown.

Henry also wrote Kendrick proposing he move his agency to Fort Defiance for the winter, provided the major would have him, Juan Anaya and Manuel Vallejos. He did not mention George Carter, who apparently had taken a leave of absence. He also failed to mention his family. On the 23rd, Major Kendrick responded enthusiastically. It was precisely what he had advocated from the start.

> "I have always thought that the system heretofore pursued of making the presents to the Navajoes at no fixed time or place to be a bad one, & have had occasion to write elsewhere that these presents should be made at this Post by the Indian Agent, & with the exception of tobacco at some fixed time or times, such as he should establish.

Kendrick had three sets of vacant officers' quarters and agreed to set Dodge up in one of them. It was doubtful that all the officers would actually show up, but the major cautioned that he couldn't guarantee Dodge's continuous use if in the outside chance they did. Kendrick hastened to add that "it would hardly be right" to build a place for the agency with Army money. Meticulously avoiding anything smacking of impropriety, Kendrick urged Dodge to pay him a visit.

> "If you were here so that we could have a free conversation touching this subject, I think it could easily be arranged to the satisfaction of both of us.
> "You speak of a herder; should you come I trust you will not find it necessary to bring many animals with you, on account of the scarcity of grazing here in the winter season."[12]

On September 30th, Agent Dodge filed his reports and returns for the Navajo agency with Meriwether, who then sent them on to Manypenny for reconciliation. Once again, the auditors found fault. Dodge failed to itemize travel expenses—voucher suspended. Dodge had failed to account for the salt on Voucher No. 2, the 522 loaves of bread on Voucher No. 6, and the twenty-one burro loads of hay listed on Voucher 8. Mr. Dodge had also neglected to enter his salary on his reports.

Apparently, Dodge did pay himself, cashing his salary with a Mr. F. Cunningham for $387.50, directly contrary to the dictates of the power of attorney he'd given his father earlier.[13] If Henry had any misgivings about this sham, they would soon be eclipsed by more pressing concerns.

On the morning of October 7th, a handful of soldiers were some two miles from Fort Defiance on a hay cutting detail. That wasn't unusual. Navajos had agreed to let the garrison use the meadows around the fort, so the cutting and grazing crews came and went without incident. Indeed, there was a prevailing feeling of security and friendship, or at the very least mutual respect, between the Americans working in the fields and the curious Navajo onlookers. In contrast to the previous year, John and Harriet Shaw hadn't the least hesitation about leaving the post for a ride and picnic. The arrival at Defiance of fellow missionaries Frederick Tolhurst and his wife had noticeably brightened Harriett's mood. When Milton and Frederick left to cut hay about a mile from Defiance, she didn't think twice about taking Mrs. Tolhurst out later for a stroll. It was a crisp and refreshing fall day, perfect for a lark. In retrospect, Harriett thought twice as to her wisdom in such a frivolity.

> "We were very imprudent to go so far, but our husbands were off cutting hay & we were expecting them & went to see if we could see them coming. I shall not do it again . . ."

The first hint the something had gone horribly wrong that Saturday came with a sudden commotion on the parade ground. A crowd was forming in front of the hospital. It seemed a soldier with the hay detail, Private Nicholas Hefbiner of Company B, 3rd Infantry, had been brought in gravely wounded. A Navajo man had appeared at the cutting fields and, for no comprehensible reason, had shot an arrow deep into Hefbiner's chest. The post surgeon, Jonathan Letterman, concluded that the young man would not survive.[14]

The apparently unprovoked attack confounded everyone. Edward Bennett, then stationed at Taos, had heard that the Navajo had asked Hefbiner for some smoking tobacco and when the private told him he had none, the Indian shot him.[15] Harriett Shaw provided a more detailed explanation in a letter on October 10th, just three days after the incident. The morning of the killing, the Navajos had come to the fort to sell peaches. Harriet recalled she had actually purchased some fruit from the very Navajo accused of killing Private Hefbiner.

> "After leaving the fort he went up to this soldier who was loading hay, & asked him for his pants which of course the soldier refused whereupon the Indian drew his bow & shot him near the heart with an arrow then ran jumped upon a horse and fled."

Had Hefbiner been killed for a pair of pants? It seemed unlikely, unless the outrageous request was a pretext for someone bent on homicide, but Harriet's preconceptions made it all believable. As to her fears of Indian treachery, Harriett had never actually witnessed any. There had always been some Navajo teasing, the morbid kind that really disturbed her, but it was just teasing. Once while Milton Shaw and Frederick Tolhurst were out alone among the Navajo, a headman appeared and warned them they'd be shot dead in their sleep. The missionaries replied to let the Indians come and do it if they dared. At that the old fellow laughed aloud and sauntered away. In time he returned with his family and offered to protect them by sleeping near them that night. Was it a harmless joke to test the Americans' bravery or was the headman actually protecting them? Harriett was never sure. Indians, she was convinced, were inherently perfidious.

Major Kendrick was not at Defiance the day Hefbiner was shot, but a day's ride north of the fort. The moment he got the news, he immediately spurred his horse back towards the post. After doing an initial investigation of the incident, the major found no cause for the unprovoked attack, none other than pure malevolence. He well understood the possible ramifications of the deed however, particularly if Nicholas Hefbiner died.[16] Die he did. Hefbiner lingered a day and finally expired on Sunday afternoon of the 8th. That evening Kendrick informed headquarters, fully convinced that even though there was no hint of general hostility among the Navajo, the incident would plunge them into war.

> "I am sending for the chiefs to come in here, & shall make a formal demand upon them for the delivery of the Murderer, but I have no idea that it will be yielded to in the <u>first instance</u>, for the Navajoes, however anxious a majority of them may be of peace, at this [confess] a real or fancied inability to do. They have never surrendered a guilty party, always affirming <u>that</u> to be impossible..."

Kendrick emphasized that surrendering criminals to American justice had to be vigorously enforced with military might. It was a typical Army opinion, one he'd taken once before during the Martin crisis. He informed Garland that, until he heard from headquarters, he would confine his actions to demanding the Navajos turn over the murderer and in educating them on the grim alternative if they failed to do so.[17]

As Kendrick's hand scribbled out the letter, his head was already organizing the strategy and logistics of war inevitable. Henry Dodge arrived at Fort Defiance as poor Hefbiner was breathing his last.[18] Meanwhile Harriett Shaw described the gravity of the situation.

> "All is commotion & excitement here now, & what will result from it I know not but in all probability a war unless the murderer is given up. We deeply regret it as it will necessarily put a stop to our missionary labors for the present, & Sr & Br T. were intending to do much for them this winter, but do not let this cause you anxiety for our safety. If war occurs we shall be safe here & you need not apprehend we shall stray far from the fort in future..."[19]

John Milton Shaw prophesized an equally bleak outlook. Kendrick had demanded the murderer. The Navajo would refuse to surrender him. War would be the inevitable result.

> "Bro. Tolhurst and myself were absent alone among the Indians all the week that it happened, and felt no apprehension of danger... Hitherto the good hand of Providence has protected us; but if the warlike propensities of the savages are again aroused, no one will escape who falls within their power. It is very easy to talk of courage when we are far from danger, but let one be placed a hundred miles from assistance, and be surrounded by fierce and savage Indians, and it takes a stout heart not to tremble and fear..."[20]

On October 18th, Garland ordered Kendrick to demand the unconditional surrender of the murderer. The general would ready a force to back up the demand and immediately send Kendrick forty-two fresh horses and accoutrements under the command of Lieutenant Tidball.[21]

After being briefed by Kendrick, Henry Dodge undertook the task of bringing in the killer. In the company of interpreter Juan Anaya and his herder, Manuel Vallejos, he pursued the culprit through Navajo country. Dodge found the Navajo surprisingly cooperative. The news of Hefbiner's murder doubtlessly dismayed the majority of Navajo. They understood better than Kendrick himself the potentially disastrous results.[22]

As for the killing, there could have been any number of motives. Hefbiner may have offended him or a member of his family. The Navajo may killed Hefbiner in revenge for some previous affront by another soldier, perhaps even for some offense delivered years earlier. Many Navajos had lost relatives in the slaughter by Washington's troops near Two Gray Hills in 1849 and memories were long. For that matter, the killer may have had a violent argument with his wife or her family the day before and released his rage by shooting the soldier. It wasn't unheard of. The man's motive, however, was irrelevant. In 1853, the *Bilagáana* had insisted that the Navajo surrender the murderers of Ramon Martin and were only dissuaded after considerable compensation and the passage of time. With the murder of a soldier, the Navajo understood the Americans would be adamant—no amount of promises or payments would substitute for the surrender of the perpetrator.

Clearly something drastic had to be done. On October 18th, several Navajo headmen came into Fort Defiance to invite Dodge and Kendrick to an unprecedented conclave of Navajo leaders to be held in three days in the Carrizo Mountains some sixty miles north of the fort. The sole purpose of the meeting was to peacefully resolve the catastrophe looming before them. Harriett Shaw mentioned the headmen's arrival in a letter to her mother and sister.

> "Several chiefs have been in to settle it by paying sheep & horses, but the murderer has been demanded of the tribe & the result we do not know. . . . if he is not given up a war will inevitably ensue which will materially affect our labors here . . ."

Kendrick believed little would come of the conclave, but endorsed the attempt. Henry Dodge and Juan Anaya, in company with Lieutenant Alley and twenty soldiers departed immediately for the Carrizozo. Upon their arrival, the Navajo headmen again offered to pay sheep and horses as indemnity for Hefbiner's slaying. Milton Shaw, who accompanied Dodge on the expedition, stated that Dodge and Alley refused the offer. The exasperated Navajos then offered to surrender the life of an old, blind man, since the Americans were so intent on killing someone. According to Shaw, Dodge again refused because "he could not take the innocent for the guilty."[23]

Red Shirt repeated Kendrick's demand that nothing would suffice as remedy short of surrendering Private Hefbiner's killer. He also assured the Navajos that if they declined, the Army would sweep down on them as a scythe of destruction. After some discussion, the Navajos at last capitulated. They would surrender the perpetrator to the Americans as soon as he could be apprehended. When Dodge reported the results of the meeting to Kendrick, the major was skeptical, but noted one positive aspect in his letter to General Garland on October 23rd. Henry Dodge was convinced that the Navajos would indeed comply.

> "As a result, although they affirm that it is the first instance, in their history, of a surrender, the Council promised to bring the offender to this place and have sent a chief who resides on the San Juan, with eight Navajoes, in pursuit of him. From the character of this chief and the disposition manifested by the Navajoes, Capt. Dodge is sanguine that the surrender will be affected."

The headman sent on that distasteful errand was Armijo, the influential and accommodating Navajo headman of Ojos Calientes, whose oratory had impressed Greiner at the Jemez meeting. He had become Dodge's benefactor and close friend. All the same, Kendrick believed the promise was yet another delaying tactic. True the entire Navajo Nation was thirsty for peace, particularly when faced with starvation and hardships of a winter war with the Americans, but their primitive political structure prevented any coordinated attempt to apprehend the killer. Kendrick actually wrote that the tribe was "such a complete mob" that it was all but impossible for them to comply with their promise. He then returned to thoughts of the impending war.[24]

Events soon brought some moderation to his thinking. It indeed appeared that the Navajo would do the inconceivable and surrender the killer. The headmen personally assured Kendrick that he'd have his prisoner. Dodge was convinced they would and so was Lieutenant Alley. Kendrick realized such an act would be a milestone in Indian relations in New Mexico and of immeasurable value to the Americans, and he would spare no effort in securing that result. Yet he still could not bring himself to believe it would actually happen and that "great doubt hangs on the result."

He advised Garland not to postpone preparations for a major war.[25]

The letter to General Garland was already enroute when Henry Dodge informed Kendrick the Navajo had apprehended the killer. Once again, Dodge and Alley departed with a small contingent of soldiers, the Reverend Shaw again in tow. They ranged northward through the Chuska Valley. On or about October 28th, Dodge arrived at Armijo's home. Armijo promised Red Shirt that he would personally deliver the killer to them in seven days and if he failed to do so, would surrender his own son as hostage.[26] In the meantime, the headman's band made the Americans comfortable. On November 5th, while Dodge and Alley rested idly in Armijo's camp, a sudden halloo echoed down on them. In a moment it was clear. Armijo's men were bringing in Hefbiner's murderer. Dodge later reported the amazing news to Meriwether.

> "On the 5th November he was delivered to Lieut Ally badly wounded by an arrow shot in the loins he having made fight to the last The man that shot him is a nephew of Armijo's who says that but for a shield that he had provided himself with he would have been killed that thirty-eight arrows was shot at him many of which struck the Shield in the center."[27]

The man, wounded in the bowels and hog tied, seemed utterly resigned to his fate. As Armijo's men brought him up to the camp, the prisoner apparently died. The Navajo, having a deep fear of corpses, immediately abandoned the body in horror. Incredibly, the heretofore-deceased prisoner suddenly leaped up and made a miraculous dash for the hills. His herculean attempt was unsuccessful and he was quickly recaptured and turned over to Agent Dodge. Dodge and Alley, with their prisoner and large Navajo escort, arrived at Fort Defiance on the evening of November 7th. Harriett Shaw detailed the scene.

> "The murderer was hunted in the mountains by a party of Indians who said he fought much & they had to shoot him in the side with an arrow before he could be taken & then would not go & they tied him to a horse & they dragged him along. When brought here, he was brought on a litter by the soldiers who were sent with the Indian Agent & officer, was badly wounded in the side & the skin was nearly all rubbed off his back but his sufferings here were of short duration..."[28]

Indeed. The hapless fellow was brought before the sergeant and two privates who claimed to have witnessed the murder. Without hesitation, the soldiers identified him as Hefbiner's killer. Then, at the insistence of Armijo, Zarcillos Largos and over one hundred principle men of the tribe, with the concurrence of Henry L. Dodge, Major Henry L. Kendrick had him hanged. Dodge ended his report to Meriwether in the court sentencing jargon of the day; they had "him hung until he was <u>dead, dead, dead</u>. Which I hope will meet with your approbation."[29]

Harriett Shaw proved somewhat more sympathetic to the man dangling from a noose, now truly dead. She stated that Dodge and Alley had arrived at the fort around noon on the 7th and in her words, "lynch law like" they had him hung before nightfall.

> "...All the trial he had was-the soldiers were called in to say if he was the one. Of course they all said 'yes', though not a person was within a hundred yards of the soldier when killed, 'so they say.' The poor Indian has no sympathy from the white man, all wish them exterminated, but as we wish them converted to God ... A gallows was erected just back of the buildings on the south side of the garrison & all the officers but two & a large number of soldiers & Navajoes went to see him hung. I could hardly control my feelings when I saw the poor Indian brought in here bound hand & foot with long ropes knowing he was in the hands of his enemies who would show him no mercy, but his being hung here affected me less than I had supposed it would . . ."

At least that was a relief. Harriett related that the Navajos claimed the condemned man was a devil and always managed to kill someone wherever he went. He had no friends and apparently no family of any consequence.[30] That would have been tremendously convenient for the Navajo leaders, living in fear of launching an endless feud among the executed man's kinsmen. Navajo culture provided scores of brothers and sisters, aunts and uncles, grandparents and cousins. The very idea of having no kin was incomprehensible and one of the strongest insults one Navajo could give another was to accuse him of acting as if he had no relatives. The condemned fellow doubtlessly had relatives, if he were truly Navajo.

He may not have been. Dodge's own apparent eagerness to see the deed done and his off hand, even sardonic presentation of the facts to Meriwether raises the suspicion that the man may have been a sacrificial goat. Several years later, Major Brooks, whose sympathies for the Navajo were few, claimed the hanged man was actually a Mexican captive. If so, one might expect he'd protest his innocence in Spanish, unless he had subsequently forgotten his native language during his captivity. Perhaps he had been so severely wounded that he'd been unable to utter the fact. It was unlikely, but not impossible. The suspiciousness of the circumstances elicits a queasy disquiet. Major Kendrick's official report to General Garland did little to ease that unrest.

> "On the return of their Agent to this place many of the better class of Navajos accompanied him, and seemed very anxious lest the offender

should recover his liberty; well knowing that he would then involve the Nation in fresh difficulties; for this reason, and on the recommendation of Capt Dodge Indian Agent in whose judgment myself and other officers here entirely coincided and at the earnest solicitation of the Principal Navajo Chiefs & of their people who were with them, I have thought proper to cause the murderer to be hanged, while the Indians were at this Post and in the presence of as many of them, as saw fit to witness the execution."

The fact that the man was conveyed to the gallows on a stretcher appears to preclude any possibility of escape. Furthermore, if the Navajo had so desired, they could have easily killed the man outright for the practice of witchery, thereby removing him as a source of "fresh difficulties." In his report, Kendrick specifically praised Henry Dodge for "his energy and good management in procuring the surrender of this murderer."[31]

On November 30th, David Meriwether wrote a brief report to Commissioner Manypenny, detailing at some length the incidents leading up to the execution.

"The hanging of this Indian in this summary manner, without a legal trial is to be regretted but there is no jails or other means of confining such a prisoner in this Territory until next Spring, when our civil courts are held, and it became necessary that an example should be made to impress other bad Indians of New Mexico. This I am informed is the first instance of an Indian having been surrendered to Justice in this Territory, and without fully justifying his prompt and unceremonious execution, I am of opinion that it will have a decidedly good effect upon others."[32]

John Milton Shaw, who had fully expected a devastating war, heaved a prosaic sigh of relief when he wrote "we were then in the midst of anxiety and fear but we rejoice that the clouds of war seem to have passed over, and that the dove of peace again broods over the agitated waters." It was as if the crisis had never happened. Both Americans and Navajos were anxious to consign that nasty episode to oblivion. There had been no complaint by the Navajo over the death sentence, "but all seemed satisfied and contented which we feared would not be the case." As the Reverend had dryly observed, the hanging had been an act of "stern but needful justice."[33]

The Americans were eager to hang someone and, to insure their own survival, the Navajo leaders were willing to provide a victim. All in all, it was a sordid affair.

39

TAKING UP THE CROSS

Perhaps the most remarkable thing about the execution's aftermath was that the Navajo appeared even more sociable than before. There certainly were plenty of them wandering the grounds of Fort Defiance. Henry Dodge had relocated his agency there from Pass Washington at the suggestion of Major Kendrick, and the Navajo who had once thronged to the old agency site now converged in great numbers on the garrison, a side-effect that Kendrick had failed to take into account when he first suggested the idea. Navajo horses and sheep competed with Army livestock for grazing. Navajo visitors took advantage of Army amenities, not the least of which was Army rations. The Indians were there day and night, creating a perpetual "open house" atmosphere that Kendrick believed distracted the soldiers and eroded discipline.

The effect was equally felt in the Shaw household. In a November letter to her family, Harriet Shaw described Navajos who frequented her home as exceedingly friendly and consequently were increasingly pleased to while away the hours in her tiny parlor. Harriet had a houseful while she was writing, but she remained charitable, although it was flustering to have curious Navajos peering over her shoulder as she indulged in the mysteries of literacy.

> "For several days our house was crowded with them & we visited them at their camp fires on the hills & all seemed friendly & kind offering us what they had to eat. We gave them many presents, and all seemed perfectly satisfied with what had been done, but it is such a long tedious task to get their language what would you say, mother, should I become so much attached to <u>savages</u>, that it would be painful for me to live with civilized people? But I have not exactly become a savage <u>yet</u> or lost my desire to visit my dear friends. But were not for <u>our own dear family</u>, there is little to attract me to the States.

A certain amount of sympathy was all well and good, but the woman never allowed herself to stray very far from her prejudices.

"They have but little clothing, and sometimes the poor little children have no clothes at all; but when they bring them here we give them clothes to wear, and food to eat, and then they seem very glad, and say: "Eh-keh-heh Sekiss" ("Thank you friend"). Our little Georgie is very fond of them, and they love him, "Aweh-lahki" ("the white baby"), and sometimes want him to go home with them; but Indians are very treacherous and we cannot trust him alone with them, for they often steal little children."[1]

For Reverend Shaw, the crowds of Navajo thronging the post were a veritable windfall of souls. He wrote that over one hundred Navajo at a time had been in the fort, and could have easily overwhelmed the garrison if they'd been of a mind to. He attributed their large presence and continued amiability to the fact Henry Dodge had made his winter agency there.[2]

Throughout the Hefbiner calamity, Dodge had been liberally supplying the Navajos with provisions; perhaps to reassure them of American friendship, to encourage cooperation and certainly remind them upon which side their bread was buttered. During his meeting with Armijo at Ojos Calientes, Red Shirt exchanged fourteen sheep to the fort commissary for a beef cow, which he then contributed to the Navajo. A few days after the prisoner's execution, he drew better than $350 of merchandise for Navajo gifts from Sutler Weber, including butcher knives and the ever-popular plugs of tobacco.[3] While Henry endeavored to reassure the Navajo, Kendrick was equally resolved to intimidate them. He believed a show of rockets would do the trick, so he ordered twenty-four rockets from Fort Union. On November 13th Kendrick hosted a fireworks show to wow the Indians, and wow them he did, but it remained to be seen as to how deeply his enthusiastic audience had been intimidated.

From the moment he had mounted a horse as Indian agent, Agent Dodge had focused his efforts exclusively on the Navajo. Officially he was the agent of four other tribes, the Pueblos of Acoma, Laguna, Zuni and the Hopi, commonly known as the Moqui. Each of the pueblos was relatively self-sufficient, peaceful and a proven ally of the Americans, so there was negligible risk in neglecting them. Of the four tribes, the Moqui were by far the most remote, enigmatic and, according to the Indian Service, the most destitute. Almost miraculously, they survived in a region notorious for its harsh aridity, surrounded by the belligerent Navajo, eking out a living by hunting small game and dry farming on the sandy flats below their seven mesa-top villages. It was said the name *Moqui* itself was an insult, purportedly a

Navajo rendition of the English word for "monkey." The claim is highly suspect, but well-illustrates the contempt that the Navajo often felt for their mesa dwelling neighbors.

The Moqui referred to themselves as *Hopi'sinom*, the "People Who Live Correctly", and would have been incredulous to hear such unflattering characterizations, for they believed they were neither ignored, destitute or inferior. They viewed themselves as the guardians of creation, the very caretakers of existence residing at the center of the spiritual universe, and it was no less than their complex cycle of ceremonies that kept the very universe itself ticking. Hopi religion and philosophy held an intimate understanding of the natural world and the absolute need to live in harmony with it and reverence for it. They kept a strict secrecy over such matters and therefore could appear reluctant and stand offish. Unlike other pueblos, the Hopi language falls within the Uto-Aztecan language family, as is Nahuatl, the tongue of the Aztecs. Hence, if any pueblo could claim to have guarded the fabled fire of Montezuma, it would have been the *Hopi'sinom*. Their society seemed as ancient as the country in which they dwelled, borne by countless generations stretching into an immeasurable past. Although they were known as The Peaceful People, they occasionally used violence to blunt a threat to their villages or their religious traditions. In 1701, after the Hopi village of Awatovi decided to admit Spanish missionaries, the other villages united and utterly obliterated the place.

Hence in November, with Navajo relations never better, Dodge decided it was time to look in on his most inscrutable responsibility, the Hopi'sinom. Major Kendrick was preparing a small expedition to lay out a wagon road to Hopi in hopes of supplying his command with Hopi corn instead of drawing it from the depot at Laguna, some 160 miles to the east. Kendrick also hoped that an army contract for corn would give the Hopi a much-needed economic boost after their devastating small pox epidemic. It was a perfect opportunity for Dodge to assess the pueblo's condition. Once more the Reverend John Milton Shaw would join them. Shaw's motivation was obvious, for there were perhaps hundreds of Moqui souls crying for salvation. He might have been equally motivated by the prospect of a three week vacation from the humdrum of domestic life and the constant crowds of Indians pressing through the front door. Harriet would remain dutifully behind once more, keeping house and hosting the Navajo, all while trying to suppress her perpetually upset stomach, an undying case of the blues and her hectic obsession over her children's health. Georgie and Hattie had managed to contract the dysentery with the accompanying scourge of vomiting and diarrhea. She dosed them up with mercury powder, calomel and opium prescribed by Dr. Letterman, and hovered over them like the anguished angel of distress.

> "It is as much as I know how to do to take care of my children, do all the sewing & the other various duties that devolve on me, my health is not good I have a good deal of distress in my stomach and across my breast, but am better of it now. I think perhaps it is humour. I am now taking that bottle of Whiton's anti-scrofulous syrup . . . My whole system seems out of order, and I feel like a broken-down horse, good for nothing. But my husband says I am better than two dead wives now. . . . Georgie is much better of his boils."[4]

Such was a life of a missionary wife.

Major Kendrick, Henry Dodge, Reverend Shaw and a small contingency of troops departed Fort Defiance for Hopi around November 16th. Rather than striking the direct, west-southwesterly trail over Defiance Plateau, they decided to angle north and descend into Canyon De Chelly to survey the Navajo condition there. As they followed the canyon stream westward Shaw noted the acres of peach orchards, now barren with advent of winter, lining the main and side canyons. Occasionally the groves framed ruins of ancient Anasazi pueblos tucked into the canyon walls, built by the ancestors of the people Kendrick's expedition planned to visit. That season the Navajo had extensively settled the west end of the canyon and their collected wealth in sheep and horses was an impressive reminder of their prosperity.

Emerging into the broad Chinle Valley, the column ambled its way towards the buff-colored bluffs that marked the fringes of Hopi country. It was sixty odd miles of sandy, barren, rolling country generally scattered with yucca and cactus, braced by yellow and beige mesas and punctuated by rugged buttes. The ride had been pleasant enough, although the trail was heavily sanded and the November nights bitterly cold. The countryside was devoid of firewood so each night they had to forego the luxury of a warming fire. After a sojourn of six days, the expedition arrived at the first of the seven Moqui towns, probably Walpi, set on a bluff some two hundred feet above them. The ravages of small pox were immediately apparent to the travelers. While riding along the foot of the mesa, Shaw noted "the bones of the dead bleaching in the sun, left, probably by the wolves after having consumed the flesh." The disease had killed so many Hopi that the living had been forced to throw the dead over the cliffs onto the rocks below. After establishing a camp on the flats, the column ascended a precipitously narrow trail leading up to the village.

In due time and with due caution, Kendrick, Dodge and Shaw emerged at the mesa top. A crowd of Hopi men, women and children greeted them. Many of those beaming, friendly faces were covered with the scars and sores of the pox. The sight of the town behind them was, for the Reverend Shaw at least, quite a shock in itself, the cockeyed flagstone dwellings clinging desperately to one another, giving every indication they might at any moment collapse and cascade down the cliff side. He described the place as "very filthy" and the Hopi people about the place "poorly clad." Among them ran their children without a stitch of clothing on them. It was enough to rattle the most basic sensibilities of civilized folks, but it made good copy. Mrs. Shaw later tantalized her family with those particulars, accentuating the most appalling passages with bold underlining.

> "Moquis like all others [are] a most filthy degraded set of beings. Large boys & girls <u>entirely naked</u>."

Shocking, indeed. No doubt the respectable folks back home perused her letter repeatedly.

Kendrick and Dodge, with Shaw in tow, visited all seven of the villages; from east to west Walpi, Hano, Sichomovi, Shungopavi, Mishongnovi, Kykotsmovi and the largest, Oraibi. Upon their approach, women and children often ran and hid, but even so they found the Hopi unflaggingly hospitable and generous with what little they had. As a gesture of friendship, they offered them gifts of corn bread, perhaps a chicken and other trifles. Towards the end of their visit, the Americans witnessed a corn harvest dance in the Oraibi plaza.

> "In a few moments, a company of dancers appeared, and these dispersed; the performers were headed by a deformed Indian . . . they were dressed as hideous as possible, each having the skin of a wolf, wild cat, or some other wild beast, dangling behind them."

At that point Reverend Shaw confessed he had wished to have the gift of tongues. Here was, as the reverend put it, an "emphatically <u>heathen</u>" people and he had no way to communicate the Good News to them. No Hopi there spoke Spanish, and no American could speak Hopi. It was for him some consolation that there was no evidence of Catholic influence. Shaw suggested later that the Hopi "would be an interesting field for some self-sacrificing minister who has no family. . ."[5] In other words, count him out.

Doubtlessly, Major Kendrick was equally unimpressed by the people and their condition. Two years after the expedition, Kendrick would send Meriwether a lengthy description of the Moqui villages and the prospect for drawing corn from them. It was a gloomy, unflattering assessment. There were twenty to twenty-five hundred people living in seven mesa top towns. Kendrick warned that their population was in real danger of extinction. He surmised that their "vicious system of intermarriage had deprived them of all manliness", allowing the Navajo to ride rough shod over them at will. Furthermore, if the Indian Service wished to convince the Navajo to adopt a pueblo life style, the Moqui were certainly an unfavorable example. Their one hope at resuscitation might well be a fodder contract with the Army. Essentially, Kendrick echoed Harriett Shaw's conclusions, complete with double underlining . . .

> "If there be any where a <u>missionary who is really</u> anxious to practice self denial, to take up his cross and keep it up ("none other need apply") he will find an open field at Moqui."[6]

The Hopi, of course, wouldn't have appreciated Kendrick's impolite opinions, if they had even bothered to waste effort reflecting upon them. If Dodge ever expressed any particular opinions about the Hopi, they remain unknown. The party stayed at Hopi for a week before heading back to Defiance.

During their return or shortly thereafter, Henry Dodge discovered among the Navajo a young Mexican captive, a girl of ten or eleven years. The family holding her explained that the girl had accidentally fallen into the fire, but she showed all the symptoms of having been abused. Henry took the girl up, brought her into the fort and delivered her to the Shaw's front door. Harriet was appalled. The little apparition was the perfect portrait of misery.

> She had been most <u>shockingly</u> burnt. They said she had a fit & fell in the fire half of her leg from the knee to the ankle was one raw sore filled with proud flesh & <u>maggots</u>. The other leg was also badly burned also her foot, hand, back shoulders, & all of the toes on one foot had been frozen off. We took her, washed her & cleaned her sores & gave her clothes & made her a little bed in our kitchen (for we had no other place) & the Dr took charge of her burns. So filthy an object I never saw. . ."

Sister Tolhurst cleaned her up and made her a bed in the kitchen, but when the stench of her festering sores began wafting around the dinner table, they moved her into a vacant room across the post.[7] Gradually the girl's health improved. She related that she had been taken when she was very small and could recall little of her true family. Still, Agent Dodge made efforts to find her relatives, probably without success.

Slavery among the Indian could be a cruel destiny, particularly for girls and women. During a Ute treaty meeting, David Meriwether curiously commented that of the young Hispanic captives held by Indians, "boys were all willing to remain with the Indians, while the girls were anxious to leave them."[8] In defense of keeping humans as property, the Southern apologist and senator John C. Calhoun immortalized a popular euphemism for it in the early 1830s. He referred to it as "our *peculiar* institution." Most Southerners considered the use of the term slavery to be offensive, even if the institution itself was not. The word *peculiar* derived from the Latin *peculium*, meaning private property, which in turn derived from *pecu*, the term for cattle. Thus Calhoun's usage was closer to the truth than he might have suspected. Of course, he meant *peculiar* in the 19th century sense of the word "special" rather than the modern spin on it, "strange or eccentric." In describing slavery as it existed in New Mexico at that time, the later usage fit to a tee . . . for strange it was.

Upon its admission into the Union, the Territory of New Mexico had overwhelmingly rejected the Southern version of slavery. Yet it universally tolerated if not openly endorsed its own peculiar, pernicious version. The slave trade had existed in New Mexico at least since the late 16th century and although Indian tribes were co-participants, it was the Indian who was its primary victim. For every captive held by an Indian, the New Mexican held a dozen or more. Indians were seized and sold from tribes as far away as Utah, Nevada and California. Cahuilla, Paiute, Apache, Navajo and Ute captives were commonly found in well-to-do New Mexican households. New Mexicans didn't think of it as slavery per se, but as more of a humanitarian apprenticeship in Christian civilization, to teach them proper behavior and morality, the benefits of hard work, a love for Christ and a fear of God, ironically the very arguments used by Southerners to defend black slavery.

Slave raiding caused endless conflict between New Mexican and Indian. During peace treaty negotiations, provisions for an exchange of captives were always included but invariably the result was one sided, as the Navajo leader Armijo had pointed out to John Greiner. New Mexican citizens resisted surrendering Indian captives and the New Mexican civil government abhorred forcing the issue. United States Army was reluctant to send Indian captives, particularly children, back into what they decried as the debasing clutches of immoral savagery. Consequently the Navajo might surrender a dozen captives, but prying a single Navajo child out of the grip of a New Mexican household was nearly impossible, as Henry L. Dodge would soon discover.

The year of 1855 had started uneventfully enough for Dodge, but a letter received by Governor Meriwether around Christmas of 1854 would change that. It was a petition from two local attorneys, the ex-Navajo agent Spruce M. Baird and James L. Hubbell. James Lawrence Hubbell was a Connecticut man of Northern sympathies who had come to New Mexico in 1846 as a private in the 2d Regiment of Missouri Mounted Volunteers. The country and its opportunities seduced him and, after settling in Pajarito south of Albuquerque, he married a local girl and fathered six children. Among friends and acquaintances, he was known affectionately as Santiago. Both Baird and Hubbell, coincidentally, were no friends of Meriwether and, for that matter, any New Mexican who proclaimed himself a Democrat.

The petition itself was on behalf of one José Castillo, the justice of the peace for Cebolleta. In early January of 1854 Meriwether had ordered Castillo to seize two Indian captives being held in the area and return them to Agent Dodge. Rumor had it that one of the captives, a young girl, was living with a local widow, the Doña Marcelina Otero y Cháves. The following September Castillo actually managed to get both of them, but rather than returning the Navajo girl to Dodge, he took her into his own household instead. The outraged widow Doña Marcelina promptly petitioned the New Mexico courts to get the girl back, claiming Castillo had illegally seized the girl to make her a servant.

Meriwether slogged through the tangle of protracted, flowery legalese so much the trademark of ill-trained lawyers. Through Baird and Hubbell's tortured prose, Castillo admitted his guilt, that Dona Marcelina's claim had indeed been true. Yes, it was true the 12 year old Navajo girl knew only the Cháves household as her home. True, the girl thought of Doña Marcelina "by no other appellation than Mother." Yes, he had seized her by Governor Meriwether's order. Yes, he admitted, he had made the girl a servant in his own household, but weakly protested that he had done it all for purely humanitarian reasons.

> "But so it is may it please your Excellency, finding the said captive thoroughly adopted by the said Marcelina as her child, who has no offspring of her body, and thoroughly christianized and wholly ignorant and insensible of her relationship with the Navajo Indians, and horror stricken at the idea

of being forced to return among them, your petitioner naturally felt an anxiety to rescue her from so sad a fate so revolting and so horrible, and for that reason and that only paid Agent Dodge the sum of one hundred dollars as a consideration for her release from the horrid fate awaiting her..."

That must have set Meriwether back. Dodge had sold the girl? He read on. The petitioner José Castillo, being wholly ignorant of the laws and instead trusting fully in a government agent's "superior intelligence, humanity, patriotism, and disposition to comply with and never exceed their lawful powers" believed Henry Dodge had every right to do whatever he pleased in regard to the Navajo girl, including selling her. Meriwether thumbed through the petition's attachments. Good Lord. There was even a bill of sale attached. It was in Dodge's handwriting and signature all right, executed in Spanish at Cebolleta, dated September 16th, 1854. With unusual and unfortunate diligence, Henry had procured the signatures of two witnesses, Román Baca and Salvador Candelaria.

"Be it known by this so that all may know that this signed below by Agent of the Indians having in my hands an order by the Governor and Superintendent of Indian Affairs, said order is directed to the Alcalde of Sebolleta, effecting the removal of two Indians who in previous years had been sold by the Sandoval Navajos whom were not owned by the gentleman but solely to the Navajos ... They were removed from those who previously had them and delivered to me the aforementioned, as agent and I as authorized agent by said Indians which gave me the power to sell them, I sold them to Don José Castillo, resident of Sebolleta, one of the said Indians (female) by which no person has the right to intervene in the future, absolutely with said buyer."[9]

The court subsequently ordered the girl returned to her adoptive mother, causing Castillo to bring claim against Dodge. Baird & Hubbell were demanding Henry Dodge return Castillo's money, plus costs. If not, they were prepared to pursue the money through the Navajo Tribe and, that failing, through Commissioner of Indian Affairs Manypenny and even as far as the President of the United States, potentially a humiliating scandal, indeed.[10]

Meriwether laid the petition down. Here was trouble. Taking up his quill, he began scratching out a terse letter to Agent Dodge at Fort Defiance.

"Sir:

A petition has been presented to me by Mr. Hubble on the part of José Castillo, relative to a Navajo Indian captive, which it is charged that you sold to said Castillo. The petition requests me to cause the purchase money together with all costs amounting to $175 to be refunded by you, because of this captive having been recovered from Castillo by due process of law, and if you fail to refund the amount claimed, that I will transmit the petition to the Supt of Indian Affairs. I give you this information that you may act as you think proper in the premises."[11]

Judge Kirby Benedict had been the first to hear the case of *Otero Y Cháves vs. Castillo*. Remarkably, the widow Cháves was represented by none other than the law firm of Baird & Hubbell. On October 24th, Castillo and the Navajo girl appeared before Benedict. Castillo admitted the girl was in his care but denied she was a servant, that the governor of the territory had required him "to take the within mentioned Indian into his custody and keeping and return the same to Henry L. Dodge, Indian Agent." Castillo insisted that he was then ready, as he had always been, to turn her over. All Dodge had to do was request the girl.

Castillo neglected to mention anything about money changing hands.[12] That omission came to light two days later. Doña Marcelina explained through her two lawyers that she had inherited the girl "some six or seven years ago." She had named her Letrada and claimed that until last September, the girl had happily lived with her as mother and child until she was forcibly seized. The pleas of the widow not withstanding, Castillo refused to surrender the girl, and announced that he had a financial interest in the girl. He'd purchased Letrada as a household maid. It was a seriously miscalculated admission. With that, Judge Benedict slapped Castillo with a writ of habeas corpus, commanding him to release the girl to her adopted mother immediately.

Dodge probably received Meriwether's letter the second week of January. The governor couldn't have been more unambiguous. Fix it and fix it now. Henry was no political neophyte. He well understood the seriousness of the implications. Aside from sullying his own name, the issue had potentially severe political consequences for Governor Meriwether. It is therefore astounding that Henry Dodge was able to fix it as quickly as he did. On the 1st of February, roughly five weeks after receiving Castillo's petition, Meriwether got a second one from Castillo, again executed through his lawyers Hubbell and Baird. This time it was considerably shorter, but what it lacked in substance it made up for in contrition.

"Sir: I beg leave to call your attention to a petition which was presented to you on the 26th of Dec. last by the undersigned in reference to the reclaiming of a Navajo Indian by Henry L. Dodge. Since filing said petition I have communicated with Agent Dodge and discovering that there was probably some mistake about the matter, and as the affair has already been amicably settled, I desire to withdraw said petition, and stop further proceedings in reference thereto."[13]

Incredible. Castillo, Baird and Hubbell wanted to drop the whole matter—thank you very much, sincerely yours and no hard feelings. Given that the alcalde had managed to simultaneously put his foot in his mouth and his hand in the wringer of justice, his reluctance to follow through wasn't particularly surprising. What . . . or who . . . could have possibly persuaded Castillo to pursue the matter in the first place? The governor had a pretty good idea of whom indeed, and it infuriated him.

Henry L. Dodge arrived in Santa Fe on the very day Castillo withdrew his claim. The agent was in town to pay off a few agency debts and to brief Meriwether on the results of his investigation. Henry explained that the actual sale of the girl had been a gross misunderstanding. A year and a half ago, in late fall of 1853, a Navajo man had appeared at his agency and told Henry he'd learned one of his missing relatives, a little girl, was alive and being held by a New Mexican citizen. Although many little Navajo girls were held as servants in New Mexican homes, it is quite probable that the little girl was Letrada. Navajo intelligence was usually impeccable. In hopes of ransoming her, the man purchased two Paiute children to exchange for his little girl. Meriwether later explained to Manypenny, that the Paiute had been "for a great number of years in the habit of selling their children to the Mexicans of this territory, and other Indians, and a considerable number are now held as servants by those people."

The Navajo man then approached Antonio Sandoval, the Mount Taylor headman, who seemed to be the perfect broker for a deal. Sandoval consented, so the Navajo fellow left the Paiute kids with him and departed to await the outcome. Never one to pass up a business opportunity, Sandoval promptly sold the two captives to the New Mexicans and pocketed the money. Events at that point then became somewhat muddled. Instead of the two Paiute children, whose fate remained unresolved, Castillo had seized Letrada and another nameless captive. Having spent most of her childhood with Doña Marcelina, Letrada was terrified and distraught over the prospect of being surrendered to the Navajo. No man with a heart could have been untouched by such anguish, so Dodge finagled a solution. He sold Letrada to Castillo for one hundred dollars to be used as an indemnity payment to her Navajo family, whereupon Castillo would return the girl to her dear adopted mother, the widow Cháves. All his compassionate protestations aside, the alcalde had apparently neglected to do so.

Henry Dodge also discovered that Castillo's motives for filing the petition for payment as well as the petition to rescind had not been his ideas at all, but those of his two scheming lawyers. On February 2nd, the day after Henry Dodge got to Santa Fe, he sent Meriwether a brief note. Castillo had only been a marionette. Spruce Baird and Santiago Hubbell were pulling the strings.

> "Learning from the proceedings of a Whig meeting lately held in Santa Fe, that you have been censured and accused of participating in the sale of a Navajo captive, I deem it my duty to exonerate you from all participation in the matter except having requested the alcalde to have her surrendered to the parties who claimed her."[14]

Spruce Baird and Santiago Hubbell had attempted to smear Meriwether's reputation for Whig political gains. They had persuaded or perhaps even coerced Castillo, whose suspicious purposes had compromised him, to claim Dodge had participated in a slave sale with the governor's full knowledge. It was a sweet revelation for Meriwether to realize it wasn't Castillo's capitulation he had in his hands, but Spruce M. Baird and Santiago Hubbell's. It must have been a sublimely delicious moment. Withdraw the petition? Hell no. He had no intention of withdrawing the petition. He'd send it on to Commissioner Manypenny as evidence of a scurrilous Whig conspiracy to undermine the territorial government. With any luck, it would end up on the President Pierce's desk. That would turn up the heat quite nicely on the two conniving Whig barristers.

In his report to Manypenny, Meriwether completely exonerated Dodge's actions in the controversy. Judge Benedict himself had assured the governor that through the entire affair Dodge had consistently acted as a friend to the Navajo and there was no evidence that the agent had profited a single penny from the sale. He was skeptical as to how sincere Marcelina Otero y Cháves had been about her loving relationship with her so-called adopted daughter Letrada. He hadn't a shred of doubt that Letrada was as much a servant for the widow Cháves as she had been for the alcalde Castillo. Still, all was well that ended well.[15] After receiving the governor's report, Commissioner Manypenny concurred.

"I have to remark that in the opinion of this Office, Agent Dodge is excused from all censure in view of the facts forwarded by you relative to the course pursued by him in the case of the Indian Captive before mentioned."[16]

Case closed.

40

BEST FRIENDS

With the exception of dealing with Baird and Hubbell's intrigues, most of Henry Dodge's activities in January of 1855 involved the unremarkable tasks of running his Fort Defiance Indian agency. He made typical purchases on behalf of the Navajo: "sundry presents" of axes and files, shovels, brass kettles, scissors and wool cards, two strings of coral for jewelry, leather and fabric and of course tobacco. Smoking tobacco was constantly in demand by visiting Navajos, who would roll their cigarillos in dried cornhusks, squat down on their haunches in typical Navajo fashion, and smoke with serious intensity.[1]

In somewhat less than praiseworthy performance, Henry Dodge waited to the very last moment to prepare and submit his account for the 4th quarter of 1854. The traders Webb and Kingsbury notified him that although the governor had approved his salary for the quarter, a draft for it from them could not be sent until he turned in his accounts completed.[2] No accounts . . . no pay. Dodge's expenses would again fail to pass muster with the accountants in Washington. Among the contested items: Dodge filed a voucher of $75 to cover his expenses when he, Anaya and Gallegos had been on the trail of Hefbiner's killer. There were no receipts. The fact Navajos didn't issue receipts was beside the point. The General Accounting Office suspended it, noting with amazement that every trip Dodge took seemed to cost three bucks a day.[3]

Friendly relations between the Navajo and the Americans continued undisturbed. Keeping it that way was of paramount concern to David Meriwether and General John Garland. At the end of 1854, the Mescalero renewed their attacks on the settlements along the Pecos and had fought an engagement with Lt. Sturgis' dragoons. The Jicarilla and Ute soon joined the fray. On Christmas, a war party of over one hundred men all but destroyed a tiny, isolated settlement above the Huerfano River in present-day Colorado, known simply as Pueblo. An open state of war suddenly existed with three formidable tribes and the Army was hard pressed to meet the challenge. The Department of New Mexico was shockingly below strength by some 557 soldiers and Garland was compelled to ask Meriwether to call out five volunteer companies.[4]

Thus it became Dodge's task to preserve the Navajo tranquility at all costs. While Henry was in Santa Fe, Governor Meriwether advanced him $1200 for Navajo goods and agency expenses and reminded Dodge of the grave importance that he succeed.[5] Henry didn't need the reminder. Kendrick had already made that priority clear to him. Under no circumstances should Dodge allow the Navajo to be influenced by their warring Ute neighbors to the north. To expedite that goal, on February 14th Kendrick took advantage of Henry's absence from the post to make General Garland a proposition.

> "I think it advisable for the present, at least, that the Indian Agent should reside at this post; & I respectfully request permission to cause commissary supplied for the use of his family, to be sold him at contract prices so long as he resides here.

Kendrick believed having Dodge close at hand at Fort Defiance was crucial and he hoped to make the agent's stay permanent. General Garland subsequently approved Kendrick's request. Dodge could purchase Army supplies at officers' prices for himself and that mysterious family of his.[6]

At the time, Red Shirt had left Defiance to accompany two hundred Navajos to Jemez for a three-day feast. He arrived there on the 13th, pausing to write Meriwether a letter informing him of his whereabouts. In those tense times, his report was reassuringly optimistic.

> "I arrived here today with two hundred Navijos who wish to attend a feast in this Puebelo which will last three days when I will return with them to their country.
>
> "I have the satisfaction to report them at peace with but few exceptions the Utahs have made every effort to get them to join them in a

war against us but cannot succeed. I have sent out runners to all the Navijos living near the Rio San Juan to retire south fifty or sixty miles and to make every exertion to keep the Utahs from passing the aforesaid River which is recognized as the line between the two Nations. I have the extreme pleasure to say that all of the rich have obeyed promptly retireing with their flocks and herds ..."

Dodge then inserted a qualification.

"... But I have not the least doubt that many of the poor have not and will join them. If it is possible I would like very much that two companies one of Dragoons and one of Volunteers should decend the Rio San Juan on the North side eighty or one hundred miles making the starting point Arbiqu a regular officer in command if such a force should be sent it would have a most excelent effect. The Capote Utaws have joined the Utaws and Apaches—this information I have from the Navijos and the Indians of this Puebelo from whom they stole nine horses a few days since—the Puebelos pursued them and had a skirmish with them but did not recapture the horses."

In regards to reports of a recent theft of sheep by renegade Navajos, Henry assured Meriwether he was investigating.

"I have made every effort to return the sheep stolen from a Mr. Grube living in Santa Fe who has the sheep of Don Pedro Pero on the shares—The Navijos have returned all the sheep they say that was taken by the thieves one hundred and sixty two in number which they contend was all that was ever taken into their country Mr Grube by his herder has made proof before an Alcalde that he lost the number as above mentioned The Navijos say that they wish the mater refered to you and will they say will abide your decission or act as you may direct.

"Please write me by the bearer Mr. Carter the Mode in which I am to proceede."[7]

Red Shirt scrawled his signature, sealed the letter and handed it to George Carter, recently back from a lengthy absence. Carter returned three days later with the governor's reply. Meriwether deeply regretted that it was impossible to arrange a show of force for the renegade San Juan Navajo. Every soldier General Garland had available, not to mention Meriwether's volunteers, was being flung at the Jicarilla and Ute. The only thing that could be done was to keep the Navajo quiet by carefully explaining to them "the danger to themselves of associating or intermixing with the hostile Indians, and by apprising them of their ultimate punishment in the event of a union of the two tribes, in any hostile movement against our citizens."[8]

It seemed an overwhelming responsibility, but Henry was confident the Navajo would neither turn against him or the New Mexicans. While at Jemez, Dodge bought two guns and six flasks of powder from the traders I. & H. Mecure, gifts to his Navajo companions. For himself, he bought a fine Navy pistol with holster, belt and hardware, paying the extravagant price of fifty dollars.[9]

Dodge returned to Fort Defiance on or about February 25th. He briefed Major Kendrick on the doings at Jemez and repeated his proposal to send a column to the San Juan to intimidate the renegades. It seemed imperative to make some gesture, certainly. The Navajo, Dodge explained, had told him that Tamouche's band of Capote Ute, in the company of a few Jicarilla, had been spotted some thirty miles south of the San Juan, in the vicinity of the Canyon Largo and Chaco. They were rumored to be two hundred strong, most of them fighting men, in perfect position to wreak havoc on the settlements. The men of Jemez all expressed enthusiasm for joining the soldiers for an attack on the Ute. Kendrick recommended Dodge's plan for a San Juan expedition to Garland.

> "We shall use every effort to prevent a coalition between the Utahs & Navajoes, & hope to succeed in it, & even to embroil them with each other by inducing the latter to take the animals of the Utahs, of which it is said they have a large number. At the same time, if it be in the power of the Genl to send an expedition of at least two companies under a regular officer, by way of Jemez or Abiquiu, those being the nearest routes in Search of these Indians, it would be well to do so."

Kendrick stated that any attempt of making reconnaissance using the Fort Defiance garrison would be counterproductive. Sending such a miniscule force would fail to impress neither Ute nor Navajo. In the worst case, the Navajo people might see it as a sign of weakness and rise up against the Americans. That was an outside chance to be sure, but Henry Dodge concurred. It might be best to take a sounding. Kendrick and Dodge instructed a Navajo headman to seek out various bands and determine the general mood of the nation. Shortly after that, Henry rode back to

Jemez to gather information regarding Capote Ute intentions, and was under orders to send his findings by a Jemez messenger to General Garland himself.[10]

To an extent, the on-going Ute "excitement," most notably the hostile stance taken by Tamouche's Capote Ute, had been exacerbated by the vigilante actions of New Mexicans. There existed roughly a dozen bands of Ute scattered across the central and southwest Rockies. Three bands were associated with New Mexico territory: the war-like Moache of the eastern plains, the Capote of the San Luis Valley, and the Weeminuche of the San Juan River area. The Moache had long been the most hostile of the three, but the Weeminuche and Capote were fairly benign. That would soon change.

On February 18th, the Ute Agent Labadi informed Meriwether that a party of New Mexicans had raided the peaceful Capote camp of Tamouche's brother, killing him and several others.[11] That promptly turned Tamouche's people hostile. Two days later, the Ute agent reported additionally disturbing news. José Rafael Lucero, a man held as captive by the Navajo since November of 1854, had confided to him that the Navajo were preparing to go to war. At that very moment, he explained, the rich were withdrawing their herds to safer regions. Four days following that letter, on February 24th, Labadi recanted. The Navajos and Ute in the west were "very peaceable, quiet, and do not intend to take up arms against any person of this Territory . . . that they wish to live quietly in their country and will not molest any person whatsoever . . ." Of Tamouche's threatening crowd nothing more substantial was heard . . . for a time.[12]

On March 27th, Red Shirt wrote Meriwether another reassuring letter from his agency in the Tunicha Mountains.

> "I have the satisfaction to report the Navijo nation of Indians at peace with our Government and the Indian tribes around them . . . The Utahs cannot induce them to join in a war against our the U. S. all effords on their part has failed.

To what extent Dodge and Kendrick's efforts persuaded or dissuaded the Navajos is a matter of conjecture. That happy circumstance could have equally resulted from the exhortations of Zarcillos Largos, Armijo, Manuelito, Barboncito and the other Navajo headmen. The Navajo had unflaggingly shown they desired friendship with the Americans, Kendrick's suspicion of the Indians' motives not withstanding. However much credit Dodge could have claimed for defusing tensions, he was nonetheless determined to do whatever he could to encourage that friendship.

"The Spring bids fair for a good croping year as much snow has fallen in the Mountains of Chuski, Tounicha, & cañon Blanco, and the Indians in the above mentioned places are much in want of about 200 hoes and one dozen axes please send me the hoes and axes if possible by Mr. Carter the Black Smith who goes to Santa Fe to visit his family."[13]

Meriwether understood the importance of materially encouraging the Navajo and when Carter delivered the letter to him, he promptly complied with Dodge's request for farm tools.[14]

By the close of the 1st quarter, March 31st, 1855, the Navajo agency was well prepared to insure the Navajo peace. Dodge had assembled his original crew, interpreter Juan Anaya, the herder Manuel Vallejos and blacksmith George C. Carter. They would have an agency on horseback, touring the broad valleys and canyons of the Navajo land, ranging from Fort Defiance, to Tunicha, to Canyon de Chelly and back. For the first time they enjoyed the luxury of having enough money to buy all the supplies needed and to draw a salary to boot.[15] Henry, however, was paid nothing. Back in Washington City, his brother Augustus had filed that power of attorney with Commissioner Manypenny. In turn, Manypenny instructed Meriwether to let Henry know that his father Senator Dodge would draw his salary until he'd paid back $1000.[16] Additionally, Dodge learned that his request to be credited for the $405 he'd spent on agency business before actually becoming agent in the summer of 1853 had been approved . . . but he would not see a cent of it. Manypenny had requested the 2nd Auditor issue Henry Dodge a treasury draft for the amount. The 2nd Auditor, P. Clayton, would have none of it, as he explained to H. L. Dodge in a letter he sent care of Governor Meriwether.

" . . . As you stand charged with moneys advanced at different periods payment cannot be made to you, but the amount will be passed to your credit on settlement of yr accs—You will therefore please charge the same in your accs current—"[17]

Dodge probably shrugged it off. It figured.

As March passed into April, Dodge's prediction that many of the San Juan Navajo would ally with the Ute appeared accurate. Captain Charles Deus of the New Mexico Volunteers, one of Meriwether's companies formed to fight the Jicarilla and Ute, reported from Taos that on April 7th an Indian war party composed of Capote

Ute and Navajo warriors had raided the stock of one Juan Trujillo and his mother.[18] On April 9th the citizens of Rio Arriba formally petitioned General Garland to protect them from Navajo and Ute depredations.[19] Although the hostile acts of a few Navajo had the potential to besmirch the reputation of the entire tribe, Kendrick and Dodge remained unconcerned. As Kendrick pointed out in his report of April 16th, on the whole the Navajo were consistently cooperative and were providing important intelligence about Ute intentions.

> "I have the honor to state, that the Navajoes report to us that the Utahs, with a portion of Jicarillas, in all amounting to nine hundred (men, women & children) are at the South Western base of the Sierra de la Plata, within the Utah country. They affirm to the Navajoes that they intend to hold their ground at that point against any force that will be sent to contend with them. They declare that in one instance, by pretending to be anxious for peace, they were permitted to sleep in the camp of the Americans, & that in the night they massacred the entire command.... The Utahs further state, that some time since five Mexicans, from Abiquiu, came to their camp with corn for sale to the Utahs, who took their corn & slew the Mexicans..."[20]

Having hence arrived at Fort Defiance the day following Kendrick's report, Henry Dodge substantiated the major's assessment in a letter to Meriwether. Clearly the two men were working together as one.

> "I still have the satisfaction to report the Navijo Nation of Indians at peace and making every effort to farme more extensively this spring than they ever have since they commenced the cultivation of the soil I have furnished them with hoes spade and all the axis that could be had at this post Armijo the greates farmer in the Nation seeing the facility with which the soldiers are enabled to plant by means of the plow made application to Major Kendrick Commanding officer at this place for the loan of a plow and three yoke of oxin which he would have been very glad to have furnished if they could have been spared..."

Henry Dodge and Armijo had visited the fort specifically for agricultural tools. By this time, the two men had become fast friends, a friendship later to be proven in the worst of circumstances. As for Ute attempts to subvert the Navajo, Dodge flatly stated their efforts had been for naught.

> "The Utahs have and are still making great efforts to get them to join in making war upon our people but I feel well assured that they cannot be opperated upon by them to do anything rong as a Nation.... The Utahs has said to them that we are easy prey for them that they had killed eight hundred of our people since the war commensed and have taken a very large amount of horses, mules, and horned cattle—the Navijos replied that they would buy mules & cows if they could see them and believe that the Utahs have lied with the view of decieving them. They have beged the Navijos not to plant this year but to join them and drive the Americans from the Territory—The Navijos reply that we are the best friends they have ever had and they will not do any thing to make us enemies..."

Although the Navajo as a nation generally shunned the Ute, Dodge noted certain "individuals may join them I think is very likely but as yet I have no proof that such is the fact." He also repeated the news Kendrick had just relayed to Garland, that about one thousand Ute and Jicarilla were encamped on the southwest slope of the La Plata Mountains.

> "The Navijos represent to me that the Utahs and Apaches are in strong force on the south West side of the Silver Mountains—they say nine hundred men women and children and that a few days since five Mexicans came out to their camps from Arbiqu to sell them corn and that they killed them and got the corn for their trouble..."

Henry mentioned nothing about the supposed slaughter of American soldiers. It was not impossible that the Ute had killed the Mexican corn vendors, but the tall tale of massacring an entire American detachment was preposterous, a deception the Navajo had immediately detected.[21]

John Weber delivered Dodge's report to Meriwether, who congratulated the agent on the "favourable condition" of the Navajo, then admonished him for failing to submit his detailed monthly report as required by the Honorable Commissioner of Indian Affairs George Manypenny, to whom Meriwether would have to explain Dodge's deficit. He then turned to decidedly more serious business.

> "Mr. Weber informs me that on his road to this place he was informed, that a Navajo Indian had been killed by a Mexican, he did not learn

the circumstances attending this affair, but I hope that you will investigate the matter, and if a Navajo Indian has been killed without provocation and evidence of the fact can be produced, cause the guilty party to be arrested and dealt with according to law. In the mean time assure the Navajos that Justice shall be done them . . ."

Weber had been told that a delegation of Navajo was already headed to Dodge's agency to file a complaint. The governor concluded his letter by announcing he expected to hold a major council with the Navajo at the end of June or beginning of July. Congress had finally given Meriwether the power to negotiate treaties and reservation boundaries with the New Mexican tribes. To encourage tribal cooperation, the lawmakers had appropriated $25,000 for treaty goods and related bribes. Meriwether was gratified Congress had adopted the very policy he'd endorsed, to establish well-defined Indian reservations a good distance from the settlements and make the Indians dependent on the government. He planned to meet first with the defeated Mescalero, and then follow up with the Chiricahua, the Jicarilla and the Ute. He was saving the Navajo for last and instructed Dodge to get as many Navajos to the meeting as he could round up.[22]

On May 2nd, Dodge reported to Meriwether that he had received and distributed 150 hoes and 12 axes to the Navajo at Tunicha and Cañon Blanco. The Navajos remained at peace and had no intention of breaking it. Meriwether's complaint over missing monthly reports had Henry scratching his head.

> "I have been under the impression that the letters I wrote you monthly reporting the condition of the Navajos was all the report required but will make any that you may order please send me a form . . .

He had discovered that the raids initially blamed on the Navajo had actually been the work of the Capote Ute and confirmed that Chief Tamouche was indeed leading them to avenge his brother's murder by New Mexicans near Taos.

> "The depredations committed on the Rio Purco was the Capote Utahs also at Arbique and they have within sixty mile of this place the captives taken and stock at the Silver Mountain—Tamuchi who heded the party says that a Brother of his was killed in a fight above Tews—The Navijos protes that they had no part in these depredations and will not buy anything of them—The Spring has been unusually wet and bids fair to be

a good cropping year and this Nation have planted four thousand acres of land and cannot be induced to go to war. Major Kendrick will confirm this statement . . . Respectfully your Obdt Servt H L Dodge Indian Agent for the Navijos"

Henry enclosed a voucher for what he had to pay the freighters for shipping those farm tools from Santa Fe to Tunicha . . . sixty bucks. Meriwether later explained to Manypenny that he didn't doubt Dodge paid the entire amount, for "the price for freight is extravagant."[23]

Notably, Dodge made no mention of the alleged murder of the Navajo man, nor of any Navajo delegations meeting with him seeking justice. Apparently the issue never surfaced. All the same, Dodge continued to nourish the relationship with plenty of gifts purchased from fort sutler John Weber: cloth domestic brown, red and blue drill, blankets and coats, yarn and indigo dye, handkerchiefs, bells and adzes, axes, hoes, rasps and shovels, pocket knives, butcher knives, a roll of brass wire and 150 pounds of tobacco.[24]

In the meantime, the Army had begun to see some progress in their war against the Ute and Jicarilla. During the previous winter and early spring, General Garland had thrown a force of regulars and volunteers roughly a thousand strong against the hostiles. Initially, they had made little headway. The Ute had continued sporadic attacks around the San Juan Mountains and the San Luis Valley while the troops had to contend with bitter cold and snow in efforts to catch the hostiles. Yet if winter had become Garland's antagonist, it concurrently proved to be a potent ally. Constant harassment and the fear of being overtaken kept the Indians on the run. Cold, starvation and fatigue inevitably wore them down.[25] At the end of April, Colonel St. Vrain and his volunteers caught up with the Jicarilla just below the Huerfano River. In two days the New Mexicans killed or captured a dozen and forced the Indians to abandon all their possessions. Two days after that, American regulars under Colonel Fauntleroy launched a night attack on Chief Tierra Blanca's Moache Ute camp at Poncha Pass, just north of the San Luis Valley. General Garland later crowed the attack had been "a triumph over these Indians seldom if ever equaled in the United States."[26]

On May 24th Meriwether informed Dodge that once he planned to treat with the Navajos at or near Fort Defiance around July 10th. In the intervening six weeks, he instructed Agent Dodge to assemble the entire Navajo nation, including the San Juan Navajo.[27] When he received the letter, Henry was getting ready to head for Santa Fe to wrap up 2nd quarter business. After discussing Meriwether's proposed parley with Major Kendrick, both men questioned the wisdom of having the treaty meeting at Fort Defiance. Kendrick wrote Meriwether with an explanation.

> "These Indians are extensively aware that something of moment to them is to take place, when you come here, and if proper notice be given, there will doubtless be a large collection of them; from their form of government, or rather of no government, it is desirable that it should be so. They know that it will be the most important treaty that has been made with them-perhaps the most so, that the Americans have ever made with any Indians in New Mexico.

The foreseeable difficulty, the major noted, would be the immense turnout of Indians and the resulting hordes of ravenous Navajo horses and sheep mowing through the fort grazing grounds. There were already Navajos camped near the fort in anticipation of the parley and their animals were in the fort hay fields.

> "There will probably be a thousand horses at the point where the treaty is made, besides which, many of the flocks will be driven near to that place, to avoid theft by other Navajoes. Should the treaty be made immediately at this Post, the Indians will be forced to bring these animals upon our grazing and haying ground, and we shall be <u>obliged</u> to drive them off by <u>force</u>. ..."

Kendrick didn't need to point out the effect that act would have on the Navajo. In addition the Indians were likely to be on edge to start with. Holding the meeting at the fort might be seen by Navajo as an attempt to intimidate or coerce them. A rumor was already spreading that the Army intended to lure the Navajos into Defiance to imprison and murder them. Navajo who remained leery of American friendship would be hesitant to show up for a meeting in the American stronghold.

> "For these reasons the Indian agent and myself, have informed the Indians that the treaty will be made at Laguna Negra, a point some twelve or fourteen miles north of this place, with which we are in easy communications. In that place there is plenty of water in the driest season, both in the lake and in the stream which feeds it. The grass is abundant in an extensive meadow by the margin of the lake, and wood at hand on the slopes near by. It is the prettiest and most eligible locality in the Navajoe Nations, and is nearer to the wealthy Indians than we are."

Kendrick offered to store Navajo presents and goods at Defiance for Meriwether until he needed them sent to Laguna Negra. As for presents, Kendrick suggested the governor bring what the Navajo referred to as "soft goods" such as bayeta wool cloth, cotton manta, indigo and leather. The Navajo cared "very little for trinkets or luxuries." The major also suggested that when Dodge left Santa Fe he proceed directly to Laguna Negra to prepare for the distribution of annuity goods.

"They have already received from Capt. Dodge all the hoes, axes and spades which he could get at the Post Sutlers, which they are putting to a good use. They all represent to me, that they are cultivating more extensively this year than ever before, which is to be attributed to the very often-repeated advice of their agent and myself, as well as to the existence of this Post, which has taught them the advantages of planting . . ." [28]

Both Dodge and Kendrick knew that amicable Navajo relations could easily go sour with a single misstep, a fact conveyed to Meriwether. An early drought was threatening the hopes of a good harvest. The New Mexicans, despite repeated warnings, continued to graze their herds on Navajo lands. The Navajos knew all too well that the American troops had been stretched dangerously thin fighting a war with the Ute, Jicarilla and Mescalero and that if they decided to rise up, it would be no small task to put them down.

41

LAGUNA NEGRA

At the end of June, Henry Dodge and a small delegation of Navajo and Pueblo leaders arrived in Santa Fe. Henry dutifully penned out a comprehensive report of the Navajo Agency for Commissioner George Manypenny, his task made easier by the news he was reporting. Dodge had never been more optimistic, particularly considering the ominous events of the previous autumn. Private Hefbiner's murder in October had portended utter catastrophe for his agency and for the Navajo in general. The Americans' ultimatum and the determination to carry it out were unalterable. Surrender the killer or suffer complete annihilation. None believed the Navajo would surrender the murderer and that a subsequent conflagration was inevitable.

Yet, to the amazement of everyone, they did. With that crisis resolved, another emerged.

> "At the commencement of this fiscal year war was raging on our borders with the Apaches and Utahs and every effort that was possible for me to make had to be put forth to prevent the poor, viciously disposed parts of the tribe from joining with the enemy. During the year [several outrages] have been committed upon the property of our citizens and murder perpetuated upon the body of a soldier near Fort Defiance by the party anxious for war thinking that it would be inevitably forced upon the nation by such acts of bad faith."

Yet, at Dodge's urging, the Navajo took prompt and extraordinary measures to defuse the situation. They paid out or restored hundreds of head of stolen livestock and rejected repeated Ute enticements to join in their war against the Americans. Since then, the tribe had enjoyed an unprecedented period of peace and prosperity, a direct result, Dodge noted modestly, of Meriwether's "liberal policy extended to them" and "a little extra exertion on my part." That was not to say there hadn't been some troubles. The Navajo had recently paid an unanticipated price for cooperating with the Americans. After being soundly trounced by Garland's troops the previous spring, the Moache Ute avenged their defeat by attacking the ranches of two rich Navajo headmen on the southern banks of the San Juan River.

> "... killing them both capturing their children and running off one hundred head of horses. ... This has produced a panic in all their farming [endeavors] for the present and caused the rich to flee to the mountains with their women children flocks & herds where they have concentrated in a body for mutual protection..."

Dodge feared that if a full-scale war between the two tribes erupted, the Navajo would be routed. The Ute had fine rifles, were highly mobile and aggressive. The Navajo, Henry observed, had a few dilapidated firearms, lived by farming and raising livestock, and were generally "not war like."

> "A treaty will be made in the early part of next month with them by Gov. D. Meriwether at which Genl Garland the Commanding officer of this military department has assured us he will be present, & that the Navijos shall have every assistance against their enemies that it is possible for him to give...."

Privately, Henry probably doubted that American troops would defend the Navajo against the Ute. Although the Army was always eager to enlist Indian auxiliaries for a campaign, putting soldiers in the field to defend one tribe from another was unprecedented. On the other hand, it is surprising that Dodge would assert the Navajo were not warlike, given their history in the territory. They could handle themselves. The Ute had temporarily set the Navajo back on their heels. Once they recovered, they'd settle all debts with the Moache. Dodge concluded his report in a sanguine, almost sentimental tone.

> That a friendly visit to the heart of their country by the Governor and the Genl commanding the military arm of our government in this territory will have a happy influence upon these people and secure a treaty of limits and friendship which will last for years I have reason to believe.

It was the type of statement heretofore unvoiced by any American, yet Dodge believed that, as long as the Indian Service continued its "enlightened policy" for at least a year, the Navajo could not fail to succeed and to succeed quickly. Concluding, Henry apologized for spending so much money on contingencies, although they were all unquestionably justified for the cause of peace. He closed his report with a note of minor contrition.

> "P.S. I will make monthly reports in future as requested by the department"[1]

Dodge certainly believed things were going as well as he had portrayed. For the first time, he had all the money he needed to meet his agency's needs. Dodge had already received a total of $2,760 from Meriwether, including a lump sum of $1,500 he'd received from the governor that morning. Meriwether must have appreciated the potential danger of giving Henry such a bankroll, for His Excellency himself frequented the gambling salons of Santa Fe.[2] Agent Dodge was a but a quick stroll from the monte parlors, but he didn't have time for such frivolity. Meriwether would leave in a few days for his parley with the Navajo and he expected Dodge to have a large gathering of Indians there when he arrived. That gave Henry about a week and a half. So when the agent and his Navajo delegation departed Santa Fe, they did so with a sense of urgency.

The Governor and his official retinue left Santa Fe on the afternoon of July 5th. There were five in the party: the governor and his son, two servants and his secretary, William Watts Hart Davis. Overall, the trip was a monotonous but uneventful one, with two exceptions. The first was Meriwether's failure to meet up with Garland and his military escort as planned, missing them first in Santa Fe and later at Albuquerque. Undaunted, the governor and his small party bravely continued on to Laguna without protection. A more disquieting incident came two days out of Laguna. Meriwether's party had camped at Agua Azul, a shimmering lake set like a turquoise jewel in the Zuni Mountains, some fifty miles west of Laguna. Late that night Juan Anaya came into their camp, sent by Dodge to guide them to Defiance. The following morning the exhausted travelers awoke to find, in the middle of July, a biting cold and a heavy frost. Meriwether had a fire kindled, then decided to get some breakfast. He'd seen some ducks down on the lake. Invigorated by the cold and the promise of a warm breakfast, he snatched up a rifle, marched resolutely down to the shoreline and began picking his way through the rushes along the shore.

> "I had gone but a few hundred yards through the high grass and weeds... when I came upon the skeleton of a man, over which I nearly fell. He had evidently been dead a year or more, as the flesh was all gone and the bones bleached white. I suppose it was the skeleton of some poor fellow who had been killed by the Indians or who might have starved to death..."[3]

Not much shocked David Meriwether but that incident had, so much so that, in dictating his memoirs nearly forty years later, he described it with chilling clarity. The party broke camp and continued down the trail. If it had been an omen, Meriwether pondered, it wasn't an encouraging one. As the carriage jolted along, no further signs appeared to reassure the governor and ease his suddenly depressed thoughts. Late in the evening of July 12th they at last arrived at Fort Defiance. It was nine o'clock at night, but Kendrick gave the Governor a warm reception. Meriwether was due to meet the Navajo the following day and there was still no sign of Garland.

Meanwhile, Henry L. Dodge waited on the shores of Black Lake. The Navajo had responded to his appeal in breathtaking numbers. Most had camped in the surrounding foothills and forests where there was adequate wood, water and grass, but many had settled in the fields around Laguna Negra. There they waited, their makeshift shelters dotting the meadows and the smoke of their morning cooking fires masking the valley in a serene blue veil. Red Shirt pitched his own tent on a hillock overlooking the lake. July 13th found him there, with Zarcillos Largos and the Navajo delegation, waiting for Meriwether's scheduled arrival. A handful of mounted warriors were nearby, watching the women prepare a feast of roast mutton and corn bread for their anticipated guests, while below groups of seemingly indifferent men passed the time horse racing and wrestling.

It was late morning when a column of dust was spotted rising from the south. It was the Meriwether party. Trundling into camp, the Governor and Major Kendrick exchanged greetings with Dodge and the headmen. Meriwether explained he'd come that morning to arrange the final details for the actual treaty, to be held on July 16th. He also expressed his disappointment at what he saw as a small number of Navajo at Laguna Negra. It was hardly the entire nation. Both Henry and Zarcillos Largos assured him that on the appointed day he'd see more Navajo than he could count and he would indeed have his great council. Dodge then invited the delegation to sit and eat, an essential element of Navajo good manners and hospitality. Obligingly Meriwether's party sat on blankets spread over the ground and dined Navajo style. W. W. H. Davis, for one, was unimpressed.

> "We dined with the agent. A dirty squaw, who seemed to be the mistress of the kitchen, baked a corn cake in the ashes, roasted the side of a sheep on a stick before the fire, and made a pot of coffee. These we ate sitting upon the ground, and, as soon as we had done, our red brethren took our places and finished the repast. We returned to the fort the same afternoon."[4]

The next day General John Garland and his dragoons finally arrived at Defiance to a thunderous artillery salute, courtesy of Major Kendrick. On the morning of the 15th, the major assembled the entire garrison for the general's inspection. Garland was impressed—the boom of the cannon, the rattle of musket, the glint of polished insignia, the tight, machine-like discipline among the troops, even if the uniforms were outdated. If the display was meant to equally impress the Navajo, it doubtlessly did, stirring up old fears of treachery and slaughter.[5]

The following morning, Meriwether and a cavalry escort departed Fort Defiance for Laguna Negra. Garland had decided to remain behind, deferring to the Meriwether's civil jurisdiction over such matters. As they moved leisurely up the valley, groups of excited Navajo warriors, boldly painted and bristling with weapons, fell in with the column. The procession's ranks rapidly swelled as they lurched along until it seemed Meriwether's party was being swept along in a flood of boisterous Indian warriors. The image of that anonymous, bleached skull may have flashed through Meriwether's mind. After all, their impromptu Navajo escort could, if they so desired, massacre them all on a whim.

When at last Meriwether's wagon dipped down into valley of Laguna Negra, a breathtaking sight opened before him. Dodge hadn't exaggerated. It was truly something no American had before seen. There were hundreds, nay, apparently thousands of Navajo warriors armed for war, galloping to and fro, their hair untied and flowing freely in the wind. The fact that the Navajo unbound their hair in preparation for war may have been lost on Governor Meriwether, but being the old Indian hand he was, he surely must have noticed there were almost no Indian women and children to be seen... a sure sign the Navajo expected trouble. It was a 19th century frontier version of Dante's Hell and Meriwether was descending into the thick of it.

The Governor pitched his tent along the lakeshore and had the dragoons picketed a few yards away. After getting settled, Meriwether called the Navajo leaders into conference. It was shortly after noon. Henry had arranged to have a large circular cedar arbor and ramada built to hold the Navajo and American dignitaries, but as the crowds pressed in it became obvious it wouldn't be big enough. The Navajo and American delegates entered, and throngs of the less notable surged in after them, filling every nook and corner. Once the crowd settled in and the delegates were seated, Henry Dodge handed out tobacco to Zarcillos Largos, Manuelito, Aguila Negra, Delgadito and the others. No less than an unprecedented twenty-seven principal Navajo headmen were in attendance. They immediately rolled cigarettes and smoked with, as Davis described it, "great gravity and gusto."[6]

With the preliminaries completed, Meriwether addressed the council. It was a time-consuming process; requiring him to communicate through two interpreters, from English to Spanish and from Spanish to Navajo, then back again.

> "I have come here to meet the Navajos and am glad to see as many present. I am glad the Navajos and the whites have been at peace so long a time, and hope they will remain at peace. I have come to see you to agree upon a country the Navajos and whites may each have, that they may not pasture their flocks on each other's lands. If we have a dividing line so that we know what each other's country is, it will keep us at peace."

It was a proposal the Navajo hadn't heard before. The *Bilagáana* leader wished to mark their country with strict but imaginary boundaries. Furthermore, they would be required to surrender all country outside of those phantom borders. Meriwether assured them that the Great White Father in Washington would compensate them for any loss.[7]

In conformance to Navajo custom, the headmen's expressions betrayed none of the unease rising in their hearts, but one treaty provision did elicit comment. Meriwether explained that the treaty required the Navajo to surrender suspected criminals to American justice. In reply, Zarcillos Largos stated he preferred paying the injured party or their family for the harm done. Meriwether's response was blunt. Under no circumstances would blood money be an option. Largos said nothing more. After some silence, the governor concluded the parley by asking the Navajo leaders to consider the treaty in its entirety and to give him their answer the following morning. He then adjourned the council.[8]

If Meriwether initially felt satisfaction over the first meeting, his confidence would soon be shaken. Sauntering back to the lakeshore, he discovered his personal tent overrun by warriors belonging to Delgadito's band. Delgadito's reasons for staging such a demonstration were unclear, but the posture and expression of his warriors was notably antagonistic. The sergeant of the guard had earlier discovered the warriors occupying Meriwether's tent. He moved to drive them out until one of the squatters coolly notched an arrow and drew a bead on his sternum. The sergeant wisely backed out. Dodge and Meriwether were probably not overly upset. Clearly, the Navajo were toying with them. Davis, on the other hand, was outraged.

> "When we returned to our camp we found it surrounded by hundreds of Indians, and some dozen or more greasy fellows were occupying our tent, and smoking in a manner ridiculously cool and independent, but they soon made tracks after our arrival."

To Dodge's relief, no other incident marred the remainder of the afternoon. Gradually dusk cast the countryside in a cool, soothing shadow and the first stars emerged in the azure sky. Almost all of the Indians remained in camp that night, keeping Henry Dodge, his agency staff and several Navajo ladies busy cooking. Nevertheless, a welcome sense of serene security had descended.

Late that night a rumor drifted through camp . . . like some malevolent spirit . . . that the Navajo were preparing to murder all the Americans in their sleep.[9]

Writing afterwards from the safety of Santa Fe, Davis shrugged it off as "an idle tale" and claimed he had slept "with the same feeling of security as though there had not been an Indian near us." Distance encourages bravado. Davis doubtlessly felt less plucky that night, lying wide-eyed in his tent, surrounded by the murmurings of a multitude of Indians. By strange coincidence, the seemingly ever-present Private James Bennett was also in camp that evening. He'd been attached to Lieutenant Ewell's escort and the rumor soon reached his ears as well. Decades later he described that night, and although his account was badly corroded by the years, he did clearly recall Henry Dodge.

> " . . . At 11 P.M., Mr. Dodge, the Indian Agent, came crawling into our camp and informed us that we were to be attacked at daylight in the morning. Capt. Ewell at once had a man mounted upon a horse and gave him the following instructions: "Go as soon as God will let you, and tell the Commanding Officer at the fort to send me some help or we will all be killed in the morning." At least 1000 little fires were to be seen about us. The first signs of day had just begun to appear when was heard a more welcome sound than music: the rumbling of cannon wheels over the solid rock road. When it was just light the full 75 men of the Artillery Company came charging into our camp. *No attack was made.*"[10]

Although melodramic, Bennett's rendition was nevertheless pretty accurate. According to Davis, the rationale for the massacre was to preempt an American attack on them. There were those among the Indians who believed that once Garland and the artillery arrived, the soldiers intended to slaughter them all.[11]

It was unlikely that such a thing was ever seriously contemplated. Still, Dodge's initial optimism had probably shriveled some. Things seemed to be going sour. More worrisome developments attended the morning. The Navajo had met early to discuss the treaty provisions among themselves. Contrary to Bennett's description, General Garland, Major Kendrick and the battery of artillery arrived at around nine o'clock. The Navajo showed no overt anxiety about that, but shortly afterwards an Indian messenger appeared at Meriwether's tent. He held in his hands a ribbon-festooned medal and a walking cane. Meriwether and Dodge recognized them immediately. They belonged to Zarcillos Largos. Meriwether had given them to the headman a year earlier as symbols of his position as principal chief of the Navajo Nation.

Zarcillos Largos, the messenger explained, wished to resign. He was too old to continue and was unable to govern his people any longer. Largos had steadfastly been an ally of peace and a friend to the American. Now, suddenly, he'd had enough. Dodge may have not known precisely why *Naat'áani Náádléél* wished to resign, but he probably had a good idea. It obviously wasn't age or infirmity, for the man at his age was a vital force and would remain so for several years. On the other hand, Meriwether's abrupt rejection of his suggestion at the treaty meeting the day before could have been the catalyst. Equally possible was that Largos was expressing his mortification over the brouhaha with Delgadito's men in Meriwether's camp. It was more likely that Zarcillos Largos had realized the honor of being head chief had become, like ill-fitting shoes, increasingly uncomfortable.

There was growing skepticism among the Navajo leaders as to the benefits of cooperating with Americans in general. They could rightfully claim that the partnership had been one sided. The Navajo had proven both generous and cooperative, while, other than handing out a few tools and kind platitudes, the Americans had not. The Army had not crushed the Ute for the murder of their headmen along the San Juan. They'd yet to punish New Mexicans mercenaries for raiding Navajo homes. They had never so much as detained, much less tried and jailed, a New Mexican guilty of killing a Navajo. Not a single enslaved Navajo woman or child had been returned. The Americans had not driven New Mexican stockmen off of Navajo land. Now the *Bilagáana* obviously intended to whittle down Navajo country and give the balance of that territory to those presently and illegally occupying it. A chasm among the headmen was opening up, a chasm which Zarcillos Largos straddled. It was time to step aside.

Reluctantly, Meriwether accepted the resignation and asked the Navajo leadership to elect a new head chief. They soon presented Manuelito, the son of Cayetano, a prominent local headman. Henry Dodge knew that Manuelito could be a challenge. He was a relatively young man, both physically and verbally imposing. Better than six feet tall, well-muscled with a barrel chest boasting several war wounds and a deep, booming voice, Manuelito had a remarkable intensity. Among his own people he was known at *Hastiin Ch'ilhaajinii*, or Man of the Black Plants Place. From an early age, he had proven himself a captain of daring and valor, having successfully fought with his father-in-law Narbona against the New Mexicans. Although experience had done little to dampen his fiery disposition, it had taught Manuelito some finer points of diplomacy. He was nonetheless passionate and proud and boasted of how his enemies feared him.[12]

Meriwether presented Manuelito with Zarcillos Largos' cane and medal.

Hastiin Ch'ilhaajinii demurred, protesting that accepting the elder headman's insignia would drain him of any influence he might have over his people. Unflustered, the governor handed his own cane to Manuelito and had the medal restrung before draping it over the young leader's shoulders. Satisfied, Manuelito and the Navajo delegation retired to hash out the remaining treaty provisions. Just before noon, a messenger announced that the headmen had reached consensus.[13] Dodge, Meriwether and Davis started up to the cedar arbor, noting as they walked the multitude of Navajo warriors congregating around them.

> "They were galloping to and fro along the valley in tens, and twenties, and fifties, and on the border of the lake, half a mile distant, large groups were collected together as though engaged in deliberation. Our camp was again surrounded by hundreds, who would sit so immovable upon their horses that man and beast seemed but one animal."[14]

It was noon when the treaty delegates reconvened. Present for the Americans were Governor David Meriwether, W. W. H. Davis, Henry Dodge, General John Garland and Major Henry Kendrick with Captains O. L. Shepherd 3rd Infantry and R. S. Ewell of the 1st Dragoons. Representing the Indians, Manuelito and twenty-six principal men of the Navajo nation, among them Aguila Negra, Dodge's friend Armijo, Mariano Martinez from the Washington Treaty of 1849 and of course Zarcillos Largos. Once the usual smoking ritual was completed, *Hastiin Ch'ilhaajinii* formally announced that the headmen had endorsed the treaty and apologized for the incident at Meriwether's camp the day before. Meriwether politely noted that older men were disposed to listen while "the boys only behaved badly." He then asked the council for a show of hands if they approved of Manuelito taking Zarcillos Largos' place as principal chief. Juan Anaya translated. Only one in every four hands went up. Seemingly unperturbed, Meriwether turned to the treaty itself. As he read each article, he had it explained through a chain of interpreters. The headmen approved the first three articles, which established eternal friendship with the United States and an end to all hostilities, an acceptance of a reservation with clearly marked boundaries and the willingness to the surrender all lands beyond those boundaries.

Meriwether then pulled out a map to illustrate the specific boundaries of the Navajo reserve, as described in Article 4. Manuelito protested. They had always claimed a much larger area than represented on the map. Furthermore, the boundaries would prevent Navajos visiting many of their spiritual shrines and forbid them a pilgrimage to Salt Lake south of Zuni to gather sacred salt. It was unacceptable. Meriwether reassured him that the sacred spots were within the reservation boundaries and that he would allow the Navajo to leave their reserve to gather sacred salt below Zuni. After conferring, the headmen agreed that the boundaries were adequate. Surprisingly, other provisions of Article 4 remained uncontested and there is some suspicion they were never sufficiently translated. Article 4 also allowed the Army to claim exclusive right to fifty square miles of Navajo land around Fort Defiance, a vast tract of prime grazing country. It empowered the President, at his whim, to divvy up reservation lands held in common into sixty-acre parcels and allot them to individual Navajo families as private property, in effect taking tribal lands from tribal control. The President also "at his discretion" had the right to dispose of such lands as he saw fit, to adjust boundaries to accommodate "any vested rights," to carve out wagon roads, railroads and additional military posts. Significantly, he could arbitrarily substitute any parcel found to have valuable ore for non-mineral bearing lands, insuring that potential mining profits went into American rather than Navajo pockets.

Even if Article 4 had been accurately translated, the mystifying habit of the Bilagáana for parsing and vivisecting the land would have baffled the Navajo.

Having safely leaped that hurdle, Meriwether proceeded to Article Five and Six, defining the yearly amount of annuity money to be paid the Navajo. The United States agreed to pay the Navajo a total of $98,000 in successively decreasing annuities for the next twenty years, until 1875. Control of those annuities would remain in the frugal hands of the Indian Service, who would expend it on behalf of the Navajo for training, civilizing and morally educating them. Once translated, the Navajo again conceded. The headmen then endorsed Articles Seven and Eight. Both prohibited the sale or distribution of liquor "until other wise ordered by the President" on or in the vicinity of the Navajo Reservation. Liquor was an anathema to the headmen. They'd seen the damage it had done in the settlements.

At some point in the negotiations Major Kendrick's artillery began noisily drilling outside the meeting grounds. W. W. H. Davis noted that about the same time the crowd of mounted Navajos outside the arbor had become rather rowdy and that once or twice their horses stampeded. The two disruptions may have been related. The decision to run the big guns through their paces was clearly calculated to prick Navajo anxieties. It wasn't the first time Kendrick had resorted to that tactic. It must have seemed to the Navajo that the Army was once again rattling sabers to encourage cooperation. They were, of course, quite correct in that assumption.[15]

Some two hours into the treaty recital, Meriwether reached Article Nine.

Article 9th: The Navajoes do further agree and bind themselves to make restitution or satisfaction for any injuries done . . . and to surrender to the proper Authorities of the United States when demanded any individual or individuals who may commit depredations to be punished according to law. And if any Citizen of the United States shall at any time commit depredations upon the Indians the Navajo agree that they will not take private satisfaction or revenge themselves but instead thereof they will make complaint to the proper Indian Agent for redress . . ."

By treaty, the Navajo would not only be required to pay indemnity for damages, as Zarcillos Largos had suggested, but to surrender wrongdoers to American justice as well. *Hastiin Ch'ilhaajinii* objected. The one time the Navajo had surrendered one of their own, Private Hefbiner's alleged killer, the Army had hanged the man. The entire affair had been repulsive to them. Furthermore, it was inordinately dangerous for one Navajo to attempt to apprehend another. If the Americans absolutely insisted on the provision, Manuelito requested that they seize perpetrators themselves. In response, Meriwether reasoned that since Americans were strangers in Navajo Country, they wouldn't know the innocent from the guilty and hence all Navajo would end up shouldering the blame. The provision must remain. There was a prolonged discussion, but the Navajo leaders finally agreed to that article as well.[16] At that point, Meriwether recited the 10th and final provision requiring all signatories to adhere to the treaty "as soon as the same shall be ratified by the President and Senate of the United States . . ."[17] The delegates for both sides then solemnly signed the treaty, although, interestingly, Henry L. Dodge did not.

It had been a typical treaty, written in typical jargon. Typically, Congress would never ratify it.

With the conclusion of negotiations, Dodge and Meriwether prepared to distribute the wagonload of gifts and annuity goods among the Indians. The headmen asked the governor to allow them to "make a proper division." Meriwether didn't see any harm in the concession and agreed. At the appointed time, the distribution commenced. According to the highly bemused Secretary Davis, what little decorum existed at the outset rapidly disintegrated into complete pandemonium. Rather than hand out items with sober respectability, the headmen embraced an invigorating Navajo tradition and began flinging the items helter-skelter into the surging crowd.

". . .The reader can imagine the scene, when a wagonload of goods is thrown among nearly two thousand wild horse-men, and each one bent upon getting all he can. What riding and pitching there was! Here you would see a fellow, with a piece of muslin, riding toward the mountains at full speed to hide his prize, and two or three others in hot pursuit, with their knives flashing in the sun. The fugitive being overtaken, a severe struggle takes place for the spoil. The muslin has become unwrapped and stretched to its full length, each party tugging to obtain the lion's share, when, as the opportunity offers, each horseman cuts off as much as he can, and gallops away with his well-earned prize, after leaving the original possessor but a small portion. Some were seized and made to disgorge by main force, while others affected a safe retreat with what they obtained in the first instance, and returned to the scene of contest for more. Others were unhorsed in the struggle, and both parties contended . . . until one or the other proved victorious. Brass kettles, knives, tobacco, muslin, looking-glasses, and various other articles changed owners with a magic quickness . . ."

It was glorious fun, even given the appalled expressions on the American faces. As the exuberant Navajo crowds began to depart with their prizes, Kendrick treated them to another light artillery maneuver, which Secretary Davis stated completely "astonished the natives." Before returning to Fort Defiance on the morning of July 18th, Davis took an opportunity to ask Henry Dodge for a short list of Navajo words. As he had earlier for John Shaw, Dodge and headman Armijo's son prepared a list that later appeared in Davis' book, *El Gringo*, published in 1857.[18]

Governor Meriwether returned to Fort Defiance that morning, and departed the fort that afternoon, under sheets of chilling rain. They managed twelve miles that day before camping at a spot where, as Davis noted, they sank "shoe-top deep in mud at every step." Henry Dodge eventually returned to his agency, evidently satisfied with his own efforts and the outcome of the treaty meetings. It had all gone very well, in spite of a few tense moments. On August 2nd, Red Shirt penned the required monthly report to Manypenny. To say his praise for Meriwether and the Treaty of Laguna Negra was inflated was, in itself, an understatement. Henry was nearly maudlin, stating that the Navajo were "very much delighted with the liberal treatment in territory and presents gave them by the Governor," that the land granted them was both "amply sufficient" and "larger than they anticipated." Henry was also confident that, despite the failure of the Army to intercede, Meriwether's liberal policies would end the war between the Navajo and Ute.

Dodge clearly had his audience in mind when he wrote. Whether he actually believed what he was writing was another matter. Notably, Henry neglected to mention Delgadito's persnickety behavior, the invasion of Meriwether's camp by his contentious warriors, and uttered not a word about Zarcillos Largos' resignation or the Navajo headmen's lukewarm endorsement of Manuelito. He did have one request of Manypenny.

> "The Navijos are greatly in want of a few or at least two mills built after the Mexican fashion which would not cost including the transportation of stones from the Rio Grande to this point more than one hundred and fifty dollars each. This would enable them to have flour and meal instead of using the grain in its entire state at present they grind a small quantity by a very laborious process by hand. All of which is respectfully submitted."[19]

Meriwether supported Dodge's plan when he sent the agent's report on to Manypenny on August 11th. He felt Henry had underestimated the cost for each mill by about one hundred dollars, but the expense could be paid out of the special appropriation made in the previous year for the Navajo by Congress.[20] In the meantime, Meriwether basked in the radiance of a long-sought tranquility that seemed to be settling over the territory, prodding the Santa Fe Gazette on September 1st, 1855 to report that nearly all Indian hostilities in New Mexico had at last ceased.[21]

42

FOR AMIGOS

The provisions of the Laguna Negra treaty were so unfavorable to the Navajo that it is surprising they conceded each article so willingly. Perhaps Manuelito and the other headmen decided to let the gun toting, cannon hauling Americans have their way. Paring down Navajo land on paper was one thing. Actually doing it was another.

The new Navajo Reservation flawlessly reflected the psyche of the white man. It was a giant rectangle, its precise ninety-degree corners firmly bolted into that psyche like angle iron, the boundary lines surgically slicing through every natural feature in its path, large or small. Starting in the north where present day Chinle Wash meets the San Juan, the boundary extended eastward past Shiprock several miles, then plunged southward some hundred miles to just above the Wingate Valley before turning westward to Hopi. At that point the line turned northward up the Chinle Valley and back to the San Juan.

True, the reservation preserved for the Navajo the Carrizo and Chuska Mountains, half of the Defiance Plateau, Canyon de Chelly and the Chinle Valley. Nevertheless, the meticulously etched lines had cut away two-thirds of Navajo country, areas inhabited by Navajos for decades if not centuries. Black Mesa, the Shonto uplands, Navajo Mountain and the broad plateau sloping away towards the canyon of the Colorado, the forested slopes of the sacred mountain of the west, the San Francisco Peaks, all were excluded. Even so, many New Mexicans were outraged, as Dodge observed, "that the limits assigned the Navajos by the late treaty is entirely too liberal." He dismissed the complaints as a product of ignorance. If those eager farmers and stockmen believed the reservation was a peach ripe for picking, they were deluding themselves. Proportionately, the amount of arable land existing in Navajo country was miniscule.

Irrespective of lingering doubts over the treaty, feelings between the Navajo and Americans remained amicable. Turning aside the growing hue and cry by New Mexican citizens over his "liberal" Indian policy, the Governor reported to Manypenny that nearly all the tribes were at peace, and he characterized the Navajos as in a "highly flourishing condition," despite a few minor incidents by "bad men" of the tribe.[1] Late summer passed into fall, and a reassuring aura of peace held sway over the territory. On August 31st, Garland reported to Thomas that he had nothing to report. A month later, on September 30th Garland again had little to say; only noting, "the Indians during the past month have been unusually quiet." It was downright spooky.[2]

Taking advantage of the lull, Henry Dodge showed up in Santa Fe at the end of August. The Gazette's September 1st issue noted his arrival in the capital.

> "Capt. Dodge, agent for the Navajo Indians, arrived in town, with a delegation of some 70 of the tribe, last Wednesday afternoon. He reports every thing quite (sic) in the nation, and that their crops generally look well . . . "[3]

On September 5th Dodge embarked on what could only be termed a shopping spree. He first made purchases for the Navajo from Henry Mercure, including a three-dollar pistol, four rifles and lead for shot. He also bought himself a coat and a hat, a handkerchief, and a pair of shoes and socks. Interestingly, he also bought a pair of boy's pants and a coat.[4] Subsequently, two days later he strode into Webb & Kingsbury's establishment and again bought several items in small amounts—two pitchers for example. Again the mysterious young lad is conspicuous on Red Shirt's shopping list, which included "1 boy's hat, 3 boys' fancy hats . . . 1 pr. Boys Shoes" and, of all things, two red umbrellas. If one wished to pursue the idea Dodge was buying for a family, then one might also note the relatively small yardages of cloth included on the list. Henry returned on the 13th, the 15th, and the 17th, racking up a total of nearly five hundred dollars in purchases. True to his Navajo nickname, Henry bought himself another red flannel shirt and drew five dollars cash. It was a fairly lavish outing, considering Henry's father was at that time drawing on his salary back in Washington.[5]

At the close of September 1855, Henry Dodge continued his optomistic depiction of Navajo affairs in his report to Manypenny.

> "It is a source of great satisfaction to me to be able to state in this my annual report that the condition of the Navajo tribe of Indians during this year and at present is prosperous in a degree heretofore unknown to them. They are in the full enjoyment of peace with all of its blessings and have raised fine crops of corn, wheat, and vegetables their flocks and herds are rapidly on the increase [which] furnished them with the means of supporting their families with all the absolute necessaries of life in food and raiment . . .
>
> "This tribe of Indians manufacture a great variety of woolen goods and of a more substantial kind than any other people in this Territory and their horses and sheep are esteemed the best raised in New Mexico. The late treaty made with them by you if confirmed by the Senate of the U.S. will secure to them a home and country free from the inroads of the New Mexicans which has been from time immemorial one of the causes of difficulty between them."

Once the treaty was ratified, Dodge hoped to hire an agency farmer for at least a year, perhaps longer. The government had given the Indians plows; consequently they needed a farmer to instruct them. With the departure of George Carter the previous March, the agency needed a blacksmith as well, and four sets of blacksmith tools and a thousand pounds of iron. There were already eighteen smiths among the Navajo, fashioning bridle bits and buckles with painfully primitive tools and a hand bellows. Moreover, the purchase of two modern mills to grind Navajo wheat and corn would be a great benefit. The Navajo were, in Dodge's words, "extremely anxious" about having them built.

Surprisingly, the Navajo had also mentioned another new interest—that of education.

> "I have frequently had the rich and intelligent men of this tribe to ask me to take their boys of five and six years of age and learn them to read and write in the English language a school established amongst them I think would be productive of much good."

Ever the practical folk, the Navajo headmen saw the importance of teaching their people the skills get along with and to get things from the Americans, and the need to deal directly with them, rather than depend on intermediaries who, at times, could not be trusted.[6]

Meriwether echoed Dodge's warm assessment. The Navajo were thriving and "that judicious management and the fostering care of the government will soon make them a prosperous, happy, and contented people."[7] If only he could say as much for Steck's Apaches. Agent Michael Steck was making some progress among the Mimbres Chiricahua, but it was slow. To complicate matters, age-old tension continued to simmer between the Apaches and New Mexicans, ever-threatening to rupture the uneasy peace. There were less-known, aggressive bands of Apache, the Mogollon, Coyotero, Garrotero and Tonto, ranging northwest of the Gila into modern day Arizona. Meriwether knew little of them other than they had a reputation as troublemakers. He had no doubt they'd soon prove to be source of real irritation.[8]

Still, Governor Meriwether must have felt satisfaction at having executed treaties with all the major tribes of the territory, a satisfaction heightened by his impending exit from New Mexico. He was returning to the States on business, and subsequently planned to travel to Washington City to lobby lawmakers for the ratification of all those Indian treaties, including the essential Navajo treaty of Laguna Negra.[9] He would be gone six months at least. Before departing in early October, he appointed his secretary William Watts Hart Davis as acting governor and Indian Affairs superintendent.

Unlike his previous stint as acting governor, Davis had every indication that the most recent assignment would be a cushy one. October of 1855 had passed in a state of tranquility all but unknown to New Mexico. Nothing was going on at all.

423

General Garland's October and November reports reflected his previous ones. There hadn't been a serious act of Indian hostility for months, with the one exception that Mogollon Apaches had allegedly... allegedly... run off some stock in the Sabinal vicinity—a minor affair. It could have as easily been rustlers. Garland noted that New Mexicans from Cubero and Cebolleta, rather than Indians, had been responsible for a single instance of robbery in November. He admitted there had been a few small incidents, an Apache raid here and there, but they had been reprisals for New Mexican offenses, and in no way indicated the Apache desired war.[10] As for the Navajo, they had remained so imperturbably quiet that in early December, General Garland decided to reassign a portion of Fort Defiance's garrison, Major O. L. Shepherd's Company B 3rd Infantry, to Albuquerque to forestall an increase in Apache thefts along the Rio Grande and keep the citizens content. The move instantly cut the number of troops at Fort Defiance in half, doubtlessly giving the ever-anxious Major Kendrick the jitters.[11]

As luck would have it, the winter of 1855-56 would test that tranquility. Stories trickled in to Santa Fe of blizzards blasting the Plains, stranding supply trains, swallowing up mail parties, and leaving seasoned buffalo hunters to exclaim they had never seen such ferocious storms. Temperatures plummeted and snow locked up everything from the main roads to hunting trails, making travel for everyone nigh impossible. The freeze was taking a grim toll on the Navajo, stranding and killing off entire herds, yet the Indians appeared determined to hunker down and ride it out without complaint.

The same could not be said for the Apache, who depended solely on the harvest of the hunt. With the trails buried and the animals scarce, the remote bands of the Gila were soon in dire circumstances. To stave off starvation, they had but once viable choice and that was to raid the settlements. The howls of outraged citizens soon reached the New Mexico Legislature, which began turning up the heat on Davis. Representatives bitterly derided the acting governor's claim that the territory was free of Indian depredations and demanded action. Barely concealing his contempt, Davis responded that the New Mexicans themselves were to blame for the recent Apache infractions, retaliations for a raiding expedition against the Gila Apache by Cebolleta and Cubero men the previous fall.[12]

Still, reports of fresh outrages soared, threatening to force a referendum on Meriwether's entire territorial Indian policy, now under Davis' stewardship. On January 23rd, the Pueblo of Acoma claimed losses from Gila raids amounting to nearly two thousand dollars, claims submitted to Davis on their behalf by the law firm of

Baird & McCarty. Baird never let an opportunity slide. Uncle Sam's compensation for claims of Indian thievery, whether true or false, was a lucrative feeding trough, and every New Mexican knew it.[13] However, complaints became frequent enough that Garland reluctantly concluded that something had to be done, and that a quick military expedition might serve to cow the Gila Apache and quiet the critics. The efficient and capable Apache agent, Michael Steck, hesitantly endorsed the idea, but worried that the expedition would sweep the peaceful Chiricahua living along the Mimbres River into the dustbin along with the hostile. To prevent just such a misunderstanding and perhaps head off a tragic mistake, Steck petitioned Garland to allow him to accompany the Army on their incursion.[14] His request was granted.

Long before the advent of winter, Governor Meriwether had determined the Navajo had become so self-sufficient they wouldn't need the usual Indian Service handouts. Consequently he instructed Henry Dodge to limit his gifts to a little tobacco now and then. Any further distribution would have wait until Meriwether returned from the States in the spring. When Dodge informed Davis on December 26th that he'd purchased one hundred dollars of tobacco, shirts and other provisions for the Indians, the acting Indian superintendent reminded the Navajo agent of the governor's directive.

> "As they are both well clothed and well supplied with grain and other articles of food of their own raising, there can be no necessity of issuing to them any more shirts and provisions during the winter."[15]

Cutting back on generosity could well sow dissatisfaction among the Navajo. Paradoxically, Davis' order also seemed to ignore the bitter cold gripping the country that December, a fact of which he was well aware. On Christmas Day the temperature at Fort Defiance stood at an incredible thirty-two degrees below zero.[16] Concurrently, Davis may have also missed a warning in Dodge's letter, that the poorer Navajo, those most victimized by the winter, had of late committed several small robberies. In October, someone had actually stolen the agency mule and a horse. Although it was true most of the thefts had been solved with the cooperation of the Navajo leaders, the fact that such incidents had increased was significant.

In fact, Dodge added, the five hundred dollars Meriwether had given him was already gone. He used some of the money to replace the mule and horse. He'd also had to pay Anaya and other agency employees their salary out of that money, then had drawn sixty dollars for travel expenses hunting down his own purloined property, and had purchased supplies for the beleaguered Navajo. For the first time since becoming agent, Henry L. Dodge complained that the job and the weather were slowly grinding him down.

> "My agency has been a traveling one this winter I am afflicted with rheumatic pains in the back and piles or I would visit you at this time. The snow is in this section of New Mexico is two feet deep at this time and exceedingly cold."

Two feet, and it was only December. Poverty, rheumatism and hemorrhoids aside, Dodge had some more troubling news.

> "I regret to have to report that on or about the 18th day of the present month a Navajo Indian killed an Indian said to belong to the Pueblo of Isleta who was acting as head shepherd for Juan Chavis of Sabinal.
> "The facts as related to me both by the Mexicans and Navajos are as follows the Navajo was hunting in the Mountain near the blue waters on horseback with a boy when they encountered two herders. The Navajo asked the Indian of Isleta for powder, which he refused him.
> "The Navajo said I am hunting and have but one charge of powder and that is in my gun give me two charges more for Amigos.
> "The other replied I will not give you a grain."

The scene Dodge described would have seemed comical, had it not turned tragic.

> "The Navajo grabbed the hat of the Isleta but did not attempt to run thinking that he would get the powder by returning hat in this he was sadly disappointed for the powder he received was from the gun of the Isleta accompanied with a ball which wounded him in the hand and lodged in his thy. At the same time the other shepherd knocked the boy from the horse with a stick. When the Navajo recovered he discharged his gun at the Pueblo wounding him mortally."

Upon hearing the news, Dodge met with the Navajo headmen. He believed them to be sincerely horrified by the incident, knowing they'd be required to deliver the killer to Agent Dodge and American justice. The headmen requested Dodge refer the issue to Davis, promising to abide by the acting governor's decision.[17]

Davis' response to the news was surprisingly mild. He regretted that the Isleta man had acted rashly and had consequently been killed. Clearly both parties were at fault.

> "... Under the circumstance I think, if the thing is practicable, you had better have a meeting of the Navajo Chiefs, and a few of the head men of the Pueblo, examine into the matter well, and let the council determine what punishment, if any, should be inflicted upon the Navajo; but in the first place both parties must agree to abide by the decision of the council. If the Indians can be brought together for this purpose, without a difficulty occurring, I think it the best course that can be pursued...."[18]

The ultimate outcome of Dodge's efforts is unknown. No other communication indicated a resolution, though one was probably finagled. Davis' divergence from the American mantra of justice may have taken Manuelito and the Navajo leaders by surprise, but so much the better. They preferred settling such ugliness with a discreet indemnity payment to the victim's family. Conversely, Manuelito probably did appreciate the fact that if the victim had been an American, Davis would have demanded justice paid in Navajo blood.

At the end of January 1856, P. Clayton of the office of the Second Auditor for the United States Treasury wrote to Henry L. Dodge not once but twice. It seemed that Dodge was piling up substantial debt to the United States. During his tenure as Indian agent, he'd dispersed some $12,175.74 but had come up short by roughly fifteen hundred bucks. Clayton had sent him a staggering list of deficiencies: expenses disallowed, vouchers suspended, expenses without vouchers—and overcharges ... blatant overcharges ... too.[19]

> "Sir, Your Indian property act as Indian Agent for the 3rd & 4th qrs 1853, the year 1854, 1st & 2nd 1rs 1855 have been adjusted and a balance found due the United States of $357.38 besides one mule recd of Late Gov. Lane, also one saddle, you do not say who the saddle was from or the cost will you please inform this office the cost of the Mule & Saddle...."[20]

Clayton sent the letters care of David Meriwether, so it isn't certain when Henry L. Dodge actually saw them, if ever. More than likely they would have arrived in Santa Fe at the beginning of March. By then, Henry had bigger problems than a mere Treasury audit.

Having begun early and in earnest in 1855, winter held an unmerciful grip on the territory through January and February of 1856. A harsh winter invariably brought an unsettled spring.[21] Dodge and Kendrick fully expected the poorer Navajos would begin to raid out of desperation, as had the Apache. Kendrick viewed such thievery as acts of Navajo *pelados*—the lower class poor or literally the "skinned ones." A pelado had lassoed and killed a stray cow belonging to the fort herd. Another pelado, believed to be Navajo, had sent an arrow into one of the fort mail party's mules, wounding it so badly that it had to be destroyed. In both cases, the Navajo had promised to pay for the damages. It was quite likely pelados had also stolen Dodge's mule and horse.[22]

So, on February 5th, when an express from Major Carleton in Albuquerque brought Kendrick news that Navajo raiders had run off stock belonging to one Manuel Barela, the major was not particularly surprised. He did feel it was serious enough to warrant Agent Dodge's immediate attention. At the time, Dodge was at Hopi on agency business.[23] Kendrick quickly penned a note to him on the back of Carleton's dispatch.

> "Captain—The above was brought me by special express after dark this evening, & I immediately forward it to you. In a subsequent letter, of the same date however, Maj. Carleton says that he finds "that Barela is a reliable man" & that he does not understand Miguelito said that he would give up the animals to an "armed force" in any unfriendly spirit.
>
> "I fear the bad men are beginning to think of their usual stealing in the spring, & the quicker it is arrested the better. I do not know where Miguelito is, but have no doubt that if you were to see him, from yr. old acquaintance, he would readily restore the stock. The Navajoes have been doing some other things, which they must settle for, of which I will tell you when you come in, which it is <u>important that you should do at **once**</u>..."

Although the major realized that recovering property stolen by "treaty Indians", as opposed to "wild ones", was the exclusive task of the civil agent rather than the military, Kendrick remained anxious that they work together.[24]

Red Shirt looked over Kendrick's instructions, and then carefully read Carleton's report. It seemed Manuel Barela of the Ranchos de Albuquerque reported that a party of Navajo had run off fourteen of his animals, mostly mules, from along the Puerco, on the 27th or 28th of January. They had also taken his herders' weapons, which Barela also owned. He had then tracked the raiders to a Navajo settlement just west of Cebolleta, where he spotted some of his animals. He demanded their return. According to Manuel, the headman Miguelito snootily replied that he'd surrender the stock only if Barela would return with a force large enough to seize them. Oddly enough, Miguelito then returned Barela's stolen weapons. Dodge knew Miguelito as both cooperative and trustworthy. He'd recently interpreted for the agent. He didn't believe for a moment that Miguelito had actually dared Barela to take the animals by force, but rather meant that when the stockman returned with enough herders to take possession, he could have them. By the tone of his report, Carleton didn't appear to believe it either, indicating that it had all been a misunderstanding.

Barela also mentioned that once he'd discovered the identity of the thieves, he would send Antonio Sandoval to Carleton with the information. As it turned out, Sandoval had never met with Carleton.[25]

While awaiting Dodge's arrival, Kendrick sent Armijo to Miguelito to learn the circumstances of the theft and persuade the headman to bring the stolen stock to Defiance. If need be, Kendrick and Dodge could journey to see Miguelito and adjust the issue themselves, but only if absolutely necessary. Given the wintery conditions, such a trip would take better than six days. There was also some question as to the actual status of the stolen property itself. According to Navajo informants, some of the animals had been killed for food or lost to a Ute raid, or both. If true, the statement indicated that the Ute were once more raiding the Navajo, a most unfortunate development. The Navajo had also informed Kendrick six of the animals had already been returned to Barela. In actuality, the major believed none of it, instead supposing the stock had merely been scattered. He wrote Carleton and suggested he accompany Mr. Barela with a detachment and see if they could not be rounded up. He also cautioned Carleton to keep a wary eye on Sandoval.[26]

Once Henry Dodge arrived at Fort Defiance, he and Kendrick decided to meet with Navajo leaders at Bear Springs to settle the issue. They dispatched runners across the snow-laden landscape and hoped for the best. On the morning of February 16th, Kendrick and Dodge rode out of Defiance, their expectations as chilled as the weather. The Navajo had requested more time to gather their headmen, pleading the hardship of traveling through deep snows, but Kendrick and Dodge insisted.[27] How many Navajo leaders appeared at Bear Springs is unknown. It is possible none showed. Neither Kendrick nor Dodge made any reference to the meeting other than having met the headman Delgadito along the way there, who assured them he was friendly, unlike his previous disposition at Laguna Negra. They also spoke with a principal leader of Navajos residing around Bear Springs who admitted his people had been "ill-disposed" towards the Americans, but insisted he wished peace and was looking forward to a good spring planting.[28]

Good news welcomed Kendrick and Dodge's return to Defiance. Armijo had brought word that Miguelito and Barela had reached an agreement, and at that moment the two of them were driving Barela's livestock back to the Rio Grande. As a bonus, the Navajo had also replaced both the stolen Army cow and the murdered mail mule, allowing Kendrick to report that the outstanding thefts had been resolved. He and Dodge hoped it would stay that way, but they probably knew better.[29]

43

MADNESS IN THE EXTREME

Although the Navajo had settled several claims against them, there nevertheless remained an atmosphere of disquiet in the territory as the winter of 1856 finally eased its stranglehold. Many Indian tribes were left all but destitute and none felt it more profoundly than the isolated Apache bands of the Gila. Whether spurred by necessity or expediency, fleecing the settlements was becoming increasingly popular with the enigmatic Mogollon and Coyotero bands. To further complicate the situation, Garland's military expedition launched against them had managed to accomplish just about everything Michael Steck dreaded it would.

In early March, a column of 3rd Infantry under Brevet Major Daniel Chandler, late commander at Cebolleta, departed Fort Craig for the headwaters of the Gila River, the heart of uncharted Apache country. Rendezvousing with Chandler's force near the Mimbres River was Major O. L. Shepard's command, having marched from Fort Thorn on the Rio Grande. Accompanying Shepard was Apache Indian agent Michael Steck, who had joined the campaign with Garland's endorsement. He was to serve as Chandler's liaison with the friendly Mimbres Apache, guiding him to the hostile Apache bands and away from the friendly ones.

After weeks on the march and only one brief skirmish with the hostiles to show for it, the perturbed Chandler attempted to pursue the Apache into their rugged mountain lair, but was stymied by the swollen Gila River. Exasperated, the major then retreated to The Copper Mines and ... strangely ... proclaimed the expedition was over. The two columns then separated, Chandler and his troops trotting off to the southeast for Fort Craig, leaving Steck and Shepard's column to march back to Fort Thorn. Shortly after departing, Chandler and his men reached the Mimbres River where, to his utter elation, they discovered a band of Apache encamped there.

Of course, the major ordered an immediate attack.

The abrupt popping of musketry telegraphed news of the battle back to Steck and Shepard's troops, who promptly wheeled about and came galloping at the double time to Chandler's support. Once on the scene, a wave of dismay washed over Steck. The purportedly hostile Apache Chandler had assaulted were none other than Delgadito and his friendly Mimbres band, who had decided to camp there and faithfully wait for Steck's return from the campaign. The so-called battle had lasted for twenty minutes. The horrified agent surveyed the damage done. One Mimbres woman was dead—another woman wounded. Three children had been shot and seriously injured, while a fourth child was missing. In his subsequent report, Steck was furious. Not only had the shrieks of dying and wounded women and children, as Steck put it, potentially shattered any trust and good will the peaceful Mimbres once had for the Americans, the expedition's painful ineffectiveness had only emboldened the hostile Apache.

> "Firing upon them at the time he did and without a provocation known to me was so unexpected and may be productive of <u>so much evil</u> that I deem it my duty to report the circumstances in detail."

Yes, indeed. Chandler's fiasco would help inaugurate a chain of events that would envelope many in the territory, including Henry Dodge.[1]

Yet at the end of March, oblivious to the ominous potential of Chandler's campaign, Henry was in Santa Fe closing out the quarter and buying farming tools for the Navajo. The winter had given him time to think up a plan to accelerate Navajo progress towards civilization. Dodge suggested to Davis that they encourage the Navajo to become more sedentary by building them a pueblo of their own, near Bear Springs. In truth, it was an idea neither new nor proven successful, as the Spanish friars of Cebolleta had discovered a century before. Whether Henry was ignorant or merely ignored the fact, he seriously believed the idea would work.

Grandiose plans would have to wait, however. The Ute had renewed their attacks on the Navajo. One Navajo man had been killed already. A retaliatory strike would surely result, followed by reprisal raids, which could easily escalate into an all out war.[2]

Dodge departed Santa Fe for Defiance on April 6th, perhaps reassured there had been no news of Navajo reprisals . . . yet. He was on the road toward Laguna when he spotted a rider coming up strong behind him. It was an express from Santa Fe. Such hurried appearances invariably heralded bad news. The express man pulled up and handed him two letters, one from Garland to Kendrick, the second one hastily addressed to Agent Dodge. Henry broke the dispatch seal and unfolded it. It was from Davis.

"I have just received notice that on the 27th of March the Nabajo Indians stole from José Antonio Parea and others, of the Rio Abajo, 11,000 head of sheep, and killed the herder. The sheep are said to have been in the Nabajo country when taken. I desire you, as soon as possible, to investigate the matter, and, in connection with Major Kendrick, whom the general will instruct in the premises, take the proper steps to have the sheep returned. As this is a grave offence you may apprise the chiefs and head men of the tribe, that they <u>must</u> surrender the thieves or take the consequences. . . ."[3]

While Dodge was with Davis in Santa Fe, the acting governor had received a letter from the alcalde of Vallecito, stating that two Jemez Indians returning from Navajo land had found a substantial sheep trail leading towards the Tunicha Mountains and that they had later come across a corpse, presumably that of the New Mexican herder. Therefore, the news of the raid wasn't a total surprise, but the number of stock taken was breathtaking.

The raid had occurred more than a week ago along the Puerco River. Henry Dodge had just passed the place. Could Antonio Sandoval and the Mount Taylor Navajo have been so bold? Henry suspected not. They were far too vulnerable. Was the raid incited by recent losses Navajos had suffered from the Ute? Perhaps. It wasn't altogether impossible that New Mexicans had been the culprits and counted on the Navajo to take the blame. Dodge had one certainty, however. His return to the agency at Fort Defiance had been delayed. So, too, would be Garland's dispatch to Kendrick, which Henry pocketed, doubtlessly knowing the contents.[4]

As it turned out, Major Henry Kendrick learned of the raid without the benefit of Garland's dispatch. The Navajo themselves had notified him and, although the details were muddled, it seemed certain at least two herders had been killed. Kendrick met with several headmen to arrange restitution. On April 17th, in a letter describing his actions to Garland, Kendrick left the onus of investigation on Dodge's shoulders.

> "The Indian Agent, in going to Santa Fe & on his return, will have passed very near the scene of the raids. I have been expecting his return for some time, supposing he would have full information upon the subject, & probably come with instructions in relation to it. . . . I have not thought proper to allude to the course which may be taken with the evil doers themselves, presuming that Capt. Dodge will have his instructions upon that point. I suppose it belongs to the Indian Dept. . . . to take the initiative in that matter.
>
> "I deem it necessary for me to leave for Moqui in the morning. Should the Indian agent return during my absence, he will have quite enough to do until my return, in making known to the Indians the determination of the authorities in relation to them."[5]

Predictably, Dodge arrived at Fort Defiance the day after Major Kendrick's departure for Hopi. Henry promptly sent Garland's dispatch ahead with a runner. Kendrick received it while encamped along the trail. The facts as related by Garland differed slightly from the Navajo account, but not by much. A band of Navajo had run off eleven thousand sheep belonging to Antonio José Otero, Juan Andrés Romero and others on March 27th west of the River Puerco in Navajo land. They had killed not one but three herders. The stock trail led unmistakably into Navajo country. Garland's prognosis was grim.

> "This must lead to war unless the murderers and sheep are given up. If war ensues, I will muster in service all the Mexicans who desire either to recover their herds or make reprisals."

At the very least, Garland concluded, the Navajo "will of course receive no annuity until this affair is settled." Kendrick sent the freight wagons ahead to Hopi with Lieutenant Symonds and promptly returned to Defiance.[6]

When Kendrick got back, Henry Dodge corroborated both the Navajo account and the details in Garland's letter. He had visited the scene of the crime, examined two of the three corpses left behind, and then scrutinized the livestock trail moving out of the Puerco River valley and into the Tunicha Mountains. The evidence was irrefutable and Navajo leaders acknowledged some of their young men had taken the livestock, but that the animals were in plain sight there in the mountains and could easily be recovered. The headmen had also admitted that the young men had indeed killed three herders. From that point, as Dodge later explained to Davis in his report of April 19th, the situation became precarious.

> "The Navajos that committed this depredation are rich and influential men, the son of Narbona two sons of Archulet and two sons in law of Cyotanos they live with the Capote Utahs and say they perpetrated this outrage to revenge the Utahs for the loss of 8 horses stolen from them by the Navajos in the early part of March last.
>
> "They drove the sheep into the heart of the Navajo country and are selling and giving them away, and have procured the return of the horses stolen from the Utahs who they say have promised to aid and assist them in defending themselves against all enemies."

Unlike Private Hefbiner's killer, these young men were no outcasts. They were all kin to influential headmen. Dodge and Kendrick subsequently demanded the Navajo return all 11,000 sheep stolen from Otero and Romero and to surrender the murderers to justice, but they knew there would be no surrender. The headmen promised to restore all the stolen animals, but would risk annihilation by the Americans rather than surrender the accused men and spark a civil war, one in which the Ute would ally with the killers' families. The whole affair had left Manuelito in an uncomfortable position. He was a son of Cayetano. Two of his clan sisters were married to men he was expected to help arrest. So, understandably, Manuelito and the headmen pressed on their agent and the fort commander.

> "They say that they do not wish to have a war with the Government of the U. S. that they will return all of the sheep and give three servants in place of the herders killed or pay for them in horses and sheep to the satisfaction of the relatives of the men killed, that this has been the custom amongst them and the Mexicans [since] time immemorial."

Kendrick and Dodge rejected the offer outright. The headmen then asked to present their proposal to Davis and Garland, as well as to the families of the men killed, before war was to be declared. In the meantime, they would continue efforts to recover the sheep. Armijo and Ganado Mucho had already recovered about half of the sheep and would send them immediately back to the owners, just as soon as they were done lambing. Henry's response to that offer is unknown. He confided in his report to Davis that he believed the Navajo would never return such a vast number of stock unless strong military expedition forced them to do so. Even with a major campaign, "they will never give up the offenders until severely chastised if ever."

"It would be madness in the extreme to attempt to effect any thing with the small force at this post at present as any small party going out to collect sheep or attempt to capture the murderers could be surrounded by 1000 warriors before going 25 miles."

Henry L. Dodge had never sounded so pessimistic. He warned Davis that he had recently observed a few Navajos near Hopi sporting fine silver-embellished rifles. The Navajo told him that they had traded horses with the Mormons for the guns. Furthermore, the Mormons had asked them why they hadn't driven the Americans out of Fort Defiance and their country, that letting them stay would allow them to seize all of Navajo land. Dodge was convinced that the Mormons were stirring up the Navajo and Ute.[7]

The members of the Church of Jesus Christ of Latter Day Saints, commonly known as Mormons, had little affection for the United States, and with good reason. In a manner tragically similar to Indians, they had been stripped of their property, driven from their homes, harried, assaulted and murdered from Missouri to Illinois by Americans. After enduring all that, their founding prophet, Joseph Smith, had been shot to death while confined in an American jail, under the protection of American law. Under Brigham Young's leadership, the Mormons finally found refuge in Utah in 1847, on the wild western slopes of the Wasatch Mountains overlooking the Great Salt Lake. Unimpeded in their New World Zion, they forged a rapidly expanding nation, the State of Deseret, and established economic and political relationships with Indians across the West. As they had in Missouri and again in Illinois, the United States government considered the Mormons in Utah a growing threat.

In the meantime, Governor David Meriwether returned from Washington. In sizing up the crisis, the Governor appeared to be considerably less concerned than Garland. First of all, he'd been informed that the number of stock stolen was considerably less than eleven thousand. Secondly, Dodge assured him that the raid was the act of a few disaffected Navajos who had abandoned their tribe rather than an act of the Navajo Nation proper. Although the principal tribal leaders had refused to surrender the guilty parties, they had sworn to pay for the losses.[8]

In contrast to Meriwether's rather offhanded assessment, Major Kendrick's wordy reports to General Garland left no doubt he was mentally strapping on his saber, and the more the major wrote, the more militant and gloomy he became.[9] At that moment, he regretted the reduction in his garrison's number more then than at any time previous. He was certain that the Navajo had interpreted the withdrawal of Shepard's company from Defiance as a sign of American weakness, contributing directly to the present difficulties. War was inevitable and should the Army fail to hit the Navajo hard, no one in the territory would be safe from Indian aggression.

> "The expeditions heretofore made by the Americans into the Navajoe country have been so abortive that a repetition of such ones will do more harm than good. I am certain that if inadequate attempts against them are made at this time, the Utahs will make common cause with them— If however we succeed in humbling the Navajoes known, as they are to be rich and proud, the example will tell on all the other tribes in New Mexico."[10]

On May 2nd, Major Kendrick reported that, even after several more meetings with the Navajo leadership, nothing had changed. Major Kendrick and Agent Dodge had used every approach to get the guilty parties short of issuing an ultimatum. They brought up the promises the Navajo made in the most recent treaty. They warned that the Navajo would lose all their annuities to pay for losses. Damages could be so great, Kendrick threatened, that the Navajo would lose a good chunk of their reservation along the eastern border, just to pay for it all. In the worst case, General Garland would view their refusal as a national act and wage upon them unrelenting war. Kendrick confessed to Garland that the only reason he and Dodge hadn't issued an ultimatum was that he believed the Navajo would see it as justification to strike first. In truth, neither Kendrick nor Dodge had been authorized to issue any ultimatum, something that the major neglected to mention.

It was absolutely maddening. All the persuasion, cajoling and threats were for naught. The Navajo steadfastly refused to bend, commenting only that the Capote Ute had precipitated the crisis. Why, then, must the Navajo nation be punished? Kendrick was unimpressed by their logic. The rich Navajos desired peace, of that he was certain, but he suspected the "majority of the pelados, constituting the larger part of the nation, deem their power altogether superior to that of the United States."[11]

Although appreciative of Kendrick's frank if perhaps alarmist suggestions, General Garland was nevertheless hesitant about going to war. Perhaps it would be best to not press the Navajos but "temporize" with them about turning over the accused killers, at least until Garland knew if the Senate would finally ratify the Laguna Negra Treaty. Additionally, Garland's thinly spread troops had just come off a campaign against the Gila Apaches. Reflecting on the impressive turn out of Navajo warriors at Laguna Negra the previous July, Garland surmised giving them a telling blow would take considerable preparation. It promised to be no simple Apache escapade.

> "They number over two thousand stout warriors, and I should hesitate to invade their country with less than Eight hundred men, which number I cannot put in the field, without drawing off too many from the different garrisons."[12]

General Garland replied to Kendrick on May 3rd. One can imagine the major's brow furrowing as he read it. He instructed Kendrick to tell the Navajo leaders that the whole episode had given the General "much disquiet" over the damage done to the mutual friendship of the Americans and Navajo, and that both he and the governor had taken up the issue. Rather than press the issue of surrendering the perpetrators, Kendrick was to then to focus on getting the sheep back, at least enough to satisfy Otero and Romero, and to encourage the Navajo to plant. The general noted that if there were war, the Army would do the harvesting later. He concluded by encouraging Kendrick to continue sending his suggestions. In a word, Garland had directed Major Kendrick to do precisely what the Navajo leaders had requested him to do. That must have been particularly galling.[13]

At least there was some good news for Henry L. Dodge. Davis informed him that his accounts had never arrived in Washington. The mail had been robbed in transit. Would he please redo them as quickly as possible? It was a reprieve of sorts, insomuch as it would delay receiving another harping letter from Clayton, and the crisis at hand prevented him from dropping everything and rushing to Santa Fe to comply. Politely, Henry replied that his account papers were with John Ward in Santa Fe and suggested Ward could make copies of the copies, sending the first set on to Washington and holding the second set until he could get to Santa Fe to sign them.[14]

It did not appear Dodge would be able to get to Santa Fe soon. On April 23rd, Davis informed him that the inevitable had happened. According to Lorenzo Labadi, the Ute agent, a Navajo raiding party had stolen twenty Capote Ute horses. Davis asked Dodge to assist the Ute "with all the aid in your power to recover said animals."[15] It was preposterous. The Navajo were declaring war on the Capote, Garland and Kendrick were preparing to obliterate the Navajo, and W. W. H. Davis was telling Dodge to aid the enemies of the people he was assigned to represent. The crowning incongruity, however, rested in the wooden crate before him. It contained seed packets, dozens and dozens of them. Dodge thumbed through the box: corn, peas, cabbage, turnips and cauliflower, spinach and celery, as well as the more exotic cresses and mushroom spawn, even Italian crimson clover and mignonette for God's sake. Meriwether had just sent them out to Defiance. They were for the Navajo. Would Dodge to "instruct them in the proper mode of cultivation?"

It was folly. Meriwether must have surely appreciated that in a matter of weeks the Army would be obliterating those neatly planted gardens sprouting from the governor's gay little seed packets. Nevertheless, Dodge dutifully distributed the more common vegetable seeds to the Navajo—the exotic he donated to the Fort Defiance gardens. In addition to his gardening instructions, Meriwether directly addressed the crisis at hand.

> "I have seen your report relative to the late depredation of the Navajos, and I desire you to inform the head men as you see them, that this circumstance has given me great pain; say to them that I am sorry to learn, on my return, that whilst I was at Washington endeavoring to get their treaty ratified, a portion of their tribe were breaking one of the articles of this treaty.
>
> "You will insist upon the surrender of the murderers if you are still satisfied that a murder has been committed, and you will cause as many of the stolen sheep to be restored as practicable. You will also endeavor to ascertain the actual number of sheep taken by them, as there seems to be some doubt on this point. Report to me fully upon all these points."[16]

Of course, for Meriwether the Navajo situation may have seemed a mere distraction compared with the ruckus over his Indian policy in Santa Fe. He'd been hanged in effigy in the Plaza over it before his departure in the fall of 1855 and, from the tone of the Legislature and the editorials of the Gazette, he would be hanged again. At the same time as, some old adversaries were collecting interest on his political misfortunes. Samuel Gorman notified Meriwether that Spruce Baird was in Laguna stirring up trouble over that unending land and water dispute between Acoma and Laguna.[17] Baird & McCarty had also filed suit against him and Steck over Indian depredations, a weighty petition ten pages long, described by the district attorney as "exceedingly profuse and ridiculous."[18]

Dodge and Kendrick spent the first two weeks of May arranging an indemnity payment of livestock with the Navajo headmen before reaching an agreement. The Navajo agreed to deliver payment in the form of sheep and horses at

Laguna Negra on May 31st. On May 16th, in response to Meriwether's question as to the circumstances and number of stock taken, Dodge stated his estimation as to the number stolen was considerably less than 11,000.

> "You ask for information as to the actual number of sheep stolen this is a difficult question to answer as the Mexicans always exaggerate and the Navajos under estimate I have visited the ground and from the size of their trail and the enclosures from which the sheep were taken and the knowledge I have acquired in ten years experience in this county in relation to the mode of the Mexicans in taking care of ewes when they are lambing I believe that 6000 sheep is a large estimate for the amount taken."

Henry also mentioned that the Navajo had supposedly returned the 20 horses Agent Labadi had reported stolen and assured Meriwether that he and Kendrick were doing everything they could think of to expedite Navajo reparations. Kendrick was taking a detachment into Canyon de Chelly the following morning to gather contributions, while Dodge would ride northward beyond Black Lake and the Chuska on the same mission.[19]

In a dispatch to Garland, Kendrick remained more pessimistic than Henry, but pursuant to the general's instructions, he had softened his demands a bit. He didn't believe the Navajo would ever pay for the stolen stock, in any amount, whether four, six or eleven thousand in number. Although the murderers had clearly fled past the north banks of the San Juan into Ute country, Kendrick had continued to demand their surrender. Yet in meetings with the headmen he had hinged the question of war solely on paying for the lost sheep rather than bringing the culprits to justice. Consequently, Kendrick suggested attacking those Ute and Navajo along the San Juan who sheltered them. Why Kendrick or Garland did not earlier propose such a move in itself—assaulting the offending band rather than the entire Navajo nation—is worthy of some contemplation. Garland's reply was simple and reassuring. Stay the course. Stay the course. Presently Defiance would be reinforced.[20]

On May 22nd, the situation suddenly deteriorated. A report reached Meriwether's desk stating that Navajo warriors had driven off four hundred sheep from José Ignacio Montoya near Peña Blanca northwest of Santa Fe. Three New Mexican herders had been wounded, two of them mortally. The local citizens had pursued the raiders into the Valle Grande, in the mountains above Jemez, killing two Navajo men and recovering about one fourth of the number of stock. Francisco Tomás Baca, who had written the report, couldn't resist a sarcastic slap at the governor by suggesting that his Excellency Governor Meriwether guard the valley entrance with a respectable force, lest he have wild Indians in the suburbs of the capitol, "a visit as pernicious as disagreeable to many of the Citizens of Santa Fe."[21] Meriwether may have wondered if the Navajo were gathering stock to satisfy Otero by robbing other citizens. The fact that two Navajo had been killed at Valle Grande bode badly. There would be retaliation, the killings would escalate and the territory would be plunged into war. Meriwether also thought the Navajo were being particularly sluggish in making reparations. Capt. R. L. Ewell, commanding at Los Lunas, announced that he had determined the number of sheep stolen at about 10,000 and that the Navajo had delivered up to him seven hundred head, having lost one hundred animals along the trail.[22] Taking that with the thousand head of sheep the Navajo had surrendered at Cebolleta earlier, it was a weak beginning, a mere 1700 head. Things looked grim.

When the prearranged day for payment at Laguna Negra arrived, Major Kendrick and Henry Dodge once more climbed into the saddle. Henry was beginning to feel the toll that constant travel and consternation was exacting on him. He hadn't been feeling well for some time to start with and their latest journey would further damage his health.

Once they arrived, they found roughly 120 Navajo, including several principle headmen. All they were able to offer was thirty horses and four hundred sheep, all of the animals contributed by various Navajo bands desirous of peace. The headmen reiterated that under no circumstances would they be able to surrender the accused murderers, but they again offered Dodge and Kendrick three peons as reparation for the three dead herders. Kendrick and Dodge refused to accept them. They then offered the three as partial payment for the stolen sheep. Once more, Kendrick and Dodge refused. Exasperated, the Navajo decided they would present them to Otero and Romero directly, hoping they would be more reasonable than the two Americans standing there before them. Accordingly, they sent the three captives to Cebolleta under the care of the headman José Miguel.

Before closing, the Navajo leaders once more emphasized they desperately desired peace and that, should war erupt, they would see their own homes and property destroyed or run away, before firing a shot in anger at the Americans. They would pay whatever was required if they could. But they were tired. They were tired of making constant contributions on behalf of those they could not control. They themselves seriously doubted any more stock would be given up unless extracted under the threat of American guns.[23]

So concluded the meeting, shrouded in foreboding. Henry L. Dodge and Major Kendrick returned to Fort Defiance the following day. As he wearily pulled his feet from the stirrups, Dodge must have realized that he had exhausted the good will of even those headmen he'd once counted as fast friends, such as Zarcillos Largos, that those fast friends had come to perceive him less as a friend himself and more as a mouthpiece for the Americans' incessant demands.

It was the darkest times Henry had yet experienced. And it was going to get worse.

44

AN OUNCE OF FEAR

Dodge and Kendrick returned to Defiance on June 1st. On June 2nd, Henry dutifully scribbled out his report to Meriwether. The trip had accomplished little other than aggravating his health and darkening his mood.

> "On yesterday I returned in company with Major Kendrick from the Black Lake where we met the Navajoes on the last of May by previous arrangement.... They have turned over to me in all fourteen hundred sheep and thirty horses, which I have sent to Mr. Otero, the person who lost the flock of sheep in March last.... They also tendered Major Kendrick & I three peons in payment for the three Mexicans killed by them as we declined receiving them they were sent to the owner of the sheep by the Nation by a chief by the name of José Miguel who speaks Spanish well.
>
> "Except about one thousand sheep of the original flock, there have been raised both sheep and horse by contribution the head men say they will pay any amount of sheep and horses that you may demand but that they cannot give up the murderers as they have left their country and gone to the Capote Utas."

The Navajo contributions had been far short of the requirement. Indeed, given the headmen's resigned attitude, Henry didn't believe they'd ever willingly make up the loss. Dodge closed his report on a rare personal note.

> "I am quite unwell and think it quite probably that I will not be able to visit Santa Fe this month.... I have drawn on you in favor of Mr. J. C. Weber for six hundred dollars to pay the contingent expenses of my agency which please pay and I will account for the same in my next quarters accounts."[1]

Kendrick's report to Garland perfectly reflected Dodge's, observing tersely that, of all the livestock contributed by the Navajo, not one head had come from "the culprits" themselves. For the first time the major had noted the headmen's growing frustration.

> "The chiefs who have been most efficient in collecting these contributions say that they are tired out in making them, that they think it quite improbably that any more collections can be made-without the exhibition of a respectable force, ready to strike. I quite agree with them. With such an exhibition, unaccompanied by a demand for the murderers, I think it <u>probable</u> that even the number claimed may be obtained.[2]

The territory was again rife with rumors of war and it was already apparent there would be no shortage of citizens anxious to take part. In early June, Don Diego Archuleta of Los Luceros, Rio Arriba notified General John Garland that he had raised a militia to fight the Navajo.[3] The general thanked Archuleta and assured him he would call should he need them. Garland was quite prepared to invade Navajo land and use volunteer companies, but he sincerely hoped he wouldn't have to. His concerns were more practical than pacifist. Garland knew full well that companies of citizen volunteers such as Archuleta's were notoriously undisciplined, hard to manage and easily panicked. Regular Army officers who had served with volunteer units on the field of battle generally scorned them.

Garland didn't have that luxury. The Department of New Mexico was desperately understaffed, and even with volunteer units, he wouldn't have enough soldiers to field an expedition unless he pulled troops from several garrisons around the territory, weakening them and presenting an irresistible temptation for the Ute and Apache to resume hostilities. He believed, as did Kendrick, that pulling troops from Fort Defiance in December to suppress the Gila Apache had done just that with the Navajo ... emboldened them. To avoid repeating the error, Garland considered limiting his war to the Navajo sheltering the killers, the San Juan band led by Archuleta, the testy headman who several years before had showered Lieutenant

Ransom in a blizzard of flour.[4] True, his own policy forbade waging war on only a portion of a tribe to the exclusion of the whole, but desperate times occasionally justified desperate backpedaling.[5]

Consequently, General Garland suggested that very remedy to Kendrick in his dispatch of June 11th, adding that he acknowledged and appreciated the Navajo gesture of sending the captives to Otero, but it would not dissuade him from pursuing Archuleta and his gang of rapscallions.

> "The General will be pleased to receive suggestions from you as to the best route into their country, and the best method of getting at this refractory band."[6]

David Meriwether was likewise clinging to hopes that a Navajo war could be avoided. He knew Garland was planning an assault and that it would probably come in July or August. As that fateful date approached, the governor entertained quixotic thoughts of going to Navajo country personally "to settle our difficulties with this tribe" and convince the Indians to peacefully surrender the murderers. All political and humanitarian motivations aside, he must have known that even his presumed stature as the supreme civil officer of the territory wouldn't persuade the Navajo. Quite the contrary; from all reports the Indians appeared to be going about business in a more time-honored way. On June 6th, a Navajo raiding party ran off eight of Antonio Baca's horses. Two days later at San Ysidro, raiders led by Aguila Negra injured one cow and captured three others. Meriwether reported the incidents to Dodge, who doubtlessly welcomed the news with dejected resignation.

On top of it all, there was the real possibility that Meriwether's entire Indian policy would be gutted. There was a plan afoot in Washington to separate the positions of territorial governor and superintendent of Indian affairs. The superintendency would consequently become a separate and independent position, with autonomous powers. The idea hadn't been hatched in New Mexico, but Meriwether had no doubts many in Cíbola were ecstatic over it, for in their thinking it would end the insult of having a governor, an outsider and East Coast political toady, favoring the savage Indian over civilized New Mexicans, who, all agreed, had more practical experience in properly dealing with savages to begin with. The most mortifying thing about it was that the man most likely to get the new position was Meriwether's greatest gadfly, the editor of the Santa Fe Gazette, James L. Collins. It seemed that, in addition to railing about unpunished Indian outrages and Meriwether's pampering of the red man, Collins had been energetically promoting himself back in Washington as the best man for the job.[7]

A letter landing unexpectedly on Meriwether's desk momentarily brought him out of his funk. It was from Agent Dodge, dated June 13th. Breaking the seal, he unfolded it. Dodge had written four pages. Four pages! The man never wrote more than a paragraph or two. As the Governor read through each hastily scrawled page, a sinking feeling crept in.

> "Since my last communication things have taken an entire change in the feelings of the Navajos. They say that four of their men went upon a stealing expedition and but two have returned and that they have good reason to believe that the Mexicans have killed them."

That, Meriwether realized, was the ncident at the Valle Grande.

> "In consequence of which they refuse to pay any more sheep or horses to the owner of the flock stolen by them March last. They say they are tired of such business and as the Mexicans have killed two of their people they would as soon go to war as not and that they can do the Mexicans and Americans more injury that they can do them."

Unbelievable. The Navajo actually thought they could win a war against the United States. Manuelito himself, appointed by Meriwether as head chief, had adopted a sharply bellicose attitude.

> "Manuelito the head chief in the last conversation had with him by Major Kendrick and myself—when asked if he did not intend to respect the treaty made by you in August last by keeping his herds and flocks off of the grounds ceded to the U. S. for the purpose of maintaining this Post, said he did not, that he had owned the places where the hay had been cut since the establishing of the Fort [from the time he was] a boy—that Major Kendrick had wagons and soldiers and could go to the Celites thirty miles distant from this place to cut grass or drive him from the grounds that he was occupying if he thought he had force sufficient.
> "That he Manuelito was a great captain, that he could call around him in quick time one thousand warriors, and from [what] he had seen here and at Santa Fe he had more braves than the Gov. or Genl. of the Americans.

That when they were at Laguna Negra it was as much as he could do and other good men of this nation could do to keep his people from running over them both, they were so small in numbers."

At that point, Dodge noted, Manuelito's tone had turned somewhat contemptuous.

"Mexicans they had always robbed and killed and that we could not prevent it that we had several times attempted to do so but had always failed that the Americans were too fond of <u>sleeping eating drinking</u> and had white eyes and could not see the road to catch them when they chose to keep out of their way. In short all of their reminiscences of the wars in which they have been engaged for many years past are of the most pleasing kind. They have made themselves rich and have become haughty and proud."

According to Henry, the head chief's feelings were widely shared by his fellow Navajo.

"In my late visits to different parts of their country collecting sheep they have taken great pleasure in pointing out to me one of their mountain passes in which they say they put to rout one thousand Mexicans and Pueblos and killed Capt Inohos & the Father of Don Tomas Baca the rich man of Pena Blanco and forced the Capt of the Pueblos of Jemez to jump off a precipice and kill himself."

It wasn't mere bragging. In February of 1835, Captain Blas de Hinojos led a large military expedition into the Chuska Mountains. Composed mostly of volunteers, the New Mexicans were scattered along in disorganized bunches, joking and guffawing, brash in their bravado and boisterous in their revelry when they entered a wide canyon leading to the heights above. The soaring canyon walls gradually closed in on them, mocking the men's careless laughter as they clamored upwards. Suddenly from the cliffs above broke a perfect storm: musket shot, arrows, boulders, tree trunks and stones, all rained down onto the panic-stricken revelers, sending them reeling pell-mell back down the canyon. Although the Navajo usually exaggerated the casualties, the Mexican losses that day, though never accurately reported, were without a doubt staggering.[8]

"I cannot account for this sudden change in their feelings but in two ways the late killing of two of their people which is considered by all Indians that have not been taught to feel the power of our Government however justifiable we may think the killing has been done. That they have to revenge all such offences committed against them upon the innocent or guilty as they may have the opportunity.

"The second cause is that a report became rife among them in the early part of December 1855 that this post was to be abandoned that the commanding officer had left and many soldiers were to return and that the balance would soon follow. . . . This report was started by Sarcillos Largo . . . who also said that the Americans could not keep up the Fort any longer that it cost [too] much.

"They are no fools and see at a glance of the eye that the troops at this place cannot affect or stop their killing and robbing and that [the soldiers] are barely able to protect themselves and herds without attempting an offensive movement against them."

It was also no coincidence the rumor sprang to life shortly after Garland had pulled O. L. Shepard's command from Defiance. If Zarcillos Largos was carrying a grudge and purposely subverting American peace efforts, could any of the Navajos be trusted to remain friends of the American?

"That I deprecate the present state of things with these deluded people as much as it is possible for any person to do and have done as much as it was possible to have been expected of an Indian agent I think you and all the officers at this Post will do me the justice to admit.

"They are the owners of large flocks and herds and have at this time finely cultivated lands in wheat and corn and have received great encouragement from the Government of the U. S. to keep at peace and I have had great hopes the large interest they have at stake and the kind treatment received from the U. S. would make them an exception to the general rule . . . laid down for the government of Indians which is that an ounce of fear is better than pounds of love . . . that their thieving and murdering propensity could be corrected without the dreadful scourge of war.

"But alas I cannot see at this time any other alternative but war and that of the harshest kind."[9]

Meriwether paused to lean back in his chair. It had all gone to pieces. Yet even so, he rationalized, things could be worse . . . and, of course, in returning to Dodge's concluding page, he discovered things indeed were.

> "I have this moment received information from a Navajo that a war party headed by the son of José Largo a rich man of the tribe who lives at or near the Hot Springs to steal and kills all persons that may be so unfortunate as to fall into their hands. They are relatives of the two Navajos killed at the Valle."

Major Kendrick's letter to Garland, written the same day as Dodge's, was equally pessimistic. The Navajo disposition had taken a dramatic turn for the worse at the worst possible time.

> "Whatever causes of complaint Indians out of New Mexico may have had, the strictest good faith, & the most exact justice have ever been observed towards the Navajoes by the Americans. They do not even allege the slightest wrong, but base their notions entirely upon their supposed power. The Indian Agent & myself have lost no opportunity of impressing upon them the ability of our government to punish their wrong acts, while at the same time we have been equally anxious to demonstrate to them its beneficent intentions in their behalf.
> "From all this, as well as from their having everything to lose & nothing to gain by a war, I had hopes-at times with many misgivings-that we might ultimately, solely by peaceful means, succeed in enlightening these people in relation to their true interests-& I am disappointed." [10]

Learning of the war party at about the same moment as Dodge, Kendrick dashed off an express to Carleton at Albuquerque, stating he believed the Navajo were headed for Laguna and advising him to sound the alarm. Word of the raiding expedition spread rapidly. Towns up and down the Rio Grande drew their livestock in, barred the gates, posted sentries and collectively held their breath, waiting for the eruption of fighting.

Undeterred by a growing feeling of futility, Dodge and Kendrick continued to work for some kind of compromise; anything to avoid what they both acknowledged was unavoidable. On June 13th, the very day Dodge had reported events to Meriwether, he and Kendrick learned that an immense number of Navajo were convening near the Bear and Carrizo Springs, doubtlessly to discuss the potential impact the arrival of troops and a subsequent war might have on them. Once more and somewhat more reluctantly, Dodge shook off his lingering sickness, swung into the saddle and embarked on another seemingly useless mission. The results of their trip to Bear Springs were not recorded, but whatever happened apparently did little to remedy the rapidly deteriorating situation. Reports of Indian outrages continued, some verifiable, others not. In late June Dodge received word from Samuel Gorman that a group of Mount Taylor Navajo had murdered a prominent citizen of Cubero.

> "Dear Sir, Lest in the excitement of our present consternation, others should neglect it, I feel it to be my painful duty to tell you that four Navajos, said to be of Sandobal's party, on the 25th which was Wednesday of this week, came upon Juan de Dios Ballegos of Covera, in the mountain a little above Enseñal, and shot him in two places, one ball entered his back, low down & came out at his left side. The other an arrow entered high up between the shoulders, and another one was shot in the back of his shepherd. The shepherd made his escape & told the news. The friends went as soon as possible up the mountain, & found Juan still alive, and so far recovered, as to be sane and able to talk. They took him to the house of Don Marcos Vaca where he lived till yesterday morning, he died. You no doubt know him. He was one of the best men in my estimate"

Peons of the headman Mariano had committed the murder, with the headman's complacency, to avenge the killing of Mariano's sister by Comanche over a month before. To Reverend Gorman and most other Americans, it was an incomprehensibly malicious, barbaric act.

> "Now I think it is time that some thing were done with these fellows. The blood of Juan De Dios cries in the ears of our government for the execution of justice for cold-blooded murder. How long shall it cry in vain? We look to the officers of our government for that protection of person and property, which is guaranteed to us in our federal compact. May we not look in vain."

"Yours truly, S. Gorman
P.S. Juan leaves a wife & 7 small children to mourn his loss."[11]

Would the month of June never end?

By the close of the month, Henry L. Dodge had recovered enough of his strength to travel to Santa Fe for the quarter's end. He had little but bad news to report to Meriwether, information that the governor was obliged to report to Commissioner Manypenny on June 30th.[12] If what Dodge told him was true, Meriwether was convinced "that we cannot too soon teach these Indians to feel our power and ability to chastise them." Yet his misgivings lingered. The old Kentuckian remained acutely skeptical of the circumstances surrounding the Otero robbery. He had seen New Mexicans inflate their losses to Indian depredations and blame Indians for stealing livestock they'd actually stolen themselves. Publicly pointing out those facts out had earned Meriwether the enmity of many a New Mexican stockman. The Governor remained undaunted and he was convinced the Otero claims were grossly inflated.

First of all, there had been two independent investigations of the theft, one by Henry Dodge for Meriwether and another done by Captain Ewell for General Garland. Based on his examination of the crime scene, Dodge had estimated the sheep taken at between six and seven thousand. Ewell drew his estimates from interviews with the victims and their neighbors. To no one's surprise, least of all Meriwether's, Ewell's tally was much larger—forty percent or three to four thousand head higher—than Dodge's. Upon further investigation, Meriwether discovered that Otero's contractors had shorted their employers 150 head of the 1,900 Navajo animals Dodge and Ewell had collected by under-reporting the actual number they'd received. That drew Meriwether to one conclusion: if a majordomo would lie about the number of sheep returned, he could conversely lie about the amount of the original loss to cover up some personal larceny.[13]

As the governor labored over his report to Manypenny, word arrived from Ute Agent Lorenzo Labadi that the Navajo had stampeded his Indians' livestock. On the heels of that came a second complaint from Reverend Gorman, announcing the death of yet "another good citizen." It seemed the previous Friday Navajo raiders had run off the Cebolleta cattle herd. The alcalde and twenty-six men had successfully given chase and recovered the stock, but were later ambushed by the Indians as they returned home. The Navajo shot the alcalde dead and another man in the face before putting the rest of them to flight.[14]

Lieutenant John Trevitt, with O. L. Shepard's 3rd Infantry camped at the time near Laguna, mentioned the tragedy facetiously in his journal.

"We are getting along very slowly: weather hot: water bad and scarce. So far as we can learn the Navajo War is all 'in my eye'. Some few of Sandoval's band under Mexicans are cutting up their shindys, and popped a Mex from Cuvero who was up in their country the other day. The people say that Kendrick's Indians are all as friendly as ever and have no intention of fighting. So we go. . . . "[15]

Garland had come to the conclusion that he'd have to strike the Navajo, but he approached the task almost diffidently. One of the foremost concerns rattling in his head was what the practical result of a Navajo war would be. Once the soldiers destroyed the farms and flocks of "these misguided people . . . this will make them, again, a marauding band." Rather than stifle the violence, it could spread it. Nevertheless, the territory was clamoring for action, so he took the first few tentative steps. He notified all companies to be ready to take the field at a moment's notice. He cautioned Ewell at Los Lunas and Carleton at Albuquerque to be especially vigilant, directed that warnings to be sent out to the settlements up and down the river to take precautions.

On June 26th Garland ordered Shepard's Company B, 3rd Infantry at Albuquerque to reinforce Fort Defiance, which was precisely where Trevitt and company camped at Laguna were headed.[16] Garland's instructions were explicit. Shepard's command was to move without delay into Navajo country, and to proceed with equal amounts of caution and discretion. Shepherd was under strict orders to show no hostility whatsoever to the Navajo, to steer clear of confrontations at all costs and, most critically, under no circumstances to launch an attack. Do not assault the Indians. The last thing Garland wanted was to spark a war he wasn't yet ready to fight.[17]

As Trevitt had noted, Garland's Navajo war seemed simply "in one's eye." They encountered no hostiles whatsoever, while those few Navajo brave enough to approach the column were, if not cooperative, at least amiable. Company B trundled into Fort Defiance on July 10th, having made the trip without a single incident. For Kendrick and Dodge, the benefits of the reinforcement preceded its actual arrival. Two days before, a delegation of headmen appeared at the fort. Gone was the belligerency Dodge had experienced earlier. The Navajo expressed a fervent desire to remain the Americans' friends and pledged to comply with American demands. Not only did they want to continue making reparations, the headmen promised they'd make a large payment there at the fort in three days. The payment took place as scheduled, in front of Shepard's newly arrive company, and was marked, as Kendrick later noted, by the "largest collection of Indians ever at this Post." The

Navajo delivered three hundred sheep and twenty horses, insisting that the whole crisis had been a big misunderstanding. The Navajo vigorously desired peace and were willing to do anything to avert a war... except to deliver up the murderers. Kendrick responded to that stipulation with mild sarcasm.

> "In other words, they pretend to be more afraid of some 20 or 30 bad men of their own tribe & of the Capote Utahs than of the whole force of the U. S. Government. I am persuaded that until this feeling is changed by coercing them to place the evil doers, in some way, in our hands or by suffering from us what they will deem an equivalent amount of injury no lasting peace can be hoped for with these people."

Although he appreciated the encouraging turn of events, the major still believed a hard lesson was called for, but even in that his stand had mellowed. If General Garland displayed an overwhelming show of force, it could be enough to get the Navajo to guide them to the murderers' refuge north of the San Juan. The apocalyptic vision of massive columns of soldiers obliterating Navajo settlements, farms and herds up and down the river might even persuade Archuleta to surrender them himself. And if he didn't, well... the troops would be in a perfect position to press the point.

> "...we ought to inflict such an injury upon the Navajos with whom the wrong doers are more or less connected, as will make them the keepers of the peace hereafter. This can be most humanely done (perhaps not the most effectively) by levying upon them a heavy contribution in the way of stock, particularly of horses..."

Kendrick had gradually arrived at the same position as Garland, endorsing a surgical strike against a part of the tribe rather than the whole nation. Nonetheless, should that fail and Garland declare war on the entire tribe, the major suggested using a three-prong attack employing tactics familiar to the Navajo. Wage a rapid, hit and run war. Scour the countryside with small, mobile units, driving out and harassing the Indians at every point. It was a strategy that would be adopted against the Navajo five years later, with devastating effectiveness.[18]

Feeling as gratified as his sickness might allow, Henry L. Dodge composed a long report of his own to Meriwether, laboriously scratching out one copy, making several corrections and then rewriting it.

"Sir: Since my last communication all of the head men of the Navajo tribe of Indians have met Major Kendrick and myself at this place and disclaimed all intention of going to war with our Government. Manuelito & all others say that the Interpreters have misstated their intentions.... That actions speak louder than words, that they have quit the grazing grounds of this place and are willing to comply with the treaty made with you in everything except the delivery of the murderers that it would produce war among themselves but are willing to deliver their families' flocks and herds to any force sent against them.

The Navajo knew well that, in a civil war, the Capote Ute would ally with the San Juan Navajo.

"That there is but twenty eight bad men amongst them and that they live near the Capote Utahs and they are sorry that our Government should make them accountable for their acts. On the tenth of the present month they turned over to me without being forced or any display of troops in their country whatever 300 sheep and twenty two horses and say that they will pay any amount of sheep and horses that you may demand."

Furthermore, Dodge reported, they were willing to lose all before taking up arms against the Americans, that "if we commence a war upon them, they will not run and we may take their flocks, herds, and families if nothing else will satisfy us."

Dodge did not note as much in his letter, but evidence increasingly suggested that the initial Navajo position in the crisis had been correct all along, a fact that General Garland and Major Kendrick were beginning to appreciate. The Otero raid had been exclusively the work of a few miscreants among the San Juan Navajo and any subsequent raids could be laid at their feet or at those of Antonio Sandoval and the Mount Taylor Navajos.

Echoing Kendrick's words, Henry suggested concentrating a large force in Navajo country.

"I give it as my opinion founded upon many years of experience with these people that if a strong force is concentrated at different points in their country and that they have to pay the expenses of the war if the offenders are not delivered they will give any assistance that may be required of them in their apprehension..."

In the meantime, Dodge had sent his herder Manuel Gallegos and the headman José Miguel to Cubero with the surrendered sheep and horses. Miguel would deliver them to the alcalde Juan Durán, who would wait for Meriwether's instructions to distribute the stock. Henry apologized for not doing it himself.

> "I am quite sick or would go in myself I believe that this sudden change has been produced in their conduct by the arrival of an additional company of troops at this post and a belief that war is to be waged against them."[19]

On July 24th, David Meriwether replied, expressing satisfaction over the Navajos' "favorable alteration in deportment" and their payment of stock. He regretted Dodge had been too ill to go to Cubero himself. Skeptical as he was of New Mexican honesty, Meriwether thought turning Otero's stock over to Durán instead of overseeing the delivery himself was a bad idea. Aside from that, the Governor expressed a hope that, if all went well, he'd get out to visit the Navajo in September.[20]

Hope had been resuscitated, but Governor Meriwether knew its condition remained critical. By coincidence, he had in his hands a letter from the Alcalde of Cubero, Don Juan Durán one and the same, notifying him that Dodge had made him receiver of the surrendered livestock. The alcalde, in a haughty and somewhat insulting manner, availed himself of the occasion to list everyone of the vicinity who had claimed a loss . . . there were several . . . and Durán demanded the Navajo pay them all in full. Then he went on.

> "Be it understood also, that we the citizens of the U. S. & Territory of N. M. are unwilling to receive <u>animals</u> to compensate for the murder of our fellow citizens. We value our fellow citizens more than we do animals. We have laws. They require the execution of murderers. We ask of your Excellency, that these laws be enforced."[21]

It was certainly a sudden and dramatic turnabout from the previous three hundred year tradition. Durán's statement, as with so many other of Meriwether's detractors, was doubtlessly crafted less from an appreciation for the life of a peon or two than for the opportunity to make a political statement.

Dodge had told Meriwether that the Navajo blamed the Capote Ute for stirring up the present difficulties. Meriwether doubted that, believing that the

Capote band had demonstrated consistent friendship with the Americans. The critical issue, as Durán had insolently pointed out, was that Navajo still refused to turn over the killers. Until they did, Meriwether conceded, there could be no satisfactory resolution. Clearly, some amount of force would have to be used.[22] It was precisely that which General John Garland was preparing to administer. The preliminary groundwork for an attack on the San Juan Navajo was well underway, provender for the troops in the field secured, armaments polished and oiled, ordnance stockpiled, units assigned and tentative dates for the invasion set. All that was needed was the order to go.

Then, in late July, Garland learned that Army Command in New York had issued General Order Number 6. Effective immediately, General Order Number 6 had transferred the 1st Regiment of United States Dragoons from New Mexico to the desert garrison of Tucson and to California, dooming Garland's war plans. The 1st Dragoons under Ewell and Carleton were the key component of his Navajo expedition. Suddenly they had been pulled right out from under him. In its wisdom, the War Office had scheduled replacement troops to be sent to New Mexico . . . the operative word being 'scheduled.' Garland could expect they would arrive long after the 1st Dragoons had departed, leaving a gaping hole in New Mexico's defenses for potentially months.[23]

The General gave Kendrick the news on July 26th. The expedition was off. Now was not the time to plunge into a conflict. Temporize. Stall. Coddle, if need be, but arrange things "in such a way that the necessity may not be forced upon us to take up arms at once."[24]

Thus, the latest Navajo crisis was ended not by shrewd diplomacy or bold action, but by a simple fluke of bureaucracy.

45

A MOOT POINT

Early in September, Henry Dodge and a delegation of seventy Navajo appeared in Santa Fe. It was a trip designed as much for diplomacy as for picking up farming tools and treaty annuity goods. The very fact the visit took place at all illustrated how abruptly tensions between the Navajo and Americans had eased. In addition to meeting with Meriwether, Dodge, Manuelito and the headmen made a point to visit General John Garland to express their gratitude for his forbearance, to reaffirm their desires for peace and their promises to pay for Otero's losses. The meeting was so cordial, with warm embraces and expressions of lasting friendship all around, that Garland felt confident the Navajo would keep the peace. On September 30th, Henry sent Commissioner Manypenny his formal report. In it he apologized for having failed to transmit his 2nd quarter papers on time, as he was perpetually on horseback retrieving stolen livestock, searching out the killers of Otero's shepherds, and battling his own ill-health.

> I am happy to inform you that I have succeeded in getting part payment from the tribe for the sheep. The Nabajoes have paid Mr. Otero two thousand sheep, fifty-two horses and three servants and all the principal men say they are willing to pay him until he is satisfied. . . . The Navajos have raised fine crops of corn and wheat this year and they are at this time friendly disposed toward the government and citizens of this territory and a large majority of them have always been so, and say they will do all they possibly can to prevent their bad men from pilfering and committing depredations. I am sir,

Very Respectfully,
Your Obdt. Servt.
Henry L. Dodge, Indian Agent"[1]

In the month and a half since they'd all stood on the brink of war, Dodge and his agency had settled back into an old and comfortable routine, something Henry would have thought impossible the previous July. Things were, but for some minor details, almost back to normal. He had drawn his full salary and actually had a little leisure time to spend it, visiting the card salons of Santa Fe, apparently fortified by the five hundred dollars cash Meriwether had given him earlier to purchase farming implements for the Navajo. It seems Henry lost it all in one sitting. A. G. Mayers, the Pueblo Indian Agent, was the big winner that evening.[2] On September 27th, Dodge filed a claim for 160 acres of bounty land to the Commissioner of Pensions in Washington City, earned for his service in the Navajo Campaign of 1849. Whether Henry intended to claim cash, sell the claim or to apply it for land in New Mexico is anyone's guess. Given his nature, he probably took the money.[3] Dodge lingered in

Santa Fe before returning to Fort Defiance in early October. He had been gone from his agency for nearly a month.

Major Kendrick likewise observed that through early autumn the Navajo coming in to the fort had remained friendly and cooperative.

> "They profess to be very anxious for the preservation of peace, & I presume that they are sincere, for they well know that the authorities have not abandoned our causes of complaint against them."

According to Garland's instructions, Kendrick and Dodge kept the Navajo headmen in a state of, as the major put it, "wholesome anxiety" by continually pressing them for payments of stock. In truth, both men knew the Navajo would never pay Otero the full amount, much less surrender the fugitives to justice. The Navajo remained adamant that seizing them was impossible. In an essentially empty gesture, Manuelito did promise to deliver the killers up to Dodge at the first opportunity . . . if the opportunity ever came. But as long as the Indians remained affable, that didn't seem to matter anymore. Both sides had accepted the fact that the issue was, in General Garland's own words, a moot point.[4] There would be no expedition against either the San Juan Navajo or the entire nation. The foremost advocate of the Navajo expedition, General Garland himself, had taken a temporary leave of absence, leaving the department under Colonel Benjamin L. E. de Bonneville, a well-worn if not well-weathered career soldier. He took command on October 11th. While he stood at the helm, the portly, squinty-eyed and whiskey-faced Bonneville had no intention of doing anything more dramatic than filing reports.[5]

Relations with the Navajo remained so amiable that, in early November, Major Kendrick and Henry Dodge were able to draw up a formal contract with the Navajo headman, El Gordo, brother of Zarcillos Largos, to lease grazing lands and hay fields for the sole use of the Defiance garrison, from April 1st until "the Government is done cutting its grass and grazing its animals there for each year." Gordo and his people were to receive manta cloth as payment for each hay load up to twenty loads. If more than twenty loads were cut, the Army would pay him one rawhide, one axe, one hoe and "two planches of Tobacco." However unsophisticated the agreement seemed, it was the first formal contract executed between the United States and the Navajo Nation.[6]

Shortly after Bonneville assumed command, Henry Dodge and David Meriwether both received subpoenas to appear in the district court at Tomé, courtesy of Antonio José Otero through his law firm, the indefatigable Baird & McCarthy.

Antonio Otero was suing the alcalde of Cubero, Juan Durán, the man Dodge had assigned to take responsibility for returning Otero's stolen livestock, for "contriving and fraudulently interceding craftily and subtly to deceive and defraud" him. As Meriwether had earlier predicted, Durán had apparently shorted Otero two thousand dollars worth of sheep. When the subpoena was issued, Dodge was at Fort Defiance at the time. The marshal, Charles Blumner, had to travel some 350 miles to deliver it.[7]

It is unlikely that Henry actually showed up for the court date. The distance not withstanding, he had plenty to keep him busy at Defiance. There had been one or two minor hiccups in the newly restored Navajo tranquility that needed his attention. Around September 12th, while Dodge and his delegation were still in Santa Fe, a Kiowa party of two hundred warriors was spotted ranging along the Rio Grande just south of the city. As with the Comanche expedition a few years previously, the Kiowa were reportedly headed for Navajo country on a raid, perhaps wishing to cash in on the general war the whites were rumored to be waging. Their disappointment didn't prevent them from invading Navajo land. Notably and contrary to the resurrected spirit of friendship with the Navajo, the soon-to-be-relieved General Garland did nothing to stand in their way. Still, this failure ended up wreaking havock on the enterprising war party, for once the Kiowa arrived in Navajo country, the Navajo tore them up first rate, routing them and seizing a good number of their horses. The only time Garland became concerned was when he learned of their defeat, fearing that the Kiowa would make up their losses by looting the settlements. To everyone's relief, the war party left New Mexico without further incident.[8]

On October 20th, Lorenzo Labadi informed Meriwether that a Navajo party had killed three principle Capote Ute and that the Ute had killed two Navajo in retaliation. It seemed that, under the pretense of peace, the Navajo were settling up old debts.[9] Happily, nothing more apparently came of that particular event, but a few days afterwards, a contractor bringing in a herd of cattle for Kendrick's garrison arrived at Fort Defiance with a disturbing story. A gang of Navajo had attacked him outside of Cubero, he explained, and had run off 16 head of the Army cattle. Because of that, he only had 119 cattle out of the original 140 to deliver to Kendrick.

Some quick math revealed that the man's explanation left a difference of 21 head rather than 16. Kendrick and Dodge asked where the remaining five head were. Well, the majordomo explained, thirteen cows had actually run back to Tecalote, another had died, and that the Indians had stolen seventeen, not sixteen. Kendrick then pointed out that his new figures accounted for ten cows too many. The man, at a loss, stammered that well . . . perhaps he'd misspoken. He had meant to say three cows had run back to Tecalote, one died, and seventeen stolen.

Although amused, neither Kendrick nor Dodge believed him for a moment. The following morning Henry and a detachment of soldiers dutifully escorted the majordomo back to the scene of the crime outside of Cubero. When they reached Bear Springs, the increasingly nervous majordomo finally confessed that there had been no Navajo raid. They had actually left Cubero with only 122 head. Three cows had given out on the road. As for the remaining 18 animals; the majordomo and his men had simply lost them. Dodge was gratified.

"I had information to be relied upon before leaving this place, that they passed Cubero with but 122 cattle, and I have since heard that they killed a beef in Laguna and sold the meat and hide for deer skins, corn cakes & chili. I was much pleased, I can assure you, when I found the Navajoes guiltless of the charge of stealing from this herd of beef cattle, guarded as they were by two Mexican men and two boys, which was a temptation so great to the thieves and rascals of the tribe, if I had been asked my opinion on the subject, I should have at once said they will not reach Fort Defiance with fifty.[10]

Those scattered, minor incidents still provided sufficient grist for the Santa Fe Gazette's continuing attacks on Meriwether's policies. James L. Collin's editorials claimed to serve the interests of the people of New Mexico, but were rather designed to serve his own interests. In Washington, the positions of territorial governor and Indian superintendent had been split and, within the year, newly elected President James Buchanan would grant Collins the prize peach he had desired, the Superintendency for New Mexico. The man was already pontificating about his plans for the Indians. He'd permanently isolate all the wild tribes and prevent them from fraternizing with the citizenry. He'd congregate the Navajo in a few towns and slash their huge reservation by hundreds of thousands of acres, all for the benefit of New Mexican stockmen. The same fate awaited the Ute and the Apache. They would be collected and reduced like indolent cattle, even if it took brute force to do so. Collins even toyed with the idea of subduing the distant Mogollon, Pinal, Coyotero and Tonto of Western Apachería in a like manner. His grandiose plans not withstanding, the Western Apache would soon demonstrate to Collins and all New Mexico they had no desire to oblige him.[11]

46

RECONNAISSANCE

The Western Apache of the soon-to-be-created territory of Arizona owed no allegiance to any authority other than their own, a fact they frequently demonstrated to the woe of the settlers and stock raisers on either side of the United States—Mexican border. The Coyotero had long waged war with Mexico, often allying with the Mogollon and Chiricahua for raids deep into Sonora. Indeed, the principal Chiricahua leader, Mangas Coloradas, had daughters married into Western Apache bands and was in frequent contact with them. Concurrently, the Mogollon and Coyotero hadn't the slightest reticence about raiding New Mexican settlements as well. Whether it was out of ignorance or careless bravado, they neither respected nor feared the Americans. The Mogollon in particular were keen to avenge Colonel Chandler's attack on one of their bands the previous spring in the Almagre Mountains, in which one person was killed, several others wounded and the band's livestock seized.

In October of 1856, a Coyotero war party, possibly including Mogollon allies, emerged from their sanctuary in the White Mountains of eastern Arizona and headed northward. They planned to raid the outlying farms and herds of Zuni Pueblo. They soon discovered a large number of sheep poorly guarded by a few pueblo shepherds . . . easy pickings. Seizing the opportunity, the Coyotero attacked, routed the shepherds and seized their stock. The exhilaration of victory quickly evaporated when Zuni warriors overtook them. In the skirmish that followed, the Zuni recovered the entire sheep herd, killed one Apache raider and sent the rest of them fleeing for their lives. The Coyotero returned home empty handed, utterly humiliated but equally determined to inflict a greater revenge on the Zuni . . . just as soon as they got the chance.

News of the Coyotero defeat eventually reached Major Henry Kendrick at Defiance, but since it had resulted in a Zuni victory, there was no need for further action. True enough, for almost two months after the incident, there wasn't a single report of hostile Apache activity in the area. Nonetheless Kendrick's anxieties gnawed at him. He knew very well that the Coyotero's mortification would prod them to strike Zuni again. It might be judicious, he thought, to reconnoiter the vicinity south of the pueblo, bordered as it was on the west by the White Mountains of the Coyotero and on the south by the Gila Wilderness of the Mogollon. If the Apache were around, the signs would be there. Subsequently, Kendrick detailed a scouting party of men from his 2nd Artillery and men of the 3rd Infantry, commanded by 2nd Lt. Richard V. Bonneau. The major asked Henry Dodge to join the scout, and to bring the headman Armijo and several Navajo guides with him.

Dodge's health had improved markedly and he hadn't had a break from the drudgery of agency routine all summer, so he jumped at the chance to get out. They departed Fort Defiance on the morning of November 16th. It was capital riding weather. The air was sharp in its purity and the sky overhead cerulean blue. A cool wind brushed gently through the piñon boughs as they ambled along, evoking wistful memories of the year and times gone past. The intense autumn sunlight cut harsh shadows across landscape, but felt pleasantly warm, almost reassuring, falling across Dodge's shoulders as he leaned back easily against the cantle, the reins draped lazily from a hand, swinging in time with the rhythm of creaking saddle leather. He couldn't recall a time when he felt more at ease.

They arrived at Zuni on the evening of November 17th, where Kendrick enlisted the Zuni war captain Salvador and several of his men to join the reconnaissance. The column departed the following morning, better than forty men strong, following the sacred Salt Trail towards Zuni Salt Lake, a two-day march to the south. The weather remained temperate and the trail well marked, so even with broken and steep terrain, they made excellent time. The stars were gathering over a brilliant crimson sunset as the column descended into the Jaralosa Valley. There Kendrick called a halt and they camped amid the cedar and piñon at the base of basaltic cliffs. Kendrick would later refer to the spot as Cedar Springs. Rations were meager that night: salt pork and hard tack, warmed over a smoldering campfire or two.

It may have been the paltry provisions as well as a sense of adventure that inspired Dodge and Armijo to leave early the next morning in search game. Henry Dodge always enjoyed the hunt. With luck, their next meal would be complemented by fresh venison. Sometime after Henry and Armijo disappeared into the vast Jaralosa, Kendrick and his men moved out. Eventually Armijo rejoined the column later that morning. He was alone, the carcass of a buck hoisted over the rump of his horse. The headman explained that Henry Dodge had gone ahead to follow a promising track and would meet them later after making the kill. Major Kendrick and his scouting party moved on, first ascending then crossing Santa Rita Mesa. The dwindling afternoon had turned quite cold and for the first time a disconcerting breeze hinted the possibility of snow, but the day's travels remained pleasant. The Americans descended the southern flank of Santa Rita, and emerged onto a broad and barren plain that sloped gently down towards their destination, the Sacred Zuni Salt Lake, already a faint apparition in the gathering dusk.

Such a glorious autumn, such an agreeable, tranquil journey in which the world itself seemed altogether right and secure, could delude the most cautious of men into a casual complacency. Such may have been the case with Kendrick and Dodge, who couldn't have known but probably should have at least considered, that all was neither right nor secure.[1]

47

ZUNI SALT LAKE

Oddly, that critical revelation came first not to Major Kendrick, but to Major Enoch Steen, a week earlier as he camped with his company of 1st Dragoons in the middle of the Sonoran desert of southern Arizona. They were a few days on the trail due west of the Copper Mines, having departed Fort Thorn on the Rio Grande for their new post in distant Tucson, in accordance with General Order Number 6. They had settled into their camp for the evening when a ragged and half-starved Mexican boy stumbled out of the dark and into their firelight. Through an interpreter and mouthfuls of rations, the boy explained that he had been a Coyotero captive and had managed to escape from their village because most of the Apache men had left on a raid. The sudden concern furrowing Steen's brow encouraged the boy to elaborate. The war party was very large, he said, up to two hundred warriors . . . composed of Coyotero and Mogollon fighters. He believed they were headed northward to fight the Navajo.

Major Steen immediately realized the importance the boy's information, but there was little his company could do other than send an express to Agent Steck at Fort Thorn. That accomplished, Steen took up the Mexican boy and continued on to Tucson. As fate would have it, when Steen's express arrived at Thorn, Michael Steck was at Fort Stanton meeting with the Mescalero. He wouldn't learn of the Apache expedition for better than a week. The only other individual potentially in a position to alert the territory of the danger was Mangas Coloradas, who at the time was on a trading rendezvous at Lemitar on the Rio Grande. Mangas probably knew of the Coyotero expedition, even if he hadn't known the exact targets. There was very little he didn't know and from having campaigned with the Mogollon and Coyotero in Mexico as recently as September, he was certainly aware they planned to wage war against Zuni and the New Mexicans. A number of the warriors in the expedition were probably his in-laws. In any case, he was either unable or unwilling to warn the Americans. In the meantime, the Coyotero and Mogollon force had divided into at least two raiding parties, which were then descending Zuni Plateau into the Jaralosa. They couldn't possibly have missed Kendrick's trail.

In fact, the Apache were not more than a few miles from Kendrick's column. A small group of Mogollon had arrived at Salt Lake prior to the Americans, and was camped at a sheltered freshwater spring in the nearby hills. They'd come to collect salt at the lake. Of the group, there were several men, a woman and three captives. One of the captives was a boy of about fifteen years of age named Refugio Corrales. The Apaches had kidnapped him over a year before as he herded his father's cattle near Galeña in Chihuahua, Mexico. Suffice it to say, he had been abysmally treated and was desperate for any opportunity to escape.[1] The arrival of the American soldiers came as a shock to the Apache, but a vision of salvation to Refugio. The Mogollon instantly abandoned their salt gathering, covered all evidence of their presence and retreated into the woods.

At nearly the same time, a detachment from the Coyotero expedition had also spotted Kendrick's column. Hidden in the uplands overlooking the Jaralosa Valley, they had observed every movement the Americans made after decamping earlier that morning. The two men who led the party, Isano and Cautivo, both had personal scores to settle. As a Coyotero, Isano was anxious to revenge his brother's death at the hands of the Zuni in the failed raid the previous September. It was he who had actually organized the latest expedition. The other leader, a Mogollon named Cautivo, had joined the expedition with several of his people in hopes of avenging their defeat by Chandler and the American soldiers that previous spring.

Unaware of the presence of either group, Kendrick's column arrived at the lake in the twilight. With no sign yet of Henry Dodge, the major gave the order to camp. Having seen absolutely no evidence of hostile Indians, the major ordered their horses sent out to graze in the meadow below for the night. Hobbled, the animals wouldn't wander far. The men kindled campfires and gnawed wearily on their rations as an intense darkness closed in, matched only in its depth by the profound silence that embraced the land. An hour passed. Still Henry Dodge failed to appear. The wind rose slightly, sending temperature down sharply. It would be a cold night.

Where the hell was Dodge? Obviously the agent must have lost his way in the darkness. After a time, Kendrick ordered the men to light several bonfires along the tops of the surrounding hills, hoping to guide Dodge in. Of course, the signal fires caught the attention of the Mogollon salt gatherers, still hunkered down in the shadows some distance away. Intrigued, the warriors left the woman and their captives under the care of one or two men and crept towards the American camp.

The bonfires blazed long and brightly, but failed to guide Henry Dodge to their camp. After what seemed eternity, Kendrick concluded that, for whatever reason, the agent had been unable to see the signal fires. He ordered his men to discharge their carbines into the air, thinking the racket wouldn't fail to draw Dodge to them. With the first discharge, the few Mogollon remaining at the spring panicked, certain they were under attack, and took to their heels. It was the chance Refugio Corrales had waited for. He dashed pell-mell through the darkness, stumbling blindly over stones and through cedar and cactus, tearing his feet and gashing his legs. So desperate was he, he hardly noticed when the volleys of musketry eventually ceased. Exhausted, he finally found a deep crevice between some cliff boulders and squeezed into it, barely daring to breath. There he remained that entire, numbingly cold night.

Kendrick figured Dodge, an accomplished tracker and woodsmen, had heard the shots and would be in by morning, but the chilling dawn of the 20th revealed no trace of Dodge. There was another unpleasant surprise. Several of the horses sent out to graze the previous evening were missing. For the first time, Major Kendrick felt real apprehension. He immediately sent Armijo and a party of Navajo back along the previous day's trail to try and locate Dodge. At the same time he ordered Lt. Bonneau to find the missing horses, or at least the trail of the thieves who'd taken them. Bonneau and his dragoons failed to recover the horses, but they did discover, cowering in the rocks, Refugio Corrales, who had never been happier in his life to see an American.

After some questioning by Kendrick, Refugio confirmed what the major had feared. The Apaches were, or at least had been, close at hand and were obviously responsible for stealing the horses. Consequently, Kendrick concluded that they were likely responsible for Henry Dodge's disappearance as well. If that were true, it essentially guaranteed Dodge had been killed. The major queried Refugio and asked if he'd seen an American man at any time, dead or alive. The boy had not. Dodge was missing, but at least he wasn't confirmed dead. It was also notable that Kendrick's men hadn't been openly attacked. Chances were they would not be . . . strength in numbers. With no idea of Dodge's location or condition, nothing remained for

Kendrick but to follow Armijo and his men back up the Salt Trail to Cedar Springs. Perhaps after some searching, they'd be able to pick up Dodge's track, a path Kendrick thought gloomily that could very well lead to Henry's mutilated corpse.

Kendrick and Bonneau overtook Armijo's search party the following day. Dodge was still nowhere to be found. Armijo suggested following the path Henry had taken the morning he and the headman had separated. At around noon they discovered not one but several sets of moccasins footprints and pony tracks in the sand. Armijo and the Zuni war captain Salvador immediately interpreted the prints as Apache, not Coyotero but probably Mogollon or Gileños. Among the moccasin prints was the unmistakable impression of a pair of boots . . . Henry Dodge's boots. There was no sign whatsoever that there had been any kind of struggle. The ground around was undisturbed, the prints clear and unmarred. There was no evidence of violence . . . no blood, no hanks of hair, no discarded clothing and, fortunately, no stray body parts. Rather than being killed, it looked for the entire world that Dodge had been standing around having a casual conversation with the Indians.

Seemingly after some discussion, the entire party had mounted their horses and headed off towards the southeast. Armijo and his guides swung onto horseback and galloped off along the trail off towards the Datil Mountains in the hazy southeast. Some twenty miles along they came to a small spring where tracks indicated the Apaches had stopped, perhaps to rest and eat. The head of a deer rested among a set of jagged rocks, staring back at the scouts with glazed, dispassionate eyes: perhaps the buck Dodge had stalked and killed. Just beyond the spring, the pony trail divided. A small group turned westward back towards the Laguna Sal. The larger group angled southeastward towards the Gila wilderness and Mogollon country. With the trail confused and pursuit impracticable, Armijo and his men returned to Kendrick.

Taken all together, the evidence indicated that the Mogollon had done something extraordinary for the Apache, who invariably killed captive men on the spot. They had taken Dodge prisoner. Kendrick had to admit that Dodge himself was extraordinary. Perhaps the Indians had recognized him as a government agent and an old trading partner of Mangas Coloradas, and planned to hold him for ransom or as some kind of bargaining chip. Refugio Corrales offered the opinion that since Dodge hadn't been killed right away, the Apache probably wouldn't harm him at all, adding that once Mangas learned of Dodge's kidnapping, he would certainly arrange for his release. Major Kendrick had to give the boy's assessment some credence. Henry knew the Apache and Mangas Coloradas and they knew him from his days at The Copper Mines. He'd be able to communicate with them. He spoke Spanish, as did many Apache. Dodge probably had learned a smattering of Apache language as well, to facilitate trading.²

If anyone could talk himself out of a fix, it was Henry L. Dodge.

48

EVERY EXERTION

In the early afternoon of November 27th, Brevet Major J. Van Horne in Albuquerque received an urgent dispatch from Major Kendrick at Zuni, dated November 22nd. Due to intervening snowstorms, it had taken five days to arrive, a delay that took on real significance as Van Horne read it.

> "I regret to inform you that H. L. Dodge Indian Agent while hunting on the 19th Nov. some 35 miles south of Zuni was taken captive by the Apaches and carried southward entirely beyond our reach or negotiation. These Apaches are believed to be the Mogollones or the Gileños probably the former. From appearances he was treated kindly. A Mexican captive who came into us says Mangus Colorado or his brother will get information of Captain Dodge being captured, and if so it is presumed that he may be ransomed, which the boy thinks will be the object of the captors.
>
> "The object of this note is to ask you to get this information to Dr. Steck Ind. Agent at Fort Thorn as <u>quickly as possible</u> by whom it is presumed Capt Dodge's liberation can be effected.
>
> "I have also to ask that this information be at once sent to the Governor. . . .
>
> "P.S. Please also to send this information to the Colonel comdg the Department. The Indians who are supposed to have Capt Dodge are said to go into Limitar Doña Ana etc. to trade frequently."¹

Van Horne immediately sent the dispatch on to Bonneville and sent an express with the news of Dodge's capture to Michael Steck at Fort Thorn.² Bonneville received the news that evening and immediately passed the dispatch on to Meriwether. The Governor had been seriously ill for three days, but rose from his sick bed to write Steck.

> "A note from Maj. Kendrick dated on the 22d inst. at Zuni informs me that a party of Indians either Mogollon or Gila Apaches, has captured Agent H. L. Dodge and taken him towards the Gila, and the object of this letter is to instruct you to endeavour to procure his release as soon as possible.
> "You will therefore without delay send out one or more parties of Mimbres Apaches or Mangas Colorada's people, to communicate with the Mogoyone and Gila Apaches, and try if possible to procure the release of Agent Dodge; . . . You are authorized to pay to the parties sent out a reasonable compensation for their services, and also pay to those having him in captivity a ransom if necessary to procure his release, and should any other means than those pointed out to procure his release, suggest themselves to you, you can employ them, of which and the result you will apprise me as soon as practicable."[3]

The long-time Santa Fe trader James J. Webb, heard of Dodge's abduction the same day as Meriwether, and he received the news with a mixture of hopefulness and skepticism.

> "News has arrived today that Captain Dodge has been taken a prisoner by the Apache Indians. He had gone some 20 miles south of Zuni hunting and while out the Indians came upon him and took him prisoner. I think they must have known that he was an officer of the Gov't or they would have killed him. I have never before heard of these Indians taking a grown man prisoner. . . . "[4]

On November 29th, both Meriwether and Bonneville filed reports to their respective supervisors regarding Dodge's capture. Meriwether remained hopeful stating that Henry would be "reserved for ransom" but in a remark betraying his underlying unease added, " . . . although Col. Chandler made an expedition into the country of the Mogoyones last spring and killed several of this band."[5] Colonel Bonneville's report to Army headquarters the same day was brief and businesslike, also pointing out that Dodge's captors were the same band Chandler had attacked the previous spring. His otherwise dryly-worded, professional report concluded with an unexpected touch of emotion.

> "His Excellency Governor Meriwether was immediately advised of the fact, and he was instructed Dr. Steck to use every exertion for the release of the Captain, who he believes is alive and even treated kindly having been seized merely for the ransom. I do really hope so. . . . I can only promise that in case any harm is done him, if necessary the whole strength of the Department shall be used to punish and break up this people."[6]

While search efforts were being launched to locate Dodge, the Coyotero and Mogollon war party was wreaking terror throughout the region, from Zuni to the banks of the Rio Grande. They bushwhacked a party of New Mexicans on the road between Belen to Cubero, a mere fifteen miles from the river, badly wounding a man and abducting two women. The same band drove off Luna's cattle herd after stripping the herders of their possessions and their clothing. Later they surrounded the Los Lunas army post's wood cutting detail and dared the soldiers to attack them. Sensibly, the woodcutters fled.[7]

On December 5th, a full sixteen days after Dodge had vanished, Michael Steck finally returned to Fort Thorn, having been delayed at Fort Stanton by the snow, and found Kendrick's dispatch and two urgent directives from Meriwether. In his absence, Captain Thomas Claiborne, the commander at Fort Thorn, had sent Ammon Barnes, a local citizen who ran a ferry across the Rio Grande, and two Chiricahua men, Costates and Ratón, to meet with Mangas Coloradas at the Copper Mines. They had left on December 1st with Claiborne's authorization to spend up to $1000 for Dodge's ransom.[8] After conferring with Claiborne, Steck met with Delgadito, who wasn't optimistic about their chances of getting Dodge back alive, especially if his captors were Pinal or Coyotero Apache, as he believed they were. Nevertheless, he agreed to send another scout to the Almagre Mountains and the southern Mogollon villages in search of information. Should no information surface within a few days Steck fully intended to send Apache runners to Coyotero country in the White Mountains.

Out of the blue, in the first week in December, splendid news arrived at Fort Defiance. Captain William Gordon, in command while Major Henry Kendrick was absent on general court martial duty in Santa Fe, had received word the Apache had brought Henry L. Dodge to Zuni to surrender to the Americans. Gordon immediately sent a detachment thundering off to get Dodge, but upon their arrival, they discovered no Apaches and no Dodge. It seemed nobody at Zuni had heard any such news. It had been nothing but a rumor.⁹

On December 12th, Barnes, Costates and Ratón returned to Fort Thorn with similar results. There was no sign of Dodge. It was as if he had simply evaporated. Steck therefore concluded that Dodge's abductors must have been the more remote Pinal or Coyotero. Although there had been no new information on Dodge's fate, Mangas Coloradas assured Barnes that he would find out what had become of him.¹⁰ Five days later Mangas confirmed Steck's fears. The Coyotero and Mogollon Apache were indeed waging war on the white and had divided into two parties. The western party had struck the Navajo, Zuni and Acoma, seizing sheep, horses, mules and two wagonloads of provisions, while the eastern group had raided the roads and settlements along the Rio Grande. As for Henry L. Dodge, Mangas confessed he had discovered absolutely nothing, but had sent his brother José Mangas and a companion, Tinaja, into the Gila to make further inquiries. It would be no small quest, requiring José to traverse the Gila Wilderness, the Mogollon and the Almagre Mountains in winter conditions that would severely test his legendary Apache toughness, in an uncertain attempt to locate and meet with the warring faction of Mogollon. The odyssey would take two weeks.¹¹

Meanwhile, the Apache war parties continued their rampage, seemingly immune to the deep snow and biting cold, culminating on December 22nd, when the Coyotero exacted their long-awaited revenge on the Zuni by slaughtering ten of the pueblo. Then, without any apparent reason or warning, the Apache raids stopped, and an eerie silence descended, inaugurating a two-week vacuum of any news whatsoever about the fate of Henry L. Dodge. Christmas passed quietly, then the month of December and New Year's Day of 1857, without incident or information, as winter kept its grip locked on the land.

Then on January 2nd, José Mangas and Tinaja, weary and weather-beaten, appeared at Fort Thorn.

49

A WANTON ACT INEXPLICABLE

June 1st, 1883 was a warm and humid one, as late spring days could be in Burlington, Iowa. The heavy air enveloping the First Congregational Church hadn't discouraged the people from gathering there for the signature event of the season, the Commemoration of the Fiftieth Anniversary of the Settlement of Iowa. A thousand or so Iowans would attend, among them several of the old pioneers themselves. Inside, seated at the dais discreetly fidgeting with the notes for a speech was seventy-one-year-old Augustus Caesar Dodge, the foremost pioneer of them all. The venerable old Democrat had been appointed Chairman of the Executive Committee and President of the Day in recognition of his contributions to Iowa. The executive committee had awarded him a nostalgic souvenir for the occasion, an ornate hickory cane "cut from the precincts where sleeps the immortal Jackson."[1]

It was a token of a more glorious time. Plaudits had come infrequently for Augustus and the Democrats over the last decade or two. Iowa itself had been steadfastly Republican for nearly thirty years.

But it was his due. Augustus Caesar Dodge had spent his entire life in public service. He had schools, streets and counties named for him. His political successes had started early in life and his rise rapid. In 1838, at the age of 26, he was Registrar of Public Lands for the Iowa Territory, was appointed general of the Iowa militia, and later served four terms as his territory's delegate to Congress. In 1848 when Iowa matriculated to statehood, he became its first senator, having influential roles in passing both the Compromise of 1850 and the Kansas-Nebraska Act. Although the stream of Northern immigrants gradually shifted the balance of power in Iowa from Democrat to Whig, Augustus continued to enjoy political success. After losing his senate seat in 1856, the following year he was appointed by President Franklin Pierce as Envoy Extraordinary and Minister Plenipotentiary to Spain . . . all this before he'd reached fifty. As it turned out, that was to be the high mark.

Augustus' loyalties eventually proved his undoing. He had always been seen as an apologist for the South. When his appointment as United States Minister to Spain ended in 1859, he returned to Iowa to find his constituents, horrified by the sectional violence in Kansas, firmly Republican. Augustus was defeated in a bid for governor that year by a Republican, Samuel J. Kirkwood, and in 1860 similarly rejected for senator. The calamity of the Civil War effectively extinguished any remaining hope for national aspiration. In 1874, he managed to get himself elected for a two-year term as mayor of Burlington, but as an independent rather than a Democrat. In his later years, Augustus resigned himself to promoting the causes of temperance and education and in giving guest lectures at Iowa pioneer gatherings . . . all fairly benign and uncontroversial activities.

Dr. Salter, the pastor and master of ceremonies, introduced him, and Augustus rose from his seat, slowly and deliberately. Polite applause rippled through the audience. His features, the receding chin and fading hairline, the down-turned mouth and a beaked nose framed by bushy eyebrows, inspired the image of a paunchy old eagle. He began to speak in the same manner in which he moved, slowly and deliberately. No rambling or fussing; the old fellow was still plenty sharp. After disposing of the requisite gestures of appreciation, Augustus spoke of the earliest days of Iowa, extolling the sacrifices and contributions of those dwindling pioneers "fast falling like ripened grain before the reaper."

> "They leave behind the glory of the well fought battle, which has reclaimed an immense wilderness from the occupancy of savages and beasts of prey, converting it into productive fields; thus facilitating the onward march of improvement, and dispensing comfort and happiness to civilized man."[2]

Surpisingly, his narrative unexpectedly turned to the pioneering days of his Wisconsin youth, extolling the triumph of Christian civilization over the brutal savages, who during the Blackhawk War had burned homes, slaughtered livestock, and had kidnapped the virgins Rachel and Silvia Hall to be subjected to unimaginable abuses, while the rest of the Hall family received no mercy.

> "All the victims were carefully scalped, their bodies mutilated and mangled; the little children were chopped to pieces with axes, the women were tied up by the heels to the walls of the house, their clothing falling over their heads left their naked persons exposed to public gaze."

Such barbaric acts, Augustus intoned, were not isolated anomalies or vicious traits peculiar to the Sauk, Fox and Winnebago tribes, but rather an ingrained quality of the entire Red Race, that from the "first landing of our forefathers . . . down to and including the bloody events of the present day, truly does history repeat itself." Cruelty was a universal trait of the Indian.[3]

Augustus then paused, reaching deep into the gloomy tomb of his reminiscences, and brought out an apparation, one long lost and all but forgotten...

"My own brother, Henry La Fayette Dodge, U. S. Indian agent in New Mexico, by appointment of President Pierce, was captured by the Appaches in 1857, and burned to death at the stake. Before his sad fate became known, as it did through friendly Indians, large rewards of every kind were offered in vain, for his ransom. Besides the tender of money; he might have successfully pleaded (for he could speak ten different dialects) before any tribunal, other than the infuriated Appache, the preservation of the lives of two of their race, an Indian woman and her child, snatched by his own hands, from the jaws of death in the heat of battle at Bad Axe, exposed as he was to the fire of friends and foes when he accomplished the deed."[4]

Lafayette's selfless valor at Bad Axe had made his gruesome destruction at the hands of the Indians all the more monstrous. It was, as the *Milwaukee Sentinel* had stated thirty years earlier a "wicked and wanton act inexplicable" and that the treacherous savage had "Joel like, smote the benefactor of their race."[5] Burned at the stake, a vision of Hell itself, of shrieking red devils dancing as Lafayette stood stripped and bound upon the pyre, his brave but desperate demeanor finally shattering into agonized screams as the flames peeled the living skin from his shins.

Some in the audience looked down or away, as if to block the grotesque vision. Others nodded their heads sympathetically. Augustus had the crowd spellbound, for even to that day, such was the mystique of the American Frontier, imbedded like an iron spike in the American psyche.

Augustus' tale wasn't precisely true to the facts, of course, and the old codger knew it. But the truth could be freely sacrificed to perpetuate that mystique, that sacred spring from which the very values of America flowed: self-reliance and ambition, industriousness and perseverance, piousness and bravery. The Indian played a fundamental part in that myth and A. C. Dodge would be damned if it were to be sullied, even by the truth. Two years earlier, Helen Hunt Jackson had written *A Century of Dishonour*, a scathing indictment of the United States' treatment of the Indian race. It had become a national best seller, rattling the locks of American's conscience and for many, desecrating the Myth of the Frontier. Now in its defense Augustus had resurrected his own brother, had even uttered his name, La Fayette, a name so shrouded in scandal that for years it had hardly been whispered, even among the Dodge family.

In five short months, Augustus C. Dodge himself would succumb to the Grim Reaper, slain by pneumonia brought on by a severe November cold. At the funeral, three hundred Iowan children showered the old man's casket and his memory with garlands of flowers. He was buried at Burlington in Aspen Grove Cemetery, among friends and family and the old pioneers, beside the tomb of his father Henry Dodge, who had died sixteen years earlier. Engraved on his headstone an epitaph consistent with the temperament of the proper and important man entombed within;

> *"Life is not a pleasure nor a pain,*
> *But a serious business*
> *Which it is our duty to carry through and terminate*
> *With honor."*

His older brother, Henry Lafayette Dodge probably couldn't have disagreed more.[6]

There had been no magnificent epitaph etched on a granite obelisk to mark Henry Lafayette's life, no mantle of perfumed flowers draping his casket to sweeten recollections of him. What remained with the family for three generations was the mystery... a nagging miasma of melancholy floating just beneath the consciousness. As Charles Wentz observed when he wrote Augustus Dodge from Navajo country in 1864, a painful ambiguity had always shrouded Lafayette's last moments for "no living white man saw him fall." Certainly there was a lingering suspicion that his supposed friends, the Navajo themselves, had murdered Henry.

For a century after he had left Kendrick's camp at Cedar Springs and ridden into oblivion, accounts of Henry's fate were short on fact and long on romance. In 1941 Richard Van Valkenburgh related that, according to an old Navajo informant, Red Shirt had joined the annual Navajo antelope hunt south of Zuni. While the medicine men of the tribe were conducting a ceremony to insure a successful hunt, Henry slipped away through a curtain of lightly falling snow. He never returned. The following morning, his Navajo friends traced his tracks to the peak of a ridge. When they looked down, they discovered his corpse outlined in a pool of gore with "his body was so filled with Chiricahua Apache arrows that it looked like a porcupine."[7]

At roughly the same time an Old West hobbyist and amateur writer, Mrs. White Mountain Smith, offered a version told her by the venerable Henry Chee Dodge, Navajo entrepreneur and first tribal chairman. Chee acknowledged Captain

Dodge was both a fine soldier and man, that he had "treated the Navajos like they, too, were men," but denied he was Dodge's son. He did relate that one fall day Lafayette, Armijo and other Navajo companions rode down to Wide Ruins to search for a lost silver mine. Dodge's party looked in vain up and down the ravines, and when it began to snow they gave up the search. Lafayette suggested they head over towards Zuni and hunt until the snow melted, at which time they'd return to continue prospecting. Once they had pitched camp south of Zuni, Dodge and Armijo went out to hunt up some venison for dinner. Armijo was the first to bring down a buck, so he remained with it. Lafayette continued up over a hill and into history.

> "After awhile the Navajos followed his tracks in the snow and found him killed. He lay face down in the snow, his clothing gone, and his body mutilated. The tracks of the murderers were those of Apaches with the turned up toes on Apache moccasins. The Navajos ran quickly away and left him because he was no longer their friend when he was dead, but evil spirits were around him to harm the Navajos. It was many months before soldiers found out what had happened."[8]

On August 23, 1901, Mr. William F. Fox wrote to Mr. T. R. Woodward, a Dodge family historian in Chicago, offering him information on Lafayette's fate. William Fox was the husband of Mary Therese Dodge-Fox, Henry L. Dodge's daughter. William, Mary and her mother, Adele Bequette-Dodge, who was by then a cranky 89 years old, were living together in Chicago. It may have been Mary's tenacious desire to soothe her lingering sorrow that prompted her husband's letter, to discover not so much the details of her father's death, but the hushed circumstances, that conspiracy of silence, of why he had abandoned her in the first place. She had been but six when her father left them. As a small girl herself, Mary Therese's granddaughter, Elizabeth, understood that her grandmother had never really come to terms with that heartbreak.

> "She always, all her life, had a feeling of sadness and longing where her father was concerned. It was undoubtedly because of this intense feeling that she made me promise that I would someday find his grave at Fort Defiance and take some earth from his grave and put it on her own. She lived to be 93."[9]

With Mary's consent, William wrote a synopsis of the particulars concealed in the crumbling yellow leaves of some ancient letters, written by a man named Wentz in 1864, and sent it to Woodward. Lafayette had been slain by Apaches. The soldiers had searched for his body in vain. All they had found was his skull, placed between two rocks, "thirty miles from Zuma towards the Giles rivers."[10] The Apache had burned him at the stake and all that remained was his charred skull.

It was explanation the family came to accept. In 1886, three years after Augustus' death, Robert Dodge formally enshrined that explanation in his Dodge genealogy, titled *Tristram Dodge and Descendants*.

> "The eldest son, Henry L. Dodge, who had achieved distinction in the Indian Wars under his father, and had served as High Sheriff by election, and also as Clerk of the United States District Court for Iowa County, Wisconsin, was appointed agent for the Navajos, whose language he spoke as he did that of some ten other tribes, was captured by the Zuni savages and burnt to death at the stake. This shocking act of savage barbarity was perpetrated near Fort Defiance, New Mexico, in 1856. He left a widow and four children."[11]

Zuni, Navajo or Apache, it didn't matter. All that mattered was that they were Indian.

Augustus Dodge had long known the truth of his brother's fate. He'd had access to the complete reports filed with the Secretary of War and the Secretary of the Interior. Yet as early as 1858, the gnawing disquiet prodded him into making inquiries. He wrote Samuel M. Yost, the editor of the *Santa Fe Gazette* at the time, and asked him to travel to Fort Defiance to get information about his brother. One didn't dismiss a request by the Envoy Extraordinary and Minister Plenipotentiary to Spain, so in early autumn of that year Yost obliged him.[12]

Upon arriving at Fort Defiance, Yost obtained the facts from John Weber, who had been sutler at the fort during that period. Weber related that Lafayette and Navajo chief Armijo had left Kendrick's camp to go hunting. Armijo shot a deer. Lafayette spotted a second deer in the distance. Moving up over the rise after it, he disappeared, never to return. Weber then guided Yost to a grave on a sandy slope outside the fort. Someone had erected a crude headboard.

> "To the Memory of H. L. Dodge
> Aged 45 years
> Agent of the Navajos,

*Killed by Apache Indians on the 15th of Nov. 1856
A portion of his remains rest beneath this spot . . ."*

On September 29th, 1858, the inscription appeared in the Santa Fe Weekly Gazette, nearly two years after Lafayette's disappearance.[13]

Apparently Yost's explanation hadn't been sufficient for A. C. Dodge. Six years later he asked Charles W. Wentz, a German immigrant and member of Company G, 1st Cavalry of New Mexico Volunteers, to investigate Lafayette's fate, to locate the grave and procure a fitting tombstone for it. Wentz was stationed at Fort Canby, originally Fort Defiance, in the latest and final Navajo war. In response, Wentz, or the "Old Dragoon" as he styled himself, interviewed several career soldiers at Fort Canby and wrote three meandering and pedantic letters to Augustus C. Dodge. He was clearly pandering to the old politician, yet through his suffocating verbosity, something vaguely similar to the truth managed to escape.

Lafayette had departed Fort Defiance on November 9th or 10th with twenty-five men of Company B 2nd Artillery under Major Kendrick and Lieutenant Alley to map a road between the fort and Zuni Salt Lake. The priest of Cebolleta, Padre Rafael Cháves, ten Zuni and fifteen Navajo men as well as "five Navajo squaws", accompanied the column. After five days in the saddle, the party camped at Cedar Springs. The following morning Lafayette left the camp alone to hunt antelope and wild turkey, telling the Navajo and Zuni to remain behind. Kendrick's command resumed their march two hours after his departure. When Lafayette failed to show up at Salt Lake that evening, Major Kendrick had signal fires set on the surrounding hills, then ordered his men to fire their rifles into the air, all in vain. The next morning Kendrick discovered a number of their horses had been stolen. While searching for them, the soldiers found a Mexican boy hiding in the rocks. The lad told Kendrick that about fifty Apache had taken their animals and that they had also "killed the Captain (meaning your brother)."

"I have just been informed by an Old Soldier who was present with Major Kendrick when Capt. H. L. Dodge was killed. He says it was Mangas Coloradas' (Red Sleeve) band of Apache who killed him."

Supposedly, Mangas had Lafayette killed out of jealousy because the agent had been the "Great Father of the Navajo", and was nearly worshipped by all the Indians of the tribe.

Acting on the boy's information, Kendrick had sent out a search party, but there was no living sign of Captain Dodge. The soldiers did find his tracks in a sandy canyon and followed them for nine miles, where the trail ended and Lafayette "must have had a rough and tumble fight with the Apaches on foot." An imprint in the sand was clearly visible of a man lying on his back, as if the Apache had lassoed Lafayette, dragged him off his horse then picked him up and carried him away on foot. That was as far as the searchers got. According to Wentz, Kendrick was completely unstrung over having lost his good friend.

> "Major Kendrick and Padre Chavez and the Navajoes wept like children at the loss they sustained in your brother's demise."

Subsequently, it was Kendrick who personally led the search party to find Henry's body the following February. After a thorough search, all the men found was his skull, seven miles from where they believed he'd been slain.

> "... the skull had been placed between the points of two projecting rocks. Dr. Leatherman, Surgeon of the 3rd Infy. Examined it with great care and from internal evidence afforded by the teeth and the circumstance, pronounced it to be that of your brother."[14]

Wentz assured Augustus that Lafayette's head had been solemnly interred at Fort Defiance and that "every soldier and Navajo Indian has dropped a tear over the sacred spot, a tribute of respect to the brave and manly qualities of Capt. H. L. Dodge." The Old Dragoon added with gratification that Mangas Coloradas was later captured and shot to death by soldiers. "Thus the murderer of your brother fell by the hand of White Men."[15] In his last letter to Augustus, Wentz included a clipping from the Santa Fe Gazette, a three-part heroic ode to the trapping and killing of that bloodthirsty Chiricahua chief Mangas Coloradas.[16] Wentz stated that he had actually seen Lafayette's grave, strewn with wild flowers and promised Augustus he would procure a proper tombstone for his brother's final resting place.

He never did.

50

THE WORST OF NEWS

In Santa Fe, Governor Meriwether must have felt he was living on the doorstep of hell. He'd been sick for most of November and into December and still wasn't well. Henry Dodge had been kidnapped by Apaches, and every subsequent effort to get information about his fate, much less having him ransomed, had proved fruitless. In defiance of the harsh winter, the Apache had continued terrorizing the territory and Meriwether feared their successes had inspired the San Juan Navajo to resume robbing the settlements. A citizen, Pedro Armijo had filed a complaint that in November the San Juan Navajo had stolen about thirty mules and horses. Fortunately, he was able to recover all but four of the animals.[1] God only knew what other tribes would resume raiding.

Governor Meriwether expected the imminent eruption of a wider Apache war. Costates and Ratón, the two Mimbres Apache men who had faithfully assisted Ammon Barnes in sleuthing out Dodge, had been brutally murdered, the result of a sublimely perverse coincidence. On the night of December 29th, New Mexican raiders stole sixteen horses from the Mimbres Apache camp on the west bank of the Rio Grande. The following day, Costates and Ratón pursued and overtook the raiders, but they escaped southward on the fastest horses after abandoning eleven of the Apache ponies. At Agent Steck's urging, Costates and Ratón then tracked the horse thieves as far south as Mesilla. With darkness gathering, the two Apaches decided to spend the night at the San Diego ferry house along the Rio Grande, and then continue their pursuit in the morning. They apparently asked and received permission to sleep there from the two New Mexicans running the ferry.

The following morning, a group of passing U. S. soldiers noticed the ferry house was mysteriously deserted. Upon entering, they discovered the floor and walls of the ferry house splattered with blood and globules of human flesh. After some probing around the scene, the troopers found Costates' mutilated body bobbing in the Rio Grande. His head had been split open with an axe and his entire scalp torn off. They never located the corpse of his companion, Ratón. The two New Mexicans in charge of the ferry house had also vanished, murderers presumably fleeing for the safety of Chihuahua. A quick investigation revealed that one of the ferrymen was named Martín Corrales. That in itself was of little significance, except that Martín happened to be the older brother of Refugio Corrales, the very lad Kendrick's men had discovered shivering among the rocks near Zuni Salt Lake the morning after Dodge had vanished. After rescuing Refugio, Kendrick had sent him to Santa Fe, where he was doing chores for the Army while waiting to be sent home. Refugio told the soldiers he had a mother and a brother José in El Paso and another brother Martín living at Las Cruces. Martín, knowing nothing of Refugio's rescue, had killed Costates and Ratón to avenge his little brother's kidnapping.[2]

Ordinarily Meriwether would not have lost much sleep over the lives of two Apache, but the territory was already at war with the Coyotero and Mogollon. Now it seemed likely they'd shortly be fighting the Mimbres as well, "for notwithstanding the promise of Delgadito, who is the head chief of this band . . . I doubt his ability to restrain his people from retaliating upon some of our innocent people."[3]

In regards to the Navajo, the state of affairs with that tribe was touchy. Since Dodge's disappearance, the Navajo Agency had ground to a halt and would have collapsed altogether had it not been for Major Henry L. Kendrick's assumption of the more critical responsibilities. At the close of December, Kendrick had visited Meriwether to update him on the condition of the agency. The Navajo, he explained, were completely destitute of tobacco "and other little necessaries usually obtained from their Agent." The governor dutifully gave him 122 pounds of tobacco, believing that Kendrick would make the best temporary replacement until Dodge had been liberated. Juan Anaya, the agency interpreter, Gallegos the herder and the blacksmith George Carter hadn't been paid yet. Meanwhile, a variety of creditors had presented Meriwether with bills yet unsatisfied for personal and Indian goods Dodge had purchased, not the least of whom was John Weber, the sutler at Fort Defiance.[4] Much to Meriwether's consternation, not one but two traders had presented him with drafts on Henry Dodge's 4th quarter salary. He dismissed it in his report to Manypenny as clearly an error.

> "I presume that he must have drawn these two Drafts for the same quarter through mistake, as I understand that the one in favour of Speigelburg, Buithner & Co. was drawn several months before the other, and he could not have expected that I would approve of you to pay both."[5]

On January 2nd, 1857, the very day that José Mangas and Tinaja had returned to Fort Thorn, Meriwether's initial report of Dodge's kidnapping arrived on Commissioner Manypenny's desk in Washington. The following day Manypenny forwarded it to his supervisor, Secretary of the Interior Robert McClelland, who in turn sent an urgent letter to Secretary of War Jefferson Davis, requesting that the

Army assist in redeeming Dodge. Remarkably, at that moment Jefferson Davis was sending his own letter to McClelland, having received Bonneville's report of Dodge's capture in the same mail.

> "Sir:
> I have the honor to transmit, herewith, for your information copies of letters arrived yesterday, from Colonel Bonneville and Brevet Major Kendrick and Van Horne reporting the capture, by the Mogollon Apaches, of Captain Dodge, Indian Agent for the Navajos.[6]

A messenger was promptly dispatched to locate Senator Henry Dodge, who was in Washington at the time. The senator's stern and frontier-hardened features betrayed none of the many emotions that swept over him at hearing the news, but a feeling of helplessness could well have been one of them. The Apache had kidnapped his son at the end of November, well over a month ago. Senator Dodge understood painfully well that, in these matters, what might happen to Lafayette had probably already happened, be it joyful or tragic. In the end all Senator Dodge could do was to wish for the best and send some gesture of concern . . . perhaps of love . . . for his long exiled son. For that, he pulled from his coat pocket the two letters from his teenage granddaughters, Mary Therese and little Christiana, nicknamed "Kitty." They were Lafayette's girls, daughters he hadn't seen in more than a decade. The letters themselves were of no real importance other than as a memento of hearth and home and family affections. Kitty didn't remember her father, but Mary did, quite clearly and poignantly.

Senator Dodge solemnly folded the letters, sealed them into an envelope, and firmly addressed it.

> "Capt. Henry L. Dodge, U. S. Indian Agent, Santa Fe, New Mexico, Care of Gov. Meriwether."

With luck it would arrive on the Meriwether's desk by the middle of February and with the blessing of God's hand and acquiescent fortune, he would be able to deliver it.

José Mangas and Tinaja crossed the dusky parade ground of Fort Thorn, their expressions betraying nothing of what they had learned after two harrowing weeks beyond the Gila Wilderness. They waited outside of the commandant's office in inscrutable silence. Presently, they were ushered in by Captain Claiborne and Michael Steck. In the lantern glow, the two Americans listened intently as José

Mangas reported what they'd learned. The news was, to say the least, disheartening. After several days traveling from the Copper Mines westward and traversing both the Burro and Peloncillo mountain ranges, the two Apache had managed to locate the renegade Mogollon near the arid Dos Cabezas Mountains, seventy-some miles east of Tucson. There were eight to ten families under the leadership of Cautivo and Isana, and they were indeed the band that Chandler had attacked the previous spring, the same band that had just returned from their raiding expedition with the Coyotero.

José and Tinaja found Cautivo and Isana resolutely unrepentant and defiant, so much so they bragged out the details of their exploits. They had entered Zuni country to avenge their losses in previous American and Zuni victories. After killing nine New Mexicans near Cubero, they divided their forces. The Coyotero headed for Zuni to settle an old score, while Cautivo and Isana's party ranged up and down the Puerco River valley, seizing sheep and better than one hundred head of horse and cattle. Doubling back, the two victorious war parties reunited at the headwaters of the Rio San Francisco. After dividing the booty among them, the Coyotero returned to the White Mountains with the bulk of the captured stock, while Cautivo and Isana's people made their way southward towards the Gila. As evidence of the truth of their tale, the Mogollon showed José and Tinaja mutton from some of the sheep they'd captured and threatened that, if by some coincidental misfortune the Americans found their location and attacked them, they would hold both men and the Mimbres bands responsible.[7]

None of that came as a surprise to either Steck or Claiborne, but it begged the question—what had they learned of Henry L. Dodge? Skirting the point, José Mangas and Tinaja replied they had seen no American, and were convinced that none had been captured or was being held captive by the Mogollon or any other Apache group. Steck realized the evasive response foreshadowed tragic news. José Mangas continued. It seemed Cautivo and Isana had mentioned that early in the expedition, as they scouted the Jaralosa along the north face of the Zuni Plateau, they'd come across an American hunting alone.

They had shot him dead.

The following day, Michael Steck wrote Governor Meriwether.

"As I have heard of no American being killed and from the fact of Agent H. L. Dodge having been out hunting at the time there is but little doubt He is the American referred to by those Indians and that he was killed."[8]

In his subsequent report to Commissioner Manypenny on the 27th, David Meriwether accepted the obvious.

"I have the honor herewith to enclose you a letter from Agent M. Steck relative to the fate of Agent Dodge, and the murder of Costales and Ratton a Mimbres Apache Indian, also copies of two letters from Capt Claiborne, and a report of Leiut, Steen on the same subject.

"I very much fear that the information contained in these seals the fate of poor Dodge"[9]

Meriwether would journey to Fort Defiance himself and collect the late agent's books and papers. In the meantime, he requested Colonel Bonneville commanding the department to recover Henry Dodge's remains.

51

WITH DUE SOLEMNITY

On January 28th, a raiding party of San Juan Navajo attacked Pedro Armijo's sheep near Laguna; it was the second time in three months. The bandits seized several hundred sheep, along with several donkeys, four guns, two dogs and the shepherds themselves. After driving the animals two days, the raiders stopped, butchered four of the sheep and packed the meat on four of the donkeys. They then stripped the pastores, tied them up and, abandoning the flock of sheep, rode away with the herders' dogs, their guns and their clothes. Armijo didn't find out about the theft until after the shepherds had untied one another with their teeth and made their way to Cebolleta. Guided by Juan Anaya, Pedro Armijo tracked his animals into Navajo country. There he met several sympathetic Navajo headmen, who returned 275 of his animals and promised to help him get the balance. In the course of conversation, the headmen told Armijo they had heard a rumor that their agent Red Shirt was dead, but believed he was still alive and that they planned to send five hundred men into Mogollon country to rescue him when spring arrived.[1]

A dispatch Major Henry L. Kendrick received at about that same time was substantially less hopeful. It was from Colonel Bonneville in Santa Fe, dated January 30th, 1857. In it were orders simple and straightforward.

> "The Department Commander directs that you send two officers and forty men to search for the body of Captain Dodge, and, if found, to have it interred at Fort Defiance.
>
> "As you are more familiar with the place or point where Captain Dodge left your camp, it is thought you are more capable of giving the necessary instructions in regard to the search than any one else and the Colonel Commanding therefore leaves this matter entirely to yourself - From the letter of Dr. Steck, of which you have been furnished with a copy, there appears to be no doubt that Captain Dodge was killed at or near the place of his capture."[2]

Kendrick detailed Lieutenant J. Howard Carlisle to lead the recovery effort. The major was thorough in his instructions. He realized he was sending the recovery party into potential danger. The Apache had again been active, raiding Laguna as recently as the week before.

> "The object of the expedition being to recover the body of Captain Dodge, you will seek to avoid hostilities, so far as it can be done with propriety, until after that object is attained, or from necessity abandoned. Although we are at war with the Mogollones you will not proceed farther than the object for which you are sent requires, unless circumstances should render it manifestly proper to do so. Under these limitations, should you find yourself in the vicinity of hostile Indians, you will act as you would were you in an Indian enemy's country under any other circumstances."

He instructed Carlisle to do a detailed search, at least as far as the small spring where they'd found the deer head, and to keep his search within 60 miles of where Dodge had apparently been seized. The extra rations provided were to allow the soldiers to make a thorough search, not a lengthy march. There he left it, encouraging Carlisle to use his own best judgment to accomplish the mission.[3]

Lieutenant John W. Alley, who had known Henry Dodge at Cebolleta, was assigned to accompany Carlisle in the recovery effort. With them came Dodge's longtime interpreter Juan Anaya, his friend the headman Armijo, and several Navajo warriors. The expedition, complemented with a string of pack mules and two rumbling supply wagons, left Fort Defiance at noon on February 5th under a fast falling curtain of snow that showed no intention of letting up. It continued to snow all that day, all that night and all of the following day. It was still snowing when Carlisle's chilled detachment trudged into Zuni in the late afternoon of February 7th. They found the welcome there as about as warm as the weather. The Zuni were decidedly set against helping Carlisle, either in supplies or manpower. The lieutenant proposed hiring the war captain Salvador and a few of his men who had been with Dodge in November, but they begged off, insisting that it would be impossible to find the body—the snow was too deep and their starved horses would never survive such an exacting trip. The Navajo Armijo suspected the Zuni were afraid, and derisively announced he would go on inspite of them. Salvador retorted that Armijo's horse would probably give out. The headman merely replied that he would persevere on foot if need be, until he found Red Shirt's body.

Armijo's comment may have shamed the Zuni some, for Carlisle later reported that Zuni guides had indeed accompanied him on the search. Nevertheless, the pueblo was reluctant to even help the Americans with provisions and preparations for the search. It was an annual feast day, they explained, and people were much too busy. Lieutenant Carlisle astutely deduced the real reason for their refusal to assist him.

> "... But the fact that the bodies of the ten Zuni Indians killed by the Apaches within ten miles of the Pueblo were allowed to remain for some time where they were killed and were at last brought in by stealth in the night, & that their sheep were left for some two or three days without herders, rendered it extremely doubtful whether the reasons assigned were the true ones."

Their bitterness over this inequity was understandable.

Carlisle and Alley had the two freight wagons unloaded, rations and equipment prepared and loaded onto the pack mules. While preparations were underway, Sergeant Fallon and four soldiers arrived from Defiance with a follow-up dispatch from Kendrick. The major had received new information from Steck indicating Dodge had probably been killed near Cedar Springs where Kendrick's men had camped that first night out. It was initially thought Dodge had been captured and taken a short distance, then killed after the Apache had interrogated him about Kendrick's party. In retrospect, it was a very un-Apache scenario. It was more likely

Dodge had been shot outright, after which an Apache had put on Dodge's boots and led the agent's horse around and about to confuse any trackers. Kendrick suggested Carlisle search some three or four miles south along the route that Armijo and Dodge had taken that morning after leaving Cedar Springs, particularly between the places where Kendrick and Bonneau had thought the agent had had a "friendly talk" and where Dodge had apparently been captured.[4]

Carlisle and his detachment left Zuni on the 9th, plowing their way along the Salt Trail in snow better than a foot deep and getting deeper. They arrived at Cedar Springs the following morning, where winter had lightened its assault. Spread below them, the Jaralosa was a vast glittering sheet of snow. That sight alone seemed to confirm the Zuni position that finding Dodge's remains, lying somewhere out there for almost three months, would be nearly impossible. In truth, there was no proof other than an Apache tale that his body was even out there.

All the same, Lieutenant Carlisle immediately got the search underway. After organizing a system of signals for an emergency, he split his command. Carlisle, Alley, and twenty-five soldiers continued along the trail into the snowbound Jaralosa, guided by Armijo and his Navajo trackers. The balance of the command remained in camp. In time they arrived at the place where Armijo claimed he had parted with Henry Dodge. Following Kendrick's instructions, they then moved towards Zuni Plateau and Cantalero Springs, wedged in one of the many canyons cutting into the plateau. Carlisle's search party eventually discovered the point where Dodge was supposedly captured. Amazingly, three months after the fact they were still able to discern evidence that people had been there.

> "... some four or five Apaches had evidently been seated for some time & apparently an American with them. We searched in the vicinity for the remainder of the day without finding anything that could aid us in our search except the heel of one of Captain Dodge's shoes which was found at the place where he was supposed to have been taken prisoner..."

Heels were an irritation to the Apache. If one of them had claimed Dodge's boots, they would have removed the heels. It was a sure sign that Dodge was dead, that the Indians were already wearing Dodge's clothes. Logically then, Dodge's body should be directly behind them, back up the trail they'd just come down. Finding the remains wouldn't be easy. The entire area was a convolution of hillocks and arroyos, some filled with several feet of snow. Armijo's first attempts to backtrack Dodge's trail failed. The signs were so confused Armijo was convinced that Red Shirt was wandering aimlessly lost. Carlisle doubted it. Dodge had probably never been lost in his life. Even under the insightful scrutiny of Navajo trackers, the Apache were proving to be masters of deception. In the end, the day produced nothing other than frostbite and frustration. The exhausted searchers retired to camp.

The following morning, Lieutenant Carlisle decided to approach the problem differently. He and Alley led the search party back down the Salt Trail to where Armijo and Dodge had originally parted. If the trails were too confused to track, the lieutenant concluded, then they would do a blanket search of the terrain. Man for man, they would spread out in a skirmish line, each man easy hailing distance from the next, in order to search as much ground as possible. He instructed Lieutenant Alley and his fifteen men to form their line there and slowly work their way southward. Carlisle then took Armijo and the remaining men a few miles south towards the base of Zuni Plateau, where Dodge's boot heel had been discovered. They would sweep to the northwest, back towards Alley's line. If Henry L. Dodge's body were anywhere at all in the vicinity, it would lie between the two converging lines.

Slowly their ranks moved towards one another in a meticulous search of the immense and snow-hushed tableland, bathed in a tepid and uncomforting winter light. The morning crept by in an eerie quietness broken only by the crunch of snow under foot and the infrequent remark of a soldier or two. One hour slipped by and then two, as the sun arched towards noon.

Then, out of the steep silence, a holler went up.

> "About 11 o'clock a.m. a portion of his remains was found, in an arroyo about one mile northwest of the point where it appeared to you Capt. Dodge had been captured & about one mile nearly west from the place where Armijo parted with him. The snow at the place was stained with blood & on the reverse side of the arroyo where the snow was melted, were distinct points of Captain Dodge's shoes as though he or someone wearing his shoes had stood there for some moments."

Carlisle's hunch had been right. He tactfully avoided reporting the nature of the remains, but his men had probably stumbled across poor Henry's head.

> "From all we could see & learn from the tracks &tc we were led to believe that Captain Dodge was waylaid, murdered & <u>scalped</u> & deprived of his clothes at or near the place where the snow was stained with blood; that

one of his murderers put on the clothes & shoes of Captain Dodge & that his tracks were mistaken for those of Capt. Dodge & that it is probably that subsequent to Capt. Dodge's death his horse was led or ridden in various directions to render it difficult for anyone who might come in search of him to trail the horse back to where Capt. Dodge was killed."

The Apache had stumped everyone, including Armijo.[5]

Rather than being satisfied with what little they'd found, Carlisle had his men shovel snow away from around the site and search the surrounding area for miles in hopes of finding the rest of the body, but discovered nothing further. What the coyotes and crows hadn't stolen was undoubtedly buried under several feet of snow.

With the grim detail completed, Carlisle's detachment turned their horses onto the trail home, carrying with them a bundle of meager and sad remains. On February 16th they buried them at Fort Defiance, on a lonely slope towards the back of the canyon. Colonel Bonneville dutifully reported those facts to headquarters in Washington, DC a month and a half later.

> "The detachment sent from Fort Defiance in compliance with Department Orders to search for the body of Captain Dodge, late Agent of the Navajoe Indians has returned, and brought his remains with them to that station. They were there interred with due solemnity. Believing that the friends of the deceased would be desirous to know all the facts connected with this sad occurrence, I have enclosed the Report of Lieutenant Carlisle, Commander of the detachment, which I hope may prove satisfactory to them."[6]

Armijo's loyalty to his friend Red Shirt had clearly touched Carlisle. In his official report, he praised Armijo in terms seldom reserved for any Indian. The headman's shrewdness as a tracker was "only equaled by his indefatigability in the search & his long tried devotion to Americans in this country, he was invaluable to me as a guide in that broken country as well as being the only one with me who could follow the track of the Apaches under such unfavorable circumstances."[7] In a letter to Meriwether, Kendrick concurred with Carlisle and suggested that the governor make a point of rewarding Armijo for his exemplary service when he came to Fort Defiance.

"He is the most reliable Indian, & throughout the occurrences in connection with the loss of the Agent of these people, he has acted, & is now acting, in a most praiseworthy manner, & to his cost. A pair of red blankets, a good rifle, a good box coat (black if possible) a black hat, besides a share of things mentioned in my list, would not be too much."[8]

On March 14th, Commissioner of Indian Affairs George Manypenny in Washington received Meriwether's report stating that Henry L. Dodge had been killed and that troops were endeavoring to bring in his remains.[9] Certainly the War Department must have received Bonneville's report at about the same time and that Senator Dodge was notified of the tragic news shortly afterwards. Three weeks after that, the news hit the papers. The National Intelligencer made the news public on April 11th. Seven days later the Milwaukee Sentinel ran the article.

"The Fate of Henry L. Dodge.
-Information has been received at the Department of the Interior confirmatory of the painful rumors that have been circulated respecting the fate of Henry L. Dodge, United States Agent for the Navajo Indians, in New Mexico, who has been missing for some time past. Major Kendrick, commanding at Fort Defiance, sent out a command to search for Mr. Dodge, and his corpse was discovered at a point about thirty miles south of the Zunia, and towards the head-waters of the Gila river.

"Mr. Dodge being a great favorite among the Navajos, and devoted to their interests, renders this wicked and wanton act inexplicable. The writer states that the Indians "struck off the hand that fed them, and Joel like, smote the benefactor of their race."

"It is stated that so soon as grass is sufficiently advanced to sustain horses, 1,000 troops will take the field against these Indians, and chastise them so that they will learn the miseries of retribution upon treachery and murder.

"The victim of this cruel act is the son of the Hon. Henry Dodge, the venerable ex-Senator from Wisconsin.-National Intelligencer, April 11."[10]

On May 18th, Secretary of War John B. Floyd wrote a letter to Senator Dodge, then retired and residing at Dodgeville, enclosing details of the efforts made to recover his son's body.

"Sir:

From the enclosed copy of a report of Lieut. J. Howard Carlisle, 2d Artillery, which is herewith transmitted to you at the suggestion of Lieut. General Winfield Scott, you will perceive that orders were promptly given, on the receipt of the melancholy intelligence of the murder of your son, the late Captain Dodge, by the Apache Indians, and an expedition dispatched in search of his remains. Believing that it would be soothing to the feelings of his relatives to know that they had been recovered, I have now the honor to give you the gratifying information that the search was not fruitless, but that they were recovered, brought to Fort Defiance, New Mexico, and interred with due solemnity."[11]

Senator Henry M. Dodge received it a week later. It was a meager epitaph for his oldest son that he held in his weathered hands, a discordant measure of formal letters and copies of hastily written reports, putting an end to the macabre rumors that for weeks had preceded the facts.

Or at least it should have.

52

OF GREATER USE TO THE INDIANS

Today take away your spell from me
Away from me you have taken it
Far off from me you have taken it
Happily I recover . . .

As the bleak winter sun ushered in February, David Meriwether sat at his desk in the Governor's Palace, surrounded by clammy adobe walls resolutely unaffected by the feeble fire in the hearth. Wearily he examined the envelope in his hands. He'd received it in January and had been saving it—possibly as charm of sorts—a wish for a fortunate outcome, a wish now thoroughly extinguished. It was from the Honorable

Senator Dodge in Washington, DC to his son Captain Henry L. Dodge, U. S. Indian Agent. The Senator had hoped Meriwether could deliver it. Sadly, he could not.

Inside the envelope were two letters from Henry's young daughters, a touching expression. Meriwether wondered what to do with them. Unable to bring himself to throw them away, he tucked them in his coat pocket. Once he got out to Fort Defiance, he would include them in the papers and records Henry Dodge had left behind.

Meriwether arrived at Defiance in early March to pick up the pieces of the Navajo Agency. He found pitifully little to pick up. Dodge's agency and quarters, one and the same, were empty. There wasn't a scrap of paper that indicated what the agent had been up to. Dodge had always been notoriously remiss on paperwork, but this was a nightmare. Kendrick had warned Meriwether about the situation two days after Dodge had been buried.

> "Although he lived here for some time before his death, he left very little if any property at this Post. I am told however that he had some animals—a few—in the charge of certain Navajoes. But it will be very difficult to arrive at the number, & more difficult to identify them. I do not suppose that those animals are known to any one here that can be relied upon."

Kendrick also suggested appointing Mr. Clarke of Albuquerque to administer Dodge's estate since there was no one at the fort who could serve in that capacity. The major did promise to "give, so long as I am here, all the aid I can in recovering any property that may belong to the estate."[1]

Of course, there was no estate—not so much as a tin cup. Henry apparently had worn all his life's possessions or had them stashed among the Navajo somewhere. There had been three agency horses listed on his property returns. The Apaches had stolen one of the animals. Meriwether hadn't a clue where the other two were. Most of the tools he'd given his agent . . . five-dozen hoes, spades and axes . . . were unaccounted for. He knew Henry had distributed them, but damn it, there were no vouchers or receipts. Furthermore, a number of vendors were clamoring to be paid, all purchases by Dodge, unsubstantiated, of course. Foremost in the pack was John Weber, the fort sutler, who informed the governor that Dodge had run up a large bill, all for Navajo goods. The auditors back in Washington were sure to throw a clot.[2]

Meriwether wasn't the only one concerned about Dodge's books. His sureties, those businessmen who had signed Henry's bond, found themselves losing sleep over what outrageous amount of debt they could be responsible for. When James Josiah

Webb wrote his trading partner William Messervy indicating he thought Messervy was on Dodge's $1500 bond, his nervous partner replied:

> "I was surprised when I read in your letter, that I was on Dodge's Bond. If I went as one of his sureties I had wholly forgotten it, for I have always refused to go security for anyone, yet it is possible I may have been fool enough to have put my name upon his bond . . ."

He begged Webb to investigate further and confirm "if I am on & if I am really on." Much to Messervy's relief, he discovered he wasn't. The businessmen Duvall & Beckwith were the sureties, poor fellows.[3]

Lastly, the Navajo Agency desperately required a new agent. Kendrick's had done an admirable job, but troubles had begun brewing almost immediately upon Henry's disappearance. There had been the San Juan raids against Armijo's sheep at the end of January, and then in the first week of February, when the same Navajo band ran off a flock near San Ysidro. Fortunately, the Navajo leadership resolved both issues. On February 13th, two days before Dodge was buried, four or five Navajos had attempted to take a flock of sheep from along the Puerco. The unfortunate fellows were caught in the act and pursued by fifteen New Mexicans, who first captured and then killed one Navajo man. As with the Apache, Meriwether feared a Navajo revenge raid was bound to follow.[4]

U. S. soldiers had of late been targets as well. On the night of February 14th, twelve discharged Fort Defiance troopers on the road to Albuquerque were camped at Bear Springs when, reputedly, fifty Navajos slipped into their camp and robbed them as they and their only sentry slept: harnesses, bridles and saddles, three muskets with cartridges and knapsacks and even the soldiers' clothing. At least that was the story. A corporal with the group later stated that the back of a wagon cover had been slit open and three clothes trunks and five knapsacks taken. He estimated the number of Navajos as no more than eight.[5]

There were also rumors of a general Navajo-Ute war, the conventional product of a Ute war party having killed eight Navajo and the Navajo retaliating by killing five Ute. The prospect of the two tribes going at one another didn't particularly disturb either Meriwether or Major Kendrick. If the Navajos were victorious, so much the better, but if the Navajo were defeated, there was a real danger they would strike the settlements to make up for their losses. Kendrick suggested it would be wise if "the Mexicans were induced to keep their flocks out of the way of the Navajoes, at least until those difficulties are over."[6] Of course, that wasn't going to happen.

The New Mexicans continued to encroach upon land the Navajo claimed as their own and, until the sluggish Senate acted on Meriwether's late treaty and affixed boundaries for a reservation, there would be a perpetual state of crisis over it.

Chances were that whoever took the agency job wouldn't be nearly effective as either Kendrick or Dodge. It would be only a matter of time before some outrage occurred, another Navajo calamity would grip the territory and there would be no one to intercede who wielded the kind of influence that Agent Dodge had exercised among the Navajo.

> *Happily my interior becomes cool*
> *Happily my eyes regain their power*
> *Happily my head becomes cool*
> *Happily my limbs regain their power*
> *Happily I hear again . . .*

The most pressing issue at hand however was the impending military campaign to eradicate the Apache. Colonel Bonneville was already getting preparations underway for a May expedition. On January 26th, he informed Major O. L. Shepherd at Fort Defiance that his company would be assigned to the expedition, scheduled to assemble at Acoma on May 1st. They would be part of the largest American force ever sent against the Indians.[7]

> "The depredations committed by the Mogollones are of too outrageous a character to be passed over—they must be punished—I am preparing to have in their country all troops that can be spared from other portions of the territory, and expect them to remain in the field during the summer and fall and until they shall have accomplished the object proposed."[8]

Continued Apache raids in February only strengthened Bonneville's resolve. A raid at Laguna on February 17th outraged Reverend Gorman, who had lost more than one or two acquaintances to the Apache, among them Captain Dodge. Echoing the words of Henry's father from the Black Hawk War years before, the preacher prayed the Army would "take measures to give those thieves their long & well earned dues . . . to hunt them out as pray hounds do the foxes, who like these savage thieves only live to plunder & destroy."[9] That was precisely Bonneville's intentions, to send a thousand regulars against the Indians in "a perfect deluge" of men and to so utterly obliterate the Mogollon and Coyotero they would "not be heard of again as a distinct people." He expected to fortify that deluge with Pima and Pueblo fighters, all anxious to plunder their inveterate enemy the Apache.[10]

It was a foregone conclusion to Colonel Bonneville and Governor Meriwether that the Navajo would be eager to join the campaign and avenge the murder of their agent Red Shirt. In fact, Bonneville was depending on Meriwether to enlist them.[11] Meriwether presented the proposition to Navajo leaders during his March visit to Fort Defiance and to his pleasure found the headmen enthusiastically endorsed the idea. Once Meriwether had returned to Santa Fe, however, that initial enthusiasm rapidly withered. On April 10th, John Weber sent the governor a list of items Dodge had purchased at the sutler store. In the cover letter he confirmed that, in spite of every effort by the officers to enlist the Navajo to fight Dodge's killers, "not a single Navajo will go."[12] A week before the expedition was to rendezvous at Acoma, Sandoval and 141 Mount Taylor fighters arrived in Santa Fe and asked Bonneville's permission to join the expedition. The Colonel gave them rations and invited Meriwether to "come and interview them if you wish." Ironically, in the end they would be the only Navajo to serve as avengers of Dodge's death . . . a minor concern for them at best.[13]

In early May, John Garland returned to New Mexico to assume command of the department, freeing Colonel Bonneville to pursue his war. For the first weeks of May, the Colonel's grand invasion force saw little or no action. The huge, plodding expedition was about as effective against the Indians as shooting a howitzer at a mosquito. The Apaches simply stayed out of Bonneville's way.[14] Nevertheless, the expedition did score two telling victories against the Apache. Colonel William Loring and his forces attacked Cuchillo Negro's band, implicated in livestock thefts. They killed him and five others, took several women and children captive and recovered a thousand sheep.[15] Near the end of June, after penetrating the recess of the White Mountains in present day Arizona, American forces attacked a Coyotero village, killing forty Apache and capturing forty-five.

Among the Apache dead that day lay the man who had allegedly shot Henry L. Dodge, himself shot to death by musketry.[16]

> *Happily for me the spell is removed*
> *Happily I walk*
> *Impervious to pain I walk*
> *Feeling light within I walk . . .*

It was the final victory for Bonneville's war of annihilation. In August,

Garland ordered the expedition concluded. On September 2nd, a Coyotero delegation sued for peace, expressing bewilderment as to why the soldiers had attacked them. They admitted that some of their people had accompanied the Mogollon on raids the previous November and that the man who had murdered Henry L. Dodge happened to be in their village the day Bonneville had attacked. All that not withstanding, the Coyotero protested that they had always desired peace with the Americans.[17]

Meriwether's abortive attempt to enlist Navajos in Bonneville's expedition was one his last acts as New Mexico's Governor and Superintendent of Indian Affairs. In a three-way contest for president the previous November, the Democrat James Buchanan had defeated first time Republican candidate John C. Fremont and the nativist American Party candidate, Millard Fillmore. Now the anticipated heads were starting to roll. Buchanan replaced David Meriwether as governor with North Carolinian Abraham Rencher and, fulfilling Meriwether's fears, appointed James L. Collins Superintendent of Indian Affairs for New Mexico . . . a veritable fox in the hen house. Meriwether left New Mexico for Washington on May 1st, long before his successor's arrival, appointing his faithful secretary, W. W. H. Davis to again act as interim governor. Davis' time in that capacity was limited, for he had also been replaced, but while he occupied the governor's mansion, he took every opportunity to disparage, antagonize and aggravate Collins.[18]

At about the same time, Major Henry Lane Kendrick learned he'd been offered the professorship of Chemistry, Mineralogy and Geology for the United States Military Academy at West Point. Kendrick had been in New Mexico for eight years; he had commanded at Fort Defiance for six. In that time, working hand in hand with Henry Dodge, he had been able to forge a dependable peace with the most powerful tribe in the western United States. He was an intelligent, dependable and prudent career officer, with a thorough knowledge of New Mexico and its people and an uncanny intuition regarding Indians, above all the Navajo—a priceless resource for any commander of the 9th Military District. There was never any doubt as to Kendrick's decision.

He accepted the professorship without hesitation. On May 17th, H. L. Kendrick relinquished command of Fort Defiance, paused in Santa Fe long enough to brief James Collins on the state of Navajo relations, and then left for New York on the Hudson, never again to return to New Mexico.[19]

Major Kendrick's successors would be found critically wanting. Brevet Major William Gordon, 3rd Infantry, one of Kendrick's junior officers, first assumed command at Defiance. Having held temporary command before, he knew something of the Navajo situation. Despite that, he proved woefully untalented in crisis management. In June, after the Navajo drove their undernourished livestock onto the fort grazing grounds, Gordon summarily dispatched Lieutenant Carlisle with thirty dragoons and some cannon to drive them off. They were met by an incensed Manuelito and as many as five hundred Navajo warriors. When Carlisle demanded they withdraw, Manuelito flatly refused, saying that since losing their agent Red Shirt and their trusted friend Major Kendrick, they didn't give a damn for anyone else. Carlisle wisely retreated.[20]

That incident proved to be prologue for troubles innumerable. As a result of the grazing field incident, General Garland sent Colonel Loring and his force of 300 riflemen to Defiance. Loring assumed command and with Garland's authorization, delivered an ultimatum to the Navajo; abandon the fort grazing grounds or suffer the consequences.[21] Seeing the fort so heavily reinforced, Manuelito backed down and withdrew the stock. In September, confident that the Navajo desired peace, Colonel Loring relinquished command and departed with his riflemen. On November 26th, Brevet Major William Brooks, who had no affection for the Navajo and had once called Henry L. Dodge a liar and purveyor in stolen public animals, took command. During his tenure, his bull-in-a-china-shop diplomacy would quickly unravel all that Dodge and Kendrick had accomplished and set the stage for years of war.[22]

> *His feet, my feet restore*
> *His limbs, my limbs restore*
> *His mind, my mind restore*
> *His voice, my voice restore*
> *His plumes, my plumes restore . . .*

If insightful skills had become scarce at Fort Defiance, they were nonexistent in the Navajo Agency. The appointment of James Collins to the Superintendency of Indian Affairs in New Mexico was an abject lesson as to why a local politician should not have been appointed to such position in the first place. By allying with settler and rancher interests, Collins' administration was not only unable but also unwilling to represent the Indians' welfare. The natives were to be confined and shoved aside, and just as quickly as possible. Any reluctance by the Indians to acquiesce would be met with force. It was a philosophy guaranteed to ignite conflict, but one the new Navajo agent would be expected to support.

Whether for better or worse, a new Navajo agent would not appear on the grounds of Fort Defiance for nearly a year after Dodge's disappearance. In the wake of the crisis at the fort grazing grounds, Collins fidgeted about sending the new agent for the Gadsden Purchase Indians, a Mr. Walker, to Fort Defiance to calm things down, but dropped the idea after Loring's arrival cowed the Navajo.[23] Like Brooks, Collins may have held Henry L. Dodge as a scoundrel and Indian lover, but he had to concede one point in his favor.

> "It may be some time before we get an agent for those Indians that will have the influence with them that their late agent, Captain Dodge, had . . ."[24]

On July 30th, 1857, William R. Harley of Hernando, Missouri, was appointed agent to the Navajo. He would not arrive in the territory until September 24th and not actually occupy his agency until October, when he accompanied Collins out to Defiance for the annuity giveaway.[25] The Navajo immediately noticed an unfavorable contrast between Harley and Red Shirt. Dodge had been easy-going, hospitable and generous. Harley seemed standoffish, cold and stingy. For his part, the new agent was piqued by that famous Navajo friendly familiarity. Barely hiding his contempt, he noted the Indians "when visiting the agency expect to be treated as they were by Capt. Dodge—that is, to sleep and eat with the agent." Not surprisingly, Harley wouldn't last a year. In the following three years there would be five more agents, all equally unsuccessful.[26]

On July 16th, 1858, the argumentative Major Brooks wrote Superintendent Collins. There had been another incident at Fort Defiance. A Navajo had killed his black servant and slave, Jim, there on the very parade ground just outside his office. Clearly a premeditated execution, it was most likely to avenge Brook's order to shoot seventy of Manuelito's animals, once again found grazing on fort pastures. Brooks' handwriting was typically ragged and nearly undecipherable, but in no way inhibited his righteous outrage in his report to Collins, who had expected to visit the fort with Samuel Yost, editor of the Gazette and the latest Navajo agent.

> "I think you have well decided not to come out here—although Capt Dodge was of great use to us when we had a similar difficulty in 1854, yet I conceive he was of greater use to the Indians—I think the time for talking to and advising them has passed. They feel too self-confidant to appreciate any advice that we can give them . . ."[27]

By September there would be escalating clashes between Navajo and American, followed by a major military expedition against the tribe, which after four months, ended in yet another treaty. Within a year, that treaty of peace would crumble, igniting a guerrilla war by soldier and mercenary alike, an interlude between wars known among the Navajo as *Naahoondzood*, or *The Fearing Time*. Increasingly desperate, the Navajo launched reprisal attacks on the Fort Defiance cattle herds and wood cutting details, even massing an estimated force of one thousand in the predawn light of April 30, 1860 to attack the fort itself. It was a mere demonstration and the Navajo quickly withdrew. In 1863 General James Carleton, assigned to command the Department of New Mexico, directed Kit Carson commanding at Fort Defiance to launch the long-threatened apocalyptic invasion of Navajo land. Carson's fast moving Army units, in conjunction with independently marauding New Mexican, Pueblo and Ute raiders, utterly laid waste to Navajo country. The harried, stricken and starved Navajo had no choice but to surrender. Surrender they did, in the thousands, and were exiled, driven like cattle, to a tiny reservation on an alkali infused plot of land in eastern New Mexico, just southeast of Santa Rosa. The Americans knew the site as Fort Sumner, named in honor of old Bullhead Sumner. The Navajo called it *Hwéeldi*, *The Fort*, a word that became synonymous with disease, starvation, hopelessness and death.

And through the catastrophe, the Navajo would yet remember Red Shirt with increasing esteem as an American they had respected, trusted and counted as a friend. It was to be Charles W. Wentz who perhaps best eulogized Henry L. Dodge in 1864 when he stated that had Agent Dodge lived, " . . . I am of the opinion that the subsequent Navajo War would never have occurred."[28]

And so it was that Red Shirt, Henry L. Dodge, had indeed been of greater use to the Indians.

> *With beauty before him, with beauty before me*
> *With beauty behind him, with beauty behind me*
> *With beauty above him with beauty above me*
> *With beauty below him, with beauty below me . . .*
> *With beauty around him, with beauty around me*
> *With pollen beautiful in his voice, with pollen beautiful in my voice*
> *In beauty it is finished. In beauty it is finished.*[29]

NOTES

Chapter 1-A Turn of Fortune, November 1856

1. Meriwether to Manypenny, December 29, 1856, *Letters Received by the Office of Indian Affairs 1824-1880, New Mexico Superintendency,* National Archives Record Group 75, Records of the Bureau of Indian Affairs, M234 (Washington, DC 1980), Microfilm Reel 546.

Chapter 2-I Regret to Inform You . . .

1. Kendrick to Nichols, November 26, 1856, *Letters Received by the 9th Military District, 1848-1853,* National Archives, *Records of U.S. Army Continental Commands,* Record Group 393, M1102, Washington, DC 1980, Microfilm Reel 5, frames 875-877.

Chapter 3-A Matter of Honor

1. Kennedy, David M. *The Brief American Pageant: A History of the Republic,* (D. C. Heath and Company, Lexington, 1989), 235-237.
2. Pelzer, Louis, *Henry Dodge,* (The State Historical Society of Iowa, Iowa City, 1911), 188.
3. Pelzer, *Henry Dodge,* 191.
4. Davis to McClelland, January 3, 1857, *Letters Received by the Office of Indian Affairs, 1824-1880, New Mexico Superintendency, 1824-1880,* Record Group 75, M234, Microfilm Reel 546, 1857, N241-W385.
5. McClelland to Davis, January 3, 1857, *Letters Sent to the Indian Division of the Department of the Interior, 1849-1903,* National Archives, Records of the Bureau of Indian Affairs, Record Group 75, M606,(Washington, DC 1956), Microfilm Reel 2, frame 11.
6. Mary T. Dodge to Mrs. Henry Dodge, November 27, 1856, *Records of the New Mexico Superintendency, 1849-1880, Agencies, Records of the Santa Fe Agency,* National Archives, Records of the Bureau of Indian Affairs, Record Group 75, T21, Microfilm Reel 2.
7. Christiana A. Dodge to Mrs. Henry Dodge, December 6, 1856, *Records of the New Mexico Superintendency, 1849-1880, Agencies, Records of the Santa Fe Agency,* T21, Microfilm Reel 2.
8. Fox, Mary Dodge, "The Grove—Recollections of Mary Dodge Fox, as Dictated to Her Daughter in April, 1918," Mary Dodge Fox Papers, Wisconsin State Historical Society Archives, (University of Wisconsin, Madison).

Chapter 4-Damn'd Rascals

1. Pelzer, *Henry Dodge,* 1.
2. Draper, Lyman C., ed., *Collections of the State Historical Society of Wisconsin, Vol. 4,* (Democrat Printing Company, Madison, 1906), 429.
3. Alvord, Clarence W., *The Illinois Country, 1673-1818,* (A. C. McClurg & Company, Chicago, 1922), 352.

4. Pelzer, Louis, *Augustus Caesar Dodge*, (The State Historical Society of Iowa, Iowa City, Iowa, 1908), 3.
5. Alvord, Clarence W., *Kaskaskia Records, 1778-1790, Collections of the Illinois State Historical Library 5*, (Illinois State Historical Library, Springfield, 1909), xvii.
6. Alvord, *The Illinois Country*, 352-353.
7. Alvord, *Kaskaskia Records*, 236-238.
8. Alvord, *Kaskaskia Records*, 238.
9. Alvord, *Kaskaskia Records*, 429.
10. Alvord, *Kaskaskia Records*; 160, 273.
11. Alvord, *Kaskaskia Records*; 397-398.
12. Alvord, *Kaskaskia Records*, 426. John Rice Jones was born an Englishman on February 10, 1759. Having studied medicine and law at Oxford, he practiced law in London before moving to American in 1784. An acquaintance of Benjamin Franklin of Philadelphia, he joined George Rogers Clark's expedition and later earned the distinction of being the first English-speaking lawyer in Indiana Territory. Jones was a classical scholar, well trained in mathematics and spoke Greek, Latin, French, Spanish and Welsh. He became the first attorney general of the territory and was a member of the legislative council. Shortly after his confrontation with John Dodge, he moved to Kaskaskia where he practiced law and speculated in real estate. He too ended up an émigré to Missouri. See Williams, Walter, *Missouri, Mother of the West*, (The American Historical Society, Chicago, 1930).
13. Alvord, *Kaskaskia Records*, 436.
14. Foley, William E. *The Genesis of Missouri: From Wilderness Outpost to Statehood*, (University of Missouri Press, Columbia, 1989), 41.
15. Foley, *The Genesis of Missouri*, 61.
16. Alvord, *Kaskaskia Records*, 515-516.

Chapter 5-The Devil Take All

1. Ekberg, Carl J., *Colonial Ste. Genevieve, An Adventure on the Mississippi Frontier*, (Patrice Press, Gerald, Missouri, 1985), 60, 72.
2. Pelzer, *Augustus Caesar Dodge*, 271. One suspects that the phrase 'nits make lice' was not the chief's choice of metaphor, but that of the American historian, as it can be found frequently in accounts of American and Indian relations. See Chapter 14, note 10 for further discussion.
3. Schaaf, Ida M., *Sainte Genevieve Marriages, Baptisms and Burials from the Church Registers*, (Missouri Historical Society, Jefferson Memorial, St. Louis, 1918), 25-33.
4. Ekberg, *Colonial Ste. Genevieve*, 452.
5. Goodspeed Publishing Company, *The Goodspeed History of Southeast Missouri*, (Goodspeed Publishing Co., Chicago, 1888), 410.
6. Pelzer, *Henry Dodge*, 9. See also Carter, Clarence, E., *The Territorial Papers of the United States, Vol. 13: The Territory of Louisiana and Missouri, 1803-1806*, (Government Printing Office, Washington, DC 1948), 292.
7. Ekberg, *Colonial Ste. Genevieve*, 118.
8. Foley, *The Genesis of Missouri*, 77, 79.
9. Foley, *The Genesis of Missouri*, 140, 163.
10. Governor Henry Harrison commissioned Israel Dodge as sheriff of Ste. Genevieve District on

October 1, 1804, to be done "during our pleasure." See *Henry Dodge Papers*, the State Historical Society of Iowa Archives, Des Moines. See also the *Ste. Genevieve Archives*, State Historical Society of Missouri, Western Historical Manuscripts Collection, Columbia State University, folder 514.
11. Goodspeed, *History of Southeast Missouri*, 310
12. Carter, *Territorial Papers, Vol. 13*, 138-139. John Smith T was born in 1770, the fifth generation of an old Essex County, Virginia colonial family. After attending the College of William and Mary, he moved to Tennessee, where he served as a judge and dabbled in land speculation. Smith T arrived in Louisiana territory in 1804. He opened mines at Shibboleth and had several confrontations with Frederick Bates regarding the legitimacy of his claim. He was also an impassioned competitor of Moses Austin of Potosi. When Austin's mines went broke, Smith T bought the lands up. John Smith T was granted a license to trade with Indian tribes in 1811. Apparently he and a party of men attempted to occupy lead country around Galena, Illinois, but were driven off by Indians. Eventually he returned to Tennessee, where he died in 1836. Never shy to resort to violence, John Smith T left a legacy of intimidation, fear and murder. He was credited for killing more than a dozen men, including Lionel Browne, a nephew of Aaron Burr, in 1819. When Smith and Browne drew their dueling pistols, Smith's bullet struck Browne square in the forehead. Needless to say, he died instantly. In 1830, Smith was tried for murdering Samuel Ball in a drunken brawl at William McArthur's tavern in Sainte Genevieve. See Goodspeed, *History of Southeast Missouri*, 313.
13. *Conveyances of Deeds 1804, Book C*, Ste. Genevieve County Courthouse, Ste. Genevieve, Missouri, 229.
14. Goodspeed, *History of Southeast Missouri*, 310.
15. Carter, *Territorial Papers, Vol. 13*, 548.
16. Gracy, David B., *Moses Austin: His Life*, (Trinity University Press, San Antonio, 1987), 114.
17. Pelzer, *Henry Dodge*, 19-20.
18. Carter, *Territorial Papers of the United States, Vol. 14: The Territory of Louisiana and Missouri, 1806-1814*, (Government Printing Office, Washington, DC 1949), 120.
19. Goodspeed, *History of Southeast Missouri*, 311.
20. Carter *Territorial Papers of the United States, Vol. 14*, 174-176.
21. Goodspeed, *History of Southeast Missouri*, 408.

Chapter 6-Sainte Genevieve

1. Foley, *The Genesis of Missouri*, 80-81.
2. Basler, Lucille, *Pioneers of Old Ste. Genevieve* (published by author, 1983), 54.
3. Goodspeed, *History of Southeast Missouri*, 311.
4. Lowrie, Walter, *The American State Papers; Public Lands, Vol. 3, Documents, legislative and executive, of the Congress of the United States, in relation to the public lands: from the first session of the first Congress to the first session of the twenty-third Congress, March 4, 1789, to June 15, 1834 / selected and edited, under the authority of the Senate of the United States, by Walter Lowrie*. (Duff Green, Washington, DC 1834), 580.
5. *Index #0 Conveyances of Deeds-Indirect 1804-1880, Book B*, Ste. Genevieve County Court House, Ste. Genevieve, Missouri, 303. In 1818, Dodge also purchased the house lot of Walter Fenwick, who had perished in the famous Moreau Island duel with Crittenden. See Ste.

Genevieve County Court House *Index #0 Conveyances of Deeds-Indirect 1804–1880, Book C,* 242.

6. *The Missouri Gazette,* date unknown. See also State Historical Society of Missouri, *Ste. Genevieve Archives,* folder 674 and Carter, *Territorial Papers, Vol. 14,* 636.

7. Schoolcraft, Henry R., *A View of the Lead Mines of Missouri: Including Some Observations on the Mineralogy, Geology, Geography, Antiquities, Soil, Climate, Population and Productions of Missouri and Arkansaw,* (Charley Wiley & Co., New York, 1819), 33. Henry Rowe Schoolcraft was born in 1793 near Albany, New York. He left the family business of glassmaking and journeyed down the Ohio to Louisiana country. In 1819, he completed *A View of the Lead Mines of Missouri,* a volume of geological and geographical studies of Missouri. He later explored the Mississippi River, Northern Michigan and the Upper Great Lakes as General Lewis Cass' geologist, and produced a book of his explorations. His greatest contribution would be to American Indian ethnology. The extent and thoroughness of his work was impressive, particularly for the times. After being an author, Indian agent to the Ojibwa and a territorial legislator, Schoolcraft moved back east in 1841. Between 1851 and 1857, he produced a six-volume study on American Indian Tribes. He died in 1864. The Columbia University Press, *Henry Rowe Schoolcraft,* Columbia Electronic Encyclopedia, Sixth Edition, Columbia University Press, 2008, http://www.encyclopedia.com/doc/1E1-Schoolcr.html (accessed August 29, 2009).

8. Foley, *The Genesis of Missouri,* 11. In 1787 Louis Tonnellier from Paris became the schoolmaster, but then went into lead mining and farming. In 1795 Augustin-Charles Frémon de Lauriére succeeded him, stressing proper conduct and practical skills, but couldn't make a go of it.

9. Phillips, Claude A., *A History of Education in Missouri: The Essential Facts Concerning the History and Organization of Missouri Schools,* (Hugh Stephens Printing Company, Jefferson City, 1911), 5.

10. Bryan, William S., *A History of the Pioneer Families of Missouri,* (Bryan, Brand & Company, St. Louis, 1876), 74. Timothy Flint was born in 1780 in Massachusetts. After graduating from Harvard in 1800, he entered the ministry and served as a missionary in the Mississippi Valley between 1815 and 1825. He wrote several books, his most important contributions being *Recollections of the Last Ten Years,* published in 1826, and *Biographical Memoir of Daniel Boone* in 1833. Timothy Flint died in 1840. See *Timothy Flint,* Columbia Electronic Encyclopedia, Sixth Edition, Columbia University Press, 2008, www.encyclopedia.com/doc/1E1-Flint-Ti.html, (accessed August 29, 2009).

11. *Probate File # 33-850,* Ste. Genevieve County Courthouse, Ste. Genevieve, Missouri, Swiss citizen, Joseph S. Hertich arrived in Baltimore in 1796, then moved to Danville, Kentucky, where he opened a school. Sources indicate that Dr. Hertich moved to Ste. Genevieve in 1810 to open a store, though the Israel Dodge probate records show he was teaching in the area prior to that year. The Asylum was to provide a balanced curriculum of moral and religious training as well as that of abstract knowledge. See Williams, *Missouri, Mother of the West,* 293. The school produced several luminaries, including Augustus C. Dodge and George Wallace Jones. Henry Dodge himself was represented by Mary Rozier Sharp as having been one of five United States Senators to have attended the school, though given his age that would have been improbable. It may have actually been his son, Lafayette Henry Dodge. See Sharp, Mary Rozier, *Between the Gabouri: A History of Ferdinand Rosier,* (published by author, 1981). See also Goodspeed, *History of Southeast Missouri,* 599.

12. Foley, *The Genesis of Missouri*, 118-120. Henry Marie Brackenridge was born in 1786 in Pittsburgh, Pennsylvania, the son of the Scottish-American writer Hugh Henry Brackenridge. As a young man, he moved to St. Louis in 1806, where he pursued law and journalism. His works included *Views of Louisiana*, written in 1814, *South America* and *Voyage to South America* and *Recollections of Persons and Places in the West* published in 1834. Returning to Pennsylvania, he served as a judge and as that state's representative to Congress. He died in 1871 at the age of 85. See *Henry Marie Brackenridge*, The Columbia Electronic Encyclopedia, Sixth Edition, http://www.encyclopedia.com/doc/1E1-BrackenrHM.html (accessed August 29, 2009).
13. Williams, Walter, *Missouri, Mother of the West*, (The American Historical Society, Chicago, 1930), 298.
14. Bryan, *A History of the Pioneer Families of Missouri*, 77.
15. Bryan, *A History of the Pioneer Families of Missouri*, 76.
16. Schoolcraft, *A View of the Lead Mines of Missouri*, 39, 114.
17. Bradbury, John, *Travels in the Interior of America, 1809-1811*, (University Microfilms Inc., Ann Arbor, 1966), 251-252.
18. Ekberg, *Colonial Ste. Genevieve*, 154.
19. Schoolcraft, *A View of the Lead Mines of Missouri*, 30-31.
20. Schoolcraft; *A View of the Lead Mines of Missouri*, 134-149.
21. Yealy, Francis J., *Sainte Genevieve: The Story of Missouri's Oldest Settlement*, (The Bicentennial Historical Committee, Ste. Genevieve, 1935), 94-95. John Scott was born in Hanover County, Virginia in 1785. After graduating from Princeton, he moved to Pennsylvania, where he became a licensed lawyer. He moved with his wife to Sainte Genevieve in 1805, being one of the first lawyers in town. After his wife died, he remarried. As well as practicing law, he was involved in mining and real estate. He became attorney general of the territory in 1807. Later a member of the Missouri territorial legislature and delegate to Congress he also became Missouri's first congressman. Lucille Basler, in her work *Pioneers of Old Ste. Genevieve*, described Scott as "of very nervous temperament, quick and active in his movements and very rapid in his speech. He used profanity, the presence of ladies not affecting him in the least, and was very eccentric in his dress and manners. He always wore pantaloons four or five sizes too large for him, a little black cloth cap pulled down over his eyes, and invariably carried a big green bag in which he kept his books and papers . . . He also was in the habit of carrying the assortment of pistols and knives . . ." John Scott died in 1861 at the age of eighty. When shortly before his death John Scott was urged to seek religion, his answer was, "I have served the devil all my life and it wouldn't be right to desert him now." See Basler, *Pioneers of Old Ste. Genevieve*, 97.
22. Marshall, Thomas M., *The Life and Papers of Frederick Bates, Vol. 2*, (Missouri Historical Society, St. Louis, 1926), 278-279.
23. Carter, *Territorial Papers of the United States, Vol. 14: The Territory of Louisiana and Missouri, 1806-1814*, (Government Printing Office, Washington, DC 1949), 481.
24. Schoolcraft, *A View of the Lead Mines of Missouri*, 116.
25. Marshall, *The Life and Papers of Frederick Bates, Vol. 2*, 20.
26. Schoolcraft, *A View of the Lead Mines of Missouri*, 128.
27. Carter, Clarence E., *Territorial Papers of the United States, Vol. 15: The Territory of Louisiana and Missouri, 1815-1821*, (Government Printing Office, Washington, DC 1949), 4-7.
28. Goodspeed, *History of Southeast Missouri*, 313.

Chapter 7-A Nasty Little War

1. Switzler, William F., *Illustrated History of Missouri From 1541 to 1877*, (C. R. Barns, Saint Louis, 1879, reprinted by Arno Press, New York, 1975), note 189.
2. Foley, *The Genesis of Missouri*, 120-121.
3. Waldman, Carl, *Atlas of the North American Indian*, (Facts on File, New York, New York, 1985), 19-22.
4. Wayman, Norbury L., *Life on the River: A Pictorial History of the Mississippi, the Missouri, and the Western River System*, (Crown Publishers, New York, 1971), 2.
5. Foley, *The Genesis of Missouri*, 5.
6. Foley, *The Genesis of Missouri*, 64-65.
7. Foley, *The Genesis of Missouri*, 90. See also Ekberg, *Colonial Ste. Genevieve*, 155.
8. Foley, *The Genesis of Missouri*, 92.
9. Foley, *The Genesis of Missouri*, 145.
10. Foley, *The Genesis of Missouri*, 1989; 156. In his autobiography, Black Hawk later claimed that the Sauk and Fox delegation had gone to Saint Louis to pay blood money for the release of a young tribe member jailed for murder. According to his version, Harrison demanded land and let the Indians know the prisoner would then be released. Harrison later claimed, rather than being released, the prisoner had attempted escape and was shot dead. One can understand Black Hawk's skepticism. He also insisted that the four Sauk had been "drunk the greater part of the time they were in Saint Louis." See Blackhawk, Makataimeshekiakiak, *Black Hawk, An Autobiography*, edited by Donald Jackson, (University of Illinois Press; 1964), 53-54.
11. Foley, *The Genesis of Missouri*, 193.
12. Foley, *The Genesis of Missouri*, 203, 216.
13. Foley, *The Genesis of Missouri*, 220.
14. Parrish, William E., *Missouri: The Heart of the Nation*, (Forum Press, St. Louis, 1980), 40.
15. Foley, *The Genesis of Missouri*, 222-224. William Clark was born on August 1st, 1770, the son of a Virginia plantation owner. After moving to Louisville, Kentucky he fought Indians in the Ohio Valley. He enlisted in the regular army in 1792 but retired at the age of 26 to manage his family's plantation. In 1803 an army comrade, Meriwether Lewis, invited him to join the expedition to explore Upper Louisiana. After his return, Thomas Jefferson appointed Clark both Indian agent and brigadier general of the militia for Louisiana Territory. In 1813, after Meriwether Lewis' suicide, Clark served as Missouri governor. In 1820, he unsuccessfully ran for the governorship of the new state of Missouri. He became Superintendent of Indian Affairs in 1822 and remained in that position until his death in 1838. See *William Clark*, The Virginia Center for Digital History, (University of Virginia), www2.vcdh.virginia.edu/lewisandclark/biddle/biographies_html/clark.html (accessed September 19, 2009)
16. Blackhawk, Makataimeshekiakiak, *Black Hawk, An Autobiography*, edited by Donald Jackson, (University of Illinois Press; 1964), 67.
17. Waldman, *Atlas of the North American Indian*; 115-117.
18. Goodspeed, *History of Southeast Missouri*, 245.
19. For Dodge's appointment, see Carter, *Territorial Papers of the United States, Vol. 14*, 614. See also Pelzer, *Augustus Caesar Dodge*, 38, for Dodge's earlier militia activities and Marshall, *The Life and Papers of Frederick Bates, Vol. 2*, 252, for Dodge's 1813 reconnaissance.

20. Foley, *The Genesis of Missouri*, 230-231.
21. Goodspeed, *History of Southeast Missouri*, 489.
22. Pelzer, *Henry Dodge*, 24-25.
23. Shoemaker, Floyd C., *Missouri and Missourians: Land of Contrasts and People of Achievements*, Vol. 1, (Lewis Publishing Company, Chicago, 1943), 303. See also Marshall, *Life and Papers of Frederick Bates*, 283.
24. Foley, *The Genesis of Missouri*, 233-235.
25. Parrish, *Missouri: The Heart of the Nation*, 41-42, 45.
26. Foley, *The Genesis of Missouri*, 252.
27. Carter, *The Territorial Papers of the United States, Vol. 14*, 473.
28. Foley, *The Genesis of Missouri*, 291.
29. Goodspeed, *History of Southeast Missouri*, 312.
30. Parrish, *Missouri: The Heart of the Nation*, 51.
31. Switzler, *Illustrated History of Missouri*, 203-204.
32. Parrish, *Missouri: The Heart of the Nation*, 56. At this time John Rice Jones was sixty-one years of age. He had relocated to Missouri shortly after helping to drive John and Israel over the river. He became a close ally of Moses Austin and worked with him as a business partner to develop the first reverberating furnace in the region. In 1813, he donated the land upon which Austin's town of Potosi was built. Elected in 1814 as a representative of Washington County for Missouri Territory's second General Assembly, he served as president of the legislative council in 1816. He was a candidate for one of Missouri's seats in the Senate, but was defeated by David Barton and Thomas Hart Benton. Appointed as the first Supreme Court justice for Missouri, he died in Saint Louis in February of 1824 at the age of sixty-five. It is perhaps ironic that one of his sons, George Wallace Jones, would become a life-long friend and ally of the Dodge clan. See Williams, *Missouri, Mother of the West*.

Chapter 8-Non Est

1. Switzler, *Illustrated History of Missouri*, 218.
2. Williams, *Missouri, Mother of the West*, 402.
3. Foley, *The Genesis of Missouri*, 257.
4. *The American State Papers, Public Lands, Vol. 3*, 580.
5. Foley, *The Genesis of Missouri*, 245, 247.
6. Bryan, *A History of the Pioneer Families of Missouri*, 75.
7. Pelzer, *Henry Dodge*, 1911, 29.
8. *U.S. Survey 358, Sainte Genevieve County Court House Index #0 Conveyances-Indirect 1804–1880, Book C*, 447, 449.
9. *U. S. Survey 150; Sainte Genevieve County Court House Conveyances, Book C; 455* See also *Sainte Genevieve County Court House Index #0 Conveyances-Indirect 1804–1880, Book C*, 264.
10. *Sainte Genevieve County Court House Index #0 Conveyances-Direct 1804–1880, Book D*, 61.
11. *Sainte Genevieve County, Deeds*, Missouri State Archives, Jefferson City, *Vol. D*, 156.
12. Pelzer, *Augustus Caesar Dodge*, 1908, 39.
13. Petersen, William J., *Steam Boating on the Upper Mississippi, The Water Way to Iowa* (The State Historical Society of Iowa, Iowa City, 1937), 215, 222.
14. Wayman, *Life on the River*, 252.

15. Petersen, *Steam Boating on the Upper Mississippi*, 222.
16. Flint, Timothy, *Recollections of the Last Ten Years Passed in Occasional Residences and Journeying in the Valley of the Mississippi*, edited by C. Hartley Grattan, (New York: Alfred A. Knopf, 1932), 85.
17. Petersen, *Steam Boating on the Upper Mississippi*, 212.
18. Foley, *The Genesis of Missouri*, 93-94.
19. Pelzer, *Augustus Caesar Dodge*, 40-41.
20. Pelzer, *Augustus Caesar Dodge*, 41-42.
21. *Iowa Series 74*, University of Wisconsin, Platteville, Wisconsin Room.

Chapter 9-Fever River

1. Petersen, *Steam Boating on the Upper Mississippi*, 204-205, 206. See also Nesbit, Robert C., *Wisconsin: A History*, (University of Wisconsin Press, Madison, 1989), 110.
2. Buley, R. Carlyle, *The Old Northwest, Pioneer Period, 1815-1840, Vol. 2*, (Indiana University Press, Bloomington, 1978), 56.
3. Petersen, *Steam Boating on the Upper Mississippi*, 206-207.
4. Buley, *The Old Northwest, Pioneer Period, 1815-1840, Vol. 2*, 56.
5. Petersen, *Steam Boating on the Upper Mississippi*, 212.
6. Draper, Lyman C. ed., *Collections of the State Historical Society of Wisconsin, Vol. 5*, (Democrat Printing Company, Madison, 1907), 343.
7. Petersen, *Steam Boating on the Upper Mississippi*, 207-208. William S. Hamilton would become a long-time resident of southwest Wisconsin. Born August 4th, 1797, he was but a lad of seven when Aaron Burr killed his father in the infamous duel of 1804. He entered West Point in 1814, but resigned three years later. At the age of twenty-three, he had relocated to St. Louis where he served as a deputy surveyor general. In 1822 he migrated to Springfield, Illinois as the United States Surveyor of public lands. In 1824 he was elected to the fourth General Assembly of Illinois Legislature and practiced some law. Hamilton moved to the lead county in 1827. The following year he partnered with two other men to stake a lead claim near the present day town of Wiota, Wisconsin. Hamilton's Diggings, as the claim became known, proved to be very profitable. See "Billy Hamilton and Hamilton's Diggings," *The Old Lead Region Historical Society*, www.geocities.com/old_lead/wiota.htm, (accessed September 5, 2009).
8. Clark, James I., *Life on Wisconsin's Lead Mining Frontier*, (The State Historical Society of Wisconsin, Madison, 1976), 8, 13, 15-16.
9. Waldman, *Atlas of the North American Indian*, 31.
10. Sturtevant, William C., *Handbook of North American Indians, Vol. 15 Northeast*, (Smithsonian Institution, Washington, 1983), 691-692, 695.
11. Waldman, *Atlas of the North American Indian*, 118.
12. Sturtevant, *Handbook of North American Indians, Vol. 15 Northeast*, 697.
13. Derleth, August, *The Wisconsin, River of a Thousand Isles*, (Rinehart & Company, Inc., New York, 1942), 51-52, 59.
14. Sturtevant, *Handbook of North American Indians, Vol. 15 Northeast*, 697. See also *Dictionary of Wisconsin Biography*, (The State Historical Society of Wisconsin, Madison, 1960); 299.
15. Buley, *The Old Northwest, Pioneer Period, 1815-1840, Vol. 2*, 58. The events described are according to John A. Wakefield, in his book on the Black Hawk War, written in 1834. Given the

popular sentiments of the time, his version must be looked upon with some skepticism.
16. Waldman, *Atlas of the North American Indian*, 118.
17. Buley, *The Old Northwest, Pioneer Period, 1815-1840, Vol. 2*, 58.
18. Pelzer, *Henry Dodge*, 42.
19. Parkinson, Daniel M., "Pioneer Life in Wisconsin," *Collections of the State Historical Society of Wisconsin*, edited by Lyman C. Draper, vol. 2, 326-363, (Democrat Printing Company, Madison, 1908), 329.
20. Pelzer, *Henry Dodge*, 42, 45.
21. Draper, Lyman C. ed., *Collections of the State Historical Society of Wisconsin, Vol. 10*, (Democrat Printing Company, Madison, 1888), 397. James D. Doty was a circuit judge from Green Bay. James Duane Doty was born in Salem, New York in 1799. Educated in law at Lowville Academy, he began practice at Detroit in Michigan Territory in 1819 at the age of twenty. He also served the territory in a variety of legal and legislative positions. In 1820 he accompanied Governor Lewis Cass as his expeditionary secretary on Cass' birch bark canoe exploration of present day Wisconsin. After returning to Washington, DC in 1821, Doty was admitted to practice before the Supreme Court. President Monroe appointed him judge of the northern Michigan judicial district in 1823. That same year he married Sarah Collins of New York and relocated to Green Bay. James D. Doty was a Yankee, a Whig and a man of considerable financial and political aspirations. In succeeding years, he and Dodge, who was a Missourian and passionate Democrat, maintained a straight forward relationship. They utterly hated one another. More than ten years Dodge's junior, James Duane Doty would die on June 13, 1865. His nemesis Henry Dodge survived him by two years. See Smith, Alice E., *The History of Wisconsin, Vol. 1: From Exploration to Statehood*, (State Historical Society of Wisconsin, Madison, 1973), 167, 194.
22. Pelzer, *Henry Dodge*, 42-43.
23. Draper, Lyman C. ed., *Collections of the State Historical Society of Wisconsin, Vol. 1*, (Democrat Printing Company, Madison, 1903), 331, note.
24. Pelzer, *Augustus Caesar Dodge*, 42-43.
25. "A Notable Pioneer Woman," *The Gazette*, Burlington, Iowa, clipping circa 1895, in the Mineral Point Room, Mineral Point, Wisconsin.
26. Waldman, *Atlas of the North American Indian*, 118. Henry Atkinson was born in 1792 in Person County, North Carolina. After joining the army in 1808 and serving in the west, he moved to New York, where he was promoted to colonel. He subsequently saw action in the War of 1812 and became commander of the 6th U. S. Infantry in 1815. He led two explorations of the Yellowstone River, one in 1819 and the second in 1825, when he assisted in negotiating peace and trade agreements with a variety of Plains tribes. He commanded federal forces during the Winnebago Uprising of 1827 and Black Hawk War, five years later. Atkinson also oversaw the eviction of the Winnebago to Iowa. His busy military career did afford him a family. He wed Mary Ann Bullitt in 1826, subsequently having a son Edward. Henry Atkinson died on June 14, 1842 at the age of 60 years. See Ghent, W. J., "Atkinson, Henry," *Dictionary of American Biography, Vol. 1*, (Charles Scribner's Sons, 1928).
27. Western Historical Company, *History of Iowa County, Wisconsin*, (Western Historical Company, Chicago, 1881), 464.
28. Derleth, *The Wisconsin, River of a Thousand Isles*, 66-67.
29. Western Historical Company, *History of Iowa County, Wisconsin*, 464.
30. Derleth, *The Wisconsin, River of a Thousand Isles*, 66.

31. Western Historical Company, *History of Iowa County*, 464.
32. *Dictionary of Wisconsin Biography*, (The State Historical Society of Wisconsin, Madison, 1960), 299.
33. Buley, *The Old Northwest, Pioneer Period, 1815-1840, Vol. 2*, 59.

Chapter 10-Captain of an Aggressive Civilization

1. Parkinson, "Pioneer Life in Wisconsin," 332.
2. Crawford, George and Robert M. Crawford, *Memoirs of Iowa County, Wisconsin from the Earliest Historical Times Down to the Present*, (Northwestern Historical Association, 1913), 177-178.
3. Western Historical Company, *History of Iowa County*, 465, 467, 738.
4. Schafer, Joseph, *The Wisconsin Lead Region*, (State Historical Society of Wisconsin and Antes Press, Evansville, 1932), 118.
5. Clark, *Life on Wisconsin's Lead Mining Frontier*, 6.
6. The Gazette, "A Notable Pioneer Woman."
7. Pelzer, *Augustus Caesar Dodge*, 44.
8. *Ste. Genevieve Archives*, (Missouri Historical Society, West Manuscripts, Columbia), *folder 843*.
9. Clark, *Life on Wisconsin's Lead Mining Frontier*, 5.
10. Pelzer, *Henry Dodge*, 33.
11. Hagan, William T., *The Sac and Fox Indians*, (University of Oklahoma Press, Norman, 1958), 106.
12. Clark, *Life on Wisconsin's Lead Mining Frontier*, 6.
13. Western Historical Company, *History of Iowa County*, 472.
14. Petersen, *Steam Boating on the Upper Mississippi*, 243.
15. Western Historical Company, *History of Iowa County*, 472.
16. Davidson, W., "Personal Narratives of the Black Hawk War," *Collections of the State Historical Society of Wisconsin*, edited by Lyman C. Draper, vol. 5, (Democrat Printing Company, Madison, 1907), 318.
17. Western Historical Company, *History of Iowa County*, 467. See also Crawford, *Memoirs of Iowa County, Wisconsin*, 178.
18. *History of Southeast Missouri, Biographical Index, 598-599*, Arizona State Archives folder.
19. Crawford, *Memoirs of Iowa County, Wisconsin*, 178.
20. Clark, *Life on Wisconsin's Lead Mining Frontier*, 16-17.
21. Western Historical Company, *History of Iowa County*, 741.
22. Clark, *Life on Wisconsin's Lead Mining Frontier*, 16-19.
23. Parkinson, Daniel M. "Pioneer Life in Wisconsin," 335.
24. Clark, *Life on Wisconsin's Lead Mining Frontier*, 19-20.
25. Crawford; *Memoirs of Iowa County, Wisconsin*, 179.
26. *Dodge, Henry, oversize folder*, Iowa State Historical Society, Des Moines.
27. Smith, Alice E., *The History of Wisconsin, Vol. 1: From Exploration to Statehood*, (State Historical Society of Wisconsin, Madison, 1973), 241.
28. Schafer, *The Wisconsin Lead Region*, 77.
29. Carter. Clarence E., *Territorial Papers of the United States, Vol. 12: Michigan Territory, 1829-1837*, Government Printing Office, Washington, DC 1949, 136-137.
30. Clark, *Life on Wisconsin's Lead Mining Frontier*, 23.

Chapter 11-A Nastier Little War

1. Buley, *The Old Northwest, Pioneer Period, 1815-1840, Vol. 2*, 126.
2. Sturtevant, *Handbook of North American Indians, Vol. 15 Northeast*, 598-599, 648-649.
3. Waldman, *Atlas of the North American Indian*, 118-119.
4. Sturtevant, *Handbook of North American Indians, Vol. 15, Northeast*, 650.
5. Hagan, *The Sac and Fox Indians*, 126-127, 131, 133.
6. Waldman, *Atlas of the North American Indian*, 119.
7. Hagan, *The Sac and Fox Indians*, 135-136.
8. Blackhawk, *Black Hawk, An Autobiography*, 17-18, 116, 118-119.
9. Smith, Henry, *The Expedition Against the Sauk and Fox Indians, 1832*, (Military and Naval Magazine Reprint, New York, 1914), 5.
10. Hagan, *The Sac and Fox Indians*, 145.
11. Braun, Robert A., "Black Hawk's War, April 5-August 2, 1832-A Chronology," *Old Lead Region Historical Society*, September, 2001, http://www.geocities.com/old_lead/bhwchron.htm (accessed September 7, 2009)
12. Parkinson, "Pioneer Life in Wisconsin," 336.
13. Blackhawk, *Black Hawk, An Autobiography*, 119-122.
14. Pelzer, *Henry Dodge*, 66. Ironically, his squadron included a local Oneida Indian man, whose tribe the Americans had ejected from New York. See Draper, *Collections of the State Historical Society of Wisconsin, Vol. 2*, 334.
15. Pelzer, *Henry Dodge*, 55.
16. Dodge, Adele, Pension Claim, Oct.22, 1892, *Index to the Compiled Service Records of Volunteer Soldiers Who Served During Indian Wars & Disturbances, 1815-1858*, National Archives, Records of the Adjutant General's Office, Record Group 94, M629, Washington, 1965, Microfilm Reel 10.
17. Hagan, *The Sac and Fox Indians*, 153-155.
18. Western Historical Company, *History of Iowa County*, 479.
19. Thwaites, Rueben G., "The Story of the Black Hawk War" in Thwaites, *Collections of the State Historical Society of Wisconsin, Vol. 12*, (Democrat Printing Company, Madison, 1892), 245.

Chapter 12-A Soft Shelled Breed

1. Braun, "Black Hawk's War, April 5-August 2, 1832-A Chronology," 2.
2. Jackson, *Black Hawk, An Autobiography*, 123-124, 127.
3. Western Historical Company, *History of Iowa County*, 480-481.
4. Pelzer, *Henry Dodge*, 53.
5. The Gazette, "A Notable Pioneer Woman."
6. Salter, William, *The Life of Henry Dodge, from 1782 to 1833: With Portrait by George Catlin and Maps of the Battles of the Pecatonica and Wisconsin Heights in the Black Hawk War*, (Burlington, Iowa, unknown publisher,1890), Illinois Historical Digitization Projects, Northern Illinois University Libraries, 2001. http://lincoln.lib.niu.edu/file.php?file=dodge.html, 28, (accessed June 9, 2011).
7. Blackhawk, *Black Hawk, An Autobiography*, 128, 132.

8. Eby, Cecil D., *"That Disgraceful Affair," The Black Hawk War*, (W. W. Norton & Company, New York, 1973), 150. See also Hagan, *The Sac and Fox Indians*, 164.
9. Jackson, *Black Hawk, An Autobiography*, 128.
10. Eby, *"That Disgraceful Affair," The Black Hawk War*, 167.
11. Braun, "Black Hawk's War, April 5–August 2, 1832-A Chronology," 2.
12. Eby, *"That Disgraceful Affair," The Black Hawk War*, 168. See also Hagan, *The Sac and Fox Indians*, 161.
13. *Dodge, Henry, oversize folder*, Iowa State Historical Society, Des Moines.
14. Parkinson, "Pioneer Life in Wisconsin," 339.
15. Braun, "Black Hawk's War, April 5–August 2, 1832-A Chronology," 2.
16. *Letters Sent by the Office of Indian Affairs, 1824–1881, Records of the Michigan Superintendency, 1814–1818, Letters Received*, National Archives, Record Group 75, M1, (Washington, DC 1940), frames 129-130.
17. Braun, "Black Hawk's War, April 5–August 2, 1832-A Chronology," 2.
18. Salter, *The Life of Henry Dodge, from 1782 to 1833*, 53.
19. Pelzer, *Henry Dodge*, 55. See also Draper, *Collections of the State Historical Society of Wisconsin, Vol. 2*, 342.
20. Western Historical Company, *History of Iowa County*, 128.
21. Pelzer, *Henry Dodge*, 55, 56.

Chapter 13-Army of the Frontier

1. Hagan *The Sac and Fox Indians*, 166.
2. Eby, *"That Disgraceful Affair," The Black Hawk War*, 184.
3. Draper, *Collections of the State Historical Society of Wisconsin, Vol. 2*, 371.
4. Pelzer, *Henry Dodge*, 57-59.
5. Blackhawk, *Black Hawk, An Autobiography*, 131, note.
6. Eby, *"That Disgraceful Affair," The Black Hawk War*, 191.
7. Salter, *The Life of Henry Dodge, from 1782 to 1833*, 43.
8. Western Historical Company, *History of Iowa County*, 483-484.
9. Eby, *"That Disgraceful Affair," The Black Hawk War*, 192. See also Hagan, *The Sac and Fox Indians*, 169 and Blackhawk, *Black Hawk, An Autobiography*, 129-130.
10. Blackhawk, *Black Hawk, An Autobiography*, 130-131.
11. Thwaites, *Collections of the State Historical Society of Wisconsin, Vol. 12*, 246.
12. Salter, *The Life of Henry Dodge, from 1782 to 1833*, 53.
13. Salter, *The Life of Henry Dodge, from 1782 to 1833*, 44. There had long been a less than amicable competition between the settlers of Illinois and western Michigan Territory. The Badgers, who nearly all derived from Missouri, referred to the miners of northwestern Illinois as Suckers. The nickname was probably first applied in 1827 at Galena among Missouri and Illinois miners. There are various renditions as to origin of the term. One version maintains that the name Sucker derived from the suckerfish, one of the few fish of the region that migrates upstream each spring. Missourians noted that the Illinois folks, who nearly all hailed from the southern part of the state, resembled the sucker. Lacking the toughness to survive harsh winters, they left the lead fields each fall and returned each spring. A second version implies that the Illinois folks were nothing better than the suckers on a tobacco plant that must be stripped off to

insure the main plant matures robustly: in other words, they were Southern poor white trash compelled by their lower class poverty and sloth to move to Illinois to make a living. Either way, the term was distinctly vulgar and derisive. Not to be undone, the Illinois miners answered with their own nickname for the Badgers from Missouri. They referred to them as Missouri Pukes. The Pukes were low class ruffians and rowdies that Missouri had vomited up to the northern lead mines to be rid of the worst of her population. See Ford, Thomas "The Winnebago War and Why Illinoisans are Suckers" in *History of Illinois, 1854*, www.illinoishistory.com/winnebagowar.html, (accessed September 19, 2009)

14. Braun, "Black Hawk's War, April 5–August 2, 1832-A Chronology," 2.
15. Pelzer, *Henry Dodge*, 60. Not surprisingly, William Hamilton little resembled the image of sophistication and refinement presented by his statesman father, Alexander Hamilton. Although contemporaries described him as a congenial and able gentleman, they remembered him as a coarsely clad eccentric who shunned social contact, never married and lived in a humble style more reminiscent of a monk. In 1849 the lure of California gold drew him to Sacramento. Cholera cut his ambitions short and he died there on August 7th, 1850 at the age of fifty-three. He was buried with other cholera victims in a mass grave marked simply with the number 50. In 1877, a family friend Cyrus Woodman reburied his remains and put up a headstone in part reading "Colonel W. S. Hamilton . . . In size and features, in talent and character, he much resembled his illustrious father." In 1887, the city of Sacramento renamed the section in the cemetery around the grave Hamilton's Square. Relatives later erected a larger monument bearing Billie's name and a bronze relief of Alexander Hamilton, the father he had hardly known. See "Billy Hamilton and Hamilton's Diggings," *The Old Lead Region Historical Society*, www.geocities.com/old_lead/wiota.htm, (accessed September 19, 2009).
16. Thwaites, *The Life of Henry Dodge, from 1782 to 1833*, 248.
17. Bracken, Charles, "Further Strictures on Ford's Black Hawk War" *Collections of the State Historical Society of Wisconsin,* edited by Lyman C. Draper, vol. 2, (Democrat Printing Company, Madison, 1908), 404. See also Thwaites, *The Life of Henry Dodge, from 1782 to 1833*, 248.
18. Hagan, *The Sac and Fox Indians*, 171-172, 174. From fingers to hearts to heads, the practice of taking body parts as trophies of war is as old to humanity as it is widespread. Scalping was a common practice among many American Indian peoples, a practice later encouraged, supported and adopted by European immigrants to the New World and their American descendents. Once an enemy was felled, the warrior rushed up and pressed a knee firmly between the shoulder blades of the prostrate adversary, whether dead or alive. Jerking the victim's head firmly back by the hair, he swiftly slit the skin across the forehead, drew his knife blade completely around the circumference of the head and violently yanked the scalp free. Scalping itself was not fatal, though complications from blood loss and disease often were, and there are harrowing tales of folks who survived the painful act. Traditionally, scalping was uncommon in 16th and 17th century Europe. Usually the entire heads would be severed and displayed as trophies.

Archaeological evidence seems to support the existence of scalping among native peoples before European contact. European explorers as early as 1535 made note of the widespread practice. By 1688, both the French and British were encouraging the practice by offering generous bounties for the scalps of their enemies, both native and European. In American Indian cultures, scalps had significance in war, religion, society and aesthetics. Americans in the 19th century took scalps almost exclusively as souvenirs. It was a macabre notion of the times that a variety of body parts could be taken for conversation pieces and not exclusively from vanquished

Indian warriors. In 1864, Colonel Chivington and his Colorado Volunteers slaughtered Cheyenne men, women and children at Sand Creek, taking away scalps, fingers, genitalia and breasts for knickknacks. After being lynched in 1881 in Rawlins, Wyoming, the outlaw known as Big Nose George Perrot was flayed and his skin made into a pair of shoes. Such was the common lure of morbid curiosity. See Axtell, James, "Scalping: The Ethno History of a Moral Question," and Axtell, James, and William C. Sturtevant, "The Unkindest Cut, or Who Invented Scalping? A Case Study," *The European and the Indian: Essays in the Ethnohistory of Colonial North America*, (Oxford University Press, New York, 1981).

19. Smith, *The Expedition Against the Sauk and Fox Indians, 1832*, 13. See also Hagan, *The Sac and Fox Indians*, 173 and Thwaites, *The Life of Henry Dodge, from 1782 to 1833*, 249.
20. Thwaites, *The Life of Henry Dodge, from 1782 to 1833*, 249.
21. Hagan, *The Sac and Fox Indians*, 175-176.
22. Eby, *"That Disgraceful Affair," The Black Hawk War*, 210-211.
23. Hagan, *The Sac and Fox Indians*, 175-176.
24. Thwaites, *The Life of Henry Dodge, from 1782 to 1833*, 250.
25. Hagan, *The Sac and Fox Indians*, 177-178.
26. Hagan, *The Sac and Fox Indians*, 178 and Chapman, C. B., "Early Events in the Four Lake Country" *Collections of the State Historical Society of Wisconsin*, edited by Lyman C. Draper, vol. 4, 343-349, (Democrat Printing Company, Madison, 1908), 345-346.
27. Thwaites, *The Life of Henry Dodge, from 1782 to 1833*, 252-253.
28. Hagan, *The Sac and Fox Indians*, 179.
29. Thwaites, *The Life of Henry Dodge, from 1782 to 1833*, 254. See also Western Historical Company, *History of Iowa County*, 434.
30. Chapman, C. B., "Early Events in the Four Lake Country" *Collections of the State Historical Society of Wisconsin*, edited by Lyman C. Draper, vol. 4, 343-349, (Democrat Printing Company, Madison, 1908), 346.
31. Hagan, *The Sac and Fox Indians*, 180.
32. Parkinson, "Pioneer Life in Wisconsin," 360.
33. Thwaites, *The Life of Henry Dodge, from 1782 to 1833*, 255-257. See also Hagan, *The Sac and Fox Indians*, 181.
34. Hagan, *The Sac and Fox Indians*, 182. See also Blackhawk, *Black Hawk, An Autobiography*, 18-19.
35. Thwaites, *The Life of Henry Dodge, from 1782 to 1833*, 256-257.

Chapter 14-Kill the Nits, Then You'll Have No Lice

1. Thwaites, *Collections of the State Historical Society of Wisconsin, Vol. 12*, 258.
2. Blackhawk, *Black Hawk, An Autobiography*, 137.
3. Hagan, *The Sac and Fox Indians*, 186. See also Smith, *The History of Wisconsin, Vol. 1: From Exploration to Statehood*, 139 and Thwaites, *Collections of the State Historical Society of Wisconsin, Vol. 12*, 258.
4. Eby, *"That Disgraceful Affair," The Black Hawk War*, 244-246.
5. Hagan, *The Sac and Fox Indians*, 188. For the Iowa County Volunteer, Michigan Militia companies involved that day, see Alderfer, William K., *The Black Hawk War, 1831-1832*, (Collections of the Illinois State Historical Society, 1975), 969.

6. Blackhawk, *Black Hawk, An Autobiography*, 138. See also Thwaites, *Collections of the State Historical Society of Wisconsin, Vol. 12*, 25.
7. Eby, "That Disgraceful Affair," *The Black Hawk War*, 252.
8. Hagan, *The Sac and Fox Indians*, 189.
9. Blackhawk, *Black Hawk, An Autobiography*, 138.
10. Eby, "That Disgraceful Affair," *The Black Hawk War*, 252-254. The saying 'nits breed lice' neatly sums up the prevalent attitude of frontier whites towards their red brethren, an attitude that precipitated one scandalous massacre after another throughout the 18th and 19th centuries. Though its meaning is clear, its source and width of application among English speaking conquerors is unknown. Oliver Cromwell purportedly used it as early as 1649 to justify the slaughter of Irish Catholics. An early American reference is found from around the time of the Puritan Indian wars of the mid 1600s, when the English settlers recited a ditty regarding the Indians, "A swarm of Flies, they may arise/a Nation to annoy/Yea Rats and Mice or Swarms of Lice/a Nation may destroy." See Churchill, Ward, *A Little Matter of Genocide: Holocaust and Denial in the Americas, 1492 to the Present*, (City Lights Books, San Francisco, 1997), 178-179.

Louis Pelzer claimed a malevolent Piankeshaw chief, seeing the infant Moses Henry Dodge in his cradle, remarked "nits make lice; this little nit may grow to be a big louse and bite us . . ." See Pelzer, *Augustus Caesar Dodge*, 271. In this case it is probable Pelzer, having himself heard the phrase, misapplied it in the purported quotation. H. L. Hall, the murderous exterminator of native peoples of Mendocino County, California was quoted by a neighbor, William T. Scott, as having said that he didn't want any man going with him on an Indian killing expedition who would not kill all Indians because a "nit would make a louse." See Lynwood Carranco and Estle Beard, *Genocide and Vendetta, The Round Valley Wars of Northern California*, University of Oklahoma Press, Norman, 1981.

The most familiar instance of the phrase's use was by Colonel John Chivington in the 1864 slaughter of Cheyenne families at Sand Creek, Colorado who asserted that he would "kill and scalp all, little and big, that nits make lice." See David Svaldi, *Sand Creek and the Rhetoric of Extermination*, (University Press of America, Lanham, MD, 1989). An aged veteran of the Sand Creek affair, Morse Coffin, explained that the expression 'nits make lice" meant to make a clean thing of it, that it was commonly heard among both Denver gentlemen and ladies supporting a war of Indian extermination.

In 1851, Charles Bennett, soldiering in New Mexico noted that a group of them had heard noises in the dark just outside their camp one night and after searching the willows by the streamside discovered a Jicarilla Apache baby strapped to a cradleboard. "An old gruff soldier stepped up and said, 'Let me see that brat.' I handed it to him. He picked up a heavy stone, tied it to the board, dashed the baby and all into the water . . .The soldier's only comment was, 'You're a little fellar now but will make a big Injun bye and bye. I only wish I had more to treat the same way.'" Earlier that day, the soldiers had buried Mrs. White, a captive white woman purportedly killed by the Jicarilla. See Bennett, James A., *Forts and Forays: James A. Bennett, a Dragoon in New Mexico, 1850-1856*, edited by Clinton E. Brooks and Frank D. Reeve, (University of New Mexico Press, Albuquerque, 1948), 25.

In defense of the Michigan and Illinois militiamen's actions, if it can be so construed, they were a product of their times and their atrocities against the helpless were traditional acts of vengeance passed down from the earliest English colonists.

11. Frank McNitt to Elizabeth Sheridan Spearman, March 10, 1972, *The Frank McNitt Collection*,

New Mexico State Records and Archives Center, Santa Fe. See also Pelzer, *Henry Dodge*, 63-64. Eyewitness accounts of events recalled ten, twenty or thirty years after the fact are regularly fraught with errors, either mistakenly or intentionally. One chronicler of the Black Hawk War insisted that the campaign was undertaken in the autumn of 1832 under the leadership of General Scott. In relating his journey through southwest Wisconsin, he stated: "Arriving at Mineral Point, met a son of General Dodge, from whom I engaged a good supply of smoked side pork, not needed for the troops, as the war had closed. I engaged flour at $14 per barrel. During our journey the weather had been warm and smoky, but the night of our arrival a terrible snow storm occurred, continuing thirty-six hours, with drifts fifteen to twenty feet high ..." He had probably met Henry L. Dodge, but most assuredly long after the Black Hawk War had closed. See the *Report of the Pioneer Society of the State of Michigan Vol. 3*, (W. S. George & Co Lansing 1881).

12. Waldman, *Atlas of the North American Indian*, 120.
13. Thwaites, *Collections of the State Historical Society of Wisconsin, Vol. 12*, 261.
14. Hagan, *The Sac and Fox Indians*, 190.
15. Pelzer, *Henry Dodge*, 64.
16. Jones, George W., "Robert S. Black and the Black Hawk War," *Wisconsin State Historical Society Collections*, edited by Lyman C. Draper, vol. 10, (Democratic Printing Company, Madison, 1895), 229-230.
17. Smith, *The History of Wisconsin, Vol. 1: From Exploration to Statehood*, 139.
18. Blackhawk, *Black Hawk, An Autobiography*, 151.
19. Sturtevant, *Handbook of North American Indians, Vol. 15, Northeast*, 653. Among the Americans, there was never doubt as to the ultimate outcome. During a brief visit to Galena in the fall of 1832, Colonel Charles Whittlesey described throngs of adventurers lining the east shore of the Mississippi in anticipation of the United States wresting from the Sauk valuable Dubuque mineral lands on the west bank. Soldiers had been assigned as guards to prevent squatters from crossing and taking illegal possession. Although not completely unsympathetic with the settlers, Whittlesey ventured to state that squatters who were killed while encroaching on Indian property got what they deserved. See Whittlesey, Charles, "Recollections of a Tour Through Wisconsin in 1832" *Collections of the State Historical Society of Wisconsin*, edited by Lyman C. Draper, vol. 1, 64-85, (Democrat Printing Company, Madison, 1903), 82.
20. Smith, *The Expedition Against the Sauk and Fox Indians, 1832*, 19.
21. Blackhawk, *Black Hawk, An Autobiography*, 22-24.
22. Jones, "Robert S. Black and the Black Hawk War," 229-230. Black Hawk nurtured his disgust for Keokuk to the last. In 1836, during the sale of Sauk lands, the frontier artist George Catlin noted that the chief, dressed in "an old frock coat and brown hat on, and a cane in his hand ... stood the whole time outside of the group, and in dumb and dismal silence." Makataimeshekiakiak died two years later, on October 3, 1838, at roughly seventy-one years of age. An Illinois doctor spirited off his corpse, doubtlessly justifying it for the furthering of scientific elucidation. His bones were eventually returned to Governor Lucas at Burlington, Iowa in 1840, but were never reburied. Bundled in a box, they were moved to Iowa City and stored in a law office until 1853, when they and the building were destroyed by fire. See Catlin quoted by Blackhawk, *Black Hawk, An Autobiography*, 151 and Thwaites, *Collections of the State Historical Society of Wisconsin, Vol. 12*, 262-263.

Chapter 15-Politics Again

1. Woodward, Gilbert Mortier, *James Duane Doty*, 134.
2. Woodward, *James Duane Doty*, 407, note 30.
3. Schafer, *The Wisconsin Lead Region*, 78-79.
4. Bounty Land Warrant No. 51557 for 160 Acres 155 Wed Oct. of 1855.
5. Fox, "The Grove."
6. Neil Giffey to author, 1995. See also Western Historical Company, *History of Iowa County*, 757, 881.
7. Pelzer, *Augustus Caesar Dodge*, 44.
8. Dodge, Henry oversize folder, *Iowa State Historical Society*, (Des Moines, Iowa). See also Goodspeed, *History of Southeast Missouri*, 245.
9. Pelzer, *Henry Dodge*, 81-85.
10. Davis never forgot Mary. In 1883, the old and frail Confederate president wrote her fondly, "Widely and long we have been separated, but your image has not been dimmed by time and distance. . . . If you have preserved enough of the pleasant memories of one springtime to care for one who flitted with You over the flowers of youth's happy garden, it will give me sincere gratification to hear from you . . ." Jefferson Davis to Mrs. John Dement, February 4, 1883, *D. Rowland, Papers, 12*, 203. See also Monroe, Haskell M., ed., *The Papers of Jefferson Davis, Vol. 1, 1808-1840* edited by Haskell M. Monroe, Jr. and James T. McIntosh, (Louisiana State University Press, Baton Rouge, 1971), 286-287.
11. Iowa State Historical Society, "Letters of Henry Dodge," *The Annals of Iowa, Vol. 3*, 1897-98, (Iowa State Historical Society, Des Moines), 221-222, 292, 294.
12. Dodge, Henry oversize folder, *Iowa State Historical Society*.
13. Smith, *The History of Wisconsin, Vol. 1: From Exploration to Statehood*, 250.
14. Confirmation of Marriages, Church Records, 1836, *Ste. Genevieve County Court House*.
15. Western Historical Company, *History of Iowa County, Wisconsin*, 776, 881.
16. Palmer, Strange M., "Western Wisconsin in 1836," *Collections of the State Historical Society of Wisconsin*, edited by Lyman C. Draper, vol. 6, (Democrat Printing Company, Madison, 1908), 298. See also *History of La Fayette County, Wisconsin*, author unknown, 1881, 617.
17. Pelzer, *Henry Dodge*, 137-138.
18. Way, Royal Brunson, *The Rock River Valley: Its History, Traditions, Legends and Charms*, (S. J. Clarke Publishing Company, 1926), 177-178.
19. Smith, *The History of Wisconsin, Vol. 1: From Exploration to Statehood*, 254-58. See also *History of La Fayette County, Wisconsin*, 1881, 621.
20. Western Historical Company, *History of Iowa County*, 475, 754.
21. *The Henry L. Dodge Family Bible*, The Mineral Point Room, Mineral Point Public Library, Mineral Point, Wisconsin.
22. *Mineral Point Miners Free Press*, April 16, 1839.
23. *Mineral Point Miners Free Press*, August 28, 1838.
24. *Mineral Point Miners Free Press*, November 20, 1838.
25. Kennedy, *The Brief American Pageant: A History of the Republic*, 162-163.
26. Johnson, Allen, ed., *Dictionary of American Biography, Vol. 5*, (Charles Scribner's Sons, New York, 1959), 172-173. See also Nesbit, *Wisconsin: A History*, 126. Jones briefly served as surveyor general of Iowa and Wisconsin in 1840, and then was removed in 1841. In 1844, he

was in Mineral Point, serving as clerk of the district court for Iowa County. Finally, in 1845, George Jones moved permanently to Dubuque, Iowa. There his political career would resurrect most robustly.

27. Smith, *The History of Wisconsin, Vol. 1: From Exploration to Statehood*, 263.
28. Pelzer, *Henry Dodge*, 150, 153. Such reasoning was common contrivance to usurp Indian lands bordering the white settlers. Failing to destroy a tribe, frontier leaders often proclaimed that the influence of white civilization, particularly that of alcoholism and disease, was so destructive to Indians that it was for their best to be "removed from the settlements." During those times, it was not seen as base hypocrisy to assert the superiority of white Christian society on one hand, and proclaim it evil and corrosive to Indian peoples on the other, irrespective of how acculturated a tribe had become. There is no doubt the degenerating influence of disease and liquor weighed heavy on the Indian, as it does on all disinherited and defeated peoples. The Stockbridge band of New York had already experienced one expulsion. As Iroquois, they had fought alongside the colonists against the British during the Revolution. With the war won, the Americans soon dismissed that loyalty and deemed their presence a nuisance and had the band relocated to Wisconsin, purportedly for their own good. The tribe rapidly degraded. Demoralized, diseased, poverty stricken and ravaged by alcohol, they were eventually forced to move again.
29. *Milwaukee Sentinel*, March 19, 26, 1839 and September 17, 1839, November 3, 1840 and December 15, 1840.
30. Nesbit, Robert C., *Wisconsin: A History*, (University of Wisconsin Press, Madison, 1989), 112.
31. Thwaites, Rueben G. ed., *Collections of the State Historical Society of Wisconsin, Vol. 15*, (Democrat Printing Company, Madison, 1900), 365.
32. Smith, *The History of Wisconsin, Vol. 1: From Exploration to Statehood*, 331.
33. *Milwaukee Daily Sentinel*, March 19, 1839. John P. Sheldon **was** a newspaperman and politician originally from Massachusetts. After serving during the War of 1812, he became involved in newspapers in both New York and Detroit. After becoming a Democrat, he dabbled for a time in Michigan territorial politics. In 1833, Sheldon moved to Dubuque, Iowa to serve as the federal agent for the Dubuque lead-mine area. He was appointed register of the Mineral Point federal land office the following year. An ardent Dodge supporter, his tenure was marred by scandal. John Sheldon moved to Madison in 1843 then left Wisconsin for Washington, DC in 1845, where he served as a clerk in the U.S. Treasury Department at Washington, DC for fifteen years. He eventually returned to Wisconsin to retire and died in 1871.
34. *Mineral Point Miners Free Press*, November 12, 1839.

Chapter 16-The Devil's Foothold

1. Pelzer, *Augustus Caesar Dodge*, 63.
2. Smith, *The History of Wisconsin, Vol. 1: From Exploration to Statehood*, 365. See also Beckett, Eugene, *Becquet, Bequette, Beckett Family History: From Cambrai to Cambria*, (Eugene Beckett, 1991), 75.
3. *Mineral Point Miners Free Press*, April 16 and April 23, 1839.
4. *Mineral Point Miners Free Press*, June 11, 1839.
5. Nesbit, *Wisconsin: A History*, 100, 201-202. Byron Kilbourne later had a part in founding the city of Milwaukee and served as its mayor in 1848 and 1854. As railroad speculator he was

accused in 1858 of using over $600,000 in bribes to facilitate federal land grants. He survived that scandal and remained an influential Milwaukee citizen until 1868, when he moved to Jacksonville, Florida for his failing health. He died there two years later at the age of seventy. See "Kilbourne, Byron, 1801-1870," *Dictionary of Wisconsin History,* Wisconsin Historical Society, www.wisconsinhistory.org, (accessed September 15, 2009).

6. *Mineral Point Miners Free Press,* July 2, 1839.
7. *Mineral Point Miners Free Press,* July 9, 1839.
8. *Mineral Point Miners Free Press,* August 6, 1839.
9. *Mineral Point Miners Free Press,* August 24, 1839. See also Pelzer, *Henry Dodge,* 154.
10. *Mineral Point Miners Free Press,* June 16, 1840.
11. *Mineral Point Miners Free Press,* July 14, 1840.
12. *Mineral Point Miners Free Press,* August 3, 1840, excerpting a speech by the Honorable A. Duncan of Ohio.
13. Nesbit, *Wisconsin: A History,* 129-130.
14. Strong, Moses, *A History of the Territory of Wisconsin, 1836-1848,* (Democrat Printing Company, State Printers, Madison, Wisconsin, 1885), 346-347.
15. *Mineral Point Miners Free Press,* June 9, 1841.
16. Smith, *The History of Wisconsin, Vol. 1: From Exploration to Statehood,* 620.
17. Schafer, *The Wisconsin Lead Region,* 55.
18. Rodolf, Theodore, "Pioneering in the Wisconsin Lead Region," *Collections of the State Historical Society of Wisconsin, Vol. 15,* edited by Rueben Gold Thwaites, (Democrat Printing Company, Madison, 1900), 376-377.
19. The marriage of Nancy Adeline Dodge and Joseph Ward was a curious match, insomuch as Ward was a Whig and avid Doty supporter. Nancy was 37 years old at the time and had been married twice, by her first husband, George W. Scott, and by her second Lt. Gaines P. Kingsbury, who left her widowed in 1836. Joseph and Nancy moved to California in 1852, where Joseph died a year later. After marrying P. G. Sanders, Nancy Adeline herself expired in 1854 at the age of 49 years. Although she had been married four times, there is no evidence of any surviving children.
20. McNitt, Frank, *Navajo Wars: Military Campaigns, Slave Raids and Reprisals,* (University of New Mexico Press, Albuquerque, 1972), 98. See also Spearman to McNitt, November 8, 1971, *The Frank McNitt Collection.*
21. Goodspeed, *History of Southeast Missouri,* 245. Lewis Fields Linn heralded from one of those storied Kentucky pioneer families. He was born on November 5, 1785 near Louisville, Kentucky. His father was Ashael Linn and his mother Nancy Hunter Dodge, Israel Dodge's ex-wife. Ashael Linn himself endured tribulations both fantastic and legendary. Captured by Shawnee Indians, he and his brothers were adopted into Indian families and held for up to three years before making their escape. Ashael and Nancy were married sometime before 1795 and had three children, Mary, Lewis and William. Orphaned at age ten or twelve, Lewis made his way to Ste. Genevieve around 1812 in much the same manner as Henry Dodge had as a boy. Dodge took his frail-looking half brother in. Lewis undertook the study of medicine there then relocated to St. Louis to start a practice in 1833. While treating cholera victims, Linn contracted the disease and never completely recovered from it. His senatorial seat came quite by accident, as he was selected to replace the deceased Senator Buckner. He was again elected for a full term and became known as The Boy Senator and The Father of Oregon for a bill he introduced in

1838 authorizing American occupation of the Columbia River country. Lewis Linn remained a senator until his untimely death in 1843 at the age of 48. See Goodspeed, *History of Southeast Missouri*; 574. See also *The Frank McNitt Collection,* Spearman Genealogy chart, 1972; Basler, *Pioneers of Old Ste. Genevieve,* 126 and Rozier, *Between the Gabouri: A History of Ferdinand* quoted in Basler, 127.

22. *G. B. Billon v. Henry Dodge, 1843, Iowa Series 27, Judgment Book,* (Wisconsin Room, University Archives, University of Wisconsin, Platteville), Box 3, Folder 37.
23. *George Fay vs. H. L. Dodge No. 66 Appearances 1843,* Iowa Series 27, Judgment Book, Box 9, Folder 34,
24. *Wisconsin Territorial Papers, Proceedings of Iowa County Board of Supervisors, Vol. 2,* (Wisconsin Historical Records Survey, Madison, Wisconsin, 1942), 76.
25. *Iowa County Court Cases, Iowa Series 23,* (Wisconsin Room, Archives, University of Wisconsin, Platteville).
26. *United States v. Henry Dodge et al, No 35, Issues 1846, 28-36,* Iowa Series 27, Judgement Book, (Wisconsin Room, University Archives, University of Wisconsin, Platteville).
27. Rodolf, "Pioneering in the Wisconsin Lead Region," 378.
28. Pelzer, *Henry Dodge,* 165-167.
29. Nesbit, *Wisconsin: A History,* 130.
30. Western Historical Company, *History of Iowa County, Wisconsin,* 682. See also Thwaites, *Collections of the State Historical Society of Wisconsin, Vol. 15,* 381.
31. Woodward, *James Duane Doty,* 286.
32. Smith, *The History of Wisconsin, Vol. 1: From Exploration to Statehood,* 400.

Chapter 17-Mineral Point

1. Crawford, *Memoirs of Iowa County, Wisconsin,* 194.
2. Taylor, Stephen, "Mineral Point in Days of Yore" in Draper, *Collections of the State Historical Society of Wisconsin, Vol. 2,* (Democrat Printing Company, Madison, 1903), 486-487.
3. Smith, *The History of Wisconsin, Vol. 1: From Exploration to Statehood,* 186-187.
4. Palmer, "Western Wisconsin in 1836," 300.
5. Draper, Lyman C. ed., *Collections of the State Historical Society of Wisconsin, Vol. 1,* (Democrat Printing Company, Madison, 1903), 144-145.
6. Nesbit, *Wisconsin: A History,* 114.
7. Smith, *The History of Wisconsin, Vol. 1: From Exploration to Statehood,* 186, 400.
8. Theodore Rodolf recalled the spectacle of seeing one at Mineral Point shortly after the election of 1840. "A poor fellow, named William Caffee, had, while under the influence of liquor, about two years before stabbed and killed a man at a ball given at Berry's Grove. He fled, but was finally caught at St. Louis, and brought back to Mineral Point, where he had his trial. He was convicted of murder, and Judge Charles Dunn sentenced him to hang. When the fatal day arrived, the crowd of morbid sightseers that poured into the village was something wonderful. They began to arrive before daylight, and from as far as forty miles; they came by wagonloads, on horseback, and on foot, in a continuous stream. Old men and young women and children and babies were there, whole settlements were for a day abandoned, many brought their provisions with them, and camped upon the hill sides. Considering the sparsity of the populations, the gathering was larger than any circus nowadays can bring together. The stores and shops of

all kinds did that day a very large and profitable business." See Rodolf, "Pioneering in the Wisconsin Lead Region," 367.
9. *Mineral Point Miners Free Press*, November 24, 1840.
10. Rodolf, "Pioneering in the Wisconsin Lead Region," 366-367. See also *Mineral Point Miners Free Press*, November 17, 1840.
11. Rodolf, "Pioneering in the Wisconsin Lead Region," 358.
12. *Mineral Point Miners Free Press*, March 16, 1841
13. Rodolf, "Pioneering in the Wisconsin Lead Region," 369.
14. Rodolf, "Pioneering in the Wisconsin Lead Region," 362. See also Palmer, "Western Wisconsin in 1836," 299.
15. Rodolf, "Pioneering in the Wisconsin Lead Region," 378.
16. Western Historical Company, *History of Iowa County*, 666.
17. Rodolf, "Pioneering in the Wisconsin Lead Region," 380.
18. *Mineral Point Miners Free Press*, September 22, 1837.
19. *Mineral Point Miners Free Press*, August 14, 1838.
20. Rodolf, "Pioneering in the Wisconsin Lead Region," 364.
21. Rodolf, "Pioneering in the Wisconsin Lead Region," 371.
22. *Mineral Point Democrat*, May 30, 1845.
23. *Mineral Point Democrat*, June 5, 1845.
24. *Mineral Point Democrat*, August 20 and November 19, 1845. See also *Iowa Series 24 License Book 1839-1859: Marriages*, 212 and photo copy of an original document provided by Dean Conners of Foundry Books, Mineral Point, Wisconsin.
25. *Mineral Point Democrat*, April 11, 1845.
26. *Mineral Point Democrat*, August 6, 1845.
27. *Mineral Point Democrat*, April 25 and May 2, 1845.
28. Nesbit, *Wisconsin: A History*, 184-185.
29. Wisconsin Historical Records Survey, *Wisconsin Territorial Papers, Proceedings of Iowa County Board of Supervisors, Vols. 1-2, Executive Journal 1836-1848*, (Madison, Wisconsin, 1942), 112.
30. Bloom, John P., *Territorial Papers of the United States, Vol. 28: The Territory of Wisconsin*, (The National Archives and Records Service, General Services Administration, Washington, DC 1975), 788-789.
31. Bloom, *Territorial Papers of the United States, Vol. 28: The Territory of Wisconsin*, 876. See also *United States vs. Dodge*, (Special Collections, Wisconsin Room, University of Wisconsin, Platteville).
32. *United States vs. Henry Dodge et al*, (Special Collections, Wisconsin Room, University of Wisconsin, Platteville).
33. *Records of the Department of Treasury*, Record Group 56, M236, Microfilm Reel 17, frame 214, National Archives and Records Administration, Denver Regional Center, Denver, Colorado.
34. *Iowa Series 5*, folder 9, (Wisconsin Room, University of Wisconsin, Platteville).
35. *Records of the Department of the Treasury*, M236, Microfilm Reel 17, frame 218.

Chapter 18: Absquatulated

1. *Letters Received by the Adjutant General's Office*, National Archives, Records of the Adjutant General's Office, 1780-1917, Record Group 94, M567, R319 K173, 1846, frames 168, 171.

2. McNitt, Frank, ed., *Navaho Expedition, Journal of a Military Reconnaissance From Santa Fe, New Mexico to the Navaho Country, Made in 1849 by Lieutenant James H. Simpson* (University of Oklahoma Press, Norman, 1964), xlvii, note.
3. Underhill, Ruth, *Here Come the Navajo*, (U. S. Department of the Interior, Haskell Press, Haskell, Kansas, 1953), 145.
4. Elizabeth Sheridan Spearman to Frank McNitt, January 6, 1972, *The Frank McNitt Collection*.
5. Neil Giffey to author, 1995.
6. Eugene Beckett to author, February 2, 1996.
7. Stephen Watts Kearny was born August 20, 1794 in Newark, New Jersey, the son of an Irish Tory. He was well educated, attending Columbia University. He never attended West Point, but his military talents rapidly matured during the war of 1812. His first engagement at Queenston Heights was a serious defeat for the American troops. Wounded, Kearny was captured and held by the British in Quebec, along with Winfield Scott and other officers, until 1813. Between 1819 and 1824, Kearny served with the Army in the west. He was adjutant for Colonel Atkinson at Council Bluffs and was a member of the first and second Yellowstone Expeditions and had made several councils with the Ponca, Cheyenne, Ogallala and Mandan tribes. Brevetted Major in 1823 for faithful service, Kearny helped construct Jefferson Barracks and became the post's first commander. He received command of Fort Crawford in 1828, but was arrested shortly thereafter by the local sheriff for having the audacity to seize some lumber that settlers had illegally cut from Indian lands. Kearny was tried, but nothing came of it. Once Zachary Taylor assumed command there, Major Kearny returned to Jefferson Barracks. He was sent to New York City in 1832 as superintendent of recruiting, thereby missing the Black Hawk War.

In 1833, Kearny was appointed second-in-command of the 1st Dragoons under Henry Dodge. The regiment was later split to more effectively protect the frontier. Kearny and 113 soldiers were stationed at the new Fort Des Moines in Iowa. When Dodge resigned in the spring of 1838, Kearny took command of the 1st Dragoons at Fort Leavenworth. Known by 1842 as an efficient and upstanding officer of unbending principle, Stephen Kearny was assigned command of the 3rd Military Department, providing military escorts for traders along the Santa Fe Trail. Indeed, it was his command that defeated Jacob Snively's band of bandits, the so-called "Texas Invincibles", who were preying on the Santa Fe caravans. In 1845, just before the outbreak of hostilities with Mexico, Kearny and his dragoons reconnoitered the mountain regions as far as South Pass, Wyoming and along the Oregon Trail, returning via Bent's Fort. A proven organizer, commander, explorer and fighter, possessing an intimate knowledge of western trails and peoples, Kearny was the perfect pick to lead an American expeditionary force into the province of New Mexico. In the end it would bring him considerable grief.
8. Elizabeth Sheridan Spearman to Frank McNitt, January 6, 1972, *The Frank McNitt Collection*.
9. *Andrew J. Hewitt vs. Henry L. Dodge, 1847*, (Wisconsin Room, University Archives, University of Wisconsin, Platteville), Box 12, Folder 63.
10. Western Historical Company, *History of Lafayette County, Wisconsin, containing an account of its settlement, growth, development and resources; an extensive and minute sketch of its cities, towns and villages ...* (Western Historical Company, Chicago, 1881), 612, 615.
11. *Mineral Point Miners Free Press*, February 5, 1839.
12. Curiously, the census identified her as having been born in Iowa rather than Wisconsin. In the 1846 territorial census for Belmont, four people, two male and two female, were listed in

the Holtshouser residence. The identity of the additional couple is unknown. In a subsequent enumeration done in 1847, Oliver's surname was mistakenly represented as Owlsouser, with a total of three people in the household, presumably he, his wife, and infant Mary.
13. Dodge Genealogy Chart, Mineral Point Room, Mineral Point Public Library, Mineral Point, Wisconsin.
14. *Democrat Tribune*, July 2, 1964.
15. Neil Giffey to author, 1995.
16. Fox, "The Grove."
17. Beverly Finlay to author, August 20, 1997.

Chapter 19: Army of the West

1. Sunder, John E. ed., *Matt Field on the Santa Fe Trail*, (University of Oklahoma Press, Norman, 1960), 37.
2. Chalfant, William Y., *Dangerous Passage: The Santa Fe Trail and the Mexican War*, (University of Oklahoma Press, Norman, 1994), 3.
3. *The Missouri Republican*, June 20, 23, 25, 26, July 3, 1846. Manuel Armijo was a native of New Mexico, born at Albuquerque in about 1793. In 1822 and 1824 he served as alcalde for Albuquerque and as a lieutenant in the militia. He first rose to the position of governor of the province in 1827. Armijo again earned the governorship in 1837, but by less than democratic means. Governors habitually had been picked from the local upper classes until 1835, when the Mexican government appointed an outsider, one Albino Perez, to take the position. The locals viewed him with a great deal of suspicion and later blamed him for sweeping new and unpopular taxes imposed the following year. In the summer of 1837, a band of poor peons and Pueblo Indians overthrew and decapitated Perez, then elevated one José Gonzalez to governor. In response, Manuel Armijo and a small army occupied Santa Fe and defeated the insurgents. He had Gonzalez shot. In 1845, Armijo was reappointed as governor. See Simmons, Mark, *The Little Lion of the Southwest: A Life of Manuel Antonio Chaves*, (The Swallow Press Inc., Chicago, 1973), 45-46, 51-52. See also Wroth, William H., "Manuel Armijo" *New Mexico Office of the State Historian*, New Mexico State Record Center and Archives, 2004-2009, www.newmexicohistory.org/filedetails.php?fileID=549 (accessed September 25, 2009).
4. Barry, Louise, *The Beginnings of the West: Annals of the Kansas Gateway to the American West, 1540-1854*, (Kansas State Historical Society, Topeka, 1972), 593.
5. Chalfant, *Dangerous Passage: The Santa Fe Trail and the Mexican War*, 5.
6. Barry, *The Beginnings of the West*, 587-588, 590.
7. Sunseri, Alvin R., *Seeds of Discord: New Mexico in the Aftermath of the American Conquest, 1846-1861*, (Nelson-Hall, Chicago, 1979), 74.
8. Barry, *The Beginnings of the West*, 430.
9. Edwards, Frank S., *A Campaign in New Mexico With Colonel Doniphan*, (Carey and Hart, Philadelphia, 1847, reprinted by the University of New Mexico Press, Albuquerque, 1996), 26.
10. Barry, *The Beginnings of the West*, 600.
11. Magoffin, Susan Shelby, *Down the Santa Fe Trail and into Mexico: The Diary of Susan Shelby Magoffin, 1846-1847*, edited by Stella M. Drum, (Yale University Press, New Haven, 1926), 63-64, 68.
12. Magoffin, *Down the Santa Fe Trail and into Mexico*, 10.

13. Abert, James William, *Abert's New Mexico Report, 1846-'47*, edited by William A. Keleher, (Horne & Wallace Publishers, Albuquerque, 1962), 126.
14. Crutchfield, James A., *Tragedy at Taos: The Revolt of 1847*, (Republic of Texas Press, Plano, 1995), 159.
15. Barry, *The Beginnings of the West*, 620.
16. Magoffin, *Down the Santa Fe Trail and into Mexico*, 12.
17. Chalfant, *Dangerous Passage: The Santa Fe Trail and the Mexican War*, 11.
18. Edwards, *A Campaign in New Mexico With Colonel Doniphan*, 30-31. See also Clarke, Dwight L., ed., *The Original Journals of Henry Smith Turner with Stephen Watts Kearny to New Mexico and California, 1846-1847*, (University of Oklahoma Press, Norman, 1966), 64.
19. Chalfant, *Dangerous Passage: The Santa Fe Trail and the Mexican War*, 17.
20. Brown, William E., *The Santa Fe Trail, The National Park Service 1963 Historic Sites Survey*, (The Patrice Press, St. Louis, 1988), 181-182.
21. Chalfant, *Dangerous Passage: The Santa Fe Trail and the Mexican War*, 18.
22. Calvin, Ross, ed., *Lieutenant Emory Reports: A Reprint of Lieutenant W. H. Emory's Notes of a Military Reconnaissance*, (University of New Mexico Press, Albuquerque, 1951), 34.
23. Magoffin, *Down the Santa Fe Trail and into Mexico*, 80.
24. *Milwaukee Sentinel & Gazette*, August 27, 1847. See also Clarke, *The Original Journals of Henry Smith Turner*, 70.
25. Clarke, *The Original Journals of Henry Smith Turner*, 132.
26. *St. Louis Republican* quoted in *Milwaukee Daily Sentinel & Gazette*, August 27, 29 1847.
27. Barry, *The Beginnings of the West*, 624.
28. By the time Kearny had arrived at Bent's, he knew that Manuel Armijo and the New Mexicans would not oppose his invasion force. To insure they didn't, Colonel Kearny arranged a comprehensive tour of his entire command for three captured Mexican spies, and then gave them a reassuring circular proclaiming Kearny's promise to protect the people's property and civil and religious rights provided they did not resist the American occupation. He then sent them on their way. Kearny also dispatched Captain Philip St. George Cooke, Susan Magoffin's brother-in-law Don Santiago Magoffin and twelve dragoons to Santa Fe. He instructed Magoffin to meet with Armijo and arrange a mutually advantageous understanding. Santiago was the perfect mediator. He had been the U. S. Consul to Chihuahua, an influential trader and an in-law of Governor Armijo. It is possible that President Polk himself had authorized Magoffin to bribe Armijo.
After abandoning Apache Pass and Santa Fe to Kearny, Armijo fled south to Chihuahua in search of reinforcements. After surviving an inquest regarding his role in the loss of New Mexico, he returned to New Mexico and lived out his days in the comfort fitting an old caudillo. He died in 1853. See Wroth, William H., "Manuel Armijo", www.newmexicohistory.org/filedetails.php?fileID=549 (accessed September 25, 2009).
29. Simmons, *The Little Lion of the Southwest*, 92-94.

Chapter 20-Montezuma's Fire

1. Edwards, *A Campaign in New Mexico With Colonel Doniphan*, 43-44.
2. Davis, W. W. H., *El Gringo or New Mexico and Her People*, (Rydal Press, Santa Fe, 1938 reprint of Harper & Brothers, New York, 1857). William Watts Hart Davis authored several books, his

most notable being *El Gringo or New Mexico and Her People*, probably the most comprehensive American study of New Mexico life at that time. He was born in 1820 in Southampton Township, Pennsylvania, graduated from Norwich University in 1842 and subsequently taught at the Virginia Military Academy. Davis returned to Pennsylvania in 1844 to practice law and was admitted to the bar and to the Harvard Law School in 1846. He left Harvard after his first semester and enlisted to fight in the Mexican War with the First Regiment of the Massachusetts Infantry. He was stationed in a variety of locations in Mexico, including Saltillo, Buena Vista and Mexico City, though he apparently never saw battle. He was mustered out as captain in 1848 and returned to his law practice.

Davis accepted an offer to become the United States District Attorney for New Mexico Territory and arrived in Santa Fe in November of 1853. His duties kept him in the saddle for a great amount of the time, traveling to U. S. District Courts through present day New Mexico, Arizona and Colorado. Between 1853 and 1857, Davis served as the United States District Attorney, attorney general, superintendent of public buildings, secretary and acting governor of the Territory of New Mexico, concurrently publishing the *Santa Fe Gazette* in partnership with James Collins. Davis was discontented in New Mexico, believing his talents were being squandered. After purchasing the *Doylestown Democrat* in 1857 he returned to Pennsylvania. During the Civil War W. W. H. Davis was captain of Company I 25th Regiment of Pennsylvania Volunteers. He served in the Army of the Potomac and was later brevetted brigadier general for his service at the siege of Charleston, during which time a Confederate shell blew off most of the fingers on his right hand. He mustered out in 1864. A lifelong Democrat, Davis ran unsuccessfully for Congress in 1882 and 1884. He later served under Grover Cleveland as the United States Pension Agent in Philadelphia. He took a great interest in Pennsylvania historical societies. William Watts Hart Davis died in Doylestown, Pennsylvania, in 1910 at the age of 90 years. See Twitchell, Ralph E., *The Leading Facts of New Mexican History, Vol. 2*, (Horn & Wallace, Albuquerque, New Mexico, 1963), 313, note 221.

3. Sunseri, *Seeds of Discord*, 80. Josiah Gregg was an explorer, trader and one of the first Americans to write about the Santa Fe Trail. Born in Tennessee, he moved with his family to Illinois in 1809 and then to Missouri in 1812. His first trip to Santa Fe was made in 1831, followed by several expeditions to New Mexico. His recollections were published in 1844 under the title *Commerce of the Prairies*. After serving with General Wool in the Mexican War, he joined the gold rush to California in 1849, where he died while leading prospectors across the mountains during winter.
4. Davis, *El Gringo*, 71, 73, 891.
5. Davis, *El Gringo*, 40, 51-52.
6. Allison, W. H. H., "Santa Fe in 1846," *Old Santa Fe Magazine*, April 1915, 395-396, 401-406.
7. Gardner, Mark L., ed., *The Mexican War Correspondence of Richard Smith Elliot*, edited and annotated by Mark L. Gardner and Marc Simmons, (University of Oklahoma Press, Norman, 1997), 87-88.
8. Abert, *Abert's New Mexico Report, 1846-'47*, 37. James William Abert was born in 1820 in New Jersey. His father, Major John J. Abert, was chief of the Bureau of Topographical Engineers. James graduated from Princeton University in 1838 and promptly entered West Point. He was first assigned to the 5th Infantry in 1842, and then transferred to the Corps of Topographical Engineers the following year to conduct a survey of the northern lakes. At about that time he married Jane Stone and had one son. In the summer of 1845, Abert joined the quirky and

unpredictable Charles Frémont on his third expedition to explore the Canadian River country. Frémont preferred to take his men to California, and turned the reconnaissance over to Abert and a party of civilians. Abert's reconnaissance led him through eastern New Mexico and across the Texas panhandle, noting the flora, fauna and landmarks, meeting Comancheros and Kiowa along the way. The expedition eventually disbanded at Fort Gibson and Abert returned to St. Louis.

Upon arriving in Santa Fe with Kearny, he made a thorough survey of New Mexico as far south as Socorro, taking copious notes for a report he would later submit to Congress. He joined the faculty of West Point in 1848 and taught drawing. In 1853 he was promoted to first lieutenant and then to captain in 1856. In the wake of his first wife's untimely death, he married Lucy Taylor, and had several children. Abert traveled to Europe in 1860 to study military affairs, and then served the Union during the Civil War from 1861 to 1862 on campaigns in the Shenandoah Valley. He was promoted to major in 1863 but had to resign after suffering a severe injury falling from his horse. Abert first entered the mercantile business in Cincinnati, Ohio, and then became a patents examiner in Washington, DC. From 1877 to 1879 he taught English literature at the University of Missouri. He later became president of the Examining Board of Teachers for the Kentucky public schools. James William Abert died on August 10, 1897 at the age of 77 years. See "James William Abert, 1820-1897" *in U. S. Corps of Topographical Engineers*, Topographical Engineers Homepage, 1995-2006, www.topogs.org/b_abertjw.html (accessed September 29, 2009)

9. Magoffin, *Down the Santa Fe Trail and into Mexico*, 163.
10. Allison, "Santa Fe in 1846," 396-397.
11. Davis, *El Gringo*, 174-175, 189.
12. Abert, *Abert's New Mexico Report, 1846-'47*, 46.
13. Webb, James Josiah, *Adventures in the Santa Fe Trade 1844-1847*, Southwest Historical Series, edited by Ralph P. Bieber, (The Arthur H. Clark Company, Glendale, California, 1931), 97. James Josiah Webb was a life-long freighter and businessman of the Santa Fe Trail. He was born in Connecticut in 1818 and during the early 1840s managed general stores in Georgia and later St. Louis. In 1844, at the age of 26, he took his first load of merchandise over the trail to Santa Fe, where he subsequently set up a store. Through the years he took several partners, first George P. Doan of St. Louis and then William S. Messervy of Salem, Massachusetts. In 1853 he and John Kingsbury partnered to form the firm of Webb and Kingsbury, reputedly the largest such company in Santa Fe. Government contracts made his company prosperous. Webb himself habitually resided in New Haven, Connecticut where he ordered and shipped goods to Kingsbury in Santa Fe. This did not prevent him from maintaining close relationships with the people of New Mexico. In 1856 he was elected to the New Mexico Territorial Legislature. He adopted a young Hispanic boy, José M. Hernandez, in 1849 and raised him to adulthood. After his relationship with Kingsbury ended in 1861, he remained in Connecticut where he died in 1889 at the age of 71 years. See *The James Josiah Webb Correspondence, 1852-1864*, University of New Mexico Center for Southwest Research, Albuquerque, New Mexico, in The Rocky Mountain Online Archive, University of New Mexico, 2006, rmoa.unm.edu/docviewer.php?docId=nmu1mss232sc.xml (accessed September 30, 2009)
14. Edwards, *A Campaign in New Mexico With Colonel Doniphan*, 64.
15. Webb, *Adventures in the Santa Fe Trade 1844-1847*, 96-97.
16. Magoffin, *Down the Santa Fe Trail and into Mexico*, 121-124. Gertrudes "Las Tules" Barcelo was

an independent businesswoman at a time when such a thing was unusual. Gertrudes Barcelo was born in Valencia near Santa Fe, at the beginning of the 19th Century. She earned notoriety as the proprietress of a gambling hall and as an adept monte dealer. Her establishment ran several tables at once, each one with a banker, at which thousands of dollars might change hands. La Tules managed to build both a large retinue of admirers and a tidy fortune, sinking her winnings back into the business to create a sophisticated gambling palace along San Francisco Street. She also invested in real estate around the capitol, traveling from one place to another in a fine carriage attended by personal guards. Gertrudes "La Tules" Barcelo did not survive much longer after the Americans took New Mexico. She died in February of 1852 at the age of 47. Her funeral resembled a state function, with hundreds in attendance and the Bishop of Santa Fe presiding over the ritual. See Ken Keinman, "Rags to Riches: The Gambling Lady's Lost Gold," *Treasure Cache Magazine*, January 2002, www.losttreasure.com/ newsletter/1-6-2004/ tale.html. (Retrieved September 30, 2009).

17. Davis, *El Gringo*, 54.
18. Rice, Josiah M., *A Cannoneer in Navajo Country: Journal of Private Josiah M. Rice, 1851*, edited by Richard H. Dillon (Old West Publishing Co, Denver, 1970), 52-53. The veracity of Rice's accounts of his experiences in New Mexico published as *A Cannoneer in Navajo County: Journal of Private Josiah M. Rice, 1851* is suspect, insomuch as a cursory comparison of his work and Frank Edward's 1847 journal *A Campaign in New Mexico with Colonel Doniphan*, show that Rice freely plagiarized Edwards, sometimes paragraphs at a time. There's no doubt Rice was in New Mexico, but probably used Edward's work to build up and fill in the gaps of his own work, published a few years after Edward's work.
19. Clarke, *The Original Journals of Henry Smith Turner*, 74.
20. Bennett, *Forts and Forays*, 19-20.
21. Webb, *Adventures in the Santa Fe Trade, 1844-1847*, 96-97.
22. Gardner, *The Mexican War Correspondence of Richard Smith Elliot*, 188.
23. Abert, *Abert's New Mexico Report, 1846-'47*, 57.
24. Davis, *El Gringo*, 185-186.
25. Magoffin, *Down the Santa Fe Trail and into Mexico*, 120, note 44.
26. Allison, "Santa Fe in 1846," 402. Francisco Perea was born on January 9, 1830 in Las Padillas, New Mexico of a prominent New Mexican family. He attended private schools in New Mexico until the age of 13, when he attended a Jesuit college in St. Louis. He would later attend the Bank Street Academy in New York City. Following his education, he was engaged in stock raising and gradually took an interest in politics. In 1846, at the age of 16, he served as translator for his uncle Don Jose Leandro Perea and other influential citizens to Kearny and the Americans, a task he considered "one of the greatest triumphs of my life." Perea supported the American annexation of New Mexico, an opinion he held throughout his life ". . . for I knew it would ultimately result in making our people freer and more independent . . ."

Perea was elected to the Territorial Council in 1858 and later was commissioned as a lieutenant-colonel of a pro-Union volunteer regiment during the Civil War, commanding a post at Albuquerque and participating in the Confederate defeat at Glorieta. He was subsequently elected as New Mexico Delegate to Congress in 1863. Apparently Perea was one of President Lincoln's friends and had the dubious distinction of being seated near Lincoln the night he was assassinated. Perea eventually returned to New Mexico to continue his interests and was elected again to the Council in 1865 and in 1884. Perea died on May 31, 1913, in Albuquerque, at the

age of 83. See "Francisco Perea," *Hispanic Americans in Congress, 1822-1995*, The Library of Congress Hispanic Reading Room Online Collections, 2009, www.loc.gov/rr/hispanic/congress/pereaf.htm. (accessed September 30 2009).
27. Rice, *A Cannoneer in Navajo Country*, 47.
28. Bennett, *Forts and Forays*, 14-15.
29. Davis, *El Gringo*, 89-90.
30. Magoffin, *Down the Santa Fe Trail and into Mexico*, 95.
31. Gardner, *The Mexican War Correspondence of Richard Smith Elliot*, 100-101.
32. Rice, *A Cannoneer in Navajo Country*, 47.
33. Calvin, *Lieutenant Emory Reports*,78-79.
34. Rice, *A Cannoneer in Navajo Country*, 118.
35. Magoffin, *Down the Santa Fe Trail and into Mexico*, 130-131. The white woman as a frontier symbol of civilization is repeated throughout period chronicles. Reminiscences of old pioneers in Wisconsin were somehow remiss if they did not include a sentence describing so-and-so as the first white woman to live at such-and-such a place. Insuring the safety and more pointedly the sanctity and purity of white women was a popular rationale for eliminating the Indian, although evidence of white women being raped by Indian men is nearly non-existent, which sadly cannot be said for white men. The fascination of the dark skinned for light skinned peoples is a theme as old as Cortez and the conquest of the Aztecs. Predictably Susan and her contemporaries believed the women's interest in her complexion was from admiration and perhaps jealousy, whereas it could have as easily come from the kind of fascination that appears when scrutinizing a particularly pale and lethargic slug. Susan obviously didn't pause to ask and, had she, they probably would have told her what she wanted to hear anyway.
36. Davis, *El Gringo*, 54, 85-86, 88, 430.
37. Gardner, *The Mexican War Correspondence of Richard Smith Elliot*, 106.
38. Abert, *Abert's New Mexico Report, 1846-'47*, 46.
39. Davis, *El Gringo*, 29 and Abert, *Abert's New Mexico Report, 1846-'47*, 37.
40. Magoffin, *Down the Santa Fe Trail and into Mexico*, 131.
41. Sunseri, *Seeds of Discord*, 101-102.
42. *Records of U. S. Army Continental Commands, 1784-1821, Department of New Mexico, Selected Letters*, National Archives, Records of the Office of the Secretary of War, Washington, 1980.

Chapter 21-Rebellion

1. Clarke, *The Original Journals of Henry Smith Turner*, 146.
2. *Records of the Office of the Quartermaster General, Reports of Persons & Articles Hired, 1846-47*, National Archives, Record Group 92, Washington, DC, Box 30 A-S.
3. Crutchfield, *Tragedy at Taos: The Revolt of 1847*, 161. Donaciano Vigil was born on September 6, 1802. He participated in expeditions against the Navajo during the 1820s and 1830s and was briefly jailed during the 1837 insurrection. Vigil was elected to the New Mexican Assembly and then appointed by Armijo as Military Secretary in 1839. There followed several promotions, including one brevetting him as captain for his role in capturing the Texas invaders in 1842. After serving Armijo on his general staff, he was among the defenders at Apache Pass when the governor disbanded the militia and departed. Rather than retreat with Armijo, Vigil resigned his

commission and arranged for Kearny to enter Santa Fe peacefully. For his efforts, Vigil became Secretary of the Territory of New Mexico. With the establishment of United States military governorship, he continued serving as Secretary of the Territory until 1851. Vigil served in the Territory Legislative Assembly on several occasions up through 1865, then as school director for San Miguel County in 1871 and 1872. Donaciano Vigil died on August 11, 1877 at the age of 75 years. See Vigil's biographical sketch in Twitchell, Ralph E., *The History of the Military Occupation of the Territory of New Mexico From 1846 to 1851*, (The Smith-Brooks Company, Publishers, Denver, Colorado 1909).

4. Crutchfield, *Tragedy at Taos: The Revolt of 1847*, 95.
5. Reducing his force nearly got Kearny and his command obliterated in California, where things were not as rosy as the dispatches had indicated. After passing through friendly Apache country, Kearny's column followed the Gila across the vast Sonora and Mohave deserts. Exhausted and nearly starved, they reached Warner Ranch, California on December 2nd. Four days later on December 6th, a regiment of Californian Lancers cut his puny detachment of dragoons to ribbons. Kearny was speared three times, including one ignoble wound in the buttocks, while his homesick guide Kit Carson was nearly killed. Kearny and his men eventually recovered and in the end, Stockton, Fremont and Kearny defeated the Mexican forces at San Gabriel de Los Angeles. After a brief tenure at the Presidio of Monterrey, Kearny headed home, never to return to New Mexico or the West. Ordered to Veracruz, he arrived that spring of 1848 to take command. He was greeted by an epidemic of yellow fever and dysentery and soon became ill. Although he recovered enough to serve as military governor of Mexico City and take command of the 6th Military Department at New Orleans that July, he never fully recovered. He died in St. Louis on October 31st, 1848 at the age of 54 years. See Clarke, Dwight, *Stephen Watts Kearny, Soldier of the West,* (University of Oklahoma Press, Norman, 1961).
6. Magoffin, *Down the Santa Fe Trail and into Mexico*, 170-171.
7. *Records of the Office of the Quartermaster General, Consolidated Correspondence Files*, National Archives, Record Group 92, National Archives, Washington, DC, Entry 225, Box 987.
8. Gardner, *The Mexican War Correspondence of Richard Smith Elliot*, 98, 108.
9. Jacob Hall to Mary, January 29, 1847, National Frontier Trails Center Manuscript Collection, National Frontier Trails Center, Independence, Missouri. Calornel, more commonly known as calomel, is the mercurous chloride Hg_2Cl_2 and was taken orally as a purgative to purge perceived impurities in the body. Overuse in a patient, which was common, could cause both hair and teeth to fall out.
10. *Missouri Republican*, November 28 and December 5, 1846.
11. Herrera, Carlos R. "New Mexico Resistance to U. S. Occupation during the Mexican-American War of 1846-1848," in Gonzales-Berry, Erlinda, ed., *The Contested Homeland-A Chicano History of New Mexico*, 23-42, (University of New Mexico Press, Albuquerque, 2000), 31.
12. Twitchell, *The History of the Military Occupation of the Territory of New Mexico From 1846 to 1851*, 314.
13. Abert, *Abert's New Mexico Report, 1846-'47*, 116, note 24.
14. Crutchfield, *Tragedy at Taos: The Revolt of 1847*, 98, 166.
15. Abert, *Abert's New Mexico Report, 1846-'47*, 117, note 2.
16. Crutchfield, *Tragedy at Taos: The Revolt of 1847*, 97.
17. Twitchell, *The History of the Military Occupation of the Territory of New Mexico From 1846 to 1851*, 124-127.

18. Crutchfield, *Tragedy at Taos: The Revolt of 1847*, 103.
19. Abert, *Abert's New Mexico Report, 1846–'47*, 117, note 24
20. Twitchell, *The History of the Military Occupation of the Territory of New Mexico From 1846 to 1851*, 132, 141-144.
21. Crutchfield, *Tragedy at Taos: The Revolt of 1847*, 129, 160. See also Torrez, Robert J., "1846-The Mexican American War," *New Mexico Office of the State Historian*, 2004-2009, www.newmexicohistory.org/filedetails.php?fileID=21394, (accessed October 5, 2009).
22. *The William G. Ritch Papers*, Microfilm Edition, Henry E. Huntington Library and Art Gallery, San Marino, California, at the Center for Southwest Research, University of New Mexico, Albuquerque, Microfilm Reel 2, entries 247, 286.
23. McNitt, *Navajo Wars*, 99.
24. *The Santa Fe Republican*, September through December 1847.
25. *The Santa Fe Republican*, October 16 and 30, 1847.
26. McNitt, *Navajo Wars*, 125, note 2.
27. Murphy, Lawrence R., "The United States Army in Taos, 1847-1852," *The New Mexico Historical Review* 47, no. 1 (1972): 34-35. Major Beall and his 1st Dragoons relieved Reynolds, the locals having become so alienated that they refused to lease buildings to Uncle Sam unless Beall could absolutely guarantee payment.
28. Certificate of War Service, H. L. Dodge, Missouri State Archives and Museum, Jefferson City, Missouri.
29. *Index to the Compiled Service Records of Volunteer Soldiers Who Served During Indian Wars & Disturbances, 1815-1858*, Microfilm, Microfilm Reel 10.
30. Photocopy of original certificate, courtesy of Eugene Beckett.
31. *The Santa Fe Republican*, Wednesday, Nov. 15, 1848.
32. *The Santa Fe Republican*, Nov. 25, 1848.
33. *Letters Received by the Adjutant General's Office*, National Archives, Records of the Adjutant General's Office, (Washington, DC), Microfilm Reel 319, frame 20. See also *Territorial Archives of New Mexico, Journals and Ledgers of the Treasurer of the Territory, Receipts & Disbursement Journal*, New Mexico State Record Center, Santa Fe, New Mexico, 1971, in the Center for Southwest Research, University of New Mexico, Albuquerque, Microfilm Reel 46.
34. *Territorial Archives of New Mexico, Journals and Ledgers of the Treasurer of the Territory, Receipts & Disbursement Journal*, Microfilm Reel 46. See also *The William G. Ritch Papers*, Microfilm Reel 5, entry 1533.
35. *Andrew J. Hewitt v. Henry L. Dodge, 1847*, (Wisconsin Room, University Archives, University of Wisconsin, Platteville) Box 12, Folder 63. See also Neil Giffey to author, February 16, 1996.

Chapter 22-Indians

1. Cremony, John C., *Life Among the Apaches*, (A. Roman & Company, Publishers, New York, 1868).
2. Clarke, Dwight L., *Stephen Watts Kearny, Soldier of the West*, (University of Oklahoma Press, Norman, 1961), 147.
3. Clarke, *The Original Journals of Henry Smith Turner*, 86-87.
4. Calvin, *Lieutenant Emory Reports*, 101.
5. Clarke, *Stephen Watts Kearny, Soldier of the West*, 153.
6. McNitt, *Navajo Wars*, 97-100.

7. Barry, *The Beginnings of the West*, 635-636.
8. Gardner, *The Mexican War Correspondence of Richard Smith Elliot*, 156.
9. Abert, *Abert's New Mexico Report, 1846-'47*, 120, note 30.
10. Locke, Raymond F., *The Book of the Navajo*, (Holloway House Publishing, Los Angeles, California, 1976), 210. Zarcillos Largos, whose name in Spanish meant Large Earrings, was known among his people as *Naat'áanii Náádleel* or *He Becomes a Leader Again*. For being such an influential headman, very little is known of him. His was probably born in the last quarter of the 18th century. He belonged to the Navajo *Tábaaha* Clan. Zarcillos Largos would become a staunch defender of his people's rights and a steadfast advocate of diplomacy and peace with New Mexican and American. As with so many of his compatriots, his efforts towards peace didn't preclude his own violent death at the hand of enemies. He was killed at about the age of seventy by New Mexican and Zuni raiders sometime between 1858 and 1860. See Virginia Hoffman, *Navajo Biographies, Vol. 1*, (Navajo Curriculum Center Press, Rough Rock, Arizona, 1974).
11. Gardner, *The Mexican War Correspondence of Richard Smith Elliot*, 121-122. Richard Van Valkenburgh, in his work *Navajo Place Names*, cites three different terms Navajos used specifically to designate soldiers as opposed to Americans in general, terms that reflect the typical Navajo ability to see humor in everything. Soldiers became known as *Bijaa'yeenjahi* or *Those Who Sleep on Their Ears*, *Bigod dook'ali* or *Those Who Scorch Their Kneecaps*, due to crouching too closely to their campfires, and simply *Sha bidiilchii* or *The Sunburned Ones*. The term *siláo* was also later used, derived from the Spanish term *soldado* or soldier. Presently the term *siláo* refers to policemen. See Van Valkenburgh, Richard, *Dine Bikéyah*, (Department of the Interior, Navajo Agency, Window Rock, Arizona, 1941), 169.
12. Gardner, *The Mexican War Correspondence of Richard Smith Elliot*, 122. See also Magoffin, *Down the Santa Fe Trail and into Mexico*, 109, note 40. See also Abert, *Abert's New Mexico Report, 1846-'47*, 128.
13. *The William G. Ritch Papers*, Microfilm Reel 1, entries 1814 to 1821.
14. McNitt, *Navajo Wars*, 106.
15. Abert, *Abert's New Mexico Report, 1846-'47*, 78, 81. Originally from the mesa country around Jemez, the *Diné Anaa'í* inhabited lands skirting the Navajo sacred mountain of the south, Mount Taylor. For more than a century the Enemy Navajo had the dubious honor of living in often uncomfortable proximity to the Spanish settlements. As a result, their survival demanded a certain amicable relationship with the New Mexicans under both Spanish and Mexican regimes. The separation from the main body of Navajo occurred officially in 1818, when the Enemy Navajo headman Joaquín informed the cacique of Jemez and the Spaniards that the Navajo were planning a war and that he had determined to forsake them. It is thought that soon afterwards, his people moved south towards Old San Mateo and Cebolleta. When it became apparent that they were being blamed for raids actually conducted by Navajos in more remote regions, the Enemy Navajo began collaborating with New Mexicans, aiding them in strikes against hostile Navajo groups. Not only did their collaboration bolster the security of *Diné Anaa'í*, but the profit in slaves and booty was lucrative enough that they independently conducted raids against their brethren in the west. Of the Enemy Navajo headmen, the most memorable was Antonio Cebolla Sandoval.

Chapter 23-Expedition

1. Fisher, Kelly, "The Forgotten Dodge," *Annals of Iowa* 40, no.4 (1970): 296-305, 297.
2. McNitt, *Navaho Expedition*, xliv-xlv. John Macrae Washington was born in Virginia in October of 1797. After graduating from West Point in 1817, he was assigned to artillery units in the South. Lieutenant Washington was appointed captain in the Creek conflict of 1833-1834 and subsequently saw action against the Seminoles in 1836. When war broke out with Mexico he was brevetted major and accompanied Wool's army into Saltillo. He received a promotion of lieutenant colonel for gallantry at the battle of Buena Vista and became acting governor of Saltillo before being ordered north into California. He served as both the civil and military governor of New Mexico until October of 1849. On December 23, 1853, the steamboat San Francisco, carrying him and his regiment, was wrecked off the Cape of Delaware in the Pacific. Washington and over 180 soldiers drowned. See McNitt, *Navaho Expedition*, xliv-xlv and Keleher, William A., *Turmoil in New Mexico, 1846-1868*, (The Rydal Press, Santa Fe, New Mexico, 1952), 123-124, note 41.
3. McNitt, *Navajo Wars*, 134.
4. *Returns from U. S. Military Posts, 1800-1918, Taos, New Mexico, September 1848-March 1861*, National Archives, Record Group 94, Records of the Adjutant General's Office, M617, Microfilm Reel 1254, (Washington, DC 1967).
5. *The Frank McNitt Collection*, New Mexico State Records and Archives Center, Santa Fe, New Mexico.
6. Abel, Annie H. ed., *The Official Correspondence of James S. Calhoun*, (Government Printing Office, Washington, DC 1915), 340-341.
7. *Letters Received by the 9th Military District, 1848-1853*, Microfilm Reel 1, frame 533.
8. *The William G. Ritch Papers*, Microfilm Reel 1, after entry 1828, also 1812. Although the claims present fairly damning evidence, many of the thefts probably never occurred. Many of the accusations actually came to light in depositions given to government agents in 1853, when the United States was paying aggrieved citizens for property allegedly lost to Indian depredations, and many of them were unsubstantiated. Navajo reputation alone served nicely to extract a dollar or two from Uncle Sam.
9. McNitt, *Navajo Wars*, 128.
10. McNitt, *Navaho Expedition*, 253-256.
11. *The Santa Fe Republican*, July 8, 1848 in McNitt, *Navajo Wars*, 131.
12. *Letters Received by the 9th Military District, 1848-1853*, Microfilm Reel 1, frame 491.
13. *Letters Received by the 9th Military District, 1848-1853*, Microfilm Reel 1, frame 569.
14. *Letters Received by the 9th Military District, 1848-1853*, Microfilm Reel 1, frame 495.
15. *Letters Received by the 9th Military District, 1848-1853*, Microfilm Reel 1, frame 499.
16. McNitt, *Navaho Expedition*, 3.
17. Canyon de Chelly is a corruption of the combined Spanish Navajo terms Cañon de Tséyi' or Canyon among the Rocks—literally "Canyon Canyon." The precipitous red rock canyon served as a home and refuge for the Navajo people. It provided a temperate climate and dependable water as well as an easily defendable homeland. There were tales that the Navajo had actually constructed a fortress there, though the towering walls of the canyon would have dwarfed the grandest Roman rampart or European castle. The canyon was composed of petrified sand dunes laid down 230 million years ago and carved out by several streams flowing into Chinle

Wash. Wind worked over millennia to carve many caves and alcoves into the walls of Canyon de Chelly, its northern branch Canyon del Muerto and numerous side canyons, creating a perfect home for ancient Anasazi cliff-dwelling Indians. Prehistoric farmers inhabited the canyon for a thousand years. The Navajo were relative latecomers, estimated to have settled there in the mid 1700s. When intermittent war began between the Spaniards and Navajo, Canyon de Chelly became legendary as the Navajo stronghold. See "Canyon de Chelly, Arizona" edited by John D. Grahame, and Thomas D. Sisk, 2002, *Canyons, Cultures and Environmental Change: Land Use History of North America*, Northern Arizona University, Flagstaff, www.cpluhna.nau.edu, (accessed October 13, 2009).

18. McNitt, *Navaho Expedition*, 11.
19. Keleher, William A., *Turmoil in New Mexico, 1846-1868*, (The Rydal Press, Santa Fe, New Mexico, 1952), 129, note 56. James H. Simpson would become the chief historian of Washington's expedition, creating one of the most thorough documentations of a military move against the Navajo. He was born in New Brunswick, New Jersey on March 9, 1813. After being appointed cadet to West Point 1828, he graduated on July 1, 1832 and served the Army as a topographical engineer and in other capacities until his retirement in 1879. In 1849 he explored and mapped the route from Fort Smith, Arkansas to Santa Fe. From 1859 to 1861, he also explored and reported a new route from Salt Lake to the Pacific. During the Civil War Simpson helped plan the defense of Washington, DC. At the close of the war he was appointed brigadier general. James H. Simpson died of pneumonia in St. Paul, Minnesota on March 1, 1883 at the age of 70 years.
20. Although they all died relatively young and in tragic circumstances, the Kern Brothers left a permanent mark on both 18th Century American art and western history. There were three of them: the oldest Benjamin, Richard and finally Edward. Benjamin was born in 1818 and became a physician. Richard H. Kern was born in Philadelphia in 1821 and took an early interest in art, exhibiting his landscape and figure studies around Philadelphia beginning roughly in 1840. He was also a member of the Academy of Natural Sciences and taught art at the Franklin Institute. His brother Edward M. Kern was born in 1823 and like Richard took an interest in art. Of the three, Edward Kern appears to have been the most adventurous. When John Fremont needed an artist and cartographer for his next expedition to California in 1845, acquaintances back east suggested Edward Kern, who was hardly 23 years old. After Fremont became involved in the Bear Flag Revolt in upper California, he left Edward Kern in command at Sutter's Fort with the rank of lieutenant in the California Battalion. Shortly after that, Kern was involved in relieving the stranded Donner Party in the Sierras. Fremont was so impressed with his young protégé that he named the Kern River after him.

Thus in 1848 Edward convinced his older brothers Benjamin and Richard to join John C. Fremont's 4th expedition into the Rocky Mountains to scout out a transcontinental railroad route. Edward and Richard served as the expeditionary artists and Benjamin as the company doctor. Fremont injudiciously made the trip in late autumn and got his entire entourage snowbound at South Park. Facing cold and starvation, the Kern brothers decided to head for Taos. Before leaving, they cached their sketches, studies and equipment in the mountains, intending to retrieve them once the snows receded. In February, Benjamin Kern, the mountain man Old Bill Williams, and a handful of Mexican packers headed back into the mountains for the cache. Although the packers returned, Benjamin and Old Bill Williams were never seen again. Whether they were murdered for their goods by the packers or killed by the Ute is still a matter of speculation. Benjamin Kern had been about 31 years of age.

After recovering from that tragedy, Richard and Edward accompanied Colonel Washington's expedition into Navajo country, describing the geology and rendering detailed sketches of heretofore unknown country, ancient Anasazi ruins, and portraits of Pueblo and Navajo life and leaders. They chose to remain in New Mexico for a time. Richard joined the Sitgreaves exploration of the Little Colorado River in 1851 while his brother Edward accompanied Lieutenant John Pope in an effort to find an improved road from Santa Fe to Fort Leavenworth. Richard returned to Pennsylvania in 1852, but turned west again the following year to again help survey a railroad route through the Rockies. On October 26, 1853, the Pahvant Indians, seeking revenge for the killing of their chief, killed Richard Kern and eight others near Sevier Lake, Utah. Richard had been about 32 years old.

The sole remaining brother Edward apparently decided to exchange land exploration for that of the sea. Between 1853 and 1860, he served on the U.S.S. Vincennes in the North Pacific in an expedition that circled the globe and later assisted in surveying sea routes between California and China. During the Civil War, Edward had the opportunity to serve with John C. Fremont once more, who commanded the Army of the West. Edward died suddenly of an epileptic attack on November 23, 1863 at the age of 40 years. See "Kern Drawings of the Southwest, 1849," *Ewell Sale Stewart Library, Academy of Natural Sciences*, 1900 Benjamin Franklin Parkway, Philadelphia, www.acnatsci.org/library/index.html, (accessed October 13, 2009).

21. Horn, Calvin, *New Mexico's Troubled Years, The Story of the Early Territorial Governors*, (Horn & Wallace, Publishers, Albuquerque, 1963), 22-23. Calhoun had been an ambitious businessman and politician, having served as mayor of Columbus, as a lawmaker in the Georgia legislature, and the operator and director of a steamship line, two banks and the Chattahoochee Railroad. He had also previously served as an Indian agent. Love for the dusty wilderness and the dusky Indian was not what lured Calhoun to leave the States. In truth Calhoun aspired to command a regiment of cavalry on the frontier, a dream he'd never fulfill. As with many who would follow him, Calhoun expected his service would reap more prestigious and lucrative political returns later. He was born near Abbeville, South Carolina in about 1803 and purportedly related to the famous congressman John C. Calhoun. He married Caroline Ann Simmons in 1822. After she died prematurely in 1826, he wed Annie V. Williamson four years later. One of his daughters, Carolina from his first marriage, married William E. Love in 1843. Love would accompany his father-in-law to New Mexico. After 1830, Calhoun relocated to Columbus, Georgia and went into the shipping business. He commanded a company of Georgia volunteers during the Mexican War but never saw action. Calhoun was a devoted Whig and greatly admired General Taylor. Although Calhoun knew nothing of New Mexico per se, President Taylor appointed him Indian agent for New Mexico. He would later suffer a rocky tenure as governor of the territory.

22. McNitt, *Navaho Expedition*, 14, 19, 24-25. Henry Lane Kendrick and H. L. Dodge would later form an effective team in working for peace with the Navajo, although professionally they were strikingly dissimilar. One of nine children, Henry L. Kendrick was born a year after Dodge, on January 20th, 1811 in Lebanon, New Hampshire. He entered West Point Military Academy in 1831 and after graduating in 1835, he spent twelve years serving as assistant professor of chemistry, mineralogy and geology at West Point. His first active service occurred in the Mexican War, where he was assigned to the 2nd Artillery and in June of 1846 made a captain. Kendrick would take part in several battles, including the siege of Vera Cruz, the battle at

Cerro Gordo, a skirmish at Amazoque, and was involved in the defense of Puebla, when he was brevetted major in October of 1847 for gallant and meritorious conduct.

23. Linford, Laurance D., *Navajo Places: History, Legend, Landscape,* (The University of Utah Press, Salt Lake City, 2000), 180.
24. McNitt, *Navaho Expedition,* 27-29.
25. McNitt, *Navaho Expedition,* 31-32, 35, 53. Simpson referred to Sandoval by the English rendition of his Navajo name, *Tus-ca hogont-le.* Antonio Sandoval was of the *Tótsohnii'* Clan, or *People of the Large Waters* and it is possible this name was derived from that. In the course of a lifetime, a Navajo might be referred to by several names. The New Mexicans knew him as Antonio Cebolla Sandoval; his middle name derived from his Navajo boyhood nickname of *tl'ohchini,* or onion. Sandoval was born around 1807, possibly around Mount Taylor but more likely north of there in the San Juan River drainage region. During his boyhood his father brought a captive Hispanic girl into the family. From her he gained a rudimentary understanding of Hispanic language and customs. During a period of heightened conflict around 1816, his people took refuge from Comanche raids on fortified mesa tops. After peace returned in 1819, the family located near Cebolleta. In time Sandoval came to frequent the settlement to trade. When hostilities again broke out between New Mexican and Navajo, Sandoval adroitly played both sides. While assisting New Mexicans in raids against western Navajos, he also worked with Navajo leaders, most notably Narbona, to forge peaceful relationships with them, serving the headmen as interpreter to the Mexican governor Vizcarra in 1829 and 1830. When these efforts eventually failed, he allied himself firmly with the New Mexicans against his more warlike kin. That relationship changed very little after the Americans took over. Antonio Sandoval died of internal injuries after being thrown and kicked by an unbroken horse in roughly 1859 at the age of 52. See McNitt, *Navaho Expedition,* 248 and Hoffman, *Navajo Biographies,* 29.
26. McNitt, *Navaho Expedition,* 42-56, 59, 61-62, 63.
27. Unlike the lighter and sturdier Indian ponies, the heavy mounts favored by the cavalry could not survive on desert brush. Adequate grass for cavalry mounts usually meant plenty of it. American military would repeatedly have troubles fighting Indians, whether Navajo, Apache, Jicarilla or Ute, precisely due to the vulnerability of the American horse. The success of any expedition depended on whether the horses survived.
28. McNitt, *Navaho Expedition,* 62-64, 65.

Chapter 24-Into De Chelly

1. McNitt, *Navaho Expedition,* 71-72.
2. McNitt, *Navaho Expedition,* 66-67.
3. McNitt, *Navaho Expedition,* 68. Narbona was born in 1766 in the Chuska Mountains of present-day northeastern Arizona. His childhood and teen years were marked by frequent conflict with various traditional tribal enemies and New Mexicans. He demonstrated remarkable prowess at a young age and soon took a position of leadership on raids, including strikes in 1804–1805 against new Spanish settlements around Mount Taylor. In 1818, Narbona took a principle role in uniting Navajos against Spanish encroachments on their lands, resulting in the treaty of 1819. Fighting flared again under Mexican administration in 1823, inflicting severe hardships on Navajo people. Now in late middle age, Narbona actively worked to establish peaceful relations with the Mexican government by cooperating with them in redeeming New Mexican captives

and property taken in war. In 1835, however, he orchestrated an ambush of several hundred New Mexican raiders, at *Bééshlichí'ii Bigiizh* or *Copper Pass*, later renamed Washington Pass, inflicting heavy losses and routing the entire force. He continued efforts for peace in the early 1840s. When the Americans seized New Mexico, he was anxious to secure a peace with them as well, counseling and persuading his people to cooperate with the Americans, though other Navajo groups were not so willing to show restraint.

4. In being fair to the Kerns and the nature of the times, such morbidity was neither unusual nor seen as particularly disgusting. Lopping off body parts and robbing the graves of notorious Indians, bank robbers and desperados was a relatively common and accepted way of both conducting scientific research and picking up a memento or two of history.
5. McNitt, *Navaho Expedition*, 69.
6. McNitt, *Navaho Expedition*, 72-74.
7. McNitt, *Navaho Expedition*, 75-76.
8. And thus it would remain named for years. Pass Washington, or later Washington Pass, was also referred to as Copper Pass, Navajo Pass and Cottonwood Pass. The Navajo Nation later renamed it Narbona Pass to commemorate the old headman.
9. McNitt, *Navaho Expedition*, 78.
10. McNitt, *Navaho Expedition*, 80.
11. McNitt, *Navaho Expedition*, 82-85. In 1804 a Spanish expedition penetrated the north fork of Canyon de Chelly, killing over one hundred Navajos in two days. During that assault, the soldiers slaughtered a group of women and children hiding in an unreachable canyon wall alcove high overhead by sending shots ricocheting off the ceiling. The alcove became known as Massacre Cave and the canyon took its macabre name, *Cañon del Muerto*. See Grahame, "Canyon de Chelly, Arizona" www.cpluhna.nau.edu, (accessed October 13, 2009).
12. McNitt, *Navaho Expedition*, 88.
13. McNitt, *Navaho Expedition*, 89.
14. McNitt, *Navaho Expedition*, 90.
15. McNitt, *Navaho Expedition*, 91, 92.
16. McNitt, *Navaho Expedition*, 95-96.
17. McNitt, *Navaho Expedition*, 98-99
18. *Letters Received by the 9th Military District, 1848–1853*, Microfilm Reel 1, frame 947.

Chapter 25-El Morro

1. McNitt, *Navaho Expedition*, 96, 101.
2. McNitt, *Navaho Expedition*, 107-108, 110.
3. McNitt, *Navaho Expedition*, 111, 113.
4. McNitt, *Navaho Expedition* 120, note 138. The village was actually named Hálona, the last of six original villages encountered by Coronado in 1540. In fear of Spaniard retaliation after killing their priests during the Pueblo Revolt of 1680, the Zuni abandoned their villages for the safety of Corn Mesa. After the Spaniards retook New Mexico in 1690, Don Diego de Vargas persuaded the Zuni to leave Corn Mesa and gather at Hálona to live in the spirit of peace and cooperation. They have lived there and in a few surrounding farm settlements ever since.
5. McNitt, *Navaho Expedition*, 115.
6. McNitt, *Navaho Expedition*, 119.

7. McNitt, *Navaho Expedition*, 126-127, 139. The rock itself is today known, appropriately, as Inscription Rock, located at the El Morro National Monument along New Mexico Highway 53, roughly 13 miles east of present day Ramah.
8. Juan De Oñate was born around 1550, the son of a prominent Zacatecas miner and rancher, a true child of New Spain. He saw early military service against the Chichimec Indians, helped establish new missions along the northern frontier and also prospected for silver. He married Isabel de Tolosa Cortés y Moctezuma, a direct descendant of both Hernando Cortez and the Aztec king Montezuma. In 1595, King Philip II of Spain granted Oñate a contract to establish a colony in New Mexico. He made his entry with a sizeable army of colonists in early 1598 and soon subdued the Pueblos he encountered. After making his headquarters at San Juan Pueblo 25 miles north of Santa Fe, Oñate explored a considerable amount of the Southwest, including the Great Plains a far as central Kansas in 1601, followed by the expedition to the Gulf of California, as noted in his inscription of 1605. The year after that King Philip ordered Oñate to Mexico City to explain the deterioration of the New Mexico colony and to answer charges about his alleged cruelty to the Indians there. Before knowing about the order, Juan de Oñate resigned his governorship over financial problems. In 1613 he was accused of using excessive force to subdue Acoma as well as a host of other charges. As a result, he was fined and barred from New Mexico. Ironically, Juan de spent the remainder of his life in Spain trying to clear his name. He died in about 1626. See "Oñate, Juan de" in *The Handbook of Texas Online*, The Texas State Historical Association, 1997-2002, www.tshaonline.org/handbook/online, January 18, 2008,(accessed October 26, 2009).
9. McNitt, *Navaho Expedition*, 140.
10. McNitt, *Navaho Expedition*, 143-145, 148.
11. Atrisco on the west banks of the Rio Grande was founded in 1703, three years before the Villas de Albuquerque. The name is not Spanish but rather from the Aztec language of Nahuatl, *atlixco* meaning "upon the water." Although Atrisco is identified with the Atrisco Land Grant made by Don Diego de Vargas to Don Fernando Duran y Chávez in 1692, the name itself proclaims yet another lasting effect the Aztec had on the colonization of New Mexico. It is quite certain that Nahuatl speaking Indians accompanied both Coronado and Oñate into New Mexico and had contact with the Indian peoples there early on, including apparently the Navajo, whose term for pig, *bisóodi*, is likely derived from a Nahuatl term *pitzotl* or *cuapitzotl* for wild boar. See Simmons, Mark, *The Little Lion of the Southwest*. See also *The Nahuatl-Spanish Online Dictionary*, aulex.ohui.net, (accessed October 26, 2009).
12. Abel, *The Official Correspondence of James S. Calhoun*, 47.
13. *Territorial Archives of New Mexico, Muster Reels 1847-1897*, Microfilm Reel 85, page 32. A notation was made on the muster roll beside Baca's name in what appears to be Henry Dodge's hand "supposed to have been killed by Indians while on Express duty about the 8th of September, '49 near the Cañon de Cheille."
14. Abel, *The Official Correspondence of James S. Calhoun*, 38.
15. Abel, *The Official Correspondence of James S. Calhoun*, 32-33.
16. Calhoun to Medill, October 29, 1849 in Abel, *The Official Correspondence of James S. Calhoun*, 65.
17. Bender, A. B. "Government Explorations, 1846-1859" *The New Mexico Historical Review* 9 (1934): 258.

18. *Letters Received by the 9th Military District, 1848–1853*, National Archives, Record Group 393, M 1102, (National Archives and Records Administration, Washington, DC 1980), frame 869.

Chapter 26-Cebolleta

1. *Letters Sent by the 9th Military District, 1849–1890, Records of U. S. Army Continental Commands, 1821–1920*, Record Group 393, M1072, (National Archives and Records Administration, Washington, DC 1980), Microfilm Reel 1, frame 19.
2. *The Frank McNitt Collection*. See also *Records of the New Mexico Superintendency of Indian Affairs, 1849–1880*, National Archives, Records of the Bureau of Indian Affairs, Microcopy T21, (Washington, DC 1954), Microfilm Reel 1 frame 3, in the Center for Southwest Research, University of New Mexico, Albuquerque.
3. John Munroe was born in Scotland in about 1796. He graduated from West Point in 1814 and entered the service as a 3rd lieutenant of the 1st Artillery during the War of 1812. After the war he saw numerous stations in both the North and South. Promoted to captain of the 4th Artillery in 1825, he saw several posts of duty, including service in the Black Hawk War, the Seminole conflict and the infamous Trail of Tears, the forced relocation of the Cherokee Nation to Oklahoma. Much of his service revolved around teaching gunnery. He was brevetted major for his service in the Seminole War. After a decade of teaching artillery at several places, he became a full major of the 2nd Artillery in 1846. He served General Taylor as chief of artillery during the Mexican War, was brevetted as lieutenant colonel for bravery at Monterey, then as colonel for his gallantry at Buena Vista.
After the end of the war he served stints at Fort Columbus in New York and Fort Marion in Florida before being appointed military governor of New Mexico and commander of the Ninth Military District, a position he held until summer of 1851 when relieved by Colonel Edwin Vose Sumner. Back east once more, he was given command of the Department of Florida from 1853 to 1856, when he took a two year leave of absence. He returned to command the Department of the Platte headquartered at Fort Randall, Dakota Territory from 1858 to 1861, serving a year as commandant of Fort Laramie, Wyoming. He was given leave of absence to return to the States on January 10th, 1861, probably for medical reasons. On the eve of the Civil War John Munroe died in New Brunswick, New Jersey on April 26, 1861 at the age of about 65 years. See *U. S. Mexican War, The Zachary Taylor Encampment at Corpus-Christi, 1845–1846*, Corpus Christi Public Libraries, Corpus Christi, Texas, www.library.ci.corpus-christi.tx.us/MexicanWar/munroej.htm, (accessed February 19, 2011).
4. Reeve, Frank D., "The Navaho-Spanish Peace, 1720s–1770s," *The New Mexico Historical Review* 34, (1959): 9-40. Initially the Navajos welcomed the mission. Hostility between the relocated Navajo and neighboring Acoma and Laguna pueblos and the uninviting prospect of mind-numbing mission life soon changed the Navajos' minds. They explained to the padres quite succinctly that they had no need for fathers, as they had already grown up. Furthermore they had no desire to live in pueblos or to become Christians because "they had been raised like the deer" and could not stay in one place. However, they offered to remain friends with the Spaniards and would do the priests no harm if they remained, and would even allow some of their children to be baptized Catholic, although they, themselves, would never be Christians. The priests later learned that the Navajos had come in for the promise of gifts more than salvation, and had no intentions of lingering once the offerings shriveled up. Shortly after that,

the padres abandoned the mission. See Kelly, Henry W., "Franciscan Missions of New Mexico, 1740-1760" *The New Mexico Historical Review* 16 (1941): 41-69, 60.
5. *Territorial Archives of New Mexico; Land Records of New Mexico; Surveyor General Records*, Microfilm Reel 17, Report 46, Town of Cebolleta, New Mexico State Records and Archives Center, in the Center for Southwest Research, University of New Mexico.
6. Simmons, *The Little Lion of the Southwest*, 25.
7. Peña, Abe, *Memories of Cíbola: Stories from New Mexico Villages*, (University of New Mexico Press, Albuquerque, 1997), 2, 4.
8. Simmons, *The Little Lion of the Southwest*, 35.
9. Peña, *Memories of Cíbola*, 22. Stories of perseverance through such severe injuries, almost unbelievable by today's standards, are common in the annals of the West. Both Indian and hardened European westerners seemed capable of enduring incredible suffering and pain. A surgeon during the Plains Indian wars of the 1860s and 1870s noted once that the soldiers had brought him a young Indian boy, probably no older than 8 years, who had been shot in the gut. While the doctor gouged and probed to remove the deep-seated slug, he was astounded the boy made neither a sound, nor a twitch of discomfort and sat unmoving through the excruciating procedure.
10. Simmons, *The Little Lion of the Southwest*, 30-31.
11. *Letters Sent by the 9th Military District, 1849-1890*, Microfilm Reel 1, frame 11. Little is known of Croghan Ker. He was appointed 2nd Lieutenant of the 2nd Dragoons upon its creation and apparently saw service during the Seminole Wars. After stint with the 2nd dragoons patrolling the Texas-Mexican boundary and protecting the Santa Fe Trail, in the spring of 1845 Ker was present during the fighting at Palo Alto and Resaca de la Palma that ignited the Mexican War. He was severely wounded at the Battle of Molino del Rey outside of Mexico City on September 8, 1847 but recovered sufficiently to accompany the regiment to New Mexico. Ker was stationed at Abiquiu during Colonel Washington's expedition of 1849.
12. Abel, *The Official Correspondence of James S. Calhoun*, 101. See also *Letters Sent by the 9th Military District, 1849-1890*, Microfilm Reel 1, frame 22.
13. *Letters Received by the 9th Military District, 1848-1853*, M 1102, frame 797.
14. *Records of the Office of the Quartermaster General, Consolidated Correspondence Files*, Box 513, Entry 225, NM-81, Dodge, H. L. 1850.
15. *Records of the New Mexico Superintendency of Indian Affairs*, Microfilm Reel 1 frame 5.
16. *Records of the Office of the Quartermaster General, Consolidated Correspondence Files*, Box 513, Entry 225, NM-81, Dodge, H. L. 1850.
17. *Letters Sent by the 9th Military District, 1849-1890*, Microfilm Reel 1, frame 103. Dr. William Alexander Hammond was born in Annapolis, Maryland in 1828. After moving to Harrisburg, Pennsylvania, he began his study of medicine at the age of 16 years and in 1848 graduated from the University of New York. After a year working in Philadelphia at the Pennsylvania Hospital, he joined the Army and was ordered to New Mexico, where he remained for three years. A heart condition exacerbated by the rigors of frontier service forced him to retire briefly, but once he regained his health he was posted at Florida, then at West Point.
By 1854 he was at Fort Riley, Kansas. His four-year stay again exacted a serious toll on his health and he returned to the States and subsequently took a lengthy European tour to restore his vitality. While there he studied European military medical organization and toured several medical facilities. In 1860 he was appointed Professor of Anatomy and Physiology at the University

of Maryland. He resigned his commission with the Army but remained at the University until the start of the Civil War. During the war Hammond oversaw the running of military hospitals at Hagerstown, Fredericksburg and Baltimore. President Lincoln appointed young 34 year old Hammond Surgeon-General on April 25th, 1862. Unfortunately for Hammond, constant strife with the contentious Secretary of War Edwin Stanton brought him to a court martial for irregularities in purchasing medical supplies, where he was found guilty and dismissed from the service in 1864. Stanton had obviously stacked the court and fifteen years later he was vindicated by an act of Congress. After his conviction, a poverty-stricken Hammond went to New York and set up a practice in neurology. He quickly regained his fortunes. From 1867 to 1873 he was professor of diseases of the mind and nervous at both Bellevue Hospital Medical College and at the City University of New York. Hammond remained at the University of the City of New York until 1882, when he helped found the New York postgraduate medical school. Aside from making several important contributions to medical science, Hammond's disease, a neurological affliction of young infants characterized by slow writhing and contractions, is named for him. He was one of seven who founded the American Neurological Association. He wrote extensively on subjects from the role of insanity in crime to male sexual impotence. He was also a novelist, a playwright and a lecturer and it was said that his voice was so powerful he could make himself heard upwind in a hurricane. William Alexander Hammond died in Washington, DC on January 5, 1900 at the age of 72. See "Dr. William Hammond, Surgeon General" in *Son of the South* 2003-2008, www.sonofthesouth.net, (accessed January 22, 2010).
18. *Records of the New Mexico Superintendency of Indian Affairs*, Microfilm Reel 1 frames 12-13. See also *Records of the Office of the Quartermaster General, Consolidated Correspondence Files*, Box 513, Entry 225, NM-81, Dodge, H. L. 1850. These military records detailing Henry Dodge's activities while at the Cebolleta post were originally and mistakenly filed with the Indian Office records.
19. *Letters Received by the 9th Military District 1848-1853*, Microfilm Reel 2, frames 891-892.
20. *Letters Received by the 9th Military District, 1848-1853*, Microfilm Reel 2, frame 895.
21. *Letters Sent by the 9th Military District, 1849-1890*, Microfilm Reel 1, frames 110-111.
22. *Letters Received by the 9th Military District, 1848-1853*, Microfilm Reel 2, frames 783-784.
23. *Letters Sent by the 9th Military District, 1849-1890*, Microfilm Reel 2, frame 1038, Microfilm Reel 1, frame 114. Croghan Ker's career slipped downhill from that point. He remained under arrest in Albuquerque for a time awaiting court-martial for a mysterious infraction regarding a sword that occurred prior to his unauthorized excursion. He apparently lived there with his wife and children, requesting Colonel Munroe to grant him leave in September of 1850 to take his children back to the care of relatives in Texas and Louisiana. He also continued to complain about perceived harassment by Major Howe. He remained in Albuquerque through 1853, at one point attempting to rescind his resignation as captain. Ker continued to stir up trouble for himself. On September 6, 1853, he complained to the Ninth Military District Commander General John Garland that the prefect of Bernalillo County, Rafael Armijo, was trying to have him killed and that the local sheriff Juan Sanchez had "repeatedly fired a pistol at me." Apparently Ker had yet another long-standing feud that had become so threatening he requested to surrender himself to the Army for his own protection. He was yet living in Albuquerque by November of 1854, but apparently his days were numbered. His date and cause of death is unknown, but Croghan Ker died as a captain of the 2nd United States Dragoons and was buried at the old Albuquerque post cemetery. Eventually his remains were moved

to the Santa Fe National Cemetery at Fort Marcy, plot B 722. See *Letters Received by the 9th Military District, 1848-1853*, Microfilm Reel 2 frames 815, 826-827, Microfilm Reel 3 frame 709, Microfilm Reel 4 frame 198, 720 as well as Microfilm Reel 6, frame 288 and "Santa Fe National Cemetery," *Internment.net Cemetery Records Online*, www.interment.net/data/us/nm/santafe/ santanat/santa_fe_kemko.htm, (accessed January 24, 2010).

24. *Letters Received by the 9th Military District, 1848-1853*, Microfilm Reel 2, frames 328-329.
25. Little is known of John R. Tullis. According to the 1850 Census, he originally hailed from Maryland. At the age of 22, he briefly served in Ceran St. Vrain's company during the Taos Rebellion, then as alcalde in Santa Fe and as deputy clerk to the U. S. District Court during the Taos treason trials of March 1847. He is also mentioned in the May 3rd 1848 *Santa Fe Republican* as having an interest in gold mining at Placera just southwest of the capitol. Later in the year he became a Santa Fe County representative to the territorial legislature, but resigned in 1851. He served Governor James S. Calhoun as a negotiator to settle the seemingly never-ending water and land dispute between Acoma and Laguna Pueblos. Apache Indian Agent Michael Steck mentions him in a report in the summer of 1853 as having his wagon train attacked south of Albuquerque by the Mescalero and had "narrowly escaped with his life." See *The William G. Ritch Papers*, Microfilm Reels 1 and 2. Also see the *New Mexico Territorial Archives, Records of the Adjutant General of the Territory, Muster Reels, 1847-1897*, Microfilm Reel 85, the *New Mexico Territorial Archives, Records of the Secretary of the Territory, 1851-1911*, Microfilm Reel 1, *Journals and Ledgers of the Treasurer of the Territory, Receipts & Disbursement Journal*, Microfilm Reel 46, the *State Department Territorial Papers of New Mexico, 1851-1872*, National Archives, State Department Records, T17, (Washington, DC 1954), Microfilm Reel 1, March 3, 1851-Dec. 8, 1860, and lastly *Letters Received by the Office of Indian Affairs*, M234, Microfilm Reel 546.
26. *Records of New Mexico Superintendency of Indian Affairs*, Microfilm Reel 1 frame 27.
27. New Mexico Genealogical Society, *New Mexico Territorial Census Vol. 1, 1850*, (New Mexico Genealogical Society Inc. Albuquerque, 1976).
28. *Records of the Office of the Quartermaster General, Consolidated Correspondence Files*, Box 513, Entry 225, NM-81, Dodge, H. L. 1850.
29. Buford to McLaws, July 5, 1850, *Letters Received by the 9th Military District, 1848-1853*, Microfilm Reel 2, frame 356.
30. *Letters Sent by the 9th Military District, 1849-1890*, Microfilm Reel 1, frames 120-121.
31. Abel, *The Official Correspondence of James S. Calhoun*, 237-246.
32. Tyler to McLaws, June 9, 1850, *Letters Received by the 9th Military District, 1848-1853*, Microfilm Reel 2, frame 1191.
33. *Letters Received by the 9th Military District, 1848-1853*, Microfilm Reel 2, frames 331-332, 337-341, also frames 342-345. Manuel Antonio Chávez was known as New Mexico's Little Lion, or *El Leoncito*, for his toughness and perseverance. He was born in Atrisco around 1818, a descendent of an original conquistador of Juan De Oñate's colonists. When Manuel was about seven years old, the family moved to Cebolleta. At an early age Manuel became involved in trading expeditions and slave raiding expeditions into Navajo country. In one expedition his party was overrun by Navajos. Manuel was severely wounded, but managed as the only survivor of fifty to get home. He later served in the army with his cousin, the future governor Manuel Armijo and helped quash a rebellion in Santa Fe.

Chavez appears to have been well-traveled early in life, having hooked up with German traders as a muleteer and ending up in New Orleans for a time, later in 1839 forced to flee to St. Louis after being implicated in an assassination plot against his cousin Armijo. At that time he began a woodcutting business there and later entered the fruit business with a Cuban partner Alfonso Fernandez. After Fernandez absconded with the business assets, Chavez followed his trail to New York and then Cuba without finding him. Upon learning that his disgruntled cousin Armijo had pardoned him, Manuel returned to New Mexico. Chavez is said to have negotiated the surrender of the ill-fated Texas invasion of 1841 and received the cross of honor from his government for performing that service. During the early 1840s Chavez was living in Santa Fe. He married Maria Vicenta Labadie of Tome in 1844.

After the American invasion, Chavez was jailed for a time under suspicion of plotting rebellion. He had been a proponent of resisting the Americans, but he subsequently pledged loyalty to the United States and served as a private during the Taos Rebellion, supposedly saving Ceran St. Vrain's life during the siege of the Taos Pueblo. The next several years he spent as a rancher, trader, businessman, and Indian fighter. In 1855 he guided an expedition against the Ute and Jicarilla and served as a captain under Ceran St. Vrain. In 1860 he became a lieutenant colonel in the Second New Mexico Mounted Volunteers formed to fight Apaches and Navajos and became commander of Fort Fauntleroy in 1861. In that year he was implicated in the killing of several Navajos after an argument over the outcome of a horse race at the fort. Kit Carson arrested him, but charges were later dropped. Chavez saw action for the Union during the Civil War at Valverde and Glorieta Pass and further action against the Navajos from 1863 through 1868. He remained a rancher on the slopes of Old San Mateo and died in January of 1889 at the age of about 71. See Simmons, *The Little Lion of the Southwest*, 33.

34. *Letters Sent by the 9th Military District, 1849–1890*, Microfilm Reel 1, frame 128.
35. McLaws to Buford, July 25, 1850, *Letters Received by the 9th Military District, 1848–1853*, Microfilm Reel 2, frames 348-350.
36. *The Frank McNitt Collection*. See also Buford to McLaws, July 18, 1850, *Letters Received by the 9th Military District, 1848–1853*, Microfilm Reel 2, frames 363-367. During his career John Buford would later see action against the Sioux and the Mormons, but would become best known for his chance presence on July 1st, 1863 at an insignificant Pennsylvania town called Gettysburg. There his 1st Division Cavalry Corp held off Robert E. Lee's Confederates until General Meade could bring up reinforcements, thereby perhaps saving the Union itself.

John Buford was born on March 4, 1826 near Versailles, Kentucky of a family already known for military service. Buford's first attempt at entering West Point failed, so he attended Knox Manual Labor College in Galesburg, Illinois. He left college for Cincinnati, Ohio in 1843 and attended Cincinnati College. Finally he was admitted to West Point in 1844, graduating in the middle of his class. He was brevetted 2nd Lieutenant in the 1st Dragoons stationed at Jefferson Barracks, Missouri. In 1849, he was promoted to full 2nd Lieutenant while stationed at Fort Scott, and then transferred to the 2nd Dragoons. Rather than joining that outfit, which had earned a scandalous reputation for debauchery, he was sent to Santa Fe on detached service and reassigned to the 1st Dragoons as regimental quartermaster. Buford returned east and was stationed at Fort Mason, Texas in 1852 where he finally joined the 2nd Dragoons. Again he was regulated to paper work and failed to see military action.

In 1853 John Buford was promoted to 1st Lieutenant and on May 9th of the following year married Martha McDowell Duke of Kentucky. They had two children, a boy and a girl, but both died at relatively young ages. 1855 finally provided him with some action against the Sioux. Later he participated in the invasion and seizure of Utah from the Mormons. In 1859 he was promoted to Captain and placed in command of green cavalry recruits at Carlisle Barracks, Pennsylvania. The outbreak of the Civil War found him as Captain in the 2nd Cavalry shoring up Washington's defenses. In July 1862 he was made Brigadier General of Volunteers and saw some action at Thoroughfare Gap, Antietam and Richmond. A month before Gettysburg, he was made Major General of Volunteers commanding the 1st Division of Cavalry Corps. Having survived the Confederate assault at Gettysburg, Buford would not survive the typhoid. In November of 1863, he contracted the fever. He died in a hospital at Washington, DC on December 16th at the age of 36. See "A Brief Biography of John Buford" by Eric Wittenberg in *The Gettysburg Discussion Group*, www.gdg.org/Research/People/Buford/bufbio.html, (accessed January 24, 2010). See also "Union Generals" in *US Civil War Generals*, sunsite.utk.edu/civil-war/ung_b.html, (accessed January 24, 2010).

Chapter 27-An Extremely Violent Contest

1. The Field House Foundation, *Iowa County Heritage, Vol. 1*, (The Field House Foundation Inc., Dodgeville, Wisconsin, 1967). See the last will and testament for Henry Dodge dated Sept. 4, 1866.
2. *Henry Dodge Papers*, State Historical Society of Iowa, Des Moines, Iowa, Folder 39.
3. Western Historical Company, *History of Iowa County*, 600-601.
4. Pelzer, *Augustus Caesar Dodge*, 136.
5. Pelzer, *Henry Dodge*, 190.
6. *Milwaukee Daily Sentinel*, Oct. 17 and 25, 1850.
7. *The Benjamin Read Collection*, entries 138-139, New Mexico State Records and Archives Center, Santa Fe.
8. *New Mexico Legislative Journal*, Center for Southwest Research, University of New Mexico, Albuquerque, December 2nd, 1850.
9. Chávez, Thomas E., *Manuel Alvarez, 1794-1856, A Southwestern Biography*, (University of Colorado Press, Niwot, 1990), 5.
10. Twitchell, *The History of the Military Occupation of the Territory of New Mexico*, 149, 152.
11. *The Santa Fe Republican*, January 22, March 11, 1848.
12. Larson, Robert W., *New Mexico's Quest for Statehood, 1846-1912*, (University of New Mexico Press, Albuquerque, 1968), 127.
13. Prince, L. Bradford, *New Mexico's Struggle for Statehood: Sixty Years of Effort to Obtain Self Government*, (The New Mexican Printing Company, Santa Fe, 1910), 9-10.
14. Twitchell, *The History of the Military Occupation of the Territory of New Mexico*, 155.
15. *The Santa Fe Republican*, November 15, 1848. Spruce McCoy Baird was born in Glasgow, Kentucky on October 8, 1814. After a brief career teaching school, he moved to Texas and eventually began a law practice at Nacogdoches. Governor George T. Wood appointed Baird judge for Santa Fe County, Texas on May 27th, 1848. Texan efforts to annex New Mexico were met with nearly universal derision, but apparently Baird enjoyed a modicum of respect and success during his failed attempt and he remained in New Mexico after abandoning the Texan cause. He eventually settled in Albuquerque. Baird took up the law practice again, served as an Indian agent to the Navajo and was a member of the New Mexico territorial legislature. He also apparently farmed and raised sheep. In 1857, Spruce M. Baird was major general of

the southern division of the New Mexico militia. In September of that same year, he ran for New Mexico's territorial delegate to Congress, but was defeated by Miguel Antonio Otero. A southern sympathizer, in 1861 Baird resigned his position as Attorney General for New Mexico and left the territory. Shortly after that, he was branded a traitor and his property confiscated. Baird commanded a Confederate regiment, the Arizona Brigade of the 4th Regiment, during the war and, rather than seeing Arizona, saw uneventful service in Texas. After being paroled for his part in the War of Rebellion, he moved to Trinidad, Colorado in 1867 and opened a law office there. Spruce M. Baird died five years later at the age of 58, on June 5, 1872, at Cimarron, New Mexico. See the *Territorial Archives of New Mexico, Secretary of the Territory Executive Record Books, 1851-1912*, Microfilm Reel 21. See also *Letters Received by the Department of New Mexico, 1854-1865, Records of U. S. Army Continental Commands, 1821-1920*, National Archives, Record Group 393, M1102, (Washington, DC 1980), Microfilm Reel 4, frame 124 and Microfilm Reel 6, frame 2397. See also "Baird, Spruce McCoy" in *The Handbook of Texas Online*, www.tshaonline.org/handbook/online/articles/BB/ fba18.html, (accessed January 28, 2010).

16. Larson, *New Mexico's Quest for Statehood, 1846-1912*, 18-19.
17. Davis, *El Gringo*, 109.
18. Manuel Alvarez was born in 1794, a native of Abelgas, in the Leon region of northern Spain. In 1818 at the age of 24 years, he immigrated to Mexico. In 1823, during the Mexican Revolution, he removed to Cuba, then New York, and finally to Missouri. In 1824 he opened a store in Santa Fe, but was forced to leave after Mexico expelled citizens of Spain in 1829. He trapped furs for a time before being able to return to Santa Fe in 1834. Secretary of State John Forsyth appointed him Consul to Santa Fe in 1839, but his relationship with the Mexican administration under Governor Manuel Armijo was tempestuous. Alvarez claimed both United States and Mexican citizenship, but was regarded with distrust by Armijo as an American agent. Manuel Alvarez officially became a United States citizen in 1842. He later served as consul in Santa Fe for the United States and was appointed U. S. Commercial Agent at Santa Fe in the Mexican Republic by President Buchanan in March of 1846. He clearly favored American over Mexican administration prior to the outbreak of war in 1846.

Alvarez was a member of the lower house of the Kearny government upon its first meeting in December of 1847 and played an influential role in politics and worked diligently with other Santa Fe businessmen to end the taxes imposed upon them by Price's Order Number 10. In June of 1850, Alvarez was elected lieutenant governor and served as acting governor during governor-elect Henry Connelly's absence in the States. Although Alvarez had powerful American allies, for whatever reason he was never able to rise as far as he might have. He was a leading candidate for Secretary of the Territory under Calhoun's governorship, but politics pushed him aside in favor of the American John Greiner. On the eve of his departure to the States at the close of March, 1852, Calhoun nominated Alvarez as acting governor but withdrew his name three days later. Calhoun's successor, William Carr Lane, appointed Alvarez Commissioner of Public Buildings for the territory in 1852. During these trying times, Alvarez continued his mercantile businesses, served as financial advisor to several businesses, practiced law, managed Santa Fe real estate and was bonded as an Indian trader. Manuel Alvarez died on July 5, 1856 at the age of 62 years. See Chávez, *Manuel Alvarez, 1794-1856, A Southwestern Biography*. See also The *Benjamin M. Read Collection I*, New Mexico State Records and Archives Center, Santa Fe, Document 99 and 106.

19. Larson, *New Mexico's Quest for Statehood, 1846-1912*, 28. See also Abel, *The Official Correspondence of James S. Calhoun*, 163.
20. Twitchell, *The History of the Military Occupation of the Territory of New Mexico*, 162, 165, 175. Like so many of the early New Mexico territorial politicians, Richard Hanson Weightman was an American Army officer. He was born December 28, 1816 in Washington, DC, educated in private schools, graduated from the University of Virginia in 1834 and attended West Point from 1835 to 1837. He was living in Saint Louis when the Mexican War erupted. Weightman enlisted as a volunteer and was unanimously elected as captain of Battery A of the Missouri Light Artillery. The battalion left Fort Leavenworth with Kearny's Army of the West on June 30th, but without Weightman, who had taken ill. He eventually overtook his command at Las Vegas, New Mexico, bringing with him Kearny's commission as Brigadier General of the Army. Weightman later saw action with Doniphan in Chihuahua at the battle of Sacramento, February 28th, 1847. Weightman also served as Army paymaster until his discharge in 1849. He then returned to Santa Fe to practice law and publish a small newspaper, which has since been lost to history.

    Weightman became immediately active in local politics. Paradoxically, he was an outspoken critic of military rule and representatives of the civil government that supported it. Hugh N. Smith was a favorite target. After his failed attempt at entering Congress as the State of New Mexico's first senator, he was elected in 1851 to a two year term as the Territory of New Mexico's first congressional delegate. At that time he was also appointed Indian agent for New Mexico.

    Weightman was not adverse to resorting to violence upon being insulted. He was nearly killed in a duel with Houghton in 1850. In 1852 he stabbed a prominent trader and pathfinder, Felix X. Aubrey, to death in a Santa Fe bar over an insult. Weightman claimed self-defense and, other than being slightly stained by the scandal, apparently suffered little in consequence of his act. In 1858, he moved to Kansas and then in 1861 to Independence, Missouri. When the War Between the States erupted, Weightman sided with the Confederacy and commanded a battalion of the Missouri State Guards. He was killed by a federal artillery barrage at the battle of Wilson's Creek, near Springfield, Missouri, August 10th, 1861. Ironically, the ball that killed him came from a battery commanded by Captain Barkoff, who had served with Weightman during the Mexican conflict. See Twitchell, *The History of the Military Occupation of the Territory of New Mexico*, 381-394. Also see "Weightman, Richard Hanson" in *The Biographical Directory of the United States Congress, 1774 to Present*, http://bioguide.congress.gov /scripts/biodisplay.pl?index=W000255, (accessed January 31, 2010).
21. Abel, *The Official Correspondence of James S. Calhoun*, 213, 219-220. The conflict between the pro-state and pro-territorial factions became so impassioned that at one point Judge Houghton, a territorialist, challenged Weightman to a duel after the major accused him of graft and favoritism on the bench. It is certain that Weightman was motivated less by his outrage over judicial impropriety than by his wish to become the congressional representative for the new State of New Mexico. The two met in an arroyo just outside of Santa Fe. Upon the order to fire, Weightman aimed and pulled the trigger. The ball whizzed harmlessly past Houghton's ear, leaving the judge standing there with a befuddled look on his face. Houghton, who was somewhat deaf, later claimed he hadn't heard the command to fire. No slacker to fair play, Weightman raised his arms over his head and invited Houghton to shoot. Judge Houghton instead chose to leave the field rather than commit cold-blooded murder. Bloodshed had been

avoided, but the rancorous debate raged on. See Larson, *New Mexico's Quest for Statehood, 1846-1912*, 31.

22. Henry Connelly was born in Nelson County, Kentucky in 1800. As a youth he attended medical school at Lexington, Kentucky and graduated in 1828. Shortly afterwards, he immigrated to Missouri, settling in Liberty, Clay County, to practice medicine. He soon moved to Chihuahua, Mexico, where he eventually entered the mercantile business and partnered with Edward J. Glasgow and in 1838 married a local girl. Their union produced three sons. Connelly was in Santa Fe during the American invasion and acted as a liaison to the Americans for Governor Armijo. Even during the war, he pursued business in Chihuahua and was arrested by Mexican authorities on suspicion of aiding American forces. He was eventually released and remained in Chihuahua during the term of the war. With the armistice, he returned to New Mexico. After the premature death of his first wife, he married again to Dolores Perea, the widow of Jose Chavez, and settled at Peralta south of Albuquerque, where he kept a successful trading business. Congress ended his administration and the so-called State of New Mexico in September of 1851, when they voted to admit New Mexico as a territory. Henry was elected as a representative for Bernalillo County to the upper house of the territorial council in 1851, and served as such for nearly ten years. Connelly did get a second chance at the governorship when Abraham Lincoln appointed him territorial governor in 1861. Connelly was an avid opponent of slavery and a stout Union man. During the Civil War he was instrumental in preventing a Confederate takeover by Sibley's Texans. Poor health plagued him during this administration, and in June of 1866 he resigned the governorship. Henry Connelly died on August 12, 1866 in Santa Fe, purportedly of an opium overdose. He was sixty-six years of age. See Twitchell, *The History of the Military Occupation of the Territory of New Mexico*, 365-366. Also see "John Connelly" in *The Civil War in New Mexico, 1861 to 1862*, Palace of the Governors, Museum of New Mexico, www.nmculturenet.org/heritage/civil_war/sketches/connelly .html, (accessed on January 31, 2010).

23. Prince, *New Mexico's Struggle for Statehood*, 18.

24. Twitchell, *The History of the Military Occupation of the Territory of New Mexico*, 386-391. Even after leaving the government, John Tullis in company with Judge Houghton, A. W. Reynolds and others continued their grudge match with the Alvarez faction. As late as March of 1852, Richard Weightman, who by then was the New Mexican delegate to Congress, wrote from Washington City that the Houghton faction had presented the President with a twenty-pages of accusations against "Governor Calhoun and myself" replete with outrageous lies defaming New Mexico as being composed of a "corrupt and brutal people." He claimed Tullis, Houghton and Reynolds were conspiring to reinstall the military regime in New Mexico. The truth of the matter was that even at that late date Assistant Quartermaster A. W. Reynolds still lusted for Weightman's seat in Congress and was doing all he could to undermine the man.

25. Abel, *The Official Correspondence of James S. Calhoun*, 234.

26. Pelzer, *Henry Dodge*, 188.

Chapter 28-Chupadero

1. *Records of the Office of the Quartermaster General Consolidated Correspondence Files*, Box 513, Entry 225, NM-81, Dodge, H. L. 1850.

2. *Records of the New Mexico Superintendency of Indian Affairs, 1849-1880*, T21, Microfilm Reel 1, frames 21-23, 25.
3. *Records of the New Mexico Superintendency of Indian Affairs, 1849-1880*, T21, Microfilm Reel 1, frames 19-20, 23.
4. *Records of the Office of the Quartermaster General, Consolidated Correspondence Files*, Box 513, Entry 225, NM-81, Dodge, H. L. 1850. See also *Records of the New Mexico Superintendency of Indian Affairs, 1849-1880*, T21, Microfilm Reel, 1, frame 9, and Center for Southwest Research, *New Mexico Superintendency, Miscellaneous Papers, 1857*, T21, Microfilm Reel 3.
5. *Territorial Archives of New Mexico, Journals and Ledgers of the Treasurer of the Territory, Receipts & Disbursement Journal*, Microfilm Reel 46, Territorial Auditor, 1851-1889, Taxes Collected, Exp. 7, Folder 14.
6. McNitt, *Navajo Wars*, 167. See also *1850 Federal Census for New Mexico, Cebolleta*.
7. Chandler to McLaws, September 3, 1850, *Letters Received by the 9th Military District, 1848-1853*, Microfilm Reel 2, frames 409-410.
8. Saunders to McLaws, October 16, 1850, *Letters Received by the 9th Military District, 1848-1853*, Microfilm Reel 2, frame 1153. Little is known of Daniel T. Chandler, particularly surprising considering his pivotal role in New Mexican Indian affairs during this period. It appears he was born either in Maryland or Virginia in 1820. The Census of 1850 listed him as born in Washington, DC. He served in the Mexican War in Smith's Brigade of Twigg's Division and saw action at Contreras and Churubusco in 1847. Much later, he achieved some prominence as the Assistant Adjutant and Inspector General for the Confederate Army of America, during which time he inspected the infamous Andersonville prison, recommending the officers in charge be dismissed. His letters and testimony were important evidence in the subsequent trial of Andersonville's commander, Heinrich Wirz, who was later hanged over his protests that he had "only followed orders." There are indications that Chandler served on General Robert E. Lee's staff and was captured himself by the Union in the spring of 1863 and then paroled. He died in 1877.
9. McNitt, *Navajo Wars*, 168.
10. McLaws to Chandler, October 9, 1850, *Letters Sent by the 9th Military District, 1849-1890*, Microfilm Reel 1, frames 166-167.
11. Saunders to McLaws, November 1, 1850, *Letters Received by the 9th Military District, 1848-1853*, Microfilm Reel 2, frame 1160.
12. *The William G. Ritch Papers*, Microfilm Reel 1, entries 1813 to 1816.
13. Bailey, L. R., *Indian Slave Trade in the Southwest*, (Westernlore Press, Los Angeles, 1973), 95-96. See also *The William G. Ritch Papers*, "Muster Roll of Captain Antonio Lucero for December of 1850," Microfilm Reel 1.
14. Chandler to McLaws, December 4, 1850, *Letters Sent by the 9th Military District, 1849-1890*, Microfilm Reel 1, frame 377.
15. Saunders to McLaws, Feb. 2 and Feb. 5, 1851, *Letters Received by the 9th Military District, 1848-1853*, Microfilm Reel 3, frames 306-307.
16. Tolin to Chandler, Feb. 5, 1851, *Letters Received by the 9th Military District, 1848-1853*, Microfilm Reel 3, frame 309.
17. *Letters Received by the 9th Military District, 1848-1853*, Microfilm Reel 2, frames 1162-1166.
18. *The Frank McNitt Collection*, Letters Sent and Received, Adjutant General's Office, AGO C-3-1851, National Archives.

19. Dodge to Chandler, *Letters Received by the 9th Military District, 1848-1853*, Microfilm Reel 3, frame 281.
20. Saunders to Jones, Feb. 14, 1851, *Letters Received by the 9th Military District, 1848-1853*, Microfilm Reel 3, frames 406-40.
21. *Letters Received by the 9th Military District, 1848-1853*, Microfilm Reel 3, frames 907-908.
22. *Letters Received by the 9th Military District, 1848-1853*, Microfilm Reel 3, frame 368.
23. Chandler to McLaws, June 20, 1851, *Letters Received by the 9th Military District, 1848-1853*, Microfilm Reel 3, frame 402.
24. Bloom, Lansing B. "The Rev. Hiram Walter Read, Baptist Missionary to New Mexico," *New Mexico Historical Review* 17, (1941): 113. The Baptists had made an early and relatively strong showing in New Mexico, courtesy of the United States Army. There were at least two missionaries active at that time. In 1849, Hiram Read and Henry W. Reed arrived in Santa Fe, where both served consecutively as chaplain at Fort Marcy. Two others would follow: John Milton Shaw in 1851 and Samuel Gorman in 1852.

Hiram Read was born in Connecticut in 1819. In 1844, after his ordination, he began his work in the Madison, Wisconsin area, serving for a time as the Wisconsin State Senate chaplain. Having weathered the long trip on the Santa Fe Trail in the "dreary wilderness, exposed to the cruelties of the hostile Indians . . ." the Reverend Read enjoyed some success founding a Baptist school in Santa Fe before striking out on his missionary tour. One January visit to Taos, Read solemnly observed the fabled Fire of Montezuma.

"Here, for the first time, I saw the fire of Montezuma, which, as tradition says, he requited his people to keep constantly burning until he returns again. It is a slow, smoldering fire, covered with ashes, kept in a small pit three feet square, curbed with flat stones. I asked the Governor how long it had been burning in this place; to which he replied, that he did not know, but long, long before he was born . . . . The greatest calamity that could befall the Pueblo would be to have the sacred fire extinguished. . . . I am informed that whenever this fire, at any Pueblo, by any means becomes extinguished, the place is at once and forever deserted."

Read returned east in 1851 due to his wife's failing health, but soon returned west. In 1853 he accompanied the Texas Western Railroad Survey through Tucson to Fort Yuma, doing evangelical work along the way. He eventually returned to his wife and family back East and settled at Falls Church, Virginia, serving both as a minister and a clerk for the First Comptroller's Office of the Treasury Department.

Upon the outbreak of the Civil War, he took leave to minister to Union troops in the field. He was subsequently captured by Confederates in 1862 and held in Richmond for six months before being paroled. Read was appointed postmaster by Abraham Lincoln for Arizona Territory and accompanied the newly appointed government to Fort Whipple in 1864. He was to serve at Tucson, but when the new town of Prescott was chosen as territorial capital, he served there. Aside from those duties, Read continued evangelizing and conducted Arizona's first census of the region. He departed Prescott a year later, in 1865, then relocated to California until ultimately returning east, where he settled in Hannibal, Missouri. It is unclear how long he remained there, but by 1880 he was back in the West again, serving as a pastor of the Baptist Church in yet another sinkhole of inequity, Virginia City, Nevada. In 1882, he returned to Arizona, settling in Tucson, then moving to El Paso, Texas. There he served out his remaining years as a bible preacher. He was known as the "Bishop" Read, a title some say he "appropriated unto himself in order to exert a stronger influence over the Mexican Catholics he was seeking to convert." Hiram Walker Read died on February 6, 1895 at the age of 75 years and is probably buried in El Paso. See Gorby, Richard, "Prescott's First Post Office" *Sharlot Hall Museum Days Past*, www.sharlot.org/archives/history/dayspast/text/ 1998_09_13.shtml, (accessed February 7, 2010). See also "Hiram Walter Read" *Arizona Genealogy and History, Hayden Arizona Pioneers Biography Collection*. www.arizonagenealogy.com/bio.htm, (accessed February 7, 2010).

25. Bloom, "The Rev. Hiram Walter Read, Baptist Missionary to New Mexico," *New Mexico Historical Review* 17, (1941): 129-133.
26. Bloom, "The Rev. Hiram Walter Read, Baptist Missionary to New Mexico," *New Mexico Historical Review* 17, (1941): 153.
27. Simmons, *The Little Lion of the Southwest*, 125.
28. *Letters Sent by the 9th Military District, 1849-1890*, Microfilm Reel 1, frames 241, 248.
29. *Letters Received by the 9th Military District, 1848-1853*, Microfilm Reel 3, frames 832-839.
30. *Letters Sent by the 9th Military District, 1849-1890*, Microfilm Reel 1, frame 250.
31. *The William G. Ritch Papers*, Microfilm Reel 1, frame 656.
32. *Letters Sent by the 9th Military District, 1849-1890*, Microfilm Reel 1, frames 260-261.
33. Chandler to McLaws April 24, 1851, *Letters Received by the 9th Military District, 1848-1853*, Microfilm Reel 3, frames 356-359.
34. Dodge to Munroe, May 12, 1851, *Letters Received by the 9th Military District, 1848-1853*, Microfilm Reel 3, frames 425-427.
35. McLaws to Chandler, May 17, 1851, *Letters Sent by the 9th Military District, 1849-1890*, Microfilm Reel 1, frame 284.
36. *The William G. Ritch Papers*, Microfilm Reel 1, entry 656.
37. Chandler to McLaws, April, 1851, *Letters Received by the 9th Military District, 1848-1853*, Microfilm Reel 3, frames 352-354.

Chapter 29-Fort Defiance

1. Senate Executive Documents, 31st Cong., 2nd session, no. 26, pg 2-5.
2. Van Valkenburgh, Richard, *Dine Bikéyah*, (Department of the Interior, Navajo Agency, Window Rock, Arizona, 1941).
3. Chandler to McLaws, June 2, 1851, *Letters Received by the 9th Military District, 1848-1853*, Microfilm Reel 3, frames 40-41.
4. Graham to McLaws, May 6, 1851, *Letters Received by the 9th Military District, 1848-1853*, Microfilm Reel 3, frames 566, 603.
5. McNitt, *Navajo Wars*, 183-184.
6. Chandler to McLaws, June 28, 1851, *Letters Received by the 9th Military District, 1848-1853*, Microfilm Reel 3, frames 413-414.
7. McNitt, *Navajo Wars*, 186-188.
8. Chandler to McLaws, July 24, 1851, *Letters Received by the 9th Military District, 1848-1853*, Microfilm Reel 3, frames 420-424.
9. McLaws to Howe, July 19, 1851, *Letters Sent by the 9th Military District, 1849-1890*, Microfilm Reel 1, frame 320.

10. Edwin Vose Sumner appeared the epitome of soldiering, but in reality was at best of modest ability. He was born on January 30, 1797 in Boston, Massachusetts. As a youth he attended West School, Billerica School and later the Milton Academy but did not attend West Point. As a young man he took up a mercantile career in Troy, New York then entered the army as a second lieutenant in 1819 at the age of 22 years. He served in the Black Hawk War in 1832, was promoted to captain in 1833 and assigned to the First Regiment of United States Dragoons under the command of Colonel Henry Dodge. By 1838, Sumner was in Carlisle, Pennsylvania, where he superintended the cavalry school.

During the Mexican War, Edwin Vose Sumner served under General Winfield Scott and saw action at Vera Cruz and Cerro Gordo, where he was seriously injured. After being brevetted lieutenant colonel, he was in command of the cavalry at Molina Del Rey, where he saw the hottest action, having at one point his horse shot out from under him. For his bravery, he was brevetted colonel. Having survived the fortunes of war in Mexico, Sumner gained, if not actually an appreciation, then an exposure to New Mexico on Stephen Watts Kearny's staff.

In the wake of James S. Calhoun's sudden departure and death, Sumner served a tumultuous and controversial stint as the acting territorial governor of New Mexico from May to September of 1852, at one point recommending that the United States give the territory back to the "Mexicans and Indians." Regardless of that, he was promoted to the rank of colonel on March 3, 1855 and assigned command of the First U.S. Cavalry Regiment stationed at Fort Leavenworth in what was then known as "Bleeding Kansas." There he labored to pacify both the savage Cheyenne and the even more savage Abolitionists and Fire Eaters slaughtering one another over slavery. He was later posted to St. Louis.

In 1861, with the outbreak of the Civil War, Sumner was promoted to brigadier general and was appointed to command the Department of California. At his own request to see action, he was again transferred back east to the Army of the Potomac, where he was assigned, among other duties, to guard President Elect Abraham Lincoln on his inaugural journey from Springfield to Washington, DC. At the age of 64, he had the dubious distinction of being the oldest general in the Union Army. Sumner saw action in the Battle of Seven Pines and Malvern Hill in McClellan's Peninsular Campaign and later at Antietam, as well as the Union debacle at Fredericksburg and in the Seven Days Battle, where he was again wounded. As to the old war dog's military attributes, McClellan diplomatically described him as a model soldier but of a capacity that nature had limited "to a very narrow extent." The Comte de Paris, a military advisor with McClellan, was less diplomatic. He characterized him as a bearded old man with an "air of stupidity that perfectly expressed his mental state." In truth, as a commander Sumner's still booming, intimidating voice showed more courage and audacity than he actually displayed in battle.

After Hooker assumed command of the Army of the Potomac, Sumner resigned, probably in response to withering criticism of his actions or inactions. He was soon reassigned to the Department of the Missouri. Before journeying to St. Louis to take command, he headed home to visit a son-in-law in Syracuse, New York. He apparently contracted pneumonia during his trip and it quickly killed him. Sumner died on March 21, 1863. He was 66 years old. However much the old soldier was criticized, none less than Robert E. Lee took note of his passing in a letter to his wife, stating that "Genl Hooker sent me yesterday the account of the death of Genl Sumner. He died at Syracuse after a week's sickness from a cold." Sumner's last words were said to be "God save my country, the United States of America!" His obituary appearing in *The New*

York Times for March 22, 1863 was absolutely profuse in praise: " . . . He sleeps now with our bravest and truest, and no braver or truer has his country or its army ever lost."

See "General Edwin Vose Sumner" in "Union Generals," *Historycentral.com*, 2010, www.historycentral.com/bio/UGENS/USASumner.html, (accessed February 13, 2010).

See also "Edwin Vose Sumner, Obituary and Editorial" in *The New York Times*, March 22, 1863, library.morrisville.edu/local_history/sites/gar_post/sumner2.html and library.morrisville.edu/local_history/sites/gar_post/sumner4.html. See also "Edwin Sumner" in *Territorial Kansas Online, 1854–1861*, University of Kansas, www.territorialkansasonline.org, (accessed February 13, 2010).

11. McNitt, *Navajo Wars*, 191-192.
12. Sumner to Bliss, August 3, 1851, *Letters Sent by the 9th Military District, 1849–1890*, Microfilm Reel 1, frame 328.
13. Sumner to Chandler, August 16, 1851, *Letters Sent by the 9th Military District, 1849–1890*, Microfilm Reel 1, frame 500.
14. McNitt, *Navajo Wars*, 194. See also *The Richard A. Kern Diary*, 18-19. The term sutler referred to a camp follower who made money selling both necessities and luxuries, including liquor, to the soldiers. Its original meaning is less than complementary. The term derived from the Middle Dutch term *zoetelaar*, originally meaning a lackey who does dirty work, from the word *zoetelen*, to foul or sully. The sutler was an unofficial position, but one that many lonely and ragged recruits found indispensable. Hence, wherever one found an Army post, a sutler was not too far away. He depended on the acquiescence of the commanding officer to run shop, however, and was scrutinized with a certain amount of suspicion. Dodge probably served as the sutler for Cebolleta before the Sumner expedition and continued in that capacity after the closing of the post.
15. A cursory comparison of the two texts side by side provides all the evidence any outraged historian might possibly desire to secure an indictment. Edward's work, *A Campaign in New Mexico with Colonel Doniphan*, was originally published by Carey and Hart of Philadelphia in 1847, shortly after Edwards chronicled his experiences, and was subsequently reprinted by the University of New Mexico Press, Albuquerque, in 1996. Rice's journal, held in its original form by the Denver Public Library and only published in 1970 by Old West Publishing Company, details the private's purported experiences beginning in 1850. Any suspicion that Rice carried Edward's book with him on his tramps through New Mexico is confirmed when the discerning reader compares the two books. After a quick review, this author found at least ten instances where Rice had copied Edward's work word for word and paragraph for paragraph, going so far as to even lift a stanza of the poet Bryant's work, quoted by Edwards.

"And a sight of these prairies would often cause Bryant's beautiful lines to rise to my lips, and I would picture to myself the magnificent plains peopled by the almost extinct red man—his leaving for a wider hunting-ground—and fancy, with the poet and his murmuring bee—The sound of that advancing multitude which soon shall fill these deserts. From the ground come up the laugh of children, the soft voice of maidens and the sweet solemn hymn of Sabbath worshippers." See Edwards, 1847, 24.

Josiah Rice relates the identical. Note that the notations within brackets are those of the book's editor: "And a sight of these prairies would often cause [William Cullen] Bryant's beautiful lines to rise to my lips and I would picture to myself the magnificent plains peopled by the almost extinct red man, his leaving for a wider hunting ground, and fancy with the poet and his murmuring be, that with the sound of the advancing multitude which soon shall fill these deserts from the ground comes up the laugh of children, the soft voice of Sabbath worshipers."

Rice's journal was written by hand, so any differences in wording can be attributed more to bad penmanship and grammar than the flow of creative juices. On page 30, describing Kearny's march across the plains, Edwards writes "A volunteer from one of the St. Louis companies was drowned during our stay at Pawnee Forks. He received a prairie burial." Compare that with page 36 of Rice, who wrote "A soldier from one of the New Port companies was drowned during our stay at Pawnee Forks. He received a prairie burial . . ." The same can be observed in comparing, in pairs, Edwards' words on pages 26, 38-39, 40-41, 42-43, 60-61, 62-63, and 147 with Rice's work on pages 35, 41, 42, 43, 53, 54, and 57. What is most disturbing is that Rice relies on incidents that happened to Edwards, changing the names and places to make them incidents he claims he himself experienced. Compare the following:

Edwards describes his march with Kearny towards Armijo's forces rumored to be entrenched at Apache Pass: "I accompanied the serjeant [sic] to General Kearney's tent, where we left our prisoner. The stranger was a young handsome Mexican, and declared himself to be a son of General Salazar. This young man's object was, apparently, friendly, as he stated that he had come out in order to inform us that the Mexican army, which had numbered four thousand men under the command of Governor Armijo, had been strongly entrenched at the Pecos Pass . . ."

Rice recounts his march with Sumner towards Las Vegas: "I accompanied the Sergeant to Colonel Sumner's tent, where we left our prisoner. The stranger was a young and handsome Indian, and declared himself to be a son of the Chief Sandoval. This young man's object was apparently friendly, as he stated that he had come out in order to inform us that the Indians, which had numbered four thousand warriors under the Chief Carvajal, had been strongly entrenched in the mountains at Pecos Pass . . ."

Frank Edwards eventually continued south into Mexico with Doniphan. Five years later, Josiah Rice headed west to Canyon de Chelly with Sumner. One might be tempted to think that Rice's liberal lifting of Edward's words would have stopped once he and Frank had parted ways and experiences, but unfortunately such was not the case. Rice's description of a drama society started by the soldiers at Fort Defiance almost perfectly reflects Edward's story of the same at Fort Marcy, right down to the plays they presented, *Pizarro, Bombastes Furioso* and *The Scottish Shoemaker and His Wife*. See Edwards, 1847; 70 and Rice, 1970; 88. One can only conclude that Josiah Rice's own experiences were so painfully mundane that he had to spice them up for the admiring folks back home. See Edwards, Frank S., *A Campaign in New Mexico With Colonel Doniphan*, Carey and Hart, Philadelphia, 1847, reprinted by the University of New Mexico Press, Albuquerque, 1996 and Rice, *A Cannoneer in Navajo Country: Journal of Private Josiah M. Rice, 1851*, (Old West Publishing Co, Denver, 1970).

16. *The Richard A. Kern Diary*, 26-27. See also Weber, David J., *Richard H. Kern: Expeditionary Artist in the Far Southwest, 1848-1853*, (University of New Mexico, Albuquerque, 1985), 317 note 16.
17. *The Richard A. Kern Diary*, 27.
18. Rice, *A Cannoneer in Navajo Country*, 67.
19. Electus Backus was born on February 17th, 1804 in New York, the son of Sabra Judson Backus and Lt. Colonel Electus M. Backus, who had tragically been killed in 1813 at Sackett's Harbor.

Losing his father at the age of seven didn't dissuade Electus from pursuing a military career. After attending West Point, he entered the 1st Infantry as a 2nd Lieutenant and was garrisoned at Sackett's Harbor during his first year of service. He served in Florida and at Jefferson Barracks, Missouri for the next few years, reaching the rank of 1st lieutenant 1831 and captain in 1837.

Backus saw brief and undistinguished service during the Black Hawk War as an officer to Brigadier General Hugh Brady, whom he served from 1827 through 1837 and managed to marry not one, but two of the general's daughters: Sarah who after a year of marriage died apparently childless in 1828 and then two years later Mary, who would give him a daughter and eventually outlive him by twenty-eight years. From 1837 to 1840 Captain Backus served in the Seminole War. Severe and lingering sickness compelled his reassignment to Fort Columbus, New York, followed by a four-year stint at Fort Snelling in Minnesota and a year at Jefferson Barracks. Backus saw action during the Mexican War and was brevetted major for his gallant conduct at Monterey. With the close of the war, he was assigned to recruiting service at Buffalo, New York. On June 10th, 1850, he was promoted to a major of the 3rd Infantry, relieved of recruiting and ordered to report to Colonel John Munroe at El Paso, Texas. By July of 1851, Backus was in command of the El Paso garrison.

After building Fort Defiance, Electus Backus commanded there for a brief period then was assigned command of Fort Fillmore, some six miles south of present day Las Cruces. He remained there for about a year before being ordered back east to resume recruiting duty, this time at Newport Barracks, Kentucky. He served there as superintendent of general recruiting until 1856. The year 1858 found Backus back in New Mexico, serving in the latest Navajo war, remaining at Fort Defiance through 1859. While at Rengold Barracks, Texas he was promoted to lieutenant-colonel, 3rd Infantry. After Texas left the Union, he brought his command safely to Jefferson Barracks via New Orleans on the steamship *Star of the West*.

Due to his deteriorating health, Backus saw no action during the Civil War, but continued to serve as a mustering and recruitment officer in Detroit. In 1862, he was promoted to full colonel, but shortly afterwards that lingering infirmity finally ended his life. He died at Detroit in June of 1862 at the age of 58 years and was buried in Elmwood Cemetery. He was known as an efficient and responsible officer and, though he saw little action, it could be said he did his father proud. See *Letters Sent by the 9th Military District, 1849–1890*, Microfilm Reel 1, frames 316, 807, and 903 and *Letters Received by the Office of Indian Affairs*, Microfilm Reel 6, frame 524. See also "Electus Backus Jr.," Brady, Quigley, *Backus Family*, http://Ancestry.com, freepages.genealogy.rootsweb.ancestry .com/~palmfronds/ 2006 WEBSITE/ electusbackusjr.htm, (accessed February 13, 2010).

20. Abel, *The Official Correspondence of James S. Calhoun*, 418.
21. Rice, *A Cannoneer in Navajo Country*, 72, 74.
22. Bennett, *Forts and Forays*, 30-31.
23. Rice, *A Cannoneer in Navajo Country*, 75-76.
24. Bennett, *Forts and Forays*, 30-31.
25. Rice, *A Cannoneer in Navajo Country*, 75-76.
26. Sumner to Jones, October 24, 1851, *Letters Sent by the 9th Military District, 1849–1890*, Microfilm Reel 1, frames 515-518.
27. Rice, *A Cannoneer in Navajo Country*, 77, 78.
28. Sumner to Jones, October 24, 1851, *Letters Sent by the 9th Military District, 1849–1890*, Microfilm Reel 1, frames 515-518.

29. Abel, *The Official Correspondence of James S. Calhoun*, 419.

Chapter 30-Wild as Hawks

1. *Records of the New Mexico Superintendency of Indian Affairs, 1849–1880, Records of the Santa Fe Agency,* Miscellaneous Documents, Microfilm Reel 1.
2. Paschal Bequette was born in Ste. Genevieve, Missouri on October 24, 1804. As a young man, he learned merchandising in the store owned by Rosier and Valle. He later moved to Mine La Motte to run a store and smelt lead. After lead was discovered in southwest Wisconsin, Bequette moved to Mineral Point. After serving under General Dodge in the Black Hawk War, he was appointed Receiver of Public Monies at Mineral Point by President Van Buren. The Bequettes were infamously close to the Dodges. Paschal married Elizabeth Peity Dodge on November 25, 1832 in Dodgeville. The Census of 1850 shows Paschal headed a large household, including Elizabeth, six children, his widowed mother Marie Louse Mesplay-Bequette and his sister Eupheme Bequette, as well as four other unrelated individuals who were doubtlessly employees.
Having been appointed Receiver of Public Monies for California by President Pierce, Paschal packed up his family and property and moved west in April of 1852. They stopped on their long journey at Salt Lake City, where they were hosted by an old friend, one Captain Hooper. A yarn common for that era had it that, while in Utah, an Indian chief was so smitten by Paschal's young daughter, Kitty, "whose flower-like beauty always attracted attention," that he offered a fine horse for her. See Beckett, *Becquet, Bequette, Beckett Family History*, 68.
The Bequettes refused the horse, retained their daughter and moved on to Sacramento, California, where Paschal invested in groceries and livestock. A promising start was almost immediately swept away by the great Sacramento fire and subsequent great Sacramento floods of 1852. Wiped out but not defeated, Paschal and family relocated to San Francisco, then across the bay to Benicia in 1856, and in 1859 relocated south to Visalia, California. Fortunately, he received further appointments as Receiver of Public Monies by Presidents Pierce in 1854 and Buchannan in 1858. In 1861, Paschal served as Recorder of Tulare County. Bequette passed away at the age of 74 years on December 2, 1879 and is buried in the Visalia city cemetery. See "Bequette, Paschal, Col." in *Our Family History, the Abercrombie Family Tree*, (www.lgabercrombie.com, accessed February 16, 2010).
3. Bartlett, John R., *Personal Narrative of Explorations and Incidents in Texas, New Mexico, California, Sonora and Chihuahua*, (D. Appleton & Company, New York, 1854), 233.
4. Van Valkenburgh, *Dine Bikéyah*, 44.
5. *Letters Received by the 9th Military District, 1848–1853*, Microfilm Reel 5, frame 303. See also *Letters Sent 9th Military District*, frame 547.
6. *Rio Abajo Press*, April 28, 1863.
7. Sunseri, *Seeds of Discord*, 27.
8. Mansfield, Joseph F. K., *Mansfield on the Condition of the Western Forts, 1853–54*, edited by Robert W. Frazer, (University of Oklahoma Press, Norman, Oklahoma. 1963), 25, note.
9. Bartlett, *Personal Narrative of Explorations*, 235-236.
10. Bartlett, *Personal Narrative of Explorations*, 227-230.
11. Sturtevant, William C., ed., *Handbook of North American Indians, Vol. 10 Southwest*, (Smithsonian Institution, Washington, 1983), 401. There were three somewhat amorphous

bands of Chiricahua: the Central Band living in present day southern Arizona, the Southern Band residing in northern Mexico and the Eastern Chiricahua straddling the border of Arizona and New Mexico.

12. Thomlinson, M. H., "Forgotten Fort," *New Mexico Magazine*, vol. 23, no. 1 (January 1945): 14-41, 39.
13. Cremony, *Life Among the Apaches*, 29.
14. Cremony, *Life Among the Apaches*, 61-62.
15. Bartlett, *Personal Narrative of Explorations*, 352-355.
16. *The William G. Ritch Papers*, Microfilm Reel 1, after entry 540.
17. *Letters Received by the 9th Military District, 1848-1853*, Microfilm Reel 5, frame 360.
18. Morris to McFerran, March 16, 1852, *Letters Received Ninth Military District*, Microfilm Reel 5, frames 353-355. There was no mention of John Tullis at Santa Rita. After the store broke up, Tullis may have immediately returned to trading along the Rio Abajo, something he would do for the next several years.
19. Sumner to Morris, 1852, April 1, *Letters Sent by the 9th Military District, 1849-1890*, Microfilm Reel 1, frames 588-590.
20. *Letters Received by the 9th Military District, 1848-1853*, Microfilm Reel 5, frame 429.
21. Thomlinson, "Forgotten Fort," 39-41.
22. Mansfield, *Mansfield on the Condition of the Western Forts, 1853-54*, 25, note.
23. Henry Carpenter Affidavit Nov. 11, 1852, *Letters Received by the 9th Military District, 1848-1853*, Microfilm Reel 5, frame 1041.
24. *Letters Received by the 9th Military District, 1848-1853*, Microfilm Reel 5, frame 1038.
25. Maj. Rucker, Albuquerque, to Headquarters, May 27, 1852, *Letters Received by the 9th Military District, 1848-1853*, Microfilm Reel 5, frame 696.
26. Abel, *The Official Correspondence of James S. Calhoun*, 538-540.
27. Abel, Annie, H., "The Journal of John Greiner," *Old Santa Fe Magazine*, July 1916), 214.
28. Abel, "The Journal of John Greiner," 216.
29. Judge Baird, as he was widely known, had come to New Mexico to help organize a Texan takeover of the territory. Baird, marginalized by New Mexicans and unpaid by Texas for his efforts, took up law in Santa Fe and was later hired by James Calhoun to prosecute tax dodgers. He soon entered politics and ironically became a representative in the New Mexico State House in 1851. At about the same time he demonstrated some interest in Indian affairs by requesting permission from Colonel Sumner to start a trading post for the Navajos at Fort Defiance. He was appointed Indian agent to the Navajo on January 22, 1852. As agent, Spruce remained in Albuquerque, living in a rented house, though he claimed he intended to move out to Navajo country that fall. He never did. See Sunseri, *Seeds of Discord*, 8-9. See also *Territorial Archives of New Mexico, Secretary of the Territory Executive Record Books, 1851-1912*, Microfilm Reel 21, and *Territorial Archives of New Mexico, Records of the Secretary of the Territory, 1851-1911*, Microfilm Reel 1, as well as *Letters Received by the 9th Military District, 1848-1853*, Microfilm Reel 4, frame 91, and *The William G. Ritch Papers*, Microfilm Reel 1, entry 511 and as well as *Letters Received by the 9th Military District, 1848-1853*, Microfilm Reel 5, frame 761.
30. *The William G. Ritch Papers*, Microfilm Reel 1, entry 531.
31. *Letters Received by the 9th Military District, 1848-1853*, Microfilm Reel 5, frame 429.
32. *Records of New Mexico Superintendency of Indian Affairs*, Microfilm Reel 1. Americans seldom failed to be impressed by their first and subsequent meetings with Mangas Coloradas and

many were effusive in their praise for him as a picturesque and noble leader. Although Bartlett described the Chiricahua Apache in general as an "ill formed, emaciated and miserable looking race" he praised Mangas Coloradas as rather handsome, as were their children. Indian Agent Edward Wingfield called him "a noble specimen of the genus homo. He comes up nearer to the poetic ideal of a chieftain, such as Homer in his Iliad would describe than any person that I have ever seen. No feudal Lord in the . . . days of Chivalry ever had his vassals under better subjugation. His manners are stern, dignified and reserved, seldom speaks, but when he does it is to the point, and with great good sense. You may be assured he is the master Spirit among the Apaches." See Bartlett, *Personal Narrative of Explorations*, 327 and *Letters Received by of Office of Indian Affairs, New Mexico Superintendency*, Microfilm Reel 547, S493-W435.

Cremony described Mangas as "undoubtedly, the most prominent and influential Apache who has existed for a century. Gifted with a large and powerful frame, corded with iron-like sinews and muscles, and possessed of far more than an ordinary amount of brain strength, he succeeded, at an early age, in winning a reputation unequalled in his tribe. His daring exploits, his wonderful resources, his diplomatic abilities, and his wise teachings in council soon surrounded him with a large and influential band, which gave him a sort of prestige and sway among the various branches of his race . . . His height was about six feet; his head was enormously large, with a broad, bold forehead, a large aquiline nose, a most capacious mouth, and broad, heavy chin. His eyes were rather small, but exceedingly brilliant and flashing when under any excitement— although his outside demeanor was as imperturbable as brass . . ." See Cremony, *Life among the Apaches*, 47-48.

Mangas was a consummate diplomat, forging alliances with the far flung bands of Coyotero and Mescalero Apaches, as well as with the Mexican and Americans. Years later the prominent Navajo headman Manuelito told Cremony that Mangas had given him one of his daughters as a bride, so it is certainly probable he counted the Navajo as potential allies, as well. See Cremony, *Life Among the Apaches*, 51. Although in early years he professed friendship with the Americans, continual encroachment upon Apache lands made him take up arms against the settlers and the Army. As with many other noble Indian leaders, such admiration would not save Mangas from a tragic fate at the hands of his purported admirers. In January of 1863 during the Apache War, Mangas was captured by members of the 1st California Volunteers. There were several versions of what actually happened. Some state Mangas surrendered willingly. There are others who insist that he was promised a truce and safe passage if he would come in alone, then was seized after he had dismissed his armed escort. That version holds that later the officer in charge told his sentries he expected Mangas delivered up dead or alive, uttering an "unmistakable emphasis on *dead*." When one of the guards bayoneted the shackled chief in the leg, he jumped up and the two sentries emptied their revolvers into him. A second version of Mangas' death is even less dignified. The night Mangas was killed his guards were entertaining themselves by burning the bound chief's feet and legs with heated bayonets. When Mangas protested that he was not a child to be toyed with, they shot him dead. The official Army explanation was that the old chief had been killed trying to escape. See Fugate, Francis L., *Roadside History of New Mexico*, (Mountain Press Publishing Company, Missoula, 1989), 427.

33. Sweeny, Edwin R., *Mangas Coloradas, Chief of the Chiricahua Apaches*, (University of Oklahoma Press, Norman, 1998), 258-259.
34. Abel, "The Journal of John Greiner," 227-228.
35. *Letters Sent by the 9th Military District, 1849-1890*, Microfilm Reel 1, frames 754-755. See

also *Letters Received by the Office of Indian Affairs, 1824-1880, New Mexico Superintendency*, M234, Microfilm Reel 546.

36. *Letters Received by the 9th Military District, 1848-1853*, Microfilm Reel 5, frame 481. See also Wingfield to Lane, December 20th, 1852, *Letters Received by the Office of Indian Affairs, 1824-1880, New Mexico Superintendency*, Microfilm Reel 547, S493-W435.

Chapter 31-Hearth and Home

1. *Santa Rosa News*, May, 1966.
2. United States Federal Census 1910, New Mexico, Guadalupe County, Precinct 9-Puerto de Luna, page 3.
3. Padilla y Baca, Luis Gilberto, *Libro de Bautismos 1862-1902, Extracted from the Church of San José, Church of Jurisdiction, Anton Chico, Territory of New Mexico, The Archdiocese of Santa Fe*, 1996.
4. United States Federal Census, 1860, New Mexico Territory, Santa Fe, County, Galisteo, M653, Microfilm Reel 714, page 392.
5. Padilla y Baca, *Extractions of Marriages for Puerto de Luna and Surrounding Settlements, 1864-1927, La Iglesia de San José Marriage Book*, LDS Family Library, Microfilm 016-627, 1998, 10.
6. United States Federal Census, 1880, New Mexico Territory, San Miguel County, Galisteo/Puerto de Luna, Census Series T9, Microfilm Reel 803, page 441.
7. United States Federal Census, 1930, Guadalupe County, Puerto de Luna, 1930, T626, Microfilm Reel 1393, page 247.
8. United States Federal Census, 1870, New Mexico Territory, San Miguel County, Puerto de Luna, Series M593, Microfilm Reel 895, page 177.
9. Padilla y Baca, *Libro de Bautismos 1862-1902, Extracted from the Church of San José, Church of Jurisdiction, Anton Chico, Territory of New Mexico, the Archdiocese of Santa Fe*, 1996.
10. United States Census, 1860, New Mexico Territory, Valencia County, Seboyeta, M653, Microfilm Reel 716, page 695.
11. United Status Census. 1900, New Mexico Territory, Guadalupe County, Puerto de Luna, District 62, page 15.
12. Danielson, Betty, *Blood Brother of Pueblo Land: The Angel from the East, Samuel Gorman Among the Lagunas*, (Published by the author, Albuquerque, 1998).
13. Danielson, *Blood Brother of Pueblo Land*, quoting Home Mission Review, vol. 4, No. 6, from Gorman at Laguna, Nov. 10, 1852.
14. Gorman, Mrs. Samuel, "Rev. Samuel Gorman: Memorial" in *Old Santa Fe*, vol. 1, no. 3, (1914): 319-320. Sanon became closely identified with the mission and, although he refused baptism for two years, faithfully assisted them by translating Gorman's sermons from Spanish into Keresan and serving as liaison between Gorman and the pueblo. However, Samuel's sole reliance on Sanon might have actually frustrated attempts to forge good relations with the pueblo leadership. Often the first sociable, obliging native to appear at the tent door is an attention-seeking ego smarting from being rejected by his own folk, an understandable behavior that later confounded many an eager ethnologist. If indeed Sanon had little status in the Laguna community, the pueblo leaders may have believed the Gormans to be trivial and of no account, when considering the kind of company they kept.

15. Danielson, *Blood Brother of Pueblo Land*, quoting Home Mission Review vol. 4, No. 6, Gorman letter, Nov. 13th.
16. Danielson, *Blood Brother of Pueblo Land*, quoting Home Mission Review vol. 4, No. 6, Gorman letter, Nov. 22nd.
17. *The Frank McNitt Collection*, National Archives, Record Group 75, *Letters Received by the Office of Indian Affairs, 1824-1880, New Mexico Superintendency*, T21-1.
18. Danielson, *Blood Brother of Pueblo Land*, quoting Home Mission Record, July 1853, from Gorman letter of March 7, 1853 and Oct. 1853, from Gorman letter of April 12, 1853.
19. Myers, Lewis A., *A History of New Mexico Baptists, Vol. 1, 1849-1912*, (The Baptist Convention of New Mexico, 1965), 59-60.
20. Gorman, "Rev. Samuel Gorman: Memorial," 316-320.

Chapter 32-Navajo Agent

1. *Schaaf Collection, 70-0069*, Missouri Historical Society, St. Louis, Missouri. William Carr Lane was born in Fayette County, Pennsylvania in 1789. He arrived in New Mexico just short of the age of 53. In his youth, Lane acquired legal, military and medical training. In 1811, he studied medicine under Dr. Collins in Louisville, Kentucky. He later joined the army to fight Tecumseh, but saw no action other than tending soldiers sick with bilious fever. Lane moved to St. Louis in 1816 and saw medical service at several military outposts. After a move to Vincennes, Indiana he married Mary Ewing in 1818. Mary hated military service, but despite that fact, Lane accepted a position as an army surgeon. Mary must have finally asserted her preferences, for he resigned his commission in 1819. They settled in St. Louis permanently and William went into private practice. From that time, William Carr Lane was noted by people of influence. In 1821, Missouri Governor Alexander McNair made him his aide-de-camp with the rank of colonel. By 1822 at the age of 33 years, he was quartermaster general of the state. In 1823 he was elected the first mayor of St. Louis and served for several terms. See Twitchell, Ralph E., "Historical Sketch of Governor William Carr Lane, Together with Diary of His Journey from St. Louis, Mo., to Santa Fe, N. M., July 31st to September 9th, 1852," *New Mexico Historical Society Publications*, no. 4, (The Historical Society of New Mexico, Santa Fe, 1917), 5-7.
   Identifying himself as a loyal Democrat certainly helped boost his career. He was elected to the state House of Representatives in 1826 and, amazingly, was probably as popular and well known as the venerable Senator Thomas H. Benton. When he was passed over for a congressional seat in favor of Benton, Lane became a Whig.
   In 1832 military service called again. William Carr Lane served General Atkinson as troop surgeon during the Black Hawk War. At the war's conclusion, Lane returned to politics in St. Louis and again served as mayor from 1837 to 1840. He became restless, perhaps due in part to the untimely death of his 16-year-old son, Victor, in 1846, and spent some time in Washington lobbying for a position with government. Finally his friends in St. Louis and Whig supporters in Washington persuaded President Fillmore to appoint him as territorial governor of New Mexico in 1852. With Calhoun's sudden departure and eventual death, Lane rushed back to St. Louis from Washington to make hasty preparations for his departure to New Mexico. See Horn, *New Mexico's Troubled Years*, 37.
   Given the fact he had become a Whig, it is perhaps surprising that the Dodges supported Lane. In December of 1852, concerned over an upcoming change in the presidency that would

probably have him ejected as governor, William Carr Lane wrote to Congressman John Darby in Washington inquiring about his chances. "I have seen both the Senators from Iowa, Dodge & Jones & Governor Henry Dodge of Wisconsin, now also a Senator," Darby replied on February 7th, "And so far as they are concerned you must be retained in your place." If, however, the new Democratic administration demanded his replacement, as they probably would, "these gentlemen will advise me of it in time to let me inform you of it, that your resignation may be handed in. They all stand high with the Democratic Party, and are much courted." See Twitchell, "Historical Sketch of Governor William Carr Lane," 8-9 and the *William Carr Lane Collection*, Missouri Historical Society, St. Louis, Box 6.

During Lane's tumultuous tenure as governor, he became embroiled in a controversy over the Mesilla Valley near El Paso, a territory disputed between the United States and Mexico. After touring the area in February of 1853, he issued a proclamation claiming the valley for the United States. Mexican officials were outraged and President Franklin Pearce, concerned over deteriorating relations with Mexico, asked Lane to resign. He did, explaining he'd quit to allow him to run for a seat as New Mexico's representative to Congress. He subsequently lost the election, returned to Saint Louis, and swore off politics. Lane chose the occupation most sympathetic to his skills, and practiced both medicine and law until he died in 1863 at the age of 74 years.

2. *William Carr Lane Collection*, Box 6.
3. Twitchell, "Historical Sketch of Governor William Carr Lane," 7-9.
4. Twitchell, "Historical Sketch of Governor William Carr Lane," 44-52.
5. Horn, *New Mexico's Troubled Years*, 39.
6. *Letters Sent by the 9th Military District, 1849-1890*, Microfilm Reel 1, frames 674, 677-678 and 684-685.
7. *Charles Bent Letters: Department of New Mexico*, Adjutant Generals Office, Old Letter Book No. 1, National Archives, Washington, DC.
8. Abel, *The Official Correspondence of James S. Calhoun*, 84, 180.
9. *Missouri Liberty Tribune*, April 22.
10. *Letters Sent by the Office of Indian Affairs, 1824-1881*, National Archives, Records of the Bureau of Indian Affairs, Record Group 75, M21, (Washington, DC), Microfilm Reel 47, frame 0108. See also *The Frank McNitt Collection*, National Archives, Record Group 75, *New Mexico Superintendency* T21-1.
11. McNitt, *Navaho Expedition*, 185. See also letter excerpt, Messervy to Webb, June 19, 1857, *James Josiah Webb Collection*, State Historical Society of Missouri, Saint Louis.
12. Sumner, Albuquerque to H. L. Dodge, May 29, 1853, No. 268, *Letters Sent by the 9th Military District, 1849-1890*, Microfilm Reel 1, frame 756.
13. *The William G. Ritch Papers*, Microfilm Reel 1, entry 456.
14. *The William G. Ritch Papers*, Microfilm Reel 1, entry 460. See also McNitt, *Navajo Wars*, 201.
15. Abel, *The Official Correspondence of James S. Calhoun*, 451. See also Calhoun to Sumner November 10, 1851, *Letters Received by the 9th Military District, 1848-1853*, Microfilm Reel 4, frame 467.
16. McNitt, *Navajo Wars*, 202-206.
17. Sumner to Jones, Jan. 1, 1852, *Letters Sent by the 9th Military District, 1849-1890*, Microfilm Reel 1, frames 539-540. See also McNitt, *Navajo Wars*, 207.

18. Greiner to Calhoun, January 1, 1852, *Letters Received by the Office of Indian Affairs, 1824–1881, New Mexico Superintendency*, M234, Microfilm Reel 546.
19. McNitt, *Navajo Wars*, 209-210. See Sumner to Secretary of War Conrad, March 27, 1852, *Letters Sent by the 9th Military District, 1849–1890*, Microfilm Reel 1, frames 583-584.
20. Sumner to Jones, April 22, 1852, *Letters Sent by the 9th Military District, 1849–1890*, Microfilm Reel 1, frames 600-601. See also, Sumner to Jones, April 24, 1852, frame 602 and Sumner to Jones, April 28, 1852, frame 606.
21. Sumner to Lane, Santa Fe, October 24, 1852, *Letters Sent by the 9th Military District, 1849–1890*, Microfilm Reel 1, frames 684, 687.
22. *Letters Received by the Office of Indian Affairs, 1824–1880, New Mexico Superintendency*, M234, Microfilm Reel 546.
23. Baird, Jemez Agency to Calhoun, February 22, 1852, *The William G. Ritch Papers*, Microfilm Reel 1, 496.
24. Home Mission Record, November, 1853, vol. 5, no. 2, Letter 16, *Dorothy Woodward Collection, Documents Series, Harriet Bidwell Shaw Letters*, Box 17, Folder 289. See also Baird to Luke Lea, April 12, 1853, *Letters Received by the Office of Indian Affairs, 1824–1880, New Mexico Superintendency*, M234, Microfilm Reel 546.
25. Greiner to Lane, May 7, 1853, *Letters Received by the 9th Military District, 1848–1853*, Microfilm Reel 7, frames 536-539.
26. McNitt, *Navajo Wars*, 218-221.
27. Lane to Donaciano Vigil, May 9, 1853, *Letters Received by the 9th Military District, 1848–1853*, Microfilm Reel 7, frames 541-542. See also *Letters Received by the Office of Indian Affairs, 1824–1880, New Mexico Superintendency*, Microfilm Reel 546, N80-N128.
28. *Letters Received by the 9th Military District, 1848–1853*, Microfilm Reel 7, frames 533-534.
29. Sumner to Lane, May 12, 1853, *Letters Sent by the 9th Military District, 1849–1890*, Microfilm Reel 1, frame 749.
30. McNitt, *Navajo Wars*, 223.
31. *The Frank McNitt Collection*, National Archives, Record Group 75, *Letters Received by the Office of Indian Affairs, 1824–1880, New Mexico Superintendency*. See also Lane to Sumner May 25, 1853, *Letters Received by the 9th Military District, 1848–1853*, Microfilm Reel 7, frames 544-545 and 562-563.

Chapter 33-On the Brink

1. *Letters Received by the Office of Indian Affairs, 1824–1880, New Mexico Superintendency*, Microfilm Reel 547, frames N131-N171.
2. McNitt, *Navajo Wars*, 214 and *Navaho Expedition*, 62-64. Kendrick arrived in New Mexico, leading an artillery battalion from Leavenworth, just in time to join Washington's expedition. He remained stationed in New Mexico until serving as escort for the Sitgreaves expedition to the Colorado River. He was without a doubt the most conscientious officer to command at Fort Defiance.
   Kendrick left the territory in 1857 after accepting an appointment as a full professor of chemistry, mineralogy and geology at West Point. In 1859, he sat on the board of assay commissioners at the United States Mint in Philadelphia. When the Civil War began, he was commissioned brigadier general of volunteers, but declined the honor. Henry L. Kendrick was promoted to

colonel in February of 1873, retiring seven years later in the winter of 1880 after forty-five years of military service. He was remembered as being one of the kindest and most popular professors to ever serve at the United States Military Academy. Among both soldiers and students, he was fondly known as Old Hanks. The Navajo reserved a special place in their hearts for Kendrick, and in March of 1885, 27 years after the major had left Navajo land, a Navajo delegation visiting Washington, DC made the trip to New York for the expressed purpose of visiting their old friend and advisor.

Henry Lane Kendrick died on May 24th, 1891 at the age of 80, the ultimate result of a cold he'd caught the previous February while serving as one of the pallbearers for General William Tecumseh Sherman. Ironically, in the same manner Sherman's funeral killed another pallbearer and former adversary, Confederate General Joseph E. Johnston. In 1918, a training camp for chemical warfare was established and named for "Professor L. Kendrick of the United States Military Academy." It was closed in March of 1919, a dubious honor for Old Hanks, to say the least. See National Archives, *Records of the U. S. Army Continental Commands*, Record Group 98, T912, Microfilm Reel 1. Also for general background see "Henry Lane Kendrick" in *The Virtual Museum of History, Evisium Inc.*, 2000, www.famousamericans.net/henrylanekendrick, (accessed on April 2, 2010). See also Tillman, Samuel E., *Colonel Henry L. Kendrick, U. S. A.: an Address by the Rev. Marvin R. Vincent, D. D. and Obituary by Prof. Samuel E. Tillman*, (U.S.M.A., E. P. Dutton & Company, New York, 1892). See also in this text Chapter 23, note 22.

3. *Letters Received by the 9th Military District, 1848-1853*, Microfilm Reel 7, frames 48-50.
4. Danielson, unpublished manuscript.
5. Danielson, *Blood Brother of Pueblo Land*, quoting Reverend Shaw letter 14, Home Mission Record, vol. 5, Number 1, October 1853, and Shaw letter 15 and 16, November 1853, vol. 5, Number 2.
6. Danielson, *Blood Brother of Pueblo Land*, quoting Home Mission Record vol. 5, Number 3, December 1853 from Shaw letter "Tour Among the Navajos."
7. Stapleton, Ernest S., *The History of Baptist Missions in New Mexico, 1849-1866*, (Master of Arts Thesis, University of New Mexico, Albuquerque, 1954), 140.
8. Danielson, *Blood Brother of Pueblo Land*, quoting Home Mission Record, vol. 5, Number 3, December 1853 from Shaw letter "Tour Among the Navajos."
9. Danielson, *Blood Brother of Pueblo Land*, quoting Home Mission Record, vol. 5, Number 3, December 1853 from Shaw letter of May 18, 1853, "Tour Among the Navajos."
10. Danielson, *Blood Brother of Pueblo Land*, quoting Reverend Shaw letter 19 in Home Mission Record, vol. 5, Number 4, January, 1854.
11. Kendrick, Ft. Defiance to Sturgis, May 25, 1853, *Letters Received by the 9th Military District, 1848-1853*, Microfilm Reel 7, frames 52-61.
12. McNitt, *Navajo Wars*, 222.
13. Sumner to Lt. Col. Thomas, AAG HQ New York, June 1, 1853, *Letters Sent by the 9th Military District, 1849-1890*, Microfilm Reel 1, frame 760.
14. Lane, Santa Fe, to Sumner, Albuquerque, June 8, 1853, *Letters Received by the 9th Military District, 1848-1853*, Microfilm Reel 7, frame 567.
15. Sumner to Kendrick, June 5, 1853, *Letters Sent by the 9th Military District, 1849-1890*, Microfilm Reel 1, frames 761-762.
16. *Letters Sent by the 9th Military District, 1849-1890*, Microfilm Reel 1, frame 763.
17. *Letters Received by the 9th Military District, 1848-1853*, Microfilm Reel 7, frame 569.

18. *Letters Sent by the 9th Military District, 1849–1890*, Microfilm Reel 1, frames 764-765.
19. Danielson, *Blood Brother of Pueblo Land*, quoting Harriet Shaw letter 20. See also Harriett Shaw Letter 21, *Dorothy Woodward Collection, Harriet Bidwell Shaw Letters*, New Mexico State Records and Archives Center, and Danielson, *Blood Brother of Pueblo Land*.
20. Manuelito would become an influential leader in both war and an ultimate, lasting peace with the American. He was born in about 1818 into the *Bit'ahnii* Clan. Throughout his life, he was known by several names, including *Hastiin Ch'ilhaajinii*, Man of the Black Plants Place, *Ashkii Diyin*, Holy Boy, *Nabaah Jilt'aa'*, or Warrior Grabs the Enemy. Manuelito had participated in the ambush of Mexican forces at Pass Washington in 1835, had signed the treaty with Doniphan at Bear Springs in 1846, and had witnessed the killing of Narbona in 1849. By 1853, he was a prominent headman, the son of headman Cayetano and one of Zarcillos Largos' son-in-laws. After Zarcillos Largos retired his honorary standing among the Americans as principal chief of the Navajo Tribe, Manuelito was given the honor. From that time onward, Manuelito's actions would have a significant effect on events in Navajo history, first as a fiery antagonist of the American government, then as an ally.
21. Kendrick to Sturgis June 14, 1853, *Letters Received by the 9th Military District, 1848–1853*, Microfilm Reel 7, frames 71-72.
22. Kendrick to Sturgis, June 14, 1853, *Letters Received by the 9th Military District, 1848–1853*, Microfilm Reel 7, frames 71-74.
23. McNitt, *Navajo Wars*, 226-227.
24. *Letters Sent by the 9th Military District, 1849–1890*, Microfilm Reel 1, frame 767.
25. Sumner to Lane, June 19, 1853, *Letters Sent by the 9th Military District, 1849–1890*, Microfilm Reel 1, frame 768.
26. Sumner, HQ, Albuquerque, to Lane: No. 304, June 15, 1853, *Letters Sent by the 9th Military District, 1849–1890*, Microfilm Reel 1, frames 767-768. See also Sumner to Maj. G. Morris, Ft. Union, June 17, 1853, *Letters Sent by the 9th Military District, 1849–1890*, Microfilm Reel 1, frame 768.

Chapter 34-Unfit for Civilized Man

1. *Letters Received by the Office of Indian Affairs, 1824–1880, New Mexico Superintendency*, M234, Microfilm Reel 546. See also Missouri Historical Society, St. Louis, *William Carr Lane Collection*, Box 6-13.
2. Keleher, *Turmoil in New Mexico*, 62-64.
3. *Letters Received by the Office of Indian Affairs, 1824–1880, New Mexico Superintendency*, M234, Microfilm Reel 546.
4. William Carr Lane effectively left politics after this humiliation. Not the ablest administrator, he nevertheless had the best intentions for the New Mexican people and indeed the Indian. He was also quite the sentimentalist as his touching letters to his grandchildren, found in the collections of the Missouri State Historical Society Library, St. Louis, give testament to his love and affinity if not for New Mexico, then for home and family. An excerpt from one is given below, written by him to his grandson Willie, shortly after the Vallecito killing.

My dear Willis,
How thankful you little boys, in St. Louise, ought to be-you have kind parents and relations and

good homes-you have an abundance of good things to eat-you are well clothed, & you sleep in comfortable houses- [in fine?] warm beds, with many, many other blessings-compare your situation with that of the poor little shepherd boys, called pastores, in this country. These boys rarely sleep in a home-They have no bed but the base ground; no covering but a single course Blanket. They are badly clothed; & worse fed. Their food consists of coarse cornbread in mush & sheep and goat milk. ... But these are not the worst of it; for the Indians sometimes surprise them & if they do not kill them, they make captives of them-sometimes never to see their families again.

"Don Ramon Martin had a cattle Ranch, as it is called, in the Chama river, about 40 or 50 miles northwest of this place; and, in the 3d of this month, he was surprised in the evening & killed at his ranch by Navaho Indians; and his nephews, named Labrado & Claavis Martin; lads of about ten years of age, were taken prisoner, & carried into the Navaho country ... I immediately sent out forty of men to recover the captives, & to demand surrender of the murderers; and to day my men returned, with the little shepherd boys, worn out with fatigue and nearly naked. ...

"When the poor little captive boys were found, they were entirely naked, with only a breech-cloth on; and when they arrived here, a little shirt with no pants, coat, jacket, shoes, socks or hat. The Indians had not given them half enough to eat; & had whipped one boy 4 times & and the other Boy twice, because they couldn't understand the Indian language-and one of them was lame from a hurt in his Hip, which made walking painful to him.

"I have had the little fellows washed, combed & clothed, from head to foot-from the hat to the shoes; and then I sent them to see the Bishop, who gave each one a Catholic medal, & a half dollar of which they were very proud and after that I gave each one another half dollar & a knife, which made the little fellows as happy ... for they never were so well clothed & had so much money in their pockets before, in their whole lives.

"Let the fate of these two pretty little manly Mexican shepherd boys make you thankful to Almighty God for his bountiful Goodness to you, & to your sister & little Brother-for preserving you all from cruel captivity & sorrow; from hunger, thirst & nakedness; and for inferring upon you so many other blessings. Adieu my dear little boy." See *Territorial Archives of New Mexico; Governors Papers, 1846-1878*, New Mexico State Records and Archives Center, Microfilm Reel 98, frames 232-235.

Lane also sent poetry and prose to the children.

He campaigned for the New Mexican seat in earnest but subsequently lost the election that September to the Albuquerque priest José Manuel Gallegos. His defeat by Gallegos was by a surprisingly narrow margin, a mere 445 votes. Even so, Lane contested the election. After 4400 illegal ballots were tossed, the votes were recounted. This time Lane lost by nearly one hundred more votes, 539. In the end, he was chivalrous about the whole affair, noting what the common folks in Las Vegas had told him "they have no personal objection to me, but that they are determined to elect one of their own race-God bless them." William Carr Lane abandoned the quest for the House and returned to Saint Louis and his medical practice. He would die there ten years later. See *The William G. Ritch Papers*, Microfilm Reel 1, entry 600. Also see Horn, *New Mexico's Troubled Years*, 44, 48.

5. *The Frank McNitt Collection*, National Archives, *Letters Received by the Office of Indian Affairs, 1824-1880, New Mexico Superintendency*, Record Group 75, T21-1.

6. *Letters Received by the Office of Indian Affairs, 1824–1880, New Mexico Superintendency,* M234, Microfilm Reel 546.
7. *Mississippi Valley French Research,* Eugene Beckett, Genealogist, Cambria, Illinois, photocopy of original.
8. *Settled Indian Accounts, 1817–1922,* National Archives, Record Group 217, Records of the Accounting Office of the Department of the Treasury, Records of the Second Auditor, (National Archives, Washington, DC), Box 634, Folder 3386-A.
9. Missouri Historical Society, *William Carr Lane Collection.* See also *Settled Indian Accounts, 1817–1922,* Box 634, Folder 3386-A.
10. *Records of the New Mexico Superintendency 1849–1880, Records of the Santa Fe Agency,* Microfilm Reel 1, 1849–1850.
11. *Settled Indian Accounts, 1817–1922,* Box 634, Folder 3386-C.
12. *Settled Indian Accounts, 1817–1922,* Box 634, Folder 3386-A.
13. *The Frank McNitt Collection,* National Archives, Record Group 75, New Mexico Superintendency, T21-2 statement of Dodge accounts dated 12-15-55.
14. *Settled Indian Accounts, 1817–1922,* Box 634, Folder 3386-A Voucher No 3, Abstract A. See also *Records of the New Mexico Superintendency 1849–1880, Records of the Santa Fe Agency,* T21, Miscellaneous Documents, Microfilm Reel 1.
15. Danielson, *Blood Brother of Pueblo Land,* quoting Home Mission Review, December 1853, from Gorman letter dated July 17, 1853.
16. Danielson, *Blood Brother of Pueblo Land,* quoting "Reverend Samuel Gorman—Memorial," *Old Santa Fe,* January, 1914, 319-32. See also Gorman, Home Mission Review, July 1853, in Stapleton, *The History of Baptist Missions in New Mexico* 158-159.
17. Cremony, *Life Among the Apaches,* 94.
18. *Records of the New Mexico Superintendency, 1849–1880,* Microfilm Reel 2, Miscellaneous 1855.
19. Miles, AAG, HQ, Albuquerque, to Kendrick: No. 309, July 3, 1853, *Letters Sent by the 9th Military District, 1849–1890,* Microfilm Reel 1, frame 769.
20. Miles, HQ, Albuquerque, to Lt. Robert Ransom Jr., Abiquiu, No. 311, July 4, 1853, *The Frank McNitt Collection,* National Archives, *Records of U. S. Army Continental Commands,* No. 311. See also *Letters Sent by the 9th Military District, 1849–1890,* Microfilm Reel 1, frame 770.
21. As it turned out, the crisis evaporated when Trias was forced to leave El Paso to put down a rebellion by French and American citizens in Chihuahua. *The Frank McNitt Collection,* National Archives, *Records of Army Continental Commands,* No. 313. See *Letters Sent by the 9th Military District, 1849–1890,* Microfilm Reel 1, frame 771. See also Miles, HQ, Los Lunas to Kendrick: No. 317, July 9, 1853, *Letters Sent by the 9th Military District, 1849–1890,* Microfilm Reel 1, frames 773 and 803.
22. Kendrick, Ft. Defiance, to Sturgis, July 12, 1853, *Letters Received by the 9th Military District, 1848–1853,* Microfilm Reel 7, frames 84-86.
23. McNitt, *Navajo Wars,* 231.
24. *The Frank McNitt Collection,* National Archives, *Letters Received by the Office of Indian Affairs, 1824–1880, New Mexico Superintendency,* T21-1 and R13-1853, *Record of Army Continental Commands.* See also *Settled Indian Accounts, 1817–1922,* Box 634, Folder 3386-A and Folder 3386-C and *Records of the New Mexico Superintendency 1849–1880, Records of the Santa Fe Agency,* Miscellaneous Documents, Microfilm Reel 1.

25. *Santa Fe Weekly Gazette,* September 1, 1853, Santa Fe, New Mexico.
26. McNitt, *Navajo Wars,* 233. See also Ransom to Sturgis, *Letters Received by the 9th Military District, 1848-1853,* Microfilm Reel 7, frame 671.
27. *Santa Fe Weekly Gazette,* September 1, 1853.
28. *Santa Fe Weekly Gazette,* September 10, 1853.
29. *Santa Fe Weekly Gazette,* September 1, 1853.
30. Kendrick, Ft. Defiance, to Maj. W. A. Nichols, AAG, August 15, 1853, *Letters Received by the 9th Military District, 1848-1853,* Microfilm Reel 7, frames 88-92.

Chapter 35-Blessings of a Christian Civilization

1. *The Frank McNitt Collection,* National Archives, New Mexico Superintendency, T21-2 exceptions to Dodge accounts dated 12-15-55. See also *Settled Indian Accounts, 1817-1922,* Box 634, Folder 3386-A.
2. Manypenny to Dodge, August 3, 1853, *Letters Received by the Office of Indian Affairs, 1824-1880, New Mexico Superintendency,* M234, Microfilm Reel 546. See also *Records of the New Mexico Superintendency 1849-1880, Records of the Santa Fe Agency,* Miscellaneous Documents, Microfilm Reel 1.
3. Graves to Manypenny, Sept. 30, 1853, *Letters Received by the Office of Indian Affairs, 1824-1880, New Mexico Superintendency,* Microfilm Reel 546. Captain Edmund A. Graves was David Meriwether's son-in-law, having wed his daughter Catherine Meriwether on January 20, 1849. Graves was born near Lebanon, Kentucky, on November 3, 1818. After studying and practicing law, he was elected to the Kentucky legislature in 1844 and again in 1846. After being appointed Captain of Company F of the Sixteenth Infantry, he served under Taylor during the Mexican War. Graves was appointed Indian agent on May 21, 1853 and went with David Meriwether to Santa Fe. See Meriwether, David, *My Life in the Mountains and on the Plains, the Newly Discovered Autobiography by David Meriwether,* edited by Robert A. Griffin, (University of Oklahoma Press, Norman, 1965), 142, note 9.
4. *Settled Indian Accounts, 1817-1922,* Box 634, Folder 3386-A and *Records of the New Mexico Superintendency 1849-1880, Records of the Santa Fe Agency,* Miscellaneous Documents, T21, Microfilm Reel 1.
5. Meriwether to Manypenny, August 17, 1853, *Letters Received by the Office of Indian Affairs, 1824-1880, New Mexico Superintendency,* M234, Microfilm Reel 546.
6. Davis, *El Gringo,* 240-246. David Meriwether was born in Louisa County, Virginia on October 30, 1800. The Meriwether family moved to Jefferson County, Kentucky when David was three, where he attended school and helped on the family farm. By 1818 he was involved in the fur trade near present day Council Bluffs, Iowa. He'd had an early and uninvited introduction to New Mexico as well. It seems that in 1819 the daring young David, his Negro slave and a group of Pawnees had partnered to open up trade with the New Mexicans. They were instead attacked by a detachment of Spanish cavalry on the Canadian River. After killing most of the Pawnee, the Spaniards seized Meriwether and his slave, accusing them of being spies. Arrested, manacled and imprisoned, Meriwether languished for a month on the west end of the Governor's Palace before being released. The Spaniards sent them both back to the States with no more than the clothes on their back. They were forced to pass the winter holed up in a cave on the Arkansas River, barely fighting off starvation. Once the weather finally warmed enough

to cross the Plains, David and his servant were attacked by Indians. His scalp would have been on a lodge pole somewhere, but for the quick actions of his slave, who supposedly discouraged the war party by killing their chief. At least, that was the story.

After surviving his purported adventure on the Great Plains and in New Mexico, he returned to Kentucky, was admitted to the bar and put up his shingle as a lawyer. Between 1832 and 1845, Meriwether was member of the Kentucky House of Representatives, but failed in his attempt to be elected to Congress in 1846. By 1851, David was serving as Kentucky's Secretary of State when he received an appointment to fill the late Henry Clay's seat in the United States Senate until a successor was elected. He served until the end of August, 1852 and was not a candidate for the seat. Meriwether fell into the appointment for governor of the Territory of New Mexico when Solon Borland turned down the honor. The now fifty-two year old politician would serve for three years, much of it characteristically tumultuous.

Meriwether returned to Kentucky in 1857 and served again in the Kentucky House from 1858 to 1885, almost thirty years. By the close of his career he was already ancient . . . eighty-five. With the cascade of the years finally slowing him down, he retired to the farm outside of Louisville, Kentucky he'd inherited from his father. David Meriwether died at the age of 93 on April 4, 1893 and was buried in Cave Hill Cemetery in Louisville. See *American Cyclopedia of Biography*. See also David Meriwether's autobiography, *My Life in the Mountains and on the Plains*.

7. Horn, *New Mexico's Troubled Years*, 55-56
8. John Garland was born in 1792 and eventually served in five separate wars, from that of 1812 through the start of the Civil War, making a career of over fifty years in the Army. By the Black Hawk conflict, he had reached the rank of second lieutenant. It is a peculiar quirk of history that as a young officer Garland was one of soldiers to guard Black Hawk after the old chief had surrendered. During the Mexican War John Garland commanded "Garland's Brigade", composed of the 4th Infantry and the 2nd & 3rd Artillery, and was brevetted brigadier general for his performance in battle. He saw action at the battles of Palo Alto and Resaca de la Palma, and received promotions for his part in those actions. He had the dubious honor of leading the divisional charge at the Battle of Monterrey when his commander, David E. Twiggs was suddenly and urgently indisposed by an accidental overdose of laxative. Garland saw several more battles and was promoted to brevet brigadier general. Actions at Molino Del Rey and an assault on Chapultepec followed. Curiously he survived without a scratch, until actually entering Mexico City, where a Mexican sharpshooter shot him in the chest. His return to service was delayed, but return he did, with the regular rank of colonel. In 1848, John Garland became the father-in-law to a young officer, James Longstreet, who had married his daughter, Louise. After serving in New Mexico, Garland took command during the Utah War of 1857-1858. In a most amazing turn, somehow consistent with Garland's character, he remained loyal to the Union when Civil War erupted in 1861. He did not live to serve the Union long, however, and died in New York City while on duty in the middle of that year. See Eicher, John H., & Eicher, David J., *Civil War High Commands*, Stanford University Press, 2001 and Sweeny, Edwin R., *Mangas Coloradas, Chief of the Chiricahua Apaches*, (University of Oklahoma Press, Norman, 1998), 513, note 20.
9. Nichols to Lt. K. Garrard, AAAG, Albuquerque, August 29, 1853, *Letters Sent by the 9th Military District, 1849-1890*, Microfilm Reel 1, frame 812.
10. *Letters Received by the Office of Indian Affairs, 1824-1880*, New Mexico Superintendency, M234, Microfilm Reel 546.

11. *Letters Received by the Office of Indian Affairs, 1824-1880, New Mexico Superintendency,* M234, Microfilm Reel 546.
12. *Records of the New Mexico Superintendency 1849-1880, Records of the Santa Fe Agency,* Miscellaneous Documents, Microfilm Reel 1. See also *Settled Indian Accounts, 1817-1922,* Box 634, Folder 3386-A.
13. Meriwether, Santa Fe, to Manypenny, September 19, 1853, *The Frank McNitt Collection,* National Archives, Record Group 75, M234, New Mexico Superintendency, Microfilm Reel 546.
14. 1853, Oct. 29, Garland to Lieut. Col L. Thomas, Asst. Adjutant General, New York, October 29, 1853, *Letters Sent by the 9th Military District, 1849-1890,* Microfilm Reel 1, frames 834-835.
15. *Records of the New Mexico Superintendency 1849-1880, Records of the Santa Fe Agency,* T21, Miscellaneous Documents, Microfilm Reel 1.

Chapter 36 Pass Washington

1. McNitt, *Navajo Wars,* 243.
2. Records *of the New Mexico Superintendency 1849-1880, Records of the Santa Fe Agency,* Miscellaneous Documents, Microfilm Reel 1. See also *Settled Indian Accounts, 1817-1922,* Box 634, Folder 3386-A.
3. Garland to Lieutenant Col L. Thomas, Asst. Adjutant General, New York, October 29, 1853, *Letters Sent by the 9th Military District, 1849-1890,* Microfilm Reel 1, frames 834-835.
4. Meriwether to Manypenny, September 19, 1853, *Letters Received by the Office of Indian Affairs, 1824-1880, New Mexico Superintendency,* M234, Microfilm Reel 546. Graves also complained that as long as he was agent for both the Ute and Jicarilla, he would be hard pressed to serve efficiently. In a barely subdued whine, he also lamented that it was often difficult to get written receipts because the population was generally illiterate and "it is but seldom that you find or come across one who can write his name." For the same reason, travel supplies couldn't often be receipted, as few Indians of the territory spoke English. See Graves to Manypenny, September 20, 1853, *Letters Received by the Office of Indian Affairs, 1824-1880, New Mexico Superintendency,* M234, Microfilm Reel 546.
5. *Settled Indian Accounts, 1817-1922,* Box 634, Folder 3386-A.
6. September 1, 1853, *James Josiah Webb Collection,* State Historical Society of Missouri. That September the name of H. L. Dodge appeared in the accounts receivable for the store of Messervy and Webb in the amounts of $590.91 and $1735.91.
7. *Letters Received by the Office of Indian Affairs, 1824-1880, New Mexico Superintendency,* M234, Microfilm Reel 546.
8. McNitt, *Navajo Wars,* 244.
9. *Settled Indian Accounts, 1817-1922,* Box 634, Folder 3386-B.
10. Woodward, Arthur, *Navajo Silver: A Brief History of Navajo Silversmithing,* (Northland Press, Flagstaff, 1973), 18-19.
11. *Settled Indian Accounts, 1817-1922,* Box 634, Folder 3386-A.
12. Meriwether to Manypenny, November 28, 1853 and December 13, 1853, *Letters Received by the Office of Indian Affairs, 1824-1880, New Mexico Superintendency,* M234, Microfilm Reel 547. To complicate matters, a small pox epidemic was raging through Hopi and Zuni. The vaccine was available, but Meriwether had no money to buy it or to hire doctors to administer it.

13. *Settled Indian Accounts, 1817-1922*, Box 634, Folder 3386-A.
14. *The Frank McNitt Collection*, National Archives, New Mexico Superintendency, T21-2, Dodge accounts dated December 15, 1855. See also *Records of the New Mexico Superintendency 1849-1880, Records of the Santa Fe Agency*, Miscellaneous Documents, Microfilm Reel 2.
15. Henry Dodge, Senate Chambers, Washington, to C.I.A. Geo. W. Manypenny, May 1, 1854, *Letters Received by the Office of Indian Affairs, 1824-1880, New Mexico Superintendency*, M234, Microfilm Reel 547.
16. *District Court Records, Valencia County, 1854*, New Mexico Archive and Records Center, Santa Fe.
17. *Records of the New Mexico Superintendency 1849-1880, Records of the Santa Fe Agency*, Miscellaneous Documents, Microfilm Reel 1. See also McNitt, *Navajo Wars*, 245.
18. *Settled Indian Accounts, 1817-1922*, Box 634, Folder 3386-B.
19. See Letters Received from Agencies, 1854, Microfilm Reel 2 and *Records of the New Mexico Superintendency 1849-1880, Records of the Santa Fe Agency*, T21, Miscellaneous Documents, Microfilm Reel 2. David Meriwether enjoyed his gambling, according to one disapproving visitor, William J. Hinchey, an Irishman artist in town to paint murals for the Catholic Church, who spotted him one evening in November of 1854 at the Exchange Hotel. After noting the cold weather and a number of rumored Indian depredations disrupting the territory, he launched into a criticism of Meriwether.
"This is the state of the Territory and the old Governor takes it easy. . . . I saw him last evening in the exchange playing cards in a corner. He is said to be both niggardly and a poltroon." See Hinchey, William J., *Diary of an Irish Artist*, edited by A. Stephen Hinchey, unpublished manuscript, National Frontier Trails Center Manuscript Collection, National Frontier Trails Center, Independence, Missouri.
20. *Settled Indian Accounts, 1817-1922*, Box 634, Folder 3386-B. "Received at Pass Washington, Navijo Agency N. M., January the 10th 1854 of Capt. H. L. Dodge Indian Agent for the Navijos in New Mexico, the sum of Eight hundred and forty nine Dollars in full for this account. [Signed] G. A. J. Noël. I certify on honor that the above account is correct and just and that I have actually this 10th day of January A. D. 1854 paid the Amount thereof. [Signed] Henry L. Dodge, Indian Agent for Navijos."
21. McNitt, *Navajo Wars*, 247.
22. *Dorothy Woodward Collection, Documents Series, Harriett Shaw Letters*, New Mexico State Records and Archives Center, Santa Fe.
23. Kendrick to Meriwether, February 6, 1854, *Letters Received by the Department of New Mexico, 1854-1865*, Microfilm Reel 3, frame 817. The United States, in promising to protect the citizens of New Mexico from Indian raids, had accepted the responsibility of paying for lost property when they had failed to provide that protection. Agents of the government documented claims up and down the Rio Grande for losses suffered from 1846 through the early 1850s. Just as one might expect, those claims were often grossly overstated.
24. Kendrick to Meriwether, February 10, 1854, *The Frank McNitt Collection*, National Archives, New Mexico Superintendency, T21-2. See also *Letters Received by the Department of New Mexico, 1854-1865*, Microfilm Reel 3, frame 814.
25. *Letters Received by the Office of Indian Affairs, 1824-1880, New Mexico Superintendency*, M234, Microfilm Reel 547.

26. *Letters Received by the Office of Indian Affairs, 1824–1880, New Mexico Superintendency*, M234, Microfilm Reel 546.
27. Garland to Thomas, November 27, 1854, *Letters Sent by the 9th Military District, 1849–1890*, Microfilm Reel 1, frames 840-841.
28. Garland to Meriwether, January 18, 1854, *Letters Sent by the 9th Military District, 1849–1890*, Microfilm Reel 1, frames 853, 855.
29. Lt. Maxwell to Col St. George Cooke, January 28, 1854, *Letters Received by the Department of New Mexico, 1854–1865*, Microfilm Reel 3, frame 349.
30. *Records of the New Mexico Superintendency 1849–1880, Records of the Santa Fe Agency*, T21, Miscellaneous Documents, Microfilm Reel 1. William Slueman Messervy, born in Salem, Massachusetts in 1812, had been involved in the Santa Fe trade from 1830. Before the Mexican-American War he had established a merchandizing house in Chihuahua, Mexico. With the outbreak of hostilities, the Mexican government imprisoned him and other Americans there until freed by Colonel Doniphan's invading forces. In 1850 he had been elected New Mexico's first delegate to the House of Representatives. In April of the previous year 1853, President Pierce appointed him Meriwether's territorial secretary.
31. Garland to Thomas, March 29, 1854, *Letters Sent by the 9th Military District, 1849–1890*, Microfilm Reel 1, frame 872 and McNitt, *Navajo Wars*, 248, note 21.
32. Meriwether to Manypenny, January 9, 1854, *The Frank McNitt Collection*, National Archives, Record Group 75, M234, *Letters Received by the Office of Indian Affairs, 1824–1880, New Mexico Superintendency*, Microfilm Reel 547. Prior to his departure Meriwether had been using his own money to help keep the ship afloat and had to pay salaries out of a contingency fund. Messervy soon discovered to his consternation that he'd be picking up the tab for the Indian Service in the same manner as Meriwether had. While planning his April departure on a four-month stay in Kentucky, Meriwether learned that John Smith, Agent to the Chiricahua had died at Doña Ana. He ordered his son-in-law Graves south to take Smith's place, and then assigned the well known guide and mountain man Christopher "Kit" Carson as the Ute agent. Kit Carson was a superior choice for Ute agent. He'd had an intimate association with the Ute and was a long time resident of Taos. Although illiterate, his experience would prove invaluable.
33. Messervy to Manypenny, April 1, 1854, *Letters Received by the Office of Indian Affairs, 1824–1880, New Mexico Superintendency*, M234, Microfilm Reel 547.
34. Dodge to Manypenny, March 31, 1854, *Letters Received by the Office of Indian Affairs, 1824–1880, New Mexico Superintendency*, Microfilm Reel 547. S493-W435.
35. *The Frank McNitt Collection*, National Archives, New Mexico Superintendency, T21-2 Dodge accounts dated December 15, 1855. See also *Settled Indian Accounts, 1817–1922*, Box 634, Folder 3386-B and *Records of the New Mexico Superintendency 1849–1880, Records of the Santa Fe Agency*, Miscellaneous Documents, Microfilm Reel 2 and Miscellaneous Papers, 1854, Microfilm Reel 2.
36. *Settled Indian Accounts, 1817–1922*, Box 634, Folder 3386-A.
37. Kendrick, Albuquerque, to W. S. Messervy, Acting Gov., April 1, 1854, *Records of the New Mexico Superintendency 1849–1880, Records of the Santa Fe Agency*, Miscellaneous Documents, Microfilm Reel 2.

Chapter 37-House Made of Dawn

1. Van Valkenburgh, *Dine Bikéyah*, 28.
2. *Settled Indian Accounts, 1817-1922*, Box 634, Folder 3386-A.
3. Van Valkenburgh, *Dine Bikéyah*, 44.
4. Van Valkenburgh, *Dine Bikéyah*, 44. See also Underhill, *Here Come the Navajo*, 99,103-105.
5. Locke, *The Book of the Navajo*, 281.
6. Kendrick to Maj. Wm. A Nichols, Asst. Adjt. Gen. HQ Department New Mexico, February 14, 1855, in *The Frank McNitt Collection*, National Archives, *Selected Letters Received by the Adjutant General's Office*. See also McNitt, *Navajo Wars*, 246.
7. Correll, J. Lee, *Through White Men's Eyes: A Contribution to Navajo History, Vol. 2*, (Navajo Heritage Center, Window Rock, Arizona, 1976), 371-372.
8. McNitt; *Navajo Wars*, 295-296, note 13. Despite Chee's affidavit, discussion and argument as to his biological father has continued for decades. In later life Henry Chee Dodge was known as *Adiits'a'ii Sání*, or Old Interpreter. Some biographies state he was born at Fort Defiance in February of 1860, of the fort's Hispanic interpreter, Juan Cosinisas, also known as Juan Anaya, and of *Bisnayanchi*, a Navajo woman of the Coyote Pass Clan, the oldest daughter of *Tl'ah Ts'ósí*, or Skinny Left Hand. Insomuch as ages were seldom calculated accurately, Chee's birth date could have been considerably earlier. Anaya was killed in the summer of 1861 by a New Mexican raiding party. After the Americans under Christopher Carson invaded Canyon de Chelly in 1861, Chee's mother gave him into the care of a sister. Chee's mother was later slain near Hopi. When Navajo were finally defeated and relocated to Fort Sumner, New Mexico, Chee found himself alone wandering near starvation until an old man and his eight-year-old granddaughter took him under their wing. After the treaty of 1868, the Navajo were allowed to return to their homes. Chee ended up at Fort Defiance, living with yet another sister married to the fort store clerk, Perry H. Williams. Williams taught Chee to clerk in his store, thereby introducing the young lad to the skills of making money.

Chee's teen years remain a mystery. Agent Arny clearly showed an interest in the boy, as reflected in Augustus Dodge's correspondence.

"I was greatly gratified to learn from Genl. Vandever that Gov. Arny feels a deep interest in this boy and would be willing to aid in reclaiming him from the quasi condition of Slavery in which he is now held by some 'herder', so called, who is said to treat the boy cruelly."

Agent Arny understood the importance of the boy to Augustus Dodge, whether or not he himself actually believed Chee was the son of the Senator's brother. He demanded Perry Williams surrender the boy to him and Perry complied. Arny clothed and raised Chee and put him in the new Fort Defiance school, noting the boy was "a mechanical Genious." In a letter to the Commissioner of Indian Affairs, Arny requested him to inform Augustus Dodge that he would do everything in his power to have Chee cared for and educated." See Correll, *Through Whiteman's Eyes*, 371-372. Nevertheless, Chee never saw the uncle who had demonstrated such interest in his welfare, and remained with the Navajo.

Dodge later worked for a freighting company. By at least 1882 he was serving as an interpreter for Agent Eastman as well as the fort butcher. In 1883 Chee Dodge became patrol chief of the newly created Navajo police force and a year later Agent Dennis Riordan appointed him head chief of the Navajo Nation, taking over the position previously held by Manuelito. If one is to believe a birth date of 1860, Chee would have only been twenty-four years old. In that capacity, he traveled to Washington, DC to meet with President Chester A. Arthur. Chee's flair for business surfaced early. By 1890, Chee had gone into business with Stephen H. Aldrich, partnering in a trading post in the Chinle Valley at Round Rock. During his lifetime he was reputed to have had eight different wives and six children, several of who would become important in their own right. Towards the end of the century, he assisted the ethnographer Washington Matthews in his studies of Navajo legends and the Night Chant.

Chee Dodge faithfully served the Navajo agent and federal officials, including helping Agent Shipley coerce Navajo parents to allow their children attend school and arranging the surrender of *Hataalii Yázhí* or Little Singer, to government troops in 1907. At about the same time he served on committees to oversee oil land leases and explorations around the Shiprock area. During the 1930s, Chee Dodge opposed the Department of the Interior's policy of conservation through forced livestock reduction and ended up losing three fourths of his own herd.

Dodge was elected the first tribal chairman in 1923 and served until 1928. He was reelected for a second term during WWII, serving from 1942 to 1946. Dodge was elected vice-chairman of the tribe in 1946, but never served. He died of pneumonia on January 4, 1947. He was at least 87 years of age. See "Henry Chee Dodge" in *The Biography Resource Center, Biographies at Answers Corporation, 2006*, www.answers.com/topic/henry-dodge, (accessed February 19, 2007).

9. Kendrick Ft. Defiance, to W. S. Messervy, Acting Governor, May 13, 1854, *The Frank McNitt Collection*, National Archives, New Mexico Superintendency, T21-2, and K-5-1854. See also Miscellaneous Papers, 1854, Microfilm Reel 2 and *Letters Received by the Department of New Mexico, 1854–1865*, Microfilm Reel 3, frames 828 to 830.

10. Kendrick, Laguna, N.M. to Nichols, May 23, 1854, K-5-1854 and *Letters Received by the Department of New Mexico, 1854–1865*, Microfilm Reel 3, frames 824-826.

11. Danielson, *Blood Brother of Pueblo Land*, quoting Shaw, Letter 23, Home Mission Record January, 1855, vol. 6, Number 1.

12. *Settled Indian Accounts, 1817–1922*, Box 634, Folder 3386-A and 3386-B.

13. The Franciscan Fathers, *An Ethnologic Dictionary of the Navaho Language*, (St. Michaels Press, St. Michaels, Arizona, 1968), 424.

14. Kendrick, Ft. Defiance, to Messervy, Acting Governor, June 22, 1854, *The Frank McNitt Collection*, National Archives, New Mexico Superintendency, T21.

15. Fisher, "The Forgotten Dodge," quoting *The Santa Fe Weekly Gazette*, June 24, 1854.

16. *Settled Indian Accounts, 1817–1922*, Box 634, Folder 3386-A.

17. *Letters Received by the Office of Indian Affairs, 1824–1880*, New Mexico Superintendency, M234, Microfilm Reel 547, A303-L464.

18. Locke, *The Book of the Navajo*, 283. See also *Letters Received by the Office of Indian Affairs, 1824–1880, New Mexico Superintendency*, M234, Microfilm Reel 547, A303-L464 and frame 441, Dodge to Manypenny.

19. *Settled Indian Accounts, 1817–1922*, Box 634, Folder 3386-B.

20. *The Frank McNitt Collection*, National Archives, New Mexico Superintendency, T21-2. See also Miscellaneous Papers, 1854, Microfilm Reel 2.

21. *Settled Indian Accounts, 1817–1922*, Box 634, Folder 3386-B.

22. Manypenny to Meriwether, August 7, 1854, *The Frank McNitt Collection*, National Archives, New Mexico Superintendency, T21-2. See also *Letters Received from Commissioner of Indian Affairs*, 1854, Microfilm Reel 2.

23. Meriwether to Dodge "Pass Washington, N. M.," August 15, 1854, *Records of the New Mexico Superintendency 1849-1880, Records of the Santa Fe Agency*, Miscellaneous Documents, Microfilm Reel 2.
24. Meriwether to Dodge, Navajo Agency Near Fort Defiance, August 15, 1854, *The Frank McNitt Collection*, National Archives, New Mexico Superintendency, T21-2.
25. Dodge to Meriwether, August 5, 1854, *Records of the New Mexico Superintendency 1849-1880, Records of the Santa Fe Agency*, Miscellaneous Documents, Microfilm Reel 2.
26. Kendrick to Meriwether, August 19, 1854, *The Frank McNitt Collection*, National Archives, New Mexico Superintendency, T21-2.

Chapter 38-Stern But Needful Justice

1. Manypenny to Meriwether, August 8, 1854, *Letters Received from Commissioner of Indian Affairs*, 1854, Microfilm Reel 2.
2. Keleher, *Turmoil in New Mexico*, 80-82.
3. *Letters Received by the Office of Indian Affairs, 1824-1880, New Mexico Superintendency*, Record Group 546, N246-N294 and *Records of the New Mexico Superintendency 1849-1880, Records of the Santa Fe Agency*, Miscellaneous Documents, Microfilm Reel 2.
4. *Settled Indian Accounts, 1817-1922*, Box 634, Folder 3386-B.
5. Meriwether, Santa Fe, to Henry L. Dodge, Navajo Agency near Pass Washington, August 14, 1854, *Records of the New Mexico Superintendency, 1849-1880, Records of the Santa Fe Agency*, Miscellaneous Documents, Microfilm Reel 2.
6. *James Josiah Webb Collection*, State Historical Society of Missouri.
7. *Settled Indian Accounts, 1817-1922*, Box 634, Folder 3386-B.
8. Brevet Maj. W.T.H. Brooks, Santa Fe, to Capt. Landon Cheves Easton, A.Q.M., August 28, 1854, *Letters Received by the Department of New Mexico, 1854-1865*, Microfilm Reel 3, frame 287.
9. Kendrick, Ft. Defiance, to Nichols, September 9, 1854, *The Frank McNitt Collection*, National Archives, K-5-1854 and Backus, March 10, 1852. See also *Letters Received by the Department of New Mexico, 1854-1865*, Microfilm Reel 3, frames 841-843.
10. *Settled Indian Accounts, 1817-1922*, Box 634, Folder 3386-C.
11. Dodge, Chupadero, to Meriwether, September 10, 1854, *Records of the New Mexico Superintendency 1849-1880, Records of the Santa Fe Agency*, Miscellaneous Documents, Microfilm Reel 2.
12. Kendrick, Ft. Defiance, to Capt. Dodge, agent, September 23, 1854, *Records of the New Mexico Superintendency 1849-1880, Records of the Santa Fe Agency*, Miscellaneous 1857, Microfilm Reel 3.
13. *Settled Indian Accounts, 1817-1922*, Box 634, Folder 3386-B.
14. Born on December 11, 1824, surgeon Jonathan K. Letterman was credited as being the originator of the modern methods for medical organization in armies. Known as the father of battlefield medicine, his system enabled thousands of wounded men to be recovered and treated during the American Civil War. Letterman arrived at Fort Defiance from Fort Riley, Minnesota a year previous to the Hefbiner incident. In 1860 he was reassigned to Fort Monroe, Virginia. He was named medical director of the Department of West Virginia in May, 1862. A month later he was appointed the medical director of the Army of the Potomac itself. Letterman immediately set to reorganizing the medical service of the fledgling army, having obtained from Maj. Gen.

George B. McClellan permission to do whatever was necessary to improve the system. The army reeled from inefficient treatment of casualties in the Seven Days Battles in June, but by the time of the Battle of Antietam in September, Letterman had devised a system of forward first aid stations at the regimental level, where principles of triage were first instituted. He established mobile field hospitals to be located at division and corps headquarters. This was all connected by an efficient ambulance corps, under the control of medical staff instead of the Quartermaster Department. Letterman also arranged an effective system for the distribution of medical supplies. His innovative methods were eventually adopted by the United States armed services in general. Letterman died on March 15, 1872. See Musto, R. J., "The Treatment of the Wounded at Gettysburg: Jonathan Letterman: The Father of Modern Battlefield Medicine," *Gettysburg Magazine*, Issue 37, 2007. See also "Surgeon Jonathan Letterman" in *The Battle of Antietam on the Web*, antietam.aotw.org, (accessed May 9, 2010).

15. Bennett, *Forts and Forays*, 48.
16. Kendrick, Ft. Defiance, to Nichols, *Letters Received by the Department of New Mexico, 1854-1865*, Microfilm Reel 3, frames 849-850.
17. Kendrick, Ft. Defiance, to Nichols, October 9, 1854, *Letters Received by the Department of New Mexico, 1854-1865*, Microfilm Reel 3, frames 849-851. He considered an attack on the band of the murderer, in which case two additional companies of dragoon and one of infantry, together with his 195 man garrison, would be suffice, but believed a larger force and a larger conflict ought to be planned in case the war spread to the entire Navajo nation. The harvesting season would the best time to wage war on the Indians, but a winter campaign would not be out of the question, either. In a second letter to Garland penned the following day, Kendrick expanded on his war plans. If the general sent a substantial force to Defiance, it would be best to stockpile supplies, bring up a herd of sheep and lay in a "liberal supply of bacon." They'd also need guides familiar with both Navajo language and land, to "trail the Indians, sweep up their tracks, & to do other things. Perhaps they may know the hiding place of the Indians & could be made zealous by a promise of retaining all that they take."
18. *Settled Indian Accounts, 1817-1922*, Box 634, Folder 3386-C.
19. *Dorothy Woodward Collection, Harriet Bidwell Shaw Letters*.
20. Danielson, *Blood Brother of Pueblo Land*, quoting John M. Shaw, Letter 24, Home Mission Record, January 1855, vol. 6, Number 1.
21. Bvt. Brig. Gen. John Garland, cmdg. Department of New Mexico, Santa Fe, to Maj. H. L. Kendrick, cmdg. Ft. Defiance, October 18, 1854, *The Frank McNitt Collection*, 271, LS.
22. *Settled Indian Accounts, 1817-1922*, Box 634, Folder 3386-C. See also *Records of the New Mexico Superintendency, 1849-1880, Records of the Santa Fe Agency*, Miscellaneous Documents, Microfilm Reel 2.
23. Stapleton, *The History of Baptist Missions in New Mexico*, 150. See also Home Mission Record vol. 5, Number 2, February, 1855, Letter 25, November 15, 1854.
24. Kendrick, Ft. Defiance, to Nichols, October 23, 1854, *Letters Received by the Department of New Mexico, 1854-1865*, Microfilm Reel 3, frames 857-859.
25. Kendrick, Ft. Defiance, to Nichols, October 24, 1854, *Letters Received by the Department of New Mexico, 1854-1865*, Microfilm Reel 3, frame 866.
26. *The Frank McNitt Collection*, National Archives, New Mexico Superintendency T21-2.
27. Dodge, Ft. Defiance, to Meriwether, November 13, 1854, *Letters Received by the Office of Indian Affairs, 1824-1880, New Mexico Superintendency*, M234, Microfilm Reel 547, L361-N399 and

Records of the New Mexico Superintendency 1849-1880, Records of the Santa Fe Agency, Miscellaneous Documents, Microfilm Reel 2.
28. Danielson, *Blood Brother of Pueblo Land*, quoting Home Mission Record vol. 5, Number 2, February 1855.
29. Dodge, Ft. Defiance, to Meriwether, November 13, 1854, *Letters Received by the Office of Indian Affairs, 1824-1880, New Mexico Superintendency*, M234, Microfilm Reel 547, L361-N399 and *Records of the New Mexico Superintendency 1849-1880, Records of the Santa Fe Agency*, Miscellaneous Documents, Microfilm Reel 2.
30. Harriet Shaw, November 12, 1854, *Dorothy Woodward Collection, Documents Series, Harriet Bidwell Shaw Letters*.
31. Kendrick, Ft. Defiance, to Nichols, November 11, 1854, *The Frank McNitt Collection*, Microfilm Reel 3, frames 869-870.
32. Meriwether to Manypenny, November 30, 1854, *Letters Received by the Office of Indian Affairs, 1824-1880, New Mexico Superintendency*, Microfilm Reel 547, L361-N399.
33. Danielson, *Blood Brother of Pueblo Land*, quoting John Milton Shaw, November 15, 1854, Home Mission Record, vol. 5, Number 2, February, 1855.

Chapter 39-Taking Up The Cross

1. Danielson, *Blood Brother of Pueblo Land*, quoting Harriet Shaw letter 27, Home Mission Record, March, 1855, vol. 5, Number 3.
2. Danielson, *Blood Brother of Pueblo Land*, quoting John Milton Shaw, November 15, 1854, Home Mission Record vol. 5, Number 2, February, 1855.
3. *Settled Indian Accounts, 1817-1922*, Box 634, Folder 3386-C.
4. *Dorothy Woodward Collection, Documents Series, Harriet Bidwell Shaw Letters*.
5. Danielson, *Blood Brother of Pueblo Land*, quoting John Milton Shaw, Letter 26, Home Mission Record, March, 1855, vol. 5, Number 3.
6. Kendrick, Capt. 2 Artillery Brevet Maj. Commanding Fort Defiance, To Hon D. Meriwether, Governor & Sup Indian Affairs of New Mexico, Santa Fe N.M., *Records of the New Mexico Superintendency 1849-1880, Records of the Santa Fe Agency*, Miscellaneous 1856, Microfilm Reel 2.
7. John Milton Shaw Letter 27, Home Mission Record, March, 1855, vol. 5, Number 3, *Dorothy Woodward Collection, Documents Series, Harriet Bidwell Shaw Letters*.
8. Meriwether, David, *My Life in the Mountains and on the Plains, the Newly Discovered Autobiography by David Meriwether*, edited by Robert A. Griffin, (University of Oklahoma Press, Norman, 1965), 230.
9. District Court Records, Valencia County, Writ of Habeas Corpus, 1854, New Mexico State Records and Archives Center.
10. *Letters Received by the Office of Indian Affairs, 1824-1880, New Mexico Superintendency*, M234, Microfilm Reel 547, N440-443.
11. *Records of the New Mexico Superintendency, 1849-1880, Records of the Santa Fe Agency*, Miscellaneous Documents, Microfilm Reel 2.
12. District Court Records, Valencia County, New Mexico State Records and Archives Center.
13. *Letters Received by the Office of Indian Affairs, 1824-1880, New Mexico Superintendency*, M234, Microfilm Reel 547, N440-443.

14. Dodge, Santa Fe, to Meriwether, February 2, 1855, *Letters Received by the Office of Indian Affairs, 1824-1880, New Mexico Superintendency*, M234, Microfilm Reel 547, N440-443.
15. Meriwether to Manypenny, February 6, 1855, *Letters Received by the Office of Indian Affairs, 1824-1880, New Mexico Superintendency*, M234, Microfilm Reel 547, N440-443.
16. *Records of the New Mexico Superintendency 1849-1880, Records of the Santa Fe Agency*, Miscellaneous Documents, Microfilm Reel 2.

Chapter 40-Best Friends

1. *Settled Indian Accounts, 1817-1922*, Box 634, Folder 3386-C.
2. *Records of the New Mexico Superintendency, 1849-1880*, Miscellaneous Papers, 1854, Microfilm Reel 2.
3. *Records of the New Mexico Superintendency, 1849-1880, Records of the Santa Fe Agency*, Miscellaneous Documents, Microfilm Reel 2.
4. Garland to Lt. Col. L. Thomas, Asst. Adj. General, New York, January 31, 1855, *Letters Sent by the 9th Military District, 1849-1890*, Microfilm Reel 1, frames 938-939.
5. *Settled Indian Accounts, 1817-1922*, Box 634, Folder 3384-B.
6. Kendrick to Garland, February 14, 1855, *The Frank McNitt Collection*, National Archives, *Selected Letters Received by Adjutant Generals Office*. See also McNitt, *Navajo Wars*, 246 and *Letters Received by the Department of New Mexico, 1854-1865*, Microfilm Reel 4, frames 688-690.
7. Dodge, Jemez Pueblo, to Meriwether, February 13, 1855, *Records of the New Mexico Superintendency 1849-1880, Records of the Santa Fe Agency*, T21, Miscellaneous Documents, Microfilm Reel 2.
8. Meriwether to Dodge, Fort Defiance, February 15, 1855, *Letters Received from Agencies, 1855*, Microfilm Reel 2.
9. *Records of the New Mexico Superintendency 1849-1880, Records of the Santa Fe Agency*, T21, Miscellaneous Documents, Microfilm Reel 2.
10. Kendrick to AAG, February 25, 1855, *Letters Received by the Department of New Mexico, 1854-1865*, Microfilm Reel 4, frames 718-719.
11. Labadi to Meriwether, February 18, 1855, *Letters Received by the Office of Indian Affairs, 1824-1880, New Mexico Superintendency*, M234, Microfilm Reel 547, N440-443.
12. Labadi to Meriwether, February 24, 1855, *Letters Received by the Office of Indian Affairs, 1824-1880, New Mexico Superintendency*, M234, Microfilm Reel 547, N440-443.
13. Dodge, Tounicha to Meriwether, March 27, 1855, *Records of the New Mexico Superintendency, 1849-1880, Records of the Santa Fe Agency*, Miscellaneous Documents, Microfilm Reel 2.
14. *Letters Received from Agencies, 1855*, Microfilm Reel 2 and *Records of the New Mexico Superintendency 1849-1880, Records of the Santa Fe Agency*, T21, Miscellaneous Documents, Microfilm Reel 2.
15. *Settled Indian Accounts, 1817-1922*, Box 634, Folder 3386-C. Anaya and Vallejos were paid a quarter of their yearly salaries. Dodge paid George Carter, who had rejoined them at the beginning of February, one hundred dollars of his salary. The Indian Department auditor later disallowed that voucher, stating that Dodge had overpaid Carter $1.67.
16. Senator A. C. Dodge, Washington, DC to Manypenny, January 23, 1855, *The Frank McNitt Collection*, National Archives, New Mexico Superintendency, T21-2 and *Letters Received Commissioner of Indian Affairs, 1855*, Microfilm Reel 2.

17. P. Clayton, 2d auditor, Treasury Department, to H. L. Dodge, c/o Meriwether, *The Frank McNitt Collection*, National Archives, New Mexico Superintendency, T21-2 and *Letters Received Commissioner of Indian Affairs*, 1855, Microfilm Reel 2.
18. Charles Deus, Capt. NMM Volunteers, Rito to Lt. Craig, Taos, April 8, 1855, *Unregistered Letters Received, Department of New Mexico*, Microfilm Reel 28.
19. *Unregistered Letters Received, Department of New Mexico*, Microfilm Reel 28, frame 189.
20. Kendrick to Lt. S. D. Sturgis, A.A.A. Gen., HQ, Department of New Mexico, April 16, 1855, *Letters Received by the Department of New Mexico*.
21. Dodge, Fort Defiance, to Meriwether, April 17, 1855, *Records of the New Mexico Superintendency, 1849-1880, Records of the Santa Fe Agency*, Agencies 1855, Microfilm Reel 2.
22. Meriwether to Dodge, Fort Defiance, April 28, 1855, *Letters Received from Agencies, 1855*, Microfilm Reel 2. See also Meriwether to Manypenny, April 27 and April 30, 1855, *Letters Received by the Office of Indian Affairs, 1824-1880, New Mexico Superintendency*, M234, Microfilm Reel 547, N440-443.
23. *Frank D. Reeves Records*, Center for Southwest Research, Microfilm. See also *Letters Received by the Office of Indian Affairs, 1824-1880, New Mexico Superintendency*, M234, Microfilm Reel 547, N440-443.
24. *Settled Indian Accounts, 1817-1922*, Box 634, Folder 3386-C.
25. *Letters Sent by the 9th Military District, 1849-1890*, Microfilm Reel 1, frames 961-962.
26. Garland to Lt. Col Thomas, May 31, 1855, *Letters Sent by the 9th Military District, 1849-1890*, Microfilm Reel 1, frame 975.
27. Meriwether to Dodge, May 24, 1855, *Records of the New Mexico Superintendency 1849-1880, Records of the Santa Fe Agency*, Miscellaneous Documents, Microfilm Reel 2.
28. Kendrick to Meriwether, May 28, 1855, *The Frank McNitt Collection*, National Archives, *Selected Letters Received by Adjutant General's Office*. See also *Letters Received by the Department of New Mexico, 1854-1865*, Microfilm Reel 4, frames 739-741.

Chapter 41-Laguna Negra

1. Dodge, Santa Fe, to Manypenny, June 30, 1855, *The Frank McNitt Collection*, National Archives, *Letters Received, New Mexico Superintendency*, Microfilm Reel 547.
2. *Settled Indian Accounts, 1817-1922*, Box 634, Folder 3386-A, 3384-B.
3. Meriwether, *My Life in the Mountains and on the Plains*, 206-207.
4. Davis, *El Gringo*, 405-406.
5. Davis, *El Gringo*, 231.
6. Davis; *El Gringo*, 406. Conspicuously absent was the Reverend John Milton Shaw. He and his family had departed Fort Defiance for the States the previous May on extended leave. Better than a year later, Shaw tendered his resignation as fort chaplain. He and Harriett would return to New Mexico to settle and start a church in Socorro, where in 1862 Harriet died. Four years later, John Shaw wed Harriet's sister, Cornelia, who subsequently died a year or two later. Shaw then married a Hispanic lady, Maria Juana Telles. They were wed in 1869 in a ceremony performed by the ex-editor of the Santa Fe Gazette and failed gold-prospector Hezekiah Johnson. Shaw remained in New Mexico, serving in the House of Representatives and as an Indian agent between the years of 1874 and 1876. He then opened a law firm. John Shaw died on September 10, 1886 at the age of 63 years. His descendants through Maria Telles remain in New Mexico to this day. See Danielson, unpublished notes.

7. Meriwether to Manypenny, July 27, 1855, *The Frank McNitt Collection*, National Archives, *Letters Received by the Office of Indian Affairs, 1824-1880, New Mexico Superintendency,* Microfilm Reel 547.
8. McNitt, *Navajo Wars*, 262.
9. Davis, *El Gringo*, 406-407.
10. Bennett, *Forts and Forays*, 67-68.
11. McNitt, *Navajo Wars*, 262.
12. Manuelito became a central figure in the history of Navajo-American relations. He was born in about 1818 to the *Bit'ahnii* Clan and was the son of Cayetano, an influential Chuska headman. Typical for the times, he was known by several names, including Holy Boy, Black Plants Man, Warrior Grabs the Enemy and then by the English moniker, Pistol Bullet. Initially, Manuelito was a reluctant ally of the Americans, but when that friendship finally disintegrated, he led the Navajo in armed resistance to United States forces. With the incarceration of the Navajo people at Fort Sumner between 1863 and 1868, he rethought his position and advocated accommodating the Americans. He was one of the signatories of the treaty that returned the Navajo to their traditional homeland.

Manuelito returned to his home east of present day Tohatchi, New Mexico and before long was appointed principal chief of the Eastern Navajo. Four years after returning from Sumner, the United States appointed him head of the Navajo Police, essentially a mounted posse meant to enforce the will of the government. Despite this, he vigorously defended Navajo lands against encroachment by New Mexico stockmen and was active in the fight against a new plague spreading through his people, one that every subjugated tribe painfully suffered ... alcoholism. If there were significant turning points in Manuelito's life, then sending his two sons back East in 1883 for schooling was certainly one of them. Manuelito had long advocated education as the best way to preserve Navajo wealth, independence and prosperity. This enthusiasm dwindled after his boys, attending school in Carlisle, Pennsylvania, became seriously ill and died. It was during this period that he began to drink. Eleven years later, in 1894, Manuelito would to succumb to measles and pneumonia at the age of 76. See Grant, Bruce. *Concise Encyclopedia of the American Indian*, (Wing Books: New York, 2000) and Thompson, Gerald, *The Army and the Navajo: The Bosque Redondo Reservation Experiment 1863-1868*, (The University of Arizona Press, Tucson, Arizona 1976). See also Virginia Hoffman, *Navajo Biographies*.
13. McNitt, *Navajo Wars*, 263.
14. Davis, *El Gringo*, 408.
15. McNitt, *Navajo Wars*, 263.
16. W. W. H. Davis, July 27, 1855, *Letters Received by the Office of Indian Affairs, 1824-1880, New Mexico Superintendency*, M234, Microfilm Reel 547, N449-505.
17. McNitt, *Navajo Wars*, 436-439
18. Davis, *El Gringo*, 409-410, 412. In his work, Davis made some surprisingly sympathetic observations about the so-called savages, describing them as peaceful, industrious and intellectually superior to any other Indian tribe, having some of the wealthiest folks in the entire territory owning property in excess of $15,000 in value. Davis lauded their skill at weaving wool and even at that early date creating silver jewelry. He was particularly intrigued with what he drolly dubbed the Navajo "modern doctrine of Woman's Rights." The women held real power in the tribe. They were the actual owners of all the sheep. They were invariably consulted regarding property and bargain making, and were admitted to the council of leaders, where they had at times controlled the deliberations.

19. Dodge, Navajo Agency, Pass Washington to Manypenny, August 2, 1855, *The Frank McNitt Collection*, National Archives, *Letters Received by the Office of Indian Affairs, 1824-1880, New Mexico Superintendency*, Microfilm Reel 547.
20. *Letters Received by the Office of Indian Affairs, 1824-1880, New Mexico Superintendency*, M234, Microfilm Reel 547, N449-505.
21. Correll, *Through Whiteman's Eyes*, 24-25.

Chapter 42-For Amigos

1. Meriwether to Manypenny, September, 1855, *Letters Received by the Office of Indian Affairs, 1824-1880, New Mexico Superintendency*, M234, Microfilm Reel 547, N507-W533.
2. Garland to Thomas, August 31, 1855, September 30, 1855, *Letters Sent by the 9th Military District, 1849-1890*, Microfilm Reel 1, frames 1002-1005.
3. "Our Indian Relations," *The Santa Fe Weekly Gazette*, September 1, 1855. See also *The Santa Fe Weekly Gazette* "Arrival of Capt. Dodge" September 8, 1855.
4. *The Frank McNitt Collection*, National Archives, New Mexico Superintendency, T21-2.
5. Charles E. Mix, Acting Commissioner, to Senator Dodge, September 15, 1855, *Letters Sent by the Office of Indian Affairs, 1824-1881*, Microfilm Reel 52. See also *Records of the New Mexico Superintendency 1849-1880, Records of the Santa Fe Agency*, Miscellaneous Documents, Microfilm Reel 2. On September 15th, Senator Dodge was informed that, by direction of the Secretary of the Interior, $250 of his son's pay would be remitted to him from the United States Treasury.
6. Dodge to Meriwether, September 30, 1855, *The Frank McNitt Collection*, National Archives, *Letters Received by the Office of Indian Affairs, 1824-1880, New Mexico Superintendency*, Microfilm Reel 547, reference 0121-0126. See also Dodge to Meriwether, September 30, 1855, *Letters Received by the Office of Indian Affairs, 1824-1880, New Mexico Superintendency*, M234, Microfilm Reel 548, L117-N23.
7. Meriwether to Manypenny, September 10, 1855, Correll, *Through White Men's Eyes*, 25-26.
8. Meriwether to Manypenny, September 30, 1855, *Letters Received by the Office of Indian Affairs, 1824-1880, New Mexico Superintendency*, M234, Microfilm Reel 547, N507-W533.
9. Meriwether to Garland, September 29, 1855, *Letters Received by the Department of New Mexico, 1854-1865*, Microfilm Reel 4, frame 1023.
10. Garland to Thomas, October 31, 1855, *Letters Sent by the 9th Military District, 1849-1890*, Microfilm Reel 1, frame 1013. See also Garland to Thomas, November 30, 1855, *Letters Sent by the 9th Military District, 1849-1890*, Microfilm Reel 1.
11. McNitt, *Navajo Wars*, 271.
12. Davis to Manypenny, January 21, 1856, *Letters Received by the Office of Indian Affairs, 1824-1880, New Mexico Superintendency*, M234, Microfilm Reel 546, N32-N99.

On January 7th, the New Mexico Legislative Assembly issued a joint resolution praising Colonel Fauntleroy for punishing the "savage and inhuman hordes" of Ute and Jicarilla the year before. Shortly afterwards, they formally took issue with part of Acting Governor Davis' annual message to them, specifically the first part of the fourth paragraph; *"It affords me pleasure to inform you that we are at peace with the various Indian tribes of this Territory."*

The lawmakers asserted that Davis' characterization was "unfortunately contradicted by the recent and frequent depredations committed by the savage Indians," causing the citizens of New

Mexico to suffer highway robbery and murder at every turn. The resolution then enumerated the outrages in detail. Mescalero, purportedly, had killed a shepherd and run off Serafin Ramirez's stock. In October Indians drove off Anastacio Garcia's flocks then struck herds of the town of Padillas and Isleta Pueblo. In November, bands reported to be Gila Apaches, murdered a stockman and ran off scores of animals from Los Lunas, Socorro and Sabinal. The list went on. The legislators resolved to send their resolution to the President of the United States and the Territorial Delegate to Congress, Mr. Gallegos and have it printed in the Gazette. First and foremost, they resolved that Governor Meriwether correct the erroneous statement that resulted, no doubt "for a want of official information." See *Letters Received by the Office of Indian Affairs, 1824–1880, New Mexico Superintendency*, M234, Microfilm Reel 546, L117-N23. They sent Davis a detailed list of stock taken from the citizens of Socorro for the previous September onward. Davis submitted it to Manypenny. He did not dispute the veracity of the list. They were a list of petty thefts more than anything: a mule here, two head of oxen there, a bull and a cow run off, etcetera-etcetera.

13. Davis to Manypenny, January 23, 1856, *Letters Received by the Office of Indian Affairs, 1824–1880, New Mexico Superintendency*, M234, Microfilm Reel 546, L117-N23.
14. Office of Indian Affairs, New Mexico Superintendency, Miscellaneous Papers, 1856, Microfilm Reel 2.
15. Davis to Dodge, December 29, 1855, *The Frank McNitt Collection*, National Archives, New Mexico Superintendency, T21-1. See also *Letters Received from Agencies, 1855*, Microfilm Reel 2.
16. Locke, *The Book of the Navajo*, 296.
17. Dodge, Navajo Agency, to Acting Superintendent W.W.H. Davis, *Records of the New Mexico Superintendency, 1849–1880, Records of the Santa Fe Agency*, Miscellaneous Documents, Microfilm Reel 2.
18. Davis to Manypenny, December 30, 1855, *The Frank McNitt Collection*, National Archives, New Mexico Superintendency, T21-1, *Letters Received from Agencies, 1855*, Microfilm Reel 2, and *Letters Received by the Office of Indian Affairs, 1824–1880, New Mexico Superintendency*, M234, Microfilm Reel 546, L117-N23.
19. *Settled Indian Accounts, 1817–1922*, Box 634, Folder 3386-A. See also *Settled Indian Accounts, 1817–1922*, Box 634, Folder 3386-C.
20. *Records of the New Mexico Superintendency 1849–1880, Records of the Santa Fe Agency, Letters Received*, Microfilm Reel 2.
21. *Letters Sent by the Department of New Mexico, Records of U. S. Army Continental Commands, 1821–1920*, National Archives, (Washington, DC 1980), Microfilm Reel 1, frame 1033A.
22. *The Frank McNitt Collection*, National Archives, K-1-1856.
23. Office of Indian Affairs, New Mexico Superintendency, Letter from Commissioner, 1856, Microfilm Reel 2.
24. *Records of the New Mexico Superintendency 1849–1880, Records of the Santa Fe Agency*, T21, Miscellaneous 1856, Microfilm Reel 2.
25. *Records of the New Mexico Superintendency 1849–1880, Records of the Santa Fe Agency*, Miscellaneous 1856, Microfilm Reel 2. See also *Letters Received by the Department of New Mexico, 1854–1865*, Microfilm Reel 5, frames 345-346 and Miscellaneous Papers, 1856, Microfilm Reel 2.
26. Kendrick to Carleton, February 28, 1856, *The Frank McNitt Collection*, National Archives, C-4-1856. See also Letters Received by the Department New Mexico, 1854–1865, Microfilm Reel 5, frames 351-352.

27. Kendrick to Nichols, February 15, 1856, *The Frank McNitt Collection*, National Archives, K-1-1856. See also *Letters Received by the Department New Mexico, 1854–1865*, Microfilm Reel 5, frames 806-808.
28. *The Frank McNitt Collection*, National Archives, *Letters Received by the Office of Indian Affairs, 1824–1880, New Mexico Superintendency*, M234, Microfilm Reel 548.
29. *Letters Received by the Department of New Mexico, 1854–1865*, Microfilm Reel 5, frame 809.

Chapter 43-Madness in the Extreme

1. Steck to W. W. H. Davis April 6, 1856, *Letters Received from Agencies*, 1856, Microfilm Reel 2.
2. *Letters Received by the Office of Indian Affairs, 1824–1880, New Mexico Superintendency*, M234, Microfilm Reel 546, A12-K44 and Correll, *Through Whiteman's Eyes*, 35-36. See also "The Navajo Agency, *The Santa Fe Weekly Gazette*, April 5, 1856.
3. *Records of the New Mexico Superintendency 1849–1880, Records of the Santa Fe Agency*, Agencies, Microfilm Reel 2.
4. W.W.H. Davis to Manypenny, April 9, 1856, *Letters Received by the Office of Indian Affairs, 1824–1880, New Mexico Superintendency*, M234, Microfilm Reel 546, L117-N23 and N100-150. Davis made his report to Commissioner Manypenny. He hastened to add that the sheep had apparently been stolen while being grazed on land that, until the Senate ratified the Treaty of Laguna Negra, remained technically and practically Navajo. The authorities had repeatedly warned the citizens to stay off of Navajo grasslands. The seeds of their indifference to that advice had come to fruition.
5. Kendrick, Ft. Defiance, to Nichols, April 17, 1856, *The Frank McNitt Collection*, National Archives, K-3-1856. See also *Letters Received by the Department of New Mexico, 1854–1865*, Microfilm Reel 5, frames 812-813.
6. Garland, Santa Fe, to Kendrick, Ft. Defiance, April 8, 1856, *Letters Sent by the 9th Military District, 1849–1890*, Microfilm Reel 1, frame 1034.
7. Dodge, Ft. Defiance, to Act. Gov. W. W. H. Davis, April 19, 1856, *Letters Received by the Office of Indian Affairs, 1824–1880, New Mexico Superintendency*, M234, Microfilm Reel 546, L117-N23 and *Records of the New Mexico Superintendency 1849–1880, Records of the Santa Fe Agency*, Agencies, Microfilm Reel 2.
8. Meriwether to Manypenny, April 20, 1856, *Letters Received by the Office of Indian Affairs, 1824–1880, New Mexico Superintendency*, M234, Microfilm Reel 546, N100-150.
9. *The Frank McNitt Collection*, National Archives, K-4-1856.
10. Kendrick, Ft. Defiance, to Nichols, April 21, 1856, *Letters Received by the Department of New Mexico, 1854–1865*, Microfilm Reel 5, frames 818-820.
11. Kendrick to Nichols, May 2, 1856, *The Frank McNitt Collection*, National Archives, K-6-1856.
12. Garland to Thomas, April 30, 1856, *Letters Sent by the 9th Military District, 1849–1890*, Microfilm Reel 1, frames 1038-1039.
13. Nichols to Kendrick, May 3, 1856, *Letters Sent by the 9th Military District, 1849–1890*, Microfilm Reel 1, frame 1039.
14. W. W. H. Davis to Dodge, Fort Defiance, April 22, 1856 and Dodge, Fort Defiance, to Davis, May 3, 1856, *The Frank McNitt Collection*, National Archives, New Mexico Superintendency T21-2. See also Letters Received from Agencies, 1856, Microfilm Reel 2 and *Records of the New Mexico Superintendency 1849–1880, Records of the Santa Fe Agency*, Agencies, Microfilm Reel 2.

15. Davis to Dodge, Ft. Defiance, April 23, 25 1856, *The Frank McNitt Collection*, National Archives, New Mexico Superintendency T21-2.
16. Meriwether to Dodge, April 1856, *The Frank McNitt Collection*, National Archives, New Mexico Superintendency T21-1. See also *Records of the New Mexico Superintendency 1849–1880, Records of the Santa Fe Agency*, Agencies, Microfilm Reel 2.
17. Gorman to Meriwether, May 17, 1856, *Letters Received by the Office of Indian Affairs, 1824–1880, New Mexico Superintendency*, M234, Microfilm Reel 548, frame 0282.
18. Meriwether to Manypenny, May 10, 1856, *Letters Received by the Office of Indian Affairs, 1824–1880, New Mexico Superintendency*, M234, Microfilm Reel 546, N100-150 and Miscellaneous Papers, 1856, Microfilm Reel 2.
19. Dodge to Meriwether, May 16, 1856, *The Frank McNitt Collection*, National Archives, *Letters Received by the Office of Indian Affairs, 1824–1880, New Mexico Superintendency*, M234, Microfilm Reel 548. See also *Letters Received by the Office of Indian Affairs, 1824–1880, New Mexico Superintendency*, M234, Microfilm Reel 546, N100-150 and *Records of the New Mexico Superintendency 1849–1880, Records of the Santa Fe Agency, Agencies*, Microfilm Reel 2.
20. Nichols to Kendrick, May 27, 1856, *Letters Received by the Department of New Mexico, 1854–1865*, Microfilm Reel 5, frames 826-828 and *Letters Sent by the 9th Military District, 1849–1890*, Microfilm Reel 1, frame 1040.
21. Baca to Meriwether, May 22, 1856, *Letters Received by the Department of New Mexico, 1854–1865*, Microfilm Reel 5, frame 261.
22. Capt. R. L. Ewell, cmdg. Los Lunas, to Lt. William Craig, aide-de-camp May 24, 1856, *Letters Received by the Department of New Mexico, 1854–1865*, Microfilm Reel 5, frame 570.
23. Kendrick to Nichols, June 2, 1856, *Letters Received by the Department of New Mexico, 1854–1865*, Microfilm Reel 5, frames 380-382.

Chapter 44-An Ounce of Fear

1. Dodge, Ft. Defiance, to Meriwether, June 2nd, 1856, *The Frank McNitt Collection*, National Archives, *Letters Received by the Office of Indian Affairs, 1824–1880, New Mexico Superintendency*, M234, Microfilm Reel 548, ref#0289. See also *Records of the New Mexico Superintendency 1849–1880, Records of the Santa Fe Agency, Agencies*, Microfilm Reel 2.
2. *Letters Received by the Department of New Mexico, 1854–1865*, Microfilm Reel 5, frames 830-382.
3. Twitchell, *The History of the Military Occupation of the Territory of New Mexico*, 239-248. It is perhaps curious that Don Diego Archuleta would so eagerly offer the Americans his help. He was the same Don Archuleta, former commander of Mexican forces in New Mexico, who had conspired to overthrow the Americans in December of 1846.
4. Garland to Thomas, *Letters Sent by the 9th Military District, 1849–1890*, Microfilm Reel 1, frame 1042.
5. Garland to Miles, March 14, 1855, *Letters Sent by the 9th Military District, 1849–1890*, Microfilm Reel 1, frames 954-955.
6. Nichols to Kendrick, June 11, 1856, *Letters Sent by the 9th Military District, 1849–1890*, Microfilm Reel 1, frame 1042.
7. *Letters Received by the Office of Indian Affairs, 1824–1880, New Mexico Superintendency*, M234, Microfilm Reel 546, N100-150.

8. McNitt, *Navajo Wars*, 73-74.
9. Dodge to Meriwether, June 13, 1856, Letters Received from Agencies, 1856, Microfilm Reel 2. See also *Records of the New Mexico Superintendency 1849-1880, Records of the Santa Fe Agency*, Agencies, Microfilm Reel 2.
10. Kendrick to Nichols, *Letters Received by the Department of New Mexico, 1854-1865*, Microfilm Reel 5, frames 836-838.
11. *The Frank McNitt Collection*, National Archives, New Mexico Superintendency T21-2.
12. *Letters Received by the Office of Indian Affairs, 1824-1880, New Mexico Superintendency*, M234, Microfilm Reel 547, N507-W533.
13. Meriwether to Manypenny, June 30, 1856, *The Frank McNitt Collection*, National Archives, *Letters Received by the Office of Indian Affairs, 1824-1880, New Mexico Superintendency*, Microfilm Reel 548. At about this time, Meriwether noted that "I have recently been informed by Mr. Apodaca the Sheriff of Socorro County, that a Mayordomo having charge of sheep on the Puerco river had sold a portion of the herd without the knowledge or consent of the owner, that one of the shepherds threatened to expose him, when the Mayordomo killed the shepherd and threw his body into the river, but a Navajo Indian witnessed the murder from a distance and gave information, which led to the arrest of the murderer and the recovery of the sheep. Is it not probable that other herds lost and charged to the account of the Indians, may have been disposed of in like manner? . . ."
14. S. Gorman, Laguna, to Major Rucker, June 30, 1855, *Letters Received by the Department of New Mexico, 1854-1865*, Microfilm Reel 5, frame 413.
15. Lt. John Trevitt, 3rd Infantry to Asst. Surgeon David C. De Leon USA dated Camp near Laguna July 3, 1856, *Letters Received by the Department of New Mexico, 1854-1865*, Microfilm Reel 5, frame 418.
16. Garland to Thomas, June 30, 1856, *Letters Sent by the 9th Military District, 1849-1890*, Microfilm Reel 1, frames 1046-1047.
17. *Letters Sent by the 9th Military District, 1849-1890*, Microfilm Reel 1, frame 1042.
18. Kendrick to Nichols, July 12, 1856, *Letters Received by the Department of New Mexico, 1854-1865*, Microfilm Reel 5, frames 851-856. Kit Carson's campaign of 1863 utilized these guerrilla tactics. Rapid response Army units, in conjunction with Ute and New Mexican mercenary bands, kept a constant pressure on the Navajo, at last resulting in their mass surrender and exile to Fort Sumner in Eastern New Mexico from 1863 to 1868.
19. Dodge to Meriwether, July 13, 1856, *Records of the New Mexico Superintendency 1849-1880, Records of the Santa Fe Agency*, Agencies, Microfilm Reel 2.
20. Meriwether to Dodge, Ft. Defiance, July 24, 1856, *The Frank McNitt Collection*, National Archives, New Mexico Superintendency, T21-1.
21. Durán to Meriwether, July 17, 1856, *The Frank McNitt Collection*, National Archives, New Mexico Superintendency T21-1.
22. *Letters Received by the Office of Indian Affairs, 1824-1880, New Mexico Superintendency*, M234, Microfilm Reel 546, N151-W201.
23. Garland to Thomas, July 31, 1856, *Letters Sent by the 9th Military District, 1849-1890*, Microfilm Reel 1, frames 1052-1053.
24. Nichols to Kendrick, Fort Defiance, July 26, 1856, *Letters Sent by the 9th Military District, 1849-1890*, Microfilm Reel 1, frame 1050.

Chapter 45-A Moot Point

1. Dodge to Manypenny, September 30, 1856, *Records of the New Mexico Superintendency 1849-1880, Records of the Santa Fe Agency*, Agencies.
2. *Letters Received by the Office of Indian Affairs, 1824-1880, New Mexico Superintendency*, M234, Microfilm Reel 546, N151-W201.
3. *Mississippi Valley French Research*, photocopy of original, courtesy of Eugene Beckett.
4. Kendrick to Nichols, August 12, 1856, *Letters Received by the Department of New Mexico, 1854-1865*, Microfilm Reel 5, frames 863-864.
5. *Letters Sent by the 9th Military District, 1849-1890*, Microfilm Reel 2, frames 41, 42. Benjamin Louis Eulalie de Bonneville was a native of France, born near Paris in 1795. When he was eight years old, his family immigrated to the United States. De Bonneville received an appointment to West Point in 1813 and graduated two years later as brevet second lieutenant of light artillery. He participated in building military roads in the eastern and southern parts of the country, later becoming a captain in 1825.
   In 1828, after serving in posts as diverse as New England and Arkansas, he ended up at Jefferson Barracks, Missouri. While there Bonneville became interested in the Western frontier, secured a leave of absence from the Army, and in 1833 formed an expedition of over one hundred men to explore Oregon and the Northwest Coast. He explored great tracts of present day Utah, where, curiously, the extinct glacial lake, the Bonneville Salt Flats, bears his name, and subsequently explored parts of Nevada, Idaho, Wyoming and California. Due to unfortunate delays and the failure of the postal service to deliver Bonneville's dispatch to the Army requesting an extension of time for his explorations, when Benjamin returned to Independence, Missouri, he discovered his commission in the Army had been revoked. He was again commissioned in 1836. He was promoted to major in 1845, brevetted lieutenant colonel for bravery during the battles of Contreras and Churubusco during the Mexican War, only to be court-martialed for "misbehavior before the enemy" during the occupation of Mexico City.
   In 1855, Bonneville was promoted to colonel. During his service in New Mexico, he became commander of the 3rd Infantry and was commandant of Fort Fillmore, later participating in the Gila Apache expeditions and serving from 1858 to 1861 as the commander of the Department of New Mexico. Colonel Bonneville retired from the military in 1861, at the age of 65, but returned to duty during the Civil War, at which time he served as a recruiting officer and commandant of the St. Louis barracks. He achieved the rank of Brevet Brigadier General and retired again in 1866. Colonel Benjamin de Bonneville spent the remainder of his life living at Fort Smith, Arkansas and died on June 12, 1878 at the age of 82 years. See "Benjamin Bonneville" *Wikipedia, the Free Encyclopedia*, en.wikipedia.org/wiki/Benjamin_Bonneville, (accessed June 18, 2010). See also "Benjamin L. E. Bonneville" in *Classic Encyclopedia, Encyclopedia Britannica, Eleventh Edition*, 1911, www.1911encyclopedia.org/Benjamin_L._E._ Bonneville, (accessed June 18, 2010).
6. *Records of the New Mexico Superintendency 1849-1880, Records of the Santa Fe Agency*, Agencies, Microfilm Reel 2.
7. *District Court Records, Valencia County*, Civil File, 1856, New Mexico State Records and Archives Center, Santa Fe.
8. *Letters Sent by the 9th Military District, 1849-1890*, Microfilm Reel 2, frame 33.
9. Labadi to Meriwether, October 20, 1856, *Letters Received from Agencies*, 1856, Microfilm Reel 2.

10. Henry L. Dodge, Ft. Defiance, to Gov. Meriwether, November 4, 1856, *The Frank McNitt Collection*, National Archives, K-17-1856. For Dodge's rough draft, see *Records of the New Mexico Superintendency 1849-1880, Records of the Santa Fe Agency*, Agencies, Microfilm Reel 2.
11. McNitt, *Navajo Wars*, 283-284. An early Missouri trader of the Santa Fe Trail, James L. Collins had experience with New Mexico and Indians as early as 1827, including being robbed by Indians as his caravan was traversing the Great Plains. He arrived in New Mexico in 1846 as a member of Doniphan's Missouri Volunteers and returned there after the war. Politician and editor of the Santa Fe Gazette, James L. Collins would become New Mexico Superintendent for Indian Affairs by 1858 and oversee full-blown war with the Navajo tribe and its relocation to Fort Sumner six years later. Collins came to a sudden end on June 5th, 1869, when, while serving as the United States Designated Depositary at Santa Fe, he was fatally shot through the heart by thieves robbing the Depository. The bandits made off with $100,000. See *The New York Times*, June 10, 1869.

Chapter 46-Reconnaissance

1. Meriwether to Manypenny, December 29, 1856, National Archives, *Records of the New Mexico Superintendency of Indian Affairs, 1849-1880*, Microfilm Reel 546. See also Kendrick to Nichols, November 26, 1856, *Letters Received by the Department of New Mexico, 1854-1865*, Microfilm Reel 5, frames 875-877.

Chapter 47-Zuni Salt Lake

1. Sweeny, *Mangas Coloradas, Chief of the Chiricahua Apaches*, 344.
2. Kendrick to Nichols, November 26, 1856, *Letters Received by the Department of New Mexico, 1854-1865*, Microfilm Reel 5, frames 875-877.

Chapter 48-Every Exertion

1. *Letters Received by the Department of New Mexico, 1854-1865*, Microfilm Reel 5, frames 1445-1146.
2. Van Horne to Nichols, November 27, 1856, *Letters Received by the Department of New Mexico, 1854-1865*, Microfilm Reel 5, frame 1443.
3. *Letters Received by the Office of Indian Affairs, 1824-1880, New Mexico Superintendency*, Microfilm Reel 546, 1857, M240-N204.
4. Bieber, Ralph P. ed., *Marching with the Army of the West, 1846-1848 by Abraham Robinson Johnston, Marcellus Ball Edwards and Philip Gooch Ferguson*, (The Arthur H. Clark Company, Glendale, California, 1936), 289.
5. Meriwether to Manypenny, November 29, 1856, *Letters Received by the Office of Indian Affairs, 1824-1880, New Mexico Superintendency*, Microfilm Reel 546, 1857, M240-N204.
6. Bonneville, cmdg. Department of N.M., to Lt. Cl. Lorenzo Thomas, Asst. Adjt. Gen., HQ of the Army, New York, November 29, 1856, *Letters Sent by the 9th Military District, 1849-1890*, Microfilm Reel 2, frames 46, 47.
7. *Letters Received by the Department of New Mexico, 1854-1865*, Microfilm Reel 5, frame 1135. See also Randall, Los Lunas, to Lt. Roberts, December 4, 1856, *Letters Received by the*

Department of New Mexico, 1854-1865, Microfilm Reel 5, frames 1151-1153 and *Letters Received by the Office of Indian Affairs, 1824-1880,* New Mexico Superintendency, Microfilm Reel 546, 1857, N214-N236.
8. Claiborne to Barnes and Meriwether, Headquarters, Fort Thorn, N. M., December 1 and 2, 1856, *The Frank McNitt Collection,* National Archives, New Mexico Superintendency, T21-2.
9. Capt. Gordon, cmdg. Ft. Defiance, to Major Nichols, December 11, 1856, *Letters Received by the Department of New Mexico, 1854-1865,* Microfilm Reel 5, frame 718.
10. *Records of the New Mexico Superintendency 1849-1880,* Records of the Santa Fe Agency, Agencies, Microfilm Reel 2. See also December 7 and Postscript December 12, 1856, Steck to Meriwether Letters Received from Agencies, 1856, Microfilm Reel 2.
11. Steck, Apache Agency, to Meriwether, December 18, 1856, *Letters Received by the Office of Indian Affairs, 1824-1880,* New Mexico Superintendency, M234, Microfilm Reel 546, 1857, N214-N236 and Sweeny, *Mangas Coloradas, Chief of the Chiricahua Apaches,* 346.

Chapter 49-A Wanton Act Inexplicable

1. Pelzer, *Augustus Caesar Dodge,* 256.
2. Burlington, Iowa, *The Semi-Centennial of Iowa, A Record of the Commemoration of the Fiftieth Anniversary of the Settlement of Iowa, Held at Burlington, June 1, 1883,* (Burlington Hawkeye Book and Job Printing House, 1883, photocopy provided by the State Historical Society of Iowa).
3. Burlington, Iowa, *The Semi-Centennial of Iowa,* 72-73, Augustus Dodge quoting *Ford's History of Illinois,* 1854.
4. Pelzer, *Augustus Caesar Dodge,* 280. See also Burlington, Iowa, *The Semi-Centennial of Iowa,* 73-74.
5. *Milwaukee Daily Sentinel,* April 18, 1857.
6. Pelzer, *Augustus Caesar Dodge,* 258, 262.
7. Van Valkenburgh, Richard, "Captain Red Shirt," *New Mexico Magazine,* July, 1941, 44-45.
8. White Mountain Smith, Dama M., "Henry Chee Dodge, Navajo," *Desert Magazine* 1, no. 9 (July, 1938) 17, 18.
9. Elizabeth Sheridan Spearman to Frank McNitt, January 3, 1972, *The Frank McNitt Collection.*
10. Beckett, *Becquet, Bequette, Beckett Family History,* 63-64.
11. Dodge, *Tristram Dodge and His Descendants in America,* (J. J. Little & Company, New York, 1886), 171.
12. Van Valkenburgh, "Captain Red Shirt," 28.
13. *Santa Fe Weekly Gazette,* September 29, 1858.
14. Wentz to Dodge, May 1, 1864, *Charles W. Wentz Letters, 1860-1864,* Wisconsin State Historical Society Archives and Library, University of Wisconsin, Madison.
15. Wentz to Dodge, May 10, 1864, *Charles W. Wentz Letters, 1860-1864.*
16. Wentz to Dodge, May 16, 1864, enclosure, *Charles W. Wentz Letters, 1860-1864.*

Chapter 50-The Worst of News

1. Van Horne, 3rd Inf. Comdg. Albuquerque, to Nichols, November 16, 1856, *The Frank McNitt Collection* V7, 1856.

2. Nichols to Commanding Officer at Fort Bliss, Texas, December 29, 1856, *Letters Sent by the 9th Military District, 1849-1890*, Microfilm Reel 2, frames 52-53. See also Major G. Morris, Fort Fillmore, to Nichols, January 29, 1857, *Letters Received by the Department of New Mexico, 1854-1865*, Microfilm Reel 6, frame 1022.
3. Meriwether, Santa Fe, to Manypenny, January 27, 1857, *The Frank McNitt Collection*, National Archives, Record Group 75, M234, *Letters Received by the Office of Indian Affairs, 1824-1880, New Mexico Superintendency* Microfilm Reel 546, ref.#0731.
4. *Office of Indian Affairs, New Mexico Superintendency*, T21, Miscellaneous Papers, 1856, Microfilm Reel 2.
5. *Letters Received by the Office of Indian Affairs, 1824-1880, New Mexico Superintendency*, Microfilm Reel 546, 1857, N214-N236.
6. *Letters Received by the Office of Indian Affairs, 1824-1880, New Mexico Superintendency*, Microfilm Reel 546, 1857, M240-N204. Davis to Secretary of the Interior McClellaude, War Department, Washington, January 3, 1857, National Archives, Record Group 75, M234, Microfilm Reel 546 and *Letters Received by the Office of Indian Affairs, 1824-1880, New Mexico Superintendency*, M234, Microfilm Reel 546, 1857, N241-W385.
7. Claiborne, cmdg. Ft. Thorn, to Asst. Adjt. Gen William A Nichols, Santa Fe, January 2, 1857, *The Frank McNitt Collection*, National Archives, *Letters Received by the Office of Indian Affairs, 1824-1880, New Mexico Superintendency*, Record Group 75, M234, Microfilm Reel 546, ref. #0736. See also *Letters Received by the Department of New Mexico, 1854-1865*, Microfilm Reel 6, frames 408-410 and *Letters Received by the Office of Indian Affairs, 1824-1880, New Mexico Superintendency*, Microfilm Reel 546, 1857, N214-N236.
8. Steck, Apache Agency, to Meriwether, January 3, 1857, *The Frank McNitt Collection*, National Archives, Record Group 75, M234, *Letters Received by the Office of Indian Affairs, 1824-1880, New Mexico Superintendency*, ref. #0741. See also *Records of the New Mexico Superintendency 1849-1880, Records of the Santa Fe Agency*, Agencies 1857, Microfilm Reel 3.
9. Meriwether to Manypenny, January 27, 1857, *The Frank McNitt Collection*, National Archives, Record Group 75, M234, *Letters Received by the Office of Indian Affairs, 1824-1880, New Mexico Superintendency*, Microfilm Reel 546, ref. #0731.

Chapter 51-With Due Solemnity

1. Van Horne to Nichols, February 4, 1857, *Letters Received by the Department of New Mexico, 1854-1865*, Microfilm Reel 6, frames 1722-1723.
2. *The Frank McNitt Collection*, V5, 1857. See also *Letters Sent by the 9th Military District, 1849-1890*, Microfilm Reel 2, frames 60-61.
3. *Letters Received by the Department of New Mexico, 1854-1865*, Microfilm Reel 6, frames 827-829.
4. Kendrick, Defiance, to Lt. J. H. Carlisle, cmdg. Expedition, February 8, 1857, *Letters Received by the Department of New Mexico, 1854-1865*, Microfilm Reel 6, frames 831-833.
5. *The Frank McNitt Collection*, National Archives, New Mexico Superintendency, T21-3, Letters, Adjutant General's Office. It is likely that Carlisle's report of Dodge being scalped was correct. Although the Apache traditionally shared the same morbid fear of the dead as the Navajo, as with the Navajo the Apache took an occasional scalp to perform a ritual, Enemies-Against Power, by which the enemy's people are weakened. Enemies-Against Power was performed

exclusively in the country of the enemy. The scalp might be tied to a pole and a brief dance done with it, but was disposed of immediately afterwards, usually by throwing it into a tree or bush. It was never kept in camp over night, for fear of ghosts. In this case, Dodge, apparently the first American killed since Chandler's expedition, may have represented the white soldiers who killed several Mogollon the spring before, making his scalp particularly susceptible. See Basso, Keith, ed., *Western Apache Raiding and Warfare, From the Notes of Grenville Goodwin*, (University of Arizona Press, Tucson, 1971), 276-278. See also Cremony, *Life Among the Apaches*, 257-258 regarding scalping and purification ceremonies after the killing of enemies.

6. Bonneville to Thomas, March 31, 1857, *Letters Sent by the 9th Military District, 1849-1890*, Microfilm Reel 2, frame 75.
7. *The Frank McNitt Collection*, National Archives, New Mexico Superintendency, T21-3, Letters, Adjutant General's Office.
8. Kendrick to Meriwether, February, 1857, *The Frank McNitt Collection*, National Archives, New Mexico Superintendency,T21-3 Letters, Adjutant General's Office. See *Office of Indian Affairs, New Mexico Superintendency*, T21, Miscellaneous Papers, 1857, Microfilm Reel 3. See also *Records of the New Mexico Superintendency, 1849-1880, Records of the Santa Fe Agency*, Miscellaneous 1857, Microfilm Reel 3.
9. Meriwether to Manypenny, January 27, 1857, *The Frank McNitt Collection*, National Archives, Record Group 75, M234, *Letters Received by the Office of Indian Affairs, 1824-1880, New Mexico Superintendency*, Microfilm Reel 546, ref. #0731.
10. *Milwaukee Sentinel*, 1857, April 18.
11. Secretary of War John Floyd, War Department, Washington to Honorable Henry Dodge, Dodgeville, Wisconsin, May 18, 1857, *Letters Sent by the Secretary of War, Registered Series, 1801-1860*, National Archives, Records of the Office of the Secretary of War, Record Group 107, M6, Microfilm Reel 39.

Chapter 52-Of Greater Use to the Indians

1. Kendrick, Ft. Defiance, to Meriwether, February 18, 1857, *The Frank McNitt Collection*, National Archives, New Mexico Superintendency, T21-3, Letters Adjutant General Office.
2. Meriwether to Manypenny, March 27, 1857, *Letters Received by the Office of Indian Affairs, 1824-1880, New Mexico Superintendency*, Microfilm Reel 546, 1857, N241-W385.
3. Messervy to Webb, May 16 and June 19, 1857, *James Josiah Webb Collection*, State Historical Society of Missouri.
4. Van Horne to Nichols, February 14, 1857, *Letters Received by the Department of New Mexico, 1854-1865*, Microfilm Reel 6, frame 1732.
5. Van Horne to Nichols, February 19, 1857, *Letters Received by the Department of New Mexico, 1854-1865*, Microfilm Reel 6, frames 1729-1730 and *Records of the New Mexico Superintendency 1849-1880, Records of the Santa Fe Agency*, Miscellaneous 1857, Microfilm Reel 3.
6. Kendrick to Nichols, February 11, 1857, *Letters Received by the Department of New Mexico, 1854-1865*, Microfilm Reel 6, frames 812-813. See *also Records of the New Mexico Superintendency, 1849-1880, Records of the Santa Fe Agency*, Miscellaneous Papers, 1857, Microfilm Reel 3.
7. Nichols to Shepherd, Fort Defiance, January 26, 1857, *Letters Sent by the 9th Military District, 1849-1890*, Microfilm Reel 2, frame 58.

8. Bonneville, Santa Fe, to AAG L. Thomas, NY, January 31, 1857, *Letters Sent by the 9th Military District, 1849–1890*, Microfilm Reel 2, frame 61.
9. Gorman to Van Horne, enclosed in Van Horne to Nichols, *The Frank McNitt Collection*, V8, 1857.
10. Nichols to Steen, Tucson, February 17, 1857, *Letters Sent by the 9th Military District, 1849–1890*, Microfilm Reel 2, frame 65.
11. Nichols to McCooke, February 24, 1857, *Letters Sent by the 9th Military District, 1849–1890*, Microfilm Reel 2, frames 66-67.
12. Weber to Meriwether, April 10, 1857, *Letters Received by the Office of Indian Affairs, 1824–1880, New Mexico Superintendency*, Agencies, 1857, Microfilm Reel 2.
13. Nichols to Meriwether, April 22, 1857, *Letters Sent by the 9th Military District, 1849–1890*, Microfilm Reel 2, frame 77.
14. Sweeney, *Mangas Coloradas, Chief of the Chiricahua Apaches*, 353.
15. Steck to Bonneville, May 16, 1857, *Letters Received by the Office of Indian Affairs, 1824–1880, New Mexico Superintendency*, Agencies, 1857, Microfilm Reel 3.
16. Sweeney, *Mangas Coloradas, Chief of the Chiricahua Apaches*, 353-354.
17. Steck to Collins, September 4, 1857, *The Frank McNitt Collection*, National Archives, New Mexico Superintendency T21-3. See also Steck to Bonneville, September 9, 1857, the *Michael Steck Collection*, Microfilm Reel 1, frame 435, and *Letters Received by the Office of Indian Affairs, 1824–1880, New Mexico Superintendency*, Microfilm Reel 546, 1857, C1054-l674.
18. Steck to Collins, October 2, 1857, *Records of the New Mexico Superintendency 1849–1880, Records of the Santa Fe Agency*, Agencies 1857, Microfilm Reel 3. See also D. B. Clitz to Nichols, November 8, 1857, *Letters Received by the Office of Indian Affairs, 1824–1880, New Mexico Superintendency*, Agencies, 1857, Microfilm Reel 3.
19. McNitt, *Navajo Wars*, 301-302.
20. Nichols to Cooper, Washington, DC, April 25, 1857, *Letters Sent by the 9th Military District, 1849–1890*, Microfilm Reel 2, frame 78.
21. McNitt, *Navajo Wars*, 300-302.
22. *Letters Sent by the 9th Military District, 1849–1890*, Microfilm Reel 2, frames 85-86.
23. McNitt, *Navajo Wars*, 308.
24. Collins to Denver, June 29, 1857, *Letters Received by the Office of Indian Affairs, 1824–1880, New Mexico Superintendency*, Microfilm Reel 546, 1857, A134-C1053.
25. *Letters Received by the Office of Indian Affairs, 1824–1880, New Mexico Superintendency*, Microfilm Reel 546, 1857, A134-C1053.
26. Collins to Denver, September 30, 1857, *Letters Received by the Office of Indian Affairs, 1824–1880, New Mexico Superintendency*, Microfilm Reel 546, 1857, C1054-l674.
27. Brooks to Collins, July 16, 1858, *Records of the New Mexico Superintendency 1849–1880, Records of the Santa Fe Agency*, Miscellaneous, 1857, Microfilm Reel 3.
28. Wentz to A. C. Dodge, Burlington, Iowa, May 1, 1864, *Charles W. Wentz Letters, 1860–1864*.
29. Excerpts from the Navajo Night Way Ceremony.

BIBLIOGRAPHY

Abel, Annie H. ed., *The Official Correspondence of James S. Calhoun*, Washington, DC: Government Printing Office, 1915.
――― "The Journal of John Greiner," *Old Santa Fe Magazine*, vol. 3, no. 11 (July 1916):189-243.
――― "Indian Affairs in New Mexico under the Administration of William Carr Lane, from the Journal of John Ward," edited by Annie Heloise Abel, *The New Mexico Historical Review* 16, no. 2 (April, 1941): 206-232.
Abert, James William, *Abert's New Mexico Report, 1846-'47*, edited by William A. Keleher, New Edition, Santa Fe: Sunstone Press, 2014.
Alderfer, William K., *The Black Hawk War, 1831-1832*, Chicago: Collections of the Illinois State Historical Society, 1975.
Allison, W. H. H. "Santa Fe in 1846." *Old Santa Fe Magazine*, April 1915.
Alvord, Clarence W., *Kaskaskia Records, 1778-1790, Collections of the Illinois State Historical Library 5*, Springfield: 1909.
――― *The Illinois Country, 1673-1818*, Chicago: A. C. McClurg & Company, 1922.
Bailey, L. R., *Indian Slave Trade in the Southwest*, Los Angeles: Westernlore Press, 1973.
Barry, Louise, *The Beginnings of the West: Annals of the Kansas Gateway to the American West, 1540-1854*, Topeka: Kansas State Historical Society, 1972.
Bartlett, John R., *Personal Narrative of Explorations and Incidents in Texas, New Mexico, California, Sonora and Chihuahua*, New York: D. Appleton & Company, 1854.
Basler, Lucille, *Pioneers of Old Ste. Genevieve*, Ste. Genevieve, Missouri: published by author, 1983.
――― *The District of Ste. Genevieve*, Ste. Genevieve, Missouri: published by author, 1980.
Basso, Keith, ed., *Western Apache Raiding and Warfare, From the Notes of Grenville Goodwin*, Tucson: University of Arizona Press, 1971.
Bender, A. B. "Government Explorations, 1846-1859," *The New Mexico Historical Review* 9, no. 1 (1934):1-32.
――― "Frontier Defense in the Territory of New Mexico, 1846-1853," *The New Mexico Historical Review* 4 (1934): 249-272.
Beck, Warren A., *New Mexico: A History of Four Centuries*, Norman: University of Oklahoma Press, 1962.
Beckett, Eugene, *Becquet, Bequette, Beckett Family History: From Cambrai to Cambria*, Cambria, Illinois: published by author, 1991.
Bieber, Ralph P. ed., *Marching with the Army of the West, 1846-1848 by Abraham Robinson Johnston, Marcellus Ball Edwards and Philip Gooch Ferguson*, Glendale, California: The Arthur H. Clark Company, 1936.
――― *Adventures in the Santa Fé Trade 1844-1847, by James Josiah Webb*, Southwest Historical Series, edited by Ralph P. Bieber, Glendale: The Arthur H. Clark Company,1931.
Blackhawk, Makataimeshekiakiak, *Black Hawk, An Autobiography*; edited by Donald Jackson, Springfield: University of Illinois Press; 1964.

Bloom, John P., *Territorial Papers of the United States, Vol. 28: The Territory of Wisconsin*, Washington, DC: National Archives and Records Service, General Services Administration, 1975.

Bloom, Lansing B., "The Rev. Hiram Walter Read, Baptist Missionary to New Mexico," *New Mexico Historical Review* 17, (1941):113-145.

Bracken, Charles "Further Strictures on Ford's Black Hawk War," *Collections of the State Historical Society of Wisconsin*, Lyman C. Draper, editor, vol. 2, 365-392, Madison: Democrat Printing Company, 1908.

――― "Pekatonica Battle Controversy," *Collections of the State Historical Society of Wisconsin*, Lyman C. Draper, editor, vol. 2, 402-414, Madison: Democrat Printing Company, 1908.

Brackenridge, Henry, *Views of Louisiana, Together with a Journal of a Voyage up the Missouri River, in 1811*, Chicago: Quadrangle Books Inc., 1962.

Bradbury, John, *Travels in the Interior of America, 1809-1811*, Ann Arbor: University Microfilms Inc., 1966.

Braun, Robert A., "Black Hawk's War, April 5-August 2, 1832: A Chronology," *Old Lead Region Historical Society*, September, 2001, www.geocities.com/old_lead/ bhwchron.htm (accessed September 7, 2009).

Bennett, James A., *Forts and Forays: James A. Bennett, a Dragoon in New Mexico, 1850-1856*, edited by Clinton E. Brooks and Frank D. Reeve, Albuquerque: University of New Mexico Press, 1948.

Brown, William E., *The Santa Fe Trail, The National Park Service 1963 Historic Sites Survey*, St. Louis: The Patrice Press, 1988.

Bryan, William S., *A History of the Pioneer Families of Missouri*, St. Louis: Bryan, Brand & Company, 1876.

Buley, R. Carlyle, *The Old Northwest, Pioneer Period, 1815-1840, Volume 2*, Bloomington: Indiana University Press, 1978.

Burlington, Iowa, *The Semi-Centennial of Iowa, A Record of the Commemoration of the Fiftieth Anniversary of the Settlement of Iowa, Held at Burlington, June 1, 1881*, Burlington: Hawkeye Book and Job Printing House, 1883, photocopy provided by the State Historical Society of Iowa.

Calhoun, James S., *The Official Correspondence of James S. Calhoun*, edited by Annie H. Abel, Washington, DC: Government Printing Office, 1915.

Calvin, Ross, ed., *Lieutenant Emory Reports: A Reprint of Lieutenant W. H. Emory's Notes of a Military Reconnaissance, with introduction and notes by Ross Calvin*, Albuquerque: University of New Mexico Press, 1951.

Carter, Clarence E. ed., *Territorial Papers of the United States, Vol. 12: Michigan Territory, 1829-1837*, Washington, DC: Government Printing Office, 1949.

――― *Territorial Papers of the United States, Vol. 13: The Territory of Louisiana and Missouri, 1803-1806*, Washington, DC: Government Printing Office, 1948.

――― *Territorial Papers of the United States, Vol. 14: The Territory of Louisiana and Missouri, 1806-1814*, Washington, DC: Government Printing Office, 1949.

――― *Territorial Papers of the United States, Vol. 15: The Territory of Louisiana and Missouri, 1815-1821*, Washington, DC: Government Printing Office, 1949.

Chapman, C. B., "Early Events in the Four Lake Country" *Collections of the State Historical Society of Wisconsin*, Lyman C. Draper, editor, vol. 4, 343-349, Madison: Democrat Printing Company, 1908.

Chalfant, William Y., *Dangerous Passage: The Santa Fe Trail and the Mexican War*, Norman: University of Oklahoma Press, 1994.

Chávez, Thomas E., *Manuel Alvarez, 1794-1856, A Southwestern Biography*, Niwot: University of Colorado Press, 1990.

Churchill, Ward, *A Little Matter of Genocide: Holocaust and Denial in the Americas, 1492 to the Present*, San Francisco: City Lights Books, 1997.

Clark, James I., *Life on Wisconsin's Lead Mining Frontier*, Madison: State Historical Society of Wisconsin, 1976.

Clarke, Dwight L. ed., *The Original Journals of Henry Smith Turner With Stephen Watts Kearny to New Mexico and California, 1846-1847*, Norman: University of Oklahoma Press, 1966.

――― *Stephen Watts Kearny, Soldier of the West*, Norman: University of Oklahoma Press, 1961.

Cooke, Philip, *Exploring Southwestern Trails, 1846-1854: Journal of Philip St. George Cooke*, Southwest Historical Series, edited by Ralph P. Bieber, Glendale: The Arthur H. Clark Company, 1931.

Correll, J. Lee, *Through White Men's Eyes: A Contribution to Navajo History, Volume 1*, Window Rock: Navajo Heritage Center, 1976.

――― *Through White Men's Eyes: A Contribution to Navajo History, Volume. 2*, Window Rock: Navajo Heritage Center, 1979.

Crawford, George and Robert M. Crawford, *Memoirs of Iowa County, Wisconsin, from the Earliest Historical Times Down to the Present*, S. l.: Northwestern Historical Association, 1913.

Cremony, John C., *Life Among the Apaches*, New York: A. Roman & Company, Publishers, 1868.

Crutchfield, James A., *Tragedy at Taos: The Revolt of 1847*, Plano: Republic of Texas Press, 1995.

Cullum, George W., *Biographical Register of the Officers and Graduates of the U. S. Military Academy at West Point, N. Y.*, Boston: The Riverside Press, Houghton, Mifflin and Company, 1891.

Danielson, Betty, *Blood Brother of Pueblo Land: The Angel from the East, Samuel Gorman Among the Lagunas*, Albuquerque: published by the author, 1998.

Davidson, W., "Personal Narratives of the Black Hawk War," *Collections of the State Historical Society of Wisconsin*, Lyman C. Draper, editor, vol. 5, Madison: Democrat Printing Company, 1907.

Davis, W. W. H., *El Gringo or New Mexico and Her People*, Santa Fe: Rydal Press, 1938 reprint of Harper & Brothers, New York, 1857.

Davis, William C., *Jefferson Davis, The Man and His Hour*, New York: Harper Collins Publishers, 1991.

Davidson, W., "Personal Narratives of the Black Hawk War," *Collections of the State Historical Society of Wisconsin*, Lyman C. Draper, editor, vol. 5, 317-320, Madison: Democrat Printing Company, Madison, 1907.

Derleth, August, *The Wisconsin, River of a Thousand Isles*, New York: Rinehart & Company, Inc., 1942.

Dodge, Robert, *Tristram Dodge and His Descendants in America*, New York: J. J. Little & Company, 1886.

Draper, Lyman C. ed., *Collections of the State Historical Society of Wisconsin, Volume 1*, Madison: Democrat Printing Company, 1903.

――― *Collections of the State Historical Society of Wisconsin, Volume 2*, Madison: Democrat Printing Company, 1903.

——— *Collections of the State Historical Society of Wisconsin, Volume 4*, Madison: Democrat Printing Company, 1906.

——— *Collections of the State Historical Society of Wisconsin, Volume 5*, Madison: Democrat Printing Company, 1907.

——— *Collections of the State Historical Society of Wisconsin, Volume 6*, Madison: Democrat Printing Company, 1908.

——— *Collections of the State Historical Society of Wisconsin, Volume 10*, Madison: Democrat Printing Company, 1888.

Drumm, Stella M., ed., *Down the Santa Fe Trail and into Mexico: The Diary of Susan Shelby Magoffin, 1846-1847*, New Haven: Yale University Press, 1926.

Eby, Cecil D., *"That Disgraceful Affair," The Black Hawk War*, New York: W. W. Norton & Company, 1973.

Edwards, Frank S., *A Campaign in New Mexico With Colonel Doniphan*, Philadelphia: Carey and Hart, Philadelphia, 1847, reprinted by the University of New Mexico Press, Albuquerque, 1996.

Ekberg, Carl J., *Colonial Ste. Genevieve, An Adventure on the Mississippi Frontier*, Gerald, Missouri: Patrice Press, 1985.

Elder, Jane L. ed., *Trading in Santa Fe: John M. Kingsbury's Correspondence with James Josiah Webb, 1853-1861*, edited by Jane Lenz Elder and Davis J. Weber, Dallas: Southern Methodist University Press, 1996.

Field, Matthew C., *Matt Field on the Santa Fe Trail*, Collected by Clyde and Mae Reed Porter, editing, introduction and notes by John E. Sunder, Norman: University of Oklahoma Press, 1960.

Fieldhouse Foundation, *Iowa County Heritage, Volume I*, Dodgeville, Wisconsin: Field House Foundation Inc., 1967.

Fisher, Kelly, "The Forgotten Dodge," *Annals of Iowa* 40, no. 4 (1970): 296-305.

Flint, Timothy, *Recollections of the Last Ten Years Passed in Occasional Residences and Journeying in the Valley of the Mississippi*, edited by C. Hartley Grattan, New York: Alfred A. Knopf, 1932.

Foley, William E., *The Genesis of Missouri: From Wilderness Outpost to Statehood*, Columbia: University of Missouri Press, 1989.

———*A History of Missouri, Volume I: 1673-1820*, Columbia: University of Missouri Press, 1971.

Ford, Lemuel, *March of the First Dragoons to the Rocky Mountains in 1835: The Diaries and Maps of Lemuel Ford*, edited by Nolie Mumey, Denver: The Eames Brothers Press, 1957.

Fox, Mary Dodge, "The Grove—Recollections of Mary Dodge Fox, as Dictated to Her Daughter in April, 1918," Mary Dodge Fox Folder, Wisconsin State Historical Society Archives, University of Wisconsin, Madison.

Franciscan Fathers, *An Ethnologic Dictionary of the Navaho Language*, St. Michaels, Arizona: St. Michaels Press, 1968.

Frink, Maurice, *Fort Defiance and the Navajos*, Boulder: Pruett Press, 1968.

Fugate, Francis L., *Roadside History of New Mexico*, Missoula: Mountain Press Publishing Company, 1989.

Gardner, Mark L. ed., *Brothers on the Santa Fe and Chihuahua Trails: Edward James Glasgow and William Henry Glasgow, 1846-1848*, Niwot: University Press of Colorado, 1993.

———*The Mexican War Correspondence of Richard Smith Elliot*, edited and annotated by Mark L. Gardner and Marc Simmons, Norman: University of Oklahoma Press, 1997.

Garraty, John A. ed., *American National Biography*, New York: Oxford University Press, 1999.

Gibson, George R., *Journal of a Soldier Under Kearny and Doniphan, 1846-1847*, Southwest

Historical Series, edited by Ralph P. Bieber, Glendale: The Arthur H. Clark Company, 1934.

Gonzales-Berry, Erlinda, ed., *The Contested Homeland—A Chicano History of New Mexico*, Albuquerque: University of New Mexico Press, 2000.

Goodspeed Publishing Company, *The Goodspeed History of Southeast Missouri*, Chicago: Goodspeed Publishing Co., 1888.

Gorman, Mrs. Samuel "Rev. Samuel Gorman: Memorial," *Old Santa Fe*, vol. 1, no. 3, (1914): 308-331.

Gracy, David B., *Moses Austin: His Life*, San Antonio: Trinity University Press, 1987.

Greiner, John, "Journal of John Greiner" edited by Annie H. Abel, *Old Santa Fe Magazine*, 189-243.

Griffin, Robert A., ed., *My Life in the Mountains and on the Plains, the Newly Discovered Autobiography by David Meriwether*, Norman: University of Oklahoma Press, 1965.

Hagan, William T., *The Sac and Fox Indians*, Norman: University of Oklahoma Press, 1958.

Heaston, Michael D., "The Governor and the Indian Agent," *The New Mexico Historical Review*, 45, no. 2 (April 1970): 137-146.

Herrera, Carlos R., "New Mexico Resistance to U. S. Occupation during the Mexican-American War of 1846-1848," *The Contested Homeland-A Chicano History of New Mexico*, edited by Erlinda Gonzales-Berry, 23-42, Albuquerque: University of New Mexico Press, 2000.

Higginbotham, Vallé, *John Smith T-Missouri Pioneer*, published by author, 1968.

Hinchey, William J., *Diary of an Irish Artist*, edited by A. Stephen Hinchey, unpublished manuscript, National Frontier Trails Center Manuscript Collection, National Frontier Trails Center, Independence, Missouri.

Hoffman, Virginia, *Navajo Biographies*, Rough Rock, Arizona: Navajo Curriculum Center Press, 1987.

Horn, Calvin, *New Mexico's Troubled Years, The Story of the Early Territorial Governors*, Albuquerque: Horn & Wallace, Publishers, 1963.

Hughs, Willis B., "The First Dragoons on the Western Frontier, 1834-1846," *Arizona and the West*, 12, no. 2 (1970): 115-138.

Hunter, William W., *Missouri 49er, The Journal of William W. Hunter on the Southern Gold Trail*, edited by David Robrock, Albuquerque: University of New Mexico Press, 1992.

Iowa State Historical Society, *The Annals of Iowa, Volume 3, 1897-98*, Iowa State Historical Society, Des Moines.

Jackson, Ronald V., *Wisconsin 1850 Census Index*, Accelerated Indexing Systems International Inc., North Salt Lake, 1978.

Johnson, Allen, *Dictionary of American Biography*, New York: Charles Scribner's Sons, 1959.

Jones, George W., "Robert S. Black and the Black Hawk War," *Collections of the State Historical Society of Wisconsin*, Lyman C. Draper, editor, vol. 10, 229-230, Madison: Democrat Printing Company, 1888.

Keleher, William A., *Turmoil in New Mexico, 1846-1868*, New Edition, Santa Fe: Sunstone Press, 2008.

Kelly, Henry W., "Franciscan Missions of New Mexico, 1740-1760," *The New Mexico Historical Review*, 16 (1941): 41-69.

Kennedy, David M., *The Brief American Pageant: A History of the Republic*, Lexington: D. C. Heath and Company, 1989.

Kluckhohn, Clyde, *The Navaho, Revised Edition*, Garden City, New York: The Natural History Library, Anchor Books, Doubleday & Company, Inc., 1962.

Larson, Robert W., *New Mexico's Quest for Statehood, 1846-1912*, Albuquerque: University of New Mexico Press, 1968.

Lester, Paul Arnold, "Michael Steck and New Mexico Indian Affairs, 1852-1865," master's thesis, University of Oklahoma, 1986.

Lewis Publishing Company, *A Memorial and Biographical Record of Iowa*, Chicago: Lewis Publishing Co. 1896.

Linford, Laurance D., *Navajo Places: History, Legend, Landscape*, Salt Lake City: The University of Utah Press, 2000.

Locke, Raymond F., *The Book of the Navajo*, Los Angeles: Holloway House Publishing, 1976.

Lowrie, Walter, *The American State Papers; Public Lands, Volume 3, Documents, legislative and executive, of the Congress of the United States, in relation to the public lands: from the first session of the first Congress to the first session of the twenty-third Congress, March 4, 1789, to June 15, 1834 / selected and edited, under the authority of the Senate of the United States, by Walter Lowrie*. Washington, DC: Duff Green, 1834.

Magoffin, Susan Shelby, *Down the Santa Fe Trail and Into Mexico: The Diary of Susan Shelby Magoffin, 1846-1847*, edited by Stella M. Drumm, New Haven: Yale University Press, 1926.

Mansfield, Joseph F. K., *Mansfield on the Condition of the Western Forts, 1853-54*, edited by Robert W. Frazer, Norman: University of Oklahoma Press, 1963.

Marshall, Thomas M., *The Life and Papers of Frederick Bates, Volume 2*, St. Louis: Missouri Historical Society, 1926.

McCall, George A., *New Mexico in 1850: A Military View by Colonel George Archibald McCall*, edited by Robert W. Frazer, Norman, University of Oklahoma Press, 1968.

McNitt, Frank, *Navajo Wars: Military Campaigns, Slave Raids and Reprisals*, Albuquerque: University of New Mexico Press, 1990.

——— *Navaho Expedition: Journal of a Military Reconnaissance From Santa Fe, New Mexico to the Navaho Country, Made in 1849 by Lieutenant James H. Simpson*, Norman: University of Oklahoma Press, 1964.

Meriwether, David, *My Life in the Mountains and on the Plains, the Newly Discovered Autobiography by David Meriwether*, edited by Robert A. Griffin, Norman: University of Oklahoma Press, 1965.

Monroe, Haskell M., ed., *The Papers of Jefferson Davis, Volume 1, 1808-1840*, edited by Haskell M. Monroe, Jr. and James T. McIntosh, Baton Rouge: Louisiana State University Press, 1971.

——— *The Papers of Jefferson Davis, Volume 6, 1808-1840*, edited by Haskell M. Monroe, Jr. and James T. McIntosh, Baton Rouge: Louisiana State University Press, 1989.

Mumey, Nolie, ed., *March of the First Dragoons to the Rocky Mountains in 1835: The Diaries and Maps of Lemuel Ford*, Denver: The Eames Brothers Press, 1957.

Murphy, Lawrence R., "The United States Army in Taos, 1847-1852" *The New Mexico Historical Review*, 47, no. 1 (1972): 33-48.

Myers, Lewis A., *A History of New Mexico Baptists, Vol. 1, 1849-1912*, Albuquerque: The Baptist Convention of New Mexico, 1965.

Nesbit, Robert C., *Wisconsin: A History*, Madison: University of Wisconsin Press, 1989.

New Mexico Genealogical Society, *New Mexico Territorial Census, Volume 1, 1850*, Albuquerque: New Mexico Genealogical Society Inc., 1976.

Ormesher, Susan, *Missouri Marriage Before 1840*, compiled by Susan Ormesher, with an index by Robert and Catherine Barnes, Baltimore: Genealogical Publishing Co. Inc. 1982.

Padilla y Baca, Luis Gilberto, *Extractions of Church Records, Archdiocese of Santa Fe*, unpublished manuscript housed in the Moise Memorial Library, 208 5th Street, Santa Rosa, New Mexico, 2007.

Palmer, Strange M., "Western Wisconsin in 1836," *Collections of the State Historical Society of Wisconsin*, Lyman C. Draper, editor, vol. 6, Madison: Democrat Printing Company, 1908.

Parkinson, Daniel M., "Pioneer Life in Wisconsin" *Collections of the State Historical Society of Wisconsin*, Lyman C. Draper, editor, vol. 2, 326-363, Democrat Printing Company, Madison, 1908.

Parrish, William E., *Missouri: The Heart of the Nation*, St. Louis: Forum Press, 1980.

Pelzer, Louis, *Augustus Caesar Dodge*, Iowa City: The State Historical Society of Iowa, 1908.

——— *Henry Dodge*, Iowa City: The State Historical Society of Iowa, 1911.

Peña, Abe, *Memories of Cíbola: Stories from New Mexico Villages*, Albuquerque: University of New Mexico Press, 1997.

Petersen, William J., *Steam Boating on the Upper Mississippi The Water Way to Iowa*, Iowa City: The State Historical Society of Iowa, 1937.

Phillips, Claude A., *A History of Education in Missouri: The Essential Facts Concerning the History and Organization of Missouri Schools*, Jefferson City: Hugh Stephens Printing Company, 1911.

Prince, L. Bradford, *New Mexico's Struggle for Statehood: Sixty Years of Effort to Obtain Self Government*, New Edition, Santa Fe: Sunstone Press, 2010.

Reeve, Frank D., "The Federal Indian Policy, 1858-1880," *The New Mexico Historical Review* 12 (1937): 275-312.

——— "The Government and the Navaho, 1846-1858," *The New Mexico Historical Review* 14 (1939): 82-114.

——— "Navaho Foreign Affairs, 1795-1846," *The New Mexico Historical Review* 46 (1971): 101-132.

——— "The Navaho-Spanish Peace, 1720s-1770s," *The New Mexico Historical Review* 34 (1959): 9-40.

Rice, Josiah M., *A Cannoneer in Navajo Country: Journal of Private Josiah M. Rice, 1851*, edited by Richard H. Dillon, Denver: Old West Publishing Company, 1970.

Robrock, David, *Missouri 49er, The Journal of William W. Hunter on the Southern Gold Trail*, edited by David Robrock, Albuquerque: University of New Mexico Press, 1992.

Rodolf, Theodore, "Pioneering in the Wisconsin Lead Region," *Collections of the State Historical Society of Wisconsin*, Rueben Gold Thwaites, editor, vol. 15, 338-389, Madison: Democrat Printing Company, 1900.

Salazar, J. Richard, *Calendar to the Micro Film Edition of the Land Records of New Mexico: Spanish Archives of New Mexico, Series I, Surveyor General Records, and, the Records of the Court of Private Land Claims*, Santa Fe: New Mexico Archives and Records Center,1987.

Salter, William, *The Life of Henry Dodge, from 1782 to 1833: With Portrait by George Catlin and Maps of the Battles of the Pecatonica and Wisconsin Heights in the Black Hawk War*, Burlington, Iowa: unknown publisher,1890, Illinois Historical Digitization Projects, Northern Illinois University Libraries, 2001 http://lincoln.lib.niu.edu/file.php?file=dodge.html, (accessed June 9, 2011).

Schaaf, Ida M., *Sainte Genevieve Marriages, Baptisms and Burials From the Church Registers*, St. Louis: Missouri Historical Society, Jefferson Memorial, 1918.

Schafer, Joseph, *The Wisconsin Lead Region*, Evansville: State Historical Society of Wisconsin and Antes Press, 1932.

Schoolcraft, Henry R., *A View of the Lead Mines of Missouri: Including Some Observations on the Mineralogy, Geology, Geography, Antiquities, Soil, Climate, Population and Productions of Missouri and Arkansaw*, New York: Charley Wiley & Company, 1819.

Sharp, Mary Rozier, *Between the Gabouri: A History of Ferdinand Rosier*, published by author, 1981.

Shoemaker, Floyd C., *Missouri and Missourians: Land of Contrasts and People of Achievements, Vol. 1*, Chicago: Lewis Publishing Company, 1943.

Simmons, Mark, *The Little Lion of the Southwest: A Life of Manuel Antonio Chaves*, Chicago: The Swallow Press Inc., 1973.

Simpson, James H., *Navaho Expedition: Journal of a Military Reconnaissance From Santa Fe, New Mexico to the Navaho Country, Made in 1849 by Lieutenant James H. Simpson*, edited by Frank McNitt, Norman: University of Oklahoma Press, 1964.

Slater, John M., *El Morro: Inscription Rock, New Mexico*, Los Angeles: The Plantin Press, 1961.

Smith, Alice E., *The History of Wisconsin, Volume 1: From Exploration to Statehood*, Madison: State Historical Society of Wisconsin, 1973.

Smith, Henry, *The Expedition Against the Sauk and Fox Indians, 1832*, New York: Military and Naval Magazine Reprint, 1914.

Stapleton, Ernest S., "The History of Baptist Missions in New Mexico, 1849–1866," master's thesis, University of New Mexico, Albuquerque, 1954.

Strong, Moses, "The Indian Wars," *Wisconsin Historical Collections*, edited by Rueben Gold Thwaites, vol. 8, 241-286, Madison: State Historical Society of Wisconsin, 1895.

––– *A History of the Territory of Wisconsin, 1836–1848*, Madison: Democrat Printing Company, 1885.

Sturtevant, William C., ed., *Handbook of North American Indians, Volume 15, Northeast*, Washington, DC: Smithsonian Institution, 1983.

––– *Handbook of North American Indians, Volume 10, Southwest*, Washington, DC: Smithsonian Institution, Washington, 1983.

Sunder, John E. ed., *Matt Field on the Santa Fe Trail*, Collected by Clyde and Mae Reed Porter, editing, introduction and notes by John E. Sunder, Norman: University of Oklahoma Press, 1960.

Sunseri, Alvin R., *Seeds of Discord: New Mexico in the Aftermath of the American Conquest, 1846–1861*, Chicago: Nelson-Hall, 1979.

Sweeny, Edwin R., *Mangas Coloradas, Chief of the Chiricahua Apaches*, Norman: University of Oklahoma Press, 1998.

Switzler, William F., *Illustrated History of Missouri, From 1541 to 1877*, Saint Louis: C. R. Barns, 1879, reprinted by Arno Press, New York, 1975.

Taylor, Stephen, "Mineral Point in Days of Yore," *Collections of the State Historical Society of Wisconsin*, Lyman C. Draper, editor, vol. 2, 486-487, Madison: Democrat Printing Company, 1903.

Thomlinson, M. H., "Forgotten Fort," *New Mexico Magazine*, vol. 23, no. 1 (January 1945): 14-41.

Thwaites, Rueben Gold, "The Story of the Black Hawk War" in *Collections of the State Historical Society of Wisconsin*, Rueben Gold Thwaites, editor, vol. 12, Madison: Democrat Printing Company, 1892.

Thwaites, Rueben Gold, ed. *Collections of the State Historical Society of Wisconsin, Volume 12*, Madison: Democrat Printing Company, 1892.

––– *Collections of the State Historical Society of Wisconsin, Volume 13*, Madison: Democrat Printing Company, 1895.

——— *Collections of the State Historical Society of Wisconsin, Volume 15*, Madison: Democrat Printing Company, 1900.
——— *Collections of the State Historical Society of Wisconsin, Volume 18*, Madison: Democrat Printing Company, 1908.
——— *Wisconsin Historical Collections*, Madison: State Historical Society of Wisconsin, 1895.
Thrapp, Dan L., *Encyclopedia of Frontier Biography, Volumes 1-3*, Spokane: University of Nebraska Press & The Arthur H. Clark Company, 1988.
Tillman, Samuel E., *Colonel Henry L. Kendrick, U. S. A.: an Address by the Rev. Marvin R. Vincent, D. D. and Obituary by Prof. Samuel E. Tillman*, New York: U.S.M.A., E. P. Dutton & Company, 1892.
Twitchell, Ralph E., *The History of the Military Occupation of the Territory of New Mexico From 1846 to 1851*, New Edition, Santa Fe: Sunstone Press, 2007.
——— *The Leading Facts of New Mexican History Vol. 2*, New Edition, Santa Fe: Sunstone Press, 2007.
——— "Historical Sketch of Governor William Carr Lane, Together with Diary of His Journey from St. Louis, Mo., to Santa Fe, N. M., July 31st to September 9th, 1852" *New Mexico Historical Society Publications*, no. 4, 1917.
Underhill, Ruth, *Here Come the Navajo*, U. S. Department of the Interior, Haskell Press, Haskell, Kansas, 1953.
Van Valkenburgh, Richard, *Dine Bikéyah*, Department of the Interior, Navajo Agency, Window Rock, Arizona, 1941.
——— "Captain Red Shirt," *New Mexico Magazine*, July 1941, 28, 44-45.
Waldman, Carl, *Atlas of the North American Indian*, New York: Facts on File, 1985.
Way, Royal Brunson, *The Rock River Valley: Its History, Traditions, Legends and Charms, covering Jefferson, Dodge, Dane, and Rock Counties, Wisconsin, and Winnebago, Stephenson, Boone, Ogle, Lee, Whiteside, Henry, and Rock Island Counties, Illinois Volumes 1, 2, 3*, Chicago: S. J. Clarke Publishing Company, 1926.
Wayman, Norbury L., *Life on the River: A Pictorial History of the Mississippi, the Missouri, and the Western River System*, New York: Crown Publishers, 1971.
Webb, James J., *Adventures in the Santa Fé Trade 1844-1847*, Southwest Historical Series, edited by Ralph P. Bieber, Glendale: The Arthur H. Clark Company,1931.
Weber, David J., *Richard H. Kern: Expeditionary Artist in the Far Southwest, 1848-1853*, Albuquerque: University of New Mexico, 1985.
Western Historical Company, *History of Iowa County, Wisconsin, containing an account of its settlement, growth, development and resources...biographical sketches...* Chicago: Western Historical Company, 1881.
——— *History of Lafayette County, Wisconsin, containing an account of its settlement, growth, development and resources; an extensive and minute sketch of its cities, towns and villages ...* Chicago: Western Historical Company, 1881.
White Mountain Smith, Dama M., "Henry Chee Dodge, Navajo," *Desert Magazine* 1, no. 9 (July, 1938): 18-20.
Whittlesey, Charles, "Recollections of a Tour Through Wisconsin in 1832" *Collections of the State Historical Society of Wisconsin*, edited by Lyman C. Draper, vol. 1, 64-85, Madison: Democrat Printing Company, 1903.
Williams, Walter, *Missouri, Mother of the West*, Chicago: American Historical Society, 1930.
Wisconsin Historical Records Survey, *Wisconsin Territorial Papers, Proceedings of Iowa County Board of Supervisors, Volumes 1-2*, Madison: Wisconsin Historical Records Survey, 1942.

Woodward, Gilbert Mortier, *James Duane Doty*, location and publisher unknown, 1904.

Woodward, Arthur, *Navajo Silver: A Brief History of Navajo Silversmithing*, Flagstaff: Northland Press, 1973.

Wyman, Leland C., *Blessingway, With Three Versions of the Myth Recorded and Translated from the Navajo By Father Berard Haile, O. F. M.*, Tucson: University of Arizona Press, 1970.

Yealy, Francis J., *Sainte Genevieve: The Story of Missouri's Oldest Settlement*, Ste. Genevieve: Bicentennial Historical Committee, 1935.

UNITED STATES NATIONAL ARCHIVES AND RECORDS ADMINISTRATION:

Appointment of Postmasters, 1832-1971, National Archives, Records of the Post Office Department, Record Group 28, M841. Microfilm.

Index to the Compiled Service Records of Volunteer Soldiers Who Served During Indian Wars & Disturbances, 1815-1858, National Archives, Records of the Adjutant General's Office, 1780s-1917, Record Group 94, M629. Microfilm.

Index to Compiled Service Records of Volunteer Soldiers Who Served during the Mexican War, National Archives, Records of the Adjutant General's Office, 1780s-1917, Record Group 94, M616. Microfilm.

Letters of Application and Recommendation During the Administrations of Martin Van Buren, William Henry Harrison, and John Tyler, 1837-1845, National Archives, Department of State, Record Group 59, M687. Microfilm.

Letters Received by the Adjutant General's Office, National Archives, Records of the Adjutant General's Office, 1780-1917, Record Group 94, M567. Microfilm.

Letters Received by the Department of New Mexico, 1854-1865, National Archives, Records of U.S. Army Continental Commands, 1821-1920, Record Group 393, M1102. Microfilm.

Letters Sent by the Department of New Mexico, National Archives, Records of U.S. Army Continental Commands, 1821-1920, Record Group 393, M1072. Microfilm.

Letters Received by the 9th Military District, 1848-1853, National Archives, Records of U.S. Army Continental Commands, 1821-1920, Record Group 393, M1102. Microfilm.

Letters Sent by the 9th Military District, 1849-1890, National Archives, Records of U.S. Army Continental Commands, 1821-1920, Record Group 393, M1072. Microfilm.

Letters Received by the Secretary of War Relating to Indian Affairs, National Archives, Records of the Office of the Secretary of War, Record Group 75, M271. Microfilm.

Letters Received by the Secretary of War, Registered Series 1801-1860, National Archives, Records of the Office of the Secretary of War, Record Group 107, M221. Microfilm.

Letters Sent by the Secretary of War, Registered Series, 1801-1860, National Archives, Records of the Office of the Secretary of War, Record Group 107, M6. Microfilm.

Letters Sent to the Indian Division of the Dept. of the Interior, 1849-1903, National Archives, Records of the Bureau of Indian Affairs, Record Group 75, M606. Microfilm.

Letters Received from the Commissioner of Indian Affairs, National Archives, Records of the Bureau of Indian Affairs, Record Group 75. Microfilm.

Letters Received by the Office of Indian Affairs, 1824-1880, New Mexico Superintendency, National Archives, Records of the Bureau of Indian Affairs, Record Group 75, M234. Microfilm.

Letters Sent by the Office of Indian Affairs, 1824-1881, National Archives, Records of the Bureau of Indian Affairs, Record Group 75, M21. Microfilm.

Records of the Michigan Superintendency of Indian Affairs, 1814-1818, Letters Received, National Archives, Records of the Bureau of Indian Affairs, Record Group 75, M1, Washington, DC. 1940. Microfilm.

Records of the New Mexico Superintendency of Indian Affairs, 1849-1880, National Archives, Records of the Bureau of Indian Affairs, T21. Microfilm.

Records of the New Mexico Superintendency of Indian Affairs, 1849-1880, Records of the Santa Fe Agency, National Archives, Records of the Bureau of Indian Affairs, T21. Microfilm.

Records of the Office of the Quartermaster General, Consolidated Correspondence Files, National Archives, Record Group 92, Washington, DC.

Records of the Office of the Quartermaster General, Reports of Persons and Articles Hired, 1846-1847, National Archives, Record Group 92, Washington, DC.

Records of the Department of Treasury, National Archives, Record Group 56, M236, Denver Regional Center, Denver, Colorado.

Records of U. S. Army Continental Commands, 1784-1821, Department of New Mexico, Selected Letters, National Archives, Records of the Office of the Secretary of War, Washington, DC, 1980.

Register of Letters Received by the Office of Indian Affairs, 1824-1880, National Archives, Record Group 75, Records of the Bureau of Indian Affairs, M18. Microfilm.

Returns from U. S. Military Posts, 1800-1918, National Archives, Record Group 94, Records of the Adjutant General's Office, M617. Microfilm.

Settled Indian Accounts, 1817-1922, National Archives, Record Group 217, Records of the Accounting Office of the Department of the Treasury, Records of the Second Auditor.

State Department Territorial Papers, New Mexico, 1851-1872, National Archives, Record Group 59, State Department Records, T17. Microfilm.

STATE AND PRIVATE ARCHIVAL COLLECTIONS CITED:

Arizona State University Archives, Arizona State University, Tempe
    History of Southeast Missouri, Biographical Index
Center for Southwest Research, University of New Mexico, Albuquerque
    New Mexico Legislative Journal. Microfilm.
    The Michael Steck Collection
    The Frank D. Reeves Records. Microfilm.
Huntington Library
    The Richard A. Kern Diary, Henry E. Huntington Library and Art Gallery, San Marino, California.
    The William G. Ritch Papers, Microfilm Edition, at the Center for Southwest Research, University of New Mexico, Albuquerque, New Mexico. Microfilm.
Iowa State Historical Society Library and Archives, Des Moines
    Henry Dodge and Augustus C. Dodge Papers.
Mineral Point Room of Local History, Mineral Point Public Library, Mineral Point, Wisconsin
    The Henry L. Dodge Family Bible
    Dodge Genealogy Chart

"A Notable Pioneer Woman," *The Gazette*, Burlington, Iowa, clipping circa 1895
Mississippi Valley French Research, Eugene Beckett, Genealogist, Cambria, Illinois
Missouri State Archives and Museum, Jefferson City, Missouri
    Sainte Genevieve County, Deeds, Volume D
    Certificates of War Service. H. L. Dodge
National Frontier Trails Center, Independence, Missouri
    Diary of an Irish Artist
    Jacob Hall Correspondence
Neil Giffey, Iowa County Historical Society, Dodgeville, Wisconsin
New Mexico State Records and Archives Center
    District Court Records, Valencia County, 1854
    Territorial Archives of New Mexico, Governors Papers, 1846-1878. Microfilm.
    Territorial Archives of New Mexico, Journals and Ledgers of the Treasurer of the Territory, Receipts & Disbursement Journal. Microfilm.
    Territorial Archives of New Mexico, Land Records of New Mexico, Surveyor General Records. Microfilm.
    Territorial Archives of New Mexico, Muster Reels 1847-1897. Microfilm.
    Territorial Archives of New Mexico, Records of Oaths and Bonds of Territorial Officials, August 11, 1851-July 29, 1867. Microfilm.
    Territorial Archives of New Mexico, Records of the Secretary of the Territory, 1851-1911. Microfilm.
    Territorial Archives of New Mexico, Secretary of the Territory Executive Record Books, 1851-1912. Microfilm.
    Territorial Archives of New Mexico; Governors Papers, 1846-1878. Microfilm.
    The Benjamin M. Read Collection I
    The Frank McNitt Collection
    The Dorothy Woodward Collection, Documents Series, Box 17, Folder 289, Harriet Bidwell Shaw Letters
Sainte Genevieve County Courthouse, Ste. Genevieve, Missouri
    Confirmation of Marriages, Church Records, 1836
    Conveyances of Deeds 1804, Book C
    Index #0 Conveyances-Direct 1804-1880, Book D
    Index #0 Conveyances of Deeds-Indirect 1804-1880, Books B, C
    Probate Files, Israel Dodge
State Historical Society of Missouri, Western Historical Manuscripts Collection, Columbia State University, Columbia, Missouri
    Ste. Genevieve Archives
State Historical Society of Missouri, Jefferson Memorial Building, Forest Park, St. Louis, Missouri
    Ida M. Schaaf Collection
    James Josiah Webb Collection
    Lewis F. Linn Papers
    Stephen W. Kearny Diary & Letter Book, 1846-47
    William Carr Lane Collection

Wisconsin Room, University Archives, Karrmann Library, University of Wisconsin, Platteville
    Iowa Series 5
    Iowa Series 23, Iowa County Court Cases
    Iowa Series 24 License Book 1839–1859: Marriages
    Iowa Series 27, Judgment Book
Wisconsin State Historical Society Archives and Library, University of Wisconsin, Madison
    Mary Dodge Fox Papers
    Charles W. Wentz Letters, 1860–1864

SELECTED CORRESPONDENCE:

Correspondence between L. D. Sundberg and David Brugge, 1995
Correspondence between L. D. Sundberg and Neil Giffey, 1995–1996
Correspondence between Frank McNitt and Sheridan Spearman, 1971, 1972, in the *Frank McNitt Collection*, New Mexico Archives and Records Center, Santa Fe, New Mexico
Correspondence between Frank McNitt and Kathy Fisher, 1971, in the *Frank McNitt Collection*, New Mexico Archives and Records Center, Santa Fe, New Mexico
Selected notes and correspondence between L. D. Sundberg and Betty Danielson
Selected notes and correspondence of Mrs. Lucille Basler, Ste. Genevieve, Missouri

www.ingramcontent.com/pod-product-compliance
Lightning Source LLC
Chambersburg PA
CBHW030513230426
43665CB00010B/600